D0769157

A HOUSE DIVIDED: ARGENTINA, 1880–1980

EDUARDO CRAWLEY

A HOUSE DIVIDED

ARGENTINA
1880—1980

MECHANICS' INSTITUTE

1984

C. HURST & COMPANY, LONDON

First published in the United Kingdom by
C. Hurst & Co. (Publishers) Ltd.,
38 King Street, London WC2E 8JT
© Eduardo Crawley, 1984
ISBN 0–905838–74–2
Printed in Great Britain

*To María Mercedes, Mariana and Juan Pedro,
who inherit all this*

ACKNOWLEDGMENTS

I could not do justice in a few lines to the many people who aided me in putting together this book. I must, however, single out a few whose help has been invaluable: Christopher Hurst, who first invited me to put on paper an account of post-Perón Argentina, and bore patiently with me as I extended its scope to cover the whole of the last 100 years; Marcelo Diamand, who tried to teach me how Argentina's economy functions; the late Jorge Sábato, with whom the book was talked out endlessly; Rodolfo H. Terragno, who gave me the benefit of one of Argentina's most outstanding analytic minds; Andrew Graham-Yooll, without whose painstakingly compiled chronologies I would often have lost my way; and Juan Eduardo Fleming, for the twin gifts of his enthusiasm over the manuscript and the humble manner in which he suggested improvements.

August 1984   E.C.

CONTENTS

FOREWORD

In 1869, when the Khedive Ismail Pasha was ruler of Egypt, the Suez Canal was opened to navigation. Twelve years later, Egypt was occupied by the British, who assumed total control of the Canal.

In 1903, through the Hay Bunau-Varilla treaty, the United States acquired the right to build a canal across the isthmus of Panama. It also acquired title 'in perpetuity' to the adjacent land.

The Suez Canal linked the Mediterranean, via the Red Sea, with the Indian Ocean. The Panama Canal linked the Atlantic with the Pacific north of the Equator. Each canal was under the direct control of a great power: Great Britain and the United States, respectively.

From that time onwards, the world became a hemisphere; commerce and war began to be waged horizontally. The South Atlantic, once the only route to the Pacific — through the Straits of Magellan at the southern extreme of the Americas — lost the strategic importance it had had since the days of the Discovery, at the end of the fifteenth century.

For many years the southern hemisphere would lack any international significance. South of the Equator there were only colonies and, in South America, a handful of republics which, while perhaps showing some promise for the future, could still be largely ignored. Europe had no reason to pay any attention to them. From the beginning of the nineteenth century the United States began to consider the rest of the Americas as an area reserved for its own influence, although its interests were vested mainly in Mexico and the Caribbean states.

In terms of international politics, the Southern Cone of America, at the bottom of the world, was the least significant of regions. Its geographical isolation was complete in an age when the ship and the telegraph were the only means of covering long distances. Commercial aviation did not develop until the 1930s, after that historic flight in 1926 when Ramón Franco first crossed the South Atlantic in his seaplane, the *Plus Ultra*. Later, suboceanic cables made possible communication by telephone, but this remained a precarious link until the 1960s, when the artificial satellite made its appearance.

It was not only in the field of international politics that South America had little significance. Economically, the northern hemisphere could get along without it. The only autochthonous raw material to achieve vital significance was rubber, because unlike other native crops it had not been

transplanted to other continents. But Britain easily overcame that omission: it required only a single naturalist to smuggle seeds out of Brazil
and take them to Malaya, Ceylon and Indonesia.

Yet Europe, which had uprooted the people from the countryside to
man its factories, was avid for food and yearned for markets in which to
place its growing industrial production. Towards 1880, Argentina had
completed its national organisation after years of anarchy, internal wars
and a unifying dictatorship. Power was in the hands of a Europeanised,
aristocratic urban class which did not take long to realise the negotiable
value of the wealth placed in their hands: an immense territory, enjoying
a variety of climates and, particularly in the fertile and infinite pampas,
apt for rapid agricultural development.

This ruling class entered into a *contract* with Britain: Argentina would
build an economy complementary to the British economy; it would produce meat and cereals to send to London and at the same time become a
big client for British industry. The deal was a good one, but it was also
precarious. With the profits it generated, Argentina would finance mass
education, attract large numbers of European immigrants, and set itself
the task of creating a 'European' island in South America.

The truth is that the rest of the world took hardly any notice of this
venture. The Anglo-Argentine *contract* was no more than a bilateral
economic relationship linking Argentina with Britain or, to be more
precise, linking Argentina's ruling class with certain sectors of the
British economy. Because it lacked strategic importance, Argentina was
largely ignored by North Americans and Europeans alike. The country
enjoyed and suffered from its isolation. The fact of belonging to a
marginal area allowed it to enjoy peace in the century of world wars, and
granted it greater freedom of movement than that of the northern Latin
American countries, which were subject to direct intervention by the
United States. On the other hand, isolation prevented Argentina, a
country of vast human and economic resources, from becoming
'inserted' in the world economy to a sufficient extent. Its own economic
expansion remained subordinate to Britain, to whose economy it was
appended by a sort of umbilical cord.

This situation had some curious side-effects. Argentina regarded itself
as 'European', but was really marginal, and it believed that it was
developing, but actually it only enjoyed the transient benefits of a
bilateral relationship which could not be favourable in the long run. Both
illusions — Europeanness   and   development — evoked   in   the
Argentines a feeling of greatness which bore no relation to their

country's real place in the world.

Relative prosperity, mass immigration and cultural development, however, gave birth to a dynamic petty bourgeoisie, which did not take long to start demanding political power. While Europe was involved in the First World War, Argentina's aristocracy was being forced to cede ground and ultimately — after the country's first free elections in 1916 — to relinquish the reins of power to a party of the middle class, with less desire for greatness and greater desire for social equity. The *contract* with Britain remained in force, but internally the balance of power had shifted.

And after the War, it was the world that changed. The great powers needed to rebuild their battered economies, and sought the means to finance that task. They found them in the accentuation of a process already under way, for natural reasons, which came to be known as the 'deterioration of the terms of trade'. The crash of 1929, which shook the foundations of capitalism and forced the great powers into unbridled selfishness, put an end to the business of exchanging foodstuffs for manufactures. This plunged Argentina into a crisis which the old ruling class pounced upon as proof of the ineptitude and the failure of those who had succeeded them in power. Incapable of removing them through the ballot box, they turned to the armed forces. On 6 September 1930, with the ouster of Hipólito Yrigoyen, Argentina entered the era of militarism. At the time, the rest of the world found no good reason to take note of this process.

The military renewed their *contract* with Britain, though on terms less favourable to Argentina, and they adopted a hardline policy towards internal opposition.

The Second World War, far more devastating than the First, made a sharp impact on Europe's productive capacity, and forced Argentina into import-substitution. The first glimmers appeared of limited industrial development, which would enlarge and strengthen the country's working class. Juan Domingo Perón became the interpreter of this emergent class, definitively broke off the *contract* with Britain (who had already ceded leadership to the United States), and attempted to create a less dependent, more distributive model.

The armed forces again made an attempt at restoration. From 1955 onwards, civilian governments — the product of social pressure in favour of democracy — alternated with military régimes, who truncated the mandates of any and all elected authorities.

The continuous frustration of democratic experiences, added to the prevailing social inequities, created the conditions for the eruption of violence in the 1970s. Argentina lived through an internal war between extremist organisations, who hoped to impose social demands by the use of violence, and the armed forces, who ferociously repressed this attempt.

In the mean time, not only had Argentina 'drawn closer' to the rest of the world, thanks to the development of telecommunications, but the southern hemisphere as a whole had begun to recover its political value. This was a consequence of the World Wars and of the East-West conflict that followed.

World War I had its origins in Kaiser Wilhelm II's demand for a 'place in the sun' for the German empire — which meant the incorporation of Germany in the colonialist race, mainly in Africa. Britain and the United States controlled the seas through their navies and the canals of Suez and Panama, and through their colonies they held the sources of raw materials — both of which ensured their hegemony. The Germans realised that even when the confrontation was taking place in the northern hemisphere, the base of British and North American power was in the south. Significantly, one of the first major naval encounters, in 1914, was the battle of the Falklands (Malvinas), where the cruisers *Karlsruhe*, *Emden* and *Königsberg* were sunk.

Between the Wars, attention turned mainly towards Africa, where the colonial powers were engaged in a further carve-up of territory, but in the north of Latin America United States expansionism became notorious: military interventions in Mexico, Nicaragua, Haiti, the Dominican Republic and Cuba proved that the North Americans were determined to gain control of the area. South America remained on the sidelines.

After the Second World War the decolonisation of Africa and Asia, the rise of the new nationalism, the alliances between emergent nations, and (interplaying with it all) the East-West conflict changed the shape of the political planisphere. Nothing, however, was as important in its effect as the closure of the Suez Canal in 1956. A new episode in the Arab-Israeli wars had deprived Egypt of the eastern bank, and with Israelis on one side and Egyptians on the other, the waterway became impassable. The nations of the northern hemisphere retreated to a situation they had believed, back in the Victorian age, to have solved for all time. It became necessary to return to the routes of the adventurers and to go round Africa to reach North America from the Indian Ocean. And there was now a pressing need to make that voyage: the transportation of the Middle East's oil to the world's leading industrial power.

Today the Indian Ocean is, in the words of the North American journalist Donald Pareth, 'a cockpit of superpower rivalry that focuses on shipping lanes, oil supplies, regional conflicts and naval bases'. Britain emptied the Chagos archipelago of natives in order to hand it over to the United States for the construction of a powerful base on Diego García. There are North American bases, also, in Kenya and Somalia, and warships of the 6th and 7th fleets operate continuously in the area. The Soviet Union maintains bases in Ethiopia and South Yemen and a considerable naval presence in the Indian Ocean.

Quite predictably, the next stage was the South Atlantic, just around the corner. As early as 1976 the Argentine journal *Estrategia* published a prophetic analysis: 'Tension in the Indian Ocean and naval escalation by the superpowers will have repercussions in a drive to the west, to the South Atlantic, which has so far been free from tension.'

The preoccupation of the United States with the area increased as Central America and the Caribbean began to slip through its fingers. In 1979, Jimmy Carter's government thought his country's interests would be best served if it agreed to the gradual devolution of the Panama Canal Zone, deferring retrocession of the Canal itself until the end of the twentieth century. The purpose of the agreement, accepted by Panama, was to defuse the time-bomb constructed by Panamanian rancour over years of unheeded claims. Whatever the advantages may have been for Washington, the fact that the United States felt impelled to choose the lesser evil revealed its vulnerability in the area. The later firestorm in Central America, set alight after the ouster of the Nicaraguan dictator Anastasio Somoza, only reinforced US fears. From 1959 onwards, the Soviet Union had its flag planted in Cuba. In 1975 it had planted another in Angola. Now there seemed to be the risk of the Soviets planting red pennants close to the Panama Canal. Control over the South Atlantic was (and still is) felt as a very real need by the United States and its allies.

It is in the light of this reality that one must analyse the 1982 crisis in the South Atlantic. The Argentine military were driven into a *cul-de-sac* by the merciless war they waged on the internal front, in the name of the West and against the vernacular representatives of the East. In order to kill off 'subversion, a cyst in the body politic', they had destroyed much of the country's social fabric and had become isolated from the people. The re-conquest of the Malvinas — occupied by the British in 1833, and claimed back ever since by Argentina — was envisaged by the military as a means of rebuilding their relations with Argentine society. The

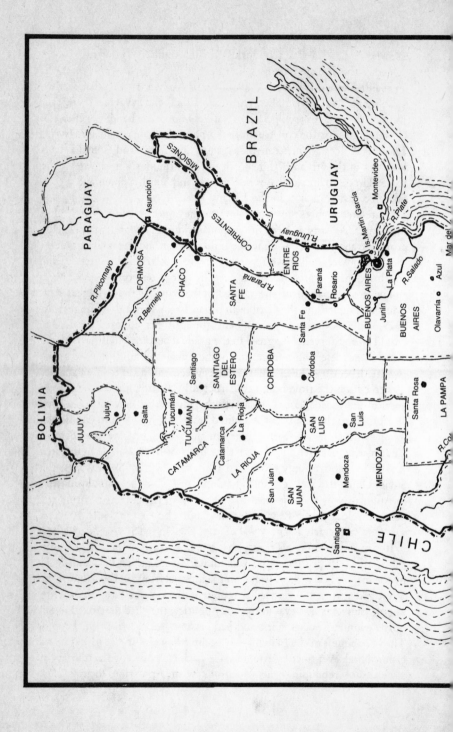

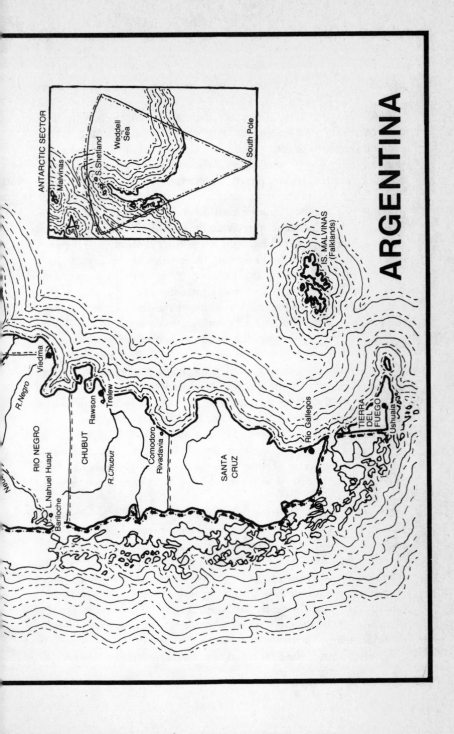

ARGENTINA

ANTARCTIC SECTOR

Malvinas
S.Shetland
Weddell Sea
South Pole

IS. MALVINAS
(Falklands)

R.Negro
Viedma
RIO NEGRO
L.Nahuel Huapi
Bariloche
CHUBUT
Rawson
Trelew
R.Chubut
Comodoro Rivadavia
SANTA CRUZ
Rio Gallegos
TIERRA DEL FUEGO
Ushuaia

attempt, however, put them on a collision course, not only with Britain but with the United States and Europe, in this stage of world evolution in which control over the South Atlantic has become an aim of the super-powers.

Rulers and strategists, historians and journalists, felt the need to take a crash course in order to understand Argentina. To think that such a crash course is possible is to betray ignorance: because, out of all the contradic-tions on which it was built, Argentina has emerged as an extraordinarily complex country. Its complexity, moreover, is suffused by the high degree of emotionalism of its people. No one could possibly imagine groups of Englishmen fighting each other in 1983 over Gladstone or Disraeli, or North Americans reviving the hatreds of the Civil War. Yet Argentines are capable of keeping alive the bitter confrontation between *rosistas* and *antirrosistas* (followers and adversaries of the dictator Juan Manuel de Rosas, ousted in 1852) and of prolonging the nineteenth-cen-tury debate between Federalists and Unitarists. The fact is that Argen-tina, which grew economically in terms of the famous *contract*, never completed its integration, its development, its consolidation.

As a result of this, whoever tries to absorb Argentine history from the vernacular historiography is bound to be frustrated: much of it is polemical, partisan and prone to generalisation. Foreign works on Argentina, meagre because of the country's relatively low strategic value for many years, do not contribute much either. Most academic works tend to over-specialise and are thus, for example, capable of dwelling on the agrarian policies of the Ortiz administration (1938–42) but incapable of providing a comprehensive overview. The available choice is mostly between the vagueness of those who say next to nothing about every-thing, and the pedantry of those who say everything about next to nothing.

Eduardo Crawley has tried to bridge the gap with this brief history, wide in its scope yet exact, fact-laden and even anecdotal. With the same combination of rigour and narrative ability that characterises *Dictators Never Die* (an indispensable book for anyone wishing to understand the evolution of Nicaragua), Crawley introduces the characters who made Argentina, paints the backdrops against which they acted, and summarises the role that each played. At times he offers a rare mix of the frivolous and the solemn (typically Argentine), which both stimulates the reader and calls attention to the seriousness of the contents. Nowhere does he succumb to the temptation of generalising, anticipating conclu-sions or spinning theories.

There is no possibility that Crawley will command a consensus among the Argentines. The *peronistas* will detect a whiff of *gorilismo* (anti-peronism), while the *gorilas* will discern an attempt to justify things they consider unjustifiable. The Left will see this history as a bourgeois account of apparent reality, while the Right will judge it as a dangerous exercise opening up old wounds and perhaps encouraging a rebellious attitude. The nationalists will think they can sense a foreign air, and foreigners will notice a passion for domestic detail.

To embark upon the knowledge of Argentina, and (for those who already have that knowledge) to be reminded and even to dissent, Crawley's work is a useful, seductive guide that confronts us with the tragedies and comedies in which the Argentines were protagonists while the world was forgetting them.

RODOLFO H. TERRAGNO

'Give armies to the countries that have no enemies, and no need to wage war, and you will create a class of industrialists which will busy itself in installing and deposing governments or — and it amounts to the same thing — in making the country wage war against itself for want of foreign wars. The army will degenerate into a ruling class and the people into a ruled or subject class.'
— Juan Bautista Alberdi, the man who drafted the bases for Argentina's Constitution, in *El Crimen de la Guerra*, 1870

1

THE LAND OF CATTLE AND
IMMIGRANTS
(1880–1895)

Between 1880 and 1980 thirty-three men and one woman occupied the
Presidency of the Argentine Republic. By stretching a point here and
there, it could be said that twenty-three of them attained power by constitutional means. Holding on to power, whether constitutional or not,
has proved to be a difficult task. Three Presidents died on the job (of
natural causes), four were forced to resign, and eleven were forcibly
removed from office. Only five managed to complete their mandatory
six-year term. Three of these — Julio Argentino Roca, Hipólito
Yrigoyen and Juan Domingo Perón — served for more than one term,
but only Roca managed to complete more than one. Yrigoyen was
deposed two years after being re-elected in 1928; Perón's second term
was interrupted by a military coup in 1955, and his third term by his
death in 1974.

In the half-century 1930–80 in Argentina, twenty-one years were
lived under military rule. Many analysts like to refer to 1930 as the
beginning of the 'era of the military coup'; since that year only one President, Perón, has managed to complete a full term of office; since then,
ten of the eleven military takeovers of this century have taken place. Just
as the three decades before 1930 were hallmarked by the rise and fall of
Hipólito Yrigoyen, the remaining half-century bears the unmistakable
sign of Juan Domingo Perón — of his rise in the 1940s; his first two Presidencies; his ouster and the long exile during which he dominated the
scene from afar; his remarkable comeback in the 1970s; his death and its
sequel of almost unimaginable violence.

Perón's image is closely linked to several of the most outstanding
features of present-day Argentina: the dominant Army, from whose
ranks he rose and, in time, his most implacable enemy; the unions, which
he welded into one of the most powerful forces ever to appear in
Argentine politics and the cornerstone of his power; and the emergence
of a nationalistic mixed economy, based on a pervasive, interventionist

1

state apparatus and the expansion of local industry.

There is, of course, far more than just that to the image of Perón. Indeed there is a whole string of mirror-images, often violently contrasted, through which sympathisers and adversaries to this day give witness to how much the changes over which he presided have been central to twentieth-century Argentina. He is seen as the embodiment of true nationalism and anti-imperialism, as the man whose social legislation and politics of mass mobilisation gave both dignity and power to the working man; as the man whose continental and indeed world vision provided a workable alternative to the rule of 'the two imperialisms'; as the wise, statesmanlike reconciler of conflicting interests in a developing country destined to become a Latin American power. Alternately, he is seen as an opportunist, a demagogue, a corrupt profiteer; the man whose irresponsible greed for power fostered terrorism and drove the country to near-bankruptcy, not once but twice in his political career. To many Argentines, Perón and *peronismo* are still either all black or all white, a sign that the changes and upheavals of the long Perón era are still incomplete, still part of a tug-of-war that is only occasionally suspended while the contenders recover their breath. Although the facts do not actually always fit the picture, much of Argentina's recent political history has been lived as a succession of attempts to eradicate or rebuild the Perón legacy, with the occasional (and so far unsuccessful) bid to find a 'third way', which has usually been no more than an attempt to steal that legacy from Perón or from his heirs.

By the end of the 1970s, many of the features of *peronista* rule had been eliminated or distorted beyond recognition, yet no-one would dare forecast that they were gone forever. But three of those features that were . closely related to the Perón image — the Army, the unions, and 'national' industry — though hardly unchanged, were still very much in evidence. It would be a gross overstatement to claim that all three are creatures of Perón. But if he did not actually create them, he certainly did grow up with them, and more than any other single person in Argentine history, was responsible for moulding them into their present form. The story of twentieth-century Argentina is not only the story of Perón and his doings, but it certainly would not make any sense without reference to them.

The old world was flat and had no plants or rivers or lakes or hills. Old Man God saw that the life his children led in this world was a sad one. So he decided to put an end to the old world. He caused the waters to rise over the earth, placing upon it a three-faced hill. He told the serpent to warn the people to climb the hill and be saved from the flood. The hill rose all the way to the heavens, where the sun beat down so strongly that people's skins were scorched brown. Once the old world was finished, Old Man God caused the waters to recede, and he planted the first tree, and then all kinds of plants which began to bear fruit. Then Old Man God shaped the rivers, the lakes, the mountains and the grass-covered prairies, and placed animals close to the people while they slept, that they might use them as they pleased.

Thus, says the Mapuche legend, did their land, the southern tip of South America which we now call Argentina and Chile, come into being. The Guaraní people also remember the flood, but in their case the chosen ones were told by Who-Are-You? to climb a palm-tree. In any case the world the Mapuche and the Guaraní found after the waters had receded was one of excellent climate, with soils of extraordinary fertility bearing much wholesome food and filled with animal life of all kinds. A more recent story has God completing his creation in Argentina, and spilling on this corner of the globe the fertile pampas and the forests, filling the undersoil with mineral wealth and peopling the territory with a wide variety of animals, until a worried angel stayed his hand, saying, 'Heavenly Father, are you not giving this part of the world too much?' To which God replied, chuckling, 'Just you wait and see what kind of people I'm about to put here!' Argentines shift easily from such self-deprecation to fierce and often abrasive pride; from a morose fatalism that depicts the country as an earthly paradise weighed down by some terrible, suicidal curse, to the almost paranoid conviction that Argentina's enormous potential and true destiny of greatness is constantly being thwarted by insidious interference from abroad.

The land is truly beautiful and most bountiful. It is also, by any standards, huge. As schoolchildren, Argentines learn that their territory extends over more than four million square kilometres. This includes the Antarctic sector and the South Orkneys, South Georgia and the South Sandwich islands, which the Argentines consider theirs by right; a claim many outside Argentina find hard to agree with. But even so, the area of continental Argentina (including the Malvinas archipelago, which the British occupy and call Falklands) adds up to 2,789,241 square kilometres, which means that you could fit in the United Kingdom, France, West Germany and Italy, and still have more than half the territory to spare. With some visual imagination, Argentina can be pictured as an isoceles triangle, its ragged base up in the tropics and subtropics, where

at its widest the country measures 1,460 kilometres across, or more than
half the distance between London and Moscow. From the tropical north
to the tip of Tierra del Fuego there are some 3,700 kilometres, about the
same as the distance between London and Cairo. Along the western side
of the country run the massive Andes that separate Argentina from Chile
and account for more than a third of the 9,000 kilometres of land
borders. The rest are, in the north, the frontiers with Bolivia and
Paraguay and, along the eastern side of the triangle, with Brazil and
Uruguay, followed by 4,500 kilometres of coastline lapped by the
Atlantic or, to be more precise, by the Argentine Epicontinental Sea, the
name given to the wide swathe of waters claimed by Argentina long
before others started thinking of a 200-mile exclusive economic zone.

A country of such dimensions is almost impossible to describe
adequately in a few words. Climates vary from the hot subtropical north,
through the ample temperate centre to the dry hot summers and bitterly
cold winters of southern Patagonia. Terrain and vegetation are even
more varied. There is Patagonia in the south with its arid steppes rising
from the Atlantic seaboard to the Andean slopes, with its icy lakes and
cool pine forests that look like Switzerland before the Swiss got at it.
Then the endless pampas of the centre; flat, fertile prairies leading west-
wards to the drier Andean foothills that nurse the world's fourth-largest
wine industry. And the green sierras of mediterranean Córdoba, and the
parched but mineral-laden mountains of Catamarca and La Rioja.
Santiago del Estero has its deserts of dust and salt, while the northwest
has mountains and forests, sugarcane and tobacco. There is the harsh
bush of the Chaco in the centre-north, and the lush rain forest of
Misiones encasing the breathtaking Iguazú falls in the northeast. Swamp
and scrubland, and sometimes palm groves, lead down to rolling *cuchillas*
in the Mesopotamia, the area between the clear waters of the river
Uruguay and the wide lion-brown scar of the Paraná, born somewhere
up in the Brazilian jungle and traversing half a continent before spilling
into the estuary of the river Plate, which is so wide that the opposite
shore can only be seen on a clear day from the top of a twenty-storey
building.

Argentina easily evokes images of waving cornfields and thick juicy
steaks, but grain and beef are just the contribution of the central pampas.
There is certainly much wheat and maize, and oats and barley and rye,
but also, in other regions, grapes and sugarcane, tobacco and cotton, flax
and sunflower, peanuts and tung, tea and *yerba mate*, hops and jute.
There are the vast citrus plantations of Corrientes and the interminable

apple orchards of the Patagonian valleys. And under the surface there is oil and gas, and iron ore, manganese, tungsten, chrome, nickel, molybdenum, copper, lead, zinc, tin, bismuth and gold. And uranium. And coal. There certainly are cows, almost two to every inhabitant, and the horse is part of the classical picture of the gaucho, Argentina's cowboy. But sheep are also to be counted in many millions, and pigs and goats. And Argentina's wilder fauna include the jaguar and the boa constrictor, the condor and the puma, the ostrich and the llama, the *guanaco* and the armadillo, the elephant seal and the penguin. The litany could continue almost forever, getting richer and stranger and more fascinating all the time. It is easy to sympathise with the angel who told God that all this seemed excessive.

The strangeness, however, does not end with the varied geography and its kaleidoscopic contents. This vast, immensely rich triangle of land is mostly empty of human beings. Argentina in 1980 had some 27 million inhabitants, just about ten people for every square kilometre of land. And that is without taking into consideration that just under half the population live in cities of more than 100,000 inhabitants, and that close to 9 million Argentines are crammed into Greater Buenos Aires, the sprawling conurbation embracing the capital. And in this urban agglomeration, and spreading along a belt that winds its way northwards to the cities of Rosario, Santa Fe and Córdoba, the Argentines have built up an industrial economy that contributes twice as much as their bountiful agriculture to the country's gross domestic product. Even more oddly, Argentina has acted for years as if it really did not have those thousands of kilometres of frontiers with neighbouring nations, and thousands more of coastline on the Atlantic — as if the country's only real door to the outside world were the silt-choked port of Buenos Aires. Political and economic decisions are made in Buenos Aires; the cultural establishment irradiates its influence from Buenos Aires; all roads and railways converge on Buenos Aires, where they meet the shipping lanes and air routes to the outer world.

Buenos Aires does not look 'typically' Latin American. True, one can find a few quarters where something remains of the Spanish colonial look of other capitals of the continent. But its downtown architecture once tried to imitate Paris, and more recently, the cities of the United States, while the suburbs are covered with low-lying, nondescript box structures much like those of Italy or Spain. Buenos Aires does not even feel very Latin American; it play-acts at being a city that really belongs somewhere in the northern hemisphere and, although it somehow drifted down to the South Atlantic, is still attached to the parental body by an imaginary umbilical cord.

Argentina was not always like this. Buenos Aires was not always the overpowering centre of everything. Indeed, Buenos Aires was nothing at all when the first Spanish colonists arrived, and no-one can remember if the place even had a name before that.

Spanish colonisation, initiated in the second half of the sixteenth century, concentrated on the northwestern corner of the country, where the colonists established settlements which amounted to a services annex to their silver-mining operations in the highlands of Alto Perú, now Bolivia. The Spaniards mixed rapidly there with the indigenous inhabitants. For a long time, Buenos Aires was no more than a minor port on the edge of the pampas, where wild cattle (the survivors of the first abortive founding of that city) were breeding at an astronomic rate, and where the Pampas Indians held sway, making overland contact with the northern settlements a hazardous affair. To a large extent it was British influence, through the indirect route of contraband, which helped to establish the future capital of Argentina as an increasingly important trading centre. Apart from legal trading and smuggling, the local economy was long based on hunting the wild cattle for their hides.

In time, the traders of Buenos Aires asserted their dominance, persuading the Spanish Crown to wrest the Argentine provinces away from the powerful but unwieldy Vice-Royalty of Perú and creating the new Vice-Royalty of the River Plate, with their own city as capital. Though not painlessly, the country was turned inside out: a peripheral port became the centre while the oldest settlements suddenly became the remote interior.

In the early nineteenth century, British forces captured Buenos Aires in an attempt to incorporate this enormous territory (then comprising Bolivia, Paraguay and Uruguay as well as present-day Argentina) into their own growing empire. Two successive defeats persuaded Britain to change its approach. Canning's policy of bringing 'the New World into existence to redress the balance of the Old' was translated into support for Argentina's bid for independence from Spain, and after this was finally achieved in 1816, into swift commercial penetration of the new republic. It took Buenos Aires long decades of fierce armed struggle to subdue the provinces of the interior, which felt cheated of their rightful share in the running of the country. Indeed their subjugation was only complete when a spider's web of mainly British-owned railways spread out from the capital, smothering the incipient regional economies under a deluge of cheap imported manufactures from Britain.

The nineteenth century saw the growth and consolidation of agricultural Argentina. Cattle ranching replaced cattle hunting as the civil war in the United States revealed that salted beef was as profitable a commodity as cowhides; while grains, first introduced under heavy tariff protection, flourished in the fertile topsoil of the pampas. The outcome of this process was highly unusual: an agricultural country without a large peasantry as a result of the extensive farming methods made possible by the fertility of the pampas; a country with highly developed forms of urban life long before industrialisation. Throughout the nineteenth century, expansion simply meant rolling back the Indian frontier and enlarging the pampas. Argentina even developed a liberal democratic form of government which, though more ostensibly fraudulent, sported roughly the same rates of voter participation as were common in Europe at the time.

When, on the eighth day of October 1895, Juan Domingo Perón was born in the small, flat and dusty pampas township of Lobos in the province of Buenos Aires, the Argentine Army, organised labour and home-bred industry were all in their infancy. It was actually only a few decades earlier that Argentina's internal frontiers had been stretched southwards, by means of a massive military effort, half-way into Patagonia, to the margins of the Río Negro. The pampas, with their legendary six feet of topsoil, were only just getting used to safety from the highly organised raids by Indian war parties, which were the sharp end of a vast cattle-rustling operation that reached across the huge emptiness of the plains to the transversal valleys of the southern Andes and into Chile. Argentine military historians regard the final 'Desert Campaign' against the Indians as the true beginning of a national army, superseding the many warring provincial forces as an instrument of a finally sovereign Argentina that had left behind the decades of federal strife when the powerful city-port of Buenos Aires was wrested in 1880 from the province bearing the same name and made a federal district; a force now acting in the name of all Argentines and extending the writ of federal authority to all corners of the Republic. The Army's task was far from finished with the defeat of the last Indian warlords on the pampas and the Patagonian steppes. Indeed in the very year of Perón's birth the country was steeling itself to meet the threat of armed confrontation with Chile, whose own forces were attempting to move into some of the remote areas vacated by the Indian but not yet controlled by Buenos

Aires. Educated youngsters were being invited to apply for commissions as officers after crash training courses in the new Colegio Militar. And another, messier internal campaign was being finalised close to the northern borders, to subdue the few forest tribes in the Chaco that remained impervious to the call of civilisation.

'Peace and Administration' had been the slogan of the 1880s, a period in which an enlightened élite, drunk with a Spencerian notion of progress, set out to put Argentina on the world map. Underpinning their project was the fertility of the pampas, newly connected to avid markets in the northern hemisphere by means of that recent invention, the refrigerated meat-packing house, and by the rapid spread of its grain-bearing fringe. A railway system, that ultimate icon of progress, was already spreading out from Buenos Aires to the 'interior', linking the port to two other poles of Argentina's 'modern' agrarianism, the sugarcane garden of Tucumán and the wine-producing region of Cuyo. The enthusiastic men of the 1880s felt that they had the formula to make the country give forth its riches. All that was needed was the magic triad of more people (their dream was an Argentina of fifty, or even a hundred million inhabitants in the following half-century), capital investment from abroad, and wholesale introduction of the fruits of European progress.

People, in that huge triangle of land spreading out from slightly north of the Tropic of Capricorn to the rim of the Antarctic, were vital to this scheme. Just as the Army that would give Perón his career was only beginning to take shape at the time of his birth, more than two-thirds of the population that would witness his arrival at the Presidency in 1946 simply were not there in 1895. Not that Argentina's population had failed to grow — it had multiplied tenfold since the Spaniards arrived in the sixteenth century. But Argentina's demographic 'take-off' had been slow in coming. There had been perhaps slightly more than 300,000 aborigines when the Spaniards came; just under three centuries later, when Argentina proclaimed its independence from Spain, its population was roughly estimated at 550,000. Acceleration began, not surprisingly, towards the middle of the nineteenth century, when the first waves of impoverished, ambitious or persecuted Europeans began to pour across the oceans. It was a period of mass migrations worldwide, and Argentina was one of their American targets. By 1855 there were more than a million people in Argentina, and they kept coming, even if political instability, civil strife and war with Paraguay persuaded many of the new arrivals to retrace their steps. By 1880, with the land pacified, immigration was in full swing, and the national census of 1895 revealed a population of 3,955,000. They were coming mainly from Italy and from Spain, from the areas left behind when those countries began to modernise their agriculture, but also from France, fleeing the failed experiment of the Paris Commune, from Central Europe, and from Britain, accompanying the railways and the many other manifestations of English capital investment. The time was drawing near when three out of every ten people in the country would be foreign-born.

They had come initially, in the words of the official slogan, to 'people the desert', attracted by the often explicit promise of a plot of land, a farm of their own. In the vision of the men of the 1880s, the immigrants would form a new community of small landowners, applying the farming skills of Europe to the most fertile soil in the world. The vision did not quite fit the reality that awaited the immigrants. Only in a few areas of the littoral, in the provinces of Santa Fe and Entre Ríos, did the new agrarian *colonias* manage to take root. Land, which had first been taken freely in county-sized portions and later — after the 'Desert Campaign' — had been distributed with equal munificence, became an object of financial speculation. Only a small percentage of the land bonds given out as prizes to the soldiers were kept by them; the rest were negotiated on an open, land-hungry market. Rapidly rising prices barred most immigrants from anything but tenant-farming and sharecropping at best, or becoming occasionally employed labourers at worst. Their role was to act as pasture improvers for the big cattle ranchers, cheaply creating a cycle with a periodic yield of useful alfalfa. Not surprisingly, many began to drift towards the cities. They had no means of knowing it, but they were repeating, on a larger scale, the exodus of the once free-ranging gaucho, who had been driven out of the open countryside by the spread of that other icon of progress, barbed wire. By 1895, only one-third of the foreigners in Argentina were engaged in agriculture; the remainder were working in industry and services.

This was not the only flaw in the dream of the 1880s. Certainly 'progress' was visible; in that decade national revenue trebled, shipping tonnage in Argentine ports increased fourfold, exports doubled in value, the banks' assets swelled by 50 per cent. A significant feature of this rapid growth was the impressive inflow of foreign investment, especially from Britain, which shot up from £25 million a year before 1880 to £45 million in 1885. Railway lines were growing by hundreds of kilometres at a time, modern port installations were appearing, and the cities, particularly Buenos Aires, were swiftly acquiring the elegant looks and sophisticated amenities of their European counterparts. Yet under this façade things were not so solid. The enlightened landed oligarchy of Argentina tended to invest their own money in the externals of progress and in dizzying speculation on the stock exchange and in land, leaving the grimier side of modernisation to the foreigner. In James Scobie's words, it was left to Great Britain to become 'the Argentine Republic's banker, stockbroker, railway builder and supplier'. What the men of the 1880s had built was an efficient machine designed on the one hand to extract and export Argentina's agricultural produce rapidly and cheaply, and on the other to introduce British manufactures equally rapidly and cheaply. Basic Ricardo. But they handed over the running of the machine to the British, and instead of ploughing back their own easy profits into technification and modernisation, they squandered them on the trappings of modernity. Purchasing the 'fruits of progress' instead of actually producing them turned out to be an expensive proposition. In spite of growing exports, the balance of trade kept running into the red, and the insatiable thirst for more 'modernity' was increasingly quenched by heavy borrowing abroad.

Before the golden decade of the 1880s was out, Argentina was hit by two severe financial crises. In 1885 the only remedy was to turn to London banks for a massive loan of £8,400,000, putting up the country's Customs revenue as collateral. A couple of years later the only solution a harrassed government could produce was to put up for sale, on European markets, some 24,000 leagues of state-owned land in Patagonia.

Local manufacturing contributed very little to the wave of 'progress' launched in the 1880s. Disregarding the experience of Britain and the United States, Argentina's rulers did little to promote its growth. Their lack of interest was justified publicly on two grounds: first, a slavish adherence to the principles of free trade which took no account of how the countries that had originally embraced this doctrine had themselves evolved; and secondly, the conviction that it was not the government's job to interfere with the workings of commerce (a notion they somehow did not feel compelled to apply to the government's very active participation in the attraction of immigrants and foreign investors, for whom they offered all sorts of incentives and concessions). 'My opinion', said President Roca in 1880, 'is that commerce knows far better than government what is in its own best interests; true politics, then, must consist in granting commerce the widest possible freedom. The state should limit itself to establishing the means of communication, linking the capital cities by means of railway lines, stimulating navigation on the great waterways [. . .], holding up high the public credit abroad [and] as for immigration, we must protect it at all costs.'

By the time Perón was born, manufacturing accounted for less than one-tenth of the country's income; according to the 1895 census there were only 22,204 industrial establishments with 2,348 machines among them, employing 145,650 people. Most of these industrial establishments were tiny shops making foodstuffs, clothing or toiletry articles, small-scale metallurgy or construction. It is worth noting, though, that the census did not classify as 'industry' the many activities that added some stages of processing to the produce of the land, such as the meat-salting plants, the distilleries and breweries, the flour and sugar mills or the wine industry. These totalled another 1,890 establishments, employing a far larger (but often seasonal) contingent of workers and attracting a far larger share of capital invesment: an average of some 92,000 pesos each, compared with an average of 13,000 pesos for the 'industrial' firms. Averages aside, the highest concentration of capital was in the meat-salting plants and the sugar mills, where a mere ninety establishments took a full fifth of all the capital.

Among the establishments classified as 'industrial', eight out of every ten were owned by foreigners; the same was true of the breweries and the wine industry, while about half of the flour mills were foreign–owned. Only among the meat-salting plants and the sugar mills were Argentine proprietors in a clear majority. The pattern was similar in the workforce: Argentines were a majority in the activities most closely linked to agriculture, but more than six out of every ten workers in industry had been born abroad.

In some cases, like the British-owned railways, it was deliberate policy not to employ natives. But on the whole the divide reflected the skills present in each segment of the community. The gaucho who had in earlier years drifted into the cities, well-versed as he was in the ways of the pampas, found little to suit his talents in the new urban activities; literature has his dexterous use of the *facón* (his long-bladed knife) leading him inexorably towards the slaughterhouses and meat-packing plants, but a colder economic appraisal finds him taking whatever unskilled job was on offer. For many the Army was the only, often unwanted, source of employment. The same, of course, held true for many of the immigrants from rural areas in Spain and Italy. Although statistics of the period show that more than seven out of every ten immigrants had a trade or craft, it must be remembered that farming skills were then considered of vital importance and were included quite naturally in this category. It has also been suggested that many would-be immigrants exaggerated their qualifications in the statements made to the Republic's agents in Europe, in the hope of receiving more favourable treatment. Yet even when this is taken into account, at least one out of every ten immigrants who arrived between 1860 and 1890 can be identified as a person with some sort of urban skills. After 1890, with the fading of the dreams of large-scale rural colonisation, their numbers began to increase sharply, until by the turn of the century they represented one out of every three arrivals. Among them were brick layers, seamstresses, dressmakers, carpenters and cabinet-makers, electricians, photographers, blacksmiths, tinkers, boiler makers, machinists, mechanics, millers, pasta-makers and bakers, stonemasons, painters, glaziers, watchmakers, tailors, haberdashers, tanners, telegraphists, printers, coopers, metalworkers, shoemakers, butchers, chauffeurs, gardeners, barbers and seamen.

The European immigrants brought with them not only their crafts and trades but also their political ideas; their Proudhon, Marx and Bakunin; their notions of how industrial societies should be organised and, above all, their unknowing acceptance of their own histories and modes of social coexistence, which the enlightened Argentine élite of the 1880s were to present to their own countrymen as models of civilisation and progress. There was, in a sense, an easy identification of the immigrant with this facet of the Argentine 'project of the 1880s', a common language built from the traditions of the immigrants and the rhetoric of the men who had enticed them across the ocean. Yet it was a common language that made for much misunderstanding. It was a mixing together of a reality inherited by the immigrants and a mirage fabricated by their hosts. In Buenos Aires the new arrivals were settling (to use a metaphor from the following century) into the fake store-fronts of a Hollywood set; they and their hosts could prefer to ignore what lay behind, beyond the reach of the cameras; to discard it as irrelevant to the civilised play they were acting out together. But it was there: the native population with its own history, forged in three centuries of colonial rule, in the wars of independence, in the long struggle between Buenos Aires and the provinces of the interior, in the war with the Indian, in the fencing of the pampas. Behind the set was a political tradition expressed not by the writings of Proudhon, Marx and Bakunin, but in the epic poem *Martín Fierro*, written by José Hernández, that tells the story of the uprooting of the gaucho, his conscription into the landowners' army, the destruction of rural family life, and the subterranean, hopeless rebellion of the erstwhile free horseman who is forced to choose between being labelled as an outlaw and a vagrant or bowing to the new servitude of paid employment. For the new Argentines from across the ocean and the local élite wearing its 'modern' mask, this was no more than a relic from a past soon to be buried forever, at best suitable to be preserved as a colourful curiosity. The newspaper *La Prensa*, which decades later would awaken to the political content of the poem, was the first to serialise it, commenting, 'It is very original for the scenes it describes in so masterly a fashion and for its profound observation of the customs and details, however insignificant but always curious, of the gaucho's way of life.'

There was another area of misunderstanding behind the common language of modernity. The ruling élite acted as if it expected the workers brought across from Europe to blend into their façade of progress quietly, without acting as working classes tended to do in their home countries. Worker associations were considered wholly unnecessary, when they were not considered demonic inventions of 'agitators and dissociators' from abroad. In at least one sense Argentina's rulers were not far from the mark. Apart from a few hardly notable attempts at setting up mutual aid associations, the first real exercises in worker organisation were of a decidedly political nature, and their avowed purpose was the dismantling of capitalism. In 1872 the pioneer 'sections' of the First International made their appearance in Buenos Aires. Reflecting the weight of the immigrant community, they chose to organise into language groups: first the French, then the Italian, then the Spanish. It was a short-lived venture which fell apart when faced with official repression. Only a year after the creation of the French section, a fire broke out in the classy, Jesuit-run Colegio del Salvador. The blame was almost instantly placed on foreign anarchists, and the police lost no time in raiding the offices of the local sections of the International and imprisoning their leaders. Ironically, this pioneering venture helped to convince the factory owners that it was in their own best interests to organise themselves, and the Club Industrial came into being.

But discontent among the workers did not need much stirring from abroad. Hardly anyone worked less than eleven hours a day, and fourteen- to sixteen-hour stints were quite common. In the interior, on the sugarcane estates and *yerba mate* plantations, in the logging camps and the vineyards, people were paid with vouchers which could only be redeemed in the company stores, where constant price increases and 'liberal' credit policies created a cycle of permanent indebtedness, almost impossible to evade in a working lifetime. Overcrowding in company lodgings, poor food and low pay fostered widespread anaemia and tuberculosis. Only by comparison with this rural scene could it be said that life in the cities was attractive. The urban working day was certainly no shorter, and a day's wage in the mid-1880s did not go very far; at best it was equivalent to the price of 8 kilos of bread; at worst, only 4. And that was when work was available round the year, a situation enjoyed by only one out of every four urban workers. Statisticians, with their love of averages, will tell you that the typical worker of the 1880s was employed for 257 days of 10 hours each out of every year; there was usually a mass of about 10,000 unemployed. Living conditions were indeed better than in the countryside, but at the beginning of the decade in Buenos Aires some 50,000 people were crowded, often five or six to a room, into just under 2,000 tenements, or *conventillos*. Seven years later both the number of *conventillos* and their population had doubled. And inflation kept eating away at people's purchasing power (according to one calculation, the real value of the average pay packet was actually halved during the late 1880s and early 1890s), while the financial straits of government often left the country's growing civil service waiting for months on end for their salaries to be paid.

The typographers were the first to organise a proper union, the Unión Tipográfica, in 1872, and the first to go on strike, protesting the fact that one of their members had had his wages cut. From then on, unionisation began to spread at a fair pace: the shop assistants were organised in 1880; the bakers, millers and bricklayers in 1881; the tailors and plasterers in 1882 (the same year as the German workers established the Vorwärts club, which was to become one of the ideological powerhouses of the labour movement); the upholsterers, river pilots, butlers and coachmen, postmen and marble-workers in 1883; the carpenters and cabinet-makers in 1885. In most cases, the formation of the union and the call to strike were almost simultaneous. Success, in spite of the firm anti-union stance taken by employers and government alike, was considerable. Nor was the movement confined to the great city-port of Buenos Aires; throughout the decade, unionisation and strikes were reported up the river in the cities of Paraná and Rosario, in the central city of Córdoba, in the pampas township of Tandil, and even as far north as the sugarcane province of Tucumán.

Blood, says the legend, was first drawn in 1888, a year after the locomotive drivers and stokers had formed their union, La Fraternidad. A rally was held at Plaza Herrera, in Buenos Aires, to launch a strike.

The assembly was dispersed by a picket of firemen (the riot-control force of the day) armed with Remington rifles. Many of the demonstrators were wounded, and at least 160 were arrested. The following year, with 3,000 carpenters and 6,000 bricklayers out on strike, the Vorwärts club despatched one of its leaders, Alejo Peyret, to attend the International Workers' Congress in Paris. On his return an International Workers' Committee was set up in Buenos Aires with a mandate to organise the First of May celebrations and to further the cause of unity among worker organisations. Threats from employers and government officials did not deter them, and only two months after a successful May Day rally, they managed to amalgamate most of the existing unions in the Federación de Trabajadores de la Región Argentina. A petition was sent to Congress, calling on the deputies to enact legislation establishing an eight-hour working day, a thirty-six-hour weekly period of rest, compulsory assurance against accidents at work, a ban on the employment of children under fourteen, and special rules for the employment of women and young people.

The growth of the Federación was interrupted soon after its creation by an attempted revolution in 1890 (of which more later). Ten worker associations were visibly involved in the anti-government conspiracy, a fact which brought down on all and sundry the ensuing police repression. The mood of the day was perhaps best captured in the name of a new journal launched by the anarchists that year: *El Perseguido* (The Persecuted). Indeed a large portion of its contents dealt with cases of police persecution and imprisonment of union militants. The anarchists were very strong in the biggest unions, yet most of the leading lights of the Federación were socialists, which made for constant squabbling over tactics, and especially over the role of political and strike action in the labour movement. The socialists felt that the government, and especially Congress, could be pressured into enacting the reforms demanded by the unions; the anarchists rejected any form whatever of dealings with the state, and advocated a build-up of strike action leading to the definitive 'revolutionary general strike'. These opposing attitudes led to the dissolution of the Federación in 1892, only months after it had managed to produce its one concrete action: a declaration of adherence to the principles of the International Workers' Congress held in Paris. Efforts to patch up differences were again interrupted, in 1894, by another armed uprising against the government, but in the following year the socialists engineered the establishment of a new umbrella body, the Federación Obrera Argentina. It too was torn apart by the same sort of dissension as before. Yet if the anarchists were proving themselves powerful enough to prevent a socialist takeover of the labour movement, they did not enjoy the same success in persuading Argentina's urban workers to try out their own revolutionary formula. In 1895, the year of Perón's birth, a call went out for a general strike: only nineteen of the thirty-six Buenos Aires unions responded.

At the time of Perón's birth, the Argentine political scene was undergoing an important change. Over the previous fifteen years the country itself had been transformed, and old confrontations were giving way to new ones. General Julio Argentino Roca, 'the conqueror of the Desert', is seen by many as the man who inaugurated a thirty-six-year period of oligarchic rule in 1880, after putting an end to the age-old confrontation between the rich city-port of Buenos Aires, with its wealthy cattle-ranching province, and the rest of the country. Indeed Roca's power was twofold. There was the budding national Army, whipped together from the many, often rival provincial forces and steeled by the victorious campaigns against the Indian. This was the force Roca used to subdue the last armed attempt by the Buenos Aires landowners, headed by former President Bartolomé Mitre, to resist the federalisation of their city, the historic capital of Argentina. Politically, his backing came from the 'League of Governors', the sum of the many provincial 'autonomist' movements which he would eventually weld into his Partido Autonomista Nacional for his successful assault on the Presidency.

It might have seemed as if the old struggle between the 'revolutionaries' of the port and the 'conservatives' of the provinces, between the 'unitarists' who wanted to centralise all power in Buenos Aires and the 'federals' of the interior, had suddenly been settled — and in favour of the provinces. Yet it was not quite so. Roca certainly did embody the demand for a share of the power hitherto wielded so exclusively by Buenos Aires, but this demand did not actually extend to sharing it out equitably with the entire Republic. His strength came from the élites of the provinces nearest to the city-port, the regions that the railways and the waves of immigration had incorporated more fully into Argentina's new role as efficient agrarian appendix of industrial Europe. The provinces of Córdoba and Santa Fe and Entre Ríos had been physically hitched up with the Buenos Aires bandwagon, and were now demanding, through Roca, a greater say in the running of the country. They got their share, but Buenos Aires was hardly defeated. The city-port and its attendant pampa powerbase would eventually absorb Roca and

his men, converting them and the provinces of the Littoral to the outlook of the *porteño*, the man of the port. Exegetes have found in the
thinking of some of Roca's men, and especially in Carlos Pellegrini, the
wish to break away from the simple Buenos Aires formula of 'sell grain
and beef, buy manufactures'. But beyond lip-service to the ideal of a
different, more autonomous project, and a few hardly earth-shattering
government initiatives, everything was left as it was. The high concentration of land ownership remained untouched, local industry was
ignored, and money was allowed to flow unchecked towards conspicuous consumption and all forms of speculation.

Small wonder, then, that many of the 'autonomist' elements who had
backed Roca against Mitre should have begun to drift away, disappointed, from the ruling party. And when it became clear that Roca
was in the business of perpetuating the rule of a clique (his brother-in-
law Miguel Juárez Celman was already being groomed for the highest
office through a spell in the governorship of Córdoba, followed by a stint
in the Senate), the split began to deepen until, by the time the country
was preparing for the 1886 elections, a large number of former *roquistas*
were to be found in the opposition. Roca's adversaries united behind a
single opposition candidate, but to no avail. The government resorted to
wholesale electoral fraud and violence, arresting prominent members of
the opposition, wrecking their houses, and breaking up their rallies and
demonstrations. In the northwestern province of Catamarca the authorities boasted openly that they had killed thirty adversaries, wounded
eighty and arrested 240 to ensure electoral victory. In Buenos Aires,
Customs workers were trucked around from one polling station to
another to cast their votes many times over in favour of the government's candidate.

Miguel Juárez Celman became President. With him fraud became the
established practice in local elections; the threat of federal 'intervention'
was used as a deterrent to independent action by provincial administrations; and there was a clear attempt to turn the Army into a political
force. Fraud was not new in Argentine electoral experience; the novelty
lay in the scale on which it began to be applied. Argentina's democracy
had previously been exclusive, but not much more so than its European
counterparts in their early years. Indeed it was pointed out at the time
that voter participation was much the same on both sides of the Atlantic.
The people who got elected to Congress or appointed to the more
political posts in the administration were likely to belong to the same
small circle. In all probability their families had been settled in

generations, and there would be a history of family association with
political power.

The country's growth in the second half of the nineteenth century was
not limited to the massive inflow of immigrants and the phenomenal
increase in the country's export earnings. There was inordinate expansion of the cities and, within the cities, of government and private
services designed to facilitate and administer the working of this
lucrative agrarian money machine. The rulers of nineteenth-century
Argentina had been great believers in education, and had ensured the
spread of the written word, first through an early primary schools
system, then through the Colegios Nacionales, the secondary institutions established to turn out cadres of *bachilleres*, young men trained for
positions of leadership in the growing state apparatus. Some would go
on to university, to emerge later with a doctorate, preferably in law,
which would ensure their access to the higher echelons of the administration. In a rapidly growing country, these were mechanisms that made
for great social mobility. Rising in social status was visibly possible, and
the immigrant's dream of *'M'ijo el dotor'* ('My son the Doctor') was the
driving force behind many a career.

Long before it had much of an industry of its own, Argentina had
spawned a huge middle class. Members of the liberal professions, traders,
shopkeepers, small farmers, the hosts of *bachilleres*, factory owners — all
shared to an extent in the expansion of Argentina's agriculture and trade,
all shared the ideals of civilisation and progress embraced by the ruling
élites. But beyond the right to vote, for what it was worth, they were
not given a real share of political power. The organisation which was to
begin to offer this marginalised middle class a political expression of its
own started to take shape in the mounting opposition to the Juárez
Celman régime. Outspoken youths of the middle strata, bent on
demanding respect for the democratic principles enshrined in the Constitution, formed the Unión Cívica de la Juventud, whose driving force
was a firebrand called Leandro Alem. Because their demands had a
target — the abuses of the Juárez Celman administration — their cause
soon became a focal point for all forms of opposition to the government,
and it was not long before they had formed an alliance with Bartolomé
Mitre, the old standard-bearer of the Buenos Aires oligarchs in their
struggle against Roca's autonomists, and their organisation lost part of
its name, becoming simply the Unión Cívica.

Alem believed that nothing short of revolution would further their
aims; Mitre, on the other hand, saw the Unión Cívica as a springboard to

his comeback as a presidential candidate, a credible power base from which he could negotiate effectively with the ruling clique. Indeed he was aware that Juárez Celman's excesses had actually estranged him from his brother-in-law, General Roca, thus opening a number of avenues for compromise. So when it became clear that Alem was embarking on preparations for an armed uprising, Mitre took himself off for a long trip to Europe. Juárez Celman's use of the Army for his own political ends had created much unease among sectors of the military, and they too began to conspire, in secret *logias* (lodges), of which the most important met frequently in the house of a young sub-lieutenant, José Félix Uriburu. Prominent among the young militants of the Unión Cívica who threw themselves wholeheartedly into preparing the downfall of the régime was one Hipólito Yrigoyen. The paths of both these men, Uriburu and Yrigoyen, would cross again, in very different circumstances, but now they were on the same side. It was not a hard task to enlist support, civilian and military, for the conspiracy: the economy was in a mess, the collapse of the wool market in Britain had deprived Argentina of much-needed hard currency earnings, and with a rising foreign debt the country was rapidly reaching the point at which default seemed to be a very real option. Inflation and social discontent were running high, and the administration seemed to be getting more desperate and more arbitrary as time passed.

In July 1890 the revolutionaries massed their forces, civilian and military, near the centre of Buenos Aires. Juárez Celman left the capital, while Roca and Carlos Pellegrini rushed to take charge of the régime's defence. For an unexplained reason the insurgents did not strike early, when their superiority was undisputed. Instead they gave the government time to muster its own forces, and by the time hostilities broke out, the balance had shifted in the other direction. The revolution was short-lived; after recording more than 1,000 casualties, the rebels capitulated. Yet, as a Congressman commented days later, the government had not emerged victorious. In August Juárez Celman resigned and handed over power to his Vice-President, Carlos Pellegrini. The new ruler lost no time in sorting out the country's financial difficulties, mainly through deals with its main creditors in London; deals which nationalists would describe later as a complete sell-out of Argentine economic sovereignty.

But Pellegrini was not to have much peace. In 1891 another uprising took place, in the central province of Córdoba, to be suppressed only after twenty-three people had died and 171 had been injured. No sooner had the shots faded away than Catamarca — the province where Juárez

Celman's partisans had imposed themselves so bloodily — rose in arms, temporarily wresting control of the governorship from the régime's appointee. As foreseen by Mitre, the régime then began to seek some formula for an orderly, agreed succession, and called in the Unión Cívica as party to the negotiations. Inevitably this led to a split in the Unión Cívica: Mitre opted for agreement with the régime while Alem stuck to his demands for open, free elections. His opposition to the 'agreement' proposed by Pellegrini and Mitre, said Alem, was 'radical' and 'intransigent'. Both terms would become part of the folklore of his wing of the party, which regrouped under the name of Unión Cívica Radical. Mitre's faction riposted by calling itself Unión Cívica Nacional, a rather cruel irony coming from the man who had so stubbornly resisted the establishment of national rule over the capital city of Buenos Aires. Pellegrini was not easily put off his course; after all, experience had shown the ruling oligarchy that the best way to deal with forceful new-comers to the political scene was to absorb them.

So he insisted on seeking out the ideal compromise candidate and calling on the recalcitrant Radicals to join all others in an agreed formula. Wooing the Radicals did not prove easy; they absolutely refused to be tempted with participation in kingmaking or with the promise of slices of power, obstinately repeating that it was not the President's task, or theirs, to impose a successor on the Republic. That, they insisted, was what elections were for. During one decisive encounter between Pellegrini and the young representative of the Radicals, Hipólito Yrigoyen, their demand was stated for the umpteenth time: 'The President must put himself in his proper place!' Pellegrini retorted, 'But how, Doctor Yrigoyen, can you expect me to put myself in my place when I can already feel on my face the heat of the revolution your party is preparing against me?' 'If the President of the Republic does his duty and guarantees the elections,' said Yrigoyen, 'he will see that no revolution is going to burn his face!' Negotiations came to an abrupt end.

The Radicals threw themselves into an organising frenzy throughout the country, but when election day came in 1892, blatant fraud ensured the victory of Luis Sáenz Peña, a seventy-year-old man who had finally been selected as the régime's heir-designate after the previous choice, his son Roque, had been vetoed as 'too much of a modernist'. Conspiracy again became the password for the Radicals, and in 1893 they launched uprisings in the provinces of San Luis, Santa Fe and Buenos Aires. Eight hundred of them were arrested and transported across the River Plate to exile in Uruguay. But from Montevideo, Hipólito Yrigoyen continued to direct the semi-clandestine organising activities of the Unión Cívica Radical, achieving almost instant success in some provincial elections. The following two years witnessed a spectacular growth of the Radical party, reflected in a succession of victories in the elections of national deputies and senators.

At the beginning of 1895 a tired and enfeebled Luis Sáenz Peña resigned the Presidency. Vice-President José Evaristo Uriburu stepped in, on 23 January, to complete the remaining three years of his term. Just under nine months later, in the pampas township of Lobos, Juana Sosa gave birth to her second son, who was called Juan Domingo Perón.

2

RISE OF THE LITTLE MEN
(1895–1916)

Perón's background was what would now be described as typically Argentine. On his father's side, he was of Sardinian stock; his great-grandfather — the son, according to Perón's own reminiscences, of a Sardinian 'dissident' or independence fighter — was a relatively early emigrant to Argentina in 1860. Perón's grandfather, Tomás Luis, followed the upward route offered by Argentina's school system and became a medical doctor. He also got involved in the provincial politics of Buenos Aires, and as a supporter of Bartolomé Mitre won a seat in the Senate. For his own son, Mario Tomás, he had wished a similar career in medicine, but the young man, an adventurous character with too many interests to be confined in the straitjacket of a profession, gave up his studies for a freer life in the countryside. He was able to use Dr Perón's considerable political influence to get an appointment as a *Juez de Paz*, literally 'Justice of the Peace', an office that combined some of the duties of a district magistrate with the more habitual task of conferring legal formality on a number of commercial and administrative transactions. It was not an occupation that would hold Mario Tomás Perón for too long.

Mario Tomás had two sons. The first, Mario Avelino, was born in 1891; the second was Juan Domingo, born four years later. Their mother, Juana Sosa, clearly showed her Indian blood in her high cheekbones, shiny black hair rising from a low forehead, and short, stocky build. Acquaintances have recalled her claim that both her parents were *indios*, and although the term was and is used loosely, embracing the many forms of miscegenation that took place on Argentine soil from the arrival of the Spaniards, this would not have been too unusual in Lobos. Though only about 100 kilometres from Buenos Aires, Lobos is close to the Salado river, which cuts diagonally across the northeast of the province and was, until well into the 1830s, the real frontier with Indian territory. Not far from there, in earlier days, passed one of the main *rastrilladas*, the Indian trails that led off southwards towards the northern Patagonian provinces. Lobos was a staging point for the columns of cavalry marching to the outer line of forts, and for the herds of cattle being driven to the Buenos Aires slaughterhouses. Laid out in the traditional Spanish checkerboard pattern around a plaza, there was little save the church and the uninspiring town hall to relieve the monotony of single-storey, U- or L-shaped houses, shuttered to the dust and heat of the streets, their true faces turned inwards to the cool shade of the tiled and often-swept patios. Politics was often discussed in the Perón household, but the memory that stuck vaguely in Juan Domingo's mind was that of the old veterans reminiscing about the war with Paraguay, which had ended painfully in 1870, a full five years after a bellicose Bartolomé Mitre had boasted, 'In three days we shall be in the barracks, in three weeks on the battlefield, and in three months in Asunción.'

When Juan Domingo was five, his father decided to try his fortune in the extreme south of the country, as a farmer. The move was almost the same as travelling to another country. Their destination, the estate known by the strange name of Chan Iaike, was near the town of Río Gallegos, in the province of Santa Cruz, practically 2,000 kilometres south of Buenos Aires. There the child Juan Domingo and his elder brother Mario would learn about chasing the *peludo*, or armadillo; about hunting those two strange relatives of the deer, the *mara*, whose tiny hooves belied its popular name of 'Patagonian hare', and the *guanaco*, that looks like a speedy llama. Where the endless pampas had earlier suggested a sea of green that would turn ochre with the heat, or golden with the ripening of some grain, southern Patagonia would present the equally endless plateaux, but clothed in a perpetual murky brown, with only the occasional splashes of yellow, white and red from the hardy flowers and berries that would sprout amid the desert shrubs. His first real friend, he would recall many years later, was a horse tamer who went by the name of Sixto Magallanes, an almost mythical remembrance of the Portuguese navigator who first found the way round those deserted shores. In his own inimitable style, Perón would claim that it was from this man that he heard the first pearl of *criollo* wisdom (one of the many he would use so frequently during his later political career): 'It is better to learn good things than to learn a lot.' Juan Domingo would tag along as his father, together with a scientifically-minded son of German immigrants, Cristóbal Sicke, set off along the steppes and gulleys of Santa Cruz to compile one of the first classifications of Patagonian flora. He must have been seven or eight when his father gave him his first truly treasured present, a .22 calibre rifle, the symbol of the pioneer's mastery over the raw wilds of the south.

Mario Tomás's first venture in Patagonian farming was not a success.

When he heard that the governor of the province of Chubut was offering land grants almost 1,000 kilometres nearer Buenos Aires, he leapt at the opportunity and moved his family northwards. They settled near Camarones (the name means 'shrimps'), a coastal location not far from Comodoro Rivadavia, which would soon become the centre of Argentina's oil industry. But in those days this was emerging as an ideal sheep-farming area, producing the finest Merino-type wool of the country. 'Ideal' should be understood in relative, peculiarly Patagonian terms. The arid, low-lying coastal steppes could only support, on average, one sheep per hectare-and-a-half (nowadays farmers in the area consider that it is uneconomic to have less than 5,000 sheep, so the region sports the unusual spectacle of 'smallholdings' covering no less than 750,000 hectares). The scenery was not all that different from Santa Cruz; the winters were bitterly cold (though the latitude of Camarones, south of the Equator, is not very far from that of the Côte d'Azur to the north), the summers were hot, and the winds were blowing all the time. There was the toughening experience of frostbite, which once turned Juan Domingo's toenails blue and withered them óff. The same *guanacos* and *maras* and *peludos* were there to be hunted; there were penguins and sea lions and killer whales to be watched off the coast.

Yet Juan Domingo was not given much time to enjoy this new location. He was very nearly ten when they settled there, and his father was well aware that the improvised schooling he had received so far would not be sufficient if the young Perón was to make headway in an Argentina that set such store on education. So Juan Domingo was packed off to Buenos Aires, as his brother had been earlier, to live with a couple of maiden aunts, doña Vicenta and doña Baldomena. Juan Domingo's destination was a school run by the priests of La Merced, whose efforts were supplemented enthusiastically by his two aunts, with whom he would remember walking through the cloisters while they taught him to read the Breviary. His elder brother Mario did not take well to the change from the parched dryness of Patagonia to the constant humidity of Buenos Aires, and fell prey to pleurisy, whereupon he was shipped back to the farm. The idea was that he would return to Buenos Aires when he was fully recovered, but his absence was to last whole decades, until Juan Domingo had become President, and Mario was appointed director of the Buenos Aires zoo.

For his secondary schooling Juan Domingo was sent to the Colegio Internacional Politécnico, in the suburban district of Olivos, nowadays one of the most exclusive areas of the Greater Buenos Aires, in those days considered quite a distance from the capital. Though not reputed to be among the 'best' schools, it was a strict, efficient institution, favoured by the up-and-coming middle class; small landowners, professionals, immigrants with ambitions for their children. A 'day-boy', Juan Domingo lived with several of his schoolmates in a *pensión*. His early years on the Patagonian farms made him a natural for sports, while on the academic side he himself would later admit to being '*un uomo qualunque*', just one of the crowd. History seems to have been the only subject that really captivated him, and especially the lives of Julius Caesar and Napoleon; not only did he devour anything Napoleonic that he could lay his hands on in the school library, but he also penned down short essays which he read to his schoolmates in the *pensión* at night.

Choosing a career was not one of his major preoccupations during most of his time at the Colegio Internacional Politécnico. He had taken it more or less for granted that he would follow in his grandfather's footsteps and study medicine; indeed in his old age he boasted that he would have made a pretty good doctor, although a deep mistrust of the medical profession had been one of his most noticeable characteristics throughout his life. It was only towards the end of his schooldays that he began to be attracted by the idea of following some of his mates into the Army. One of his uncles was a captain, and another had been assimilated with the same rank into the military as a teacher at an Army training school. But on this matter Juan Domingo made up his mind on his own, and one fine day told his parents that he intended to sit for the entrance examinations of the Colegio Militar, the already quite prestigious officer training college. They approved. Having graduated from the Colegio Internacional Politécnico as a *bachiller*, it was no great feat to tackle a curriculum which called for knowledge of arithmetic and algebra (up to first degree equations), plane geometry, lineal drawing, Spanish grammar, Greek and Roman history, general and American geography, and French. In 1911, Juan Domingo Perón was admitted into the Colegio Militar with marks that placed him forty-seventh in a class of 110.

Ahead of him lay three years of further study, one common to all cadets and two specialising in the skills of his chosen branch of the service, the infantry. These were years in which the armies of South America had chosen the Prussian military ethos as a model, and several of Perón's instructors were German officers seconded to the Argentine Army. One of these was General Wilhelm von Faupel, who was later appointed Inspector-General of the Argentine Army (and even later occupied the same position in the armies of Chile and Bolivia). Von Faupel would return to Germany shortly before the outbreak of the Second World War, and his country put his intimate acquaintance with

South American military to good use by stationing him at that notable crossroads, the German embassy in neutral Spain. Close-order drill, tactics, regulations; all were carbon copies of whatever happened to be fashionable in Germany at the time. Perón took to this environment like a fish to water. Here, unlike his previous experience at the Colegio Internacional Politécnico, he set out to be the best. But his dedication to academic excellence (more the product of taming his quick intelligence than of hard work) did not detract from his fraternising with the rest of the boys. His love of sport had not diminished; he was well on his way to being one of the Colegio's best boxers when a fractured finger forced him to concentrate instead on fencing, at which he became the undisputed champion. Although he had chosen to become an infantryman, he continued to feel at home on horseback and to practice equestrian sports. But then, infantry officers in those days did not take much to muddying their boots; they tended to direct from the saddle while the ranks did the walking. And Perón was very much a ladies' man; good-looking and charming, he was much sought after as a companion for partying and philandering. His wild oats, of course, were sown in the fashion of the time, as befitted a man who was on his way to becoming an officer and a gentleman. 'When we were young,' he was to reminisce from his exile in Madrid, 'we didn't often go to social parties, nor would it have crossed our minds to go to a private house and make love with a girl from a good family. We went dancing with hired women; it was with them that we danced and had our parties and made love. [. . .] We danced a lot, and were good dancers; we had learned in the cabarets with hired women.'

When his three years were up, in 1913, at the top of his class and still the college's fencing champion, Juan Domingo Perón received his commission as sub-lieutenant. He was immediately posted to the 12th Infantry Regiment, stationed in Paraná, capital of the province of Entre Ríos. Juan Domingo Perón was eighteen years old. As a graduation gift his father presented him with three books which would thereafter never leave his side. One was the *Martín Fierro*, José Hernández's saga of the disappearing gaucho, of which many critics say Perón would best assimilate the counsels of *El Viejo Vizcacha*, a wizened old rogue who recites to Fierro, the hero, a compendium of cunning gaucho wisdom. The other two were translations, of Plutarch's *Lives* and Lord Chesterfield's *Letters to His Son*, the collection of worldly advice which, according to Samuel Johnson, taught 'the morals of a whore and the manners of a dancing master'. On the first page of each book was inscribed his father's intentions in selecting them: *Martín Fierro*, 'So that you may never forget that, above all things, you are a *criollo*'; Plutarch's *Lives*, 'That you may always find inspiration in them'; and Chesterfield's *Letters*, 'That you may learn how to move among people'.

Juan Domingo Perón had become one of 300 sub-lieutenants in an army with 1,683 officers commanding 17,000 men in peacetime. The vast majority were conscripts, compulsory military service having been introduced in the year of Perón's birth. Argentina was not spending much on its Army by the standards of the day: its military budget, reckoned to be in the vicinity of £2 million, represented about 8 per cent of the government's revenue. At the same time, neighbouring Brazil was spending twice that proportion, as was the United States; Germany — the model for Argentina's Army — was devoting three times as much to her military. The infantry, Perón's chosen arm, was naturally the strongest in numbers — about 12,000 men, with 600 officers. His 12th Infantry Regiment was one of twenty such regiments. It had only been in existence since 1883, but had inherited the tradition of the older 12th Battalion of the Line, formed in 1865 and soon afterwards sent to fight in the war against Paraguay. In the 1870s it was active in the Desert Campaigns, first engaging the Ranqueles Indians who fought under the famous chieftain Baigorrita, then pushing down along the foothills of the Andes to secure Argentina's new internal frontier on the shores of the great lake of Nahuel Huapi, about 2,000 kilometres south-west of Buenos Aires. In the 1880s and '90s the regiment was shunted around the country, successively garrisoning Mendoza, San Juan, Resistencia, Buenos Aires, Rosario, Campo de Mayo, the federal capital, Concordia and San Lorenzo, before settling in Paraná and its twin town across the river, Santa Fe. Its conscripts were drawn mainly from the province of Entre Ríos, following the pattern set for all Argentine Army units after the unsuccessful mobilisation of the 1890s, when it was 'discovered' that recruitment from all over the country created problems of climatic adaptation for many of the men.

Perón's first two years of army life were uneventful and in 1915, as a matter of course, he was promoted lieutenant. The only outstanding feature remembered by a conscript who served as his batman in the 12th was that 'every time he sent me into town to do some shopping, it was to buy books'. But change, rapid change, was on its way. During the years of Perón's childhood and adolescence, Argentina's social and political checkerboard had become increasingly polarised. Luis Sáenz Peña had resigned in the third year of his mandate, to be succeeded by his Vice-President, José Evaristo Uriburu. Only a year later ill-health forced Uriburu to resign, and his post was taken by the President of the Senate, the old *Zorro* (Fox), General Julio A. Roca. Leandro Alem, the leading light of the Unión Cívica Radical, committed suicide that same year, leaving the leadership of the party in the hands of young Hipólito Yrigoyen, who would again oppose any form of agreement with the régime in the 1898 elections (these, following the usual pattern, were rigged to allow Julio Roca a second term as President). Roca's attempts to sort out Argentina's financial difficulties with its English creditors, and the new set of privileges offered to foreign investors would again be criticised by nationalists as a sell-out. His second Presidency witnessed the construction of even more huge infrastructural works, such as the ports of Rosario, Paraná and Concepción del Uruguay, the introduction of compulsory military service and the first official recognition of Argentina's mounting social problems.

This recognition took two forms. The first was a devastating report on 'the state of the working classes in the interior of the Republic', prepared by Juan Bialet Massé on the instructions of the Ministry of the Interior and presented to Congress. 'The claim that people are working from sunrise to sunset is false,' said Bialet Massé, 'for the working day has been extended by taking advantage of the dawn, dusk and even the moonlight.' He recorded the many cases of anaemia, fatigue and respiratory ailments in factories, and the promiscuity of the overcrowded *conventillos* in the capital city. From this report would emerge the proposal of the country's first Labour Code, regulating working conditions and formalising the existence of trade unions. The report was hailed as a breakthrough by the newly-formed Socialist Party, whose first Senator, Alfredo Palacios, also came out strongly in support of the proposed legislation. But the unions, and the majority of the Socialist Party executive, opposed it violently as a trap set by the régime, on behalf of the employers, to emasculate the workers' organisations.

It was the government's second form of recognition of its labour problems that had created this reaction. Shortly after a widespread strike spreading from Buenos Aires' huge market for perishable foods, the Mercado Central de Frutos, to paralyse virtually all port activity in the country, the government rushed through Congress the 'Law of Residence', enabling the Executive to expel any foreigner 'whose conduct compromises national security or perturbs public order' and to deny entry to Argentina to 'all foreigners whose antecedents would authorise their inclusion' in that category. The meaning of the new law became evident, in the words of a chronicler of the time, 'almost before the ink had dried on the paper': squads of the militarised security corps, Army units and firemen rounded up hundreds of known union leaders and herded them into the port of Buenos Aires, whence they were unceremoniously packed on to outgoing ships. The government decreed a state of siege, suspending constitutional guarantees and initiating systematic, wholesale persecution of the union movement.

At the turn of the century anarchists and socialists had again come together to create a new umbrella organisation, the Federación Obrera Argentina, but when the anarchists gained ascendancy in its ruling body, the socialists broke away and formed their own organisation, the Unión General de Trabajadores. This period of turbulence, marked by police harassment and the liberal use of the faculty of preventive detention, came to a climax in 1904, during the May Day celebrations, when a minor incident flared into a shoot-out, with the mounted police leaving scores of wounded and one of the early recognised martyrs of the labour movement, Juan Ocampo, a stevedore. A month earlier the country had gone to the polls, after the régime's already habitually unsuccessful attempt to coax Hipólito Yrigoyen and his Radicals to come to an 'understanding'. With the Radicals proclaiming 'revolutionary abstention' and the usual dose of chicanery, the Presidency was comfortably won by Manuel Quintana, the régime's hand-picked successor. Only months later the Radicals had a go at outright revolution. The uprising had been carefully prepared, not only by the semi-clandestine committees of the Unión Cívica Radical but also within the armed forces. Military units in Campo de Mayo (the Army's largest concentration of troops, just outside the capital), Bahía Blanca, Santa Fe, San Lorenzo and Mendoza were taken over by officers sympathetic to the Radical cause. Vice-President Figueroa Alcorta was captured by revolutionaries in Córdoba; units in the capital took over key police stations. The *coup de grace* was to come when Army units from Campo de Mayo and Bahía Blanca converged on the Buenos Aires arsenal. But the government was alerted to this manoeuvre, and managed to pre-empt it by taking over the Arsenal and preventing the link-up. When the military phase of the rebellion went awry, Hipólito Yrigoyen ordered his partisans to lay down their arms and surrendered.

Quintana's presidency was to be remarkably brief: ill-health forced him to entrust his post to his Vice-President after only a few months in office, and in early 1906 he died. Figueroa Alcorta stepped in to find that his government had lost all support, from his own partisans and from the provincial governors, to the extent that he was unable to get his budget approved by Congress. When the legislators threatened to pursue their opposition to the point of impeaching him, Alcorta ordered the security corps to close down Congress. He also decreed the federal 'intervention' of five provincial governments.

The discovery of oil in Comodoro Rivadavia, in 1907, was overshadowed by the increased militancy of the labour movement, and especially by the shift towards terrorism and political assassinations by the anarchists. The labour movement continued to be split into two factions, the socialist UGT and the anarchist FORA (the new name adopted by the earlier FOA), and a number of attempts at unification were foiled by the instransigent refusal of the anarchists to use established political channels for the pursuit of their demands. Yet some of the individual trade unions began to show signs of overcoming that divide. The printers, for example, who had divided into four factions, merged in 1907 into the Federación Gráfica Bonaerense.

That same year, union assertiveness exploded throughout the country. There were 231 strikes, involving 179,000 workers, and some of them erupted into violence when met with inordinately stiff repression. A strike of chauffeurs in the city of Rosario was put down by the mobilisation of cavalry and artillery units, while the port was blockaded by warships; yet the unions retaliated with a general strike that not only secured their original demands but also forced the resignation of the local chief of police. A strike by the riveters in the grain port of Ingeniero White, in the south of the province of Buenos Aires, was also harshly suppressed, and the ensuing response of the labour movement, supported by the Socialists, was disrupted forcibly by units of the Maritime Police, who killed six people in the process. Although the government's heavy-handedness often brought together Socialists and anarchists in strikes and protest demonstrations, formal unity continued to elude the labour movement. It was not until 1909, virtually on the eve of Argentina's hundredth birthday, that the UGT and a large number of the FORA unions put aside their differences to create the Confederación Obrera Regional Argentina (CORA).

And it had taken even more government violence to bring that about. That year, both organisations had gone their separate ways to celebrate May Day in Buenos Aires. The Chief of Police, Colonel Ramón Falcón, ordered the mounted police to disperse the anarchist rally at Plaza Lorea; when the marchers arrived they were met with drawn sabres, and later with rifle and pistol fire. Within a few minutes, eight demonstrators lay dead and close to a hundred were wounded. Fleeing workers rushed through the city streets to carry the news to the Socialists gathered at Plaza Colón. Shock quickly turned to rage, and the call went out for a general strike. Although the strike action lasted only eight days, it impressed upon the unions the need for a more concerted approach, and speedy negotiations led to the creation of CORA a couple of months later. But even more hardship lay ahead. In November 1909 a young anarchist named Simón Radowitzky took upon himself the task of avenging the May Day dead; he tossed a crude explosive artifact into the passing open carriage of Police Chief Ramón Falcón, instantly killing him and an adjutant.

Retaliation was swift and massive. The government decreed a state of siege, closed down the anarchist newspaper *La Protesta* and the socialist *La Vanguardia*, and began to arrest known union leaders by the score. Beatings and torture were used to extract the names and whereabouts of associates of the arrested union leaders; groups of civilian vigilantes set out to aid the police in unearthing 'anarchist agitators'; the 'Law of Residence' was invoked to deport the foreigners, while those deemed most dangerous among the native-born were bundled off to faraway prisons, such as the bleak penal unit of Ushuaia in Tierra del Fuego. After two months of terror, it seemed that the union movement had been decapitated, but it was not long before a reconstituted CORA was calling for a 'revolutionary general strike', demanding the repeal of the 'Law of Residence', the freeing of their imprisoned comrades and an amnesty for evaders of the compulsory military service regulations. A bomb went off in Buenos Aires' plush Colón theatre, already an internationally renowned opera house, and the deed was promptly attributed to an anarchist, whose Russian name, Romanoff, would become the cornerstone of a campaign to identify all union activity with anarchism, and *foreign* anarchism to boot. Whipping nationalist fervour to a frenzy, the government convened Congress to an emergency session and in only one day pushed through the 'Law of Social Defence', which not only stiffened the provisions of the 'Law of Residence', but also placed strict constraints on the rights of free association, assembly and expression, as well as introducing harsh sanctions for infractions, including the reestablishment of the death penalty.

It was in this atmosphere that the régime arrived at the time for its periodical exercise of 'orderly succession'. President Figueroa Alcorta had emulated his predecessors, twice attempting to persuade Hipólito

Yrigoyen to abandon his abstentionist posture in exchange for a share of power. On both occasions he was sharply rebuffed, Yrigoyen obstinately insisting that his Unión Cívica Radical would accept nothing less than 'the Cause': 'national reparation' or, in other words, guarantees of free elections, based on 'clean' electoral rolls. Yrigoyen even refused the advances of the old 'Fox', Julio Roca, who offered him an electoral pact which would almost certainly have carried him to the Presidency. Intransigent abstention it was to be for the Radicals, but even so the government resorted to electoral fraud in order to guarantee the victory of its Dauphin, Roque Sáenz Peña, the man who had been vetoed eighteen years earlier because of his excessive 'modernism'.

Events were soon to convince many of those who had cast that veto that they had been right. As soon as he was elected, Sáenz Peña called Yrigoyen with an offer of cabinet posts for members of his party. The Radical leader flatly refused, insisting that it was not a place in government that he wanted, but wide-ranging electoral reform, designed to guarantee free elections. And the 'modernist' President replied with the announcement that that was precisely what he intended. It was not so much that he, and those elements of the régime who agreed with him, had suddenly come round to share Yrigoyen's convictions; Sáenz Peña was quite sure that the high incidence of electoral abstention merely reflected the fact that people were not obliged to vote. Add to this the view, quite openly expressed in the newspapers of the day, that the workers of Argentina, the aspiring 'United States of the South', were conservatives at heart (labour strife, quite naturally, being attributed to the influence of foreign agitators), and the formula is complete. The régime felt it could afford to update its image, cast aside the worn tool of electoral fraud, and gain in legitimacy. The notion was widespread that the 'right' people would be elected in any case, and the Radicals had actually contributed to reinforce it, by selecting as their own postulants to public office men drawn from the traditional ruling élite. Yrigoyen's view was quite different; he saw widespread abstention as a sign of national protest, the demand by the nation at large that the self-perpetuating rule by a wealthy minority, or their proxies, should give way to truly democratic participation, as foreseen in the Constitution.

Indeed, Yrigoyen's movement did represent a wide demand for political participation. The country had grown; it had generated a new middle class of members of the liberal professions, of small businessmen and small farmers; it had spread out from Buenos Aires to the neighbouring provinces of the littoral; it had trained hundreds upon hundreds of people, through its *bachiller* secondary schooling system; it had expanded its state apparatus; it had spread access to culture; it had built up its capital city to look like Paris (although the effect was more reminiscent of Barcelona) and its railway network to look like part of a little England. And the people who were actually engaged in running this expanded Argentina felt acutely that they had been left out of the conduct of their political affairs. Moreover, it was they, rather than the scions of the old oligarchy, who had the expertise needed to manage this far more complex society; no longer could Argentina be seen as an extension of the pampas farms, easily run from afar by a strongminded *patrón*. It was this feeling of being marginal that had become embodied in the Unión Cívica Radical; the marginality of the new administrators and the new wealth-producing regions. Because the demand was essentially for greater participation, it was couched in general, all-embracing terms. Its rhetoric said that it was the nation as a whole that was speaking, and that it was a moral right it was claiming. This allowed for the adherence to 'the Cause' of many others, condemned to an even more marginal situation than the budding middle classes, but still far removed from positions of real influence. Because their enemies were the wealthy few, the rhetoric of 'the Cause' was anti-money, opposed to the rationale of economic progress invoked by the ruling oligarchy; it was decency and morality that moved the Radicals, against the crass utilitarianism they perceived in the régime.

The explicit aims of the Radicals were few and simple; early demands for a more detailed programme of government were rejected as diversions from their central purpose. Because 'the Cause' had to muster the support of the entire nation, it could not afford to countenance potentially divisive elements. In this attitude there were also the seeds of later rigidity. 'The Cause' became ever more identified with 'the Nation', so that dissidence from the Unión Cívica Radical, the standard-bearer of 'the Cause', became tantamount to 'anti-Nation'. The advocates of democracy began to develop an unhealthy intolerance for diversity. Moreover, the 'national' element of 'the Cause' was set up against the 'internationalism' of the dominant ideologies in the labour movement, and although many among the Radicals were sons or grand-sons of immigrants, the large number of foreign-born males in the Argentina of the Centennial had no place in the Radical demand for a guaranteed, universal franchise. The Radicals felt very much a part of historic Argentina, their roots entwined with the traditions of the Autonomists and in a way, further back, with the Federalists, though

they were a new feature in Argentine society — new classes, new
regions attached to an expanding centre — and as such they vindicated
their right to establishment. But already on the scene were the even
newer disenfranchised — the organised workers, with their 'foreign'
taint — and just over the horizon, in the interior, another wave was
waiting, manifest at the time only as a trickle of browner-skinned
workers, alien even to the Europeanised labour organisations of the
cities.

Still intransigently opposed to accepting participation in government
as a gift of the régime, Yrigoyen agreed to collaborate in the preparation
of an electoral reform law. It would take two years to make its way
through Congress, but on 13 February 1912 it was finally there: new
electoral rolls, based on the military-controlled lists of citizens of conscription age (the Army's intervention was seen as a guarantee of
'national' impartiality, superseding the pliable role played by corrupt
provincial police forces); the vote to be universal, secret and obligatory; a
form of representation that would guarantee to the minority at least one-
third of the seats in legislatures and electoral colleges. Finally, at least on
paper, there was what Yrigoyen and his Radicals had been fighting for.
All that remained was to see it put into practice.

The country had changed quite dramatically since the Radical 'Cause'
had begun to take shape in the 1890s. At the time of the passage of
Roque Sáenz Peña's electoral law, the census showed that Argentina's
population had grown to 7,888,237, twice as many as when Juan
Domingo Perón was born in Lobos in 1895. Just under one-third of the
population was foreign-born. One million children were enrolled in
schools. Thirty-three thousand kilometres of railway track extracted the
produce from almost 25 million hectares under cultivation; the country
was exporting annually 500,000 tonnes of beef and 2 million tonnes of
wheat. There were twice as many industrial establishments as in 1895;
the capital invested per establishment had increased threefold. Yet still
the country's élite shied away from any deliberate policy of industrialisation; Argentina's industry, they said, was the land; exploiting it
adequately, selling its produce abroad and correctly administering the
proceeds was clearly all the country needed in order to prosper.

But little of this prosperity was trickling down to the lower strata of
society. Unemployment was rife and working conditions were, if anything, worse than when Congress was politely shocked by the Bialet
Massé report. Rebelliousness among the workforce continued to
increase, and major incidents of violence became more frequent.

Striking quarry workers in Tandil were shot at, arrested and tortured by the local police; in the seaside town of Mar del Plata a strike by sanitation workers brought the troops out into the streets, and over 300 union members were herded into an improvised concentration camp. A hitherto passive segment of the population, the small farmers of the littoral, suddenly sprang to life with the *Grido de Alcorta* (Cry of Alcorta) manifests, launching a mass protest movement against high rural rents and extortionate contracts. Their revolt, which spread throughout the grain belt, underlined the lopsidedness of Argentina's pattern of land tenure. A mere 1,843 families owned just under one-sixth of the entire national territory. In the province of Buenos Aires the Alzaga family owned 500,000 hectares, while four others (Pradere, Anchorena, Duggan and Pereira) had holdings of more than 150,000 hectares each; in the province of Córdoba the Olmos family owned 116,000 hectares and another 123 families shared out one-quarter of the province's area; in Santa Fe there were the smaller holdings of the Anchorena, Cavanagh, Estrugamou, Perkins and Lezica families, ranging between 15,000 and 50,000 hectares each. In 1912 there were 27,000 registered owners of small farms, but more than twice as many tenant farmers and sharecroppers. It was the latter — not yet the rural *peones* and labourers — who spearheaded the protest movement of 1912, which culminated in the formation of the Federación Argraria Argentina as a rival to the powerful Sociedad Rural, which had been created by the large landowners back in 1866.

President Roque Sáenz Peña was a sick man, and even before the promulgation of his electoral law he had had to take leave from his office three times. His absences grew more frequent in 1913, until he was finally persuaded to resign in favour of his Vice-President, Victorino de la Plaza, who completed his term. In spite of the electoral law, and of the compilation of the new rolls under Army supervision, strong-arm tactics and fraud continued to be practised in provincial elections. But the tide had begun to turn, and the Radicals started chalking up victories, first in the capital, Buenos Aires, and then throughout the country. It was far from easy sailing to the Presidential elections of 1916; the UCR had to face the arbitrary annulment of provincial results, the confiscation of voting documents, and even the assassination of some of its organisers, as the ruling oligarchy grimly tried to preserve its weakening grip on power. When the time came, and Hipólito Yrigoyen, nicknamed *el Peludo* (the Armadillo) for his hardskinned obstinacy and his reclusiveness, finally accepted his nomination as a Presidential candidate, the

Radicals swept the board, collecting more votes than his three rivals put together.

An era seemed to be ending. For many Argentines, the symbol of change was the moment when a jubilant crowd unhitched the President-elect's carriage from its horses, dragging it themselves all the way from the Palace of Congress, where Yrigoyen had just been sworn in, to the Casa Rosada, the presidential palace where he would formally take office. The conservative newspaper *La Prensa* was horrified at the incident, described in its editorial columns as 'an unwonted act that runs counter to the democratic antecedents of the citizen who has now been elected President'. For others, however, a far more poignant symbol could be found in the actual handing over of the attributes of power, the Presidential sash and rod. Before the ceremony could proceed, the out-going Victorino de la Plaza had to be introduced to Yrigoyen, for the two men had never met before.

3

FROM YRIGOYEN TO THE
ERA OF THE COUP
(1916–1930)

Beyond the rejoicing and the triumphant rhetoric, however, lay the stark reality that the Radicals had only gained a shaky toehold on power. In Congress the Senate, to a man, was opposed to the President; in the Chamber of Deputies, where Yrigoyen enjoyed a majority, adversaries of all colorations coalesced in a single 'parliamentary concentration' to challenge his every initiative. Eleven provincial governments had been won by his opponents, and he found ranged against him the large land-owners, conservative big business and the militant unions. From the old Right, with its symbiotic relationship with Great Britain, he would be attacked for steadfastly refusing to let Argentina be dragged into the war already raging in Europe. In fact, Yrigoyen merely held to the policy of neutrality adopted during Victorino de la Plaza's administration, carrying it to its logical conclusions. He refused to be swayed by the entry of the United States into the conflict, calmly responded to the German sinking of an Argentine vessel by demanding — and obtaining — official apologies and reparation, and held back from the League of Nations when it became evident that some of its members were to be more equal than others. The Right would also alternately savage him for lacking any coherent programme of government, for leading the country on the road to Communism, or for failing to stamp out the threat of armed revolution. The Left, particularly the Anarchists and Socialists in the organised labour movement, saw Yrigoyen as a mere stooge of big business, who used the flowery language of democracy as a smokescreen for repression of the unions.

Indeed, during Yrigoyen's Presidency repression of the workers' organisations reached unprecedented levels, more than matching the increasingly incendiary calls of the Anarchists for complete destruction of capitalist society, which sounded even more ominous with the contemporary backdrop of the Red revolution in Russia. In spite of the lack of real contacts between the Radicals and the labour movement,

Yrigoyen's government had seemed to start auspiciously on this front, when he designated the Chief of Police to arbitrate in a strike called by the longshoremen, and he found in favour of the workers' demands. Yet he had been only a year in the Casa Rosada when the railwaymen went on strike, protesting against a clause in the law creating their pension scheme, whereby they would have had to renounce the right to strike action. The strikers ran into harsh opposition, including the shooting of some of their leaders. They appealed to the President, calling on him to nationalise the British-owned railways as well as satisfying their immediate demands. Yrigoyen responded with a decree removing the offending clause from their pension law.

Another year passed in relative peace, Yrigoyen proclaiming his identification with the 'just cause' of organised labour, before a conflict began to brew which would go down in history as the 'Tragic Week'. Although the trouble came to a head as the result of a strike in the Vasena metalworking plant on the outskirts of Buenos Aires, its roots could be traced back to the anarchist FORA's earlier declaration of support for Russian 'maximalism' and for the German revolution, and the response of the Right to this position. A number of businessmen led by Joaquín de Anchorena had organised the Asociación Nacional del Trabajo, which began to circulate blacklists of known union organisers. A more extreme line was adopted by the Liga Patriótica Argentina headed by Manuel Carlés, whose members formed themselves into armed anti-union squads. And to make matters worse, a draft bill was presented to Congress which would have had the effect of a virtual ban on unions. Feelings were thus running high when the workers at the Vasena plant, affiliated to the anarchist FORA, went out on strike. A contingent of strikebreakers was hired by the company, and their confrontation with union pickets degenerated swiftly into an armed police charge on the strikers. The incident spread to the neighbourhood, leaving a trail of dead, whose funeral the following day was disrupted by a volley of police gunfire which left even more casualties. A call for a general strike further escalated the confrontation, with the thugs of the Liga Patriótica carrying out mindless acts of violence, including the gratuitous smashing of Jewish dwellings. *La Prensa* began to rant about the threat of 'revolutionary war', striking fear into its readers with tales of the strikers being joined by 'thousands of vagabonds and criminals', of barricades going up in working-class districts and of the police having been ordered off the streets. In fact Yrigoyen had confined the police to their barracks, as well as sacking their Chief, in an attempt to curb the violence. And although elements of the extreme Right tried to entice the new Police Chief into attempting a coup, Yrigoyen finally got his Minister of the Interior to negotiate with the strikers and bring the dispute to an end. The detained FORA leaders were set free, and the Vasena workers were granted wage increases of 20 to 40 per cent. But the whole episode had left a huge death toll, calculated by some to have exceeded 1,000.

The 'Tragic Week' of 1919 in Buenos Aires was followed in late 1922 and early 1923 by the even more tragic events in the southern Patagonian territory of Santa Cruz. The anarchists of FORA had only recently begun their campaign to take unionisation to the countryside, especially to the more distant provinces, where *mensús*, *hacheros*, *cañeros* and *peones* still laboured under semi-feudal conditions. Union organisers in San Julián and Río Gallegos, in the territory of Santa Cruz, the desolate, southernmost extreme of continental Argentina, were from the outset harshly resisted by the big landowners, like the Menéndez Behety family and the many British companies engaged in sheep farming in the area. Strikes, and even the mere act of preparing petitions on behalf of the workers in the Patagonian townships and farms, were met with violent repression. This only steeled the resolve of the organisers, whose rallies got larger and larger as the list of 'Xs' and badly scribbled signatures grew longer and longer on the petitions for better working conditions. A handful of wild enthusiasts, interpreting these early successes as portents of greater things to come, formed themselves into a force of 'Red Guards' and galloped off to bring the revolution to those barren, largely empty steppes. Though never more than a chance phenomenon, this tiny band provided the excuse the landowners had been waiting for; their very presence lent credence to the litany the landowners had been reciting to the authorities in Buenos Aires, about dangerous revolution-aries and uncontrolled bandits roving the Patagonian countryside. And in the capital city there were many who were only too willing to believe, including an Army in which a peculiar brand of right-wing nationalism was beginning to take hold.

The government despatched to Santa Cruz a contingent of soldiers under Lieutenant-Colonel Héctor Varela. After a perfunctory attempt at talking to the unions, Varela switched to the use of force. He ordered all workers to register with the police and introduced what amounted to an internal passport without which travel was forbidden. Then he set about identifying the union organisers, 'troublemakers' and 'bandits'. Farmers and foremen aided the Army by pointing to the 'culprits' among their own workers and directing the soldiers towards other suspected hotbeds of sedition. The lucky ones were imprisoned or deported. But for many more it was to be summary execution, in a process which rapidly degenerated from orderly death by firing squad to mass killings in which the victims were first forced to dig their graves, and even to instances in which they were buried alive, or locked into barns that were set alight, or used for target practice by the officers. There is no accurate tally of Varela's dead, but most estimates mention 2,000 or more — in a territory with a total population at the time of under 10,000. The full import of this sordid episode was to be hushed up for many decades, surfacing only occasionally in publications for small political circles, but mostly euphemised in order to disguise or justify the sorry role played by an Army which at the time found only words of praise for Colonel Varela's conduct of a 'difficult' mission. The tragedy did not end with Varela's return to Buenos Aires; shortly afterwards 'the Hyena of Patagonia', as he had become known in union circles, was blown to bits by the anarchist Kurt Wilckens, who in turn was murdered in his cell by a prison warder. The warder's assassination by another anarchist finally brought the trail of death from Río Gallegos to an end.

All too easily the 'Tragic Week' and the events of Patagonia led anarchists and socialists to discount Yrigoyen as little more than a straw man for Argentina's capitalists, a man whose political steam had indeed exhausted itself before he reached the Presidency, when his only clear objective — a guarantee of truly free elections — was granted by his predecessor. The Right, too, castigated Yrigoyen for his alleged inefficacy, harping again and again on the fact that his Unión Cívica Radical had never had anything resembling a programme of government. Yet if Yrigoyen's rule was marred by these two unprecedented heights of anti-union repression, there is something to be said for the fact that they stand out so starkly. Violent persecution of the unions had not been absent from previous administrations; rather, it had been the rule, but during Yrigoyen's term of office the backdrop was strikingly different. Workers' wages were increased by almost 85 per cent, and existing labour legislation, mild and partial as it may have been, was actually enforced. Social security and pension schemes became, at least in the cities, a reality for many, and the working day was cut by an hour. Had Conservatives, Socialists and Communists not systematically obstructed his other initiatives, Yrigoyen would also have left the country a new Labour Code, arbitration boards for disputes in rural areas and the overall introduction of government-supervised conciliation procedures and compulsory arbitration in the case of intractable labour wrangles. The 'Tragic Week' and Patagonia were exceptions to the rule; on the whole workers enjoyed full freedom to organise, and the Yrigoyen years saw the appearance of the country's first union to be centralised nationwide, the railwaymen's Unión Ferroviaria, while the ranks of the feared anarchist FORA actually swelled to include over 200,000 paid-up members of some 500 unions.

It was also during the Yrigoyen years that the students of Córdoba gave birth to the University Reform, a movement that broke with the excessive clericalism and introverted academicism of the past and called for full involvement of Argentina's institutes of higher education in the problems of contemporary society. The Reform gave Argentina's universities a new form of self-government — by students, faculty and graduates — and a degree of politicisation which, if not always in the most enlightened fashion, was to weigh heavily in the country's affairs for the following half-century.

Yrigoyen's own brand of nationalism, quiet but as stubbornly intransigent as his struggle for free elections, became manifest in his obstinate resistance to the many pressures by the anglophile oligarchy to drag Argentina into the Great War on the side of Britain and its allies; in gestures such as his order to salute the flag of the Dominican Republic when this tiny Caribbean nation was occupied by US military forces; in the stricter fiscal control of the British-owned railways; in the creation of a merchant fleet, and in the support he gave to the state's involvement in oil production, a venture that had been entrusted to a visionary general named Enrique Mosconi. Yrigoyen managed to make enemies of the far Left, the traditional oligarchy and the ultramontane Catholics, and to judge from the editorials of most of the political press, he came to the end of his mandate isolated and with the country in a shambles.

Political reality, however, gave a different account. His popularity in 1922 was, if anything, greater than when he had been voted into the Presidency. The Constitution stipulated that he could not be re-elected, and it never really crossed anyone's mind that Yrigoyen would flout the Constitution. 'Del gobierno a casa' ('from government straight home') was his motto, and he kept to it as his party, with his blessing, triumphantly carried the candidacy of Marcelo T. de Alvear in the 1922 elections, defeating his Conservative rival two to one. Alvear, the scion of an old, well-to-do family, was one of that breed of 'respectable' politicians the Unión Cívica Radical had taken on board in its early days in order to gain a more acceptable public image. Within the party he appeared as the visible head of the 'anti-personalists' (as opposed to the 'personalist' followers of Hipólito Yrigoyen). His election was greeted with jubilation by the Conservative press, and the cabinet he appointed made it clear from the start that he intended to veer away from the more abrasive of his predecessor's attitudes.

With a friendlier disposition towards foreign business, Alvear's administration was able to take full advantage of the post-war revival of the European economies. Trade picked up, and capital and immigrants flowed in, stimulating Argentina's agriculture and pouring a balm on the social tensions of the preceding years. Alvear refurbished the country's armed forces, built new barracks, set up a submarine base and an airplane factory and, more to go along with the military than out of his own conviction, created Yacimientos Petrolíferos Fiscales (YPF), the state's own oil corporation. Oil, and the state's role in its exploitation, had made its formal entry on to the Argentine political stage.

From the outset, Alvear's 'anti-personalists' in Congress and the provincial governments began to steer their own course, ever more frequently in opposition to their party — still controlled by Yrigoyen — and coinciding with the arch-enemies of Radicalism, the Conservatives. The rift became almost irreversible only two years into Alvear's mandate, when Yrigoyen's faithful, again waving their beloved banner of 'intransigence', deliberately snubbed the President by staying away from his 'state of the nation' message to Congress. Among the absentees, signalling the gravity of the split, was Alvear's own Vice-President, Elpidio González. Alvear decided to take the bull by the horns, and promoted the creation of a new political party, the Unión Cívica Radical Antipersonalista. The latter half of Alvear's Presidency, otherwise an uneventful, prosperous parenthesis in Argentine political life, was hallmarked by an acrimonious debate between his partisans and Yrigoyen's 'intransigent' Radicals over the future of Argentina's oil, which would bring into the open the entire range of ideological disparity which the original Unión Cívica Radical had harboured within its umbrella appeal for effective democracy. While the ruling party and the Conservatives favoured a free enterprise approach — that is, whenever they reluctantly got around to admitting that it would be a good idea to extract Argentina's oil (*La Prensa* talked about an ideal government 'refusing to be overcome by the fever of opening new sources of material wealth') — the 'intransigents' insisted on enacting legislation that would make all hydrocarbons the property of the nation and pressed for rapid exploitation of the oil deposits.

The debate remained unresolved when the time came for the country to elect a new President. Early in the contest, the confident 'anti-personalists' nominated Leopoldo Melo as their candidate. The 'intransigents', on the other hand, launched forth into the campaign without naming their contenders. The reason: the struggle was on to persuade Hipólito Yrigoyen, now seventy-eight years old, to forget his promise never to return to government. Only six days before the polls his candidacy was proclaimed, and another two days were to pass before he formally accepted the nomination. When the big day arrived, the electorate eloquently reminded Alvear and his 'anti-personalists' that they had only enjoyed power thanks to the votes that rightfully belonged to Hipólito Yrigoyen: the old leader was again granted an overwhelming two-to-one victory.

Yrigoyen's enemies were not prepared to take their defeat docilely. Indeed his ouster began to be plotted almost from the moment the election result came in. A hurriedly mustered cabal of right-wingers actually attempted to prevent him from taking office by pulling off a palace coup and installing the Minister of War, General Agustín P. Justo, in the Presidency. Nothing came of this attempt, but a significant indication of the mood of the day was that General Justo did not denounce the conspiracy, and when its existence was revealed by a zealous Senator, he conceded in silence. As before, opposition to Yrigoyen came from both Right and Left, but by the time his second Presidency began there were two distinct and apparently irreconcilable strains to this opposition. On the one hand were the adversary parties: those to the Right, who were quite willing to subvert the democratic process through electoral fraud but still felt the need for a democratic façade, and those to the Left, who were committed to 'legality'. On the surface, their main objection to yrigoyenismo was that it tended, all too frequently, to identify the party with the nation, and the will of one man — however much of a majority he had obtained — with the will of the people as a whole. With age, Yrigoyen's taciturn style had turned almost to secretiveness; even more than before, he seemed to justify the nickname of Peludo (armadillo) that his enemies had given him. Old age had also weakened his health — a simple bout of influenza would prostrate him almost completely. His opponents claimed that in his isolation Yrigoyen had lost all real touch with the country; there was talk of an inner circle of sycophants who only told the aged President what he wanted to hear, to the extreme of printing dummy front pages of newspapers so that he should not know of disagreeable events.

But also among Yrigoyen's enemies was a new breed, an admixture of élitist nationalism, ultramontane Catholicism and supreme disdain for liberal democracy. They would oust Yrigoyen not only because he was Yrigoyen, but because he more than any other political figure embodied the vortex of rapid change that in only a few decades had swept away all the certainties of the old, pastoral Argentina. Not indeed the real Argentina of history, which had been changing unceasingly since its break with Spain, but a romanticised Argentina of strong, warlike patriots (the archetype was Juan Manuel de Rosas, the Buenos Aires landowner who was granted dictatorial powers in the first half of the nineteenth century) and a vision of future grandeur. Their journal *La Fronda* described Yrigoyen as 'a resentful Redskin who hates civilisation', a man whose tenderness was evoked by tyranny, 'especially if it is Central American, that is to say, run by mediocre and sickly little black men, who are of his own race and mentality'. Another periodical of similar leanings, *La Nueva República*, called quite directly for the elimination of all 'professional politics' and the foundation of a new order, the vague outlines of which reflected the influence of nascent European fascism in its several forms.

As was the case in his first Presidency, Yrigoyen counted on a Radical majority in the Chamber of Deputies but had to face an opposition majority in the Senate. This did not prevent him from pushing through Congress a belated reply to the tenant farmers' 'Cry of Alcorta' which had been so much a part of his first rise to power. He enacted a bill modifying the rural rentals law, improving the lot of those farmers who owned no land of their own. From the very beginning his second administration was prolific in public works, and especially in the mammoth expansion programme devised for the already ageing railway system, which included plans for a number of 'promotional' lines in faraway regions of the northeast and Patagonia, and in the drafting of a bill to create an autonomous federal roadbuilding authority, with enough resources of its own to complete the integration of the country's communications network.

If the political movement that Yrigoyen had led to power represented the incorporation of marginal classes to full participation in the country's political life, his second administration was clearly aiming at incorporating the marginal regions of Argentina into the country's economic life. Apart from railway and road building, this was to be achieved by granting the status of provinces, that is to say, full partners in the federal republic, to the regions that were still being ruled from Buenos Aires as 'national territories'; the areas that had been reached through Roca's

'Desert Campaign' and by the later 'pacification' campaigns in the northern Chaco.

Another key element in Yrigoyen's programme was oil. The first pipeline was built from outlying fields to Comodoro Rivadavia, and plans were drawn up for its extension to Buenos Aires, 1,800 kilometres away. The state's own oil corporation, YPF, began to regulate the domestic market for oil products, and actually managed to bring down the price of fuels. The Yrigoyen administration was determined to keep YPF out of the grasp of the 'Seven Sisters', the US and British companies that dominated the world oil market, even in those aspects in which indirect control might be exerted, like technology. So a co-operation agreement was drawn up with an unexpected partner, the Soviet Union. But still the Senate obstructed the key piece of legislation desired by the Yrigoyen administration: the declaration that all oil and gas deposits in Argentina belonged to the nation. It has often been said that the conspiracy that would eventually overthrow Hipólito Yrigoyen 'reeked of oil'. Indeed there has been speculation that the very timing of his ouster owed much to the fact that the moment was drawing near when a couple of newly-elected provincial legislatures were expected to give the 'unpopular' Yrigoyen his badly-needed majority in the Senate.

The powerhouse of the plot was the Liga Republicana, a group formed around the right-wing Catholic paper *La Nueva República*; its open calls for the downfall of the government were matched with only differences of degree by the more extreme *La Fronda* and by the newspaper *Crítica*, which had become the mouthpiece of the 'legalist' opposition. But the signal that the conspiracy might have some chance of success only came when a general on active service publicly associated himself with *La Nueva República*. This was José Félix Uriburu, the man who as a young sub-lieutenant in 1890 had been a fellow-plotter with Hipólito Yrigoyen, and now commanded not only great professional respect within the Army but also the personal esteem of many of the 'legalist' adversaries of the government. The year 1929 closed with an unsuccessful attempt on Yrigoyen's life, a sign to many that there was substance in the propaganda message that *el Peludo* had lost all control of the situation, and that it was only a matter of time before the much-vaunted revolution would take place. Yet for all the ranting and rumour-mongering from the various opposition groups, and the many hare-brained plans circulated by the civilian Right for the removal of Yrigoyen, a full six months of 1930 would pass before General Uriburu began in earnest to plan a military uprising. This episode, which inaugurated the era of military coups and counter-coups in Argentina, began towards the end of June of that year, when Major Angel Solari walked into the offices of the Army General Staff and sought out a young captain who, though fresh from the Escuela Superior de Guerra, had already begun to make a name for himself as a strategic thinker. The major did not beat around the bush. 'I can stand this no longer,' he said. 'The time has come to do something. General Uriburu intends to organise an armed movement . . . We are counting on you.' The young captain he was addressing was Juan Domingo Perón.

Perón had become a lieutenant in 1915, still attached to the 12th Infantry Regiment in Paraná. Two years later he had made his first contact with the turbulent labour scene of the time, when he was ordered to take the soldiers under his command to 'maintain order' in the logging towns of Villa Guillermina and San Cristóbal, where efforts had begun to organise the labour force against the semi-feudal conditions imposed by *La Forestal*, a huge British-owned timber company that had unsuccessfully tried to counter unionisation by a number of means, including the funding and arming of a special police force obligingly recruited for them among convicted criminals. Now that the workers had taken up arms, the Army was being called in. That repression was as swift and brutal as in many other similar incidents of the day is a matter of record. Little, however, is to be found about young Lieutenant Perón's part in these proceedings or in the many others which involved clashes between Army and workers. In the apologetic *Vida de Perón* written by Enrique Pavón Pereyra it is said that the experience in Villa Guillermina was an eye-opener; that Perón mistrusted the local *caciques* (bosses) and 'attempted' to establish contact with the striking workers. As in many other instances in Perón's life, there are also contrasting versions, as in Mary Main's violently anti-Peronist tract, *Evita — The Woman with the Whip*, which in describing the 'Tragic Week' of 1919 says, 'In one case it was Perón's voice that ordered the troops to open fire on the strikers.'

In 1918 Perón was posted to the Esteban de Luca arsenal in Buenos Aires. Apart from winning the national fencing championship, he spent much of his time discussing with his civilian friends the final phases of the Great War and its political implications for Argentina. Those who claim to remember those days say that he emerged as an admirer of the German military and a staunch defender of the neutralist stand adopted by Argentina under de la Plaza and Yrigoyen. He certainly lived through the events of the 'Tragic Week' in Buenos Aires and, shortly afterwards in February 1919, he was posted back to the 12th Infantry where he was promoted first lieutenant at the year-end. Almost immediately he was sent again to Buenos Aires, as an instructor at the Sargento Cabral school for non-commissioned officers, in the huge military complex of Campo de Mayo. There Perón was to spend six full years, leaving as a captain headed for the staff college, the Escuela Superior de Guerra. Just before entering the college he had met a girl, María Aurelia Tizón or 'Potota', as she was known to family and friends. A teacher by training, the quiet Potota was an accomplished guitarist and an amateur painter, a lover of 'culture' who also found time to spend on bouts of fundraising for good causes. They fell in love, their courtship extending even into a joint dedication to Perón's studies, as Potota used her knowledge of English to translate military textbooks for him. Very soon they decided on marriage, a decision originally scheduled to coincide with another big step in Perón's career, the publication of his first book, a treatise on operations on the Eastern front during the Great War. But the wedding had to be postponed as a result of the death of Perón's father in 1928. Once the period of mourning was over, on 5 January 1929, they married. A week later Perón graduated from the staff college and shortly afterwards was posted to the Army General Staff.

President Yrigoyen was already under heavy attack from his opponents, and the Army had not remained untouched by the division in civilian society. A large number of officers were decidedly pro-Yrigoyen; others, if not completely happy with the government, felt it was their duty to stand by the constitutionally elected authority. But among the latter the devotion to 'professionalism' started to waver when the government began to favour its friends in the forces at the time of promotions and postings. The fear that the Army might begin to 'fall apart' (right-wing propagandists said that the whole of society was disintegrating) was perhaps the leading cause of military disaffection. The nationalistic rhetoric of the Right was easy to identify with, especially when part of that rhetoric depicted the Army as the only unpolluted hope for the country, and called on its members to bring about 'the hour of the sword'. But from a nationalist viewpoint there was little to fault in Yrigoyen's policies, save perhaps what some critics have described as his lack of awareness of the dangers posed by growing US influence in South America (the North Americans had already gained an important foothold in the Argentine economy when they began to challenge the British for control of the vital meat-packing industry).

It was not that the sense of unease in political and Army circles lacked all foundation in fact. Indeed the first signs were already appearing of an upheaval that would literally overturn all the premises upon which Argentina's links with the world economy had been predicated. Even as Perón was settling into his office at the Army General Staff, Wall Street was crashing, setting in motion the first truly major crisis of the capitalist system, the great depression that would be the hallmark of the 1930s. Except by default, inasmuch as he did not readily pursue a radical modification of Argentina's economic structure (power in this field remained firmly in the hands of the landowning oligarchy), Yrigoyen's government could not be held responsible for the way this crisis affected Argentina, together with all other peripheral nations umbilically linked to the industrialised centres by their exports of raw materials. The full import of the crisis could not yet be envisaged in Yrigoyen's second year of office; no one could have foretold then that the very basis of the Ricardian international division of labour embraced by Argentina's oligarchy, the exchange of the products of the land for manufactures produced in Europe, would henceforth become rigged against the peripheral nations. From the 1930s onwards, each tonne of exports from the periphery would cost ever less, while each tonne of manufactured goods imported from the centres would cost progressively more. The mechanism described by economists as 'the deterioration of the terms of trade' came onstage as the industrialised nations sought to extricate themselves from the depression. But that was in the future; the first immediate effects were a sharp downturn in the volume of trade, and the spread of unemployment, which hit Argentina together with the onset of a new migratory wave from the countryside to the cities, and particularly to the capital, Buenos Aires. Suddenly, the overcrowed *conventillos* were no longer the most sordid aspect of Buenos Aires' lopsided development; vacant lots began to be filled with makeshift tin and cardboard shacks, the *villas miseria* where the workless, the uprooted and displaced made their homes in the hope of picking up some of the crumbs of urban prosperity.

This was the atmosphere in which Perón and some of his fellow-officers began to feel drawn to the mirage of military-led 'order' as an effective antidote to the decay rather simplistically attributed to Yrigoyen's rule. When Major Angel Solari walked into Perón's office and invited him to join the conspiratorial cabal, the young Captain did not hesitate.

He was taken along to a first meeting with General Uriburu, his son Alberto (a civilian), Majors Sosa Molina and Solari, and Captain Franklin

Lucero. There it became apparent that General Uriburu had finally decided to act on hearing that the fire brigade (still doubling as riot control police) were on the verge of attempting a coup on their own. In need of a visible head, they had invited the General to lead them; instead he persuaded them to wait until he had engaged the support of the Army. At this introductory meeting Perón heard the General explain that the revolution he wanted 'was not aimed only against the men presently in power, but also against the very system of government and the electoral laws which permitted the arrival at such a state of affairs'. Uriburu argued vehemently for a radical modification of the Constitution, leaning — says Perón — 'towards a collectivist system he did not explain clearly'. The General insisted, too, that the revolution could only be launched when the plotters had enlisted the support of at least 80 per cent of the Army's officer corps. He explained that General Justo, the former War Minister seen by many as an alternative leader of the uprising, had agreed to play no active role himself, but was willing to lend his support to the revolution when it took place. But what shocked Perón was the realisation that at that moment the conspirators only counted on the allegiance of some twenty officers, of whom the only senior men were the General himself and two lieutenant-colonels, Alvaro Alzogaray and Bautista Molina. The work, he concluded, had not even begun.

His amazement was to increase in early July, when he was told of his appointment to the Operations Section of the Revolutionary General Staff, under Lieutenant-Colonel Alzogaray. One of the first tasks given him by his chief was the assessment of an action plan which involved taking control of the Buenos Aires arsenal, then hiding ten or twenty men in a newspaper distribution van which was to drive up to the President's house, where they would charge in and take Yrigoyen prisoner. The scheme was discarded when the Captain pointed out that the assault team did not stand a chance of surviving the crossfire of machine-guns from emplacements on the rooftops of the President's house and the buildings opposite. But the incident aroused doubts in Perón's mind as to the motives that impelled Alzogaray and his colleague Molina to insist on immediate action when it was evident that very little serious planning had taken place and, even more dangerous, that very little effort had been put into recruiting the senior echelons of the Army.

In the blow-by-blow account of the preparations for the revolution which Perón penned in early 1931, he hints darkly at officers being 'personally compromised'; at 'accounts pending with military justice' and at

senior men in 'dire financial straits', but never actually spells out his
accusations. What he does say is that the two lieutenant-colonels on
Uriburu's General Staff were deliberately blocking the enlistment of
high-ranking officers in order to preserve their own positions, and that
they even kept the other members of the General Staff in the dark about
the negotiations that were taking place with civilian elements. Perón's
spirits were raised in early August when a couple of colonels (Juan
Pistarini and José M. Mayora) joined the team of conspirators, yet when
a mass meeting was called shortly afterwards, only 100 or so officers
turned up, most of them lieutenants and sub-lieutenants. Amid
grumbles from Perón and other junior staff officers that preparations
were far from ripe, by the end of that month it was clear that Uriburu
had been persuaded by his civilian mentors to act promptly; the revolutionary General Staff was disbanded and each of its members was given
an operational task. Perón was to aid in the capture of the Sargento
Cabral school for non-commissioned officers, where he had served for six
years. He was to report to a Lieutenant-Colonel Cernadas for orders.
When he did so, full of enthusiastic anticipation, he was appalled to find
that Cernadas was completely unaware of the role assigned to him by the
revolutionaries. 'Had he not been a gentleman,' writes Perón, 'he could
have ordered my arrest forthwith.' Yet the plan for the coup continued
to progress. Basically it envisaged a glorified parade, led by the officers
and cadets of the Colegio Militar, into the capital; the handful of junior
officers committed to the uprising (a second mass meeting had again
failed to raise more than 100 men) were somehow to take over their units
and join the rebel column on its way to the town centre. More credibly,
groups of armed civilians were expected to do likewise.

   Convinced that the whole exercise was doomed to failure, on 3
September Perón sought out Alzogaray and hotly resigned all commissions from the revolutionary command. However, he did state that his
ultimate support was not to be doubted, and that he would continue to
work for the revolution in the manner he though best. It soon became
evident that other officers had been thinking along similar lines. The
very next day, Perón was invited to join a group led by Lieutenant-
Colonel Descalzo, a man who had rebuffed earlier attempts to recruit
him into General Uriburu's team. Descalzo was very much in touch
with the 'legalist' civilian opposition to Yrigoyen, the despised 'professional politicians' that Uriburu wanted to sweep away together with the
ruling party. In this new group Perón found that 'we all thought that
the worst thing we could do was to enthrone a military dictatorship

which would be opposed by the nation as a whole. The students had roamed the streets shouting "no to dictatorship" and had declared that they would resist any form of dictatorship. The media were frankly against such a form of government. If the revolutionary movement gained the streets in a quest for a military dictatorship it would find itself in a vacuum.'

The overriding preoccupation of the group headed by Descalzo seemed to be to prevent General Uriburu's revolution from becoming a grotesque failure — in Perón's own words, 'an operetta uprising more fitting to some mini-republic of Central America'. One of the leading figures of this conspiracy within a conspiracy, Lieutenant-Colonel Sarobe, penned a manifesto for the revolution which they felt would be acceptable to the politicians. The following morning, while some of the plotters made the rounds of the barracks mustering support, Perón ran off 200 copies of the manifesto on an Army General Staff mimeograph. By the end of the day they had collected some 300 adherences, and armed with this backing, Descalzo set out to speak to General Uriburu. The revolutionary leader surprised them with the announcement that the uprising had been scheduled for the following morning at 7 o'clock. President Yrigoyen, bedridden again with influenza, had handed over the reins of the Executive to the acting Vice-President, Dr Enrique Martínez, with whom the revolutionaries had some sort of understanding. Martínez had declared the country to be in a state of siege. But Uriburu did not reject Descalzo's approach; instead he adopted the manifesto and appointed him representative of the Military Junta before the Civilian Junta of the Revolution, and Perón was made his adjutant.

The motley caravan of officers and cadets left the Colegio Militar on schedule. Among the incidents that remained in Army folklore was the enthusiasm of a cadet with a broken leg who insisted on being driven into the capital, plaster cast and all, in a motorcycle sidecar; the cadet was Alvaro Alsogaray, a name which was to appear again in Argentine politics. Perón was busy before dawn trying to secure, if not the adherence of the Army units within the capital, then at least promises of non-intervention; eventually he commandeered an armoured car and was among the first to arrive at the government house, the Casa Rosada, which they found with a large white tablecloth fluttering from a balcony and Dr Martínez 'wishing to resign but finding no one to whom he could submit his resignation', as Perón wrote. The young Captain missed the only armed action of the day; at the sound of cannon fire from

Congress Square he rushed through the city in his armoured car, only to find everything over by the time he arrived. A few armed civilians had attempted to resist. In *La Prensa*'s glowing version of the events, 'The shooting that took place in Congress Square between the civilian and military forces of the nation and the men lying in ambush who tried to machine-gun them was a heroic occasion of which memories will live for many years . . . There were, of course, some casualties. But the losses were almost entirely of horses of the [Colegio Militar] cavalry, whose bulk offered an easy target. As to the artillery, it was only used when they noticed aggression allegedly coming from the upper balconies of Congress . . . Then, as agreed, a 75mm. cannon was used to fire five times against this spot, upon which the aggression was silenced.' The civilian dead were never counted; Army annals remember the names of two cadets who died in that action: Güemes and Larguía.

Yrigoyen had been alerted before sunrise by his War Minister and had fled the capital to set up his headquarters in the barracks of the 7th Infantry Regiment in La Plata, some 60 kilometres away. He prepared to order a march on the Buenos Aires arsenal, which he hoped would be obeying the Minister's orders, but the revolutionaries pre-empted the move by threatening to bomb that unit, and forced it to surrender. Informed that Dr Martínez had already handed over the government to the insurgents, Yrigoyen submitted his resignation and voluntarily placed himself under arrest.

In later years Perón was to claim that he had learnt much from this, his first experience of a military revolt. At the time, however, his conclusions were brief: 'The revolution was virtually over, but in the spirits of those of us who had taken part in its preparation and execution there remained one bitter disappointment: most of the officers had not participated because they had not even been approached. Consequently, the troops had not left their barracks to support the movement save in insignificant numbers. Instead two infantry regiments in the capital had been frankly opposed to the revolution and it was a known fact that no support would be forthcoming from the Army headquarters at Campo de Mayo. People had been prepared in Congress to repel the tiny column led by General Uriburu, and their chances of success had been high. It was only a miracle that saved the revolution. That miracle was performed by *the people of Buenos Aires, who overflowed into the streets like a human avalanche to the cry of "Long live the Revolution!"*, capturing the government house and swaying the troops in favour of the movement, and co-operating in every way to secure a victory that otherwise would have proved too costly, if not impossible.' Many years afterwards, commenting on *La Prensa*'s equally enthusiastic celebration of the role played by 'the people' in the revolution of 6 September 1930, a book issued by a *peronista* union, under the title *Cien años contra el país* (A hundred years against the country), said bitingly 'As usual, *La Prensa* "confused" the people as a whole with a single class, and juridical organisation with the interests of that class.'

4

INFAMY AND THE COLONELS' DREAM
(1930–1945)

The ailing Yrigoyen was imprisoned, first on a warship and later on the island of Martín García in the River Plate. His house was set alight by a mob, as was the Radical newspaper *Epoca*; the state of siege was invoked to persecute members of the Unión Cívica Radical as well as Communists (a term already used loosely enough to cover practically anyone the government wanted out of the way). But very soon there was little left of the principles the small band of conspirators had set out to instill in Argentine political life. General Uriburu became provisional President of the Republic, swearing to uphold the Constitution he had wanted to change so radically. After threatening the Supreme Court with dismissal, he obtained juridical endorsement for his régime. His cabinet was headed by Matías Sánchez Sorondo who, under the motto of upholding 'conditioned legality', set himself the task of restoring the influence of the Conservative party; in other words, re-establishing the mechanisms for wholesale electoral fraud. From outside government, political forces rallied around the figure of General Agustín Justo, determined to place him in the Presidency either through elections or by staging another coup.

Uriburu misread the 'popularity' of his rule and in early 1931 put in motion a plan to institutionalise his régime by holding a succession of provincial elections in areas he thought he could easily carry. The first test of this policy, in the province of Buenos Aires, was a dismal failure: the Unión Cívica Radical won by a comfortable margin. Uriburu's cabinet resigned, the elections were annulled, and the following stages of the plan were suspended *sine die*. Faced with renewed threats of a coup by General Justo's followers, Uriburu announced that general elections would be held towards the end of the year; shortly after the announcement, however, he had to face a very real uprising in the province of Corrientes, led by Lieutenant-Colonel Gregorio Pomar, with military and civilian support. The revolt, explicitly aimed at 'restoring the

54

liberties that had been violated', was a flop, and Pomar had to seek asylum in neighbouring Paraguay. Justo's followers again put pressure on Uriburu, forcing him to ban the candidacy of anyone who had held office in previous Radical administrations; when the Unión Cívica Radical proclaimed the nomination of Marcelo T. de Alvear, Yrigoyen's 'anti-personalist' adversary, he too was explicitly banned, and later even physically banished to distant Tierra del Fuego.

Well before the country went to the polls, General Justo was clearly running with all the cards stacked in his favour. The conservatives, renamed 'National Democrats', nominated him as their candidate, with Julio A. Roca as his running mate; the 'anti-personalists' also nominated Justo, but substituted José Nicolás Matienzo as candidate for the Vice-Presidency. And to crown it all, Justo managed to place his own man, Octavio Pico, in the key Ministry of the Interior, whence he could preside over the details of the fraudulent procedures that would guarantee Justo's victory. The final result was never really in doubt but, fraud and all, Justo — backed by Conservatives, anti-personalists and independent socialists — did not obtain an impressive margin over his rivals, an alliance between the socialists and the Progressive Democrats, a party based in the grainbelt of Santa Fe province.

Uriburu's revolution had vanished without glory. He himself died in Paris, after an unsuccessful operation, shortly after handing over the Presidency to Justo. His ideological supporters of *La Nueva República* whined, 'If we are talking revolution, we want real revolutions, but if it is to be elections, then we prefer clean elections.' The only remnant of Uriburu's corporativist dream was the paramilitary Legión Cívica, armed by the War Ministry, which the régime would retain as a political shock force. The young Captain Perón had seen his own revolutionary career truncated at an early stage, when he was removed from the secretariat of the War Ministry and sent off to teach military history at the staff college.

In the mean time, the depression in the northern hemisphere had arrived in Argentina with all its force. Unemployment had risen steeply, the *villa miseria* next to the port of Buenos Aires had grown into a sprawling township of rickety, unhealthy shacks, tuberculosis was rampant among the ill-fed workers and destitute vagrants, and queues of hungry men and women seeking a cupful of thin soup from the 'people's pans' had become an everyday sight in the poorer quarters of the capital city. The working day was lengthened again, and the mandatory weekly day off was ignored together with the rest of Argentina's scant labour legislation. With Britain imposing protective measures in favour of the export trade of its dominions, Argentina's hard currency revenue was falling rapidly; one of Justo's first acts was to float a loan for 50 million dollars which was instantly swallowed by the servicing of a rising foreign debt. Public works were cut back sharply, with *La Prensa* thundering that it would be a cardinal sin to attempt to alleviate unemployment with make-work schemes. Fraud had been re-established with a vengeance at the heart of the political system, reinforced by the outright proscription of the country's largest political party. If the worst episode of Yrigoyen's rule had gone down in history as the 'Tragic Week', the period inaugurated by General Uriburu's coup came to be known as 'The Decade of Infamy'.

President Justo had no illusions that he was popular, and made no efforts at all to pretend that he was running a democracy. On the economic front, his main preoccupation was the recovery of Argentina's lost trading position with Britain. To this effect he despatched to London a team headed by his Vice-President, Julio Argentino Roca, to argue in favour of an exception for Argentina to the trading restrictions imposed in favour of the Empire. A member of the mission put the case very eloquently when he pleaded that, for all practical purposes, Argentina had always been like a British dominion. After long, tough talks a deal was struck, referred to officially as the London Agreement but more frequently as 'the Roca-Runciman Pact' or, in nationalist circles, *el Estatuto del Coloniaje*, the Colonial Statute. It read like little more than a list of unilateral concessions by Argentina. Britain was free to limit its imports of Argentine beef in order to maintain remunerative prices on its domestic market; it would be the British government's prerogative to allocate a full 85 per cent of the licenses for Argentina's meat trade (which meant aborting the growth of native meat-packing plants); the payments in sterling for Argentina's exports were to be applied as a whole to paying for imports from Britain, or for the remittance to Britain of profits earned in Argentina by British firms; Argentina's imports of coal and other duty-free imports were to remain unburdened by taxation; British-owned utilities — many of which already enjoyed monopoly positions — were to be granted preferential treatment; and as an added twist the creation of Argentina's Central Bank, a crucial element in the ordering of the country's financial sector, was to be supervised by a British expert.

The 'Roca-Runciman Pact' and its attendant local legislation was not implemented without opposition; the Progressive Democrats flung themselves into a fiery campaign against it in Congress. Indeed, for his unflinching denunciation of the abuses regarding British and US control of the meat-packing industry, a young Senator of that party, Enzo Bordabehere, was assassinated in the middle of a legislative session. The Socialists, most notably Alfredo Palacios, also put up a battle around the concessions in the meat trade, the railways and public utilities. But the one potentially effective opponent of the Pact and its effects, the Unión Cívica Radical, was either absent from this resistance or actually went along with the government's proposals. The erstwhile intransigents, now led by Alvear (Yrigoyen died shortly after being released from Martín García in 1933; he was then in utter poverty, although he earned the final accolade of an unprecedented mass demonstration at his funeral), were busy toning down their policy positions, abandoning such revered standards as the call for a state oil monopoly and 'principles of equality and universality' as a precondition for Argentina's entry to international organisations.

When the time came for the régime to change Presidents, in 1937, the array of fraudulent procedures (the 'open' vote, rolls purged of opposition voters, inclusion in the rolls of scores of people long dead, multiple registration of government partisans, substitution of ballot boxes, and, as an added guarantee, intimidation and outright violence) were so formidable that no one doubted that the official candidate, Roberto M. Ortiz, would be proclaimed President. So it happened, although cynics were to maintain for years to come that if the counting had been truthful, abstentions would have carried the day.

But the most carefully prepared schemes can have their flaws, and in this case the unforeseen factor was the personality of the new President, Roberto Ortiz. Soon after taking office, Ortiz publicly swung over to 'legalism'. When fraud was used to secure the continuance of the régime in the northwestern province of Catamarca, Ortiz demanded the annulment of the results. Months later he acted similarly in the province of Buenos Aires, appointing a federal trustee to take over from a governor installed by the most blatant fraud ever practiced in Argentine politics. Within his own government, Ortiz had to cope with the active opposition of his Vice-President, Ramón Castillo, a man committed to the preservation of conservative influence at any cost. In 1939 he also provoked the enmity of many in the Army; when Adolf Hitler invaded Poland and Europe was suddenly at war, Ortiz made no secret of his leanings towards the Allies, and gave his blessing to the creation of Acción Argentina, an organisation devoted to securing the country's support for Britain and its friends.

Argentina's immigratory past had blessed it with a constellation of large foreign communities, and their integration into the host society had been very variable. It was perhaps most complete among the off-spring of the largest contingents, the Spaniards and Italians from rural areas, whose first contact with 'organised culture' had taken place in Argentine schools. But even among them the links with the mother-countries remained strong; families were supported across the Atlantic by the migrants, and among the members of the older generations there remained something of that messianic dream of a return in prosperity, having *fatto l'America*. Spaniards in Argentina had weakly divided over the civil war in their homeland, for the Republic or for Franco. Italians were split, often depending on the strength of reminiscences of an anarchist forebear, between repulsion and admiration for Mussolini. This was among the more integrated; segregation remained almost com-plete still among the large British community, whose allegiance to the cause of their homeland was strengthened by the firm economic links between it and Argentina, and among the Germans, whose ties with the Army establishment were close. Argentina also had an 'old', semi-integrated community of Jews, the fruit of a fleeting Zionist dream of establishing the new state of Israel in the province of Entre Ríos, and an increasing trickle of 'new' Jews, protectively introverted in their remembrance of the more recent persecution they had escaped; the mark of the early arrivals would linger in the popular designation of the Argentine Jews as *rusos*, Russians. In a similar vein, Argentina's big Arab community, mainly Lebanese and Syrians fleeing Ottoman rule, were irritatingly called *turcos*, Turks.

As in other overseas German communities, in Argentina too there had appeared a local branch of the National-Socialist Party. In 1939 Ortiz had it banned. It is worth noting that in Argentina it was not only pro-Nazis and undiscerning germanophiles who were perturbed by Ortiz's proximity to the Allied cause. For genuine nationalists in Argentina, the truly obnoxious foreign presence, surrounded by all the privileges of the 'Roca-Runciman Pact'; the ally of the conservative rulers who retained power by undisguised fraud and violence; the enemy — was undis-putedly Britain. It is also worth remembering that in those early days Nazi and Fascist rhetoric was taken more readily at face value even in Europe, to say nothing of the United States; the horrors of the concen-tration camps, the gassing and slaughtering of millions were still in the future, to be only reluctantly accepted as reality even by those who were waging war against Hitler. What Ortiz was doing, in the eyes of many, was flirting with the true enemy.

The issue was controversial enough to keep Ortiz's leanings from being actually translated into policy: Argentina, as during the previous war, remained neutral. Moreover, Ortiz was a sick man and ever more frequently found himself having to entrust his Executive functions to his Vice-President, Castillo. By mid-1940 it was Castillo, rather than Ortiz, who was running the government, although it would take another two years before the elected President, faced with overwhelming evidence that he was medically unfit for office, was forced to resign. In the mean time, the question of Argentina's position towards the war, and towards Nazi activity within the country, was to place itself very much at the centre of political debate, creating a web of pressures and counter-pressures between the Executive, Congress and the armed forces.

In mid-1941 the Chamber of Deputies voted to establish a special committee to investigate 'subversive' (meaning Nazi) activities in Argentina. The chairman of the committee, Raúl Damonte Taborda, annouced publicly that he was acting hand in hand with his counterpart in the United States, Martin Dies, who headed a Congressional com-mittee charged with looking into 'totalitarian' activities there. Shortly after its creation Taborda's committee created a stir by stating that its investigations had revealed that the German National Socialist Party in Argentina (banned by Ortiz two years earlier) was in fact continuing to operate under the guise of the Federation of German Leagues for Culture and Welfare, and that the Congressional body had ordered the arrest of some fifty prominent members of that organisation. They were to be charged with diverting funds ostensibly collected for charity to financing Nazi propaganda in three journals, the *Deutsche La Plata Zeitung, Restaurador* and *El Pampero*. Tension was increased by the further revela-tions that a German diplomatic pouch sent from Buenos Aires to Lima, Perú, had been intercepted and found to contain a radio transmitter and inflammatory Nazi propaganda material, and that eighty-three packets of Nazi propaganda had been discovered entering the port of Buenos Aires in the Japanese ship *Nana Maru*.

While these proceedings were under way, public opinion was rocked by the news that a military uprising had narrowly been averted in the province of Entre Ríos, with the arrest of twenty-six military men con-spiring under the leadership of General Juan Bautista Molina, the man who as a lieutenant-colonel in 1930 had headed the recruitment section of General Uriburu's revolutionary General Staff, and who now styled himself the leader of a 'Supreme Council of Argentine Nationalism'.

The aborted revolt was followed by the Senate's decision to emulate

their colleagues in the Chamber of Deputies and set up their own committee to investigate Nazi activities. The first names of arrested members
of the German community became known: Herr Korn, acting leader of
the Nazi party; Herr Wieland, secretary of the Federation of German
Leagues; Herr Volberg, chairman of the German Trade Bureau. Barely a
month went by before another military revolt was nipped in the bud, this
time in the Aviation School at Córdoba, where Fascist ideological
influence was anything but discreet; twenty officers were arrested and
the head of the Air Force, General Zuloaga, was eased into retirement.

The tug-of-war between opposing forces, domestic and external,
became more intense. The Army secured from the government the
creation of its own industrial enterprise, the autonomous Dirección
General de Fabricaciones Militares, whose initial charter entrusted it
with the production of war material and prospecting for and extracting
strategic minerals, but which was to expand rapidly to other areas of
industrial endeavour. As had occurred earlier in the Great War,
hostilities in Europe had begun to squeeze Argentina's supplies of manufactured goods, and with ever more countries being drawn in, the
military had begun to view the situation with concern. Their preoccupation was at first purely military; they were becoming suddenly aware of
the extreme vulnerability of Argentina's defence apparatus as a result of
the country's almost absolute dependence on imported manufactures.
Industrialisation began to be predicated on the grounds of national
security, which overruled any considerations of economic orthodoxy to
which the Army hierarchy, aping the shallow Ricardian rhetoric of the
ruling oligarchy, had previously subscribed. Control of the country's
fuel supply, the acquisition of its own steelmaking capacity, control of its
communications systems and its public utilities; all began to be seen as
essential pieces of a coherent doctrine of national security. The influence
of German strategic thinking in all this was evident, but then similar
conclusions could be drawn from the experience of the United States,
and within the country it became suddenly possible to discover a long
tradition of political thought along similar lines, even though this was
achieved partly by stretching the imagination and incorporating some
left-overs of Spanish mercantilism and a number of examples that owed
more to narrow-minded autarkic schemes of local chieftains. Yet there is
no denying that this convergence was what gave birth to Argentina's
policies of deliberate industrialisation; indeed these unequal progenitors
are the explanation for much of the incoherence of these policies, and for
the extreme polarisation that framed them. (The oligarchy's failure to

pursue industrialisation began to be portrayed as deliberately culpable, rather than the almost inevitable outcome of its history and of current 'world' outlooks as they were imported to Argentina; because the oligarchy was mainly concerned with agriculture, preoccupation with this sector of the country's economy would become anathema.) The hard reality created by the war, as it impinged on the military mind, dictated the imperative of industrialisation. The rationale was one of national security in a very strict sense, but it would not be long before this reading of national security, as the main purpose in life of the military, was invoked to justify military intervention in the country's political life. This is not to say that it was an artificial implant in the political scene; it actually fitted the needs of the country so well that in conjunction with the demands for political and economic participation of the working class it was to generate one of the most remarkable and long-lasting political mobilisations recorded in South America.

The war produced some other fortunate coincidences. The old nationalist complaint about foreign domination of the shipping of Argentina's produce and imports, a constant 'invisible' drain on the country's income, and the demand for a national merchant marine (only minimally heeded by Yrigoyen) were to be answered by a turn of fate. A number of ships sailing under belligerent flags had been paralysed in the port of Buenos Aires by the threat of attack on high seas. The government grasped the opportunity and bought them at bargain prices, in one fell swoop augmenting Argentina's merchant capacity by almost 90,000 tonnes.

Zigzagging continued, in the mean time, on the political front. Towards the end of 1941, as acting President, Castillo decreed a state of siege and invoked its provisions to ban Acción Argentina, the pro-Allied lobby organisation. Yet the very following month, at the conference of American states held in Brazil at Washington's instigation, Argentina was formally agreeing to the 'Declaration of Rio', which although preserving its 'non-belligerent' status recommended the severance of diplomatic, commercial and financial links with Axis nations, the blacklisting of Axis-owned companies and continent-wide coordination of 'anti-subversive' operations. The Argentine government immediately created, under the Ministry of the Interior, a special police department charged with 'vigilance over and suppression of anti-Argentine activities', while a restless Army forced the government to decree the retention of the classes of conscripts who were actually serving and the mobilisation of two more classes, increasing the force's strength to 90,000 men.

In July 1942 President Ortiz was forced to resign and Castillo formally assumed office. Almost immediately the departure from Ortiz's legalism came out into the open, with the President declaring that his government enjoyed 'a unanimity of one — myself, for I am the one who makes the decisions.' An open advocate of electoral fraud as a necessity in a country where, in his view, political discernment was notably lacking in the masses, Castillo set himself promptly to the task of selecting the régime's successor. His choice fell upon Robustiano Patrón Costas, a wealthy plantation owner from Argentina's northwest. The prospective candidate ran into a series of strong objections. In surprising contrast to Castillo's own supposed pro-Axis leanings, Patrón Costas was known to sympathise with the Allies, and was particularly considered to have close ties with the United States. This made him *persona non grata* in military circles, and political gossip of the time would have had it that there had been expressions of British dissatisfaction with his selection (there was talk of an unwritten agreement to interpret Argentina's neutrality, as such things go, as flexible enough to allow both pro-German and pro-British gestures, but always to be uncompromisingly anti-United States). The fact that Patrón Costas ran his estates along semi-feudal lines also raised a number of misgivings among some high-ranking Army officers who already feared that the régime's social insensitivity might be creating a favourable atmosphere for the spread of Communism.

By the time Patrón Costas' candidacy was announced, a number of Army officers were already plotting revolution. Its preparation was much more meticulous that that of the 1930 revolution had been, and none of the previous confusion and uncertainty accompanied the mobilisation of troops to key positions on 4 June 1943 or the installation of a military government as the deposed President Castillo fled across the River Plate in a minesweeper to Uruguay. There was, however, a minor hitch as the General installed by the rebels in the Presidency, Arturo Rawson, began instantly to display signs of independence by appointing a ministerial cabinet that failed to meet the approval of the leaders of the coup. It included two civilians, one of whom was José María Rosa, the editor of *El Pampero*, the nationalist newspaper which had been accused by the Congressional committee of receiving funds for propaganda purposes from the undercover Nazi party. Rawson's deviations were corrected two days later, when the conspirators replaced him with General Pedro Pablo Ramírez, who as a lieutenant-colonel had headed the Intelligence section of General Uriburu's revolutionary General Staff in 1930. With Ramírez, an all-military cabinet was selected. Although the government included in leading positions four generals and four admirals, the real power behind the throne was a cabal of colonels who had conducted the actual orchestration of the coup. These were the members of the Grupo Obra de Unificación (GOU), whose leading light was Colonel Juan Domingo Perón, the puppet-master who for the time being preferred to keep off the centre stage, in a relatively obscure position as head of the secretariat at the War Ministry. Perón's second step, taken when the new régime was less than five months old, puzzled many at the time: he requested, and obtained, his appointment as chairman of the National Labour Department, a very minor government agency. Two months later, when he had the Department upgraded to a Secretariat (a Ministry in all but name), with himself in command, his motives had begun to emerge more clearly.

When Perón was displaced from his initial, admittedly minor position of political influence in the Uriburu régime, he settled down to what, within the Army, could be considered the closest approximation to academic life: the professorship of military history at the Escuela Superior de Guerra, the Army's staff college. As a pupil at the college he had already displayed a talent for this kind of work, which had been reflected in his first two writings, *El frente oriental en la guerra mundial de 1914* and *Estudios estratégicos* (both of 1928). Very soon he was promoted to a position on the General Staff of the college and he added to his work the essay *Lo que yo vi de la preparación y realización del 6 de Septiembre de 1930* (What I saw of the preparation and realisation of 6 September 1930) which circulated in manuscript form among some members of the officer corps and was later preserved as an appendix to the memoirs of General José María Sarobe. Almost as a matter of course, Perón became a major in December 1932. The defence he had made of military professionalism in his reflections on Uriburu's revolution, plus the name he was making for himself at the Escuela Superior de Guerra, attracted the attention of President Justo's War Minister, General Manuel Rodríguez, a man obsessed not only with modernising the Army, but also with extricating it from what he considered its excessive involvement in politics in the aftermath of the coup. General Rodríguez 'borrowed' Perón as a special adjutant, and obtained from him a stream of recommendations on the way to tackle his difficult task. The whole enterprise met much resistance, and if Perón's contributions enhanced his prestige among many of his colleagues, it also evoked reactions of envy and suspicion among his superiors. The Minister did not last in his post, and Perón soon found himself back in the Escuela Superior de Guerra teaching military history. He buried himself in military academia, churning out a number of books in the following three years: a tome on the theoretical aspects of military history (*Apuntes de historia militar: parte teórica*); a three-volume study of the Russo-Japanese war (*Guerra ruso-japonesa*); and *Toponimia araucana*, an opuscule on Indian place-names in Patagonia.

His popularity among his fellow-officers was confirmed by his election as Secretary of the Círculo Militar, the Army's social club, and it has been suggested that this popularity was at the root of the hierarchy's decision to send him abroad in 1936, during the Ortiz Presidency, as military attaché to the Argentine embassy in Santiago, Chile. While he was there he was notified of his promotion to the rank of lieutenant-colonel, and he was entrusted with a delicate labour of espionage, the task of obtaining Chile's mobilisation plans in case of war with Argentina. For this purpose he began to cultivate a retired Chilean officer, Leopoldo Haniez, and eventually got around to offering him a considerable sum of money for the plans. Haniez took the bait, but the job was a complicated one, since it involved Haniez's influencing at least one other officer on active service with access to these secret documents. Before this could take place, Perón was recalled to Buenos Aires to take up a position on the Army General Staff; the operation was left in the hands of his successor in Santiago, Lieutenant-Colonel Eduardo Lonardi. Only days after Perón's return to Argentina, Chilean counter-intelligence agents swooped on a clandestine meeting, arresting Lonardi, Haniez, another Chilean officer and a photographer. Perón's involvement was proved in a captured letter to Haniez; Lonardi was expelled from Chile.

For a few months Perón alternated between his staff job, teaching Combined Operations at the Escuela de Guerra Naval, the Navy's staff college, and putting the finishing touches to the two-volume opus *Las operaciones de 1870*, which he had been writing with Colonel Enrique Rottjer. This relatively placid existence was shattered on 10 September 1938 by the death of his wife 'Potota'. Although foreseeable, as her health had been deteriorating for some time, the event had a tremendous impact on Perón. His vivacity vanished, he took only a passing interest in his official duties and even gave up his by now consuming devotion to reading and writing. Morose and ever more withdrawn, he seemed to have lost all that drive that his fellow-officers had so admired.

President Ortiz's War Minister, General Carlos D. Márquez, came up with a solution which was both to reanimate one of his most brilliant staff officers and to put his talents to work on a task the Army, and a number of leading figures in government, considered of vital importance: the collection of accurate information on the situation in Europe. Hitler was already on the move, annexing Austria and Czechoslovakia; there was a mass of conflicting information as to the reaction of other European nations, and not a few were speaking of the possibility of war. So Lieutenant-Colonel Perón was to be posted to Rome, ostensibly as an attaché at the embassy with a particular interest in the Italian Army's mountaineering techniques, but with a private brief that called for trips all over Europe, including both Germany, where he was to contact the German officers who had been his teachers at the Colegio Militar, and Spain, where his old teacher, General Wilhelm von Faupel, had been entrusted with an important intelligence job for the Third Reich.

Perón warmed rapidly to the idea, and in February 1939 he made the crossing to Italy. The official side of his business was conducted quite thoroughly; he was successively posted to the 14th Mountain Regiment at Chieti, the *Tridentina* Alpine division and the Pinerolo Mountain Infantry division; he attended the Italian Army's mountaineering school at Aosta and the ski school at Sestriere. But it was not long before his unofficial brief took over. With the invasion of Poland and the outbreak of war, his most pressing task was to prepare an assessment of Germany's chances of success. He travelled to Germany. In old age, in his Spanish exile, he would reminisce:

In all the time I spent there I had the sensation of an enormous piece of machinery that functioned with marvellous perfection, without a single screw missing. The degree of organisation was formidable. The autobahns, another stunning marvel, were already working. The moment one entered Germany one realised that nowhere in Europe was there anything that worked so perfectly and precisely. I studied the social and political phenomenon in depth: here was a great melting-pot in which something new was coming together. The communist revolution was advancing in Russia, according to the theories of Marx and Engels, as interpreted by Lenin. But in Germany what had emerged was an unprecedented social phenomenon, National-Socialism, in the same fashion as Italy had given birth to Fascism. [. . .] Italian Fascism had given the popular organisations effective participation in the country's life, from which they had always been kept apart. Until Mussolini came to power, the nation had marched in one direction and the worker in another, and the latter had had no participation in the former. I discovered the resurgence of the corporations and studied them in depth. I began to discover that evolution would lead us, if not towards the corporations — because it was not possible to retreat back to the Middle Ages — then at least towards a formula in which the people played an active part. When I discovered this I thought that Germany was undergoing a similar process, that is to say, an organised state for a perfectly ordered community. [. . .]

That is how I created the whole doctrine. [. . .] People will say that it was a simple reflection of what was happening in Europe and I will answer that that is so, because that is the way our country has always been. What happens in Europe reaches us ten years later.

Perón's fact-finding mission took him to occupied France, to Hungary, to Yugoslavia and Albania, to Portugal ('the world's greatest centre of espionage') and to Spain ('What pain and misery! There is nothing worse than a civil war, and [for us] no effort to prevent one shall be too great'). If one accepts A.J.P. Taylor's observation that there was no such thing as a single Second World War, what Perón witnessed was the initial wave of successful aggressive wars launched by Hitler and the beginning of the harsh peace of occupation or neutrality he imposed upon continental Europe, before the Allies managed to put together their own wars of reconquest. He did not meet Hitler (the closest he got was to hear him deliver an uninspiring speech about Germany's domestic supplies) but he did make a point of calling formally on Mussolini to shake his hand ('I would never have forgiven myself if I had reached old age, having been in Rome and not having met such a great man') before he was recalled to Argentina towards the end of 1940.

Europe had certainly done marvels for the depressed, grieving widower of two years earlier. It had given him a renewed interest in his career, though with an added political slant it had lacked before. And it had reawakened in him the ladies' man of earlier years. Many decades later he would remember the 'little German girl with a complexion of flour and eggs' who was his first human contact and guide in Berlin, and the far more passionate affair he had with an Italian actress in Barcelona as he awaited the arrival of a ship to take him home. Indeed, the childless Perón was to remain obsessed with the notion that he had left her pregnant, and spent many fruitless years trying to track her down after the war.

On his return to Buenos Aires, Perón was almost immediately posted to the Instruction Centre for Mountain Troops in the province of Mendoza. There has been much speculation about this move, including the very late myth put out by one of Perón's political associates, Jorge Antonio, that the lieutenant-colonel had incurred the displeasure of his superiors by openly forecasting the ultimate defeat of Germany in the European war. No evidence has ever been offered for this argument, which indeed contradicts many of Perón's statements at the time and much later. Moreover, the new job he was given was the only natural one for an officer who had officially spent the better part of two years specialising in the command of mountain troops. There may have been something in the notion that some of his superiors wanted him far from the hub of political power, but it must be considered also that Argentine military tradition demanded of an officer destined for higher command that he must have spent some time actually in charge of some large operational unit. Perón, with most of his career spent in military training institutes and in staff or administrative positions, was certainly in need of such experience. He became Director of the Instruction Centre for Mountain Troops, was promoted to the rank of colonel a few months later, and went on to build up this relatively novel section of the Army to the point that he was appointed Commander of the Mendoza Mountain Detachment and then was attached to the General Staff as supervisor of a series of major exercises in the Andes, close to the Chilean border.

Physically he may have been far from the country's and the Army's decision-making centres. But in a very short time the centre of a new factor of power within the Army would gravitate towards him. Two lieutenant-colonels, picking up the widespread concern with the Army's division over political issues, instigated the formation of a secret organisation devoted to the 'unification' of the service's officer corps. Their creation, named Grupo Obra de Unificación (Group for the Task of Unification), soon spread upwards to attract a number of colonels, who sought out Perón as their leader. Much of this development has been romanticised, not least by Perón himself, but verifiable facts certainly point to his influence having been decisive in transforming a very loose association into a tightly organised body with objectives reaching beyond purely military concerns. The movement was secretive, and spread by means of a cell-like organisation, each new member being sworn to silence and charged with enlisting four more recruits. During the greater part of the preparatory stage, real power was kept in the hands of four colonels; Eduardo Avalos, Enrique González, Emilio Ramírez and Juan Domingo Perón. Their objective was a monolithic, highly disciplined officer corps under the orders of the War Minister; the Minister, by custom a general, would eventually be selected by the cabal of colonels. But the key feature of this dream was the purpose for which this iron structure was to be created: the dominant position Argentina would be called to play in Latin America in the new world order they believed was emerging. Many analysts have underlined that this vision coincided with Germany's plans for the hemisphere, and indeed that one of its basic premises was a victorious Germany in the war being waged in Europe.

The GOU's rationale has been presented in a document purporting to be a circular to its members in May 1943, when President Castillo's obvious preference for a pro-Allied successor, Robustiano Patrón Costas, had finally convinced the colonels that the time had come for the Army to take over the complete apparatus of political power. The circular said:

The war has proved beyond doubt that nations can no longer defend themselves on their own. Hence the insecure game of alliances which mitigate this failing without correcting it. The age of the Nation is steadily being replaced by the age of the Continent. Yesterday the feudal baronies united to form the Nation. Today the Nations must unite to form the Continent.

That is the aim of this war.

Germany is engaged in a titanic effort to unify the European Continent. The greatest and best equipped nation must rule the destinies of the newly-formed Continent. In Europe that nation will be Germany.

In America, in the North, the monitoring nation shall for the time being be the United States. But in the South there is no nation strong enough for its tutelage to be accepted without question. There are only two nations capable of assuming this role: Argentina or Brazil.

Our mission is to make our tutelage possible and undisputed.

The task is immense and fraught with sacrifices. But patriotism is impossible without sacrificing everything. The titans of our independence sacrificed their fortunes and their lives. In our days, Germany has given life a heroic meaning. These shall be our examples.

To take the first step along this hard road that will lead to a great and powerful Argentina, it will become indispensable to take Power. A civilian will never comprehend the greatness of our ideal; therefore it will be necessary to eliminate them from government and to charge them with the only mission that befits them: work and obedience.

Once Power has been conquered, our mission shall be to become strong; stronger than all the other countries together. We shall have to arm ourselves, overcoming every difficulty, struggling against internal or external circumstances. Hitler's struggle in war and peace shall be our guide.

Alliances shall be our first step. We can already count on Paraguay; we shall add Bolivia and Chile, and it will be easy to put pressure on Uruguay. Later the five nations together will easily attract Brazil, given its form of government and its large nuclei of Germans. Once Brazil has fallen, the South American Continent shall be ours. Our tutelage shall be a fact, a glorious, unprecedented fact made real by the political genius and the heroism of the Argentine Army.

Some will say, 'Mirages, utopias!' But let us cast our eyes again on Germany. Defeated, it was forced in 1919 to sign the Versailles Treaty, which was to keep it under the yoke of the Allies as a second-rate power for at least fifty years. In less than twenty years it has come a long, fantastic way. Before 1939 it was armed better than any other nation, and in peace-time it annexed Austria and Czechoslovakia. Later, in war, the whole of Europe bent to its will.

But this was not achieved without much sacrifice.

An iron-hard dictatorship was necessary to impose upon the people the renunciations this formidable programme called for.

So shall it be in Argentina. Our government shall be an inflexible dictatorship, though at the outset it will make the necessary concessions to consolidate its position. The people shall be attracted to it, but they will inevitably have to work, suffer deprivations and obey. To work more and to suffer more deprivations than any other people. Thus alone shall they make possible the arms programme which is indispensable for the conquest of the Continent. Following the German example, the radio, the controlled press, cinema, books, the Church and the education system will instill in the people the spirit to understand the heroic path along which it must march. Only thus will it relinquish the comfortable life it now enjoys. Our generation shall be a generation sacrificed for the sake of a higher good: the Argentine Fatherland, which will later shine with unequalled light for the greater good of the Continent and the whole of Humanity.

Long live the Fatherland!

Arríba los Espiritus!'

This circular, made public in 1945 by Silvano Santander, an avowed enemy of Perón's who in Congress had participated in the investigation of Nazi activities in Argentina, has been heatedly denounced as a fabrication by many *peronistas*, especially since the US State Department later resuscitated Perón's German connections in order to oppose his rise to power in the guise of an anti-Nazi crusade. The writer Germán Arciniegas, an indefatigable campaigner against dictatorship in Latin America, considered it genuine, as did a number of later analysts of the antecedents of the Perón régime. Its rhetoric certainly matches other literature put out by the GOU and its sympathisers of the day, and with modifications the general thrust of the continental policies adopted in the following years coincides with that of this document. Perón's own admiration for the achievements of Hitler's Germany was admitted quite openly by himself many years after the debate over his Nazi connections had died down. If it was a forgery, it was an exceedingly good one.

In any case, the Germans were certainly showing a keen interest in the plans of the Argentine military. Only a few weeks before the supposed date of the circular, General von Faupel had made an unpublicised visit to Argentina, secretly meeting to discuss developments with two generals (von der Becke and Pertiné) and three colonels (Brinckmann, Mittelbach and Perón) of the Argentine army.

The coup was prepared efficiently and executed swiftly. In Perón's own account: 'My immediate superior, the Inspector General, was Farrell, General Farrell. But he knew nothing about the revolution. He ignored what was going on. It was all prepared in the Instruction Centre for Mountain Troops. On 3 June we left everything prepared for the following day. The morning of the 4th was cloudy. We went around to the Círculo Militar and dragged Farrell out of bed. "General", we said, "there is a revolution under way." "What revolution?" he asked. "We are in the revolution," we replied. "I'll dress immediately," he said. We needed a general and we did not want it to be Rawson.'

The troops from Campo de Mayo were ordered to march on the capital, while Perón and some other colonels rushed on ahead to ensure that the 1st and 2nd Infantry Regiments would adhere to the uprising. The only resistance they met was put up by the Escuela de Mecánica de la Armada, the Navy's school for non-commissioned officers, which lay on the road into the city. The brief shoot-out, left almost a hundred Navy men dead or wounded. Castillo's Minister of War, General Pedro Pablo Ramírez, who had contacts with the rebels, had himself placed under arrest. Castillo fled. It was in this context that General Arturo Rawson managed to get himself appointed President of the military régime. Two days later, after Rawson had nominated his cabinet without consulting the powerbrokers of the GOU, the decision was taken to remove him. Five colonels, Perón among them, burst into Rawson's office. As Perón tells the story, the following dialogue took place:

'We have come for your resignation.'
'But why?'
'Sir, we are most surprised by the fact that you are President'.
'But *Palito* Ramírez said that I was to be President. In any case I shall make no decision until *Palito* is here.'
'You will resign before General Ramírez arrives.'
'And if I refuse?'
'If you refuse, we have orders to throw you out of the window.'
Once we had 'resigned' him, Ramírez arrived. 'You stay,' we said to him. And we left him in the Presidency.

The German ambassador wired General von Faupel in Madrid, 'Our Argentine friends have achieved their purpose with complete and secure success.' In his reply the General remarked, 'Our friend Perón is undoubtedly the strong man of the government.'

Perón was unequivocal, at the time and later, about why he did not immediately take a position of greater importance for himself. Revolu-

tions devour their children, he used to repeat; the front-line figures are bound to be worn down very rapidly by the initial political to-ing and fro-ing, so it is best to remain in a safe second-line position until the time is ripe. Not that his position was so far removed from the front line. The GOU had established as an article of faith that obedience to the Minister of War was to be unquestioned by its members. General Edelmiro Farrell had been placed in that key Ministry, and Colonel Perón was the head of his secretariat. From there, Perón immediately set himself to enlarging the scope of the GOU, and could soon boast that only 300 of the Army's 3,600 officers had failed to enlist. Each and every recruit was compelled to draft and sign a letter requesting his retirement from the service, leaving blank only the space for the date. The letters were all to be held by the War Ministry, or more precisely, by the head of the Ministry's secretariat, Colonel Perón. Perón rewrote the statutes of the GOU, placing upon its members the following obligations:
— to defend the Army, internally and externally;
— to consider serving in the Army as an apostolate;
— to defend the principle of authority, and if the chief did not live up to his mission, to arrange that the cadres should make up for his weaknesses;
— to protect the cadres through the practice of camaraderie;
— to protect oneself against politics, which by no means signifies ignoring it;
— to protect oneself against communism, mainly through the creation of an information service capable of detecting subversive agents and annihilating them at the right moment.

The GOU soon forced on the government the adoption of three decrees which were to pave the way for the construction of the new régime: one dissolved all existing political parties, another introduced mandatory religious education in schools throughout the country, and the third established controls on the printed press and on radio broadcasting. This last item was considered of vital importance by the GOU, but most officers were aware that whoever was put in charge of it would inevitably bear the brunt of political pressures from within the régime and outside it. Two colonels vied for the job: Perón and Luis César Perlinger — it went to Perón.

In the meantime, the new military government had begun to move on the international front. The Chilean Foreign Minister arrived in Buenos Aires for talks with his Argentine counterpart, Admiral Segundo Storni, and ended by signing a convention aiming at the creation of a customs union between the two nations, as a first step towards a continent-wide organisation. Storni's next step was to approach Cordell Hull, the US Secretary of State, with an official request from Argentina for the purchase of war material. Hull not only turned him down; he also published the correspondence, underlining that the North American refusal was due to Argentina's non-compliance with the agreement signed at the Rio de Janeiro conference. In the ensuing furore in Buenos Aires, Storni resigned, his position going to Colonel Alberto Gilbert, a member of the GOU. But a debate followed within the cabinet, the Finance Minister, Dr Jorge A. Santamarina, acting as spokesman for a group that demanded the severance of ties with the Axis powers, in keeping with the Rio agreement. He was successfully opposed by Colonel Gilbert, who precipitated a major cabinet reshuffle, with three ministers losing their jobs. Shortly afterwards, the government suffered another important change with the death of the Vice-President, Admiral Sabá H. Sueyro; his post went to the War Minister, General Edelmiro Farrell.

The new military régime had from the outset adopted a tough line towards the unions, regarding many of them as obvious targets in their drive to stamp out Communism. Many leaders were arrested and transported to the far-away penal colonies of the Patagonian provinces. Federal trustees were placed in charge of several unions, and the National Department of Labour, an agency hitherto devoted mainly to statistical work and administrative formalities, was entrusted to Colonel Carlos M. Gianni, who was to try out an 'open door' policy towards the unions willing to join a government-sponsored 'unification' committee. Few unions took the bait; strike action continued, and there began to circulate insistent rumours of an all-out 'revolutionary general strike' against the government. At this point Colonel Perón began to take a keen interest in developments on the labour front, holding private meetings with union leaders and inspecting the work Gianni had been carrying out at the National Department of Labour.

The union movement had not changed all that much since Hipólito Yrigoyen had been ousted by General Uriburu's revolution. True, the anarchist FORA soon withered and disappeared, and only weeks after Uriburu's takeover a number of unions again managed to sink their differences and created the Confederación General del Trabajo, an avowedly non-partisan national federation of unions. At its inauguration, the CGT's unions could only boast 60,000 affiliated workers. Throughout the 'Decade of Infamy', although the unions would occasionally put up a fight, as a rule harsh government repression kept their heads down. By the time the military took power in 1943, the ranks of the CGT had swelled only marginally, to 80,000, but their institution had split into two, the CGT-1 and the CGT-2. Moreover, many Socialist and Communist union leaders were uncompromisingly opposed to the military régime, which they saw as the embodiment of Fascism, while they had rather naïvely accepted President Ortiz's promise of free elections to come.

The union leaders were the survivors of a long, hard struggle, but many of them had arrived at 1943, through force of circumstances, almost completely out of touch with the working people they claimed to represent. The country's population had been growing relentlessly, and now numbered close to 13 million. (Immigration had lost its earlier importance; the foreign-born were now only 18 per cent of the population.) The constraints imposed on trade by the war had forced the country to start industrialising, and the number of industrial establishments had nearly doubled since the 1930s. The industrial labour force, fed now mainly by the new, internal migrants who had fled the impoverished interior during the years of depression, had doubled from 400,000 in 1935 to about 800,000 in 1943 — a number which made the size of the card-carrying membership of the two CGTs look insignificant.

Perón's personal encounters with union leaders began to suggest to him that the government's approach to the problem was completely wrong. The man who provided him with a new, practical angle was the head of the statistical section at the National Department of Labour, a Spanish-born lawyer, José Figuerola. Figuerola had been Minister of Labour in his home country during the régime of José Antonio Primo de Rivera in the 1920s, and had been largely responsible for the creation of the mixed juries in which labour disputes had been resolved under government sponsorship. After a stint as Spain's representative at the International Labour Organisation in Geneva, the proclamation of the Spanish Republic had forced him into exile in France. A fellow-countryman had secured him a job with one of the foreign-owned electricity companies in Buenos Aires, which had put his experience to good use when the government had called for consultations with the private sector over the regulation of the eight-hour working day in public utilities. Figuerola was promptly co-opted by the government into the Department of Labour, where he made it his task to compile the best available records on labour conditions and legislation in the country.

Perón, impressed by Figuerola's account of the miserable conditions in which most workers lived, asked him for a report on the role the unions were playing. Figuerola summed it up admirably: the Communists were raising the banners of improvements in the country's labour legislation which had long existed on paper but seldom been put into practice; the Socialists were basking in the glory of a combative tradition with heroic strikes and their own legislative record that had left them with many martyrs but few concrete results. The simple answer was to rescue the mass of enacted and proposed labour laws and regulations and bring it to life. Perón's request to be appointed chairman of the Department of Labour was swiftly granted, and he immediately launched into a frenzied campaign that was to produce something akin to a revolution in Argentine labour relations.

All the scheme needed to get under way was a formula to overcome the union leaders' suspicions of the 'Fascist' military régime. Perón provided this by skilful political manoeuvring. He secured the end of a strike in the meat-packing industry by releasing their Communist union leader, José Peter, from confinement in the Patagonian territory of Neuquén, then forcing their demands on management. The liberal use of compulsory arbitration procedures in favour of the workers quickly attracted the sympathy of many trade unionists. It was not all carrot, however; Perón also employed the stick to ensure that the unions he won over would join the single CGT which the government allowed to exist (CGT-2 had been banned while its main unions had undergone 'intervention'). Favourable government arbitration would be made conditional on the union's incorporation into the CGT. If a principled union boss refused to be swayed by this kind of pressure, Perón would promptly summon an up-and-coming leader from the same union and offer, on the same conditions, to aid him in the ouster of the incumbent. This put most of the union bosses in a terrible dilemma; they had to choose between loyalty to their party (Socialist or Communist, in most cases) and survival as leaders of their unions. Because Perón's promises were promptly followed by action (underlining the contrast with previous governments, he had adopted the motto, 'It is better to do than to talk, better to realise than to promise'), many chose to go along with him. Perhaps the most notable case was that of Angel Borlenghi, a former Socialist who eventually became a key political figure in the *peronista* government, indeed the longest-lasting of Perón's collaborators. Others chose party allegiance and resistance to Perón's enticements, as did José Peter. Perón put all his support behind a rival leader, Cipriano Reyes, who wrested the union from Peter after a long and bitterly violent struggle in which many, including two of Reyes' brothers, lost their lives. Symptomatic of the mood of the day was the much-remembered statement made by Reyes' mother to Perón at the funeral of her two sons. 'Colonel Perón', she said, 'if I had more sons I would offer them to your cause. I would not mind if they died fighting for you.' The conflict of conscience undergone by many of the union bosses and committed trade unionists meant very little to the masses of unaffiliated workers. Among those who remembered, the past was one of lies and unfulfilled promises; among the more recent arrivals to the ranks of urban labour the present was all that mattered, and it was a present in which, suddenly, labour legislation carried weight and hundreds of arbitral proceedings were taking place, more often than not resulting in the granting of the worker's demands; the benefits of social security were becoming tangible; and all workers were protected by law against unfair or arbitrary dismissal. And the man responsible for all this was Colonel Juan Domingo Perón.

Perón soon had his Department upgraded to Secretariat, with himself as a Secretary of State. Behind him was a loyal labour movement, organised under the umbrella of a CGT that would soon boast half a million members. At first Perón took great pains to calm the fears of the entrepreneurs, who were visibly alarmed at the decisions of this man who was granting wage increases of up to 40 per cent to the workers. He insisted both on the workers' right to organise and negotiate with employers as equals, and on the dangers of the alternative, which in his view was revolution. 'I have been in Spain shortly after the civil war,' he told the assembled members of the Buenos Aires Stock Exchange, 'and I know my country after having travelled its territory many times. The Spanish workers immediately before the civil war earned, on average, wages higher than those paid nowadays in the Argentine Republic; we must not forget that in our territory there are men who used to earn 20 centavos a day; not a few who earned 12 pesos a month; and not a few, either, who got no more than 30 pesos a month. [. . .] Nowadays we have — and, blessed be God, may it continue for many years — industrialists who can make profits of a thousand per cent. In Spain it was easy to explain the civil war. What could we not explain here if our masses of *criollos* were not as good, as obedient and as hardy as they are? [. . .] It has been said, gentlemen, that I am an enemy of capital. If you pay close attention to what I have said, you will find no more determined defender [of capital] than myself, for I know that the defence of the interests of businessmen, industrialists, merchants, is the defence of the very state itself.' Not all the entrepreneurs were willing to listen, and specially not the big landowners grouped in the Sociedad Rural, or the owners of the 'old' land-based industries grouped in the Unión Industrial. Their opposition to Perón arose first and foremost from the concessions he was granting the workers, which they claimed would destroy them economically. But it was reinforced by their distaste for the industrial policies that were emerging from the régime as a whole, based on such cardinal sins as tariff protection and wholesale state intervention. Finally, their old ties with Britain and the new ties with the United States (the former's influence having already shrunk to only 60 per cent of all foreign investment, while the latter had already carved out for itself a 20 per cent share) led them to oppose the régime, and Perón with it, on the grounds that he represented Fascism, the mortal enemy of democracy. But he did find sympathy among the country's 'new' industrialists, unconnected as they were with the traditional power centres and dependent as they were on the adoption of policies that would allow them to grow.

The Right castigated, particularly from the columns of *La Prensa*, every move of Perón as inflationary or anti-economic, and supported the lockouts and other demonstrations of the businessmen who attempted to resist the new rules of the game. But Perón pushed ahead, improving working conditions, introducing annual paid holidays and guaranteed stability in employment, presiding over the signing in 1944 alone of almost 200 agreements between employers and unions, extending the benefits of pension schemes to over 2 million people, creating labour tribunals and beginning to regulate working conditions in rural areas. Seen against the backdrop of coercion and pressure with which he built up the strength of a client CGT, it is all too easy to write off the whole operation as a mammoth exercise in demagogic bribery, as many of Perón's political adversaries did from the outset. But this is not the way it was perceived by the workers themselves. A jurist who can hardly be accused of sympathising with Perón, Ernesto Krotoschin, says in his treatise on Argentine labour law:

With the revolution of 4 June 1943 a new era begins. This revolution can be compared, from the point of view of certain aspects (pertinent to labour law) with the ones that took place in Russia in 1917, in Germany in 1918, and with the deep changes that took place in France, under Blum, in 1936. [. . .] It marks the entry of so-called labourism on to the political and economic scene, in some fashion identified with the interests and rights of the dependent workers. There is a sudden sweeping away of certain obstacles to the development of the working masses, both in the political and the juridical fields.

The workers were conscious of a distinct improvement in their lot, not only materially, but also in the more indefinable sphere of human dignity. At long last they were able to sit on opposite sides of the negotiating table with their bosses, not as inferiors with the begging bowl, but as equals who made demands. For many the argument that all this was the illegitimate child of an anti-democratic régime sounded very much like a bad joke. Among those who claimed to oppose Perón and his works in the name of democracy were the very people who had instituted electoral fraud as the mechanism for the restoration of authority, and those who had ordered the persecution of the trade unions, and the imprisonment of adversaries and even of those who spoke idealistically of the workers' rights; they had either tolerated the flouting of the country's skimpy labour legislation or had opposed its passage by Congress. This perversion of the meaning of words which allowed the anti-democratic to masquerade as democratic, on the strength not of their own political antecedents but of contemporary external alliances, would soon begin to have an insidious, long-lasting consequence: the mistrust and even, on occasions, the outright rejection by the *peronistas* of political proposals that chose to label themselves 'democratic'. And it was already leading to the creation of a whole series of unholy alliances between genuinely democratic forces and the most reactionary segments of Argentine society.

The war and the attitude of the military régime towards the belligerent nations were very much at the root of the positions adopted by the anglophile oligarchy and the parties that claimed a democratic affinity with the Allies. Pressure from the Allied camp, and particularly from the United States, for Argentina to help complete the isolation of the Axis powers by declaring war was unrelenting. Already in 1943 the issue of war crimes had come to the foreground of Allied policy, and Argentina, together with other South American nations, began to be portrayed as a future haven for Nazi war criminals once the war in Europe was over. Diplomatic moves by Britain to obtain Argentina's commitment to the eventual exclusion of such war criminals began in late 1943. The first reply from Buenos Aires was that the country would continue its tradition of offering sanctuary 'as a humanitarian institution to prevent blind acts of vengeance in moments of political passion'. The tradition was real enough; mutual respect for the right to political asylum had permitted whole generations of Latin American politicians to survive the volatility of their domestic political evolution. But the important fact was that Buenos Aires' attitude towards this issue was the

clearest indicator of changing assessments as to the eventual outcome of
the war, and of the consequent shifts in foreign policy.

In October 1943, the two leading conservative newspapers, *La Prensa*
and *La Nación*, rebelled against the strictures imposed on the press under
the state of siege regulations, and published a long pro-Allied tract signed
by 150 well-known citizens. The government officially repudiated the
publication and went on to dismiss several of the signatories who held
official positions, such as university lecturers. The propaganda war continued two months later with an announcement by the British
authorities that a German-Argentine by the name of Osmar Helmuth
had been arrested in Trinidad while travelling to take up a position as
consul in Barcelona, and had confessed under interrogation to be acting
on the instructions of agents of the Reich stationed in Argentina. Early
in 1944, a conflict arose between the US State Department and Buenos
Aires over the forcible installation of President Villaroel in power in
Bolivia. The Argentine military, amid reports that the new Bolivian
régime was both 'anti-capitalist' and in favour of 'geographic reconstruction', swiftly offered diplomatic recognition. The United States
refused to recognise the new government and set about stirring
resistance to it in the area by asserting that Bolivia intended to pursue by
force the reclamation of its outlet to the sea (which it had lost in the
nineteenth century during a war between Chile and Perú) and
suggesting that Argentina's manifestations of friendship were part of its
Nazi-inspired plan for continental supremacy.

Almost at the same time, the United States made another attempt to
sway the Buenos Aires authorities by supplying them with a mass of
documents purporting to prove the existence of a vast Nazi network of
espionage and political subversion in Argentina. The Ramírez government accepted the information as genuine and, having arrived already at
the conclusion that Germany was a loser, severed its ties with the Reich.
Weeks later the discovery of the Nazi spy organisation was announced
and among those arrested were attachés at the German and Japanese
embassies. Colonel Alberto Gilbert, the GOU member who a year
earlier had so emphatically opposed a declaration of war, now proposed it
himself, precipitating a major crisis. A number of GOU officers stormed
into the Foreign Ministry and placed Gilbert under arrest; President
Ramírez was forced to take leave of absence, and the Presidency was
'provisionally' entrusted to the War Minister, General Edelmiro Farrell.
Perón moved into the War Ministry and a close friend of his, Colonel
Filomeno Velasco, was appointed Chief of the Federal Police.

A dangerous split appeared in the ranks of the officer corps hitherto so tightly held together by the GOU. Officers loyal to Colonel Gilbert, openly supported by part of the Campo de Mayo forces and Army and Navy units in Bahía Blanca, Córdoba and Paraná, issued a demand for Farrell's resignation and either the reinstatement of General Ramírez or the transfer of the Executive to the Supreme Court, to be followed by a general election. An infantry regiment in Buenos Aires actually attempted to rise against the government, but the rebellion was crushed and Farrell held firm. Under considerable domestic and external pressure, Farrell announced publicly that elections would be held soon and that the country's foreign policy would continue to be 'based on co-operation with the United States and the solidarity of the Continent'. Washington replied by increasing the pressure, suspending its relations with the government irregularly headed by Farrell. It was not until March that normality of sorts returned, with Ramírez presenting his formal resignation of the Presidency, though not without declaring publicly that the officers who opposed him, in the belief that the whole episode of the Nazi spy ring was a US-inspired concoction, were 'deceived and misled'.

But soon Argentine diplomats in Washington and London were stating publicly, on behalf of their government, that the rumours about Argentina becoming a post-war haven for Nazi criminals were 'totally unfounded'. The ambassador in London, Dr Cárcano, said that not only would no persons accused of war crimes be allowed into Argentine territory; they would not even be allowed to create capital deposits or acquire property of any kind. The tide had turned and the actual declaration of war on the Axis powers was not far off. Perón, the War Minister at the time, has recounted that President Farrell called him in and said, 'The war is ending and nothing can change the destiny of the German nation. Therefore, our entry to the war will not affect the course of history.' Perón went off to speak to his German contacts. In his own words, 'In complete agreement with the Germans themselves, President Farrell's government, in which I was Minister of War, declared the outbreak of hostilities; in this we had the approval of the German generals and colonels who lived in retirement in Argentina, such as General Reschmer.'

In a very direct manner, the declaration of war was to aid Perón's political aims. The continuing reshuffle of the government after Ramírez's resignation had finally pushed him to the forefront of Argentine politics. When he took over the War Ministry he shrewdly held on to his earlier source of outside power, the Secretariat of Labour and Social Welfare. The next step was to add to these two positions that of Vice-President. He did not achieve this without a struggle. His colleague Luis César Perlinger, who had earlier competed with him for control of the media, rallied support in the Army for his own candidacy to the post. As before, the issue was settled by a vote in the GOU. Perón won, but by a narrow margin. Shortly afterwards the GOU was persuaded by Perón to dissolve itself, officially on the grounds that its existence could henceforth become an encumbrance to the government (the decision, it has been claimed, was precipitated by one of the GOU's last acts: an expression of concern to Perón about the increasing political involvement of his mistress, the actress María Eva Duarte). With an Allied victory now in sight, Perón created the National Postwar Council, in which he gave a central role to José Figuerola, his *éminence grise* at the Labour Secretariat. From there he began to draw up comprehensive plans for Argentina's economic development after the end of the war; these plans were to become the blueprint for his own government.

The few months that led up to Perón concentrating three of the country's most influential positions in his hands may have been dominated by the issue of the war, but they were also filled with developments that had a more direct bearing on the growth of his popularity among the people. Much of this was the result of a tragedy that took place just after the traditional year's-end festive season. On 15 January 1944 the province of San Juan, perched on Argentina's Andean backbone, was hit by one of the worst earthquakes so far recorded in South America. In less than a minute the provincial capital, also called San Juan, a city with some 80,000 inhabitants, was almost levelled to the ground. The death toll was at first reported as 2,000, but as rescue work proceeded, scores were added to that total. With the outbreak of an epidemic a very real risk, the government ordered the evacuation of the provincial capital and sent in the Army to blow up the remaining buildings. What was left of the province's hospital capacity soon overflowed, with the injured coming in by the thousand, and material losses were soon being estimated at the equivalent of some £22 million at the value of that time.

Perón took it upon himself to mobilise the public side of the relief effort, appealing to the population to contribute monetary and material aid for those affected by the earthquake and the later reconstruction of San Juan. For this he enlisted the support of Argentina's most popular showbusiness personalities and commandeered the use of the country's broadcasting networks. The man who had already come to be known as the defender of the workers appeared now as the focal point of humanitarian concern over the San Juan tragedy, his image reinforced by his very public association with the popular actors and actresses who were helping in the fund-raising effort.

It was during these events, according to tradition, that Perón met María Eva Duarte, the actress who was later to become his wife and a leading political personality in her own right, revered by the masses as their beloved Evita. The accounts of the meeting are numerous and varied, including different versions given by Perón himself at different times. The *antiperonistas* depict it as a premeditated move by a calculating woman, including a number of anecdotal references to the way she allegedly thrust herself at the Colonel during a mass fund-raising rally at Buenos Aires' Luna Park stadium. Perón's favourite version in his old age has him becoming impressed by her intelligent suggestions at an earlier meeting with showbusiness personalities, and even suggests that the mobilisation of actors and actresses was her idea. Others have one of Perón's associates, Colonel Imbert, introducing her to Perón at her request. But partisans and adversaries have on the whole agreed to accept as part of the country's political folklore that the encounter took place during the San Juan relief effort. There is, however, another, more subterranean tradition, that suggests they might have met much earlier, even before the coup of 1943. Although its final verification will have to await a competent examination of German records of the time, this tradition was picked up by very early *antiperonista* writers like Silvano Santander, and much later by people openly sympathetic to Perón, such as the Spanish journalists Torcuato Luca de Tena and Luis Calvo, and their Argentine colleague Esteban Peicovich, who together compiled what they presented as 'an autobiographical tale', based on seventy tapes of recorded conversations with Perón in his Madrid exile, called *Yo, Juan Domingo Perón*. It also appeared, with references to additional sources, as a sideline in *Aftermath*, Ladislas Farago's unconvincing attempt to prove the survival of Martin Bormann.

The common core of these versions has 'Miss Duarte' mentioned as 'our friend' by the German embassy in Buenos Aires, and actually enlisting Colonel Perón's aid in assisting a member of the local Nazi party, Herr Sandstete, to flee the country when the Congressional committee investigating Nazi activities sought his arrest. It also has her showing a member of the German diplomatic staff correspondence from

Perón immediately after the 1943 coup. In Farago's version her role is expanded to that of one of the 'straw men' heading dummy corporations allegedly used to channel funds from a losing Germany to a safe haven in Argentina.

Thus, right down to its very beginnings, the public story of Evita is almost hopelessly entwined with myth, a situation which was compounded when Perón reached the Presidency, and most of the existing records of her career as an actress were quietly withdrawn from circulation. As with Perón, there are many Evitas in Argentine political folklore. Enemies have made much of her background as an illegitimate child of a poor family, and have painted her as driven by resentment and an insatiable thirst for money and power. Her private life, and especially her sexual dalliance during the showbusiness years, have been linked to this reading of her ambitions, and embellished with the hypocrisy that was so typical of the sexual mores of Argentina's middle class, to portray her as the blackest of Messalinas. A variation of this *antiperonista* theme is the picture of Evita as the true backbone of the couple; her ambition, cunning and guts contrasting with the alleged cowardice of Perón himself. This version presents Evita as the real catalyst of Perón's rise to power, and her early death as the cause of the disintegration of the régime. There are just as many *peronista* images of Evita, almost exact mirror-images of the *antiperonista* versions. There is the saintly Eva, the woman of humble origins whose heart went out to the poor, the *Abanderada de los Humildes* (standard-bearer of the humble) of whom no wrong could be conceived. There is also the 'revolutionary' Evita, the austere militant who was in closer touch with the interests of the workers, and more intransigent in their defence, than Perón himself. This is mainly a construct of selective exegesis from her speeches, aided by her demise at an early age, that would allow later generations of the *peronista* Left to claim that 'if Evita had lived, she would have been a guerrilla fighter'. And there is Evita the proto-feminist, the advance guard of women's rights in a traditionally *machista* society, instrumental in getting women the vote and in obtaining the passage of protective legislation, but above all the person who forced Argentines to accept the presence of a female in a leading political position.

This multiplicity of Evitas, hand in hand with the multiplicity of Peróns, in the country's political folklore is hardly a unique phenomenon. To this day Argentina refuses to agree on a common version of its history. Leading figures of the past, long dead, are still the subject of fierce, uncompromising debate. As if they were still alive, there are people for and against Bernardino Rivadavia, for and against Juan Manuel de Rosas (who still lacks a monument in the country's statue-studded capital), for and against Domingo Faustino Sarmiento, to cite only a few men who led Argentina at crucial times. To make matters worse, there is a curious dualism in the way that Right and Left — if such categories can be made to fit Argentine politics — view events. In matters political the Right prefer an anecdotal approach, with great emphasis on personalities and private morality, and with consequences on a much-reduced individual plane as the ultimate tests of validity. Contrarywise, the Left prefer to distinguish trends and 'lines', concentrating on the broader significance of events; where the Right tend to disregard history and context, the Left tend to minimise the fate and significance of the individual. But when it comes to economic affairs, paradoxically, the Left, whose appeal to broad processes is based on economic assumptions, show a distinct predilection for the anecdotal, and for conspiracy theories which boil down to a multiplication of very individual decisions, while the Right adhere slavishly to 'universals', to immutable laws projected from mid-nineteenth century accidents. The Right prefer to assume an easily corruptible mass, ever prone to mobilisation by crude demagoguery; the Left erect the presence of the masses, whatever the circumstances, into a witness of underlying truth. For the Right, the true Peróns and Evitas are the sum of their anecdotes, the broader picture being their attempt to bend the laws of economics to suit their personal ambitions. For the faithful, the anecdotes are of negligible value, the crucial element being the wider meaning of the Perón phenomenon in the hearts and minds of Argentina's masses.

Against this backdrop, hidden antecedents aside, in early 1944 Argentina's political circles took public notice of the coming together of Juan Domingo Perón, Colonel, and María Eva Duarte, actress. He was forty-nine, she was twenty-five.

On 17 May 1919, three years into Yrigoyen's first Presidency and only four months after the 'Tragic Week', in Los Toldos, province of Buenos Aires, Juana Ibarguren gave birth to her her fifth child in the stable but not legally blessed union she enjoyed with Juan Duarte, a fairly prosperous travelling salesman from neighbouring Chivilcoy, where he already had an established family. When the time came to register the child's birth, just as with her elder sisters and brother, she was entered in the local registry office with his surname, Duarte. Her chosen forenames were María Eva. She came from the same part of the country as Perón; her home town's name, Los Toldos, means 'The Tents' — a sign of its own birth on the one-time frontier with the Pampas Indians, the flat, unrelieved plains whose fecundity provided the foundations for the prosperity of Argentina's rural oligarchy.

Evita was only two years old when her father died; she, her sisters Elisa, Blanca and Arminda, and her brother Juan (but not their mother) were magnanimously granted a back-row position at the burial, where his legal family held pride of place. Juan Duarte's death left Doña Juana in a difficult financial situation, and for a couple of years she and the children suffered serious deprivation, until salvation came in the form of an Italian restaurateur who fell in love with Doña Juana and persuaded her to set up house with him in the nearby town of Junín, once little more than a rough Army fort known as Federación. Junín was larger than Los Toldos, but not much else distinguished it from her former home, or from Perón's home town of Lobos. Their flat and dusty monotony were things to be fled by the youth, who thrived on the tales of the wonders of Buenos Aires, the huge, prosperous capital city, only a few hours away by train. In this atmosphere Evita went to primary school and later ferreted around for work to help her mother, whose financial stability was once again threatened by her Italian's decision to take himself off to Buenos Aires to try his luck with a restaurant there. With this example, and that of many of her friends and even her elder sisters, it was not surprising that Evita entered her teens with her mind set on finding a way out of Junín; a way that would preferably lead to everyone's Mecca, Buenos Aires.

Opportunity appeared in the form of a young, aspiring *tango* singer, Agustín Magaldi, who arrived in Junín on the mandatory tour of provincial social clubs which would make ends meet until, with luck, stardom in Buenos Aires was achieved. A precocious fifteen-year-old, Evita talked Magaldi into taking her with him when he returned to the capital. There she herself began, at his side, the tough apprenticeship of the clubs and bit parts on the stage, always on the look-out for a break into radio. It took her a full six hard years, and the lucky acquaintance with a soap manufacturer who sponsored a radio programme, to start earning the equivalent of 120 dollars a month and to move into a reasonably comfortable apartment of her own. Knowing the right people, in Buenos Aires as in the rest of the world, was essential to the advancement of many a career. Yet it is only with hindsight that it can be said that Evita cultivated the right contacts in the early 1940s. Her elder

sister Elisa had taken up with an Army major, and Evita's apartment on
Calle Posadas was the obvious choice for social gatherings to which
many of the major's comrades-at-arms were invited. These were also the
vague years in which Evita is supposed to have made contact with the
German embassy; it is certainly plausible that a young party-going starlet
with contacts in the Army should have been deemed worth approaching
by intelligence-conscious diplomats of a warring nation who were
curious about the intentions of their neutral hosts.

But her first truly important acquaintance among the military seems
to have been Colonel Aníbal Francisco Imbert, the man entrusted, after
the 1943 coup, with running the country's postal and telegraphic
systems, a job which included supervising the radio stations and thus had
a direct bearing on Evita's chosen career. Friendship with Colonel
Imbert began to make a difference very soon, her employers clearly
believing that keeping her happy was a sure way of ingratiating themselves with the man who held the fate of their radio concession in his
hands. She soon also found that other people from outside the world of
radio were interested in her. With a war on in Europe and imported
goods scarce, the obtaining of import licences and speedy (or deliberately
unseeing) treatment by the Customs became a matter of life and death for
many businesses. Over and above the established procedures, the best
way to obtain these was through a personal 'approach' to the people in
charge. And since 1943, all the people in charge were Army officers.
Evita rapidly found herself called upon to act as an influence-broker,
introducing people with 'problems' to people with 'solutions', a
position that introduced her to the world of business and especially to the
trick of turning a quick, profitable deal.

Then came the San Juan earthquake and Perón's scheme to involve
artistes in a mammoth relief appeal. Evita certainly used her influence
with Colonel Imbert to participate at par with far more famous stage and
screen personalities, and the fervour she put into her radio broadcasts and
public appearances certainly drew her close to Colonel Perón. Whether
or not they had met before, or even known each other quite well, the fact
was that their relationship soon acquired a very special nature. In her
own ghost-written autobiography, *La razón de mi vida* (The purpose of
my life), she describes it in a curiously dispassionate, almost impersonal
way; indeed there are few if any indications of romance in any of the
surviving writings of either Perón or Evita. But shortly after the San
Juan appeal they were obviously lovers, living together in an apartment
close to the first one of her own, in Calle Posadas. Her liaison with the

most powerful man in the régime worked even more wonders for her career. Her salary at Radio Belgrano increased more than sixfold, and it was not long before she was also on contract to Radio El Mundo and the state's own network, Radio del Estado, and had embarked on a new but hardly remarkable career in the movies. She showed special predilection for the portrayal of women prominent in history, and Perón would recall long after her death that 'of all those historic characters whose life she interpreted on the radio as an actress, the one she admired the most was Madame Elisa Lynch, the companion of Marshal Francisco Solano López, President of Paraguay.' Elisa Lynch wielded inordinate political power during the rule of Solano López, the 'enlightened' Paraguayan dictator who occupies a privileged position in the pantheon of South American nationalism.

But together with her rising star in showbusiness, Evita began to take a keener interest in Peron's political pursuits. It was she who, together with a scriptwriter called Francisco Muñoz Aspiri, took care of publicising on the radio every step taken by the Secretariat of Labour and Social Welfare, emphasising the identification of the Colonel in charge with the interests of the working classes. In her words, Perón became 'the People's Colonel'.

5

THE OCTOBER REVOLUTION
(1945–1946)

By early 1945 it seemed that very few obstacles remained between Perón and the Presidency — that is, except the incumbent, General Farrell, who was beginning to feel the pressure mounting against Perón from all quarters; from the United States abroad, and at home from the political parties and the student movements that were convinced he was trying to repeat a Fascist or Nazi experiment in Argentina; from a large part of the business sector, which violently resisted his pro-union policies; and increasingly from within the Navy and the Army, where his growing independent power base, the CGT, and his accumulation of crucial roles in government were viewed with suspicion, envy and resentment. Throughout 1944, as most visible opposition to Perón was conducted under the banner of pro-Allied and anti-Nazi manifestations, the government had used the excuse of preserving Argentina's neutrality to clamp down on adversaries of all coloration. The foreign-owned press media were one of the prime targets. United Press and its local subsidiary, Prensa Unida, were banned from either receiving or transmitting information; suspensions and censorship were applied to the US firms NBC, CBS and All-America Cable and Radio, as well as to the BBC. Suspensions were also dealt out to the conservative paper *La Prensa* and the socialist journal *La Vanguardia*, while the anti-Fascist Italian newspaper *Italia Libera* was closed down. Different political groups combined their propaganda themes related to the war and the resurrection of past military leaders, such as General Rawson who had been President for a few days in 1943, and General Ramírez, extolling their 'democratic' qualities in opposition to Perón's alleged pro-Nazi leanings. The result was the frequent imprisonment of participants in demonstrations organised by the Asociación de Mayo and Patria Libre, the former an association led by Socialists and Radicals, the latter an umbrella organisation that embraced almost everyone from Conservative to Communist, or by the Federación Universitaria de Buenos Aires (FUBA), the student body that claimed to embody the ideals of the university reform of the 1920s.

The Nazi taint was recalled, unremittingly, by the United States, whose official propaganda continued to attack Perón, even after there was clear evidence that his position had shifted along with the fortunes of the war, and that he had become convinced of the convenience of an accommodation with Washington. It was in keeping with this new approach that Argentina pointedly arrested as prisoners-of-war the captain and crew of the German submarine U-530 when it sailed into the port of Mar del Plata in July 1945, and immediately announced that they and their vessel would be handed over to the British and US governments. The new mood was also reflected in Perón's choice of new foreign examples to explain what he intended to achieve in the field of social relations. 'In the working sector', he said in a 1945 speech, 'we would like to achieve a professional organisation akin to that of England's trade unions. In that fashion we could efficiently contain the Communist menace and create conscientious organisations which, through collective bargaining, would establish the bases for the relations between capital and labour in each line of activity. At the same time, the study and adoption of a policy of fair wages will raise the living standards of our working classes and transform them into consumers of our own production.'

Not many of Perón's adversaries were willing to listen to the new tune, or to pay attention to the fact that the basic content of his message had been one of social appeasement. Abroad, Cordell Hull's description of Argentina as 'the headquarters of a Fascist movement in this hemisphere and a potential source of infection for the rest of the Americas', and President Franklin D. Roosevelt's claim that the country presented 'the paradox of the growth of Nazi-Fascist influence in this hemisphere at the very time that those forces are drawing closer to final defeat in Europe and the rest of the world', were revived by the Soviet Foreign Minister, Molotov, in 1945 to oppose (unsuccessfully) Argentina's admission to the United Nations Conference on International Organisation, with the added comment that 'neither the foreign nor the domestic policies of the Argentine régime in this war have met with the United Nations' approval.' Domestically, big business chose to move to all-out confrontation, egged on by the US ambassador, Spruille Braden, a businessman with a mining background in Chile who considered, to paraphrase his British colleague Sir David Kelly, that Providence had set him the mission of ousting the Farrell-Perón régime.

In June 1945 a large number of entrepreneurs issued a manifesto demanding that the government should radically change its social policies. The unions responded by plastering the walls of Buenos Aires with their own manifestos, rejecting the employers' demands and highly praising the work done by Perón's Secretariat of Labour and Social Welfare. They also began to organise demonstrations in support of Perón, in a series culminating in a gathering of thousands in front of the Labour Secretariat, where many already began to voice their backing for Perón's candidacy to the Presidency. With the active encouragement of Ambassador Braden, the anti-Perón forces carefully prepared a mass response, a procession through the streets of the capital to be named 'Marcha de la Constitución y la Libertad'. It was an impressive, and prematurely triumphalistic demonstration. Describing the event in his book El 17 de Octubre, Hugo Gambini says, 'That day [19 September 1945] antiperonistas of all colorations — Radicals, Conservatives, Socialists, Communists, Progressive Democrats and Democratic Catholics — and of all the social classes — high, middle and markedly left-wing union sectors — poured out in a compact multitude that paraded through the avenues of the city centre with an air of victory.' Pablo Giussani has commented, 'Peronismo would later refer to the event as "an oligarchic masquerade", but the objective truth is that the multitude of that day was not limited to a single class. Someone later compared it with the crowd that greeted Lonardi's victory in 1955. But the comparison is not valid. In that Marcha there was also a considerable representation of the workers alongside the aristocrats. The older generations of the Argentine working class were still standing, and the "Radical mass", though already hesitant and in the throes of dispersion, was still a fact of life.'

Much has been written about the events of those months of 1945, the prelude to the most venerated date in the peronista calendar, 17 October. Few, however, have encapsulated the transition that was already taking place as aptly as the political scientist Carlos Fayt:

The attitude adopted by the employers, who held back their collaboration and soon aligned themselves with the resistance (with the exception of the industrial sector, that adhered to peronismo out of the fear that the wartime industries might be dismantled), caused an unexpected shift and accelerated the end of the policy of social appeasement. It was the opposition of the pillars of the community and their confrontation with Perón and the Secretariat of Labour and Welfare that transformed the vacillations and doubts of the most important sectors of organised labour into adherence to the Secretariat, and support for its work and consequently for the man who was attracting all the fire from entrepreneurs and employers. The democratic political parties had not been wrong about the Fascist nature of the revolutionary government in its first stage, nor about the manifest purposes of Perón's social policies. But they did not comprehend the change of tack by the revolutionary government from 1945, or adapt their own tactics accordingly. This mistake became tragic when, in the eyes of the majority of the workers, they appeared as allies of Argentina's traditional oligarchy and of the employers' vested interests.

Events began to accelerate after the 'Marcha de la Constitución y la Libertad'. The government decreed a state of siege, then proceeded to modify the rules governing the functioning of political parties, introducing a ban on the re-election of party authorities, which would have the effect of proscribing many of the country's leading politicians. The sharp edge of opposition shifted to the universities, which were occupied by the students and turned into vociferous and highly visible centres of anti-régime propaganda. After some days the government lost its patience and sent in the Federal Police, in a violent operation that ended with more than 1,000 student protesters behind bars. This panorama of rapidly growing and, as it seemed, barely controllable opposition began to unnerve many Army officers who had hitherto resisted the pressures against Perón. Indeed the notion was already spreading from the Navy, many of whose leading figures were undisguisedly anti-Perón, to the Army, where attitudes were still widely split, that getting rid of Perón might be the way to save 'the revolution' until such time as elections were held. The unexpected catalyst was Evita. She finally persuaded Perón to obtain the appointment, as head of the Post and Telegraph Office, of Oscar Nicolini, an employee of that agency who had by then become the provider for her mother, Doña Juana Ibarguren. This meant displacing her former patron, Colonel lmbert, and was not to be achieved without overcoming much opposition. But Perón insisted, and got his way. Incidents like this had already begun to give rise, particularly among Perón's adversaries, to the legend of Evita's implacability, of her ruthlessness in disposing of those whose past association with her might make them feel entitled to a claim on her gratitude, and of her unhesitating readiness to steamroller those who dared to stand in her way. Evita herself was later to play on this reputation, portraying it as incorruptible intransigence in the service of 'her people's' interests. But on this occasion she had stepped on military toes, and for many of the undecided it was the last straw: on top of everything else, it made Perón look like a puppet in the hands of this woman who was not even his wife.

The new year in Perón's life (he celebrated his fiftieth birthday on 8

October) began with an unexpected present. The commander of the large Campo de Mayo garrison, General Eduardo Avalos, officially informed him that as War Minister he no longer had the confidence of the Army — he must resign. Perón did not take long to decide on a course of action. The very next day he walked into President Farrell's office, conceded defeat and announced that he was leaving all his government posts: the Ministry of War, the Vice-Presidency and the Secretariat of Labour and Welfare. He begged only one favour — that he be permitted to take his leave publicly of 'his people' at the Labour Secretariat. Farrell generously agreed, to the point of allowing Perón to use the state's nationwide chain of radio networks so that his farewell message might reach the provinces. In less than twenty-four hours the word had gone out to friendly union leaders that they were to concentrate as many of their members as they could in front of the Labour Secretariat; a platform was erected there and the stage was set for the transformation of the 'farewell message' into a major political coup. By the appointed time, the streets around the Labour Secretariat, only a few hundred metres from the Casa Rosada, teemed with chanting, cheering workers. Perón's speech, broadcast to the entire nation after a day-long buildup, was brief. He hinted broadly that his departure could well mean the loss by the workers of all the benefits he had obtained for them. To try to assure their position, he added, he had drafted, as his last act, a decree increasing all wages and introducing a mandatory minimum, index-linked salary. The evening edition of the *peronista* newspaper *La Epoca* had already begun to circulate with the full text of the draft decree (of whose existence no one else in government had had the slightest inkling) and the bald statement that it was this initiative that had sparked the demand for Perón's resignation. Perón rounded off his address with a trick he had learnt from Radical politicians: a pointed appeal to the workers to remain calm and to avoid 'the labyrinth of conspiracy' — in fact, a suggestion that they should do the exact opposite. Certain now that it was perhaps a matter of hours before an indignant government would order his arrest, Perón fled the city with Evita, hiding out on the island property owned by a friend in the huge Delta of the Paraná river, but not before laying a false trail by writing a note to General Avalos, telling him that he was off to a farm in San Nicolás. By buying this extra time, Perón expected that his supporters in the unions would find a way to force his return to power.

It took two full days for the new Chief of Police, Colonel Aristóbulo Mittelbach, to track down Perón and Evita. The unions had not yet

moved, but in the meantime Farrell and the military leaders had discovered that the array of pressures against the régime, far from vanishing
with the removal of Perón, had merely changed tack and continued to be
as menacing as ever. The military were themselves divided as to the most
appropriate course of action. The majority seemed to favour keeping
Farrell on with a decidedly *antiperonista* cabinet, but there were many
strong voices calling for the replacement of the entire government,
Farrell included. When leading politicians were consulted, they flatly
rejected both alternatives and, picking up an earlier call of military dissidents, demanded that Executive powers be handed over to the Supreme
Court. This solution in its turn was turned down by the military, who
decided on a minimal formula — the retention of Farrell in the
Presidency and the appointment of General Avalos as War Minister and
of Admiral Héctor Vernengo Lima as Navy Minister — while some
compromise was sought with the politicians on the composition of the
rest of the cabinet.

Consultations with the officer corps had been going on at the Círculo
Militar, the Army's social club. The Círculo was housed in an elegant
palace facing Buenos Aires' Plaza San Martín, where the city centre
proper meets the rich residential Barrio Norte. Towards noon on 12
October, the civilian opposition began to rally in front of it to press its
demand of *el Gobierno a la Corte*, 'the government to the Supreme
Court'. Admiral Vernengo Lima appeared on one of the balconies and
attempted to appease the crowd, assuring them that a complete cabinet
reshuffle was in the offing, and that he himself was a guarantee, as Navy
Minister, that the new government would be *antiperonista*. The
assembled demonstrators interrupted his address with angry demands for
Farrell's resignation and for the Executive to be handed over to the
Supreme Court. Vernengo Lima withdrew without having satisfied the
crowd, whose mood now began to turn uglier. The officers who felt that
by ousting Perón they had done precisely what the opposition wanted,
now found themselves as the targets of *antiperonista* attacks, which were
progressively becoming ever more vicious. A crudely-lettered sign was
hung on the massive doors of the Círculo Militar. It said, 'To Let'. A
colonel was badly beaten up as he tried to get in. Then the police, who
had been standing by without intervening, began to bear the brunt of the
crowd's attacks. 'Gestapo! Ge-sta-po!' was the most insistent chant, and
it was this that finally wore down police patience. A mounted unit
charged into the crowd, whacking right and left with the flat of their
sabres. Stones began to fly, then the first shot. A half-hour shooting

match ensued, and by the time the plaza was cleared, there were thirty-four injured with bullet wounds and one dead. While this was going on Perón, his susceptibility to lung ailments triggered by the sojourn in the humid Delta, was being brought back to his city apartment under arrest. In another part of the city, one of Perón's closest aides, Colonel Domingo Mercante, was attempting to persuade a gathering of union leaders that their only hope lay in mass mobilisation.

The following day a dejected Perón, who had spent most of the waiting time discussing with Evita the convenience of giving up the struggle and opting for exile, was transported to the Navy-controlled penal island of Martín García, which fifteen years earlier had been the place of confinement of Hipólito Yrigoyen. That same day, President Farrell had entrusted the Procurator-General, Juan Alvarez, with the task of negotiating the formation of a civilian cabinet. The order went out to rid government agencies of Perón's collaborators, and Colonel Mittelbach, who was held responsible for the shooting in front of the Círculo Militar, was replaced as Chief of Police by Colonel Emilio Ramírez. Army officers known to be loyal to Perón were arrested. It is worth noting at this point that the Federal Police, who had been on the front line of the encounters with *antiperonista* demonstrators, and were even now being hounded with cries of 'Gestapo!', were rather less than enthusiastic about the turn of events; indeed the officers continued to keep in close touch with their former chief, Colonel Filomeno Velasco, Perón's friend, with whom they consulted every move.

According to *peronista* myth, it was at this point that Evita sallied forth, rallying the unions and the poor to the defence of Perón. In *La razón de mi vida*, she says, 'I flung myself into the streets searching for those friends who might still be of help to him [. . .] As I descended from the neighbourhoods of the proud and rich to those of the poor and humble, doors were opened to me more generously and with greater warmth. Above I found only cold and calculating hearts, the "prudent" hearts of "ordinary" men incapable of doing anything extraordinary, hearts whose contact nauseated, shamed and disgusted one.' In actual fact, Colonel Mercante had already been hard at work trying to mobilise the workers. And when Evita set forth, her first thought was to secure Perón's release so that he could opt for exile. She was rebuffed in this quest by one of Perón's close advisers, Juan Atilio Bramuglia, who chided her for her selfishness and reminded her that both she and Perón had political responsibilities to bear. The presentation of a writ of *habeas corpus* by a group of *peronista* lawyers was aborted when a similar request, put in by a certified lunatic, was thrown out by a judge — it was felt that an insistence would not be taken seriously.

In the event, it was Perón's own initiative, aided by that of his personal physician, that began to turn the tide. Perón wrote a dignified note to General Avalos, 'informing' him that he, Perón, a senior serving officer in the Army, had been detained by the police and then handed over to the jurisdiction of the Navy, all without any indication of the charges against him. He demanded prompt action by the War Minister to clear up the matter and either order legal proceedings against him or set him free. Avalos, suddenly aware of the firm legal ground on which Perón was standing, began to protest privately that it was not he who had ordered the arrest. Simultaneously, Perón's doctor, on hearing that his patient was suffering from pleurisy, obtained permission to go to Martín García and examine him, and then returned to Buenos Aires with the firm recommendation that Perón should be transferred to the Military Hospital there. The President vacillated. In Ensenada and Berisso, twin industrial zones next to La Plata, the capital of Buenos Aires province, Cipriano Reyes was leading his meat-packing workers out on the first demonstration to demand Perón's release. Seven hundred men responded, but the limited local impact of the demonstration convinced Reyes that what was needed was a march on Buenos Aires. A first attempt was made on Tuesday the 16th, and although columns of workers were able to slip into the federal capital across the bridges on the Riachuelo (a foul-smelling river separating the capital from the industrial areas just inside the neighbouring province of Buenos Aires) thanks to the fact that the police deliberately disregarded orders to hold them back, their advance was eventually halted before they could reach the Congress building. Most of the demonstrators turned back, but others regrouped in smaller units and made their way to the square in front of the Casa Rosada, and even paraded through the fashionable Calle Florida and other streets of the city centre chanting pro-Perón slogans. Small demonstrations continued into the early hours of the morning, when the police finally dispersed the remnants with tear gas.

In the meantime, the unions were meeting at the CGT to debate a call for a general strike. The *antiperonista* unions had already openly stated their opposition, and it was only by skilful manoeuvring that the *peronistas* secured a narrow margin in favour of the motion, of 21–19. The strike, however, was not formally declared to secure Perón's release. Its motives were summarised in six points: (1) against handing over the government to the Supreme Court and against any oligarchic cabinet; (2)

for the formation of a government that would guarantee democracy and liberty for the country, consulting the opinion of the unions; (3) for the holding of elections as announced; (4) for the lifting of the state of siege and the liberation of all civilian and military prisoners who had distinguished themselves for their clear and firm democratic convictions and their identification with the cause of the workers; (5) for the preservation of the 'social conquests' and their enlargement, and for the application of the new statute governing trade unions; and (6) for the immediate passage of the decree on wage increases and the introduction of the mandatory minimum, index–linked salary. The strike was to begin on 18 October.

At the crack of dawn on 17 October Perón was transferred from Martín García to the Military Hospital in Buenos Aires. General Avalos had already tried to defuse the tension (and save his own position) by announcing officially that Perón was not under arrest — he had merely been taken into custody to protect him from *antiperonistas* who wished to kill him. Another communiqué from the War Ministry, published by the papers on the morning of the 17th, stated that Army forces would not act against the people; they would only intervene, if at all necessary, to preserve order. On the practical side, Avalos had preventively ordered the raising of the bridges on the Riachuelo, to impede the entry to the capital of the much larger contingents of workers that had by then begun to concentrate in the industrial district of Avellaneda. But the workers had found ways to begin the crossing. Some had moved upstream to find bridges that were still open. Others commandeered rowboats, and later managed to bring into service the ferry launches of the Riachuelo. Some of the more determined marchers swam across the malodorous stretch of water. Inside the capital they were met by workers coming from the west of the city, and all together they began to stream towards the Plaza de Mayo, facing the Casa Rosada, and towards the Military Hospital, as soon as the news spread that Perón had arrived there. The police stood by, without intervening; in some cases they even greeted the marchers with cries of '*Viva Perón!*' As the crowd began to swell outside, within the Casa Rosada President Farrell, General Avalos and Admiral Vernengo Lima — the entire government of the day — debated possible courses of action. Vernengo Lima pressed for swift, harsh action to disperse the workers, but Farrell vacillated again, and General Avalos refused to go back on his commitment to keep the Army out of it. The troops at Campo de Mayo waited in vain for instructions to move; a few hundred metres from the Casa Rosada, in the Central Post Office, the officer in charge had armed a company of men and stood ready to act against the crowd. But Farrell still vacillated. Soon Colonel Mercante arrived to start negotiating on behalf of Perón, who himself was torn between the two options favoured by different groups of his collaborators; while some insisted on taking over the government immediately, others, led by Mercante, favoured a more sophisticated strategy — the placement of *peronistas* in the cabinet, but keeping Perón out of government, free to conduct his Presidential campaign for the forthcoming elections. The latter line eventually prevailed, but the negotiations, fraught with tension, were to last throughout the day. At one point Admiral Vernengo Lima, disgusted at the way Farrell was giving in to *peronista* pressure, muttered to Avalos, 'I'm going to lead the Navy out in rebellion; you take care of the Army.' Avalos said nothing, but firmly squeezed the Admiral's hand. Vernengo Lima left, convinced that Avalos had given him a sign that he was on his side. News began to arrive from other parts of the Republic, where similar mobilisations of the unions were taking place. Finally Avalos gave in. An hour before midnight, Perón and Farrell appeared before an enraptured crowd on a balcony of the Casa Rosada. Farrell spoke first, announcing to the multitude that all the demands made by the CGT had been granted. Then Perón took the microphone and wove a highly emotional speech into the insistent cheering and chanting of slogans. He said:

'Workers, almost two years ago, from these same balconies, I said that I had been given three honours in my life; that of being a soldier, that of being a patriot, and that of being Argentina's First Worker. This afternoon the Executive has approved my request for retirement from active duty in the Army. Thus I have voluntarily renounced the highest honour to which a soldier can aspire: the wearing of the palms and laurels of a General of the Nation. I have done this because I wish to continue to be *el Coronel Perón*, and to place myself, with that name, wholly at the service of Argentina's authentic people. I leave the honourable and sacred uniform the Fatherland gave me, to put on the civilian's jacket and blend into this suffering, sweating mass whose work makes the greatness of the Fatherland . . .

'Thus I give my final embrace to that institution which is the buttress of the Fatherland, the Army. And I also give my first embrace to this grandiose mass which represents the synthesis of a sentiment that had died in the Republic: the true civility of the Argentine people.

'This is the people.

'This is the suffering people, representing the pain of Mother Earth, which we are to vindicate.

'It is the people of the Fatherland.

'It is the same people that in this historic square demanded from the Congress respect for its will and its rights. It is the same people, which is to be immortal, because there is no perfidy or human wickedness capable of shaking this people, grandiose in its sentiments and in its numbers. This is a true feast of democracy, represented by a people marching now to demand of its rulers that they do their duty so that the true people can exercise their rights . . .

'I have often attended meetings of workers. I have always felt deep satisfaction, but henceforth I shall feel true pride as an Argentine, because I interpret this collective movement as the rebirth of the workers' consciousness, which is the only thing that can make the Fatherland great and immortal . . .

'Two years ago I asked for trust. Many times they told me that this people for which I had sacrificed hours of my days and nights would betray me. May those unworthy dissemblers now know that this people does not deceive those who help it. That it why, gentlemen, I want to take this opportunity, as a mere civilian, of blending into this sweating mass, of embracing it deeply with my heart, just as I would with my mother . . .

'May this unity be indestructible and eternal, that our people may not only attain unity but also know how to defend it with dignity . . .

'You want to know where I have been? I have made a sacrifice I would make a thousand times over for you. I do not wish to conclude without sending kind and fraternal greetings to our brothers of the interior, who are moving and palpitating in unison with our hearts in the farthest reaches of the Fatherland.

'And now the hour arrives, as always, for your Secretary of Labour and Welfare, as I have been and will always continue to struggle at your side, to see the crowning of his whole life's ambition: that all the workers may be just a little happier . . .

'As you continue to insist, I must beg you not to ask me about what I have today forgotten nor remind me of it. Because men who are incapable of forgetting do not deserve to be loved and respected by their fellows. And I wish to be loved by you, and do not want to mar this event with any bad memory. I said the hour of counsel had arrived. Remember, workers: unite and be more fraternal than ever. Upon the brotherhood of those who work shall rise our beloved Fatherland, in the unity of all Argentines. Day by day we shall incorporate to this beautiful mass's movement each of the hapless or discontented, so that, together with us, they too shall become a beautiful, patriotic mass like you.

'I also ask all my worker friends kindly to accept my immense gratitude for the preoccupation you have shown for this humble man now speaking. That is why I just told you that I embraced you as I would embrace my mother, because you have had the same pain and the same thought as my poor, dear old lady must have felt these last few days. Let us hope that the days to come shall be of peace and construction for the Nation.

'I know that actions by the workers have been announced; now there is no need for them. So I beg you, as an elder brother, to return to your places of work and reflect. And today I beg you to return calmly to your homes, and for this once, since I was unable to do so as Secretary of Labour and Welfare, I ask you to carry out a day's stoppage celebrating the glory of this gathering of working men, who are the Fatherland's dearest hope.

'I have deliberately left to the end my recommendation that you leave this magnificent assembly with great care. Remember that among you there are many working women, who must be protected today as always by the workers themselves. And finally, remember that I am ill and that I need a rest, which I shall now take in Chubut, to restore my strength and return to struggle, elbow to elbow, with you, to exhaustion if necessary. I beg of you that we remain together for at least another fifteen minutes, for I wish to stand here contemplating this sight that has eradicated the sadness I have experienced in these last few days.'

The crowd cheered, chanted, waved its handkerchiefs and flags and torches for slightly longer than that, then began to disperse.

An unusual revolution had taken place. A government had been overthrown, not by the Army or by the threat of armed action, but by the mass mobilisation of workers whose only strength was their sheer physical presence and their fervour. It had not been entirely free from violence; earlier in the day there had been stonings and window-smashing in the provincial capital of La Plata, and later in the night the action of a handful of excited demonstrators led to a shootout in front of the *antiperonista* newspaper *Crítica*, leaving one dead. Admiral Vernengo Lima's rebellion fizzled out when the High Seas Fleet, in the knowledge that General Avalos was staying put, refused to leave its anchorage. In more than one way, the *antiperonistas* had not known how to cope with this peaceful invasion of their capital, an unusual sight in the prim and proper Buenos Aires of the day, where people just did not shed their jackets and ties, or cool their weary feet in the fountains of the Plaza de Mayo. Very many urbanites, still caught in the illusion of living in a European enclave, were aghast at the sight of this wave of browner-faced Argentines, *cabecitas negras* or *pelos duros* (literally, 'black heads', 'stiff hairs'), parading through their capital and actually dictating to government. It was, in the words of a prominent *antiperonista* politician, 'a zoological avalanche'. These newcomers were people who were just about taken for granted to do their work; as distinct from the worker of European stock, their rural, *criollo* background led them to be considered and treated with the same paternalism that ruled relations between *patrón* and *peón* on the farms; they were assumed to be simpleminded, little more than children, uneducated, unacquainted with the sophistication of 'civilised' ways. Just as the middle classes led by Yrigoyen had been considered too uncouth to cope with the complexities of political power, the new internal migrant who made up the bulk of Argentina's working class in the 1940s was deemed unprepared to understand the responsibilities and duties that went with the exercise of democratic rights. In brief, its members were denied the possibility of minds of their own, and were assumed to act only when their 'basic passions' were stimulated. Thus, the unprecedented mobilisation of 17 October could only be attributed to the effects of mass deception, of demagoguery, of deliberate political corruption. A Socialist leader attempted to cover up his amazement by stating that if the much more educated working classes of Germany and Italy had been taken in by Nazism and Fascism, it should not be too surprising that Argentina's less well-endowed workers should have fallen for the crude forms of bribery offered by Perón.

Yet they had acted when Perón was fallen, when he had lost all his positions in government, and when his original power base, the Army, was no longer unanimously behind him; when the Navy was a decidedly hostile force, and when almost all the country's traditional political parties were lined up against him. Furthermore, his original external allies, the Germans, were defeated, and their victors, particularly the United States, were set on his elimination from the continental scene. It may well have been a response to what Perón had achieved from a position of power, but the action of Argentina's workers in October 1945 was the exact opposite of seeking accommodation with those in power; it was a clear attempt, in the face of all adversity, to re-create, or to create anew, a situation in which political power and their interests coincided. Many analysts have described 17 October 1945 as more a carnival than a revolution. Indeed, in its naivety, its procedures resembled those of a carnival, but its effects were undoubtedly those of a revolution. The balance of power in the land had been decisively tilted, and henceforth power would never be held without regard to the workers. Or so it would seem for several decades.

There was more. Between leaders and followers, this still unnamed movement set in motion by Perón had somehow opted against the obvious choice: the outright capture of political power at the very moment when opposition seemed to be faltering. It was not simply another coup; Perón did not step into the Presidency, as he might have done, invoking the legitimacy conferred by this mass turnout of supporters. Here was a break with the tradition of palace coups which Argentines, and Perón himself, had experienced in previous years. Here too was a departure from the Nazi and Fascist models that had enthused Perón not long before. As a realistic politician, he would seek to extract every possible advantage from the situation, including the use of the régime's apparatus to pave his way and obstruct that of his opponents. But the avenue chosen for his accession to power was one the country had almost forgotten in the preceding 'Decade of Infamy' and its military sequel: free elections.

All that remained now was to prepare the final assault. The task ahead, even counting on government support, was a daunting one. To start with, Perón's back would have to be covered, and control would have to be reasserted over the armed forces. But even more important, a political apparatus would have to be created which would serve the purpose of this incursion into the unknown territory of electoral politics. So far, it had been a matter of attracting union support by an audacious use of officialdom. But all the skill in electoral tactics lay stored in the traditional political parties, which were Perón's enemies. Perón did not even have a party of his own, and there was the additional question of attracting to his cause the support of sectors other than the urban working classes. Attempts were made to lure the Radicals into taking up this role, against the promise that most government posts from the cabinet down to the meanest municipality would be theirs. Negotiations began with Amadeo Sabattini, leader of the 'intransigents'. In the Radicals' eyes, however, the proposal was too reminiscent of their past history, and they re-enacted their 'intransigent' rejection of similar overtures from the oligarchy, haughtily rebuffing Perón — and then proceeding to hammer out an alliance with the party of the oligarchs, and with the Socialists and Progressive Democrats and Communists. *Unión Democrática*, the Democratic Union, was the name chosen for this massive *antiperonista* entente. However, some leading Radicals, particularly drawn from among the Junta Renovadora, a splinter group that rebelled against the party executive, and members of FORJA, a youth organisation that had emerged to oppose the increasingly conciliatory policies adopted by the 'anti-personalist' party leaders during the 'Decade of Infamy', did see in Perón a figure closer to their own outlook than their party hierarchy, which was openly consorting with the conservatives. There were Hortensio Quijano, and Arturo Jauretche, and Cooke, Del Río, Reales, López Francés, Alvarado. Success had already been achieved in attracting some Socialists, like Angel Borlenghi and Juan Atilio Bramuglia. And then there were others from the ranks of Catholic nationalism who had already felt affinity for Perón through their common admiration for corporativist experiments in Europe. All this, however, did not add up to a party. The job of creating one was entrusted to Cipriano Reyes, the loyal leader of the meat-packers' union who had actually set in motion the mobilisation of 17 October. The basic idea was to adapt to Argentine circumstances the experience of the British Labour Party, which at the time had just begun to preside over the destinies of post-war Britain: a party sponsored by the trade unions, in the Argentine case those that Perón had welded into a strong CGT. Far from hiding its source of inspiration, the new organisation called itself Partido Laborista. Its charter stated that it would consist of the trade unions, professional associations, political 'centres' and individual members. Its platform called for firm policies against price increases and speculation; for monetary stability; for the establishment of a minimum, index-linked salary; for social security, paid holidays and pensions for all workers; for state and union representation on the boards of public utilities and the meat-packing plants; for the nationalisation of the country's natural resources; for agrarian reform; for the liquid-ation of the trusts controlling the trade in grain; for worker super-vision of company profits and production costs; for better working conditions.

There was not much time in which to gain the upper hand; only three clear months before the date set for the elections. Perón had married Evita in a quiet ceremony on 22 October, then spent a brief political honeymoon holed up with Colonel Mercante mapping out his strategy. While the new-born Partido Laborista began to spread to the interior, his friends at the National Post-war Council hurriedly thrashed out a detailed programme of government. Eduardo Colom's newspaper *Epoca* was virtually campaigning before Perón himself had started. In December two enthusiasts, Antonio Molinari and Mauricio Birabent, founded a newspaper, *Democracia*, which they turned into a valuable new campaigning instrument, harping constantly on their own hobby-horse, agrarian reform. They promised in Perón's name that *latifundia* would be expropriated and that land would be distributed to rural labourers. 'We have announced three fundamental reforms,' said Perón at a rally, 'an economic one, a social one and a political one. Our economic reform will lead to an increase in production. *We shall give the land to those who work it!*' And the peasants flocked to meet his campaign train when he went on a tour of the country's rural northwest. Perón had on his side the power-ful media control apparatus he had set up while himself in government, and which was now manned by his friends. It became difficult to distinguish the government's own communiqués from Perón's electioneering, and even more difficult for the opposition to get time on the state's air waves, but Perón would discover that the private radio networks were not at all eager to let him spread his gospel.

Not that opposition lacked propaganda instruments of its own. The conservative newspapers *La Nación* and *La Prensa*, the country's most prestigious dailies, worked hard at creating an image of a Perón who was getting nowhere while the candidates of the Unión Democrática, José Tamborini and Enrique Mosca, were attracting ever more support. Tamborini and Mosca had also obtained the public support of the Buenos Aires Stock Exchange and the slightly more discreet backing of the Sociedad Rural, the association of landowners, and the Unión Industrial, the organisation of 'traditional' industrialists. Big business was decidedly against Perón, although he did not lack support in some entrepreneurial sectors. Jorge Abelardo Ramos, the Trotskyite ideologue, has summed up in his own inimitable style the complex relationship between *peronismo* and industry:

Perón appears as the historic representative of the industrial bourgeoisie, though not as its political expression, since this [bourgeoisie], cowardly and chaotic, unconscious and semi-foreign, is hostile to him. In a growing semi-colonial country like Argentina, social sectors can be divided into two large groups, those who obtain their profits on the international markets and those who produce for our domestic market. Among the former one can find mainly the privileged cattle-breeders and -fatteners of Buenos Aires, the exporters of raw materials, the importers of industrial goods from the imperialist nations — mere agents of the metropolis — , the agrarian bourgeoisie of the littoral (well-off small farmers and peasants), the financial sectors that speculate between production and distribution, in association with foreign corporations. This tangle of interests has its dominant nucleus in the farmers of Buenos Aires, the true leaders of this oligarchy whose lack of national spirit is due to its externally-linked economic interests.

In the other group one finds mainly the industrialists of Greater Buenos Aires and Rosario, whose maintenance and expansion can only be achieved through the growth of the domestic market, Customs barriers, banking protection and adequate overall legislation. Quintessentially protectionist, this industrial sector lacked support in the media, since all the press was in the hands of the free-trading oligarchy and its agents . . .

Vis-à-vis his *criollo* workers, the foreign or xenophile industrialist tended to identify with the whole of the dominant class, and servilely imitated the imperialist model not only in the goods he produced, but also in the thought-patterns, habits and anti-Argentine prejudices of the parasitic oligarchy. He would send his children to English boarding schools; his only preoccupation being to become a *Señor* and quickly amass a fortune; indifferent to the country's cardinal problems, he shied away, as had the cattle-breeding oligarchy, from investing his capital in high-flying enterprises, such as the heavy industry which only calls for expenditure in its early stages. He preferred light industry, the improvised production of articles suddenly running scarce on the market, immediate profits, defrauding the exchequer and even speculating with raw materials; he was thus largely a profiteer and an improviser, an *antiperonista* and a 'Sepoy', brutally disregarding the wave that was enriching him and the historic significance of his own existence.

Although this may be a caricature, the point is well made. Electioneering was hardly a gentle affair, with a large number of violent clashes between *peronistas* and *antiperonistas*, the police intervening more often than not on the side of the *peronistas*, and organised harassment of the Unión Democrática (Tamborini's campaign train was stoned, and a rally held to welcome him back to Buenos Aires was fired on by the police, leaving three dead). Nor was violence one-sided; guns were carried and used by Unión Democrática supporters, and there was at least one foiled attempt on Perón's life. Among Perón's nationalist partisans, there were those who took it upon themselves to give their campaign an anti-Semitic bent, terrorising the Jewish quarters of Buenos Aires until Perón publicly disowned them. Yet the incidents of violence and of undue government or police interference in those three months can virtually be recounted one by one; they stand out sharply, in contrast to the countrywide exercise of violence and intimidation and the catalogue of fraud that were the hallmarks of most of the elections held since the beginning of the century. Even Perón's adversaries would concede in time that they were hardly decisive.

The biggest of Perón's assets in his campaign was his arch-enemy, Spruille Braden. In the few months in which he had been US ambassador in Buenos Aires, Braden had openly campaigned for the ousting of Perón. He had returned to his country before the events of October 1945, to become an Under-Secretary in charge of Latin American affairs in the US State Department. As soon as he had taken up this post, he was announcing a renewed campaign to prevent 'a new outbreak of Fascism in the hemisphere'. Braden's every statement was loudly echoed in Buenos Aires by *La Prensa*, and his attempt to stop Perón reached its peak with the official publication by the State Department of the *Consultation among the American Republics with respect to the Argentine Situaton*. Better known as the *Blue Book*, this purported to reveal Perón's wartime role as a Nazi agent. As recounted in *Cien años contra el País*:

More than three pages were devoted by *La Prensa* to the news of the *Blue Book*'s publication. A number of headlines made reading easy for those who did not wish to tire their eyes going through so much material: 'The Union has published its investigation of the Argentine government's action towards the war effort of the United Nations. It will be called the Blue Book' — 'Aid given to the Axis by the government of R.S. Castillo and the present régime' — 'The conclusion is reached that Argentina did not collaborate with the Allied victory' — 'Why our country was admitted to the Conferences of Mexico and San Francisco'. 'Argentine rulers made votes for a totalitarian victory' — 'Colonel Juan D. Perón's intervention in negotiations with German agents in Buenos Aires' — 'The GOU considered Argentina to be in a position similar to that of the Reich' — 'Perón was one of the main directors of the American conspiracy against the Allies' —'Argentine military men promoted a movement of Nazi agitation in neighbouring countries (the main Argentine conspirator was Perón)' — 'Perón ordered the Nazi secret service to be informed of the break with the Axis'.

Braden's open interference, which had been sharply criticised by diplomats of other nations stationed in Buenos Aires, gave Perón a wonderful propaganda weapon. While the opposition insisted on accusing him of a Fascism that few of his supporters could readily identify with the events they had experienced, Perón coined a slogan that effectively touched people's patriotic and nationalistic feelings: *Braden o Perón*. The choice, he was more than hinting, was not between Perón and the candidate of the Unión Democrática, José Tamborini, but between Perón and an openly interfering foreign power.

Only slightly less important to Perón's campaign was another asset he had inherited from the 1943 coup: the support of the Catholic church. Catholicism was the state religion; the vast majority of Argentines were at least nominally Catholic, and profession of the religion was laid down in the Constitution as one of the conditions of eligibility for the office of President. Indeed, as the heir of Spain Argentina enjoyed the privilege of the *Patronato*, which entitled the President to nominate candidates to the episcopate. The relationship of church and state was a symbiosis, a temporal *modus vivendi* which had, among other effects, that of keeping the church's efforts at evangelism confined to the sphere of private morality and far removed from political or social (other than 'charitable') concerns. The hierarchy were jealously protective of this relationship, and their rare incursions into the political sphere were usually motivated by the concern lest this privileged status might be eroded. Thus they had opposed Roca's moves towards secularisation, particularly the institution of civil marriage, and in 1931 had actually issued a pastoral letter forbidding Catholics to vote for any party that advocated the separation of church and state, the suppression of any of the privileges enjoyed by the church under the law, the secularisation of education, or divorce. At the time, this meant the alliance formed by Socialists and Progressive Democrats to oppose the candidacy of Agustín P. Justo (who in any case preferred to rely on electoral fraud to secure his victory).

When the GOU-inspired coup took place in 1943, one of its early acts was the establishment of compulsory religious education in schools throughout the country. This earned the régime the gratitude and support of the church hierarchy. Soon after Perón launched his election campaign, a priest called Leonardo Castellani called on him to commit himself to ratifying that decision in case of his election. Perón wrote out a note to that effect, and the following day it appeared on the front page of the newspaper *Tribuna*.

The full hierarchy of the church — that is to say, the Primate, Cardinal Santiago Luis Copello, and all the archbishops and bishops — had only recently revived the 1931 pastoral letter and given orders for it to be read in every church in the country. Some bishops, preferring not to leave anything to individual interpretation, added more explicit pastoral letters of their own. Such was the case of Zenobio Guilland, Archbishop of Santa Fe, who said, 'Catholics cannot vote for the Socialist and Communist parties, which have been condemned by the church, nor for the parties that form alliances or collaborate with them.' In this particular election campaign, this could only mean the Unión Democrática. Perón himself reinforced the message by claiming, 'Our social policies have largely arisen from the papal encyclicals, and our doctrine is the Christian social doctrine.'

The backing of the church was a tremendous boost, though it must be mentioned that at least one prominent group of Catholics, priests and laymen, openly opposed the hierarchy's electoral dictates from the beginning. Like all genuine democrats, they were wary both of Perón's Fascist associations and of the ambiguity shown by the hierarchy towards an influential sector of Catholic nationalists, who flaunted their disregard for Pius XI's explicit condemnation of Nazism in *Mit Brennender Sorge* by proclaiming their own admiration for Fascism, for the Middle Ages as the embodiment of the correct ordering of society, and for theories that attributed the evils of contemporary society to Judaism, Freemasonry, Liberalism and Marxism. It is almost impossible to determine how much of the popular vote was influenced by the church's position, but the fact remains that its political message was the only one to continue to be publicised, from the pulpit, after the contending parties, in accordance with electoral law, had put an official end to their campaigns.

Perón's last appeal was an emotional call to all Argentines of voting age to leap over farm gates, cut through barbed-wire fences and overcome any obstacles in the way of performing their civic duty.

The country went to the polls on 26 February 1946. By everyone's admission, the elections were free and fair. But for a number of reasons the count proceeded very slowly, and many of Perón's opponents leapt to the conclusion that this meant they were winning. On the morning of the 27th, *La Prensa* confidently printed a long report, based on early but incomplete returns from two provinces, exulting that 'the count in San Luis and San Juan has begun with a majority for the candidates of the Unión Democrática.' But electoral arithmetic soon said otherwise. Throughout the country Perón collected 1,400,000 votes, against his rival's 1,200,000; 55 per cent of the electorate had pronounced in his favour. As soon as the breakdown was known, it became clear that he had not only taken the Presidency but also the Legislature, with an absolute majority in both chambers, and the governorships of all the provinces save one, Corrientes. Perón was the constitutional President-elect of Argentina for a six-year period starting on 4 June 1946.

6

PERÓN FULFILS
(1946–1951)

Perón's first government started, for all practical purposes, in the period
between his election and his inauguration, when he prevailed upon the
outgoing President Farrell to pass a number of decrees, mainly in the
economic sphere, that would lay the foundations for his own programme, already developed under the supervision of José Figuerola in the
National Post-war Council. This first government somehow remains in
the memory of many Argentines as the period of Perón's greatest
achievements; all of what is widely accepted as 'good' in Perón's contribution to the construction of modern Argentina is quite readily attributed to his first six years in the Presidency. In this, there is coincidence
between *antiperonistas* who have belatedly wished to acknowledge the
positive aspects of the Perón régime while retaining the justification for
their opposition, and *peronistas* who have, *ex post facto*, tried to come to
terms with those facets of the régime that aroused legitimate dissidence
in the Republic. It is a convenient fiction.

The first presidency began in the midst of abundance, at least in the
paper balances of the national accounts. It was in this period that the
Perón régime nationalised the Central Bank and all the country's bank
deposits (the Roca-Runciman Pact had practically left the Argentine
banking system, from the creation of money downwards, under British
supervision) and the public utilities from railways and ports to telephones
and urban transport (they were still mainly in foreign, usually British
hands); that it created the Instituto Argentino de Promoción del Intercambio (IAPI), a state agency controlling all the country's foreign trade;
that the country acquired a sizeable merchant fleet, a national airline, and
new sources of energy; that labour legislation was consolidated, and an
income distribution policy was adopted which would give the salaried
workers slightly more than half of what the nation generated; that
capital goods were massively introduced after a decade and a half of
Depression- and war-induced neglect; that hospitals and schools were
built throughout the land; and that the gaps in the social security system
were covered by *ad hoc* methods from the Eva Perón Foundation. The

second Presidency, on the other hand, is remembered for economic crisis, the death of Eva Perón, the surfacing of corruption and the intolerability of government intrusion in private lives, and the breakdown of the relationship between the government and the unions, between state and church, and between practice and the staunchly nationalist precepts that formed the basis of the régime.

But most of this has been constructed with the benefit of hindsight. The achievements have been grouped, almost in programmatic order, as if they had been from the outset the product of a master plan of genius; the failings have been segregated into another group, as if they were barnacles essentially unrelated to the positive aspects of the régime. Arguments galore have been printed about the blindness of adversaries, who allegedly let minor and inessential flaws hide from their view the more radical and permanent benefits of *peronismo*; and also about the partisans who were supposedly blinded to wholly unnecessary and incidental perversions which ended by devaluing the central goodness of Perón's contribution. Hindsight and the urge for ideological tidiness, plus the all too natural need for self-justification, are to blame for this complacent distortion. Context was left out for the sake of convenience because, as is usually the case, contexts are far too complex to render into politically efficacious slogans. Yet the circumstances of Perón's first government, both domestic and international, go a long way towards explaining why the good and bad of *peronismo* came together, almost from the first day.

And if contexts are hard to explain in Argentina itself, with its inheritance of Spanish and French ideological thinking, they become almost impossible abroad, particularly in the militantly non-ideological Anglo-Saxon world that emerged victorious from the Second World War and accepted without much reflection the transition to the Cold War, still engrossed in the *realpolitik* of big power rivalry while the Third World was struggling to come into its own. The outlook from the periphery would only begin to impinge on North American and European awareness in the decades still to come, as colonies made the passage to formal independence. There was no category yet — other than the North American stereotypes of the banana republic and the operetta coup — in which to fit the forerunners of the Third World, those colonies of Spain and Portugal that had emerged to political independence in the early nineteenth century but were still wrestling in the 1940s with economic bonds not unlike those which in future would hold the European colonies in Africa, the Middle East and Asia. However Argentina's emergent working classes appeared in the eyes of the displaced oligarchy, the very notion that they might have a different world view of their own was inconceivable.

Yet to understand the peculiar ordering and apparently incoherent realisation of Perón's economic policies, it is essential to take note first of what he expected from the post-war world. Perón was convinced that peace was transitory; that the victorious Allies would soon discover the threat posed by an expanding Soviet Union, and that a third world war was at best only a decade away. Argentina had emerged from the war years immensely rich thanks to its beef trade, mainly with Britain. But for Argentina, most of that wealth was only a risky paper asset, since it remained blocked by a British government starved of hard currency and in urgent need of post-war reconstruction. Even if the coming world conflagration were to be delayed, common sense pointed to the danger of Britain deciding on devaluation, slashing Argentina's earned but undisbursed income for the sake of its own domestic requirements. This situation, in either of its alternatives, called for quick action; first, to preserve the value of Argentina's wartime earnings, and second, to refurbish Argentina's armed forces and industry before a new war, like the two that had preceded it, led to a cut-off in supplies. As seen by Perón in the nine months that elapsed between the end of the war and his accession to the Presidency, there was much to justify these fears. Both the Soviets and the North Americans were frantically snatching up all available German technological talent, conveniently overlooking its owners' previous associations with the Nazi régime, even as the Nuremberg trials were getting under way. Washington seemed especially willing to forget a man's Nazi past whenever it was allied to expertise or knowledge that could be used against the Soviets; absorption of German experts in Eastern intelligence into the CIA-controlled Gehlen *apparat* was a clear example. And with this backdrop, the persistent use of the Nazi taint against a staunchly anti-Communist Perón appeared as the grossest form of hypocrisy, apart from being an indication of continuing hostility.

'What was going on at Nuremberg at the time', Perón would recall in his Spanish exile, 'was in my own view an infamy and a sombre lesson for all mankind. [. . .] I became convinced that the Argentines as a whole also considered the Nuremberg trials an infamy, unworthy of the victors, who were behaving as if they had not won.' And Perón decided to compete with the Soviets and the North Americans by despatching government officials to Europe to recruit any available German scientists or technicians. 'What better deal for the Argentine Republic', he argued, 'than to bring in scientists and technicians? What cost us no more than the airplane ticket had cost Germany millions of marks!' Thousands of Germans found their way to Argentina with official assistance, provided 'on humanitarian grounds', some to make an important contribution to the development of the aircraft industry, others to make a more doubtful contribution to the beginnings of nuclear research; many more to blend into local industry and commerce as had previous generations of immigrants. There was also help for 5,000 anti-Tito Croats, whose leader Ante Pavelić would enter Argentine politics through the Fascist-oriented Alianza Libertadora Nacionalista, and for many Poles who had fought the Nazis only to find themselves unable to return to a Communist Poland after the war. Their common denominator, in the words of the friends of Perón who compiled his testimony on this matter, was that all these people were 'cultured, disciplined and absolutely anti-Communist'.

The insistent domestic echoes of Washington's Argentine 'anti-Nazi' campaign also sowed in *peronista* minds the fear that with foreign support the opposition would sooner or later attempt to oust him by force. It was this not entirely unjustified fear that led Perón, in the second month of his Presidency, despite an overwhelming legislative majority that guaranteed the execution of his will, to proclaim in a public address, 'I will make a revolution a week earlier [than the opposition]. It will be simply a matter of giving every *descamisado* [literally 'shirtless one', i.e. worker] two metres of rope. Then we shall see who hangs whom!'

The picture is not complete only with this collection of perceived threats — the imminence of another world war, or at least a devaluation of sterling, the hostility of the Unites States abroad and the threat of subversion, or 'de-stabilisation' in later Kissingerian jargon, at home. Also decisive was the man chosen to co-ordinate Perón's economic *blitzkrieg*; Miguel Miranda. This man, whom Argentines would come to know as '*el mago de las finanzas*' (the financial wizard) was almost the exact opposite of the highly ideological and organised José Figuerola, the author of the programmes that would soon be popularised as the First Five-Year Plan. Miranda was also an immigrant from Spain, but he had arrived at an early age and had worked his way up from poorly paid jobs. His first 'killing' came during the Great War, when he scented scarcity in the air and decided to put all his money into hoarding tin. The venture paid off handsomely, and Miranda moved into the food business. Perón recalled that by the time he met him at the National Postwar Council, Miranda 'was fifty-five, owned thirty factories and was personally worth about 300 million pesos'. It was not only Miranda's success as a businessman that impressed Perón, but also his ability to cut through jargon and come up with practical, if almost always audacious and unorthodox, solutions to policy proposals. His first impact was made when the Council was discussing the possibility of nationalising all banks. Miranda suggested instead the nationalisation of deposits. Not surprisingly he was charged with responsibility for the Central Bank and the introduction of a system whereby the state, as nominal owner of the deposits, allocated the distribution of credit. The régime transformed private banks into mere agents of the Central Bank, and to this extent placed a corset on the development of the banking system, but it also freed banks from preoccupation with the adequacy of interest rates: apart from the use of their own capital, their profits were made from the difference between the borrowing and lending rates, and these were set by the state.

Miranda was also entrusted with the rapid exploitation of Argentina's external accounts: the sizeable outstanding debt and the enormous reserves trapped abroad. His efforts led to one of the most unusual processes of nationalisation of foreign-owned concerns, and to massive importation of transport material and machinery. His first target was the network of British-owned railways.

Renovation of rolling stock and track had been virtually halted since before the war, and returns to British holders of stock in the Argentine railways were declining rapidly and inexorably. From a purely commercial point of view, and without even contemplating the injection of large hard-currency investments (an impossibility for post-war Britain), transforming these enterprises again into profitable concerns would have called for drastic cuts in staffing levels and sharp increases in tariffs. These were a political impossibility in post-war Argentina. Furthermore, at the beginning of 1947 the railways would have to face the burden of the expiry of one of the most important concessions they had obtained from friendlier Argentine governments: the exemption from payment of all federal, provincial and municipal taxes. The obvious alternative for the British owners was to unload a substantial share of their stock on the Argentine government, saddling it with the problem of dealing with local political and social constraints and making it responsible for at least part of the necessary investment. Miranda negotiated just such a deal against the release of Argentina's sterling holdings in London. For the British railway entrepreneurs it was a handsome proposition: Argentina would guarantee British stockholders a minimum return of 4 per cent annually, and a liquid profit of 80 million pesos a year, apart from committing itself to investing 500 million pesos in the ageing network. But this final deal did not materialise — it was vetoed by Washington. Britain was at the time the recipient of massive North American financial aid, granted *inter alia* with a view to recovering the money lent to the British during the war. So when the British attached to the railway deal a rider confining the use of the released sterling holdings to the sterling area, the US State Department gently reminded London that this violated one of the conditions under which North American aid had been granted. American nations, so went Washington's rationale, should be free to shake off their financial and trade dependence on Britain; the corollary, of course, was that their custom would be shifted to the United States.

So Miranda returned to the negotiating table, and after much tough talking emerged in January 1947 with a new deal, this time for the outright purchase of the railways. The cost of the acquisition, originally calculated at 1,000 million pesos, first doubled to 2,000 million ('for sentimental reasons and debts of gratitude with England', Miranda said), and was finally fixed at 2,700 million, as the Argentine government took over the legal and administrative costs of the operation and the debts the railways still owed the pension funds and the workers. The Socialists sneered in a clandestine publication: 'Italy paid 325 million dollars as the sum total of war reparations, while we have paid a 375 million dollar surplus only for sentimental reasons.'

Another massive purchase was that of the Unión Telefónica, a subsidiary of the US firm International Telegraph and Telephone (ITT) that ran the telephone service. Some 319 million pesos (95 million dollars at the time) were paid; according to the government this was equivalent to the difference between the company's assets and its liabilities, but opposition legislators insisted on criticising the government's arithmetic and the fact that, with the purchase, it had granted ITT a ten-year monopoly for the supply of materials and technical assistance. Institutionally, the organisation carrying out the purchases was the Instituto Argentino de Promoción del Intercambio (IAPI), a creation of Miranda's which was primarily aimed at monopolising Argentina's exports, holding out for high prices (which it often obtained in the first few years), and its imports, seeking out the best available deals abroad. In fact it functioned as a mechanism to transfer income from the agricultural to the industrial sector. Surplus war material was bought by IAPI at rock-bottom prices wherever it was on offer. Much of it went to refurbishing the armed forces: 150 million pesos' worth of Sherman tanks, 4,000 jeeps, 100 Gloster Meteor and 45 Fiat fighter planes, 30 Avro Lincoln bombers, 90 De Havilland Doves, 14 Catalina flying boats, an entire British aircraft plant and assorted equipment. But there were purchases in even larger quantities for public services and industry as well: 5,000 Empire tractors, 600 Mack buses and the new trolley-buses urgently needed by Buenos Aires' chaotic and deficit-ridden public transport service, 3,000 railway carriages, mining equipment, power generators and machinery of all kinds. The time came when the Buenos Aires port authorities begged Miranda not to buy any more, for there was no more storage space available; he replied that the answer was to stack imported goods two or three high. This purchasing fever owed much to the expectation of a new war, and indeed Miranda was able to boast of a number of unbelievably good deals, both purchases and sales. He was also taken for a ride more than once, as when he was almost sold a non-existent Italian aluminium factory or when rolling stock turned out to be of the wrong gauge, or when there were no buyers for obsolete goods; and the speed and improvisation with which he conducted operations left much leeway for minor officials to engage in shady transactions with import licenses and foreign currency deals.

Miranda also made some tragic mistakes. He gambled on Argentina's future role as a grains supplier to Europe, within the framework of the Unites States' Marshall Plan, and indeed managed to store away almost two entire harvests in expectation of the coming bonanza. But the United States virtually cut Argentina, with other non-dollar-area countries, out of the juicier parts of the Plan's purchases. The country lost heavily, and was left at a disadvantage that was to prove lasting, particularly as the expected war did not materialise and as the world prices for Argentina's imports continued to rise beyond the IAPI's capacity to compensate.

Perón's first government was responsible for strengthening the country's merchant fleet and for creating the national airline, Aerolíneas Argentinas. In both cases, the operations arose from the take-over and merger of failing private enterprises. The river and high seas merchant fleets were formed after the purchase of the firm owned by Alberto Dodero, a wealthy businessman who became the target of many accusations of having cultivated Perón and Evita and showered gifts on them to secure the deal (although after Perón's fall Dodero's heirs would claim in court that they had been cheated by Perón). Aerolíneas Argentinas emerged from the failure of three mixed enterprises, Fama, Zonda and

Alfa. Although the air carrier, like most of its kind throughout the world, continued to be a money loser well beyond the end of the Perón régime, the creation of a national shipping enterprise gave Argentina the opportunity to claw back at least part of the constant draining away of hard currency represented by freight charges for its exports and imports.

The country's dependence on imported oil and coal was another problem which the Perón administration tackled on a grand scale. Hydroelectric plants were built or enlarged throughout the country; work began on an enormous gas pipeline from Comodoro Rivadavia, in faraway Patagonia, to Buenos Aires (eventually halving the price of gas to consumers in the capital); money and work was ploughed into the development of the coal deposits in Rio Turbio, in the southernmost extreme of the country; and oil exploration was intensified, to be rewarded by the discovery of new fields in Tierra del Fuego, Neuquén, Mendoza and Salta, increasing almost tenfold the country's known reserves and creating a new major political issue: the expectation of self-sufficiency and the choice of means to achieve it.

Not all the effort was concentrated in economic infrastructure. Perón had inherited a country with a dramatic housing deficit, estimated at over 600,000 units; his government reactivated the Banco Hipotecario Nacional (the national mortgage bank) with direct injections of funds from the Central Bank, and launched into a massive house-building campaign. At the end of the First Five-Year Plan, more than 200,000 houses had been completed, in impressive contrast with the mere 1,000 built by the Comisión Nacional de Casas Baratas in the preceding three decades. Hospitals were also erected by the score, and the Public Health Ministry introduced mass vaccination campaigns and managed to eradicate a number of diseases previously considered endemic. Hundreds of schools completed the array of publicly-funded buildings, all in the same, typically Perón-era mock-Californian style, that sprouted all over the country bearing the slogan '*Perón cumple*', 'Perón fulfils [his promises]'. Attached to this slogan was another one, '*Evita dignifica*', 'Evita dignifies'. The low-cost houses, the new schools and hospitals, the pension schemes, all came nominally from the 'social cost' paid by employers; mandatory contributions amounting to almost 40 per cent of the salary, which, added to the steadily increasing wages, constituted a direct and indirect transfer of income towards the salaried classes, giving them, towards the end of the Perón era, more than half of the national income. But even this enormous transfer was unable to wipe out the effects of disparities and disadvantages accumulated over decades; the lowest wages were still very low, there were numerous intractable pockets of poverty and unemployment, and a myriad cases of hardship, which were never reached by Perón's breakneck, improvised version of the welfare state. It was this large collection of gaps in the system that Evita set herself to cover.

The story has been told many times of how the high-society ladies who ran the Sociedad de Beneficencia, a church-sponsored charity that undoubtedly did much good work while trumpeting with classy chic the virtues of its benefactresses, decided to break with custom and deny Evita, as the President's wife, their honorary chairmanship. The official excuse was that she was too young (twenty-seven at the time), but it was a transparent snubbing of this former actress who was already the butt of much malicious and even slanderous gossip. Evita never forgot the insult. Her response was not only to set up her own charitable institution with government backing, on a far grander scale than the Sociedad de Beneficencia had ever managed, but also to conduct a war of attrition that would effectively destroy the good ladies' association. Formally, Evita was not entrusted with any official position. But she was given office space in the Secretariat of Labour and Welfare from which to run the Fundación Eva Perón, and from that unpaid post she created what amounted to a new, unofficial branch of government which was as involved in politics as in charitable works. Her own explanation was that she was acting as a 'bridge' between Perón and his people; that her attention was concentrated on the many minor, day-to-day problems of the small people that the Líder, occupied with the greater destinies of the nation, could not be expected to heed in any detail.

The work of the Foundation ranged from the small, direct handout to the construction of major hospitals. Its functioning was completely unplanned; beneficiaries were chosen at random, or by instinct, by Evita herself from among thousands of applicants with the most diverse demands. Its funding was equally haphazard; there were contributions — at times very small ones, but at times running to hundreds of thousands of pesos — voted by the different unions; there were the quite large contributions in money or in kind, exacted often by unsubtle means near to extortion from big business; there were the proceeds of expropriations conducted by the State and, irregularly at first, made over with judicial acquiescence to the Foundation; and there were some truly massive injections of funds, such as the officially enforced contribution of two days' earnings from the wages of every worker in the country.

Accounting was virtually non-existent, as Evita made a virtue of cutting through red tape and providing solutions wherever the state apparatus was too cumbersome and slow to act, or even prevented from doing so by law. In time, the Foundation became a forerunner *sui generis* of the wholly autonomous state corporation; Congress voted for a law allowing it to receive official funding, including the proceeds of tax revenue, but enabling it to dispose of these funds with the same freedom and absence of supervision as a private company.

With this sort of set-up it is hardly surprising that the Foundation became the object of much suspicion, as the alleged source of illicit enrichment for the Peróns themselves (Perón and Evita had already been accused by the opposition of pocketing a large portion of the monies collected for the San Juan earthquake relief operation, before he reached the Presidency). But by the end of the First Five-Year Plan the Foundation could point to a number of very concrete achievements: twelve hospitals (including the 600-bed Policlínico Presidente Perón), a chain of hostels (for working girls, for women transients and the like), a huge estate devoted to the aged plus a number of old-age homes, just under 160 schools and a chain of low-price food stores.

From her position at the head of the Foundation, Evita also built up a considerable power base of her own. She influenced the creation of the Feminine Branch of the ruling party, and was instrumental in obtaining for women the right to vote. On a more personal level, she placed within the apparatus of government a network of people who were completely loyal to herself. Some of them were relatives: one of her brothers-in-law was in the Senate, another was the head of Customs and the third became a Justice of the Supreme Court. Her brother Juan was Perón's secretary, and her mother's paramour, Oscar Nicolini, was back in charge of the Post and Telegraphs office. But her influence extended beyond this circle of nepotism, and included the president of the Chamber of Deputies, Héctor Cámpora, and a host of other well-placed personalities. At different times her influence became evident in the form of an arbitrary power of veto. She has been credited with an important say in the eventual ousters of Miguel Miranda from economic czardom, of José María Freire from the Labour Secretariat, and of Juan Atilio Bramuglia from his post as Foreign Minister.

Evita also saw herself as responsible for spreading the gospel of *justicialismo*, as Perón's doctrine had come to be known, to the rest of the world. The Foundation conducted a wide-ranging propaganda campaign throughout the Americas, as well as disbursing funds for social causes beyond Argentina's borders (a drive that included the malicious remittance of aid 'for the needy children of Washington DC'). The apex of Evita's foreign campaign was reached in 1947, during a much-publicised tour of European nations. She received a delirious welcome in Franco's Spain, grateful as that country was to the Perón régime for having kept it supplied with foodstuffs during the virtual embargo dictated by the United States. Italy was less enthusiastic; Evita obtained an audience with the Pope, Pius XII, but failed to receive the expected Papal decoration. Switzerland was pointedly uninterested, France was frigid, and the British stop was called off when it was made clear to Evita that she would not be received by the royal family. Although in Argentina itself the tour was portrayed as an unmitigated success, its obvious failure depressed Evita and indeed cost the job of the Foreign Minister, Bramuglia, who had advised against the tour.

In a sense, the European tour marked the divide between two public images of Evita. From the moment she joined Perón on his election campaign, she had appeared publicly as the pinnacle of glamour, always dressed in the best and latest that European *haute couture* could provide, always bedecked in stunning and expensive jewellery. The European trip gave her the opportunity to show off the most impressive, ever-changing array of finery. The effects of this ostentation on public opinion were paradoxically mixed. Argentina's higher classes sneered at it as an expression of the crassness of the *nouveau riche*; middle-class adversaries of *peronismo* picked on it as clear proof of their allegations of corruption (where had all this wealth come from?) and chuckled in anticipation of the rejection it would inevitably evoke among the *descamisados*, the humble and poor whom Evita claimed very particularly to represent. Yet no such rejection was forthcoming from Argentina's poor; instead they adored her. There has been much speculation about this 'Cinderella effect'; Evita, it is said, was somehow embodying the rise from rags to riches, a poor girl's dream. Since, in real life, they knew they could never attain those heights, they revelled vicariously in her success; in her the oligarchy's monopoly of social achievement had been broken by the dispossessed.

Yet after the trip to Europe a new public Evita began to emerge, slowly taking over from this early glittering image until it completely displaced it. She lost the slight plumpness of before and began to show a trimmer figure and gaunter look, no longer draped in silk and diamonds, but in an austere tailored suit, her hair drawn tightly back into a severe bun. She appeared to work harder, for longer hours. Her rhetoric lost much of its honey and became tougher, more aggressive. Evita the militant was surfacing, and beneath the new image, unknown to all and with creeping implacability, leukaemia was taking over her body.

In the same year as Evita's failed European victory tour, Perón chose to commemorate the country's Declaration of Independence by proclaiming that Argentina was finally on its way to adding economic emancipation to the political independence achieved by the founding fathers 131 years earlier. The government and representatives of the unions and other civic organisations converged on the historic northwestern city of Tucumán, where the first declaration had been signed, to give their approval to Argentina's 'Declaration of Economic Independence'. The document, loaded with the triumphalistic enthusiasm and hope of early *peronismo*, said:

In the meritorious and most worthy city of San Miguel de Tucumán, on the ninth day of the month of July of 1947, in celebration of the 131st anniversary of the political Declaration of Independence, sanctioned by the Congress of the United Provinces which met in 1816, the representatives of the Nation, its governnment forces and its popular and working forces, meet solemnly to reaffirm the Argentine people's purpose of consummating their economic emancipation from the foreign capitalist powers that have exercised their tutelage, control and dominion, under the form of reprehensible economic hegemonies, and from those who within the country might be linked to them.

To that effect the undersigned, in representation of the people of the Nation, commit the energies of their patriotism and the purity of their intentions to the task of mobilising the immense national productive forces and to work out the foundations of a true economic policy, so that in the field of international trade the products of Argentine labour may have a firm base for discussion, negotiation and marketing, thereby guaranteeing for the Republic the economic fate of its present and future. So they understand it and so do they wish it to be, that the people who produce these commodities and the peoples of the Earth who consume them may find a higher level of prosperity and welfare than ever achieved in earlier ages, and above those recorded at present. Therefore, they reaffirm their will to become economically free — just as they proclaimed, 131 years ago, their political independence.

The forces of production and industrialisation now have a range and scope without precedent, and can be enlarged even more by the action and effort of the people of the Republic. Trade and distribution figures demonstrate that commerce and industry are expanding jointly. Co-operation, which contributes to consolidate permanently the possibilities of human action, shall be activated to the point of achieving that complete development which is demanded by the new conceptions of commerce and of the worldwide use of energy.

In conclusion, once this declaration was read and they were asked if they wished the provinces and territories of the Argentine Republic to recover and free their economy from foreign capitalism and from world economic hegemonies or from the nations associated with them, they acclaimed and reiterated their unanimous, spontaneous and determined vote for the economic independence of the country, determining the following Preamble:

> We, the representatives of the people and government of the Argentine Republic, gathered in a Congress open to the will of the Nation, invoking Divine Providence in the name of and by the authority vested by the people here represented, do declare solemnly to the face of the Earth the justice on which the peoples and governments of the Argentine provinces and territories have based their decision to break the dominant links of foreign capitalism inserted in the country, and to recover the rights to dispose of their national economic resources. The Nation attains its economic liberty to remain, *de facto* and *de jure*, with full and complete powers to give itself the forms demanded by universal justice and economy in the defence of human solidarity.

> So do the people and government of the Nation gathered here declare and ratify, committing themselves to the fulfilment and maintenance of this decision, which they ensure and guarantee with their lives and honour.

This economic independence was what the First Five-Year Plan was meant to achieve. It has been said, with some justice, that the real content of *peronismo* is not to be found in its public utterances; the very *ad hoc* nature of the decisions taken, and the rapidly changing world environment which governed initial expectations, have made *peronista* literature very much a spontaneous response to fleeting circumstances. This accounts for much of the artificiality, incongruity and incoherence of later attempts to collect all these utterances into a single body of doctrine. The writings and declarations of the *peronista* régime do, however, offer an indication of the aspirations to which a majority of the Argentines of the day offered their allegiance, independently of whether or not these aspirations were fulfilled. The declaration of economic independence dovetailed with the official slogan of making Argentina a nation 'socially just, economically free and politically sovereign'. *Justicialismo* (a construction from *justicia social*, social justice) was the name given to the path chosen by the Perón administration to achieve those aims. Perón claimed that it represented a 'Third Position', equidistant from both capitalism and Communism, which he described as 'the two imperialisms'. It is part of *peronista* folklore that the articles Perón wrote on this subject while President, under the pseudonym of 'Descartes' (published locally by the newspaper *Democracia* but also reproduced abroad as part of *peronismo*'s international propaganda campaign), were to find their way to a young Egyptian colonel, Gamal Abdel Nasser. Thus, the story goes, Perón became one of the original sources of inspiration for the Non-Aligned movement, and his 'Third Position' was to be at the root of the later notion of a 'Third World'.

There is no doubt that Perón did achieve for Argentina independence from the power that had virtually controlled the country's economy since soon after it was born, namely Britain. Ownership of the country's public services was taken into Argentine hands. Whether or not an excessive price was paid for these takeovers, as in the case of the railways, is not an easy question to answer. It was clearly not part of the Perón government's formula to attempt straightforward expropriations, and many analysts have doubted that the country had the political strength to withstand the consequences of such an action. It must be remembered that most of the hard currency Argentina had earned during the war years — the wealth Perón's opponents accused him of having squandered — was blocked in Britain, and its release required the acquiescence of a currency-starved British government, which furthermore had to operate within the constraints laid down by its largest creditor, the United States. With hindsight it is perhaps possible to imagine a number of other feasible and more profitable deals for Argentina, but at the time, given Perón's own expectations of the way the world was moving, it was one of the very few options available. Similarly, the Perón administration badly needed an accommodation with the United States, the country which, even in the GOU's dreams of Argentine supremacy, was granted a prime role in hemispheric affairs, and which in the post-war years was an unavoidable trading partner. Hence the kid-glove treatment meted out to ITT when the Unión Telefónica was nationalised; hence, too, the hands-off attitude towards US-owned companies in other areas of the economy.

The diminution of British influence was not confined to the nationalisation of formerly British-owned utilities. It also affected Britain's position as Argentina's overwhelmingly dominant trading partner. The Perón administration managed to diversify a sizeable share of Argentina's foreign trade, finding markets elsewhere for Argentine produce. Much of this new trade was conducted on a bilateral basis, again reflecting the post-war constraints on the convertibility of world currencies. Some operations were little more than glorified barter deals, and the benefits to Argentina were measured primarily in terms of the industrial products and capital goods the Perón government felt compelled to obtain at maximum speed. Even in those terms, some of the new links did not pay off; there was, for example, no useful counterpart to Argentina's massive grain supplies to Franco's Spain. It was inevitable, also, that the United States should steadily augment its role as a supplier. Many factors were responsible for the difficulties encountered in Perón's relationship with Washington, in spite of his repeated overtures. For one, wartime memories were kept alive: Perón was seen as belonging to the same category as Franco, a 'hostile neutral' who had not contributed to the Allied victory, and was treated only slightly less harshly than the Spanish *Caudillo*. And even in purely post-war terms, Perón was refusing to play the North American game. He was keeping Argentina's foreign trade and its exchange markets under strict government control, 'artificially' building up the country's industrial base, instead of opening the Argentine economy to the new international monetary order and accepting the new international economic orthodoxy, which would have returned Argentina to its 'natural' role as a supplier of grains and beef and an importer of manufactured goods, only now with the United States, not Britain, as the main supplier. He insisted on a bilateralism which he felt Argentina could control, instead of accepting a multilateralism which everyone knew would operate to the advantage of the United States. This obstinate refusal to accept the 'laws of the market' cut him off from US credit, and eventually left Argentina out of the Marshall Plan. With its own growing merchant fleet and the consequent capacity to create its own trade routes, with its willingness to negotiate bilateral deals, and above all with its aspirations of a greater say in hemispheric affairs, Perón's Argentina also managed to inaugurate a number of trade links with other Latin American nations, an area which had remained untapped since the days in which Spain, as colonial master, had banned commercial intercourse between its American provinces. The leading partners, from the sheer weight of economic circumstances, were naturally Brazil and Chile. The GOU's old proposal of a ring of alliances with the Spanish-speaking republics in order to achieve a strong bargaining position *vis-à-vis* Brazil was not entirely forgotten, but a number of variations were to be introduced during Perón's tenure of office, in line with the changing political fortunes of the neighbouring countries. One such variation was the possibility of a much swifter entente with Brazil, in tandem with a special understanding with Chile. Perón had been led to believe that Brazil's populist leader, Getúlio Vargas, was amenable to such a project, and it was on that understanding that Perón revived his predecessors' scheme of an economic alliance with Chile. Indeed the bases of an agreement were hammered out with Chile's President, Gabriel González Videla, during a visit he paid to Argentina early in Perón's mandate. The ultimate aim, as before, was to be a customs union, eventually to be extended to other South American nations. There were provisions for industrial complementarity, with Argentina aiding the development of industries in which Chile had a head start. The project, put on paper with much enthusiasm, fell apart almost as soon as theory collided with practice, and particularly with Argentina's reluctance to accept Chile's leading role in the steel industry, a sector so dear to Argentine military planners. Its further development was also aborted by Vargas' change of heart, on similar grounds. Nonetheless, what survived of the original plan was sufficient to multiply trade links between Argentina and Chile.

Bolivia's Gualberto Villaroel received a sympathetic hearing for his proposal of an alliance between Buenos Aires, La Paz and Asunción, but on this occasion it was the premature end of Villaroel's rule that aborted the scheme. However, Perón did offer much support to Bolivia's Movimiento Nacionalista Revolucionario, which took Víctor Paz Estenssoro to power, and in the early years forged close ties with this régime that nationalised Bolivia's tin mines and presided over one of the continent's earliest agrarian reforms. Perón also provided support for Paraguay's Presidents Cháves and Stroessner, including the seconding of an aide, Epifanio Fleitas Méndez, who first became Chief of Police and later a director of that country's Central Bank. Perón's Latin American diplomatic initiatives included an attempt to create, around the CGT, a continent-wide association of trade unions, called ATLAS, and a whole range of interventions, political and financial, all the way up to Central America and the Caribbean. Liberal politicians have underlined, time and again, that Perón made friends most easily with military dictators; indeed he did become close to the Dominican Republic's Rafael Leónidas Trujillo, Nicaragua's Anastasio Somoza García, Venezuela's Marcos Pérez Jiménez, Colombia's Gustavo Rojas Pinilla, and elected autocrats like Ecuador's José Velasco Ibarra and Chile's Ibáñez. Perhaps it would be more accurate to say that the commonest traits among Perón's chosen allies were autocracy and populism, though in some cases it was almost all autocracy and only a smattering of rhetorical populism. It can be argued that at the time there were few if any national leaders answering any other description on the Latin American scene. But it is true that the Perón régime offered no comfort or support to the continent's anti-dictatorial movements with the sole exception of Bolivia's MNR, a fact mitigated perhaps by the circumstance that in most cases the members of these movements were allies of his own domestic opposition. It is also true that most of Perón's chosen friends were protégés of the United States, although in this respect the association did not work in favour of Perón's continental projects.

7

POWER, CRISIS AND FEAR
(1946–1951)

Perón had come to power with an advantage few of his elected predecessors had enjoyed: a comfortable majority in Congress, which ensured that all government initiatives received prompt, unquestioning treatment. One of the first acts of this Congress was to annul his renunciation of 'wearing the palms and laurels of a General of the Nation' by overriding his decree of retirement and reincorporating him in the service, simultaneously promoting him to the rank of General. Control of the national executive and Congress, and of all provincial governorships but one did not, however, make the régime feel completely safe from its opposition. The threat of a conspiracy, aided by the ample financial resources of the oligarchy at home and by a hostile United States abroad, was perceived as very real. Within the state apparatus, all possible remaining power bases of the opposition were preventively targeted for complete takeover. The Federal Police and its provincial counterparts were purged; Army officers of doubtful loyalty were transferred to innocuous desk jobs; the Presidency was endowed with all-powerful secretariats to oversee the work of the ministries, in the political and economic spheres as well as in the new area of 'state control'. The Supreme Court, which had been chosen by the opposition in 1945 as a possible repository of *antiperonista* executive power until elections were held, was cleaned up, ironically by accusing most of its members of having perverted its function by legitimising the military régimes which paved the way for Perón's political career.

The universities had long been a thorn in the side of the emerging *peronista* movement, and early in the day Perón had attempted to ridicule their association with the oligarchic opposition by adopting as one of the slogans for his movement, '*Alpargatas sí, libros no!*' The *alpargata*, a rope-soled espadrille, was the footwear of Argentina's poor; concern for the poor was thus erected in contrast to the affluent university students' allegedly unfeeling preoccupation with *libros*, books. Once in power, Perón attacked the autonomy which the universities had so jealously defended since the reform of 1920, appointing government trustees to run their affairs and setting up, with government support, the Confederación General Universitaria, a student organisation intended to steal the thunder of the reformist Federación Universitaria Argentina.

Having won the elections, Perón soon turned also to the political apparatus that had made that victory possible, still divided as it was into the Junta Renovadora formed by dissident Radicals, and the Partido Laborista whose creation had been engineered by Cipriano Reyes. The first step was an announcement that both forces would be merged into a Unified Party of the Revolution. Reyes fiercely resisted the move, and with a mere handful of supporters attempted to keep the Partido Laborista alive. It was a futile protest, and in early 1947, indicating already the increasing personalism of the régime, the ruling party was renamed Partido Peronista.

The arch-symbol of everything the *peronistas* were against, the visible seat of oligarchic power, was the Sociedad Rural, the association of large landowners dedicated to breeding and fattening cattle. The *'Rural'* had undisguisedly supported the Unión Democrática against Perón in the 1946 election, and its president, José María Bustillo, was responsible for much of the most vitriolic *antiperonista* prose of the time. Perón's electioneering slogan of 'The land to those who work it' was hardly likely to augur good relations once he was in the Presidency, but surprisingly, the period of conflict was brief, and the ensuing *modus vivendi* was by any standards favourable to the hated oligarchs. Perón's first attitude towards the *'Rural'* was a firm refusal to grant audience to its president, a clear break with a tradition in which the representative of the country's landowners had almost free access to the Presidency. And when, during the annual cattle show, a landmark event in the social life of Buenos Aires, the governor of Buenos Aires was jeered by the elegant sophisticates of the *'Rural'*, the Federal Police promptly arrested a few score of the gentlemen and ladies, adding insult to injury by locking up the latter in the prison normally reserved for prostitutes.

The response of the *'Rural'* was to ease Bustillo out of the presidency of the institution, appointing in his stead a man who was willing to reach an understanding with the government, José A. Martínez de Hoz. The new head of the landowners' association was remarkably effective in his task. He persuaded Colonel Mercante, Perón's close friend who had been elected governor of Buenos Aires, the heartland of cattle-ranching Argentina, to annul a law recently passed by the provincial legislature inaugurating the much-heralded expropriations of *latifundia*. Through Mercante he was able to persuade Perón to drop the whole idea of agrarian reform, much to the despair of its sponsors, who in their later protests ended by losing their newspaper, *Democracia* (they were bought out by ALEA, a holding company set up by Miguel Miranda which was virtually to play the role of the régime's private enterprise arm). Martínez de Hoz also arranged for Perón to attend the next annual exhibition at the showgrounds of the *'Rural'* and even elicit cheers for him from the assembled gathering. Henceforth, in Martínez de Hoz's own words, contact with the President was frequent, 'because any president of the Sociedad Rural goes every fortnight to government house'. A later Minister of Agriculture of the régime, Carlos A. Emery, would claim, 'Our relations with the *"Rural"* were extremely cordial; not a single farm was expropriated nor were the cattle-breeders' interests affected. On the contrary, they made as much money as before, or even more.'

The problem posed by Cipriano Reyes's resistance, in spite of his visible lack of substantial backing, was paradoxically to occupy much more of the régime's attention. In September of the second year of Perón's mandate, it was suddenly announced to the public that a plot had been discovered. The Peróns, Juan Domingo and Evita, were to be assassinated by means of a bomb placed in the presidential box of the Colón theatre, where they were scheduled to attend a gala performance the following month. The instigators were 'North American imperialists'; the local executants, already under arrest, were allegedly Cipriano Reyes, a politician called Walter Beveraggi-Allende (who had become something of a nuisance with his denunciations of corruption in high places), two priests (who had defied the hierarchy of the church and preached against Perón since the election campaign) and a blind doctor. The fortuitous frustration of this dastardly scheme became the occasion for a mass mobilisation of the faithful. The CGT decreed a one-day strike in condemnation of the plot and thousands of workers were trucked to the Plaza de Mayo, filling the square in front of the Casa Rosada as it had never been filled even on the historic 17th of October 1945, to hear Evita claim that she was willing 'to die a thousand deaths' for the sake of Perón, and Perón himself to preach both retribution and constraint. The church obliged by celebrating thanksgiving masses throughout the country. No publicity was given at the time to the fact that Reyes and his alleged co-conspirators were brutally tortured by the police in a bid to get them to sign a confession. Only a few months later a judge was to set the 'plotters' free for lack of evidence against them; the judge lost his job, Beveraggi Allende fled to exile in Uruguay, and Reyes was rearrested on the improbable charge of infringement of the gaming laws, to remain imprisoned for years.

Between the beginning and the end of this sordid affair, the *peronista*-dominated Congress instructed the Executive to call for special elections to choose a constitutional assembly. Argentina's Constitution, which had suffered only minor changes since 1853, was in need of updating. Technicalities were later invoked by the opposition to invalidate the call for elections, but no one could seriously dispute the results of the polls, which gave the *Peronista* Party 109 representatives in the assembly to only forty-eight for the opposition Unión Cívica Radical. Such arithmetic, of course, made debate superfluous, and the government's proposed amendments were duly enacted three months later. The changes introduced can be grouped into three categories, each of which was to be the object of much acrimonious dispute in years to come, and each of which was to be claimed by different groups as the crucial item which would eventually lead to Perón's overthrow.

The first category was the expansion of the bill of rights guaranteed by the Constitution, previously written on the liberal, individualistic pattern of its US counterpart and now enlarged by *peronismo* to include 'special rights'; the rights of people as belonging to groups or categories. The central contribution of this section was the incorporation of the 'rights of the workers'. These were:

1. *The right to work.* Work is the indispensable means for the satisfaction of the spiritual and material needs of the individual and the community, the cause of all the advances of civilisation and the foundation of general prosperity; therefore the right to work must be protected by society, considering it with the dignity it merits and providing employment for those who need it.

2. *The right to fair remuneration.* Because wealth, income and interest on capital are fruits exclusively of human labour, the community must organise and reactivate the means of production in such a fashion as to guarantee to the worker moral and material remuneration that will satisfy his vital needs and compensate for the yield obtained and the effort made.

3. *The right to training.* The improvement of the human condition and the pre-eminence of the spiritual values impose the need to favour the elevation of culture and of professional skills, in an endeavour to orient all intelligences towards all the directions of knowledge, and it is society's duty to stimulate individual effort by providing the means so that, given equal opportunities, every individual may exercise the right to learn and to perfect himself.

4. *The right to worthy working conditions.* The consideration owed the human being, the importance attached to work as a social function and the reciprocal respect between the concurrent factors of production consecrate the right of

individuals to demand worthy and fair conditions for the practice of their activities and society's obligation to make sure of the strict observance of the
precepts that institute and regulate them.

5. *The right to the preservation of health.* The care of the physical and moral health
of the individual must be a primordial and constant concern of society, which is
charged with making sure that working conditions fulfil the necessary requisites
of hygiene and safety, that they do not exceed the normal possibilities of effort,
and that they give adequate opportunity for recuperation by rest.

6. *The right to wellbeing.* The right of the workers to wellbeing, the minimum
expression of which is the possibility of having adequate housing, dress and food
to satisfy his own needs and those of his family without anxiety in a fashion that
enables him to work with satisfaction, to rest free from worries and to enjoy in
moderation spiritual and material expansion, imposes the social need to raise the
standards of living and of work with the direct and indirect contributions made
possible by economic development.

7. *The right to social security.* The right of individuals to be cared for in case of
diminution, suspension or loss of their ability to work creates for society the
obligation to take charge unilaterally of the necessary expenditures or to
promote the institution of systems of mandatory mutual aid, both destined to
cover or supplement the insufficiencies or disabilities proper to certain periods in
one's lifetime or those that may emerge from misfortunes caused by eventual
risks.

8. *The right to the protection of the family.* The protection of the family responds to
a natural design of the individual since in it are born his highest affections, and all
efforts aimed at assuring its welfare must be stimulated and favoured by the community, as the best means to tend towards the improvement of the human race
and the consolidation of the spiritual and moral principles that constitute the
essence of social coexistence.

9. *The right to economic improvement.* Productive capacity and pursuit of excellence both find a natural incentive in the possibilities of economic improvement,
so society must support and favour individual initiatives ordered towards this
end, and stimulate the formation and use of capital, inasmuch as they constitute
active elements of production and contribute to the general prosperity.

10. *The right to the defence of professional interests.* The right to free association and
participation in other licit activities which tend to the defence of professional
interests are essential attributes of the workers which society must respect and
protect, ensuring their free exercise and repressing any acts that may obstruct
and impede them.

This set of rights is supplemented by 'the rights of the family', 'the
rights of old age' and 'the rights of education and culture'. Though far
more enunciative than prescriptive, this catalogue represented at least a
formal attempt to give the socially disadvantaged the protection of the
highest law of the land.

The second category of innovation was of a more hard-hitting practical nature. The amended Constitution's Article 40 said:

The organisation of wealth and its exploitation is aimed at the welfare of the people, within an economic order that conforms to the principles of social justice. The State, by law, may intervene in the economy and monopolise certain activities in safeguard of the general interest and within the limits established by the fundamental rights ensured by this Constitution. With the exception of imports and exports, which will be in the charge of the State according to the limitations and the régime to be determined by law, all economic activity will be organised according to free private initiative, as long as it does not aim, overtly or covertly, to dominate the domestic markets, eliminate competition or increase profits by usury.

Minerals, water courses, deposits of oil, coal and gas, and other natural sources of energy, except vegetables, are the imprescriptible and inalienable property of the Nation, with the corresponding participation in their produce to be agreed with the provinces.

The public services belong originally to the state, and under no circumstances may they be sold or given in concession for the purpose of their exploitation. Those at present in private hands shall be transferred to the State by means of purchase or expropriation with prior compensation, when a national law so determines . . .

The limits of the mixed economy already being constructed by *peronismo* were here set out, including the thorny issue of Argentina's oil and its future development.

The third category of amendments had the greatest immediate political impact. Sweeping away all precedents, it allowed for the re-election of the President.

Whatever the workers' rights enshrined in the new Constitution, the very year of its enactment brought to the fore an uncomfortable fact of life which the régime had been trying hard to ignore or push into some unlit corner: most of Argentina's workers had been unionised and most of the unions had dutifully joined a pro-government CGT, but there still remained a number of unions that clung doggedly to their independence. In many such cases, like that of the telephonists, the government had engineered an 'intervention' of the union by the CGT. Now the rank and file of the telephonists' union were rebelling and openly demanding an end to 'intervention'. As the clamour grew louder, the government responded by sending in the Federal Police's new 'Special Section', which was in charge of political affairs. A number of leading activists in the telephonists' union were arrested. In a dependency of the Special

Section they were tortured, their later testimony reading like a grim pre-
monition of the catalogue of barbarities which in the decades ahead
would be committed on a much larger scale. There were beatings, and
the yanking out of handfuls of hair. There was what the torturers called
'scientific *grippe*': prisoners drenched in ice-cold water and placed in a
draught made by open windows, or electric ventilators, or both. And
the *picana eléctrica*, a version of the electric cattle prod that was applied
to the most sensitive parts of the body, nipples, gums and genitals. And
the deliberate induction of a miscarriage in a pregnant woman. As for
purpose, there was the merest formality of an interrogation, a quest for
details of a political conspiracy in which no one really believed. The
arrested workers were held for a time, then released, only to be suspended from their jobs and finally sacked.

The impact of the telephonists' frustrated revolt, with whisperings of
their treatment at the hands of the police already reaching the streets, was
reinforced by the far more militant action in the northwestern province
of Tucumán by the workers on the sugarcane plantations, whose unionisation had originally been fostered by Perón in his days as Labour Secretary, but who had steadfastly refused to align themselves with the
pro-government CGT leadership. The canecutters' union decided to go
on strike in pursuit of a 60 per cent wage rise. The government riposted
by declaring the strike illegal; the provincial police raided the union headquarters and arrested the leaders, while the CGT promptly appointed a
trustee to carry out the usual 'intervention'. Tales of beatings of the
strike leaders began to circulate, and leaders of other Tucumán unions
started to discuss the possibility of declaring a general strike in support of
the canecutters. They too were raided by the police, and arrests and
beatings followed — with the tragic result of the death of the secretary
of the local waiters' union, Carlos Antonio Aguirre. An attempt was
made at covering up the incident, and Aguirre's body was furtively
carried across the provincial border and dumped in a rubbish bin. Its
prompt discovery, however, aroused such a degree of public indignation
that in a rapid chain of events the police officers responsible were identified and placed under arrest.

In Buenos Aires, under pressure from the opposition, Congress set up
a three-man commission to investigate the growing allegations of police
torture. The commission was formed by two *peronista* legislators, José E.
Visca and Emilio Decker, and a young Radical deputy who was already
making a name for himself as a critic of the régime, Arturo Frondizi. Yet
the functioning of this commission was rigged to allow for a quorum of

only two, thus effectively excluding Frondizi from decisive moments in its proceedings. Thanks largely to Frondizi's doggedness, the commission managed to place on record a mass of evidence substantiating the allegations, though it ultimately decided that there was not enough to build a case against the police. In Tucumán the officers accused of Aguirre's killing were soon set free. Yet the commission was to continue in existence, its original purpose deftly transformed into a brief to investigate 'anti-Argentine' activities, a category which had recently been expanded by law to include the crime of *desacato* (roughly translatable as something between disobedience and insubordination to authority) that included any offence to the dignity of government officials or patriotic symbols.

The flare-ups caused by the telephonists and the canecutters were perhaps the most serious, but by no means the only conflicts between government and unions in the first two-and-a-half years of Perón's rule. To quote José Grünfeld of the commercial employees' union, there were '320 disputes, most of them crushed by the régime, between 4 June 1946 and 31 October 1949. [. . .] Most of these disputes were declared illegal.[. . .] The CGT hired strikebreakers to suffocate the movement initiated by the municipal workers.[. . .] The police violently dispersed a rally held by the meatpackers in front of Congress; these men had been on strike for three months. The postmen's union was dissolved, its leaders were fired and several postmen were arrested.[. . .] The shipbuilders went on strike for 100 days; the seamen for ninety. The local union of Mar del Plata, with its seventeen affiliated unions, was closed down, though they continued to operate clandestinely.' In fact, union dissatisfaction had increased steadily as time passed and Miranda's economic blitz failed to pay off, leaving the country with severely depleted reserves (close to one-sixth of their value in 1946) and government spending up to almost five times the level recorded when Perón entered the Casa Rosada. Popular consumption had increased dramatically with the early wage increases and the indirect transfer of income to the salaried classes, but expectations had rocketed even further, placing enormous pressure on an industrial sector that had grown fast but haphazardly, and was plagued by a multitude of supply bottlenecks which were often compounded by the cumbersome procedures used to issue import licences. When this was added to undisciplined government spending, the result was runaway inflation. Farmers, who had grumbled earlier about the low prices paid by the IAPI (the cause, according to the North American economist Arthur P.

Whitaker, of the sluggishness of Argentina's agricultural growth in the post-war years, when other producers were increasing their output rapidly), now faced the effects of a severe drought, which was to last for nearly three years. In short, Argentina's economy was in crisis.

Miranda himself had been ditched in late 1948, and the direction of the economy had been entrusted to a triumvirate with experience as civil servants: Ramón Cereijo, Alfredo Gómez Morales and Roberto Ares. In Perón's own description, the government had moved from *phase one* under Miranda's 'assault team, which came to modify structures, causing all the inevitable changes and imbalances', to *phase two* under men whose mission it was 'to order and balance the different sectors of the national economy'. A curb was put on the growth of consumption, mainly through an attempt to rationalise banking credit and deliberately delay wage increases, but also through measures of great psychological impact, like forcing the Argentines, used as they were to their daily ration of white bread, to eat a grayish-looking mass made from wheat and millet flour. The scarcity of flour was real enough during the years of drought, but many years later Gómez Morales would chuckle remembering this measure: 'We had to convince the people that we were in trouble, and this certainly did the trick.' Measures were also taken to halt speculation on the stock exchange, and virtual war was declared on 'hoarders, usurers and speculators'. The import licence system was streamlined, and Argentina's hard currency spending was brought in line with its earnings. Most pragmatically, the régime chose to forget Perón's earlier promise that he would rather cut off his right hand than sign an application for an official loan from the United States; after a drastic budget-slashing exercise and the earmarking of a percentage of export earnings to pay off existing obligations to US banks, Cereijo made the pilgrimage to Washington and returned with a sizeable credit from the Eximbank for a consortium of Argentine banks, restoring a semblance of balance to the country's payments position.

The drought and its side-effects would contribute to delaying the success of this package of corrective measures, but three years later the government could reasonably claim to have brought the situation under control. In a way suspected by scarcely anyone at the time, this crisis and its resolution were a landmark. It was the last time a package of conventional austerity measures would prove effective against inflation in Argentina. The country's economic structure had been changing fairly rapidly since the war years, with the disorganised but nonetheless real growth of the industrial sector through import substitution. Most of the theories about such industrial development policies were still to be written, and scholarly assumptions about the level and duration of the protection needed by 'infant industries' were simply not available to the *peronista* planners. There was the observable fact that setting up manufacturing industries in a non-industrial environment was more costly than doing the same in an industrialised nation; there was also the vague expectation that once the new industries had been established for some time and had begun to interact with each other, their costs would move into line with those prevalent abroad. But this very lineal projection took little account of a number of significant details in the changes Argentina was undergoing. On the one hand, there was the fact that, even with the strict government controls applied by the *peronista* administration, the country's exchange rate (the translation of its productivity into terms the rest of the world could understand) reflected mainly the low costs of extensive agriculture in the pampas; it reflected the productivity of unaided nature far more than that of human effort. 'Protection' certainly did cover the gap between this and the much higher cost structures of industry, on the import side. But as long as the former was considered the natural state of affairs, and the latter an artificial and temporary implant, the demands placed on the performance of industry would be unrealistic, indeed quite impossible to fulfil. And there would be no parallel instrument of compensation on the export side, save the occasional timid, 'artificial' and 'temporary' recourse to subsidies. Argentina's industry would therefore be condemned to grow inwards, aimed at satisfying the needs of a relatively small domestic market.

Moreover, import-substitution in Argentina, responding as it did to circumstantial scarcities rather than to design, tended to start 'at the top', with the local production of the finished article from imported components. This was a virtual guarantee that for a long time, as the process advanced, industrial goods would become more, not less costly. As soon as the next stage 'downwards' in the production of any article (say, the assembly of a component) was attempted locally, the protection already weighing on the finished article would be augmented by the protection on the component. And so on. And to make matters more complicated, *peronismo* was already embarking on larger-scale import substitution 'from the bottom upwards', by promoting the growth of heavy industries like steel. In short, the hope of shrinking industrial costs was being sandwiched into the distant future.

The emerging pattern was that of an industrial sector which was

growing much faster that the traditional agricultural sector. Yet the
latter was responsible for generating virtually all the country's hard currency earnings, which industry, directed exclusively towards the
domestic market, consumed in ever-increasing quantities (for the
purchase of machinery, raw materials, components and fuels). Impeded
from exporting, industry contributed no hard currency earnings of its
own, and in many cases, because it relied on technologies designed for
much larger markets, it functioned well below its installed capacity,
adding to the costliness of the exercise and placing the economy in a vice.
To make matters worse, the prices of industrial inputs on world markets
were steadily rising, while those of primary products (Argentina's
source of export earnings) were decreasing. The new, semi-industrial
Argentina was a machine so put together that it would inevitably create
periodical shortages of hard currency — a new and important source of
inflationary pressures in addition to the multitude of supply bottlenecks
which would keep springing up in the country's unplanned and largely
unpredictable industrial sector. The economist Marcelo Diamand,
writing in the late 1960s, would pinpoint at least six different, interlocked sources of inflation in the Argentine economy, an array which
was impervious to treatment by the blanket conventional anti-infla-
tionary measures. All that these could achieve, as Argentina's later
governments were to discover (though rarely comprehend), was recession, more inflation, and the unwitting creation of conditions that
would make the following crisis even worse.

Naturally, none of this was on the minds of the government planners
as the 1940s came to a close. The country was taking its first steps
towards more orderly economic growth and, crisis and all, seemed to
have reason enough for satisfaction. Even eroded by inflation and with
irritating shortages, the standard of living of the average Argentine was
easily the highest anywhere in Latin America. Chaotic as the country's
productive apparatus may have been, it was at the time responsible for a
full quarter of the output of Latin America as a whole. And everyone in
the land had been made aware that the potential was available for much
greater things in the future. One of the Perón régime's most consistent
pursuits was to instill in all Argentines a sense of pride in what was their
own, in visible contrast to the self-despising attitude so characteristic of
the former ruling classes, with their unqualified admiration of anything
European and their contemptuous treatment of *criollo* achievement. The
average Argentine schoolchild could recite the names and measurements
of rivers and mountain peaks in Europe while remaining ignorant of

Argentina's geography and was familiar with the history of the peoples and institutions of the Old Continent but largely unaware of the nation's own historical heritage. Anything imported from abroad was unquestionally good, while whatever had been made locally was laughed off as the bumbling product of *flor de ceibo* industry (a reference to Argentina's red national flower).

The Perón régime's answer to this was the message that 'Argentine is best'. Hyperbole was considered necessary to break long-established habits, and some of the efforts certainly had the quality of caricature. But there was plenty to be proud of, in an age when Argentine soccer teams were earning world renown, when Juan Manuel Fangio seemed never to tire of bringing in motor racing championships (and he was only one in a constellation of drivers that included the Gálvez brothers, Farina, Marimón), when Delfor Cabrera was winning the Olympic marathon, when boxers like Pascual Pérez and Gatica were gaining international acclaim. Whatever was biggest or best was underlined: the finest polo ponies, the widest avenue (9 de Julio), the largest estuary (the River Plate). There was strict enforcement of the rule that local products should prominently bear the inscription '*Industria Argentina*' in Spanish; not a slavish 'Made in Argentina' in English. The memory of Argentina's heroic figures of the past was brushed up, including that figure so hated by the country's liberal historians, Juan Manuel de Rosas, the Buenos Aires strongman admired by nationalists for his resistance to foreign pressures. General José de San Martín, who had led Argentina's newborn Army cross the Andes to assist in the liberation of Chile, and later across the water to help Perú achieve its independence, was another favourite; 1950, the year when San Martín's remains were repatriated from France, was declared the 'Year of the Liberator General San Martín', and that phrase, by law, had to be printed under the masthead of every newspaper, every day, as well as on official stationery and as the initial entry in each schoolchild's copybook.

There was a flaw in this enterprise. Much as Yrigoyen's Radicals had tended to identify their Cause with the nation, the Perón régime tended to identify *peronismo* and its leaders as the quintessence of everything Argentine, and with the people in whose name they ruled. The corollary was similar; whoever opposed the Peróns or *peronismo* was all too easily catalogued as anti-Argentine or anti-the people. Extolling the virtues of the country and its achievements became hopelessly confused with singing the praises of the Peróns. Victorious athletes and sportsmen knew it was convenient to dedicate their triumph to Perón. Textbooks were

rewritten so that children in the first grades of school learnt to read with
sentences telling them how lucky they were to have Perón caring for
them, and about the smile on Evita's face reflecting her love for the
people. The official portraits of Perón and Evita were everywhere; any
public work in progress bore a sign with the familiar slogan 'Perón
cumple — Evita dignifica'. And a court of sycophants made sure that their
names were applied to everything under the Argentine sun: streets,
avenues, railway stations, ships, hospitals, new housing estates, a couple
of cities and eventually two provinces. Congress promoted Perón to the
rank of Division General and then, only five months later, to General of
the Army, the highest rank in the service. Protesting against the omni-
presence of *peronista* propaganda meant risking arrest and trial for *desacato*
under the new law recently passed. Its interpretation, mainly in the
hands of the Congressional committee investigating 'anti-Argentine
activities', was loose in the extreme. Dozens of newspapers were fined
for *desacato* when they failed to print the line 'Year of the Liberator
General San Martín'. And with the *peronista* party present in almost
every neighbourhood, in the government-supplied premises called
unidades básicas, dissidents and adversaries began to live in almost
paranoid fear of the *peronista* informer, the *oyente* or listener, who could
be a servant, a taxi-driver, a waiter — anyone who might overhear an
imprudent conversation.

Towards the end of Perón's first term of office, the régime had built
up an impressive media apparatus of its own; partly in the hands of the
state, partly controlled via the holding company ALEA. There were a
number of daily newspapers (*Epoca*, *La Razón*, *Crítica*, *Noticias Gráficas*,
El Mundo, *Democracia*), a host of magazines and four radio stations. The
state itself exercised control over the remaining radio stations and could
order them to join the official network at any time. The newspapers,
after a number of permanent closures and almost 100 suspension orders,
were wary of the threat of *desacato* proceedings, and the vast majority
opted for self-censorship. Buenos Aires' two major conservative dailies,
La Nación and *La Prensa*, adopted different tactics to confound the
régime. The former steadfastly refused to print any praise of the government, but published no criticism either, except what was skilfully woven
between the printed lines, and referred to Evita only as 'the President's
wife'. *La Prensa* chose to continue in open opposition, in spite of constant harassment. It was not the only newspaper to take a critical stance;
there was also the *Buenos Aires Herald*, which was able to take special
liberties because it was published in English; the authorities demanded

that the editorials carry a Spanish translation, but uncomfortable items were buried in other columns.

With a two-thirds majority in the Chamber of Deputies and a unanimously *peronista* Senate, the government was clearly strong enough to do anything it wished. With its stranglehold on the media, there seemed little to fear from public opinion. Yet if *antiperonistas* became paranoid about the government's network of informers, *peronismo* was becoming increasingly paranoid about conspiracies, and ever more intolerant of opposition in any form. Even criticism from within Congress, with the protection of parliamentary immunity, became fair game when, on Evita's instructions, the Radical deputy Enrique Sanmartino had this privilege revoked 'for gross misconduct' and had to flee into exile in Uruguay to avoid arrest by the Federal Police. Not long afterwards, another Radical deputy, Atilio Cattaneo, suffered the same fate for insisting on details of how the Peróns had acquired their wealth.

It was in this atmosphere that there appeared the first sign of a conflict, which was in later years to swell to enormous proportions, between the régime and the church. Together with the establishment of obligatory religious education in the schools (tempered by the fact that non-Catholics could opt to attend an alternative course on 'morals'), the régime had established the compulsory registration of all religious cults, curiously enough, with the Ministry of Foreign Affairs. All details of a cult's membership, its publications, premises and funding, were made subject to government approval. Some fringe organisations lost their freedom to operate legally, one such being the Escuela Científica Basilio, which could roughly be described as devoted to spiritualism, following the teachings of Allan Kardec. It is not known exactly what moved Perón in 1950 to restore legal recognition to it; but both Perón and Evita were known to take an interest in the occult, in spiritualism and in faith healing. Evita's confessor is on record as defending her views on these matters, in the hope, as he said, that the Vatican would eventually come round to recognising their validity. Perón had also given an official position, in charge of 'psychic research', to one of Argentina's most renowned mediums, John Courtney Luck. In October 1950, the Escuela Científica Basilio, having only recently resurfaced to legality, was authorised to hold a large rally in Buenos Aires' huge Luna Park stadium, under the slogan — most remarkable in an officially Catholic country — 'Jesus is not God'.

Groups of Catholic youths mingled with the attendants and, once the meeting got under way, showered the stadium with leaflets saying 'Jesus is God', and shouting 'Long live Christ the king!' The Escuela's adepts responded by chanting, 'Perón! Perón!' The meeting degenerated swiftly into a brawl, and was finally broken up by the police, who carted away many of the Catholic demonstrators. Outside, a contingent of Catholic youths marched up Leandro N. Alem avenue, then paused to pray at a corner; the police charged them, arresting 200.

This event would have vanished into the minor chronicles of the time had it not been for its timing. Five days later, in the city of Rosario, the church had scheduled the opening of a most important assembly, the Fifth National Eucharistic Congress, which was to be attended by Cardinal Ernesto Ruffini as special envoy of the Pope. Perón refused to greet the Cardinal on his arrival and excused himself from attendance at the Eucharistic Congress on the grounds that he had already scheduled a sorely needed vacation for those days. The Cardinal responded obliquely by accepting an invitation to be the house-guest of Señora María Teresa Lamarca de Pereyra Iraola, an ageing *grande dame* of Buenos Aires society whose family had had one of its farms in the province of Buenos Aires expropriated to set up Evita's 'Park for the Aged'. Acting completely out of character, Perón's Vice-President, Jazmín Hortensio Quijano, announced that he would represent the government at the Rosario Congress. When an official tried to dissuade him, he retorted, 'If I cannot go as Vice-President, I shall go as a common citizen.'

To avoid turning the incident into a major political crisis, Perón changed his mind and announced that he would be in Rosario in time to attend the pontifical mass. Ruffled feathers were smoothed, and the Cardinal stated publicly, 'When I return to Rome I shall tell the Holy Father that religion here is more alive than ever; that Argentina is marching behind its leader among the magisterial paths of true Christian civilisation.' Nonetheless, thousands of Catholics later went in procession through the streets of Buenos Aires, ostensibly to bid farewell to Cardinal Ruffini, but none-too-disguisedly to express their displeasure with the government. At the official farewell gathering, the government took good care to mobilise enough of its own supporters to neutralise the dissident slant introduced by the angry faithful. In the ensuing months Perón would outdo himself in attempts to placate the Church, by sponsoring events like the Franciscan Assumptionist Congress and by becoming the only head of state formally to request from the Vatican the adoption of a dogma — that of the bodily Assumption of the Virgin Mary.

The second half of Perón's first Presidency — the period between the adoption of the amended Constitution and the general elections, originally scheduled for early 1952 but later brought forward to late 1951 — was one of growing unease in several fields. There were still no conspiracies, but the régime had had a reminder that the Army it had so favoured, with masses of equipment, with higher salaries and a host of fringe benefits, was not an unconditional ally. Indeed it had displayed an unthinkable touch of rebellion by refusing Evita entry to the Campo de Mayo complex when she turned up, uninvited, for a surprise visit. The Peróns had retaliated by forcing the War Minister, General Humberto Sosa Molina, to exact from the Campo de Mayo garrison a formal invitation for them both to a banquet, adding as an extra twist that the officers' wives should be present too.

The unions, with inflation and the austerity measures, were also increasingly restive. There was a long, tough newspaper strike in late 1949, and the first half of 1950 witnessed a proliferation of industrial actions which the government declared illegal — by the longshoremen, the meat-packers, the builders, the seamen, the municipal workers, waiters and chefs, and dairy workers. The worst and most intractable strike came towards the end of 1950, when the railwaymen stopped work in pursuit of a wage increase. It was granted, but when a month later it had not been disbursed as promised, the railwaymen went out on strike again, and this time, even with Army intervention, persisted in their action not only until they had achieved their original purpose, but also until they had forced the resignation of their union's secretary. The conservative newspaper *La Prensa* reported that at the root of the railwaymen's strike had been a dispute between *peronistas* who were for Perón and *peronistas* who were for Eva. It was to be the last nail in the coffin of this newspaper, which had insistently been identified by Perón, together with the Communists, the oligarchy and the opposition, as one of the main enemies of the régime. The paper had already been harassed considerably in the past, through the insistent invocation of municipal health, safety and noise ordinances, and by obstructing its supply of newsprint. Now the *canillitas* (the newspaper boys — most were grown men) went out on strike with CGT and government backing. Their demands were: the exclusive handling of the entire print run, with abolition of subscription sales, and one-fifth of the newspaper's revenue from classified advertisements. In other words, distribution of *La Prensa* should be placed in the hands of loyal *peronistas*. The publishers refused to concede, strengthened by the fact that a majority of the editorial and printing staff had declared that they had no conflict with the newspaper.

After over a month of forced inactivity due to the *canillitas'* strike, an attempt was made by some staff members to march through the picket lines. They were met by gunfire, which killed one and wounded fourteen of the would-be strikebreakers. The violence was the signal for the government to intervene directly in the conflict, by sending to Congress a draft bill for the expropriation of *La Prensa*. The company was accused rather vaguely of shady foreign exchange dealings in the United States, but that was hardly the substance of the régime's case. As put in Congress by the *peronista* deputy John William Cooke:

'It may well be that the newspaper is perfectly safe on legal grounds; it may have observed the proper form in all its activities, but as a revolutionary deputy and as a man who has the habit of saying what he feels, I state that *La Prensa* owes the people of the Republic the debt of its great sins. For us *La Prensa* is a newspaper that merits grave accusations, not . . . because of its different opinions on certain aspects of national and international reality. Nor because of the insults it has aimed even at the Radical party . . . such as when it described Señor Cattaneo's revolution as 'Anarchist and Personalist elements attempting to disturb order'. If we were only dealing with this kind of insult, we would not be rejoicing so much at this opportunity of dealing it a blow through this Chamber.

'We are against *La Prensa* for much graver and more fundamental reasons. We are against *La Prensa* because we believe that newspapers of this kind have eroded the foundations of our nationality; we believe that *La Prensa* is one of the obstacles, as there are many others in the continent, that have prevented or delayed all possibility of vindication of proletarian demands in Latin America. We say so above and beyond the contingencies of the investigating committee; we say so as political men who express personal opinions.

'We are with the workers and against *La Prensa* because *La Prensa* will always be, as it has always been so far, against the workers and against us.

'This is the revolutionary position with respect to this problem of *La Prensa*. We are with our own; *La Prensa* is with its own and with its allies inside and outside the country, and with all those who, without being enmeshed in the machinations of the capitalist newspapers, believe they are defending the interests of the free press and of the freedom of expression.

From the very moment the draft bill was sent to Congress there was no real doubt as to its fate. In less than two months *La Prensa* had been expropriated. The government handed it over to the CGT; from his balcony at the Casa Rosada Perón claimed: 'This newspaper, for so many years an exploiter of the workers and the poor, a refined instrument serving the treason against our country by national and international exploiters, will now expiate its crimes by serving the workers and defending their conquests and their rights'. Above the entrance to the reopened *La Prensa* hung an illuminated sign saying 'Now it is Argentine!'

Preparations for the 1951 elections were by now well under way. All, however, was not well in the ranks of *peronismo*. For some time there had clearly been a movement afoot to proclaim Evita's candidacy to the Vice-Presidency. Sectors of the CGT and numerous party units and individuals throughout the country had begun to organise spectacular events preparing the ground for such a move. Perón himself remained silent, and Evita, caught up in a whirlwind of virtually non-stop public engagements, referred only very obliquely to the matter of taking on greater responsibilities. The opposition quickly latched on to what it saw as a possibility of driving a wedge between different factions of the ruling party, by playing insistently on the theme that had cost *La Prensa* its independence: the division between 'Perón's *peronistas*' and 'Evita's *peronistas*'. Insidious graffiti went up on the walls of Buenos Aires, proclaiming '*Viva Perón viudo!*' (Long live Perón as a widower); approaches were made to high-ranking Army officers, depicting the horrors of a hypothetical future in which a young fanatical Evita might inherit her husband's Presidency and become Commander-in-Chief of the Army. The legend began to be created of a 'good' Perón who had been bent by the consuming power hunger of 'that woman'. Not that the opposition's assumptions lacked substance; there was another clear movement in *peronista* circles to promote the candidacy to the Vice-Presidency of the governor of Buenos Aires province, Colonel Domingo Mercante, the man who had engineered most of the crucial political manoeuvring during the revolution of October 1945 and who had once been described by Evita herself as 'the heart of Perón'.

With less than two months to go before the date officially set for the inscription of the candidates, Buenos Aires was rocked by a major political scandal. As far as the public was concerned, it started with a report in the régime's newspaper *Democracia* revealing the discovery of yet another plot against the government. Involved, said the newspaper, were international Communism, the US embassy in Buenos Aires and the Unión Democrática — echoes of the trumped-up charges against Cipriano Reyes and Walter Beveraggi Allende three years before. But this time no prominent politician was detained; the newspaper account spoke only of a shoot-out with the police after which a young student called Ernesto Mario Bravo had been taken into custody. The strangeness of the episode was heightened by the fact that cryptic graffiti had already been appearing on the walls of the city, asking '*Dónde está Bravo?*'

(Where is Bravo?). And in the following weeks people involved in political affairs began to receive a mimeographed version of the events that openly contradicted the report in *Democracia*. Casting aside its habitual prudence, the conservative newspaper *La Nación* decided to publish the entire alternative version.

The story started in mid-May when a doctor, Alberto Julián Caride, was called upon to attend a prisoner who was being held by the Special Section of the Federal Police. Caride found an unconscious youth, his face so bruised as to make him unrecognisable, with a deep gash in his head, and two fingers and a rib broken. The officers explained that the youth had been beaten without authorisation, and that it was imperative to keep him under wraps at the Special Section until he was well. But Caride also heard them discussing the possibility of killing the patient off by simulating a traffic accident. The youth remained unconscious for several days. When he came to, his eyes were bandaged and Caride was addressed by an assumed name in order to hide his identity. Once he was well enough to be moved, the police transported him to a suburban house, to continue his convalescence handcuffed to a bed. After about a month of nursing the prisoner back to health, Caride was told that orders had been issued for his release. But the very next morning the news published by *Democracia*, with a picture of his patient, identified as Bravo, was not of his release but of his arrest. Very troubled, Caride told some friends of his experience and together they decided to commit it to paper and submit it to a judge known not to have pro-government sympathies. Caride was smuggled out of the country and the mimeographed versions of his testimony began to circulate, eventually landing on the pages of *La Nación*. In the ensuing furore, the government ordered Bravo's release and an investigation of the incident. Two of the officers involved were identified and arrested. Their names, Lombilla and Amoresano, became by-words for police brutality among the opposition groups.

By now a real conspiracy was afoot. Or to be more precise, two conspiracies. The first involved a number of high-ranking generals who would normally have been described as well-disposed towards the régime: Sosa Molina, Lucero, Jáuregui and a few others. Theirs was a limited objective — to prevent Eva Perón from becoming Vice-President of the Republic, going further only if Perón should refuse to bow to their will. The second one — drawn mainly from junior officers with a retired general, Benjamín Menéndez, drummed into service as their leader — had higher ambitions: the ouster of Perón and all his works.

Perón was quite aware of the hostility towards Evita in the higher echelons of the officer corps; he knew that many generals, including Sosa Molina, were still smarting at the way they had been forced to repent of the Campo de Mayo snubbing of his wife in 1949. He was also aware of their current objection to Evita's candidacy, although the Generals were still refraining from anything more than pointed hints. They were awaiting the outcome of an event which would provide them with a fairly practical means of assessing their chances of success: the mass rally which the CGT, under Evita's loyal José Espejo, was preparing for 22 August. The occasion had been billed as a *cabildo abierto*, literally an open assembly, in the sense of the event held under the same name in 1810, when the Buenos Aires *cabildo*, or city council, opened its doors to debate separation from a Spain that had fallen under Napoleonic domination. Its aim was no secret: the nomination, by popular acclaim, of Evita's candidacy to the Vice-Presidency. The organisers had been hard at work throughout the country, orchestrating a multitudinous pilgrimage to Buenos Aires from the farthest corners of the land, by offering free transport and food, and accommodation even in the city's garages. They confidently forecast a turnout of two million, and chose an appropriate venue to cope with such a crowd, the Avenida 9 de Julio, which is over 150 metres wide and dominated by the city's most conspicuous landmark, the Obelisk commemorating Argentina's independence.

When the day came, stage management required Perón to arrive alone, so that the crowd could demand Evita's presence and send for her. The first item on the agenda was little more than a formality: Perón's nomination as candidate for the Presidency and his acceptance. The second one was what they were all there for: the invitation to Evita to stand for the Vice-Presidency. She hesitated, asking for four days to think it over, but the crowd demanded an immediate response, insisting on it even when she whittled down the pause to one hour. Finally she relented, saying, 'I will do whatever the people tell me to do.' Yet the delirious reaction of the crowd was not followed two days later, as originally scheduled, by the formal inscription of the two candidacies. Both Perón and Evita had suddenly retreated into a mysterious silence. The Generals had done their head-counting at the 9 de Julio spectacular, and their arithmetic, far from showing the promised two million, revealed a figure a lot closer to a quarter of a million. The difference was large enough to give them confidence, and they issued their ultimatum. On 31 August Evita broadcast to the nation her irrevocable decision not to stand for the Vice-Presidency: 'I am not resigning from my task, but just

from the honours.[. . .] All I want history to say of me is: there was a
woman beside General Perón, a woman who transmitted to him the
hopes and needs of the people — and her name was Evita!' Perón
privately tried to play down the gravity of the confrontation, claiming
that Evita had had to be disqualified on account of her age; she admitted
publicly at the time to being twenty-nine, but was in fact thirty-two,
two years over the minimum age stipulated by the Constitution. But it
was clearly a defeat.

The Army's other conspirators, however, badly overestimated the
magnitude of the defeat. They felt that the régime's forced retreat on this
undoubtedly major issue was a sign that a mere push would send the
whole apparatus tumbling to the ground. Although they counted for
sure only on the allegiance of a few officers at the air bases of El Palomar
and Morón, the naval air base at Punta Indio, and a couple of units in the
huge military complex at Camp de Mayo, they felt confident that others
would rally to their cause at the first sign of open rebellion. They set their
revolt in motion before daybreak on 28 September. Perón was alerted to
the uprising as the first planes took off to drop revolutionary leaflets over
Buenos Aires, and his orders to suppress the revolt began to be implemented even before the disorganised rebels had managed to move out
with the units they had considered safely on their side. El Palomar was
subdued after a barrage of artillery fire ripped up the runways. At Campo
de Mayo there was a brief skirmish as the rebels attempted to take over an
armoured unit. The only casualty of the day, Sergeant Farina, died there
shouting 'Viva Perón!' Perón had declared a state of siege, imposed news
censorship, and ordered government forces to shoot the rebels on sight.
The CGT declared a strike and called its members out on the streets to
resist the takeover. But by the afternoon the rebellion had fizzled out,
with many of those involved fleeing across the river to Uruguay. From
his Casa Rosada balcony, Perón promised an enraged crowd that the
rebels 'will suffer the opprobrious penalty of a coward; as cowards they
will be executed!' He said they would be hanged 'as an example;
everyone must know that in the future those who come out to fight us
must either kill us or be killed by us.' As was the case with most of such
tough talk by Perón, nothing of the sort happened. Instead, many
officers found themselves sentenced to long stretches in distant military
penal units. Among them were names that would return to the political
scene, like Alejandro Agustín Lanusse, Julio Alsogaray and Sánchez de
Bustamante.

Between the aborted uprising and the elections there remained the celebration of *peronismo*'s greatest day, 17 October. Evita was there on the balcony next to Perón. But it was a gaunt, hoarse Evita, such as the crowd had never known before; her illness was becoming painfully visible. None of the fire, however, had disappeared. She said:

'I had to come today to tell you, as I have told the General, that it is necessary to keep an alert watch on all sides in our struggle. The danger is not past. The enemies of the people, of Perón and of the Fatherland, do not sleep. It is necessary for each Argentine worker to remain vigilant, not to fall asleep, because the enemies work in the shadows of treason, at times hiding behind a smile or a proffered hand. I had to come to thank all my beloved *descamisados* from every corner of the Fatherland for having known, on 28 September, how to risk your lives for Perón. I was sure that you would know, as you always have, how to act as a bulwark for Perón. The enemies of Perón and the Fatherland have long known that Perón and Eva Perón are ready to die for the people. Now they know that the people are ready to die for Perón.'

But there was the hint of a farewell speech. 'My *descamisados*', she said, 'there is much I would like to say to you, but my doctors have told me I must not speak. My heart remains with you, and I tell you that I am sure I will soon be back in the struggle, with greater strength and greater love, to fight for this country I love so much, as I love Perón. One thing I will ask of you. I am sure I will soon be with you, but should my health prevent my return, you must help Perón; be loyal to Perón as you have so far, because this is being loyal to the Fatherland and to yourselves. And all of you, *descamisados* of the interior, I hold you close to my heart and hope you realise how much I love you.' Three weeks later, almost on the eve of the elections, a doctor was flown in from the United States to lead a team that operated on Evita to remove a cancer of the uterus. She recovered in time to broadcast an appeal: 'For an Argentine not to vote for Perón is . . . to betray the country.'

The opposition had not had much of a chance to put its case to the electorate, thanks to the firm *peronista* grip on the mass media and the constant harassment of their rallies. But the elections were scrupulously clean. Aided considerably by the first vote ever cast by the women of Argentina, Perón saw his overall majority increased to 66 per cent. The entire Senate, 149 out of 163 seats in the Chamber of Deputies, and all the provincial governments were his.

8
DECLINE. . . .
(1952–1955)

The half-year that remained until the formal inauguration of Perón's second Presidential mandate was overshadowed by the slow, inexorable withering away of Evita. There were, of course, other events of note in the interlude. Jazmín Hortensio Quijano, who had been re-elected as Vice-President, died before taking office. The men in charge of the Republic's economic affairs submitted the Second Five-Year Plan, with 'productivity' as its keynote and a number of projects aimed at correcting the gaps and imbalances of the first Presidency. Agriculture and cattle-breeding were given pride of place, with special allocations of government credit and a new, more remunerative pricing policy, while talk of agrarian reform was whittled down to the redistribution of a mere 2 per cent of the country's cultivated land. The core of traditional Argentina not only remained untouched; it was being reinforced. One-fifth of the country's land surface, 54 million hectares, was to stay in the hands of a mere couple of thousand owners. There were high hopes of inducing private enterprise to come up with two-thirds of the investment called for in the Plan, limiting the state's participation to the remaining third. And the government was to concentrate its efforts in two areas where expansion had been made imperative by the growth of the country's light industy: steel and energy. Iron ore deposits in the northwest were to be mined and a big steel mill was to be built in the province of Buenos Aires, in an attempt to cut back on Argentina's imports of iron and steel which already totalled five-sixths of the 1.2 million tonnes consumed annually. Energy output was to be increased eightfold, with new thermal and hydroelectric plants, supplemented by an effort to speed up the extraction of oil from Argentina's newly-found fields. The new men at the helm were convinced that the Plan called for external support, in the form of credit, direct investment and new technology, mainly from the United States.

On the political front, there was an ominous ring to the quiet purchase by the Fundación Eva Perón of 2,000 rifles and 5,000 pistols, and their distribution among trusted cadres of the CGT. Whispers began to circulate about the possible formation of a workers' militia. Cipriano Reyes, who had already been locked away for four years, was sentenced to a further five years in prison.

Evita made her last public appearance at the ceremony at which Perón was sworn in for a second time as President; the occasion, also, of Argentina's first television transmission. Twenty-two days later she was dead.

Few Argentines who lived through those days will ever forget the exact time of her death; henceforth, every day at the same time, announcers on all radio stations would solemnly proclaim, 'It is 20.25, the time at which Señora Eva Perón, Spiritual Leader of the Nation, passed into immortality.' The country plunged into mourning. Opponents of the régime tend to recall a number of the nastier incidents associated with Evita's death, like the compulsory wearing of black ties and armbands, the hysterical application of the *desacato* law for real or imagined slights against her memory, the adoption of her book *La razón de mi vida* as obligatory reading material in the schools. But there was no denying the sincerity of the grief expressed publicly by an estimated two million Argentines — those who had braved the rain to pray in the streets during her last hours; those who trooped in an incessant stream past her body as it lay in state; those who lined the streets during the funeral procession; and those who would continue to turn up at the resting place she had chosen, the CGT headquarters, to gaze at the body so perfectly preserved by the Spanish embalmer, Pedro Ara. Something had gone out of *peronismo*. Although it would be simplistic to attribute the whole future course of the régime to her sudden absence from the scene, her death did mark a turning-point, partly due to its personal impact on Perón, who for the second time in his lifetime had watched a young wife waste away and die, and its repercussions in the internal politics of *peronismo*; and partly because it happened to coincide roughly with the maturation of wider, external processes.

Perón certainly did change. Suddenly his fifty-seven years seemed to start weighing more heavily, and the hard-working man everyone remembered started cutting down his working day until he was eventually putting in only mornings at the Casa Rosada. His afternoons were spent at the suburban Presidential residence of Olivos; he began to convert its well-wooded parkland and strip of beach on the River Plate into a playground for the adolescent members of the Unión de Estudiantes Secundarios (UES), the *peronista* association of secondary school students. There he would devote more and more hours to watching the young girls play basketball or to driving around with them on *motonetas* (motor-scooters). When it became known that he had begged them to abandon formality and call him by the pet-name 'Pocho', these popular two-wheeled vehicles became known throughout the country as *Pochonetas*. It was very much as if he were, on the one hand, acknowledging the passage of time by reducing his workload, and on the other, attempting to recover youth through proximity to the young. This latter course in time led him into a chain of equivocal, then visibly compromised situations which the opposition eagerly exploited.

Within the hierarchy of *peronismo*, many who had derived their standing from their personal loyalty to Evita soon discovered that her disappearance made them expendable. Among those who fell the hardest were José Espejo, who lost the command of the CGT to Eduardo Vuletich, a personal friend of General Sosa Molina who was known to have spoken openly against corruption in the higher reaches of the unions and the state apparatus; and Héctor Cámpora, who lost his position as president of the Chamber of Deputies. Nine months after Evita's death, the last of her highly-placed connections, her brother Juan, Perón's private secretary, made a dramatic exit. He was found dead in his room, a bullet-hole in his head and a gun lying beside him. The official explanation was suicide; Juan Duarte was said to have been discovered in some unspecified shady dealings and asked to resign by Perón. The opposition claimed it was murder, adding that the shady dealings in question had to do with Duarte salting away for himself some assets Evita had deposited abroad.

But the government had hardly run out of steam as a result of Evita's demise. It was in 1952 that the country's entrepreneurs were organised into the Confederación General Económica, an umbrella body led by representatives of new industries, and into which the old Unión Industrial and Sociedad Rural had been subsumed. Thus the régime rested, apart from the party, on a tripod of sectoral organisations: the workers in the Confederación General del Trabajo; the entrepreneurs, with the new generation on top, in the Confederación General Económica; and the students in the Confederación General Universitaria and the Unión de Estudiantes Secundarios. On paper a remarkable feat of unification, though in actual fact the members of the old entrepreneurial organisations still stuck together, and rival student and union groupings continued to operate semi-clandestinely. It was also in 1952 that the régime pushed ahead with some of its more ambitious international schemes, such as building around the CGT a continent-wide organisation called

Agrupación de Trabajadores Latino-Americanos Sindicalistas (ATLAS), a venture which met only with limited success in Colombia and Chile, after substantial injections of Argentine funds. It was around that time too that Perón, writing as 'Descartes', revived the notion of the 'A-B-C Alliance', between Argentina, Brazil and Chile, a large mass stretching from the Atlantic to the Pacific which he foresaw as an eventual counter-weight to the hemispheric influence of the United States. This particular scheme got nowhere.

The second Presidency also saw the régime getting harsher, though it was the schock of the aborted military uprising of September 1951 rather than Evita's death that gave its reactions a rawer edge. In April 1953, as Perón was addressing a CGT rally from his Casa Rosada balcony, a bomb suddenly exploded on the fringe of the assembly. Perón took up the cue. '*Compañeros* [comrades]', he shouted, 'these, the same people who spread rumours every day, seem to have felt even more rumorous today and have wanted to bomb us.' A second explosion shook the Plaza de Mayo. 'You can see', he added, 'that when I announced from here that this was part of a carefully prepared and implemented plan, I had my reasons . . .' The crowd responded with cries of '*Leña! Leña!* [give them stick!].' And Perón retorted, 'This business of giving them *leña*, which you are recommending; why don't you start giving it yourselves?' Groups of *peronistas* sallied forth from the square to the chant of '*Le-ña! Le-ña!*' and marched across the city to the Casa del Pueblo, the head-quarters of the Socialist party. They burst into the premises and set about wrecking everything in sight, finally setting the place on fire. Police and firemen stayed away from the scene; much later their chiefs would testify to having received orders to let the mob act freely, a clear indication that everything, bombs included, had been carefully planned. The arsonists then retraced their steps and repeated the procedure with the head-quarters of the Radical party, then moved on to the Jockey Club, which was burnt to the ground. Archives, libraries and a priceless collection of paintings were lost in the blaze.

Conspiratorial activity now began to multiply in earnest, and a number of plots were aborted by the government in their early stages. The arrest of opposition leaders, often for brief spells, became more frequent; in those days the inside of *peronista* prisons was seen by two of the most prominent figures in the Radical party, Ricardo Balbín and Arturo Frondizi, and by the Socialist leader, Alfredo Palacios, among many others. This hardening of attitudes coincided in time with the government's decision to pass a law guaranteeing foreign investment in

Argentina, and to begin negotiating the participation of North American interests in the country's oil industry. This too was pounced upon by the opposition, in some cases out of genuine concern that Perón was departing from a nationalist course, enthusiasm for which many Radicals and other adversaries shared with him despite their differences. In many other cases, however, the attitude was blatantly hypocritical, coming as it did from the same mouths that had attacked Perón's economic policies earlier precisely because of their nationalistic content.

Yet somehow Perón seemed to be braving the storm. When in early 1954 the country went to the polls, belatedly to fill the vacancy left in the Vice-Presidency by Quijano's death, the *peronista* candidate, Admiral Alberto Teisaire, raised the ruling party's overall majority to 70 per cent of the electorate. Yet this undeniable victory took place just as a number of hitherto unconnected undercurrents were merging to strengthen the hand of Perón's more determined adversaries. The re-emergence of the conflict with the church was only the tip of a huge submerged iceberg. An episode which many analysts have found difficult to explain, this conflict had many strands. There had always been a nucleus of Catholics who had refused to go along with their hierarchy's initial support for *peronismo*. Politically their views ranged widely, although perhaps the strongest strain was one that combined adherence to the church's social teachings — in which they had, on paper at least, no great quarrel with *peronismo* — and a commitment to democracy, which they saw violated by *peronismo* inasmuch as it trampled on the rights of minorities and bent institutions to suit its own purposes. During most of Perón's two Presidencies, this sector of the Catholic laity only occasionally managed to act concertedly, in small organised groups, usually around some ephemeral publication or as political debating societies. They first began to be aware of themselves as a possible catalyst for some larger movement during the events of 1950 — the demonstration against the Escuela Científica Basilio and the rallies around Cardinal Ruffini. But it took another four years for the idea of organising a political party, roughly along the lines of Christian Democracy, to germinate. However, it must be noted that not all the so-called 'liberal' Catholics, those who had resisted their hierarchy and opposed Perón from the beginning, belonged to the group that eventually established the Christian Democratic party; there were among them — as is natural in a predominantly Catholic country — Radicals and Conservatives too. All they had in common with the first group was concern over the meeting-point of church and politics and, of course, opposition to the régime.

Among the recognised political groups of the Catholic laity which had accompanied Perón from the outset, most could be described as nationalist, of the kind that combined poorly-digested Thomism with the political formulae of Action Française and who were, in the words of Marcelo Sánchez Sorondo, one of their number, 'aesthetically Fascists'. Their common ground with Perón was nationalism, and their attitude towards the worker base of the régime oscillated between tolerance for the sake of expediency and outright disdain. They had nothing in common with the 'liberal' Catholics.

Finally the hierarchy, the official voice of the church, had not only openly backed Perón in his early days but had also cruelly disciplined the few priests who had dared to continue preaching against the régime. When the incidents of 1950 had threatened to disrupt their cosy relationship with the government, they had shown themselves only too eager to heal the rift. Between the hierarchy and the government, nothing was officially disturbing that peace at least until late June 1954, when government officials thronged to the church of La Piedad to attend a requiem mass for Evita.

A multitude of events, minor in themselves, was to bring these disparate elements of the church closer together and into open conflict with Perón. *Sotto voce*, some members of the hierarchy and a number of priests had begun to complain soon after Evita's death against the campaign to beatify and eventually canonise the 'Spiritual Leader of the Nation'. One union had actually filed a formal request for Pope Pius XII to initiate the proceedings, but enthusiasts at home had not awaited the Vatican's reply; icons of Evita with a saint's halo were printed and distributed; mini-shrines began to appear everywhere; also a printed card with a prayer that began 'Hail María Eva, full of grace . . .' A Congresswoman said in the Chamber of Deputies, 'I have seen Eva Perón transforming water into wine, for there is no other comparison for the dreams-come-true of children, mothers and old people. I have seen her cure injuries and kiss the sick.'

To this was added the growing concern of the church over the UES, especially as rumours had begun to circulate about orgies at the Presidential residence of Olivos. The story was already circulating of Perón having become infatuated with a thirteen-year-old UES girl, Nelly Rivas, and having taken her as his mistress, silencing her parents with the present of a suburban house. The charge of corrupting a minor was one of the strongest levelled by the opposition against Perón at the personal level. From his later exile he derided this, saying, 'I have never

believed that it is a crime for a man to go after a woman. Only a government of pansies could consider it a defect for a man to like women. I like
women and I am pleased that I continue to like them. I have never been a
hypocrite; I was never able to live without a woman. All those stories
they put out about the girls I protected are pure hypocrisy. I protected
some *with*, and others *without*, but I do not believe, and no-one will
persuade me, that it is immoral for a man to like women. It would be
immoral if he liked men!' However, at the time, the whole UES fell
under suspicion, and priests began to include in their Sunday sermons a
call to parents 'for Christian meditation before sending your daughters
to student clubs of doubtful morality'.

Then came the matter of *Hermano Tommy*, a faith healer and evangelist
called Theodore Hicks who had obtained Perón's personal authorisation
to hold mass healing sessions at the Atlanta and Huracán soccer stadiums
in Buenos Aires. Thousands flocked to see him, and the clergy began to
worry. When Hicks moved to the province of San Luis, Bishop Emilio di
Pasquo issued a pastoral letter warning the faithful against him, and
obliquely criticising Perón's role in the affair by underlining that 'Article
77 in the Constitution establishes that the President of the Republic
must profess the Catholic, Apostolic and Roman religion.' A few days
later, in a completely independent event, the Christian Democrat Party
came into being in the city of Rosario.

The President's attention was taken up at the time by the tragic
outcome of a tough strike declared by the metalworkers' union, hitherto
one of the bulwarks of the *peronista* union apparatus. When police moved
in to break up picket lines and rallies, shooting broke out, killing two
and wounding scores of workers. But only weeks later he had to face a
sharp attack by the *Acción Católica* (Catholica Action), the official organisation of the Catholic laity, against a huge Student's Day party held by
the UES at Olivos. His advisers pointed out the series of other church-
related events, and in his mind a conviction began to form that the
church had begun to conspire against him, and that the recently-created
Christian Democratic party was the hierarchy's chosen political instrument for that purpose. He took advantage of the 17 October rally to
deliver a thinly-veiled attack on the clergy, describing them as 'infiltrated
adversaries', whose proclaimed apolitical status was 'something like
pigeon shit, because its smell is neither good nor bad'. Headed by the
two Cardinals, Santiago Luis Copello and Antonio Caggiano, and the
Vatican's Nuncio, sixteen bishops descended on the Casa Rosada for a
showdown with Perón. At the meeting, however, both sides carefully

avoided mentioning anything of substance, and the prelates left as they had arrived. But they were soon on the warpath; nine days later the episcopate marked All Saints Day by issuing a joint pastoral letter, to be read in every church in the country, with an attack on 'the aberrations of spiritualism' which, for anyone on the right wavelength, was aimed directly at Perón. Individual bishops, priests and laymen took it as a signal to become more specific at their own levels. But Perón preferred to ignore the pastoral letter and hark back to his meeting with the hierarchy, claiming publicly that 'the highest dignitaries in the church, bishops and archbishops' had declared, 'with the solemnity always used in declarations to the First Magistrate of the Republic, that they condemn those priests and those Catholics who are creating discontent [. . .], who are not only against the government but also against their own church.' He went on to make public a list of Catholic 'makers of discontent' (*perturbadores*) that included the Bishops of Santa Fe and Córdoba and twenty priests in nine provinces. Arrests began immediately, and to no avail did the episcopate request from Perón a specification of the charges against the detainees. A new pastoral letter went out, stating that 'no priest can or may take part in partisan political struggles without compromising his consecration and the church itself, [but] when it is a matter of defending the basic principles of Catholic doctrine, we are not dealing with political opposition, but rather with the defence of the altar.'

The conflict escalated rapidly. In a single month Perón pushed through Congress a package of laws that effectively disestablished the Catholic church: one decreed the separation of church and state, another eliminated obligatory religious education, yet others flagrantly gave sanction to things the church condemned, instituting divorce, doing away with the legal distinction between legitimate and natural offspring, and authorising the re-opening of brothels. Then came the administrative sequel, applied with singular viciousness all the way down the *peronista* apparatus. Priests and known Catholic militants were fired from official positions; state subsidies to Catholic schools were discontinued; the church's permission to broadcast was rescinded; paper supplies to the Catholic newspaper *El Pueblo* were suspended, a Catholic publishing house was closed down; church feasts were excised from the calendar; crucifixes and icons were removed from all publicly-owned premises.

Even before this broadside was fired against the whole church without distinction, many of the ultramontane nationalist Catholics had begun to drift away from their previous support of the régime. The visit of the

United States Assistant Secretary of State, Henry Holland, to Buenos Aires, and the creation of a number of Argentine subsidiaries of US oil firms came together in their minds as proof that Perón had finally deserted the cause of nationalism and was engaging in the same kind of 'sell-out' they had attacked in the past in the anglophile oligarchy. In this their attacks were echoed by the rising star of the Radical party, Arturo Frondizi, only recently elected leader of the UCR who, in *Petróleo y política*, would write a devastating condemnation of this turn of events. The opposition began to use for Perón the very epithet which they, and the *peronistas*, had hitherto applied to the oligarchs: *vendepatria*, literally 'one who sells the Fatherland'. Now those Catholic nationalists whose nationalist convictions, in Sánchez Sorondo's words, 'began by being religious' found not only their nationalism but also their religion under fire.

9

. . . . AND FALL
(1955)

The year 1955 began with the introduction of yet another of the régime's 'historic' achievements: a nationwide agreement between employers and workers on productivity, pay and industrial modernisation. Already in 1954 the CGE had held a congress on labour relations and organisation; now it sat down with the CGT to bring its conclusions into practice. The facts, as presented to the nation, were that since 1940 industrial output had increased by 40 per cent, employed manpower by 15 per cent and wages by 830 per cent; in other words, the increase in wages had outstripped that of productivity by 310 per cent. Of course, the starting point of wages had been a very low one, but at the moment the emphasis was on productivity, so the full import of this set of statistics was played up much in the same fashion as the workers' increased share in the national income had been highlighted in the régime's earlier years. The CGE-CGT agreement, signed in March 1955, committed both sides to: '(1) the adoption of joint methods to increase production; (2) modernisation of industry; (3) regulation of attendance at work to combat absenteeism; (4) a full, rational use of manpower; (5) direct wage increases through incentive schemes proportionate to the efficacy of work, and indirect increases by giving all remuneration greater purchasing power through the reduction of production costs. . .'

On paper, this agreement strengthened the régime's position considerably after the wave of wildcat strikes that had been plaguing government, employers and CGT leadership alike in the preceding months. It became a major propaganda theme, incessantly repeated through a *peronista* media apparatus that had become all-pervasive. The government's Information Secretary, Raúl Apold, now had at his disposal not only the state's own radio and television services, but also the much larger media empire run from ALEA (see p. 126) by Major Aloe. The private ownership of radio stations had been reallocated in favour of the régime by the simple expedient of declaring the expiry of all previous concessions. Newspapers and magazines had been bought out wholesale by ALEA, in many cases by means of 'offers that could not be refused', but mostly in the form of 'golden handshakes' to supporters who had outlived their usefulness or by financial 'rescue operations' for *compañeros* who had run into difficulties with their publishing ventures. Huge sums of money were disbursed for the creation of this empire, and on occasions (such as the case of José Agusti, the owner of *Noticias Gráficas*) the take-overs had been sweetened by the offer of a prestigious official position: Agusti got the plum job of ambassador in Moscow. The network by now included at least twenty-seven newspapers and magazines, forty radio stations, two new agencies and fifteen printing firms. The opposition had to content itself mainly with clandestine sheets, and with an increasingly efficient rumour mill, the efficacy of which was heightened by broadcasting anti-régime news through friendly radio stations across the river in Uruguay. This neighbouring state had become the main base for exiled *antiperonista* politicians, to the extent that Perón had closed the border. Measures had also been taken by the government to blunt the efficacy of any military discontent, such as strictly limiting the ammunition in the hands of units of doubtful allegiance; the Naval Air Force, for example, had had all the detonators removed from the bombs held by its operational units.

But despite the surperficial increase in the régime's strength, dissidence, both military and civilian, was spreading steadily and growing in cohesion. Moreover, it was spilling out into the open through that most corrosive of means: veiled political humour. The most memorable instance was the comic radio programme whose plots created impossibly complex situations with no apparent solution. Then a series of grunts and roars were heard amid special effects simulating jungle sounds. And the cast would break out into a joyful ditty with a refrain saying,

> *Deber ser los gorilas, deben ser,*
> *que andarán por ahí. . .*
> It must be the gorillas, it must be they,
> who are somewhere out there. . .

In the esoteric code-language of the opposition, those *gorilas* who would bring the unexplained solution were the *antiperonista* conspirators. *Gorila* became proudly identified with *antiperonismo*; the events that were to give the term its additional connotation of brutal reaction, first in Argentina and later throughout the whole of Latin America, could not yet be imagined.

The last of the chain of anti-church laws was passed by Congress in May 1955. Most priests had already abandoned the use of the soutane in

public for fear of harassment, and relations between church and government were deteriorating rapidly as police began to raid churches in search
of anti-régime pamphlets and the number of priests and lay Catholic militants under arrest increased steadily. A mass protest was organised by the
church in the form of a huge devotional turnout for the traditional fes-
tivity of Corpus Christi in June. As the church authorities decided to
shift the date from 9 to 11 June, a Saturday, in order to ensure greater
attendance, the government banned street demonstrations that day. It
also organised a rival event in order to draw the crowds away from the
cathedral of Buenos Aires: a multitudinous reception at the Luna Park
stadium for the returning flyweight champion of the world, Pascualito
Pérez. Nonetheless, the faithful (plus the not-so-faithful who took
advantage of the occasion to protest against the government) not only
filled the cathedral but also overflowed into the Plaza de Mayo. The
sermon delivered by the Auxiliary Bishop of Buenos Aires, Manuel Tato,
included a pointed call to remember 'the clergy who acted side by side
with the men of May 1810, and those who signed our Declaration of
Independence'. The religious ceremony over, a column of demonstrators
marched to Congress, chanting anti-government slogans. Despite the
official ban, the police did not intervene, and the crowd dispersed after
only a few scuffles with *peronistas*.

The reason for this passivity became apparent the following morning.
The entire *peronista* media apparatus carried the official version of the
previous day's events, including the accusation that the Catholic demonstrators had hauled down an Argentine flag and burned it, hoisting in its
place the yellow-and-white ensign of the Vatican state. While the newspapers and the radio whipped anti-Catholic feeling to a frenzy, armed
Catholic youths rushed to form a security cordon around the cathedral
and the Metropolitan Curia. The Federal Police moved in and arrested
over 400 of them. The next day a government decree dismissed the
Auxiliary Bishop, Manuel Tato, and Canon Ramón Novoa, accusing
them of having instigated the desecration of the flag. The two prelates
were unceremoniously driven to the airport and bundled aboard a plane
bound for Rome. The Vatican responded swiftly with a decree of its
own, dictating the excommunication *latae sententiae* of all the officials
involved in preventing Tato and Novoa from carrying out their duties.
Although there were no names attached to the measure, Argentina's
Catholics read it quite simply as the excommunication of Perón and the
leading figures of his régime.

Since before this latest church-régime confrontation had begun to

unfold, a large number of Navy officers had been involved in the preparation of a lightning coup against Perón. Furtively they had got hold of
munitions and bomb detonators and transported them to different bases.
Their plan hinged on a direct strike against the Casa Rosada, with Perón
inside, by the Naval Air Force, to be followed by a Marine assault across
the few hundred metres of open space that separated the Ministry of the
Navy from the back of the Casa Rosada. With Perón eliminated and the
Casa Rosada in rebel hands, the rest of the *peronista* apparatus — the
plotters expected — would rapidly come tumbling down. The planes
took to the air, their bombs primed, on the morning of 16 June, less than
a day after the expulsion of the two prelates. The régime had obviously
learned of the plot. By the time, just after noon, when the bombing and
strafing of the Casa Rosada started, Perón was no longer there, and
truckloads of *peronistas* had been mobilised to the Plaza de Mayo to
defend their *Líder*. A few of the bombs uselessly hit their intended target;
but the victims of the day were the scores of people in the square, those
who had arrived to defend Perón and those who were innocently going
about their business. The Marine company that attempted to take the
Casa Rosada from behind was mowed down by a murderous crossfire
from the War Ministry and the Central Post Office, which also claimed
civilian victims. The régime's military response was also incredibly
swift: the Navy's airbases were rapidly taken over by loyal Army units,
leaving the attackers with nowhere to land and forcing them to seek
sanctuary in Uruguay.

And there was more to come. Bands of armed *peronistas* gained the
streets, converging first on the Curia, smashing it up and setting it on
fire, and then turning their attention to Buenos Aires' other major
churches. San Francisco, San Ignacio, Santo Domingo, San Miguel, San
Nicolás, San Juan, La Merced, La Piedad, Nuestra Señora del
Socorro — all were looted, wrecked and set on fire. Only the cathedral
remained surprisingly untouched in that afternoon and evening of arson,
which coincided with a mass roundup by the Federal Police of known
antiperonistas.

All this mindless destruction shook even the most 'loyalist' elements
in the Army hierarchy, and they demanded from Perón an exhaustive
investigation and the punishment of those found responsible. The
investigation came to naught; the deeds were officially blamed on 'a
Masonic lodge', although it was later found that the government had
obtained precise reports from the investigators identifying the arsonists
and indicating the involvement of the Vice-President, Admiral Teisaire,

the *peronista* party, the Health Ministry and one of the intelligence services. But Perón did try to make amends, offering government funds to repair the damage. The Church refused the money and responded with a long pastoral letter coldly recounting the history of their confrontation with the régime.

The hundred days that followed 16 June were a period of vacillation and sudden changes of tack for the régime. Perón sacked his cabinet, and announced that the 'revolutionary phase' of *peronismo* was over. He admitted:

'We limited liberties inasmuch as that was indispensable for the achievement of our objectives. We do not deny that we have restricted certain liberties; we have always done this in the best possible manner, as far as necessary and no further. We have not established a reign of terror; we have not needed to kill anyone. Here the Argentines, as far as our action is involved, die normally in hospitals, full of injections, which is how people like to die nowadays; but we do not have any deaths caused violently by revolutionary action. Many of our people have been killed, but we have not killed anyone. Argentine citizens must keep this well in mind.[. . .] What does all this mean to me? The answer, gentlemen, is very simple: I cease to be the leader of a revolution to become the President of all Argentines, friends and adversaries alike. My situation has changed absolutely, so I must devolve all the limitations applied in the country on the attitudes and procedures of our adversaries, imposed as they were by the need to fulfil our objectives, in order to allow them to act freely within the law, with all the guarantees, rights and freedoms. This is what we are going to do.'

Prisoners were freed; opposition leaders were allowed to speak freely in public. But it was clearly too late to earn the régime any sympathy, and the freedom given his enemies only galvanised dissidence in the political arena, bringing it out into the open, as military and civilian conspiracies spread underground throughout the country. Perón then attempted another ploy: he submitted his resignation, but only, predictably, to withdraw it in face of the carefully staged demand of the *peronista* workers, and return to the tough language of earlier times: 'For each one of our people who falls', he promised, 'five of theirs will fall too.' Leadership of the *Peronista* Party was wrested from Admiral Teisaire and entrusted to that revolutionary firebrand, John William Cooke. And talk was revived of arming the CGT to form a loyal workers' militia. Perón's own friends among the military vetoed the idea, and there was not much to build on: most of the weapons distributed earlier to the CGT had already been sold on the black market. A fortnight after Perón's mock resignation, General Eduardo Lonardi (who in 1938 had succeeded Perón as military attaché in Chile and inherited his task of espionage, only to be trapped by Chilean counter-intelligence, and who in 1954 spent almost a year in prison for plotting against the régime) secretly travelled by bus to the central city of Córdoba to take charge of a military and civilian uprising scheduled for the morning of 16 September. Rear-Admiral Isaac Francisco Rojas (who had remained in favour with the régime during the June uprising by responding to a demand for a definition with the equivocal statement, 'One must be with *el Hombre* [the Man]) had already prepared the orders for the River and High Seas fleets to sail from their anchorages in support of the revolution.

General Lonardi was the revolutionaries' second choice as a leader. Their first would-be commander, General Pedro Eugenio Aramburu, still on active duty, had called a halt to all conspiratorial activity because in his view the conditions were not yet ripe. Many of his fellow-plotters, however, felt that the month of September might well be their last chance. They believed that Perón was truly intent on setting up a workers' militia, and they knew full well that there were only a few weeks left before serving conscripts would be dismissed, leaving them with much-reduced strength just as the annual round of promotions and new postings for the officer corps came up — an opportunity they were sure Perón would exploit to purge the armed forces of known dissidents.

The uprising started on time, with fierce fighting for control of Córdoba. Soon the rebel radio station in that city, *La Voz de la Libertad* (The Voice of Liberty), began to broadcast the revolutionary manifesto; the Navy issued revolutionary communiqués from its Radio Puerto Belgrano as the heavier units put to sea, and from across the river in Uruguay *Radio Colonia* completed the triad that would bombard Argentina with pro-rebel news and propaganda. There was much hard battling in Córdoba before the rebels were able to assert their superiority. 'You must proceed with maximum brutality,' had been Lonardi's order.

Throughout the rest of the country, apart from a number of skirmishes and air attacks and the guerrilla tactics adopted by the armed *comandos civiles* who supported the revolution, confusion reigned supreme. With contradictory statements from rebel and pro-government radio stations filling the air, it was not always easy to determine on which side any particular military unit was acting, especially as a number of them had left their barracks to hover deliberately around until it became clear which side seemed to be winning. The official radio station, Radio del Estado, kept on transmitting nationwide that 'loyal troops are mopping up Córdoba' while their adversaries put out an endless catalogue of real and fictitious rebel successes all over the country. It has been said that the revolution was fought and won mainly on the airwaves, but the three factors that combined to assure the rebel victory were of a far more tangible nature. The first one was their ability to capture and hold an important pair of bases: Córdoba in the centre of the country and Puerto Belgrano in the south of the province of Buenos Aires. The second was the complete paralysis that overcame Perón's own main power base, the CGT. And the third was the determined, ruthless action by the Navy; its High Seas fleet steaming up the coastline to destroy the fuel depots of Mar del Plata with cannon fire before entering the estuary of the River Plate and threatening to do the same with Buenos Aires.

Three days after the outbreak of the rebellion, Perón called in his War Minister and told him he was willing to relinquish political power if that would contribute to pacification. The generals loyal to the régime chose to consider Perón's offer as a formal resignation and to accept it. As Perón drove away to sanctuary in the Paraguayan embassy, and was later moved to a Paraguayan gunboat docked in Buenos Aires, negotiations began between the loyal military authorities and the rebel high command. The revolutionaries demanded unconditional surrender, on the strength of General Lonardi's word of honour that no one would be subjected to any indignities. Three tense days later, Lonardi arrived in Buenos Aires to a tumultuous welcome, taking over the government as Provisional President, in the name of the *Revolución Libertadora*, the Liberating Revolution. In recognition of the role played by the Navy in the revolt, the Vice-Presidency was entrusted to Admiral Rojas.

The streets of Buenos Aires rang with jubilant celebrations. In a carnival mood, the *gorilas* set about smashing busts of Perón and Evita, tearing down billboards with their names, defacing any available public sign of 'the deposed tyranny'. Again and again they chanted the revolutionary hymn, *La Marcha de la Libertad* (The March of Liberty), which began, 'With our eyes set on high. . .', but not everyone joined in the festive mood. But there was another reaction too: the painful, stunned silence of the masses. The novelist Ernesto Sábato painted a poignant picture of the contrast in *El otro rostro del peronismo*: 'That night of September 1955, while we doctors, landowners and writers noisily celebrated the downfall of the tyrant in the living room, in a corner of the kitchen I noticed that the two Indian girls who worked there had their eyes full of tears. And though during all those years I had meditated on the tragic dualism that divided the Argentine people, at that moment it struck me most movingly. What more precise portrait could there be of our Fatherland's drama than that almost exemplary double scene? Many millions of dispossessed and workers were in tears at that very moment — a dark, sombre moment for them. Great multitudes of humble fellow-countrymen were symbolised by those two Indian girls weeping in a kitchen in Salta.'

Perón own explanations of his fall suffered various changes in the course of time. One of his earliest references to the event, in a letter written in 1956 to John William Cooke, the leader of the *Resistencia Peronista*, said, 'I have not wished to tell the truth about why we did not act against the rebels. Both [General] Lucero and [General] Sosa Molina determinedly refused to let me arm the workers; their Generals and their chiefs defected miserably.' In his book *La fuerza es el derecho de las bestias* (Force is the right of beasts), written in the early years of his exile and published in 1958, he wrote, 'In the Argentine Republic there has been a clash between the parasitic and the producing classes. The oligarchy, the clergy, the parasitic sectors of professionals and military men, launched themselves with their arms against the producing classes. For such treason to succeed it was necessary to combine the money of the obligarchy, the preaching of bad priests and the agitation of professional politicians — three decidedly parasitic sectors.' Later, in his exile in Spain, in a mimeographed tract later published in *Tres revoluciones militares*, he claimed that 'when *peronismo*, in 1955, saved the country from the destruction of a fratricidal war, it did so trusting that the Army would assume the patriotic defence of the Nation, but soon the exact opposite was the case: the Navy, in the service of Great Britain, and the Freemasonry that had infiltrated the Army with similar designs, consummated the most iniquitous betrayal of the Fatherland.' Even later, in the recollections he taped for posterity in Madrid, he enlarged candidly upon this theme:

The revolution against me was pulled off by the English for economic reasons. [. . .] Argentina used to be an English colony. Consequently, our economic independence consisted in breaking the ties of dependence on England. It so happened that when in 1816 we became independent from the political power of Spain, we fell under the economic power of England. Ours was the second independence, to free us from England. The Navy played its role in this revolution. The Navy is formed by chiefs and officers who are also all Freemasons of the Scottish Celestial Rite, which is a very special rite. The English Navy belongs to the same rite. All of this gave their people [the Argentine Navy] certain leanings, although it was not enough to turn all the chiefs and officers. That called for money, and the English bought them out and turned them into mere instruments of their designs. We knew that England was directing and financing all this, and that is why we removed the Navy's munitions. We didn't even leave them with detonators for their cannons. But the English, from their bases in the Malvinas [Falklands], not only gave them the munitions but also provided them with fuels and food from Montevideo. The Navy, as a body, was alien to the other services. Not separate from the rest, but confronted with them [Admiral Isaac Rojas] was a furious *peronista*. He held receptions for the CGT and gave medals to the secretary-general, Espejo. He presented jewels to the wife of the governor of Buenos Aires. When he was Naval attaché in Brasil he wanted to teach Ambassador Cooke *peronista* doctrine, which is why they quarrelled constantly. This Rojas was a man who pretended to be a *peronista* [but was] a traitor to the movement; an individual who was lying in ambush within the movement. They paid him; they gave him money.[. . .] Had this revolution taken place in 1945, God help them! But I had been ruling the country for ten years and I was already fed up and bored with people, government, everything. Because that is the way one ends up; feeling revulsion at so much rottenness and perversion.[. . .] When we received news that something was happening in Córdoba, the strongest garrison in the country, I called the War Minister and told him, 'Look, you must go to Córdoba because the information from there is serious.' He got on a plane and went to Córdoba. This was General Lucero and the date was 14 September 1955. Lucero spoke to the commanders there, and on the 15th I got a telegram saying, 'I have been at Córdoba garrison. Only a madman can believe that these people will revolt.' Lucero returned to Buenos Aires on the 15th and Córdoba was up in arms on the 16th.

What can one do when one has to rely on guys like that? [. . .] Repression begins. The traitor was Lucero's Chief of General Staff. I was convinced that the Commander-in-Chief was also a traitor; they were all traitors; this was organised treason. This is what happened to Hitler, who acted against the traitors in a manner I could not, for I headed a legal and constitutional government and either did things according to the law or I didn't do them at all, giving up and letting everything go to hell. Because I was also somewhat tired. Furthermore, our people, who had received enormous advantages and vindications against the exploitation they had been suffering for a century, should have shown more enthusiasm in defending what they had been given. But they did not defend it because they were all *panzistas* [preoccupied with their bellies], as we say. They thought with their bellies and not with their heads or hearts. I saw this panorama and wondered if I should be more of a papist than the Pope, sacrificing my all for these gentlemen who would sacrifice nothing for themselves. This ingratitude led me to reflect that giving victories and vindications to a people that is incapable of defending them is a waste of time. All of this influenced my lack of decisiveness at the time. Had there not been so many disgusting circumstances, I would have defended the whole thing; I would have gone out with a regiment, dealt with the situation and put an end to the problem. I had the First Division with General Fatigatti — the only good general I could find. All the others failed me. Fatigatti was a man who never failed at all. Well, I could have called on the First Division, with the Regiment of Grenadiers, and gone out. What would those people have done against that? But the whole thing was horrible; the other generals were acting more like bishops; they liked to hold conferences but had no stomach for fighting. They were cowards! They were afraid of dying! That is the truth. I remember one general, one of many, whom I entrusted with a mission and he replied, 'I've got my wife in hospital.' There were deep shadows under his eyes, so great was his fear.

I could have called on the people and given them arms. But what would have happened? Was I going to send to their death thousands of men in order to defend something those same thousands were not determined to defend? The unions also disappointed me; the general strike was all ready, yet they did not come out. The leaders, headed by Di Pietro, and the whole of the CGT were ready to bring the country to a halt — yet they did not! They tried to make a deal with the new crowd. One looks at this panorama and says, is it for this that I have worked so hard and made so many sacrifices? So I arrived at the conclusion that the Argentine people deserved a terrible punishment for what they had done. There you have it: there they are now, hungry and desperate. That is the fate they deserve. Now all these years of pain are making them think again. That is the truth. All the other military events were secondary. They [the people] were a bunch of cowards who did not wish to fight on one side or the other, save a few naive ones who lost their lives. The people have the fate they deserve! That affair in Córdoba was a military episode, just like the others; like those of Bahía Blanca or Buenos Aires. Treason did not lie in any of the military episodes because there was no military struggle. Even the War Minister had defected and his command was treasonable and working for the enemy! At that juncture the Paraguayan ambassador, Juan Chávez, a great man, said to me, 'Come to my house. This whole thing is looking very bad and you must not sacrifice yourself needlessly.' So I went to the ambassador's house. I saw that the whole thing was disgusting — that the military would bring a division from the north, but did not want to fight. They would stop a day's journey short of Córdoba. At the government house I had a detachment and people willing to fight; we had anti-aircraft guns, tanks. They would not have achieved anything. So I left very calmly in my car, taking no more than two or three men with submachineguns. I went straight to the Paraguayan embassy and then on to the ambassador's house, taking no more than the clothes I was wearing. I left in civvies and later some of the boys took the things I needed to the Paraguayan gunboat. The ambassador had said, 'We are not safe here, because I have too few people to put up a fight. So let's go to the gunboat.' And we went to the gunboat. I was there for eight days.

As Perón awaited a decision from the new authorities on his request for a safe-conduct out of Argentina, President Lonardi proclaimed his motto, borrowed from a hero of the past, Urquiza, after a much tougher victory: *Ni vencedores ni vencidos*, 'neither victors nor vanquished'.

10

'NEITHER VICTORS NOR VANQUISHED'
(1955)

General Eduardo Lonardi was a unique character. For one thing, he actually believed that his motto, *Ni vencedores ni vencidos*, was practicable. He was convinced that it was basically a matter of cleansing the body politic of corruption, taking to court those guilty of misdeeds, severing the link between (*peronista*) party politics and the trade union movement and straightening out the economy. Vindictiveness was not part of his scheme; he believed that rather than eliminating *peronismo* by fiat and persecuting the recalcitrants, as recommended by a strong body of opinion within the new government, *peronismo* could be purged of its unwanted elements by persuasion, by showing the people what had gone wrong and who was responsible. To a large extent, the composition of his cabinet reflected the position of the church as an injured party in the last phase of the *peronista* régime. There were several Catholic nationalists (a description that could easily fit Lonardi himself) and members of the new Christian Democratic party. Lonardi seemed to be saying that there were many parts of *peronismo* that could be salvaged, if only the rotten element could be expunged. Very early, however, public opinion learned to distinguish two opposing factions within the government of the *Revolución Libertadora*: the 'nationalists' and the 'liberals'. Roughly, the term 'nationalist' was used to describe those of Lonardi's own persuasion; while the term 'liberal' was applied to those who wished to take a harder line towards the remnants of *peronismo* and literally eradicate it from the Argentine political scene. What was not immediately easy to ascertain, in terms which ideologues and political analysts would find comfortable, was precisely who had taken power. *Peronismo* has been described as an alliance between the Army, the workers and the country's new industrial class — an alliance with a nationalist and populist content, and therefore aligned against Argentina's traditional oligarchy and their foreign associates. It is very much an abstract description, really meaning that, deep down, *peronismo* represented the converg-

166

ing interests of the three groups in the alliance, and opposed the interests of the latter group. As was seen in earlier chapters, the actual components of the alliance were shifting constantly, and there were periods both of confrontation and accommodation with the traditional power groups and with Britain and the United States, the old and the new dominant external powers. When Perón was overthrown, Argentina was in one such period of accommodation with the United States, although it continued to stand in isolation from the international economic order, embodied in the International Monetary Fund, that Washington was willing on the post-war world. Electoral arithmetic would soon show that the traditional political expression of Argentina's oligarchy, the Conservative party, had shrunk into insignificance during the Perón era, thus making it a lot harder to determine who was representing whom.

With Lonardi in power, it was clearly the Army — one of the three pillars of the original *peronista* 'alliance' — that was calling the shots; but it was a deeply divided Army, and one that had had to concede a large share of power to its sister service, the Navy. To use the lexicon of the day, in the Army 'nationalists' and 'liberals' were very much in evidence all the way up the hierarchic ladder, while the Navy was far more homogeneously 'liberal'. It cannot be over-emphasised that both these terms, in Argentina, refer mainly to the economic policy outlook of each group; the 'nationalists' would, on the whole, have preferred to retain the nationalistic, protectionist and 'dirigiste' orientation of the Perón years, while the 'liberals' advocated a return to free trade and exchange, indeed to *laissez-faire* if possible. In the purely political sphere, however, the 'nationalist' group wished to seek some form of understanding with the majority, represented by *peronismo*, while the 'liberals' excluded the majority from any future political solution. In these terms, the 'liberals' came very close to the old attitudes of the Conservative party.

Though for different reasons, both groups coincided in the public denunciation of the evils of *peronismo*. One of the new régime's first acts was the creation of an investigating committee to unearth all the misdeeds of the Perón administration; in overall charge of this task was the Vice-President, Rojas, the most visible head of the 'liberal' group in the Lonardi government. Newspapers and the radio — the old *peronista* media empire, now turned against its creators — were filled with details of corrupt dealings, of Perón's remittances of funds to Swiss banks, of his affair with Nelly Rivas. The solid evidence of the wealth amassed by the Peróns was placed on public display, in the conviction that the sight of mass of finery (especially Evita's jewels, the scores of dresses and hundreds of pairs of shoes), as tangible evidence of the hypocrisy of a régime claiming to represent the poor and humble, would evoke revulsion among the *peronista* mass. The spearhead of the 'investigative' effort was the loose network of *comandos civiles*, the civilians who had taken up arms against *peronismo*, and who now took it upon themselves to ferret out, at every level, the most hated of the representatives of the fallen régime. During the military uprising, the *comandos civiles* had already attracted a large number of underworld figures, and when the downfall of the régime began to appear inevitable, also a large number of turncoats; former fringe elements of *peronismo* out to carve a niche for themselves in the new order. After the victory of the *Revolución Libertadora*, many people who had only taken up arms for that purpose returned to their usual activities, leaving in the *comandos civiles* a hard core of zealots and a considerable number of misfits, both borderline cases and outright criminals. This combination led swiftly to excesses in the name of aiding the investigations into *peronista* corruption; houses of former *peronista* officials and union activists were broken into without warrants, beatings were frequent, and unmitigated thievery became an alarmingly habitual component of the raids.

The new government also made much of *peronismo*'s 'mismanagement' of the economy. The Second Five-Year Plan was scrapped; new, higher prices were immediately announced for the country's farmers, together with a series of special incentives for agriculture. An economist who had once been the youngest Central Bank director in Latin America, Raúl Prebisch, was invited to prepare an overall economic plan. In announcing its outlines, Prebisch spoke of 'austerity' in public spending and the freeing of the exchange market; the rate of exchange for the US dollar, already the reference currency for Argentina, shot up from the many-tiered range of 7.50-15 pesos, to a single free rate of 18 pesos.

But Lonardi left the CGT, the base of *peronista* power, practically untouched. The very next day following Lonardi's entrance to the Casa Rosada, the CGT issued a statement saying:

As fighting among brothers has now ceased, and the Fatherland is our foremost consideration, the CGT again addresses the *compañero* workers to emphasise the need to maintain the most absolute calm and to continue at their jobs, heeding only the directives of this central body. Every worker to remain at his post, on the road to harmony, in order to demonstrate to the world that there is in Argentina a people of righteous men; for it is only in peace that it is possible to promote the greatness of the Nation, which is the way to consolidate its social advances. Let us look ahead and have faith; the rest will be done by the Fatherland.

The CGT's secretary-general, Hugo Di Pietro, rushed off with a delegation to confer with Lonardi, and came away announcing with relief that the President had given guarantees that the labour and social legislation and the CGT and its member-unions would remain untouched. Lonardi went even further by trying to appoint as his Labour Minister Juan Atilio Bramuglia, Perón's first Foreign Minister. But internal opposition was too great, and he finally settled for the appointment of Luis Benito Cerrutti Costa, a legal adviser to the powerful metal-workers' union. The CGT responded with another gesture which was sure to meet with government approval: an announcement of its wish to turn the Confederation into a body concerned exclusively with trade union affairs.

These moves towards an entente between government and CGT ran counter to the wishes of the hardliners among the 'liberals', who regarded the Confederation as one of the major symbols of *peronismo* and wanted to see it dismantled, or at least thoroughly 'de-peronised'. And some had decided to take matters into their own hands. Aided in many cases by *comandos civiles*, a number of union bosses who had been displaced during the Perón government began a campaign to 'recover' their unions, using force to occupy premises and setting themselves up as the new authorities. The CGT complained bitterly to Lonardi, adding that all the member-unions were more than willing to hold government-supervised internal elections for the renewal or confirmation of their leadership. An agreement was rapidly hammered out, the CGT leadership itself resigning and handing over the Confederation to a pair of mutually-agreed figures, Andrés Framini and Luis Natalini. A date was set for elections in the unions, but before a month was out, Framini and another 300 union leaders descended upon the Labour Minister to denounce a number of violations of the agreement, mainly through more unauthorised takeovers. Simultaneously, the 'Commission for the Recovery of Free Trade Unions' started to demand a speedier devolution of the organisations to the 'true representatives of labour'. Cerrutti Costa, the Labour Minister, came up with a new draft statute for all unions, containing also the ground rules for the forthcoming elections. The CGT responded warily, with a suspended decision to go out on a general strike.

By late October 1955 Lonardi's health had begun to falter. He was under pressure not only on the issue of the CGT, but also due to the 'demand' of the liberals that he should 'legalise' the many irregularities committed by the *comandos civiles* and take a much tougher attitude towards the *peronistas*. Differences had also begun to arise between the members of the government over one of the biggest components of the revolutionary 'booty': the *peronista* media empire.

In early November, the President's conciliatory line obtained what looked like an important victory: the withdrawal by the CGT of its threat to go out on general strike, and its acceptance of the appointment of a government trustee to administer CGT funds until the new authorities were elected. But this did not defuse the tension between 'nationalists' and 'liberals'.

The 'liberals' insisted on portraying the 'nationalists' as little better than disguised Nazis, and as people who were dangerously 'soft' on the defeated *peronistas*. And almost two months after power had been wrested from Perón, they felt strong enough to demand from Lonardi a purge of 'nationalists' from high government posts and the adoption of a much harder de-peronisation policy. The first 'nationalist' casualty was the Army Minister, General Justo León Bengoa, who resigned issuing a plea for 'tolerance of the ideas and feelings we do not share, as the only way to put behind us the hatred sown until recently by the ousted dictatorship'.

Close to midnight on 12 November, an impressive party of 'liberal' military leaders demanded to speak to Lonardi at his residence in the suburb of Olivos. The party included the three ministers of the services, Colonel Ossorio Arana, Admiral Hartung and Brigadier Abrahín; the Secretary General of the Presidency, Colonel Emilio Bonnecarrere; the head of the President's Military Household, Colonel Labayrú; the commander of the Presidential Guard regiment, Lieutenant-Colonel Alejandro Agustín Lanusse; plus four other generals and two admirals. Their opening demand was straightforward: the resignations of two Presidential advisers, of the Transport Minister, General Uranga, and of the Minister of the Interior, Luis María de Pablo Pardo. Lonardi hotly defended his collaborators, reminding Lanusse that he had been released from a *peronista* prison, and Colonels Labayrú and Bonnecarrere that it was thanks largely to the efforts of one of the advisers whose dismissal they were demanding that they were back on active duty. He also recalled that de Pablo Pardo and Uranga had better revolutionary credentials than many of those present. 'It is paradoxical', he said, 'that among their judges of today we should find men who were *peronistas* until three months ago, and who only reacted when Perón attacked the church.' Turning to one of the generals present, he added, 'Like you, for example, General Videla Balaguer, who received the Medal of *Peronista* Loyalty.' The General replied, 'Sir, I have crossed the waters of the Jordan and purified myself.' To which Lonardi retorted, 'Doctor de Pablo Pardo had no need to cross the Jordan because he was always on the other side.' Faced with Lonardi's flat refusal to countenance the dismissal of his aides, his visitors changed tack and claimed that, over and above personalities, the armed forces felt that three fundamental conditions should be met. These were: the creation of a Military Junta which would share power with the President, the takeover of the CGT and adoption of an 'energetic' policy towards the workers, and the immediate dissolution of the *Peronista* Party.

Again Lonardi rejected the impositions, saying, 'By firing broadsides the only thing you will achieve is the exacerbation of the workers and the strengthening of *peronismo*, to a point at which it would not be surprising if within four months we had Perón back in the Casa Rosada or the country submerged in civil war.'

In the meantime, Admiral Rojas had orchestrated the mass resignation of the *Junta Consultativa*, an advisory body formed by leading non-*peronista* politicians, in support of the 'liberal' demands. The idea was to create the impression that Lonardi had lost all backing, military or civilian. The following morning the War Minister, Colonel Ossorio Arana, turned up while Lonardi was dressing to tell the President that the armed forces were now demanding his resignation. 'You have five minutes to submit it. When that time expires we shall use force and there will be spilling of blood.' Lonardi said that he would resign, but was soon persuaded by his advisors to change his mind. But it was too late: General Pedro Eugenio Aramburu, the man who had relinquished the leadership of the revolt against Perón because he had considered it premature and dangerous, was already on his way to the Casa Rosada to take over the Presidency.

Only the small English-language *Buenos Aires Herald* published a statement by Lonardi saying, 'I communicate to the people that it is not true that I have resigned the position of Provisional President, or that my health is the reason for my withdrawal from Government House. This has occured exclusively as the result of a decision taken by a sector of the Armed Forces.' The rest of Argentina heard only the victor's voice, in the form of a government communiqué:

The recent crisis in the Provisional Government is exclusively due to the presence in that government of groups who influenced General Lonardi's thinking, leading his policies in the direction of totalitarian extremism, which was incompatible with the democratic convictions of the *Revolución libertadora*, and who managed, to the stupefaction of wholesome revolutionary opinion, to take over key positions in the leadership of the nation. These people, and not others, were attempting to lead the nation down a dangerous path, at the end of which there could only be a new dictatorship.

The politicians of the reconstituted *Junta Consultativa* soon added their own manifesto:

The undersigned, members of the *Junta Consultativa Nacional*, in representation of the Unión Cívica Radical, Democratic Socialist, Progressive Democratic and Christian Democratic parties, meeting after the political crisis which ended in the failure of the nationalist and totalitarian attempt to denaturalise the democratic aims of the *Revolución Libertadora*, declare: (1) that they reaffirm their collaboration with the Provisional Government, with deep faith in its clearly democratic orientation and in its determination to restore the country's institutional life, leading it towards the rule of liberty and of social justice; (2) That they reiterate their solidarity with the workers, for whose material, moral and political welfare they are striving in the light of their respective ideologies, and warn them against the maneuvres that attempt to use them for anti-democratic purposes; (3) That they affirm their unbreakable determination to prevent anyone from ignoring the rights and social conquests of the Argentine workers.

For all the rhetoric, Lonardi's ouster clearly marked the end of *Ni vencedores ni vencidos*. The unions reacted instinctively by going out on strike, but their action was swiftly aborted by the incarceration of most of the strike leaders. Three days after the palace coup, virtually at the same time as the politicians of the *Junta Consultiva* pledged their support for Argentina's workers, the government decreed the 'intervention' of the CGT.

Two days before Eduardo Lonardi arrived triumphant in Buenos Aires, Juan Domingo Perón was taken, under cover of diplomatic immunity, from the Paraguayan ambassador's residence in the suburb of Belgrano to a Paraguayan gunboat berthed for repairs in Buenos Aires's North Dock. There was a long wait until Paraguay's President, General Alfredo Stroessner, granted Perón political asylum, and then until the Lonardi government finally announced that it would be respected. Yet still the gunboat and Perón remained in the port, amid rumours that either Navy units or *comandos civiles* were preparing to storm the ship and take him prisoner or kill him. On 25 September, as an added precaution, the gunboat steamed out of port and anchored a few kilometres from the coast.

Another four days passed before it was agreed that he would be transferred to a Paraguayan seaplane, an ageing Catalina, and flown to Asunción.

In the capital of Paraguay he set up residence in the house of an expatriate Argentine, Eduardo Gayol. Almost immediately the revolutionary government in Buenos Aires began to put pressure on Stroessner to have Perón removed — so close to Argentine territory and in contact with his followers at home, he was deemed too much of a threat. Covertly, plans began to be drawn up by the Argentine military for Perón's assassination or abduction. Informers reported on his every move, and in October the Paraguayan security forces arrested a band of fifteen young Argentines who were accused of having come to kidnap Perón. When word began to spread of a secret plan to kill the former President, Stroessner had him moved to Villarica, some 170 kilometres inland, where he was lodged on the estate of a leading member of Paraguay's ruling party. Yet the pressure from Buenos Aires, overt and covert, did not ease up, and Stroessner was torn between loyalty to his friend Perón and the fact that he could not go on indefinitely defying his larger neighbour, Argentina, with whose economy Paraguay's is closely intertwined. The way out of the dilemma was suggested by one of Stroessner's aides: a bogus attack on Perón's country hideaway was staged one night by the very security men who were protecting him. The harmless discharge of volleys of gunfire into the air served the purpose of persuading Perón that he was not safe even that far inside Paraguay. So on 21 November he was quietly bundled on to a Paraguayan Air Force DC-3 which flew off for an unknown destination.

In Brazil the plane touched down at Rio to refuel, then again at San Salvador and finally landed at Amapá, on the banks of the Amazon. Only then did his intended destination become clear. A message was sent to Dutch Guiana (now Suriname), to Prince Bernhard, who was there on a visit. Perón never forgot the incident: 'He did not even reply. . . This man was in my debt. When he went to Argentina representing Philips I treated him with every honour. I made him a present of a horse and other things. Before landing in [Dutch] Guiana I sent him a telegram, but he didn't answer that either. . . Who is this Prince Bernhard? *Una mierda* [a shit], as we say!' So Perón's long flight was routed on to Venezuela, where President Pérez Jiménez sent his Chief of National Security to greet him and escort him to a hotel — but did not receive him personally. The quest for a safe haven continued. On flew Perón to Nicaragua, but there his 'old friend', the dictator Anastasio Somoza García, told him that it would be 'politically inconvenient' for him to stay on.

Turning back, Perón headed for Panama, where President Arnulfo Arias welcomed him, according to Perón's own reminiscences, 'because he thought I was worth 700 million dollars.'

The old Hotel Washington in Colón was his first Panamanian home. There he quickly penned a book, *La fuerza es el derecho de las bestias*, justifying his government and castigating the régime that had succeeded him. There he made a lasting impression on a young officer in the Panamanian National Guard, Omar Torrijos (who many years later was to lead a nationalist revolution in that country). There too he met a young Argentine dancer, a fervent *peronista*, whose troupe (financed by the Eva Perón Foundation) had been stranded by the revolution at home. Her name was María Estela Martínez Cartas; her friends called her Isabelita. Perón recalled her asking him, 'General, don't you need a secretary? I could help you with your housework as well as acting as your secretary.' 'But', Perón says he replied, 'I have no money.' 'I would work for nothing!' After Perón's death and her own expulsion from government in Argentina, Isabelita candidly told a reporter, 'From the beginning there was no doubt in our minds that we would live as lovers.'

But even in faraway Panama Perón was not completely free from the vengeful arm of the *gorilas* who were ruling Argentina. At least two teams of would-be assassins were intercepted and turned back. Interestingly, the United States forces in the Canal Zone were later blamed both by Perón (who claimed that they harassed him and forced him to leave the hotel in Colón) and by the *antiperonistas* who took part in one of the botched attempts on his life (who alleged that a hired hit man had been spirited away by the North Americans).

These first months of Perón's exile were certainly not ones of opulence. The former President claimed that he had only managed to lay hands on some of his savings, totalling about 50,000 dollars, and that his friend, the financier Jorge Antonio, had remitted him another 70,000 dollars from the royalties he was owed on Evita's book. Those who visited him at the time tend to agree that his life-style was hardly that of a wealthy man — but adversaries maintain that this simply reflected the fact that he had not yet been able to get hold of the considerable funds he had salted away abroad. His contacts with Argentina were by no means few, and although news often arrived, enthusiastically inflated, of plans to launch a 'resistance' movement that would return him to power, the overall picture was grim and far from hopeful. Lonardi's ouster had certainly steeled dissidence in the unions, but most of the best men of 'the Movement' were either in prison or in impotent exile.

11

THE 'DE-PERONISATION' EXPERIMENT
(1955–1958)

November is late in the year for a coup in Argentina, even for the kind of palace coup like the one that overthrew General Lonardi. Usually the long hot months of late spring and summer, made unbearable by the constant humidity of Buenos Aires, bring the country's political life to a complete standstill, often until late February or early March, when the children must return to school. But the summer of 1955–6 was different. For many, holidaying was prevented by a sinister menace: a rapidly spreading epidemic of polio, which kept people away from places of possible contagion. The habitual summer emptiness of the streets had an eerie quality, with most kerbs and roadside trees whitewashed with a mixture of lime and disinfectant. The powerful odour of the same disinfectant hung to the walls of public buildings and the tiled floors of private homes.

Yet behind closed doors and shuttered windows much activity was taking place. De-peronisation had begun in earnest, and its promoters had no intention of pausing for a summer break. The 'intervention' in the CGT was followed by a decree banning from union office any person identified as a 'militant' during the Perón years (although the measure soon had to be toned down when it was discovered that it affected more than 60,000 union leaders throughout the country; the ban was lifted from 'second-line' leaders, particularly in the provinces). A 10 per cent wage increase was granted in an attempt to mollify the workers, then another decree appeared with the clear purpose of breaking up *peronista* control of the large nationwide unions. All political activity in the unions was expressly forbidden, and permission was granted for the creation of new unions, even in branches of activity that were already unionised. And the *peronista* unions also became a target for the 'investigating' fury of the new authorities, bent on proving that everything connected with the 'infamous tyranny' was corrupt through and through. Many of the 'investigating commissions' were housed in the Palace of the Congress, and all wielded immense power; they peremptorily summoned people to testify, ordered arrests, and recommended interdictions and confiscations of property. There seemed to be a commission for just about everything, but three in particular were to remain etched on the country's political memory. The first of these was Commission 7, formally entrusted with looking into the legality of the *peronista* media empire. Under pressure from former newspaper owners who repudiated the sales contracts they had signed, and from a host of people from within government and outside it who saw the opportunity to take over these vehicles of influence, Commission 7 was soon involved in a mesh of sordid intrigue. Lonardi had favoured returning the newspapers to their former owners, and it is said that the struggle for *Crítica* was one of the many events that precipitated Lonardi's ouster. This particular newspaper was finally handed over to a former Radical deputy, Santiago Nudelman, for him to turn it into a mouthpiece for 'the principles of the *Revolución Libertadora*'. Nudelman also had his mind set on the purchase of *La Razón*, but there he ran into stiff resistance from the former proprietor, Ricardo Peralta Ramos, and a number of other hopefuls with powerful connections. In the ensuing months the battle for *La Razón* was to involve other 'investigating commissions', intelligence services and high-ranking government officials in a criminal spiral that proceeded from attempted extortion to murder. The case of *La Prensa* was more straightforward: in December 1955 it was taken from the CGT and returned to Alberto Gainza Paz, who without delay put it to campaigning for Argentina's entry to the International Monetary Fund and the World Bank.

The second memorable investigating body, Commission 58, began to function in the summer of 1955 under the direction of Navy Captain Aldo Luis Molinari and a weird person who called himself 'Capitán Gandhi'. Their job was to purge the police force, and their methods, mostly devised by 'Capitán Gandhi', were nothing less than spectacular. The entire personnel of a police station, or a division of the Federal Police, would suddenly be packed into black marias and carted off to the Villa Devoto prison to await interrogation. And the questioning was carried out in public sessions. An official document of the time describes the so-called Gandhi 'receiving witnesses in halls crammed with the public, with abundant picture-taking and filming, their depositions recorded on tape; often confronting them with other witnesses and even taking down statements from several persons simultaneously'. The kidnapping in Montevideo, Uruguay, of two *peronistas*, a former deputy and a former judge, was attributed to Commission 58. But its most extra ordinary exploit was the attempt to prove that Juan Duarte, Evita's brother and Perón's private secretary, had been murdered. The exhumation of Duarte's body in December 1955 was one of the events that made that a busy summer. 'Capitán Gandhi' himself helped to perform the autopsy and later took to walking around with Duarte's skull under his arm. In the end, he proved nothing. The bizarre beha viour of 'Gandhi' led to an official investigation into his own back ground by other branches of the security services, and eventually to the official announcement of his real name, Próspero Germán Fernández Alvariño. Apart from the public antics of Commission 58, their men were also involved in a number of covert operations in which the already blurred frontiers of legality soon vanished completely.

But Commission 58 was hardly the most sinister of the twilight 'investigating' bodies created by the Revolución Libertadora. It was over shadowed by the vaguely-defined Special Commission led by Juan Con stantino Quaranta. He was a retired lieutenant-colonel when he joined Lonardi's General Staff in Córdoba during the revolution. His first reward was the post of Administrator General of Customs. When Aramburu took over the Presidency, Quaranta was reincorporated to active duty with the rank of colonel, and by January 1956 he had been made general. His new official title was 'Special Commissioner of the Executive Power in All the Territory of the Republic', and the organ isation he put together was soon to be transmogrified into the Secretaría de Informaciones del Estado (SIDE), the new state intelligence service. Quaranta's team included members of the armed forces, the remnants of the comandos civiles and an inordinate number of underworld figures, who kept creating embarrassing incidents by evading arrest for car stealing and holdups by flashing their SIDE credentials. This was the Revolución Libertadora's main 'dirty tricks' department, the source of many of the failed attempts to assassinate Perón abroad, the training ground for agents-provocateurs and informers charged with infiltrating peronista 'resistance' groups, the place where torture as a method of poli tical interrogation was perfected and resorted to ever more frequently.

The summer of 1955 witnessed the announcement of Raúl Prebisch's economic plan, an orthodox package he would later disown and which at the time was criticised as 'essentially deflationary, compressive, regres sive; proposing austerity for the many and greater profits for a social minority'. It witnessed the announcement of Argentina's entry to the IMF and the International Wheat Agreement, and the virtual doubling since the revolutionary victory of the exchange rate for the US dollar, already a popular — though hardly accurate — yardstick to measure the success of economic policies. And it witnessed a steady surge of impatient disaffection among the displaced *peronistas*.

Individual acts of defiance began to be replaced by more serious plotting, spreading even into some quarters of the Army. In March 1956, the security forces uncovered a conspiracy in the wine-producing province of Mendoza, and seventy alleged plotters were thrown in prison. As Interior Minister Eduardo Busso proclaimed that 'Communism is aiding *peronismo*' (a thesis obviously designed to alienate the promoters of *peronista* 'resistance' from the traditionally anti-Communist *peronista* masses), President Aramburu put his signature to a remarkable new piece of legislation. This was Decree 4161, which formally banned the use of *peronista* symbols, slogans and denominations, and forbade the very mention of Perón, Evita and anything *peronista*. The loose wording of the decree made it applicable, at the government's whim, even to very far-fetched euphemisms. The absurdity of trying to erase by fiat a decade of Argentina's recent past was cunningly exploited by dissident humorists, who produced hilarious tracts in which possibly objectionable names and references were systematically replaced by the words 'Decree 4161'. Just as sex was for long the most noticeable component of Christianity because it was the one thing everyone studiously avoided mentioning, Perón and *peronismo* were made even more central to Argentine political life by Decree 4161.

The decree was also the last straw for many military men who had been willing to go along with Lonardi's version of the *Revolución Libertadora*, but saw the Aramburu version as creating something far more objectionable than the authoritarianism and corruption of the Perón years. They began to plot in earnest, securing the participation of two generals, Valle and Tanco, several colonels and a number of civilian 'resistance' leaders.

They rose in arms just after nightfall on 9 June 1956. In the large military complex of Campo de Mayo, Colonels Cortínez and Ibazeta led out the infantry group of the school for non-commissioned officers, and the services group of an armoured unit, while a handful of non-commissioned officers took over the Army School of Mechanics. In La Plata, a company of infantrymen under Captain Morganti, three Sherman tanks commanded by Major Pratt and 200 civilians took to the streets and laid siege to the Provincial Police Department and the headquarters of the Second Army Division. A unit in Santa Rosa, capital of the province of

La Pampa, declared for the rebels. In Avellaneda, the industrial city across the Riachuelo from Buenos Aires, military and civilian rebels attacked the headquarters of the Second Military Region, while others moved into a technical college to set up General Valle's headquarters and a clandestine radio station.

The manifesto signed by Valle and Tanco underlined 'the totalitarian monstrosity' of Decree 4161 and described the Aramburu régime as 'a cruel and pitiless tyranny'. It rejected both the proscription of the *peronista* majority and the economic policies that meant 'hunger for the workers' and 'the return of the country to the crudest colonialism through the sell-out of the fundamental sectors of the economy to international capitalism'. Its basic demand was a call for free, open general elections within 180 days.

But few people ever heard the manifesto. The attack on the Avellaneda Army headquarters was repelled by the police, who rapidly fell upon the group attempting to set up the rebel radio station. The uprising in Campo de Mayo also did not go far, the remaining units stayed loyal to the government and the rebels were quickly isolated. Only in La Plata did the rebellion seem to stand a chance, though for some reason the revolutionaries failed to take advantage of their initial superiority, allowing the loyal forces to mount an effective counter-attack. At midnight, the government decreed a state of siege and put the country under martial law; the decision had been taken to stamp out the uprising with a severity that would dissuade anyone from following the rebels' example. Before dawn the state radio was announcing that all pockets of rebellion except Santa Rosa and La Plata had been subdued, and inflated statistics of executions by firing squad were released. Less than twelve hours after the uprising started, it was all over. Twenty-seven men were summarily court-martialled, sentenced to death and executed by firing squad. Rodolfo Walsh, in *Operación Masacre*, tells the story of a group of twelve other people, detained (most of them by mistake) before martial law was declared, whose shooting was ordered, without benefit even of a court-martial, by the Chief of Police of Buenos Aires province, Colonel Desiderio Fernández Suárez. The deed, performed at night on a rubbish dump, was so badly botched that seven of these men managed to survive, and the ensuing cover-up involved the hierarchy of the régime all the way up to President Aramburu, and the shameful acquiescence of the Supreme Court. This is Walsh's summary of the twenty-seven executions carried out according to the book:

The six men led by Colonel Yrigoyen who tried to set up Valle's headquarters in

Avellaneda, and who surrendered without offering resistance, are shot at the Regional Unit of Lanús at dawn on 10 June. Colonel Cogorno, head of the uprising in La Plata, is executed in the first minutes of the 11th at the barracks of the 7th Regiment. The civilian Alberto Abadíe, injured during the shooting, is first *cured*. It is only on the 12th that he is ripe for the firing squad, which he faces in the forest. On 12 June at mid-day, Colonels Cortínez and Ibazeta and five subaltern officers are tried in Campo de Mayo. The court-martial, presided over by General Lorio, decides against the death penalty. The Executive Power leaps olympically over this judicial decision and issues Decree 10,364 condemning six of the seven men to death. The order is carried out at 3.40 in the morning on 11 June, next to an embankment. At the same time in the Army School of Mechanics the four non-commissioned officers who had taken it over temporarily are shot, and in the National Penitentiary three non-commissioned officers of the 2nd Regiment of Palermo, who were allegedly 'involved'. Some time later I spoke with the widow of Musician Sergeant Luciano Isaías Rojas. She told me that on the night of the uprising her husband had slept at home with her. On 12 June General Valle turns himself in, in exchange for an end to the killings. He is shot that very night. This adds up to twenty-seven executions in less than seventy-two hours in six different places. All of them are qualified by Article 18 of the National Constitution, in force at the time, which says, 'The death penalty for political motives is banned forever.'

The matter did not end there. Arrests of alleged conspirators in the June uprising continued well beyond the end of the year. The ill-treatment of political prisoners became so notorious that it evoked an unusual statement of condemnation from the Unión Cívica Radical. But neither the executions nor the imprisonments deterred the *peronistas*. Indeed, 'resistance' moved into the political and labour fields and began to pick up strength steadily towards the end of 1955. The state of siege remained in force, and the government responded to strikes and stoppages by promptly declaring them illegal. Aramburu claimed that 'Communists and Nazis' were threatening the state and ordered police raids on a number of organisations accused of being Communist 'fronts': the Argentine League for Human Rights, the Union of Argentine Women, the Argentine Council for Peace and the Argentine House of Culture. Conspiracies, real and fabricated, began to be seen everywhere: General Bengoa, Lonardi's War Minister, was arrested once and General Uranga, Lonardi's Transport Minister, twice. All told, some 600 people were being held in the régime's prisons without benefit of trial by the time the summer of 1956 arrived.

Again it was to be an unusually active summer. The *Revolución Libertadora* was entering a decisive political stage: the step-by-step restoration of institutional rule it had promised from the outset. A new statute was enacted to govern the political parties, clearly designed to keep the *peronistas* proscribed, and a commission was formed to study the reform of the Constitution. The leading actors began to prepare for electoral strife. A convention of the Unión Cívica Radical selected Arturo Frondizi as its Presidential candidate, but this only precipitated a split in the party. Frondizi and his followers, who favoured the 'integration' of *peronismo* in the country's political life, chose to be called Unión Cívica Radical Intransigente (UCRI), while the fiercely *antiperonista* faction headed by Ricardo Balbín renamed itself Unión Cívica Radical del Pueblo (UCRP). From afar, Perón joined the fray by appointing John William Cooke, at the time locked up in the Patagonian prison of Río Gallegos, leader of the *peronistas* in Argentina. Perón's letter said, 'I recognise in him the only chief who has my mandate to preside over the totality of the organised *peronista* forces in the country and abroad, and his decisions have the same validity as mine.'

From his cell, Cooke immediately defined his strategy. 'There is not a single case', he said, 'of a people that, having been deprived of its rights by violence, managed to reconquer them by electoral means; but there is not, either, a single case in which a people reconquered its rights by a coup, nor a single example of an insurrection that was not the result of a process in which political struggle was the main factor of organisation, exacerbation and elevation of the general revolutionary preparedness, culminating in the conquest of power and the establishment of a revolutionary order.' This was translated into a year of union agitation, sabotage of factory installations, strikes and terrorist bombings. An attempt to begin guerrilla operations in the northwestern province of Catamarca was foiled by the security forces in early 1957, but the morale of the 'resistance' was boosted in March, when John William Cooke and five fellow-prisoners (the financier Jorge Antonio, former CGT leader José Espejo, former Congressman Héctor Cámpora, Pedro José Gómez and Guillermo Patricio Kelly) pulled off a daring escape from the Río Gallegos prison and drove to safety across the Chilean border.

Aramburu announced that elections would be held for a constituent assembly in July that year, and general elections in February 1958. He would hand over the Presidency, he said, no later than June 1958. His Air Force Minister resigned in protest over the lateness of the date, harassment of the *peronistas* continued, and the Army was thrown into turmoil over the removal and later reinstatement of General Ossorio Arana; Buenos Aires was shocked by the murder of Marcos Satanowsky, a prominent lawyer and stockbreeder (as it later transpired, at the hands of one of General Quaranta's hired assassins), but Aramburu braved it out, lifting the state of siege in June and freeing over 150 political prisoners. The elections for the constituent assembly were held on time, and watched attentively by political analysts, who saw them as a dress rehearsal for the general elections of 1958. With the *Peronista* Party proscribed, its strength was measured mainly in terms of the blank protest votes cast by its adherents. They totalled just under a quarter of the electorate. Also revealing was the result of the split in the Unión Cívica Radical; Ricardo Balbín's UCRP led the field with 24.2 per cent of the vote, while Arturo Frondizi's UCRI took 21.2. per cent. All the other parties combined attracted only 30.3 per cent of the electorate. The constituent assembly itself had an unspectacular life, punctuated by angry walkouts by one group after another, but it ended by scrapping Perón's constitutional reform of 1949 and reinstating a slightly modified version of the 1853 Constitution. The ban on re-election of the President was reimposed, and the provisions for state ownership of the country's natural resources were scrapped, as were the several 'bills of rights' introduced by the *peronista* régime. In their place, however, the constituent assembly included an expanded Article 14, reiterating and even enlarging some of *peronismo*'s social innovations. The new Article 14 read as follows:

All the inhabitants of the Nation enjoy the following rights according to the laws regulating their exercise: to work and exercise any licit industry; to navigate and trade; to petition the authorities; to enter, remain in, travel through and leave Argentine territory; to publish their ideas in the press without prior censorship; to use and dispose of their property; to associate with others for licit purposes; freely to profess their religion; to teach and to learn.

Work in its diverse forms will enjoy the protection of the law, which will ensure for the worker: dignified and equitable working conditions; a limited working day; paid rest and holidays; fair remuneration; a minimum and adjustable vital salary; equal pay for equal work; participation in the profits of enterprises, with control of production and collaboration in management; protection against arbitrary dismissal; stability for the public employee; free and democratic union organisation, recognised through simple inscription in a special register.

Trade unions will be guaranteed the following: the negotiation of collective agreements; recourse to conciliation and arbitration; the right to strike. Union representatives will enjoy the necessary guarantees for the fulfilment of their unions' activities and in connection with the stability of their jobs.

The State will grant the benefits of social security, which will be integral and unrenounceable. In particular, the law will establish mandatory social insurance, which will be in charge of national or provincial entities enjoying financial and economic autonomy, administered by the interested parties with participation of the State, without any duplication of contributions; adjustable retirement pay and pensions; integral protection of the family; defence of the family's welfare; economic support for the family and access to a worthy dwelling.

But far more than the labours of the constituent assembly, it was the buildup for the 1958 Presidential elections that captured public attention. The last months of 1957 were a time of great tension. *Peronista* strategy was divided. On the one hand a number of *peronista* leaders, mainly from the provinces and with some following of their own, proposed adaptation to the new rules of the game laid down by the military régime. This meant abandoning their overt identification as *peronistas* while retaining the basic principles of *peronismo*. These *neoperonistas*, who had the blessing of Jorge Antonio, ran into stiff opposition from the party leadership under Cooke, who saw them as a factor of disintegration and debilitation of the movement. His own strategy was that of presenting *peronismo* as a united, intransigent bloc, and to drive home to everyone that no political solution would be possible without acknowledged *peronista* participation. The régime was equally divided in its response to the *neoperonista* phenomenon; while some agreed obliquely with Cooke and saw the appearance of *neoperonista* parties as a 'safe' way to integrate *peronismo* into the country's political life, others feared that the division between hardliners and *neoperonistas* was only superficial, and that the latter would ultimately be used by Perón as a Trojan horse for his return to power. Hardline *peronismo* kept up the pressure on the régime. In September the telephonists and telegraphists went out on strike and the '62' *peronista* union bloc staged a series of stoppages. The government responded by reimplanting the state of siege, ostensibly to prevent 'sabotage', and the union response was a wave of strikes by the meatpackers, bank clerks and insurance employees. As the government lifted the state of siege a month later and decreed an amnesty for the *peronistas* who had been imprisoned or had charges pending, the 'resistance' replied with a wave of terrorist bombings. The oil pipeline from La Plata to Buenos Aires, for example, was dynamited four times in rapid succession. The government refrained from returning to state of siege legislation, but began to pick up members of *peronista* cells in La Plata, Rosario and Tucumán.

In December, Argentina's centre of political gravity moved beyond its borders to Caracas, the capital of Venezuela. Perón had moved there from Panama, and several of the leading figures of the *peronista*

movement — Cooke, Antonio, Borlenghi — flew there to obtain from
el Líder an arbitral decision on the strategy to follow: stepped-up guerrilla
action or electoral participation through the *neoperonista* parties, who had
recently formed a countrywide alliance. And they were not the only
pilgrims to Caracas; there was also one Rogelio Frigerio, trusted advisor
to the UCRI's Presidential candidate, Arturo Frondizi. His job was to
propose to Perón an electoral pact.

Perón had left Panama in mid-1956. After another brief trip to Nicaragua, he flew to Caracas and, with Isabelita, settled there. Visitors say
he devoted much of his time to reading; not only his favourite Plutarch
but also Churchill's memoirs were seen open on his desk. But he also
spent much time writing letters, discussing political strategy and tactics
with Cooke, exchanging views with Jorge Antonio, and letting even
minor *peronista* leaders know that their leader still remembered and cared.
His Venezuelan exile was not a carefree one. The Argentine embassy
under General Toranzo Montero became the staging point for one
attempt after another on his life. Most of these were nipped in the bud by
Venezuelan National Security, and at least two failed because their
would-be perpetrators switched allegiances and told all they knew. Yet
the assassins came very close to success once, on 7 May 1957, when a
bomb exploded in his car only a few minutes before Perón was scheduled
to go out in it.

In spite of the full mandate Perón had given Cooke over 'all organised
peronista forces', he did not completely withdraw authorisation from
rival tendencies within the movement. Indeed he kept every possible
option open, encouraging initiatives with ambiguous statements that
gave every active leader the impression that, whatever was being said
publicly, *el Líder* was really on his side. Analysts were later to describe
this euphemistically as Perón's 'pendulum' tactics. But inevitably , direct
confrontations with him were bound to arise, such as in the conclave
held in January 1958, with Jorge Antonio pleading the case of the *neoperonista* option, and Cooke, Borlenghi and Kelly insisting on unequivocal approval of a revolutionary strategy.

Publicly the outcome of the meeting was hard to discern, as each party
returned to the fray claiming that they, and not the others, were carrying
out Perón's true will. In actual fact Perón had leapt over both options in
favour of the deal offered by Rogelio Frigerio on behalf of Arturo Frondizi and his UCRI. Essentially, Frondizi asked for the *peronista*
votes — which were bound to secure him the Presidency — in

exchange for a number of commitments: return of the CGT to the
workers, legalisation of the *Peronista* Party, enactment of a new trades
union law, revision of all the legislation enacted by the *Revolución Libertadora*, replacement of the Supreme Court, an end to the interdictions
still weighing on prominent *peronistas*. One of Perón's aides recalls
asking him if he really believed that Frondizi would honour these commitments. He says Perón slapped him on the knee, laughing, and said,
'But of course not! All political pacts are signed in bad faith!'

The conclave was virtually Perón's last act in Caracas. Towards the
end of January the régime of Marcos Pérez Jiménez was toppled by a
revolution, and the new rulers were known to be friendly to the
Argentine military. The word spread that advantage would be taken of
the general confusion to make a new attempt on Perón's life, so he took
refuge in the embassy of the Dominican Republic. On 28 January the
Dominican ambassador, wielding a sub-machine-gun, escorted Perón to
the airport and put him aboard a plane for Santo Domingo. There he was
cordially greeted by the dictator Rafael Leónidas Trujillo, *el Benefactor*,
who housed Perón comfortably for what was to be the longest stretch of
his exile in Latin America itself.

From Santo Domingo Perón continued to lay a smokescreen around
his true intentions for the imminent elections in Argentina. He told the
press that 'the interdictions and pitiless persecution unleashed on the
people render the elections completely null and void.' Then he seemed to
rule out the *neoperonista* option by stating that 'participation in these
elections by any party means that it does not belong within *peronismo*;
any *compañeros* who have accepted nominations as candidates must
resign.' Unwittingly, the newspaper *La Prensa* helped Perón by
publishing alleged letters of his, said to have been found in his Caracas
residence after his flight. One of these letters said, 'Frigerio has tried to
see me, saying that he had Frondizi's mandate, but I refused to see him,
for neither the movement nor myself are in favour of collusion. How
could I face my own people if I were aligned with the traitor Amadeo,
the arsonist Ghioldi and the weakling Frondizi? [. . .] In the eyes of
good *peronistas* the elections of the 23rd do not exist.[. . .] Every ballot
should be inscribed with the protest of free men.' In Buenos Aires,
Frondizi was singing the same tune: 'They are trying to say that our candidacies are subject to compromises and secret pacts.[. . .] I am not
bound by any commitment other than the one I publicly contracted with
the people, when I said that under an Intransigent Radical government
there shall be no persecutions or proscriptions.'

Only two days after this statement and five before the polls, John William Cooke, who had set up a '*Peronista* Tactical Command' in a house in Buenos Aires, announced that the order for all *peronistas* was to vote for Arturo Frondizi. The elections were held as scheduled on 23 February 1958. With the support of the *peronistas*, Arturo Frondizi swept the board, claiming 41.4 per cent of the vote. The runner-up, the UCRP's Ricardo Balbín, attracted 25.3 per cent. On 1 May 1958 Frondizi was installed as President. The War Minister, General Héctor Solanas Pacheco, proclaimed that 'serving the civilian power is the Army's mission'.

12

DEVELOPMENT ON BORROWED VOTES
(1958–1961)

Just a few years before Perón was born, Arturo Frondizi's parents, Julio and Isabel, emigrated to Argentina from their home town of Gubbio, in Central Italy. They settled in the province of Corrientes, where Julio became a relatively prosperous building contractor. They had fourteen children; two died and seven boys and five girls survived. Arturo, the last but one, was born in Paso de los Libres, just across the river from the Brazilian town of Uruguayana, on 28 October 1908, only a few months after Argentina's first oilwell was discovered in faraway Comodoro Rivadavia. When Arturo was four, the family moved south to Concepción del Uruguay, in the province of Entre Ríos. His formal education started there, in a small private school, but by the time he was ten his parents decided that it was time to take him to Buenos Aires. There he travelled with his mother and his sister María and was enrolled as the only boy in a school for girls. His primary school finished, he returned to Concepción del Uruguay to begin his *bachillerato* studies.

Arturo was not an outstanding student in those early years. More often than not, he barely scraped through with a 'pass' from one year to the other. He much preferred to be out playing soccer, or participating in school athletics. But then school was not the only source of intellectual food for him; round the table at home, he regularly heard his elder brothers embark on passionate debates about current philosophical and scientific issues. From his eldest brother Américo he inherited an interest in the German idealists that was to take him on a decisive intellectual journey, exploring Fichte, Schiller, Schlegel and Schelling, and finally discovering Hegel, whose dialectics were to become the pattern for much of his own later thinking. And Arturo did some reading on his own. One of his early passions was Napoleon. A Napoleonic anecdote he cherished as a lesson for his own conduct was that of the general who, fearing that his lack of physical courage might betray him, used to order his men to tie him on to his saddle before he rode into battle. In later years he would say, 'It would be terribly dangerous for me to take fright, because I am not at all brave.'

After two years at Concepción del Uruguay, Arturo was sent again to Buenos Aires to finish his *bachillerato*. When he was in his fourth year he decided to have a go at a career in the military and took the entrance examinations to the Colegio Militar. Unable to answer a question about the sphenoid bone, he flunked Anatomy. This military urge was obviously not very strong, for he did not try again. Instead he plunged back into his *bachillerato* studies, suddenly revealing himself as the possessor of a brilliant intellect. His interest in sports did not dwindle, to the point that he reached the finals in an inter-school boxing championship. But other things were occupying more and more of his time. Napoleon was forgotten, to be replaced by a more lasting idol, Niccolo Machiavelli. An essay on *The Prince* was one of the many which the young Arturo wrote and had published in student journals; 'Nationalism in the classrooms' was much commented on by his cronies, and 'What is the Fatherland?' earned him a gold medal in his last year. Politics had begun to emerge, if not yet as a vocation, at least as his overriding interest. Unusually for a young intellectual of his age, he was drawn to the Unión Cívica Radical, the ruling party at the time. And his interest was not limited to the field of political theory; he loved to learn, especially from the porter at his school, about the intricacies of political horsetrading in the neighbourhood committees.

Yet when he entered the Faculty of Law of Buenos Aires University, he made the firm commitment not to get embroiled in student politics. His target was to rush through his courses at breakneck speed, so as to emerge with his diploma as a lawyer three years later, and although he did indulge in some political writing, he stuck doggedly to this commitment. Indeed his active political life was only to begin after his graduation with honours in 1930. On 6 September 1930 he watched the troops passing his home on the way to oust Hipólito Yrigoyen. The shock spurred him into action. He rushed around trying to organise student resistance to the coup, discovering to his consternation that most of his fellows were joyfully celebrating the downfall of *el Peludo*. He made contact with Radical party leaders, attended meetings, helped organise the disruption of the University Council, and finally got himself thrown into Villa Devoto prison for wresting the reins from a mounted police officer during a street demonstration.

Prison, brief as his confinement was, did two things for Arturo Frondizi. First, it led him to decide that he would henceforth devote all his efforts to politics, and secondly, it brought him closer to Elena Faggionato, the girl with parents from Gubbio that Frondizi's mother had already chosen as his ideal bride. Frondizi had regarded his mother's matchmaking efforts as little more than a joke, but during his incarceration Elena wrote to him, revealing an unsuspected depth of feeling. On his release, Frondizi hurried to express his gratitude, but this limited purpose somehow became transmuted into the beginning of a courtship that culminated three years later in their marriage.

Arturo Frondizi took to politics like a fish to water. Within a few months he was already a delegate to the congress of the Radical youth. His professional defence of political prisoners earned him a reputation that led to his nomination as Secretary of the Argentine League for Human Rights. He embraced the cause of the Republic during the Spanish civil war, campaigned against racism and anti-Semitism, and spoke publicly against the concessions granted to foreign-owned public utilities. Within the UCR, though for a short while a protégé of Alvear's 'anti-personalists', he came to be aligned with the broader *Yrigoyenista* faction; however, he kept his distance from the more intransigent group that eventually created FORJA, the strongly nationalist intellectual powerhouse which later swung over to Perón. During the pre-war years, Frondizi was a proponent of the formation of a 'Popular Front'; when war broke out in Europe, his sympathies were openly with the Allied cause.

Yet when the colonels of the GOU took power in 1943 and decreed the dissolution of all political parties, Frondizi held back from the wave that, among Radicals as among other political parties, insisted on translating a pro-Allied stance in international affairs into 'democratic' credentials at home. Instead he set about creating a faction within the UCR that aimed at competing with nascent *peronismo* on its own ground, that of populist nationalism. When the country went to the polls in 1946, Frondizi, at thirty-eight years old, was elected Deputy for the UCR. His influence was felt in the preparation of the Avellaneda Programme, in which the Radicals set out the political objectives in terms of which the Perón régime would be judged. They called for the nationalisation of public utilities and monopolies, for agrarian reform and for worker participation both in management and in the profits of industry. Unlike other opposition leaders, Frondizi castigated Perón for not being enough of a nationalist and for being sôft on North American imperialism.

For the 1951 elections, the UCR nominated Frondizi as their candidate to the Vice-Presidency. In 1954 he was elected chairman of the party's National Committee, only to be told by an old veteran, 'What a pity that you have arrived so late. Perón's ouster is already on the cards and you will not have enough time to renovate the party before the presidential elections that will follow the revolution. You will have to split the party in order to be a candidate, and will be forced to depend on outside support to win.' That same year Frondizi published *Petróleo y política* (Oil and politics), a defence of nationalistic oil policies that became an instant success among the party's intelligentsia and even beyond the confines of the UCR. In this book Frondizi attacked the granting of concessions to foreign oil companies, on the grounds that the oil 'majors' preferred to keep them inactive as part of their worldwide pricing strategy. *Petróleo y política* became the cornerstone of the opposition to Perón's attempt to speed up Argentina's oil production through contracts with US oil companies.

Frondizi, who was to see the inside of *peronista* prisons in 1955, came out openly in support of the *Revolución Libertadora*, approving its 'reconstruction programme' and condemning the *peronista* uprising of 9 June 1956. After that fateful event and the ensuing repression, he began to lead his party on an increasingly divergent line, calling for prompt elections, denouncing the régime's attempt to reform the Constitution, and drawing public attention to the ill-treatment of political prisoners. Soon he was on a collision course, not only with the military régime, but also with the more uncompromisingly *antiperonista* faction of the UCR led by Ricardo Balbín. In November 1956 the National Convention of the UCR met in the northwestern city of Tucumán to nominate its candidates for the forthcoming elections. Balbín's followers stayed away, and the Convention duly nominated Frondizi as candidate to the Presidency of the Republic. Fulfilling the prediction made two years earlier, when Frondizi was elected leader of the UCR, this led to a deep split in the ranks of the party, Ricardo Balbín announcing (as we saw above) the formation of the UCRP while those who remained with Frondizi adopted the name of *Intransigente* and formed the UCRI. Only six months later the elections for a constituent assembly showed the full extent of the damage caused by this rift. With *peronismo* proscribed, almost a quarter of the electorate cast blank votes in protest; among the participants, Balbín's UCRP led the field with 24.2 per cent of the vote, and Frondizi's Intransigent Radicals came a close second with 21.2 per cent. More than half the party's votes had been lost by Frondizi; what he had left was insufficient to win the Presidency, even if the *peronistas* again abstained and the rest of the political spectrum remained divided.

Capturing or swaying the orphaned *peronista* vote was, of course, everyone's aim. What is not altogether clear is at what moment Frondizi switched from wooing the *peronista* electorate to the far riskier business of persuading Perón to order his followers to vote for Frondizi. Conventional political wisdom assigns an important role in the adoption of this new tack to Rogelio Frigerio, a man who had worked his way to the position of leading adviser to Frondizi. Frigerio, once a Communist, had been a leading figure in the Confederación General Económica, the employers' association controlled by Argentina's 'new' industrialists during Perón's government. After Perón's downfall he acquired a hard-hitting political journal *Qué*, around which he built a team of intellectuals to campaign along lines that rapidly converged with those of Frondizi. Retaining from his Communist past an ability for neat, well-formulated ideological argumentation, Frigerio wedded this to a technique hitherto only used (and not all that successfully) by Argentina's right-wing nationalists: the formation of a team of men identified with the ideas he proposed and qualified to execute them, and their placement next to the men in power. A former member of the *Qué* team described the early period as 'the wooing of Frondizi'. It was a highly successful courtship and it ended in marriage. In a sense, it was like the coming to life of the mental pictures built by a younger Frondizi from his readings of Machiavelli. Frondizi himself was the Prince; Frigerio was his Machiavelli, secretary and counsellor — or more appropriately, head of an entire secretariat of technocratic counsellors. Parallels have been drawn between Frigerio's relationship with Frondizi and Miguel Miranda's relationship with Perón. But Miranda was only a skilful executor of Perón's policies; the ideologue had been José Figuerola. Frigerio was both Figuerola and Miranda; ideologue and executor. The Frigerio group soon came to be known as the *usina*, the powerhouse of *frondizismo*.

It was certainly Frigerio who converted Frondizi from the nationalistic outlook proposed in *Petróleo y política* to what later came to be known as 'a nationalism of ends rather than of means' — a policy that was to open Argentina to the foreign oil companies and call for direct foreign investment on a grand scale. Few people know exactly how rapidly this conversion occurred, and although Frondizi publicly issued a few broad hints during his election campaign, the bulk of the electorate did not take cognisance of it until after he was installed in the Casa Rosada. But there is more than a suspicion that this major policy shift was not wholly unrelated to the celebration of an electoral pact between Frondizi and

Perón. Among the people with whom Frigerio discussed the new 'open' oil policy was Henry Holland, who as US Under-Secretary of State had negotiated the entry of US oil companies to Argentina during the last years of Perón's government. Holland had left his government post and gone to work for a US banking corporation with strong oil interests, Loeb Rhoades. He had also retained contact with Perón in Caracas, and has been credited with suggesting to Frigerio that an electoral agreement was a distinct possibility.

There was clearly a political price to be paid for the *peronista* votes: the legalisation of *peronismo*, an amnesty, the elimination of repressive legislation and the return of the CGT to the unions. Frondizi was willing to offer that much. But this alone did not do the trick. Perón was bribed. An emissary was sent to Caracas with a case full of dollar bills; many years later both he and one of Perón's entourage independently recalled the embarrassing moment when, after an amiable exchange of pleasantries, the emissary tried to depart discreetly, leaving behind the case — only to be interrupted by the exiled leader, who went straight to the point, asked for the case to be opened and proceeded to count the money.

Thus Frondizi was to arrive at the Casa Rosada on a wave of 'borrowed' votes, having already decided to swerve away from the policies he had previously upheld, knowing that the military were determined to prevent the fulfilment of one of his commitments — the legalisation of *peronismo*. He was to inaugurate a new era in Argentine politics with *desarrollo* (development) as his ultimate criterion. Success was to be measured in stark economic terms, according to the growth rate of the gross domestic product, the statistics of output of the 'basic industries' (iron and steel, petrochemicals, coal), the speed at which the country attained self-sufficiency in oil. This, said Frondizi, was true nationalism; not the empty talk that concentrates on ways and means. Results were the only things that mattered. With Spinoza, he ruled out 'laughing and crying'; his political rhetoric would be unemotional, cerebral. His every move would be well thought out, the costs and benefits coldly calculated. If most of the votes were not his and the power of arms was in hostile hands, his weapons had to be astuteness and skilful manoeuvring. 'Machiavellian' was to become the favourite adjective to describe Frondizi, and although the meaning was usually pejorative, he must have found it flattering. Rodolfo Pandolfi, a journalist who was very close to Frondizi, picks up the theme in his book *Frondizi por él mismo* ('Frondizi by himself'), a long paraphrase of the President's thought:

When he arrived in government Frondizi already had ready a method of political decision-making that fitted his personal traits. He was perhaps the only front-line figure with the true makings of a politician, and he became the builder of a mechanism totally lacking in naivety, Machiavellian — a genre without precedents in Argentina. And there is no value-judgment implied in saying that this mechanism must in future be analysed by every apprentice politician. Its application, however, must be understood solely within the context that made it inevitable. If Machiavelli had had the necessary force to impose his will; if his country, subjected at the time to overwhelming powers, had allowed the Prince to translate his strategy lineally into action, he would not have recommended astuteness as a system.

In later years Frondizi himself would say in response to his critics, 'The question I should be asked is why I agreed to become the President of the Republic in the circumstances. Once that problem is solved, everything else emerges as its logical consequences'.

By the time Arturo Frondizi entered the Casa Rosada, Argentina's population had grown to twenty million; it had increased by a third since Perón's accession to power in 1946, and five times since Perón's birth in 1895. The country's economic structure had also changed quite dramatically. True, just under half of the national product was accounted for by commerce and the services, with the powerful state apparatus built up during the Perón years as the biggest employer and trader. This proportion had remained almost unchanged since the turn of the century, and had provided the power-base for Argentina's huge and atypical middle classes. But the rest of the economy had been steadily altering its composition: agriculture, which in 1900 contributed one-third of the gross domestic product, had seen its share dwindle to about a quarter, while industry, and particularly the manufacturing sector, had expanded to about the same size and was clearly on its way to becoming the leading creator of wealth.

Certainly agriculture had been neglected during the Perón years, but the later attempts to boost its contribution by dismantling the complex controls introduced by *peronismo*, while partly successful, had as their main effect a transfer of income to the traditional agro-exporting sectors without a concomitant upsurge in their economic growth. The country was caught in a bind: its new manufacturing sector, mainly composed of light industries, remained trapped by its high costs within the confines of the domestic market, gobbling up most of the foreign exchange earnings generated by agriculture yet earning none of its own. The conservatives who managed the economy during the three years of the *Revolución Libertadora* attributed this to the inefficiency bred by *peronismo*'s excessively protectionist policies; they believed that industry could be forced into competitiveness by unfettering the market; by allowing the devaluation of the peso to offer an incentive to exports and using tight money policies to curb that new menace, inflation. The combination of these policies, they expected, would also encourage investment, which in turn would lead to rapid and healthy growth. It did not quite work. The formula, borrowed from the experience of the industrialised economies of the north, did not fit the peculiar traits of Argentina's economy, which Marcelo Diamand has described as an 'unbalanced productive structure'.

The farming and cattle-breeding cycle was far too long to allow for an instant reaction to the opportunities offered by devaluation, but the higher peso price for Argentina's agricultural exports did, on the other hand, tend to drag upwards the domestic prices for those same goods (and by sympathy also the prices for other foodstuffs). Almost unique in this among Third World nations, Argentina exported what it ate: beef and grains. So, far from curbing inflation, what was achieved was a further impetus to the spiral of rising prices. Similarly, most of the country's imports were essential inputs for industry; fuel, raw materials, intermediate products. For these there were no readily available local substitutes, so the higher prices caused by devaluation simply meant more expensive industrial goods within the domestic market, not fewer imports. And because industry's costs were so astronomically high when measured against those of Argentina's still extensive farming methods, even huge devaluations did not make their prices competitive on foreign markets. The US dollar had almost trebled in value on the Argentine exchange markets since Perón's ouster, yet industry was still inward-looking, agricultural output had steadied after its initial spurt, and inflation refused to go away.

The answer given by conventional economic wisdom at the time was that the country needed even more of the same in order to break out of this bind. On this there was no basic disagreement between the *frondizistas* and the conservatives. There were, however, some differences of emphasis. While the conservatives insisted on the need to eradicate inflation as an essential first step, and on relying heavily on the country's agricultural sector, Frondizi's team chose the opposite path. They held that inflation in Argentina was a 'structural' problem which would only vanish when the country had completely modified its economy. And this was to be achieved by industrialising on a grand scale, and especially by establishing heavy or 'basic' industries like iron and steel, chemicals and petrochemicals, and by attaining self-sufficiency in energy, accelerating oil production and taking full advantage of the country's hydroelectric and coal resources. Massive import-substitution was the way out of *sub-desarrollo*, underdevelopment, and a certain amount of inflation had to be tolerated as an attached evil in the early stages.

For this to come about, investment was needed on a grand scale. Somewhat simplistically, the *frondizistas* presented the alternatives in this field as a straight choice between sacrificing living standards to enforced savings, on the Soviet model, or opening the doors to foreign investment. The latter option was anathema to Argentine nationalist feeling, which ran high not only among *peronistas* but also among the two factions of the old Radical party. Yet this was the path Frondizi chose, ditching his own earlier convictions and arguing that this was a 'nationalism of ends', aiming ultimately at the attainment of true economic independence, while traditional nationalist policies were no more than a sterile 'nationalism of means', self-defeating in that they would keep the country bound by the chains of *subdesarrollo*.

The full implications of this shift in Frondizi's thinking did not really become apparent until after his election, although it is possible, with hindsight, to detect hints and rather oblique references in his campaign speeches at home, and explicit statements in interviews he granted the foreign press at the time. For many of his supporters and electoral allies, the Frondizi who had arrived at the Casa Rosada in May 1958 was the man they admired for the ideas expressed in *Petróleo y política*. Even his enemies shared this impression, and went even further, claiming that at heart Frondizi was a Communist (ever since his days as a student the right-wing political press had portrayed him as a marxist, an image often reinforced by his frequent recourse to a brand of dialectics which his friends insisted he really owed to his studies of Hegel).

Yet it was Machiavelli, rather than Hegel or Marx, that inspired the blitz launched by Frondizi as soon as he was settled behind the Presidential desk. The author of *The Prince* had strongly recommended that rulers should take all the necessary disagreeable measures as soon as possible, in a swift, sharp blow. This piece of advice was taken literally by Frondizi; in the first three months of his Presidency he produced a barrage of measures that left the country gasping for breath — and which managed to alienate a number of influential segments of the population. The CGT was returned to the unions and a new Law of Professional Associations was announced, restoring the principle of a centralised, unified labour movement. Needless to say, this enraged the *antiperonistas*, civilian and military, who felt that all their efforts of the previous three years were being wiped out at a stroke. Their anger increased when Frondizi eliminated Decree 4161 and its attendant repressive legislation and decreed a general amnesty, opening the doors for the proscribed *peronistas* to return to legality. The new oil policy, followed swiftly by a string of contracts with foreign oil companies, shocked most of those who held left-of-centre views, including many of Frondizi's own partisans, while on the Right it became the motive for allegations of corruption, mainly aimed at Frondizi's trusted aide, Rogelio Frigerio. The new, liberal rules for foreign investment evoked cries of 'sell-out!' from nationalists across the board, while a law allowing the establishment of private universities ran up against fierce resistance from most of the student body, which still adhered to the laicist and statist principles of the 1920 University Reform and saw this move as the first step towards restoration of clerical influence in education. Demonstrations, riots and street battles between rival student groups over this issue continued for months.

Machiavelli's formula of the swift, sharp initial shock was completed with the recommendation that beneficial measures should later be dosed out, a little at a time; thus anger would be concentrated in a short spell, and gratitude constantly reinforced over a long period. Here Frondizi departed from his mentor, perhaps also mindful of Machiavelli's gloomy view of the prospects of those rulers who come to power on borrowed strength. Frondizi attempted from the outset to transform and consolidate the electoral support he had received from the *peronistas* by offering the unions a 60 per cent, across-the-board wage increase. But even as he did this, the essential weakness of his position had come to the centre of political speculation. Only five days after the inauguration of his Presidency, in faraway New York the *Wall Street Journal* was asking itself how long he would last.

The question mark that hung over the return of *peronismo* to the political arena was matched by another, over the future behaviour of the armed forces, where fiercely *antiperonista* feeling still ran high. From the beginning military opinion was divided between those who were willing to accept the reappearance of *peronismo*, albeit in a 'domesticated' form, and those who felt it had been a big mistake to return to elected rule before the task of de-peronisation had been completed. Among the latter, the fact that Frondizi had been elected thanks to the *peronista* votes was itself seen as an intolerable insult. It has been suggested time and again that Frondizi was far too much in awe of the military to include them in his initial blitz and, playing on their underlying urge to leave politics and return to a professionalist role, swing them over decisively to his side. Indeed he is said to have turned down an offer, made by 'professionalist' colonels, to stage a 'preventive' coup that would have done away with the diehard *gorila* generals. General Justo León Bengoa is quoted in Pandolfi's *Frondizi por él mismo* as saying that 'Frondizi arrived at the Presidency marked by the inferiority complex felt by intellectuals towards all those who represent force, be they military men or financiers, and never discovered that those forces can be won over by a voice of command, an energetic shout; his first battle should have been fought in the very centre of power, the Army, an institution accustomed to obey orders — the habit of obedience instilled in them as cadets at the Colegio Militar, but incompatible with a deliberative technique that only unnerves it.'

Unease in the military was paired with discomfort in the ranks of *peronismo*, many of whose militants had not taken kindly to the abandonment of Cooke's earlier insurrectionist tactics. Terrorism, waves of strike action, military *planteos* (demands) and attempted coups were to succeed and overlap each other at a dizzying rate throughout Frondizi's four years as President, punctuated in public attention by Argentina's current substitute for the UFO: the appearance of mysterious submarines off the southern coasts. The first terrorist bomb went off before Frondizi had spent a full month in the Casa Rosada, placed by diehard *antiperonistas* in the offices of Cooke's Comando Táctico Peronista. Two days later the Navy reported the sighting and pursuit of the first unidentified submarine in the waters of the Golfo Nuevo. Then the second bomb exploded in the hands of a *peronista* union activist, and a third blew up an empty bus in Buenos Aires. This was followed by a month-long doctors' strike and the announcement by a group of UCRI lawyers that the military were already plotting to overthrow the government.

By the time Frondizi's policy blitz was over, there had been strikes by the bus drivers, postmen, water and sewage workers, meat packers and railwaymen; student clashes throughout the country; a police mutiny in the province of Córdoba; major upheavals in the high commands of the Air Force and Navy; and a foiled attempt on Frondizi's life (with proved participation by state intelligence agents) during an official visit to Paraguay. The cost of living had shot up by 23 per cent in only three months, and the rate for the US dollar on the exchange market had risen to 60 pesos, four times its value at the moment of Perón's fall.

Then came an important turning-point for the Frondizi administration. The workers of the state-owned oil corporation, YPF, went
out on strike protesting simultaneously at the rise in the cost of living
and the government's new oil policies. Frondizi publicly announced that
the action was part of 'a plan of strikes with insurrectionist aims', and
decreed a state of siege. It was a virtual declaration of war on the unions,
and thus on *peronismo*, although the official line was to lay the ultimate
blame on Communist infiltration. The turmoil caused by this decision
was compounded almost immediately by Frondizi's Vice-President,
Alejandro Gómez, who stated publicly that the armed forces were plotting against the government. At a stormy session in the Casa Rosada, the
military commanders demanded from Gómez some substantiation of his
claims, and specifically asked him to name his informants. Gómez
refused and a day later resigned. Frondizi's decision not to call for
elections to replace him was to have important consequences later, since
this placed the provisional president of the Senate, a colourless man called
José María Guido, next in the line of Presidential succession.

The Gómez crisis was no sooner over than the railwaymen went out
on strike. Frondizi riposted with a decree mobilising them and placing
them under military command. An attempt by the railwaymen to hold a
mass protest demonstration was broken up with gunfire, and within a
few days some 200 railwaymen were arrested and committed to military
tribunals. The state of siege regulations were tightened with an outright
ban on any broadcasts of a political nature on the country's radio waves.
As 1958 came to a close, the Argentine people heard of a frustrated attack
by insurrectionists on the barracks of the 6th Cavalry regiment at Concordia, Entre Ríos, and of a belated addition to Frondizi's economic
policy package: the decision to eliminate all exchange controls and free
the currency markets. The US dollar leapt up to 67.60 pesos.

The sense of vertigo that dominated the Argentine political scene
became even more acute in the new year. The end of the festive season
was marked by a wave of terrorist bombings in Buenos Aires. These
were mainly crude devices, known as *caños* (tubes) in militant *peronista*
circles, and they usually produced a lot of noise, minimal material
damage and — to begin with, at least — no casualties. They were used
as dangerous tools of propaganda, their purpose being simultaneously to
unnerve the régime and to bolster the combative morale of the militants.
Yet it would soon emerge that both sides could play this grim game:
SIDE agents who infiltrated militant *peronista* circles were known to

encourage the use of explosives, and even taught the militants how to make *caños*, when they did not set them off themselves, in order either to prove publicly the danger of *peronista* militancy or to flush out the more belligerent members of the opposition.

Confrontation between government and unions reached a peak in mid-January, when the meat-packers at the Frigorífico Nacional occupied the whole neighbourhood in a bid to resist the privatisation of this state-owned concern. Their action sparked off a wave of sympathy strikes in nearby factories, and shopkeepers in the *barrios* of Mataderos, Villa Lugano, Villa Luro and Liniers put up their shutters. After three days, the government sent in a 1,500-strong contingent of Federal Police, Gendarmería (the tough militarised border police) and Army troops, spearheaded by tanks, to dislodge the occupiers. As news filtered out of dozens of casualties, the leaders of the '62' *peronista* unions called a forty-eight hour general strike in protest, but the rank and file swept past this measured response, turning it into an indefinite stoppage which was even joined by the non-*peronista* unions. The protest movement did not last long. Almost immediately, the strike leaders were arrested, and police raids were carried out in most local union offices in Buenos Aires' industrial suburbs, while bus and underground drivers were mobilised and placed under Army orders. As the '62' unions lifted the strike a week after it had started, a second wave of *caño* explosions ripped through the city, signalling that there were still those who meant to continue the fight.

In keeping with the government's public reading of the situation, much of the ensuing repression was directed against the Communist Party; its newspaper *La Hora* was shut down and a number of party offices were raided amid much publicity. The point must be made that the Communists were still being kept at arm's length by the *peronistas*, and that the party line at the time was anything but insurrectionist. Indeed the most 'revolutionary' elements of *peronismo* readily described the Communists as conservatives and — remembering the days of the Unión Democrática back in 1946 as well as the more recent *antiperonista* activities of the party — as allies of the 'oligarchic reaction'.

A brief visit by Frondizi to the United States, to confer with President Eisenhower and to convince businessmen of the attractions of Argentina as an investment market, was followed in February by another pro-longed wave of bombings. The targets were now railway terminals, busy downtown street corners, the state's news agency Telam, the train carrying showbusiness personalities to the annual film festival at the seaside resort, Mar del Plata. Then came another bout of strikes, ostensibly protesting at the inexorable rise in the cost of living. Bank clerks and textile workers clashed with the police on the streets of Buenos Aires; the workers of the city's largest power utility, Segba, barricaded themselves behind overturned, blazing cars until they were dispersed by the police in a tough action that left one dead, scores of injured and 144 people under arrest. Ever more frequently the government would call on the Army to overcome the effects of strike action; to run the port of Buenos Aires and the railways, to force back to their desks the bank clerks who had virtually halted the flow of money through an indefinite strike. The prisons, which had been emptied by the amnesty, were again being filled with people held 'at the disposal of the executive power' under state of siege regulations. Recalcitrant strikers were being trucked off to military barracks to have their heads shaved and endure gruelling close-order drill until they gave in, while the more violent were taken before military tribunals for drumhead justice.

The *peronista* unions and their more 'revolutionary' militants were at the forefront of the most violent anti-government actions, but the very real pressure of unabated inflation had expanded the protest movement well beyond the confines of *peronismo*; indeed some avowedly *anti-peronista* unions were among the hardest hit by the government policy of military mobilisation. Publicly, however, everything continued to be laid at the door of the Communists. The end of Frondizi's first year of power was marked by the expulsion of three Communist-bloc diplomats, who were accused of stirring up dissent — and, as the newspapers titillated their readers with accounts of more submarine sightings off the Patagonian coast, by a decree banning the Communist Party. The day after the announcement of this ban, the government and the people of Buenos Aires took to the streets to offer a hearty welcome to a romantic official guest: Fidel Castro.

Castro's triumphant *barbudos* had entered Havana on 8 January 1959, after a protracted guerrilla war which had unseated one of Latin America's more unsavoury dictatorships, that of Fulgencio Batista. At Castro's side at the moment of victory was an equally romantic figure, Ernesto Guevara, a man the Cubans called 'Che', the term used in Central America and the Spanish-speaking Caribbean to identify the natives of Argentina (the word *che*, with almost the same meaning as *hey!*, is one of the most frequent typically Argentine colloquialisms). In those very early days of the victorious Cuban revolution, the saga of the valiant band of bearded revolutionaries who took to the mountains to defy the might of a dictator had captured the imagination of the entire continent. Castro's revolution, then identified as an idealistic nationalist crusade, was quite respectable. His victory had been applauded by liberal opinion in the United States, and in Latin America it was seen in the same light as the ouster of dictators like Venezuela's Pérez Jiménez — and Argentina's Perón. It was well known that Castro's lieutenant, Che Guevara, had been an active *antiperonista* in his student days, before he sallied forth on the Latin American pilgrimage that eventually led him to join the Cuban revolutionaries. Indeed the sympathy displayed by Argentina's *gorilas* for the Cuban revolution made it suspect in *peronista* eyes, to the extent that three prominent *peronistas* who had been living in Havana — Angel Borlenghi, Jorge Antonio and Bustos Fierro (Fierro later became one of the leaders of the *peronista* Left) — sought refuge in an embassy the very day Castro's forces entered the city.

All this did not take long to change. Within a short time Castro became the arch-enemy of the Latin American Right, and polite society in Argentina began to act as if Guevara, one of the country's most remarkable sons, had never been one of their own at all. The Cuban revolution would also become the inspiration and hope of the Argentine Left, precisely at a time when the Left was plunging into a deep revision of its previous attitudes towards *peronismo*, and the left wing of *peronismo* was cautiously considering the possibility of acting together with the non-*peronista* Left. And Frondizi's continuing contacts with Castro's Cuba became one of the reasons for his downfall. At the time, however, it was hard to imagine these developments, since Buenos Aires newspapers only fleetingly carried the image of the Cuban revolutionary leader munching *chorizo* sandwiches on the river-front before turning again to the more familiar vortex of the pressures and counter-pressures that had become inseparable from the daily business of the Frondizi Presidency: a unit of paratroopers placed under arrest for politically-motivated insubordination; the forced resignation of Rogelio Frigerio as a Presidential adviser; the expulsion of a Bulgarian diplomat; and the upsurge of the dollar on the exchange markets to an unprecedented 94.50 pesos, twice the value it had only a year earlier. The to-ing and fro-ing of military discontent led to a rapid succession of changes in the higher echelons of the Army in June 1959, and the government's ouster was narrowly averted by Frondizi's acquiescence in a complete cabinet reshuffle, the key feature of which was the appointment of Alvaro Alsogaray as Minister of the Economy.

Alsogaray, who had left the Army many years before, having reached the rank of captain in the Engineer corps and then successfully devoted his talents to business, had emerged in the political arena as the leader of the Partido Cívico Independiente, a tiny arch-conservative group that spent most of its time castigating Frondizi's economic policies. Alsogaray was a firm believer in monetary stability at all costs, and most of his criticism had concentrated on Frondizi's unwillingness or inability to curb inflation. His formula was simple: a savage cutback in government spending, tight money policies, severe wage restraint and the paring down of the bloated state apparatus, both by thinning the ranks of the bureaucracy and by pulling the state out of economic activities which were demonstrably unprofitable or could be better run by private enterprise. It would have been difficult to come up with anyone more diametrically opposed to Frondizi's and Frigerio's economic outlook.

Both sides attempted to paper over this blatant incompatibility. Frondizi was to claim later that he only appointed Alsogaray after obtaining from him a firm commitment to continue his (Frondizi's) initial economic policies. He added that Alsogaray's task was merely to be the attainment of monetary stability, which had always been envisaged in his plan. This was echoed by Alsogaray himself, who described the whole affair as a relay race in which he had simply taken over from Frigerio for the following leg, (although he actually remained in sole control of the economy until April 1961 and Frondizi himself only outlasted him by eleven months). Frigerio alone was straightforward: he stated bluntly that the military had not given Frondizi much choice.

Frondizi's bid for rapid development had indeed caused the first important spurt of economic growth since Perón's last year in power (the first year of the *Revolución Libertadora* had been one of recession, with production *per capita* dropping by 0.2 per cent, while in the second year it had only increased by 3.6 per cent). Investment had begun to pour in, particularly to the oil industry, but also throughout the manufacturing sector. Argentina, which ended the Perón era with fewer cars than it had had at the beginning, soon saw an inordinate proliferation of car factories, well beyond the ability of its small market to absorb. For the first time in many years, imports of capital goods soared, and the country's industries began to acquire a more 'modern' look. Many of the bigger new industries were subsidiaries or affiliates of North American corporations, the sign that Argentina had finally moved completely out of the British orbit and into that of the United States. However, even though export earnings were running at more than one-third higher than in the last five years of Perón's rule, the upsurge in industrial demand rapidly drained the country's holdings of foreign exchange; even after accounting for the substantial inflow of capital from abroad, Argentina's reserves shrank by some 330 million dollars. And inflation raced ahead from 32 per cent in 1958 to 114 per cent in 1959.

Alsogaray's formula for correcting the imbalance amounted to plunging the country into recession. Production *per capita* dropped by almost 8 per cent during his first year in office. This actually achieved his purpose, cutting back inflation to a quarter of its previous rate in the first year, then halving it again in the second, and building up the country's reserves to a point that allowed another two-year spurt of rapid growth. Yet, inevitably, the cycle was repeated: reserves were again run down (there was a net drop of 291 million dollars in 1961–2), production fell for two years running, and inflation again doubled. By the time this second bout arrived, however, Alsogaray had left the Ministry of the Economy. In the meantime, his harsh methods had ensured even more bitterness in the relations between unions and government, and this in turn encouraged the more militant *peronistas* to step up their bombing campaign.

Hardly a week went by between July and September 1959 without Buenos Aires being rocked by explosions, often in sequences of five or six at a time. And now the *caños* began to prove that they could be lethal as well as noisy and frightening. In July a police corporal was killed by a bomb placed near the Navy Ministry. In August a *caño* exploded in a crowded downtown tea-house, killing a customer. The police identified the author of this last gratuitous act of violence as Benito Atilio Mayo, a former *peronista* legislator, whose name would henceforth become a password among the *gorilas* for *peronista* terrorism. Strikes also became more frequent. A dispute with the metalworkers' union stretched over the entire three-month period, ending only after 800 of their members were arrested. A stoppage by the cane-workers in the province of Tucumán led to a general stoppage in the area and widespread disturbances and clashes with the police which left one man dead in their wake.

The power struggle in the armed forces matched these developments in intensity. The reshuffle in the higher echelons of the Army led a former commander, General Arturo Ossorio Arana, to attempt a rebellion against what he claimed was 'an alliance between Frondizi and Perón'. It fizzled out without violence in a week, but was followed almost instantly by a crisis in the Navy which led to the dismissal of twelve senior admirals and the successive appointment, dismissal and re-appointment of the Commander of Naval Operations. Hardly a month had gone by when the Army commander-in-chief, General Carlos Severo Toranzo Montero (a man who proclaimed publicly that the armed forces were 'the custodians of Republican life against any extremism or total-itarianism', and responsible, in view of the 'failure' of civil authority, for restoring the 'basic values' of public order and national unity), was relieved of his post, only to be reinstated two days later after he had set up a 'rebel command' and threatened to stage a coup.

The spring of 1959 began in Argentina with ninety unions out on strike, news of yet another mystery submarine off the southern coast, and the announcement of a call to partial national, provincial and muni-cipal elections in March of the coming year. Frondizi had already made a public statement to the effect that the *peronistas* would not be allowed to stand; now his Minister of the Interior, Alfredo Vitolo, announced that the Partido Justicialista (the new formal denomination of the *Peronista* Party) would be formally dissolved.

Yet what followed was a weird, tense lull during which union action and terrorist bombings disappeared and even the quarrelsome military seemed to halt their bickering. Certainly, more trouble was brewing under the surface, and at least one disquieting incident marred the peace of that year's summer. Unknown to all but a small circle of *peronista* militants, the notion of repeating the feat of Castro's revolutionaries in Cuba had already begun to gain determined adepts in Argentina. Carlos Díaz, who called himself 'Comandante Uturunco', was one of them. In the latter months of 1959, he sought out young *peronista* militants willing to follow him in the creation of a guerrilla movement of which the initial base would be Argentina's hilly, forest-covered north-west, the only region with a relatively dense and impoverished rural popu-lation — namely the workers of the sugarcane plantations. The outburst of union strife in Tucumán earlier that year and the bitterness still felt at its severe suppression suggested that this might well become Argentina's Sierra Maestra. 'Uturunco's' first coup was planned for a time — Christmas eve — when the security forces were sure to be off their guard. And the target was picked so as to reduce the chances of failure almost to nil: the small town of Frías, in the province of Santiago del Estero, an empty area just north of the country's great salt flats which was also within easy reach of Tucumán. When the day came, 'Uturunco's' small band swooped on the defenceless police station of Frías and made away with their first batch of arms 'captured in combat':

five carbines, five pistols, six revolvers and 500 rounds of assorted ammunition. But 'Uturunco' and his men did not get very far. On New Year's Day the government announced that ten members of the band had been arrested in Tucumán, and another nineteen in the small township of Cochuna. Those who got away did not give up; indeed it later became a mark of honour among revolutionary *peronistas* to have once been an 'Uturunco'. But the collapse of this particular venture put paid for some time to the dream of a guerrilla base in the north.

There were other minor punctuations of that calm summer. A brief, inexplicable spate of anti-Semitic demonstrations spread fear in Buenos Aires' Jewish community. News arrived that Perón had left Santo Domingo and flown to take up residence in Torremolinos, Spain. The Navy mobilised a task force to the Golfo Nuevo to give chase to the last of the unidentified submarines of the Frondizi administration. Helicopters were used to pepper the gulf with new depth-charges provided by the United States (Argentina's destroyers were too slow to use them and 'football teams' were used to kick them out of the helicopters' hatches), and the episode ended with confident claims that the submarine had at least been badly damaged, although it was never actually sighted again.

Then, with less than a month to go to the elections, the truce was over. The national airline and the port of Buenos Aires were paralysed by strikes; the beef trade was brought to a standstill by the meatpackers' unions; police clashed with striking workers and Communist demonstrators, arrested the editor of a *peronista* journal and raided the downtown premises of the *Peronista* Party. A string of bombs caused havoc in the Shell refinery in the province of Córdoba, and as President Eisenhower arrived on a state visit to Buenos Aires, another bomb exploded in the suburban house of an intelligence officer, Major David René Cabrera. The Major's three-year-old daughter was killed in the blast, and, riding the wave of civic and military indignation, Frondizi announced the adoption of *Plan Conintes*, a package of military-controlled security measures only just short of martial law, which had been devised by Perón for cases of 'internal commotion'. Almost instantly the police began to arrest numerous *peronista* activists and leaders, while the *peronistas* responded with a campaign of bombings and sabotage, directed mainly against the railways. When this led to the derailment of a train in the upriver port of Rosario, a state of emergency was declared in that city, and scores of *peronistas* were arrested and dragged before military tribunals which ordered their confinement in military gaols and makeshift prison camps. The Army Commander-in-Chief announced that the intelligence services had uncovered a vast plan of terrorist subversion, but Frondizi, emulating his favourite Napoleonic general who had himself lashed into his saddle, lifted the state of siege and proceeded to hold elections throughout the country.

The results showed just how much ground Frondizi had lost in his first two years in power. The *peronista* leadership, banned from putting up their own candidates, had ordered their followers to cast blank votes. They totalled 2.2 million, or just under a quarter of all votes cast. Ricardo Balbín's UCRP collected most of the 'positive' votes (2.1 million), and Frondizi's UCRI came a poor third with 1.8 million. The remaining 31 per cent of the electorate were split up into forty-one different parties, many of which had a limited, merely provincial scope. The alliance that had brought Frondizi to power in 1958 was clearly no longer in existence, and his own backing was revealed as insufficient. But although the UCRP had emerged as the most powerful of the legally recognised parties, it was clear to all — and especially to the *gorila* generals who were in despair at the evident failure of their attempts at de-peronisation — that neither alone nor in combination with other *antiperonista* forces could they ever hope to compete with whatever electoral alliance the *peronistas* should decide to enter. The balance of political power, in any conceivable electoral future, was undoubtedly held by the *peronistas*. In crude, non-electoral terms, however, it still rested with the *antiperonista* armed forces — a double-bind that dangerously heightened the temptation among the military to opt for a coup, leading to a severe dictatorship that would last for as long as it might take to remove the *peronista* toxin from the nation's bloodstream.

Formally, the armed forces rationalised their intervention in political affairs as the defence of the "basic values" of public order and national unity. In one of the most perceptive analyses of the role played by the military in Argentine politics, the book *Modernización y autoritarismo*, Guillermo O'Donnell says: 'Since it was possible to argue that these "basic values" were implicit in practically all government decisions, the military. . .became the most efficacious channel for the demands of the many *antiperonista* sectors with access to them. Consequently. . .the military became a faithful reflection of the composition, interests and demands of the *antiperonista* sectors of Argentine society. Of course, this direct participation in partisan and sectoral problems destroyed the vertical structures of intra-military authority, led to a number of internal putsches and cut short the careers of many officers.'

Frondizi himself later wrote that the armed forces 'were induced to "filter" the democratic process by those who knew they could never obtain the support of the popular majorities, and who substituted government by "democratic" minorities for government by the people. The armed forces were made the object of a persistent psychological campaign — also aimed at the middle class and the intellectuals — that tended to demonstrate that the imperfections and abuses inherent in an embryo democracy could be cured by legal statutes that only allowed the "cultured" minorities through the sieve. The military, trained in a severely regulated discipline, which works well in compact, highly evolved organisms such as their own, tend to believe that the complex social life of an inorganic community still in a formative stage can also be perfected via the magic of legislation.'

Yet Frondizi was, if anything, the exact opposite of an anti-militarist. He maintained that it was a 'universal' tendency, 'present in all modern states', for the military to demand a greater say in political affairs, in the development of the economy and in the conduct of foreign policy. He enlarged upon the 'national security' rationale that had led Argentina's military to promote industrialisation in the 1940s. Recasting this line of thinking in terms of his own proposal of *desarrollismo*, in a bid to win over to his weak-based cause that ultimate reservoir of power that lay in the armed forces, he wrote, a few years after the Army ousted him from the Presidency: 'Soldiers, sailors and airmen understand the need to participate in the foundation of a basic industry that can become a material guarantee of the sovereignty conquered by force of arms. They promote the exploitation of our energy and steelmaking resources, and install and promote plants for the manufacture of means of transport like ships, airplanes and automobiles, and communications equipment. All this fertile activity is the antithesis of the way a caste behaves. On the contrary, it shows the total identification of the armed forces with the feelings, hopes and efforts of the people to build a sovereign and prosperous nation.'

Frondizi was not alone in accepting, even favouring, an active political role for the military. Using the rhetoric of 'democracy' and eschewing his rationalisations, all the *antiperonista* forces able to find a willing military ear were constantly begging for a *coup d'état* as their only real hope of obtaining power. The *peronistas* still held to the vision of their own movement as an alliance between the workers, 'national' industry and the military, although keeping this illusion alive in face of the determined *antiperonista* stance of the armed forces called increasingly for ideological contortionism. The myth was created of a 'real' Army submerged by its current chiefs; of a batch of young colonels (a clear reminiscence of the role played by the GOU in Perón's rise to power) who felt at one with the *peronista* masses and were waiting in the wings for their chance to strike.

Even the Left, discarding its anti-militarist traditions, had begun to produce apologists for a political Army. The Trotskyist Jorge Abelardo Ramos, once a pariah of the Left for having supported the *peronista* régime because it represented the only 'national revolution' possible in Argentina at the time, regained acceptance during the Frondizi years as the Left plunged into a heart-searching revision of its earlier attitudes towards *peronismo*. Ramos produced in 1959 a much-read book entitled *Historia política del ejército Argentino* (Political history of the Argentine Army). Its central message was summarised in a later work as follows: 'The dominant presence of foreign imperialism and of a mediocre native bourgeoisie allows the Army, in certain critical circumstances, to assume the representation of the impotent national forces or, contrariwise, to become the strong arm of the oligarchy. This dualism is based on the dualism that exists in semi-colonial society, where there is not a single dominant class but two such classes: a traditional one and a weaker modern one. The struggle between both groups, the former linked to the agrarian-export sector and the latter aligned with the classes inte-rested in economic growth, is internalised in the Army and generates within it this same contradiction on another plane.' And Ramos quotes from Isaac Deutscher to claim, 'The Army took upon itself the role of leading the national revolution in Argentina because "the bourgeoisie already existed and the proletariat was still too weak to assume leader-ship." '

The old links between Argentina's Left and the working classes had been severed by the advent of *peronismo* in the 1940s. The Anarchists were already headed for extinction, while Socialists and Communists had aligned themselves with Conservatives and Radicals in the Unión Democrática, on the grounds that *peronismo* was the local incarnation of Fascism and had to be stopped at all costs. They lost. They were also heavily involved later in the struggle against *peronismo* and in the post-1955 *gorila* assault on *peronista*-dominated unions. But apart from a few Communist- and Socialist-controlled unions, their later influence on organised labour was almost non-existent. The vast majority of the *peronista* workers continued to see in the Left the allies of their enemies. The incongruity of the Left's claim to represent the political interests of the working class and the imperviousness of the workers to the Left's overtures forced many left-wing theoreticians to begin wondering if perhaps their original interpretation of *peronismo* had been mistaken. The process of self-criticism ran across the entire range of left-wing thought; it affected the Communists no less than the Socialists and Trotskyists, all of whom began to suffer endless splintering to the tune of the new insights into the nature of *peronismo* and the new strategies and tactics deduced from them.

Revision, which called for discarding a number of old ideological certainties, was surely aided by the growing popularity of Mao Tse-tung's theories of 'national liberation', which recommended an alliance of classes that could be transposed to the Argentine situation; also by the Cuban revolution, which had already moved on to a collision course with the United States, the imperialist power that attracted the enmity of the Left throughout the hemisphere. But it was not a straight translation of these influences; *peronismo* was far too uniquely Argentine for that. The many different ideological nuances of the Left's re-accommodation with *peronismo* are far too numerous and complex to recount here. In essence, they added up to granting new primacy to the 'national question' and posing the struggle for 'national liberation' as the Left's first task — Socialism would come later. At the same time, the Left demanded the setting aside of ideological absolutes in favour of taking the Argentine working classes as they were, which meant accepting that they were *peronistas*.

The annals of *peronismo*, and its public pronouncements and slogans, were scoured for elements that would reveal it as a positive force on the path to 'national liberation'. Whatever fitted the bill was eagerly adopted; the rest was conveniently forgotten. The hard core of the Argentine Communist Party was the one that allowed this new outlook to move it the least; alliance with the *peronistas* became acceptable, but nothing else. Yet splinter groups from the Communist Party, and from successive fragmentations of the Socialist Party, came up with a wide variety of more committed formulas, ranging from strategic alliances, that recognised a community of objectives but retained the Left's individuality, to 'entryism' (joining *peronismo* with the aim of accentuating its revolutionary content from within) and even outright conversion to *peronismo*.

This drift towards *peronismo* of a large segment of the Left began to be met by a leftward drift of *peronismo*'s revolutionary wing. Less evidently, the adoption by the Left, within *peronismo* and outside it, of the rhetoric of 'national liberation', by blurring the previous clearcut distinction between Left-ism and nationalism, also began to affect the thinking of Argentina's small nationalist groupings, hitherto identified with the various colorations of Fascism.

The many pressures on the military, including the increasing willingness of the country's political élite to rationalise military intervention in politics on grounds of 'national security' (though the notion was still basically an economic one), and the derivations of the Left's revised attitudes towards *peronismo*, were to become the most important formative elements of the crisis that engulfed Argentina ten years later. The intervening period would witness the rapid disappearance of the Left as an autonomous political force in the country, the conversion of right-wing nationalist groups to Marxism, the growth of a substantial left wing within *peronista* ranks and, within the military, the eventual marriage of the home-grown doctrine of 'national security' with the notions of 'total war' that emerged from the Second World War, already themselves hopelessly entwined with the ideological confrontation of the Cold War.

13

THE MAN FROM HAVANA
(1961–1962)

In the months immediately following the elections of March 1960 the terrorist bombing campaign changed tempo and style, though not its virulence. Explosions began to be spaced out and targets to be chosen much more selectively, each one becoming a political statement both by identifying the 'enemies of the people' and by showing up the vulnerability of the state's security apparatus, even when fully mobilised under *Plan Conintes*. And casualties became more frequent. A bomb destroyed the offices of the Bemberg group, an industrial and landowning conglomerate that had been expropriated by the Perón government but had later managed to recover its properties; a Bemberg employee was killed in the blast. Several other bombs left a trail of wounded policemen, and in April explosions rocked the Central Police Department in Buenos Aires. Days later a bomb went off in the UCRI party offices, and a fortnight afterwards another bomb, in the Galerías Güemes just off the classy, pedestrians-only Calle Florida, struck panic into downtown shoppers and office workers. Two men were arrested for trying to bomb the Cathedral of Buenos Aires, and towards the end of May a pair of explosions wrecked the house of General Juan Lagalaye, the current head of SIDE, the state intelligence service masterminding anti-subversive operations under *Plan Conintes*.

The sense of vulnerability created by the bombings aggravated the unease in the armed forces, increasing the rate of preventive arrests throughout the country and bringing forth all kinds of allegations about conspiracies, which peaked with the accusation that the Governor of the province of Córdoba was actively involved in subversive activities. Responding to military pressure after the bombing of General Lagalaye's house, Frondizi went to Congress with a stiffer anti-subversion law, announcing to the nation that he would re-establish the death penalty for terrorist-related crimes. Congress flatly rejected this last drastic measure, but approved the rest of the bill, which was rapidly followed by federal 'intervention' in the province of Córdoba. As on many previous occasions, far from calming people down, the stiffening of repression seemed

211

to have an exacerbating effect. Troops under General Fortunato Giovannoni attempted an uprising in the province of San Luis; members of a newly-formed Ejército de Liberación Nacional (National Liberation Army) were picked up by police in the province of Tucumán; the Federal Police were suddenly exposed to a scandal involving many of its members in 'irregularities' (a euphemism for criminal activities); and the Army was submerged in another major crisis, in which a *coup d'état* was only averted after former President Pedro Eugenio Aramburu was called in as a mediator and eighteen generals were forced into early retirement. A spate of strikes broke the fragile truce on the labour front, while *peronista* revolutionaries girded themselves for a more ambitious assault on the régime.

The re-grouped 'Uturuncos', whose attempt at guerrilla warfare in the north had been aborted earlier in the year, suffered a new blow when security forces discovered their cache of arms and explosives in a Buenos Aires suburb on the very eve of a major offensive. Yet other *peronista* groups went ahead with the planned operations elsewhere: one party attacked the guard post of the 11th Regiment in Rosario, another tried to capture the airport of the northwestern city of Salta, and militants in Buenos Aires set off another string of *caños*. But it did not swell into a countrywide uprising; decimation by arrest, lack of coordination, outright fear and the passivity of the *peronista* masses, combined to extinguish the flame almost as soon as it was lit. The most visible outcome of the failed offensive was another wave of arrests (including those of a former Governor of Santa Cruz province and the former Chief of Police of the provice of Buenos Aires).

The electoral defeat suffered by the Frondizi government in March 1960 was followed a year later by another one which sent shivers down military spines and bathed the Left in enthusiasm. Alfredo Palacios, who early in the century had become the country's first Socialist in Congress, was elected Senator for the Federal Capital after a campaign in which he openly identified with the Cuban revolution. A Socialist newspaper devoted its front page to the striking image of a pair of red footprints with the slogan '*Se viene!*' ('It is coming!').

What was coming was not precisely a Cuban-style revolution in Argentina but the visible re-insertion of the Cuban issue into Argentine politics in a way that would rapidly accentuate the vulnerability of the Frondizi government. Relations between Cuba and the United States had already soured to the point where, under Eisenhower, plans had been drawn up for a United States-backed invasion of the island by anti-Castro forces, as a prelude to direct US intervention. In October 1960 John F. Kennedy was elected to the Presidency, inheriting these plans; in March 1961 he announced the programme that would become the cornerstone of his policy of containment of Cuban influence in Latin America: an 'Alliance for Progress' in which the United States would pump billions of dollars into Latin America's economic and social development. Frondizi eagerly took up the banner of the 'Alliance for Progress' as the hemispheric counterpart of his own formula of '*desarrollismo*', but at the same time he insisted that Argentina's partnership in the venture did not imply subordination to United States policies, especially in relation to Cuba. Shortly after Kennedy announced the 'Alliance for Progress' for the first time, Frondizi travelled to the Brazilian city of Uruguayana to confer with the newly-elected President of Brazil, Jânio Quadros. From the Frondizi-Quadros meeting came the 'Uruguayana Agreement', in which the leaders of the two largest nations of South America forcefully stated their refusal to be treated as 'satellites' of the United States. Inevitably this was interpreted by many of Argentina's military leaders as a dangerous commitment to the cause of a Cuba that was clearly going Communist, and revived the old allegations that Frondizi was at heart a Communist himself. Indeed the theory began to circulate in Argentine right-wing circles (feeding on the legend of Frondizi's 'Machiavellianism', the spread of union disaffection and *peronista* insurrectionism, and even on unrelated events like the election of Palacios to the Senate) that Frondizi's true purpose was to 'accentuate the contradictions' within Argentine society, thus creating favourable conditions for the spread of Communism. The 'Uruguayana Agreement' had come only days after the complete failure of the US-organised Playa Girón (Bay of Pigs) invasion, and was followed shortly afterways by Fidel Castro's announcement that Cuba was openly adopting the form of a Socialist republic.

Frondizi felt, however, that there was still a chance of preventing Cuba's drift towards the Soviet bloc, and that this depended on keeping Cuba within the inter-American system. He saw the increasingly tough line adopted by Washington, based on the progressive isolation of the Castro régime (Latin American governments were being unsubtly pressured into severing commercial and diplomatic ties with the island), as inevitably leading Cuba into greater, and eventually exclusive, reliance on the Soviet Union. As recounted by Pandolfi, Frondizi's reasoning, as he himself put it to John Kennedy, ran as follows: Cuba's Marxist régime would not be swept away by direct US intervention, since that would imply the risk of a third world war. Consequently it was only possible to seek a solution in the field of diplomacy, within or outside the inter-American system. If agreement were to be reached outside the inter-American system, Cuba would become part of the Socialist bloc, of which it would become an exasperated expression: its survival would depend on Soviet commitments and this would place it in the area of Cold War frictions. If the solution were to be found within the inter-American system, it would strengthen, on the one hand, the continent as a whole and, on the other, the pro-Kennedy forces within the United States. Thus it would be a victory for the reformists of the hemisphere (Kennedy, Frondizi, Quadros) over the reactionaries and the revolutionaries and insurrectionists.

In Frondizi's view, only four Latin American nations were theoretically capable of acting as mediators between Havana and Washington: Argentina, Brazil, Mexico and Chile. On second thoughts he discarded Chile because of the tensions between its Conservative government and its considerable Communist and Socialist opposition, and both Brazil and Mexico because they sailed far too close to the 'non-aligned' position in international affairs. *Ergo*, Argentina was the ideal mediator. The occasion to set the mediation effort in motion would be the conference, scheduled for August 1961 in the seaside resort of Punta del Este, Uruguay, for the official launching of the 'Alliance for Progress'. And Frondizi's chosen interlocutor on the Cuban side would be that Argentine whom other Argentines had repudiated, Che Guevara.

But before this came to pass, Frondizi still had to live through another bout of acute instability at home. The Uruguayana Agreement was preceded on the domestic scene by yet another major crisis in the higher echelons of the Army, which rid Frondizi of one of the most constant thorns in his side, the coup-bent Army commander-in-chief, General Toranzo Montero, whose place was taken by General Raúl Poggi. He was also able to jettison from his cabinet the man most identified in the public mind with hardship and dwindling pay packets, his Minister of the Economy, Alvaro Alsogaray. Yet this did not ease the pressure on the labour front: railwaymen and bus drivers went on strike, disrupting transportation in the Buenos Aires area, the caneworkers of Tucumán organised a well-publicised 'hunger march', and the CGT announced a militant 'Plan of Action' that got under way with a twenty-four-hour general strike throughout the country.

And although Senator Palacios did not spearhead a revolution, he did bring to the forefront of public attention the abuses that were being committed by the police in pursuance of the *Plan Conintes* anti-subversive drive. In an impassioned speech to the Senate, Palacios produced a *picana*, the modified electric cattle-prod which, he said, was being used by the police of Buenos Aires province to torture detainees. As Congress indignantly decided to form a special committee to investigate the use of torture, the Buenos Aires police responded with an angry and menacing demonstration in Congress square. This was followed, weeks later, by a demonstration of uniformed men from the Federal Police, some of whom fired their pistols at the Palace of Congress, and shortly after that by a police strike in the province of Córdoba, which forced the government to order the Gendarmería into the streets to maintain order.

As the delegates of all American republics began their session in Punta del Este, a group of ultra-nationalist Army officers and law students attempted to spark off a coup by taking over four Buenos Aires radio stations and broadcasting a call to overthrow the government. There was no response to their appeal, and within hours the members of the small band of rebels had either been arrested or put to flight.

Seven days later, Frondizi called the Marine officer in charge of the Presidential guard and said, 'You, sir, are going to drive out to the Don Torcuato airfield. A plane, whose registration number I have written for you on this paper, will land there. A gentleman with a beard will disembark. You are to go with two cars, well armed. You shall invite that gentleman to get into one of the cars and then drive him here, to Olivos. You will protect him, but you will not allow him to speak to anyone, nor will you allow anyone to make contact with him, get near him or speak to him. You will not speak to him either. Just tell him to get into the car. No more.' The bearded gentleman who stepped off the small plane, wearing olive green battledress and a black beret with the five-pointed star that identified him as a *comandante* in the Cuban Army, was Che Guevara.

Ernesto Guevara was born in 1928 into a family that claimed to trace its forebears all the way back to one of Spain's viceroys on the River Plate. An ancestor of his had fought the dictator Juan Manuel de Rosas in the mid-nineteenth century, and failure had driven him up the continent to gold-rush California. Ernesto's grandfather, a citizen of the United States, had brought the family back to Argentina. Born by chance in Rosario, Ernesto spent the first year-and-a-half of his life in the subtropical province of Misiones, in the extreme northeast of Argentina, where his father had a plantation of *yerba mate*, from which Argentina's typical green beverage, otherwise known (outside Argentina) as 'Paraguayan tea', is made. A premature baby, Ernesto was plagued by severe respiratory ailments, to be identified as asthma some time after the family moved to Buenos Aires, where his father had decided to go into the shipbuilding business. Once his ills were recognised for what they were, the Guevaras moved again, out of perpetually humid Buenos Aires up into the dry air of hilly Alta Gracia, in the province of Córdoba.

Ernesto's father encouraged him to practice sports to counteract his asthma, and the boy took up swimming and rugby with such grim determination that he soon became, outwardly at least, the very image of health, full-faced and muscular. His ailment, however, did not leave him, and it was only by unflinching resolve that he kept going; asthma constantly interrupted his attendance at school, but he more than made up for it by working doubly hard at his studies at home, with the end result that he never failed to be top of his class. A linesman armed with an atomiser was always on hand to assist him when his breathing faltered during his rugger matches. Ernesto's father was a left-wing liberal in the European sense of the word, and a fierce anti-clerical, who by word and deed instilled in the boy an attitude of rejection of the social snobbery which was as present in smalltown Alta Gracia as in the large cities. Ernesto was only eleven when he translated his father's teaching into his first act of militancy: the organisation of a gang of youths armed with slingshots, who went out to smash the town's street lights in support of a strike declared by the provincial power workers, which the authorities had tried to break by hiring strikebreakers.

In 1941, when he was thirteen, his family moved to the city of Córdoba, the provincial capital, and Ernesto obtained his father's permission to devote his summer holidays to a solo cycle tour of the northern provinces. It was the beginning of a lasting custom, a wanderlust that would take Ernesto, often on his own and without much money, first across most of his own huge country and later across the whole continent. The toughening that had begun voluntarily as a battle against his asthma was soon to become an imposition, as his father ran into severe financial difficulties and Ernesto was forced to work his way through secondary school. Still a high achiever, Ernesto found time to work, study and even join in *antiperonista* politics, with a clear preference for action rather than speech-making.

Perón was in the second year of his Presidency when Ernesto Guevara entered the University of Buenos Aires to study Medicine. His attitude to university life was hardly that of calm academic study. Instead he aimed at finishing his studies as soon as possible. In the normal course of events, attending all the lectures and sitting for examinations as a 'regular' student, this would have taken seven years. Ernesto chose rather to cram on his own, doubling the normal speed and succesfully passing in three years the examinations normally scheduled for six.

He then interrupted his studies and took off with a fellow-student for the first of his Latin American tours. A motorcycle took them across the Andes into Chile; then they hitchhiked to Perú, crossed the Andes again to visit a leper colony in the Upper Amazon, drifted on a raft downriver to the common border of Perú, Brazil and Colombia, then flew to Bogotá, where they were briefly jailed as illegal immigrants. After an escape that led them across the border into Venezuela, they parted company. Guevara shared a flight to Miami with a cargo of racehorses, and when United States immigration officials refused him entry, returned to Buenos Aires. Within a few months Ernesto rushed through his remaining twelve exams and collected his diploma as a doctor. Four months later, in July 1953, he was on the road again.

A train took him up to Bolivia, where he joined forces with a small group of likeminded Argentine travellers to hitchhike on to Ecuador, then steam by cargo ship up to Panama, and on again by foot or hitched rides up the isthmus into Central America. In San José, the capital of Costa Rica, Guevara met for the first time some exiled members of the Cuban '26th of July Movement'. They were full of enthusiasm for revolution, in spite of having suffered a severe defeat in a frustrated assault on the Moncada barracks in Havana, and spoke glowingly of their leader, a young lawyer named Fidel Castro. They were not alone in their enthusiasm: San José was at the time the headquarters of the Caribbean Legion, an association of liberal politicians from many Latin American nations (some of whom later became Presidents of their countries) who had embarked on a crusade against dictatorial régimes in the continent. Yet Guevara was not impressed by the Cubans. A friend of his recalled that on one occasion, after listening to their ambitious plans, he scornfully turned to the speaker and said, 'Now tell us a cowboy story.' Juan Bosch, a member of the Legion who later became President of the Dominican Republic, remembers Guevara at the time: 'He was intensely preoccupied with what he saw. He seemed dissatisfied with all solutions proposed up to that time, and when he was asked specific questions, he criticised all parties, but never defined his own position.'

Guevara moved on to Guatemala, where he fell in love with the reforms launched by the government of Jacobo Arbenz, who had expro-

priated the lands owned by the United Fruit Company and was trying to
carry out a programme of agrarian reform. He attempted to offer his
services to the Guatemalan government as a doctor, but walked out of
the Health Ministry in anger when he was told that he would have to
become a card-carrying member of the PGT, Guatemala's Communist
Party, before they could give him a job. He kept alive by doing odd jobs,
and spent most of his time discussing politics with other Latin American
exiles. It was at this time that Guevara struck up a close friendship with a
Peruvian exile, Hilda Gadea, who worked in the Guatemalan government agency charged with stimulating industrial and agrarian
development.

When the United States sponsored an invasion of the country by
Guatemalan dissidents and an assortment of CIA-trained mercenaries,
Guevara leapt to the defence of the Arbenz régime. He tried to cajole his
Guatemalan friends into forming armed militias (an initiative Arbenz
quashed) and is said to have helped to transport arms to some of the few
groups that put up resistance, before he was forced to seek refuge in the
Argentine embassy. Unwanted there, he slipped shortly afterwards
across the border into Mexico and made his way to Mexico City, to meet
up with Hilda Gadea, who had preceded him.

Hilda and Ernesto set up house together, and they were married in
May 1955. Through a Guatemalan friend, Guevara had already re-established contact with the Cuban exiles of the 26th of July Movement; his
Guatemalan experience had considerably changed his mood towards
them, and he had become very friendly with their leader, Fidel Castro,
and with his brother Raúl. Raúl Castro was best man at Guevara's
wedding.

There was not much of a honeymoon. Guevara was soon involved in
the Cubans' plans to start armed insurrection in their country, and had
been accepted as their doctor. He underwent military training under
Colonel Alberto Bayo, a veteran of the Spanish civil war, and in
November 1956 embarked with them on the *Granma*, the yacht that
took them across the water to the Cuban coast. The Cuban Air Force
and Army attacked them repeatedly before they gained the sanctuary of
the Sierra Maestra, losing forty-two of the original eighty-two members
of their party. Guevara's bravery during the ensuing guerrilla war, his
rise to the rank of *comandante* in Castro's forces, his part in the drive that
cut the island in half — all are part of the legend of Cuba's revolution.
During the fighting Guevara had taken another *compañera*, the Cuban
Aleida March, and after the war he divorced Hilda to marry her.

His later career in the Cuban government is less well known. Installed in the fortress of La Cabaña in Havana as one of the few *comandantes* in the Cuban Army, he was seen initially as a military man. During the first few months Guevara was not much in the news, but speculation linked his name and that of Raúl Castro with the strengthening of PSP (Communist Party) influence to the detriment of the other constituents of the 26th of July Movement. In June 1959, immediately after the first major crisis in the new Cuban government (and only ten days after his marriage to Aleida), Guevara was sent off on a three-month tour of foreign capitals. He travelled to Egypt, Japan, Indonesia, Ceylon, Pakistan, Sudan, Morocco and Yugoslavia. There were rumours that he had been displaced because of his extreme left-wing views. Yet soon after his return, he was appointed head of the Industrial Department of Cuba's National Institute of Agrarian Reform — the spearhead of the revolution in the social and economic spheres — and then put in charge of Cuba's National Bank.

In his new role as shaper of Cuba's economic policies, Guevara came close to Frondizi in at least one area. He was convinced that Cuba's development depended on overcoming the constraints imposed by its single-crop economy; that it was necessary to leave behind the Cuba that exported sugar and imported manufactures, and to create in its place a diversified economy. Import-substitution and the building of an autonomous industrial base were at the heart of his proposals. But from there onwards he parted company with Frondizi; indeed he even parted company with Communist orthodoxy almost everywhere. Guevara not only rejected the use of US investment as the trigger of growth; in his view, the purpose of the revolution was the creation of a 'new man', and this — with all that it entailed regarding the substitution of moral for material incentives — came even before the establishment of a formally 'Socialist' economy. In pursuing this aim, he proposed nothing less than overturning all the accepted criteria for measuring the performance of state-controlled enterprises and even of budgeting the state's revenue and expenditure. On the international plane, he joined Frondizi in castigating the unequal terms on which trade was conducted between industrialised and non-industrialised nations, but Guevara readily extended this condemnation from the industrialised capitalist nations to their counterparts in the Soviet camp.

In 1960 Guevara was travelling again, to Czechoslovakia, the Soviet Union, China and North Korea, hammering out new trade links to replace those that the United States was severing. In 1961 he was appointed Minister of Industry, a position which had been redefined to make him virtually the sole controller of Cuba's efforts at diversifying its economy.

Involved as he was in Cuba's problems, Guevara had not forgotten his native Argentina. Far from it; he had placed a map of Argentina inside the door of the lavatory adjoining his office. 'You know', he told a friend, 'I've got this habit of racking my brains when I'm seated on the throne. I think of Argentina, of its unexploited economic potential, of the advantages it could bring to the Latin American revolution to acquire such a support, instead of having to rely exclusively on a small country like Cuba.' Guevara did not see that support coming from governments like Frondizi's. His scepticism about Frondizi had been with him for some time; indeed just before he began to train with Fidel Castro's small band in Mexico, a friend who was politically close to Frondizi had tried to persuade him to return to Argentina, and Guevara had said, 'Supposing your friend Frondizi should take power and you should become a minister, what could you do? You would have a government full of good intentions, proposing just a few deep changes, but the day you decide to make those changes . . .' Guevara finished the sentence by drawing his finger across his throat from ear to ear.

And that scepticism had turned to bitterness when, following the US oil companies' decision to halt shipments of fuel to Cuba, he had approached the governments of Venezuela and Argentina with a request for supplies. In his own words, 'And what did Frondizi reply? What did Betancourt propose? That we should set up joint study commissions to examine the terms under which they could give us oil. That would have taken months, while we needed oil in the following hours. It was a stab in the back that inevitably forced us into the arms of the Soviets.' And when Guevara heard of Frondizi's offer to mediate between Cuba and the United States, his comment was, 'He will fail. And not only will he fail but he will have given all the reactionaries in Buenos Aires the excuse to overthrow his government.'

On 10 August 1961 Guevara flew to Punta del Este to represent Cuba at the formal launching of Kennedy's 'Alliance for Progress', which had been heralded, somewhat misleadingly, as a US$20,000 million effort to launch Latin America on the path of rapid development. Even ardent supporters of the 'Alliance for Progress' like Frondizi would later admit its shortcomings. In his *Estrategia y táctica del movimiento nacional*, published in 1964, Frondizi wrote: 'The Punta del Este Charter set an arbitrary figure of US$20,000 million for a decade as the minimum amount of external resources needed for Latin America's development. As was well pointed out in a speech delivered in Buenos Aires by the ill-fated Peruvian politician Manuel Seoane, who was visiting us as representative of the Organisation of American States, this sum had been set without a precise study of the real needs. But, he added, ''The problem is not one of US$20,000 million. The problem is one of the security of the Western Christian world, that does not want to be assaulted by the desperation of hunger . . . the problem is not to find out how much it will cost to do things, but how much it costs not to do them opportunely. Consequently, we must influence the somewhat mechanistic thinking of the contemporary accountants of international finance, who calculate in millions what must be spent, often forgetting that they spend more for not having done things at the right time. I do not know what results would emerge from sharp statistics comparing the cost of the military and naval blockade of Cuba with the economic aid that could have been given to prevent the corrosive effects of international Communism.'' This is one of many reflections made by Latin Americans to those responsible for Washington's policies, and which I myself put to Kennedy in long and frank conversations, in which he fully shared that criterion.'

In 1961, however, this kind of criticism was muted. Only one voice was heard casting doubts on the whole project — that of Che Guevara:

'I get the impression that what is intended is to make the latrine a fundamental thing. It improves the social conditions of the poor Indian, the poor black, the poor man who leads a subhuman existence. ''Let us build him a latrine and then, once he is taught how to keep it clean, he can begin to enjoy the benefits of production.'' It should be noted, fellow-delegates, that the subject of industrialisation does not appear in the analyses made by the experts. For the experts, planning means to plan latrines. As to the rest, who knows how it is to be done?

'. . . We have come here to work, to try to fight on the level of principles and ideas, so that our countries may develop, because all or almost all of the delegates have said that if the Alliance for Progress fails, nothing can halt the wave of popular movements — I use terms of my own, but this is what they meant — and we are interested in not having it fail, insofar as it may mean a genuine improvement in the standard of living of the 200 million inhabitants of the Americas.

'. . . We have diagnosed and foreseen the social revolution in the Americas, the real revolution, because things are shaping up along other lines; because an attempt is being made to stop the people with bayonets, and when the people realise that they can take the bayonets and turn them against those who are holding them, those who hold them are lost. But if it is wished to lead the people along the path of logical and harmonious development, by long-term loans of up to fifty years at very low interest rates, as Mr Dillon announced, we are also in agreement.

'The only thing, fellow-delegates, is that we must all work together to make this figure firm here, and to ensure that the US Congress will approve it, because you must not forget that we are faced with a presidential and legislative system, not a ''dictatorship'' like Cuba . . . Things have to be ratified there in the US, and the experience of many of the delegates has been that promises have often not been ratified there.'

There was little doubt in anyone's mind that the 'Alliance for Progress' was an anti-Cuban exercise. But the Punta del Este meeting was also, behind the scenes, about the attempt to reduce tension between Cuba and the United States. Brazil's President Quadros had already conveyed to Kennedy the message that Frondizi was willing to mediate, and whatever Kennedy's expectations might have been, he gave his blessing to the initiative. Among the many people who sought private meetings with Guevara at Punta del Este was an adviser on Frondizi's staff called Jorge Carretoni. He brought with him an official invitation from Frondizi to a private meeting in Buenos Aires. There was an initial attempt to make the whole matter completely secret, but bureaucratic details — such as Guevara's need for a visa — soon spread the news across the River Plate, through the Ministry of Foreign Affairs, to high political and military circles in Argentina. In order to avoid making it look like a unilateral initiative by Frondizi — which would have instantly made him the target for a right-wing backlash — the precaution was taken of officially inviting Guevara to confer with President Quadros a couple of days later. The Brazilians also engineered a private meeting in Punta del Este between Guevara and Kennedy's adviser on Latin American affairs, Richard N. Goodwin (also Kennedy's link with the anti-Castro Cuban exiles in the United States). This signalled to all in the know that Kennedy was aware of what was going on.

On 18 August Guevara secretly boarded a light aircraft bound for the small airfield of Don Torcuato, some 30 kilometres outside Buenos Aires.

The conversation was held between Frondizi and Guevara alone, behind closed doors. Piecing together its development is no easy task, as neither participant produced a firsthand, blow-by-blow account immediately. Guevara discussed the meeting with his friend Ricardo Rojo, who in 1968 included an account in his highly personal biography of the guerrilla leader. Frondizi also discussed the encounter with the political columnist Rodolfo Pandolfi, who in the same year, 1968, published a brief version of the event in his book *Frondizi por él mismo*. In both cases hindsight has obviously affected the selection of highlights in the conversation. Rojo says they talked for an hour and twenty minutes; Pandolfi says 'several hours'. And the two authors disagree on the way the conversation started.

Discrepancies aside, there is no doubt that they discussed Frondizi's offer to mediate between Cuba and the United States. Guevara coolly stated that in his view Latin America's only hope for development and independence lay in armed struggle, based on guerrilla warfare. However, he added that he could see the need for negotiations with the United States and appreciated Frondizi's efforts to mediate in such a venture. Che later admitted to an acquaintance, a priest, that from the very beginning he was convinced that Frondizi would be unable to embark on any sort of mediation, because the military would certainly prevent him.

Yet Frondizi was clear about the limitations of any mediation effort. He told Guevara that the United States would not accept the membership of Cuba, or any other Latin America country, in an extra–continental military alliance. He added that Washington was convinced that Havana was about to sign the Warsaw Pact, which would make any return to 'the Inter-American family' impossible. This, replied Guevara, was not an option Cuba was considering of its own accord; it was being dictated by US aggression. But he went on to say that although it was undeniable that Cuba counted on Soviet military support, Moscow had not demanded a military alliance in the strict sense, nor did Cuba intend to enter such an alliance. 'The United States', he added, 'cannot conceive of one country aiding another militarily without compromising it in every possible way.'

Probing for the basis for an understanding between Havana and Washington, Frondizi tried to get from Guevara an assurance that Cuba was contemplating at least a slow restoration of electoral, parliamentary democracy. Guevara rejected the notion out of hand. He said that in Cuba that was seen as tantamount to plunging the country back into sterile partisan squabbling; two years had already been devoted to banishing that conception of politics, and under no circumstances would a retreat be considered.

Frondizi outlined his own view of how Argentina, through 'developmentalist' policies, was showing an alternative, peaceful route; one of progressive independence from US hegemony. He mentioned the advances already made in plugging the leak caused by dependence on imported oil. Guevara replied that he appreciated Frondizi's aims, but forecast that they would prove unattainable by peaceful means. Cuba shared the same aims, but its earlier experience had taught it not to rely on US investment to further them; Cuba had had one of the highest indices of US investment in the hemisphere, yet US companies had used domestic savings rather than their own funds, demanding monopoly positions in the market, and bleeding the country through inflated profit remittances back to the United States.

The President underlined that political, economic and social conditions in Cuba were hardly comparable with those of Argentina. Always the intellectual, he tried to draw Guevara into a theoretical argument.

'Tell me, Guevara', he asked, 'have you studied Marxism?'

'No, I am not well versed in the problems of Marxism,' he answered. 'I have done some sporadic and unsystematic reading. But I am a Marxist and I am committed to the struggle for power in the whole of Latin America.'

So Frondizi changed tack and began to quiz Guevara on his practical experiences as the manager of the Cuban economy. Disarmingly, Che admitted that the main problem was one of human capabilities.

'During the war', he said, 'the chief in each zone was the bravest, the most courageous, the best shot; not the most knowledgeable or the most intelligent. Once the fighting was over, these gentlemen remained as section chiefs and wished to become leaders of the economy as well as in politics. It is quite clear that the Revolution was politically unable to cast them aside and recall the old specialists. But it is one thing to know how to shoot straight and quite another to direct the economy. That has been the cause of a number of economic disasters.'

Frondizi pursued the same line of inquiry into Guevara's experience as a guerrilla leader.

'In Cuba', said Guevara, 'we knew we were on the right track because the peasants were responding to us. The peasants would feed us, give us information and encourage us. The [anti-Castro] guerrillas now appearing in Cuba will fail. Not because they are good or bad, but because they are getting no positive response from the peasantry.'

Frondizi insisted that this experience was simply inapplicable to the whole of Latin America. Neither of them could know that seven years later, both the lesson quoted by Guevara — the importance of a positive response from the peasantry — and Frondizi's assessment would be proved correct.

The encounter ended inconclusively. Frondizi drove off to the Casa Rosada, while Guevara lingered on at the Presidential residence of Olivos to savour a typically Argentine meal he had not tasted for years: *bife a caballo*, a thick, juicy steak topped with a fried egg. It was arranged that he would pay a secret visit to a sick relative before being flown out of the country.

Rumours of Che's presence in Buenos Aires had been circulating since the morning. Frondizi made a formal report of his meeting to the Minister of Foreign Affairs and the secretaries of the armed services. Once Guevara had left Argentine soil, anticipating a violent reaction from the military, he addressed the nation to make the encounter public. 'If the Cuban representative wished to discuss his country's problems with the President of Argentina, it would have been a dereliction of our duties as a ruler and as an American to refuse the dialogue. Only the weak avoid confrontation with men who do not share their views. None of the statesmen of the great Western nations refuse to speak with the leaders of the Communist countries.' In his speech, however, Frondizi only hinted obliquely at his central thesis: Cuba, a country dominated by two agrarian export crops and strongly tied to US interests, was bound to explode in a revolution such as the one led by Castro; the Cubans had every right to choose their own model of development and of political organisation, but the course of events in Cuba, particularly its increasing dependence on the Soviet Union, had been dictated more by external hostility than by the will of the Cuban people.

A couple of days later, in another speech, he remarked even more pointedly: 'Cuba has been a warning.'

The shadow of Cuba would continue to hover over Frondizi's rule, but the country's attention shifted for a time to one of the toughest labour conflicts it had ever experienced. Frondizi had long decided to uproot one of the most obstinate problems in public finances: the huge deficit of the state-owned railways. The causes of this deficit were many. There was the sheer size of Argentina's rail network, and the fact that it had been designed for a country whose economy had already undergone important changes. There was the fact that its rolling stock was ageing, and there certainly was much overmanning. But that was only part of the picture. Frondizi's 'developmentalism' had given a key role in the economy to the auto industry (more than twenty factories had suddenly grown up under the umbrella of fiscal enticements to foreign investors, and this was well above what Argentina's tiny market could support).

Motor vehicles need roads; and public funds had been poured generously into their construction and improvement. But Argentina's road network was not designed to complement the existing rail system; on the whole the roads ran parallel to the tracks. Officially fixed fuel prices became, in effect, a subsidy to road transport. Indeed, it has been suggested that if the whole complex of motor manufacturing, road construction and improvement, and fuel pricing, were to have been computed as if they were a single enterprise (like the railways), the country would have realised that it was happily supporting another huge deficit on account of a transportation system that competed unfairly with the railways. In other words, much of the unprofitability of the railways was a product of other government policies.

This broader picture, however, did not form part of Frondizi's strategy. The railways were considered in isolation, and the answer to the rail deficit was envisaged as a heroic decision to eliminate uneconomic lines, suppress unprofitable services, and dismiss redundant personnel. This policy, known euphemistically as 're-structuring' the railways, was launched only days after Frondizi's meeting with Guevara.

The many railway unions responded by striking. Their action was considered illegal, and orders were given for the arrest of strike leaders. Within days 300 railwaymen had been arrested, yet the strike continued, often combined with acts of sabotage, while the CGT called out all workers on a seventy-two-hour sympathy strike. Over the next two months the confrontation grew ever more intense and vicious; in early November, waggons were set aflame in the Laguna Paiva depot, in the province of Santa Fe, and the government ordered in the Gendarmería, the militarised border police, to control the installations. A wave of sabotage incidents followed, in Olavarría, Corrientes and Rosario, before both parties called on the good offices of Cardinal Caggiano as mediator.

Frondizi left the country on a grand international tour before a compromise was reached. The finalisation of the strike was agreed before José María Guido, the acting president of the Senate, who had been designated interim President of the Republic. Normally, this would have been the Vice-President's job, but Alejandro Gómez had resigned, and Frondizi had not risked calling elections for his replacement; as one of the Vice-President's constitutional tasks is to preside over the Senate, it was reasoned that the acting president of the Senate should logically fill in for him in his absence. A minor institutional matter, perhaps, but it was to loom much larger in the months to come.

Arturo Frondizi travelled to Trinidad, Canada, Switzerland, Greece, Thailand, Hong Kong and the United States. On his last stop, as he met J. F. Kennedy, the spectre of Cuba returned to haunt Argentina. The press published a set of documents which seemed to prove that the Cuban diplomatic mission in Buenos Aires was involved in subversive activities in Argentina. Frondizi, from afar, instantly dismissed the documents as forgeries — days later his instinct was proved right, but the propaganda effect of the incident had already further damaged his standing with the military. By Christmas Frondizi was back in Buenos Aires. The festive season brought with it the return to front-page news of another spectre: from Madrid came the report that Juan Domingo Perón, at the age of sixty-six, had married María Estela Martínez Cartas, better known as 'Isabelita', his thirty-year-old secretary and mistress.

The year that lay beyond the festivities promised to be a difficult one. Elections in most of the provinces had been scheduled for March, and for the first time Frondizi was faced with the need to honour his commitment to Perón in the electoral pact that had gained him the Presidency: the free participation of *peronismo* in the polls. Secret negotiations had been taking place between emissaries of the government and Perón, trying to impress upon him the need for a self-proscription of the *peronistas*. The alternative, it was made abundantly clear, was an *anti-peronista* military coup that would probably drag Frondizi down as well. At first Perón had seemed to agree; there was a suggestion that the *peronistas* would once again be ordered to cast a blank vote. But Perón, for all his key role as ultimate arbiter of his movement's actions, was not an entirely free agent. The years of exile had forced him to set up a two-tiered power structure within *peronismo*. He himself would decide on broad lines of strategy, and act as umpire between the different factions and leaders, but the commanders in the field, particularly the union bosses, were entrusted with the virtually autonomous conduct of day-to-day tactics. When things did not work entirely to *el Líder*'s satisfaction, or when any minor chieftain seemed likely to acquire too much political stature of his own, Perón could intervene by changing the leadership. Most of the time, however, the relations between *peronismo* and the government of Argentina were entrusted to what has been called 'black parliamentarianism' (a simile intended to evoke the black market in hard currencies); the senators and deputies of this system were the *peronista* union bosses and political leaders.

In was at best a delicate balancing act, which Perón, in the long run, always managed to dominate by keeping a 'pendulum' swinging between the right and left wings of his movement. But inevitably there were times when the movement's 'black senators' called the tune, and early 1962 was one such moment. The union bosses were adamant about running in the March elections, and Perón gave way to their decision.

But even before the elections got to dominate the internal political scene in Argentina, there appeared another ominous cloud on Frondizi's horizon. A top-level meeting of the Organisation of American States had been convened for late January in Punta del Este, Uruguay. The agenda had been set by the United States, and the crucial item was to be the expulsion of Cuba from the OAS. Most Latin American governments were willing to go along with Washington's *diktat*, and the Argentine military made it clear to Frondizi that they expected him to comply too.

Yet for once Frondizi decided to make a stand against military pressure. Although he did not instruct his delegate to vote against the resolution to expel Cuba, he did join the few independent-minded states that abstained, and emphasised that, whatever the outcome of the Punta del Este meeting, he would not feel bound to break off diplomatic relations with Castro. The expulsion was approved; only Argentina, Brazil, Bolivia, Chile, Ecuador and Mexico made the feeble gesture of abstaining from the vote. But Frondizi was determined to keep his word, and on February 3 addressed the nation in an unexpectedly violent speech to justify his position. This shocked the military, but many of the people who had become disenchanted with his Presidency rejoiced at what they felt was the re-emergence of their idol who had once written *Petróleo y política*.

Nonetheless, the military tightened the screws again, and Frondizi's newly-found resolve gave way to his more habitual Machiavellian survival tactics. Five days after his speech he announced that Argentina was cutting its diplomatic links with Cuba; in his mind he was able to find comfort in the conviction that everyone in Argentina *knew* that this decision had been imposed by the men in uniform. The same Machiavellianism governed his attitude towards the imminent provincial elections. He had his Minister of the Interior, Alfredo Vitolo, transmit to the secretaries of the armed services the President's assurances that a *peronista* victory would not be tolerated. Yet no practical moves were taken to prevent participation by *peronistas* in the contest. Frondizi's reckoning was that the military commanders would not be satisfied with these assurances, and would press for explicit proscription of the *peronistas*, thus allowing him to save face with a gesture similar to the one he had made regarding the Cuban issue. But he miscalculated badly; the military astu-

tely left the practicalities entirely in Frondizi's hands, so that he would
have no choice but to assume full responsibility for the outcome. One of
his aides complained bitterly, 'This time, when we expected the *gorilas* to
act like true gorillas, they behaved like tiny inoffensive monkeys!'

The country went to the polls on 18 March 1962. Flocking behind the
candidate for the governorship of Buenos Aires, Andrés Framini, a leader
of the textile workers' union who had acquired something of a radical
reputation, the *peronista* Left had been campaigning under the slogan,
'*On the 18th, another 17th*', a clear reference to that historic 17 October
1945 when a peaceful mobilisation of the *peronista* masses had ensured
Perón's victory over a determined *antiperonista* military hierarchy. The
results showed an impressive *peronista* triumph; they took ten provinces,
including the largest and most influential, Buenos Aires. Yet the verdict
of the nation as a whole was hardly unanimous; Frondizi's UCRI carried
six districts, including the federal capital (eight if one counts two
provinces that had voted earlier), while the UCRP took two (one of
which was Córdoba, the second most important province in the
Republic), and there were even victories for the Conservatives in
Mendoza, and for a splinter of the old Radical party in San Juan. For a
President who had first come to power mainly on the strength of
peronista votes, Frondizi could claim to have done quite well.

But the military commanders saw only the menace of the *peronista*
advances, and immediately demanded that Frondizi should keep his
word. That very day Frondizi signed a decree annulling the elections in
all the districts won by the *peronistas*, and appointed federal trustees to
take over five provinces where the incumbents had gone on record as
favouring a handover to the elected victors. With one stroke, Frondizi
had cut away from under his own feet whatever sympathy he might have
been able to command among Argentina's political leaders, including
many of his own party.

The coup, *el golpe*, was a certainty now on everyone's lips. The
military chiefs began a seemingly endless series of meetings to decide
what was to be done with Frondizi. Three options were put forward: to
keep him in power, but as no more than a figurehead for the military; to
oust him while preserving a constitutional government; and an outright
military dictatorship.

As Frondizi reshuffled his cabinet, the former military ruler Aramburu entered the scene as a self-appointed mediator, claiming to seek 'the
bridge that will carry us over the abyss'. When Aramburu stated, in a public communication to Frondizi, that 'the basis of possible coincidences

dences depends, regrettably, on your renunciation', the word spread that
agreement had been reached on the second option, namely to depose the
President while preserving constitutional rule. The very next day, however, Frondizi was told that the Navy had voted against his ouster, and
the President proclaimed, 'I shall not resign, I shall not commit suicide, I
shall not leave the country!'

The Defence Minister, Rodolfo Martínez, was busy behind the scenes
trying to rally support for the idea of keeping Frondizi in power, though
under strict military control. Then the Council of Admirals suddenly
changed its mind, and on 28 March the three Commanders-in-Chief of
the services turned up in Frondizi's office to demand his resignation. He
refused, and the military chiefs returned to their command posts to order
the mobilisation of their troops.

The President ordered his War Secretary, General Rosendo Fraga, to
take personal command of the Army and organise the suppression of the
revolt. Fraga set off to do so, but unaccountably returned to his office to
pick up some papers. There he was surprised by men loyal to the Army
Commander-in-Chief, General Raúl Poggi, and placed under arrest. Of
his own accord, the officer commanding the Presidential guard of
Granaderos ordered his men to begin the evacuation of the Casa Rosada.
Frondizi telephoned the regimental commander, ordered him to reinstate the guard, then reinforced it with police units.

As night fell, Frondizi began a series of meetings in the Presidential
residence of Olivos. The situation remained unclear as rumours flew of
troop movements and of changes of heart in the hierarchies of the Navy
and Air Force. Things began to look better close to midnight, as the
commander of the Granaderos rang the President to inform him that his
entire officer corps stood by him, and news arrived of the release of a
number of generals who had been placed under arrest by the rebels. The
Secretaries of the Navy and Air Force turned up to offer a way out: that
Frondizi should take leave of absence for a few days, while the whole
affair blew over. He refused. Then they asked him if he would agree to
Rodolfo Martínez's plan for a military-supervised continuation in
power. He acquiesced, adding, 'If in the morning I find that I still have
some force backing me, I shall go to the Casa Rosada and get on with my
job.' Soon afterwards, a busload of Granaderos officers turned up to
place themselves under Frondizi's direct orders.

In the mean time, the three Commanders-in-Chief and the Secretaries
of the Navy and the Air Force had been meeting with José María Guido,
the acting president of the Senate, to ask if he was willing to be appointed

President. Guido turned the offer down. At Olivos, Frondizi was trying to determine if he still had the force he needed to remain in office. He rang the giant military complex of Campo de Mayo where, he knew, some of the leading cavalry officers had previously resisted coup attempts. But it was too late; the reply was that all units at Campo de Mayo would obey the orders of the Army commander, General Raúl Poggi. At three in the morning, the Secretary of the Navy informed Frondizi that no agreement had been possible with the commanders of the services, and that they had decided to depose him. Frondizi called up to his bedroom the officers who had come to protect him, apprised them of the situation, and relieved them of their duties for, he said, he would otherwise be forced to give them the hopeless order to resist the coup attempt.

At eight in the morning of 29 March 1962, Frondizi was escorted from Olivos to Aeroparque, Buenos Aires' small airport, where a plane was waiting to whisk him away to confinement on the island prison of Martín García, in the estuary of the River Plate.

Later in the day, the Army Commander-in-Chief, General Poggi, convinced that he was already, *de facto* at least, the ruler of Argentina, turned up at the Casa Rosada. To his surprise, he found that the country already had a President. Defence Minister Rodolfo Martínez is credited with having persuaded Senator Guido to change his mind, given the fact that Frondizi had actually been deposed. Later in the day, Guido had turned up at the Supreme Court, demanding to be sworn in as President. The argument was the same as that used previously to justify his appointment as interim President while Frondizi was abroad: there being no Vice-President, although the Constitution remained silent on the point, the acting president of the Senate was logically the next in the line of Presidental succession. Guido's formal inauguration was scheduled for the following day at noon.

14

REDS VERSUS BLUES
(1962–1963)

Political legerdemain had narrowly averted the re-establishment of military rule. An astonished Argentina awoke to find the Presidency in the unsteady hands of an obscure Senator from the province of Río Negro, of whom little was know to the public at large, except — thanks to the political gossip columns — his predilection for red wine in abundance. The convoluted reasoning whereby Guido was deemed to have succeeded constitutionally to the Presidency (while the elected President, Arturo Frondizi, who still refused to resign, was locked up in a government prison) was rejected only by two groups — Frondizi's remaining followers and their arch-enemies, the hardline *antiperonista* generals who believed that only a harsh, unflinching military dictatorship could rid the country permanently of all vestiges of *peronismo*.

The hardline generals were perhaps the most surprised of Argentines, not only at the manoeuvre that had elevated Guido to the Presidency, but also at the sudden unanimity with which most of the country's political leaders closed ranks to prevent Guido's ouster. And not only politicians, but a considerable number of high-ranking Army commanders, were adamant that Guido should stay.

The vocally *antiperonista* UCRP, many of whose leaders had earlier been 'knocking at the doors of the barracks' to demand Frondizi's removal from office, was now proclaiming publicly that it had been wrong to annul the *peronistas'* election victories. And even among the leading figures of the *Revolución Libertadora* that had toppled Perón, those close to the former military President, General Pedro Eugenio Aramburu, were casting their vote in favour of Guido's permanence.

The paradox owed much to a cold, cynical appraisal of what had happened. The pretence of constitutionality that underpinned Guido's Presidency was interpreted as meaning two things: first, that sooner rather than later elections would again be called; and secondly, that the military were determined to prevent a *peronista* victory. This added up to the expectation of some form of proscription of *peronismo*, which would leave the *peronista* electorate either out of the counting or, as very many

232

were rapidly reckoning, available for anyone with the necessary talent and opportunity to 'do a Frondizi' — i.e. to sweep into power on borrowed votes. The clique surrounding Aramburu had a more definite plan: to take advantage of Guido's evident weakness (he clearly lacked a sufficient political base of his own) and of their own influence in military and business circles, so as to take over the real reins of power and so orchestrate events that their leader, Aramburu, would emerge as the country's next elected President.

All these calculations rested on the assumption that a large segment of the Army's officer corps were opposed to the idea of yet another bout of military rule. And for some time there had been signs that this was precisely the case. One of the strongest motives for rebellion against Perón had been his attempts to politicise the armed forces. But whereas some of the military had carried their *antiperonismo* openly into the political arena, seeing it as their mission to ensure the eradication of *peronismo*, if necessary by holding power themselves until this was achieved, others advocated a return to a 'professionalist' role for the military services.

It was not that the 'professionalists' proposed to withdraw entirely from the political scene. They defined their 'professionalism' mainly in opposition to the 'deliberative' mood that had engulfed the services during the Frondizi years, when it had come to seem as if any commander of a large unit was entitled to make political *planteos* (a term which in Argentine political jargon means something between a statement of demands and an ultimatum backed by the threat of military force). Indeed, when one such *planteo* by a group of officers prevented a newly-appointed War Secretary from taking office, the 'professionalist' commander of the Armoured Division at Campo de Mayo, General Juan Carlos Onganía, had made known to Frondizi his willingness to act against those guilty of insubordination in the name of Army discipline. Frondizi, as often before, had hesitated. But he remembered the gesture, and in March 1962, when it became clear that he was facing an outright *coup d'état*, it was General Onganía that Frondizi contacted at Campo de Mayo in an eleventh-hour attempt to organise resistance. By then it was far too late, and Onganía curtly informed the President that he would obey any orders given him by his superiors.

It was a typically 'professionalist' response. This group believed that the Army should not be in the business of ousting and installing Presidents, or of dictating the everyday conduct of government. But they held that the forces should 'gravitate' in politics; that they should have influence over the basic rules of the game. And in order to do so effectively, they believed that the Army should act as a homogeneous whole — hence their emphasis on discipline and 'professionalism'. In other words, what they advocated was an institutional political role for the Army (as the ultimate defender of national integrity and the Constitution); what they rejected was individual politicking by Army men, whatever their rank or position.

Guido's brief Presidency was to be punctuated many times by the struggle between hardline *antiperonistas* and 'professionalists' in the armed forces. Yet the opening events of his rule, which were to leave an equally lasting mark on Argentine memories, took place not in the military arena but in the equally sensitive field of the economy. Only five days after he was hurriedly sworn in as President, Guido appointed a new Minister of the Economy. His choice, Federico Pinedo, was a legendary figure in Argentine politics. In the early decades of the century he had been among the first young Socialist deputies elected to Congress. Later he had swung round in his public postures until he became the epitome of conservatism and the most outspoken advocate of economic liberalism. He came to office now as an old man, determined to translate his caustic criticisms of populist policies and of *desarrollista* pipedreams into the strong medicine needed to contain Argentina's inflation and halt its slide into a severe balance of payments crisis.

The exchange market, which had been closed during the coup that deposed Frondizi (exchange markets are always shut down during major crises in Argentina), reopened on the day that Pinedo moved into the Ministry of the Economy, a building whose brown marble façade symbolically still showed the pockmarks caused by the strafing on that fateful day of 1955 when the Navy tried to kill Perón in an air raid. One of Pinedo's first public statements was an assurance that the peso would not be devalued. The US dollar was being sold at 83.05 pesos. Argentines were already learning to be very sceptical about such assurances. In less than a week, in tune with Pinedo's austerity measures, the peso was allowed to fall dramatically, raising the quotation of the dollar (the man in the street's standard, but misleading, measure of the country's economic health) to 98.15 pesos — almost a 17 per cent devaluation. Rumours spread quickly that Pinedo's friends and associates had known in advance about the move, and that many had made a killing on the exchange markets. But alleged corruption was only part of the picture. Tariffs for public services, including the state-run railways, and the official prices for fuels were raised sharply, and a groan of protest arose from the unions, especially those under *peronista* leadership, which were still smarting from the annulment of the *peronista* electoral victories.

After only sixteen days in office, the legendary Pinedo was forced to resign. His place was taken by the man the military had previously forced upon Frondizi: Alvaro Alsogaray. The cadet who had won the high honour of being appointed standard-bearer for the Colegio Militar, who had had himself driven in a motor-cycle side-car with a broken leg in a cast because he did not want to miss the coup that deposed President Yrigoyen, who had been described by his commanding officer as 'too intelligent for the Army' and had retired after promotion to the rank of captain to become a highly successful entrepreneur, was back in the forefront of the Argentina political scene. Like Pinedo, Alsogaray was an ardent advocate of economic liberalism and the 'market economy'; Alsogaray's formula for Argentina's economic ills, which he claimed was simply the same that had been so successful in postwar Germany, was to slash public spending, tighten the money supply, free the exchange markets, eliminate excessive protection, make the country attractive for foreign investment, and let the market take care of rewarding the efficient and weeding out the inefficient. Political constraints made much of this inapplicable, at least in the drastic form Alsogaray would have preferred, but what he did manage to put into practice plunged the country into a severe recession. The next year, Argentina's gross domestic product would *decrease* by almost 4 per cent, with the cost of living surging upwards by a third. Alsogaray's slogan, 'We must get over the winter', stuck in the country's political lexicon as an expression of sarcasm.

Yet even before Alsogaray's hard winter started, trouble had begun to brew on the military and political front. A shortlived rebellion by a general, Enrique Rauch, led to the displacement of the Army Commander-in-Chief, General Raúl Poggi, the man who for a moment had seen himself as President after Frondizi's ouster. A new War Secretary was appointed, and a few days later there was a major series of transfers and promotions in the Army hierarchy. From the wings the Navy Commander-in-Chief, Admiral Gaston Clement, urged President Guido to annul by decree the *peronista* electoral gains. This Guido did, in a broad sweep that voided all election results since mid-December the previous year. The city council of Buenos Aires was dissolved, and a police cordon was thrown around Congress to impede the access of all but the ninety-eight deputies unaffected by the decree. Then Guido decreed a 365-day Congressional recess and announced that elections would be held, for legislative office, on 31 May the following year, and for the Presidency on 27 October 1963.

The Congressmen refused to accept the measure. Three days after the decree they gathered to rush the police blockade. A few made it inside, including thirty-one of the forty-seven elected *peronista* deputies. They held a 'minority session' in which they decided to appeal to the judiciary against the President's decision. Olegario Becerra, the senior congressman in the lower chamber, released a document in which he scathingly condemned Guido's action:

The Executive can only open and close the extraordinary period of sessions. It may open the ordinary period — though this is doctrinally debatable — but it cannot close it. Regarding the preparatory period, it neither opens it nor closes it. We are in the preparatory phase of the period of sessions. The act of the Executive, dictating a recess in an instance which is beyond its competence, apart from being juridical nonsense, shows that the Executive wishes to treat the Honourable Chamber of Deputies as if it were an administrative dependency of the Casa Rosada. The decree is as unsustainable as if it attempted to modify the calendar or to alter the geographic boundaries of a province. This is to say that we are dealing, not with an act of violation, but with a non-existent act. Nonsense is not a juridical category. If to this we must add the outrage of preventing access to Congress of the elected deputies, on whose election, rights and titles only the Honourable Chamber over which I preside can determine, I ask myself if we are not already facing the kind of vexatious situations that can only be aggravated by violence, corrected by justice, and judged by posterity. In my sphere of competence we shall abide by the Constitution and by the rules that are the law of the Chamber.

Becerra attempted to keep parliamentary resistance alive, organising a ceremony to celebrate the centennial of Argentina's first representative legislature. But his valiant campaign did not last. Frondizi's UCRI, the party with a majority in both chambers, held its national convention in the city of Rosario and decided to abandon its seats in the legislature and pass into open opposition to this government that claimed to be the constitutional successor to its own.

The *peronista* Governor-elect of the province of Buenos Aires, Andrés Framini, made a token gesture of claiming his office, then left the country on a flight to Madrid, to discuss the movement's future strategy with its leader in exile, Juan Perón. The CGT, facing not only political discontent but also increasing economic hardship among its rank and file, called a twenty-four-hour stoppage; the stevedores and railwaymen went out on brief strikes, while stoppages in the private bus companies disrupted transportation in the capital until the government stepped in and began to commandeer buses. The left-wing groups that were operating within *peronismo* or on its fringes, and had accompanied the frustrated electoral attempt of March with much-publicised scepticism, now called for more radical action. A serious attempt was made to organise a grass-roots campaign for the return of Perón. Tactically, apart from the obvious emotional content of such an appeal, the idea was to show up the political leaders of *peronismo* and particularly the union bosses as seeking accommodation with the régime: inasmuch as they did not explicitly pick up the banner of Perón's return, they would appear to be selling the *peronista* masses short. Or so the Left calculated. And if the *peronista* leadership did pick up that banner, the corollary was that, given the nature of military resistance to Perón's return, the objective could only be attained through popular mobilisation and eventually revolution. Some sectors of the *peronista* and non-*peronista* Left, more impatient, were already preparing for armed insurrection, stockpiling weapons and organising training in guerrilla warfare.

Perón himself, from Madrid, kept every option open. Hardly any of those who visited him, representing or claiming to represent an important faction of the *peronista* movement, came away emptyhanded. For many years, *la carta* (the letter) from the Leader was a symbol of authority, of the Old Man's approval of a particular person, policy or course of action. But at any one time there were many *cartas*, some to be used publicly, others 'privately'; although they did not often contradict each-other too flagrantly, in the last instance they offered support to opposing factions and lines of thought. And they were always sufficiently ambiguous to leave *el Líder* himself as the ultimate arbiter. By the early 1960s, *la carta* had begun to be replaced by *la cinta* (the tape recording), but the technique remained the same. Perón had put his weight behind the Union Popular's electoral bid, and especially behind the most important candidate, Andrés Framini. But he never completely disowned the *neoperonistas* who had managed to carve little niches for themselves by disobeying previous orders of abstention or 'blank' voting. And at the same time he fed the militancy of the radicals and left-wingers with *cintas* in which he spoke glowingly of 'socialism' and quoted from Mao Tsetung. Within the CGT he backed José Alonso, the veteran union leader many were slating as secretary-general of a reconstituted countrywide confederation embracing even the non-*peronista* and *antiperonista* unions. And he also backed Alonso's main rival, Augusto Timoteo Vandor, *el Lobo* (the Wolf), the powerful leader of the metalworkers' union who had become a master at the art of negotiating with *antiperonista* governments, and the man most visibly identified by the Left with the 'sell-out' of *peronista* ideals in the name of pragmatism.

The speed — and confusion — with which events began to follow each other in Buenos Aires suggested that Perón would indeed need all the options he had kept open, and perhaps even more. Guido issued a decree banning all proselytising activity by the *peronistas*, and even the display of *peronista* iconography and the playing of *peronista* marches. The government announced that only 'non-totalitarian' parties would be allowed to take part in the coming elections — a measure which, oddly, was repudiated by the national convention of the highly *antiperonista* UCRP. As August began, the CGT called out its members on a two-day protest stoppage. Only days later, high drama erupted on the military front. General Federico Toranzo Montero, a prominent hardliner, revolted against the War Secretary, setting up a 'rebel command post' in the northwestern province of Jujuy. To add to the confusion, he proclaimed publicly, 'I am not in rebellion against the President of the Republic, whose authority I obey.' The War Secretary, General Juan Bautista Loza, was replaced by General Eduardo Señorans, who immediately ordered troops to suppress the rebellion. Señorans lasted in his job for only a few hours, as the President seemed to find the solution to the crisis in the appointment of General Juan Octavio Cornejo Saravia. There was one tragic skirmish during the four-day crisis: troops stationed on the Avellaneda bridge, on the southern rim of Buenos Aires, opened fire on a fire engine, killing the driver. He was on his way to extinguish a fire in the Dock Sud power plant, which damaged the installations so badly that it left the capital with a serious shortage of electricity.

The pause in the military crisis lasted only a few days. In mid-August 120 officers mutinously walked out of the ceremony of installation of the new Chief of Staff, and the Minister of Defence resigned. Factions began to align themselves in ways that eluded definition; it was nearly impossible for the man in the street to tell who was rebelling against whom and who was loyal to which authority. Economy Minister Alvaro Alsogaray, whose links with the Army were, if anything, stronger than before (his brother Julio was one of the leading lights of the 'professionalist' group in the élite cavalry corps), managed to negotiate a seventy-two-hour truce among the warring factions. The month ended with the appointment of a new Defence Minister, while out on the streets of Buenos Aires civil servants and state employees were demonstrating against Alsogaray's decision to pay their salaries in bonds of the 'Patriotic 9th of July

National Loan', which shopkeepers were only accepting at a substantial discount in payment for their merchandise. Although it did not make news when it happened, it was at that time that the police of Buenos Aires province arrested a young metalworker, Felipe Vallese, for questioning about his connections with *peronista* revolutionary groups. For days the political grapevine had been alive with stories of how a Federal Police unit and men of the Buenos Aires provincial police, while separately staking out an alleged revolutionary hideout, had mistaken each other for their prey and engaged in a bloody gunbattle. It was in the ensuing enraged crackdown that Vallese was arrested and tortured to death. But reaction to the horror of that crime, and the elevation of Vallese to the category of martyr of the radical *peronista* cause, were to come later.

To run the quarrel-ridden Army, General Bernardino Labayrú was brought out of retirement and appointed Commander-in-Chief. Labayrú, who has been described as 'a legendary and subtle weaver of military intrigue', was clearly identified with the faction that supported the political ambitions of former military ruler Pedro Eugenio Aramburu. Indeed his appointment appeared as a masterstroke of *aramburista* strategy: with a strong Army — run by one of their own men — wielding real power over a weak President, it would be possible to negotiate with the political parties the terms on which the forthcoming elections would be held. Against the alternative of a military dictatorship, they would be offered the opportunity of agreeing on a candidate which the Army would find acceptable: a candidate such as, for example, Pedro Eugenio Aramburu, who was already demanding an 'urgent' call to elections.

Following the appointment of Labayrú, President Guido moved to put an end to what was left of his institutional conflict with the legislature: he decreed the dissolution of Congress and reaffirmed his decision to hold elections on 27 October 1963. All political parties decried the measures, but the only reply they got was a caustic remark from Alsogaray: 'The government has indicated the way out. For those who like it, well and good; for those who don't, there is always the solution of rising in arms against the government.' It is only with hindsight that these words might be read as an earnest invitation to rebellion, rather than the haughty put-down intended by Alsogaray, but events were already on the move which would lead many, including the Minister's brother, to rise in arms against the government.

Labayrú had rapidly set himself the task of reorganising the higher echelons of the Army. Key posts began to be allocated to hardline *anti-peronistas*. Those who were suspected of *peronista* sympathies, or of being lukewarm towards *peronismo*, and especially those who saw themselves as 'professionalists', were shunted away from *los fierros* ('the irons' i.e. the command of powerful combat units) and towards desk jobs or postings of secondary importance. This the 'professionalists' decided to resist. They were particularly strong in the cavalry, a corps with a special mystique and *esprit* of its own. Not only did the cavalrymen trace the history of their regiments back to the wars of independence; many of their officers came from old military families with close links to the landowning oligarchy (many of those of immigrant extraction had married into Argentina's 'old' families). Their devotion to horse-breeding and equestrian sports (polo and fox hunting, English style, were leading attractions of their private club at Campo de Mayo) strengthened these links with Argentina's high society. Traditionally the cavalry was the source of general officers and Commanders-in-Chief for Argentina's Army; although only two out of every ten graduates of the Colegio Militar entered the cavalry corps, at the top of the hierarchical pyramid they accounted for well over two-thirds of the generals. It was, therefore, not surprising that the public was more aware of who was who in the cavalry than in other Army corps. The names of the senior cavalry officers of the day — Villegas, Alzaga, López Aufranc, Sánchez de Bustamante, Uriburu, Lanusse, Alsogaray — had a familiar ring; they reeked of Argentine military history, of 'patrician' social standing and of what had come to be known as 'professionalism' in Army and political circles. To them the actions of Labayrú were anathema. And they made it quite clear that they would not tolerate any attempt to remove their corps commander, the less well-known General Juan Carlos Onganía.

Yet half way through September 1963 that was precisely what Labayrú tried to do. The 'professionalists' rose in rebellion. The confusion created by the previous adoption of labels such as 'loyalist', 'rebel' or 'revolutionary' led them to eschew any such self-description. Instead they chose for themselves and their adversaries the same names traditionally used on peacetime manoeuvres and in war games: the 'professionalists' become the *azules* (blues), and the forces obeying the Commander-in-Chief, General Labayrú, became the *colorados* (reds). The *azules* demanded the immediate resignation of General Labayrú. To back their demand they had an impressive array of might: the large military complex of Campo de Mayo; the 2nd Cavalry of Concordia in the province of Entre Ríos; the 3rd Cavalry of Tandil, in the province of Buenos Aires; the 4th Cavalry of Curuzú Cuatía, in the province of Corrientes; and a number of minor units dotted throughout the country. Labayrú did pen his resignation, but it was rejected by the War Secretary, General Cornejo Saravia, who imposed on the country the *Plan Conintes* devised by Perón and used by Frondizi and ordered that the rebellion be put down. The *colorados* had been able to muster to their cause the 1st Infantry Regiment of Palermo in the capital, and the Artillery School, as well as the Third Army Corps of Córdoba, which included the crack 7th Paratroopers. President Guido called a meeting between the Minister of Defence and the rebel chief, General Onganía, but to no avail. The Navy decided to remain aloof, though confident that Labayrú would gain the upper hand. Then the Air Force decided not to take part in the suppression of the revolt. As troops began to move against each other, differences in style quickly became evident. The *colorado* leadership directed operations from their offices, leaving their units in the field in the hands of subalterns who were far from having a clear idea of what was expected of them. The *azules* put their commanders in the field with their men, leaving no doubt in any minds that this particular military episode, despite the chosen names of the adversary groups, was not to be conducted in the usual style of a war game, nor was its outcome to be decided by the traditional arithmetic of military coups, conceding victory to the side that could count the greater number of adherents, and before shots were fired in anger. The *azules* were determined to fight. As the radio transmitters of Campo de Mayo issued a stream of communiqués laying down the *azul* doctrine, asserting that 'the armed forces should not rule, but they should carry weight in the solution of the nation's problem in order to ensure respect for the Constitution and to prevent any sort of totalitarian enterprise', the hard edge of their movement took the form of a menacing advance by the 8th Tank Regiment from Magdalena. A *colorado* force went out to intercept them just south of La Plata, capital city of the province of Buenos Aires. The tank unit, led by Colonel Alcides López Aufranc, did not halt; instead it charged ahead, firing its guns and drawing blood.

The shock caused by a rebel force actually willing to use the strength at its disposal — a highly unusual occurrence in Argentina's internal military squabbles — enabled López Aufranc to move on, unopposed, into the outskirts of Buenos Aires city. President Guido ordered a truce and the return of all units to their barracks. The *azules* paused, but when it became clear that the *colorado* leadership intended to remain at their posts, their tanks rolled again, rapidly overrunning what armed resistance remained in the capital. The *azules* were in charge. At this point the Navy tried to intervene, proposing that a junta of Commanders-in-Chief should take over from the President. The notion was rejected outright by Onganía, and a relieved President Guido was able to announce, 'The episodes that have shaken the soul of the Nation have come to an end. My prayer to God has been heard. God has protected the Republic. The country has had a terrible lesson. A new chapter of its history has been written in blood. We are at a new starting-point which must become the foundation for the future greatness of the Nation.' From Campo de Mayo, the *azules* issued communiqué no. 150, spelling out their own reading of their victory: 'The great drama we have lived in the last few days has been the culmination of the efforts and anxieties of those men who believed that, above all, the country should once again take the path of the Constitution. Our aim is to maintain the present Executive and to ensure for it the necessary freedom of action, as long as its purposes lead to the fulfilment of its commitment to the people of the Nation of returning, in the shortest possible time, to the rule of the Constitution.'

The leader of the *azules*, General Onganía, his job done, drove home. He later told friends that it had been his intention to put in a request for his retirement from active duty the following morning. But he found his wife waiting for him on the doorstep, with the news that the radio had just announced his designation as Commander-in-Chief of the Army.

The Secretaries of War, Navy and Air Force were replaced; Rodolfo Martínez, the man who had engineered Guido's accession to the Presidency, was brought back to the Ministry of the Interior, where he lost little time in announcing that the elections would be brought forward to 16 June 1963, and that the contenders would have to conform to a new Statute of Political Parties, which would effectively proscribe *peronistas* and Communists. Although President Guido announced that there would be tolerance towards the vanquished military faction, Onganía interpreted the policy in his own fashion. Only about seventy *colorado* leaders were arrested, but hundreds of officers who had embraced their cause were forced to retire in the prime of their careers. Onganía's reasoning was simple enough: keeping them in the service would have posed an unacceptable dilemma, because to have isolated them in inoffensive, secondary posts would have been tantamount to institutionalising political discrimination in the Army, while the absence of any such discrimination would have left them at liberty to attempt another *colorado* adventure in the future.

It was not that the victory of the *azules* had finally conjured away that particular threat. The Army had indeed been purged and whipped into the 'professionalist' line, but the same could not be said of the other two services. The same 'deliberative' mood that had dominated the Army continued to exist in the Air Force, which was to witness a botched attempt at rebellion in the province of Córdoba before the year was out. And the Navy did little to disguise the *colorado* leanings of many of its senior officers.

The economic crisis had not eased during these months of military up-heaval. Factories were closing down or laying off personnel by the thousands, bankruptcies were climbing to record levels, unions were striking or demonstrating in the streets, and a steady flow of militant union leaders and would-be guerrilla fighters was swelling the country's prison population. The government, which despite all the earlier 'professionalist' rationale was in the hands of *azul* appointees, was becoming engaged in something akin to a juggling act on a tightrope, attempting to reconcile a host of mutually antagonistic factors. On the one hand was its commitment to early elections, which called for distension in the political arena; on the other was its proscription of the *peronistas*, which demanded a fair share of repression. Then there was the economic crisis, which had not disappeared after Alsogaray's winter, and was breeding the kind of disaffection that in military minds was the best possible culture for that menace threatening the entire continent: Castroite subversion and armed insurrection. This called for conciliatory gestures towards the trade unions, but was tempered by the fact that the labour movement continued to be dominated by the *peronistas*, who were apt to seize any opportunity they were given to move more freely and openly into opposition.

The juggling act began with the removal of the by now highly unpopular Minister of the Economy, Alvaro Alsogaray, a move for which the new War Secretary, General Benjamin Rattenbach, deserved most credit. But Alsogaray was replaced by yet another exponent of liberal economic orthodoxy, Eustaquio Méndez Delfino, whose policies would not differ greatly from those already in force. Then came the decision to complete the task Frondizi had begun: the 'normalisation' of the CGT, that is to say its full devolution to the unions after the long period of interim arrangements inaugurated by the *Revolución Libertadora*.

In January 1963 a *Congreso Normalizador* was held, attended by 818 delegates representing close to a hundred unions. The CGT gave itself a secretariat which included *peronista* and non-*peronista* union leaders. As secretary-general they elected José Alonso, the veteran *peronista* labour leader. Just as the hardline *antiperonistas* had feared, the Congress went on to approve a 'struggle plan' under the slogan 'The Total Transformation of Economic Structures'. The plan contained a number of militant demands: the liberation of union and political prisoners, the investigation of kidnappings and torture by the security forces (the Vallese case was already public knowledge), the abolition of repressive legislation (and particularly the statute on state security which the military had foisted on Guido), legal recognition of all trade unions, and worker participation in the management of state-owned and private enterprises. Most pointedly, the CGT issued a statement of principles in which it said, 'We consider untouchable the constitutional provisions that consecrate the civic rights and liberties without whose unrestricted enjoyment democracy — the supreme form of human coexistence — and the sovereignty of the people are grotesque fictions.'

This oblique assertion of the *peronistas'* right to take part in the announced elections seemed to be taken up by the government, in the form of a statement by War Minister Rattenbach, saying that the authorities distinguished between *peronismo* and *justicialismo*; in other words, that it was acceptable to hold *peronismo*'s ideas, but unacceptable to attempt to restore *peronista* power as it had been known previously. The exact limits of this distinction were never made clear; indeed, a week later the Executive issued a decree expressly banning *peronista* participation in the elections. To accentuate the confusion, days later the government granted legal recognition to Unión Popular, which it was impossible not to recognise as the *Peronista* Party under another name.

This erratic drift of policies towards *peronismo*, compounded by the government's decision to move former President Frondizi from the island prison of Martín García to the more congenial environment of Bariloche, an Andean resort of mountains, pine forests and huge lakes, needled into action the dormant *colorado* groups. In the first weeks of the summer, nearly forty officers were arrested for plotting; in two cases to take Frondizi's life (the former President was moved to quarters guarded by the Gendarmería Nacional, the tough, militarised border police), and in one to overthrow the government.

In mid-March the Navy issued a strong formal protest to their colleagues in the Army and Air Force about the legal recognition of Unión Popular. The complaint went unheeded, and the strongly *antiperonista* Navy hierarchy began to plot rebellion. In the mean time, that elaborate schemer, Rodolfo Martínez, the Minister of the Interior, began to unfold an electoral strategy of his own. He publicly addressed the country's political leaders, telling them that the only way to come up with an effective government for the country was through electoral alliances. Instantly this was read as meaning that the proscription of *peronismo* was to be used by the government as a means of coaxing the leaders of the outlawed majority into making a deal, presumably on a mutually acceptable Presidential candidate, with Congressional, gubernatorial and ministerial candidatures open to horsetrading. The UCRP responded by unsuccessfully attempting to create an electoral entente of its own, inviting all parties to join in an 'Assembly of Civic Forces'. Others made their calculations and concluded that in the struggle to come it would be crucial to have some sort of legally recognised party structure, and to make suitably sympathetic noises towards Argentina's political pariahs, in order to be able to strike a deal — a legal avenue for electoral participation in exchange for key candidacies — when the government's proscriptive policies closed all other overt routes. Thus retired General Justo León Bengoa, who had been a minister in the short-lived Lonardi administration, registered a party under the name Unión Nacional. Colonel Juan Francisco Guevara, a recently retired Army officer who had been disciplined for rebellion the previous year, and who was now engaged in a bid to convert the *peronistas* to what he called 'communitarianism', registered an organisation under the title Fuerza Nueva. Former *peronista* official Oscar Albrieu inscribed his own party denomination, Justicia Social. And many more were to follow. Aramburu, the former military ruler who had failed to take over the Guido régime to orchestrate his own election to the Presidency, decided to go it alone, and formed a party called Unión del Pueblo Argentino, better known by its acronym 'Udelpa'.

Whatever Rodolfo Martínez's actual plan might have been, he never had the chance to carry it out. Within days of his 'alliances' speech he was forced to resign. March ended with the political scene more confusing than ever, and with the persistent economic crisis pushing the dollar quotation on the exchange markets up to 135 pesos, almost 63 per cent higher than when Guido came to power a year earlier.

The latest leap on the exchange markets, as so often, had owed much to rapidly spreading rumours of an impending upheaval in military circles. This time the rumours were well-founded. On April 1, the Navy and Air Force confined all their units to barracks. The following morning, General Benjamín Menéndez, the ageing veteran of *anti-peronista* coup attempts, broadcast a revolutionary manifesto, and most major Navy units signalled their support for the uprising. The rebels seemed to have learnt the lessons of the previous September: this time they too were determined to fight, and one of their first actions was to call for the surrender of the 8th Tank Regiment of Magdalena, whose commander Colonel Alcides López Aufranc (already known, with characteristic hyperbole, as *el Zorro de Magdalena*, the Fox of Magdalena) had decided the day in favour of the *azules*. By mid-day, Naval Air Force units were reducing the Magdalena barracks to rubble. But the tanks were no longer there; López Aufranc had led them out to take cover in woodland alongside a river, and they remained undetected. Onganía responded by ordering out a division under the command of Alejandro Agustín Lanusse. In manoeuvres that covered as much terrain as Hitler's Panzer divisions in their advance towards the English Channel, Lanusse drove his armour to the Naval air base of Punta Indio, which it proceeded to demolish; then across most of the province of Buenos Aires, to within striking distance of the Navy's major anchorage, Puerto Belgrano. By the third day Onganía's forces had positioned themselves so as to check-mate the rebels; on the fourth day the Navy surrendered. It was, at last, the end of the *colorados*.

Guido's government had survived a second time, thanks to Onganía, and it seemed only fitting to offer the victorious general the chance of becoming President himself, in the same way as the *aramburistas* had earlier envisaged for their leader, Aramburu. It is said that Onganía lectured his tempters on the fact that blood had been spilt precisely in order to keep Army and politics well apart.

Nonetheless, the government was seen by all as a government of the military *azules*. And, as the political wags of Buenos Aires put it, with the *colorados* out of the way, the blue colouring chosen by the 'profession-alists' seemed to be turning rapidly purple, as they revealed themselves just as *antiperonista* as their former adversaries. The operation to close the side and back doors to *peronista* participation in the elections became sharper: a decree was issued forbidding the 'exaltation' of *peronismo*, seemingly a sure way of neutralising those politicians wishing to woo the *peronista* voters or to offer themselves as proxies.

In the final stretch leading up to the elections a major cabinet reshuffle took place, in which the most notable events were the appointment of Osiris Villegas, a leading *azul* cavalryman, as Minister of the Interior, and of José Alfredo Martínez de Hoz as Minister of the Economy. The date for the polls was set back to 7 July.

The government's blocking tactics did not deter the *peronistas* from seeking loopholes. With the blessing of Perón and Frondizi, a 'National and Popular Front' was created, with Vicente Solano Lima, leader of the minuscule Popular Conservative Party, as figurehead Presidential candidate. Disagreement over the nomination of the candidate to the Vice-Presidency led to a deep split in the major legal component of the Front, Frondizi's UCRI: the majority of UCRI followers decamped behind Oscar Alende, a former governor of Buenos Aires province, with a view to running in their own right. The small Christian Democrat Party, which had shed most of its early *antiperonista* elements, rushed in to offer the *peronistas* another way round government obstructions, by nominating Raúl Matera, a distinguished neurosurgeon who had recently resigned his position as Secretary-General of the *Peronista* Party. By then, however, Matera had lost most of his support among the *peronista* bosses, who sarcastically dubbed him a '*neuroperonista*' (a pun on *neoperonista*, as those who had disobeyed previous orders to abstain were known). Perón had already secretly issued instructions to his followers to cast blank votes, a method of abstention that was politically measurable, since electoral statistics always included the number of blank or spoiled ballots.

Running on their own were former military President Aramburu and the UCRP. The latter, however, were virtually certain that the *peronista* vote would be swung behind some other candidate, and that therefore they did not stand any real chance of winning. So much so that their leader and perennial Presidential candidate, Ricardo Balbín, was not selected to run. Instead the party's convention had nominated a little-known doctor from the province of Córdoba, Arturo Umberto Illia.

Six days before the polls, Perón's order to cast blank votes became public. Two days later the government, as an added precaution, firmly blocked the only remaining loophole: a decree expressly banned the candidacy of Raúl Matera. On 7 July 1963 a weary, confused electorate went to vote. Actual abstention was low; 85.5 per cent of registered voters turned out. Even the *peronistas*' blank vote was unremarkable, at 17.2 per cent of the ballot. The surprise of the day was the unexpected victory of the UCRP candidate, Arturo Illia, with just under a quarter of the votes cast. The divided UCRI collected less than a sixth of the ballot, while Aramburu's Presidential dreams were shattered by a return of only 6.7 per cent.

Twice in two years Argentina had been given a President few people had actually heard of. Once again the country had a constitutional ruler, of sorts.

15

A DEMOCRATIC MINORITY
(1963–1966)

To describe Argentina at the time when Arturo Illia came to power in 1963 is difficult: not because the facts are unavailable, but because the picture that emerges from them is so complex and full of paradoxes. To make matters worse, perceptions of the Argentine situation — and particularly the Argentines' image of themselves — had become unusually distorted by the rapid economic and political changes of the past few decades. With many ups and downs, Argentina had industrialised rapidly, and the manufacturing sector was already contributing more than twice as much as agriculture to the country's gross domestic product. Important psychological breakthroughs had been achieved: the country was producing its own steel; oil production had risen while oil imports had shrunk to a very manageable trickle; motor vehicles were leaving the assembly line at a rate of over 100,000 a year; and durable consumer goods of all sorts were being produced locally. The import-substitution drive accelerated by the Frondizi administration had been highly successful, although its very success — measured by the expansion of local industry — had ended by leaving the country far more dependent than before on imports of raw materials and intermediate products for industry. As a whole, industry was still aimed mainly at the domestic market, and the hard currency needed to pay for these imports still came mainly from the export of agricultural produce.

For all the speed of this development, the rhetoric of *desarrollismo* had built up expectations that remained unsatisfied. Indeed one of the doubtful contributions of *desarrollismo* to Argentina's self-image was the generalisation of purely economic measures of success. Growth rates, rates of inflation, exchange rates — all had become standard front-page fare. And thus the fact that the country had not yet sprouted a large-scale petrochemical industry, or that giant hydroelectric complexes had as yet failed to materialise, became signs of 'slowness' in the fulfilment of the promise of development.

Many Argentines had made a lot of money. The population as a whole enjoyed the highest incomes of Latin America; indeed, in absolute terms,

248

it is provable that the minimum earnings of the poorest tenth of the population were higher than those of their counterparts in the Netherlands, Norway and France. Wealth was more evenly distributed than elsewhere in Latin America, but that did not prevent the wealthiest 5 per cent of the population from pocketing almost a third of all the income. Land ownership continued to be highly concentrated: just under half the farms, in units of more than 5,000 hectares each, were held by a mere 1.2 per cent of the landowners. If the scale is enlarged slightly, the picture is of a full two-thirds of all farms, in units of more than 1,000 hectares each, held by 5.6 per cent of the landowners. Yet the ownership of land had ceased to be the main source of income for the rich of Argentina: the people in the top 5 per cent of the income scale only took about a fifth of their revenue from the land. And one out of every five of Argentina's urban entrepreneurs had already joined the ranks of that top 5 per cent. Yet land retained its value as the ultimate source of social status, and the memory of the fantastic rates of profit produced earlier by land ownership had etched upon the psyches of merchants and industrialists a perverse notion of what should constitute an adequate reward for their efforts.

Prosperity had spread chiefly along the 'industrial belt' of Argentina's littoral, from the city of La Plata on the shores of the River Plate to the city of Santa Fe up the Paraná river, and inland to the city of Córdoba. This was also where most of the population had gathered too. In the first years of the 1960s, population growth had decelerated even more sharply than it had been doing in the 1950s, to a mere 1.25 per cent, more typical of the highly industrialised nations of the northern hemisphere than of anywhere in Latin America. Families, statisticians said, were down to an average of 3.7 members; the norm, particularly in the huge middle classes, had become only one or two children. Argentina boasted that less than nine out of every hundred inhabitants were illiterate, though it was becoming increasingly apparent that the dropout rate in primary schools was high. In fact, when these were taken into account, illiterates, semi-literates and 'functional illiterates' were seen to make up more than a third of the country's adult population. The problem was more acute beyond the 'industrial belt' in the provinces, which had also been left behind in other spheres. Statistical averages, for instance, showed that Argentina had as many doctors per thousand inhabitants as a number of European nations, but most of them were in Buenos Aires and the other large cities. While the urban dwellers enjoyed sophisticated medical techniques — the treatment of heart ailments and neurosurgery were often quoted as areas of high development — endemic diseases continued to affect a large segment of the rural population, and nutritional deficiencies were evident in several provinces in the interior.

Even in the large cities the bonanza had passed many by. More than a million-and-a-half people either had no home at all or were housed in makeshift or obsolescent dwellings — the *villas miseria*, the shanty towns that had made their appearance in the 1930s, were still very much in evidence, and although many of the earlier migrants from the provinces had moved on to better quarters, their places had been taken by droves of new arrivals, including an increasing contingent of immigrants from the poor neighbouring republics of Paraguay and Bolivia.

As Illia came to power, almost nine out of every hundred workers were out of a job. And inflation had been squeezing the paypackets of the eight-and-a-half million who held regular jobs. The mood of the unions was foul, and had been aggravated by what the *peronista* union bosses could only interpret as another frustration of their movement's rightful claim to political power.

It has long been an article of faith in Argentine politics that the UCRP is, *par excellence*, the party of the middle classes (just as *peronismo* is seen as the party of the working class). Illia's victory was widely regarded as the accidental triumph of a minority, middle-class group. Historically, of course, the old Unión Cívica Radical had appeared on the Argentine political scene as the party of the emerging middle classes. It had split once in 1957, the majority remaining with the UCRP; the splinter UCRI itself divided in two in 1963, with a minority following former President Frondizi. In the latter year, the branches from the old Radical trunk, taken together, attracted over 40 per cent of the vote; the 24.5 per cent that took the UCRP to the Presidency matched the votes of the *peronistas*, if blank votes are computed together with those that went to *neoperonista* candidates.

The social composition of the UCRP vote at the time is well known, thanks to a survey conducted by the sociologist José Luis de Imaz. More than a fifth of its followers were identified as belonging to the working classes; just under half were described as lower-middle-class; and a third as upper-middle-class. In a country where industrial and construction workers represented a quarter of the population, and those employed in the services sector just over 40 per cent, this configuration was hardly unrepresentative.

The UCRP was certainly a minority, one of many competing for power in 1963. Its minority condition, however, was heightened as a result of a change introduced in the electoral system. Had the contest been governed by the same rules that applied at the time Perón or Frondizi gained power, known as the 'selective' or 'incomplete' list, the votes collected by the UCRP would have given them 113 seats in the Chamber of Deputies — a clear, absolute majority. But proportional representation had been introduced, as one of the many instruments devised to avert a repetition of Perón's absolute control of Congress. Thus Illia's support in the Chamber of Deputies was reduced to only seventy-two seats. True enough, this was much more than any other party: the mainstream UCRI had nineteen; the dissident UCRI (soon to be known as Movimiento de Integración y Desarrollo, or MID) twenty; *neoperonistas* seventeen; and Aramburu's Udelpa fourteen (the remainder split up into seven tiny blocs). But from the outset it posed the threat of parliamentary alliances against the ruling party; a threat that would soon turn into a very real challenge.

Of course, Illia was offered many opportunities to form some sort of a coalition, sharing cabinet posts with several of his adversaries in exchange for Congressional support. But the Radicals decided to go it alone.

They had come to power, unexpectedly, with a programme their opponents described as vague. There was a commitment to nationalist economic policies, and particularly to the annulment of the oil contracts signed by the Frondizi administration with private companies, mostly from the United States, and to the rejection of the policy conditions established by the International Monetary Fund for loans to Argentina. There was a promise that all political proscription — and that meant Communists as well as *peronistas* — would be abolished. There was the commitment to that old aim of the labour movement, the minimum index-linked salary, and to that favourite of the enemies of *peronista* dominance in the trade union movement — a reform in the trade unions statute, aimed at de-centralising power and de-politicising strike action. In the military sphere, there was a promise to make some sort of reparation to the many *colorado* officers who had lost their commissions or been dishonourably discharged during the Onganía purge. In its most extreme form, this commitment went as far as the reinstatement of all the officers affected, but even before Illia took office the military leaders made it clear that they would not tolerate any such step. Over and above the matter of the *colorado* officers, it was Illia's intention to act as if everything the *azules* or 'professionalists' had said was actually true; that is, that the military were truly subordinated to the constitutional authorities.

What all this added up to was that Illia arrived at the Casa Rosada with almost every other political force opposed to him for one motive or another. The *peronistas* were not at all convinced that the proscription against them would really be lifted, and they were determined to force the government into keeping that promise. The unions, with unemployment and falling wage packets affecting their membership, did not believe in the government's economic policy, and were bent on exacting concessions as soon as possible, and on staving off any threat to *peronista* supremacy in the CGT. The followers of Arturo Frondizi were violently opposed to the government's declared oil policy, and wary of the implied threat to investigate alleged corruption in the negotiation of the Frondizi oil contracts. The Left, including the faction of the UCRI that had flocked behind Oscar Alende, felt that Illia's policies were not radical enough. The Right felt that the UCRP's penchant for economic nationalism and its rejection of the IMF's financial orthodoxy were a formula for disaster. The *azul* leadership of the military were convinced that the Illia government was plotting a *colorado* restoration, or at least a return to the days of 'political' control of the armed forces.

With this panorama, it is not surprising that some should have believed that Argentina was quietly nearing the brink of a major upheaval.

In Havana, ever since the *azul-colorado* battles of September 1962 and April 1963, Che Guevara had been taking a keener interest in developments in his native Argentina. His visitors were systematically quizzed about conditions there. He is reported to have been especially interested in the left-wing campaign for the return of Perón. One friend was asked, 'Assuming that Perón left his exile in Spain and took up residence here in Havana, do you believe that this would change the disposition of the Argentine masses?'

Guevara made no secret of his own conclusions regarding his country: 'The objective conditions for struggle have begun to appear in Argentina. There is unemployment, the people are hungry, and now the working classes have begun to react. This reaction attracts repression, which intends to crush dissidence by creating a climate of terror; but repression breeds hatred. It is at this precise juncture that the subjective conditions should intervene next to the objective conditions, that is to say, the awareness that victory is possible through violence, against the imperialists and their internal allies.' Che was sure that the moment was ripe to begin a guerrilla uprising in Argentina, starting in the country-side and progressively encircling the cities.

Unknown to the many people who heard Guevara expound these notions at the time, the veteran guerrilla leader had already set in motion a plan to bring about such an uprising. A key figure in this operation was an Argentine journalist, Jorge Masetti, who had been drawn to Che during the Cuban revolution, and after its victory had settled in Havana, where for a time he worked at his profession, helping to set up and direct the new Cuban governmental news agency, Prensa Latina. Political problems, aggravated by squabbles with his Cuban colleagues, had lost Masetti his job at Prensa Latina, but now, under Che's guidance, he was receiving training in guerrilla tactics. Masetti had been chosen by Guevara to lead a small band that was to establish itself in the extreme northwest of Argentina, in the province of Salta, close to the Bolivian border. Masetti's inexperience was to be offset by the presence of three members of Guevara's staff, the Cuban *comandantes* Hermes Peña Torres, Raúl Dávila and another known only by his *nom de guerre*, 'Papi'. Furthermore, Masetti's title was *Comandante Segundo*, Second Commander; the implication being that there would be a First Commander, a *Comandante Primero*. This was to be none other than Che Guevara himself.

The small contingent of revolutionaries arrived in Bolivia in May 1963 to start recruiting their guerrilla fighters. Masetti did not establish contact with any of Argentina's major political parties, nor even with the larger radical groups of the Left. He sought adherents mainly among dissaffected Communists and radical student groups. Recruitment, which meant attracting sympathisers in the major cities of Argentina and transporting them all the way to Bolivia, was a complex job. It was also conducted with scant regard for security, which scared off many of the by now highly security-conscious militants of the Argentine Left, while inevitably attracting the attention of the security services. While training proceeded at a farm in Bolivia close to the Argentine border, Masetti eagerly awaited news that the military, as he expected them to do, had prevented Arturo Illia from taking office.

When it became evident that nothing of the sort was to happen, Masetti in September 1963 ordered his men to begin *Operación Dorado* — their infiltration, unarmed, across the border into the Argentine province of Salta. He arranged simultaneously for the left-wing *peronista* magazine *Compañero* to publish a manifesto, calling on Illia to resign and urging the masses to rebel. He signed it 'Comandante

Segundo'. Almost at the same time as Masetti was ordering the start of the second phase of his infiltration — the smuggling of arms into Salta, which he named '*Operación Trampolín*' (Operation Springboard) — the security services were preparing a full investigation of this mysterious *Comandante Segundo* and his *Ejército Guerrillero del Pueblo* (People's Guerrilla Army). Buenos Aires was not paying much attention to these goings-on. Illia had taken office, and his government had formally announced that the oil contracts signed during Frondizi's Presidency were to be annulled. Days later, it became known that negotiations would be entered into with the oil companies with a view to seeking agreement on compensation payments. The UCRP was clearly sticking to its middle-of-the-road tradition. A couple of gestures were made in the direction of the armed forces: Juan Carlos Onganía was promoted to the rank of lieutenant-general, the highest in the Army, and a decree granted the military salary increases ranging from 20 to 40 per cent. On the economic front, import controls were introduced, and a one-year 'state of economic emergency' was declared, during which the government would control the supply and pricing of essential goods.

But the unions were already on the warpath. The CGT announced that it was embarking on a '*Plan de Lucha*' (Struggle Plan), which began with demonstrations, stoppages and a barrage of propaganda in January 1964. Soon a second stage of the *Plan de Lucha* was threatened, including the occupation by workers of their places of work. In its early days, however, the CGT's campaign was overshadowed by the spate of shoot-outs, assassinations and bombings by an extreme right-wing organisation. Its targets were Communists and Jews.

Then in early March came the news that the Gendarmería Nacional had come across a guerrilla encampment near the town of Santa Rosa, in the province of Salta. The first reports said that five of the guerrilla fighters had been arrested, and that one of them was a Cuban.

The adventure of Masetti's guerrilla band began to degenerate into tragic farce almost before it got started. Hopeful recruits did turn up, and by the time they had set up their camps in Salta province, they were a motley crew of some forty enthusiasts, mainly in their twenties. There were students of philosophy and medicine, bank clerks, unemployed mechanics and oil-drillers, evaders of compulsory military service, and even a Spanish sailor and a florist. But the critical political atmosphere in which they had expected to launch their insurrection had failed to materialise. There had been no military coup, and instead of a harsh military dictatorship in Buenos Aires there was a mild-mannered civilian President who believed in democracy. Even if the political climate had been more propitious, it is hard to imagine what this small group really expected to achieve in an area that, by Che Guevara's own precepts, was hardly ideal for guerrilla warfare. Salta's terrain might have been reminiscent of the Sierra Maestra in Cuba where Fidel Castro established his guerrilla base; mountainous and covered with forests of huge oaks, *lapacho, quebracho, palo blanco, palo amarillo* and *palo borracho*, it was certainly not the kind of theatre in which Argentina's conscript Army was trained to operate. But then there was no compelling reason for the Army to go there, even in the knowledge that a band of guerrilla fighters was roaming the region. Cuba's Sierra Maestra could have fitted several times in the forest areas of Argentina's northwest. And by comparison with Cuba, the province of Salta was empty of people: there were less than three inhabitants per square kilometre, hardly the sea of people in which the guerrilla fighters could expect to disappear like the proverbial fish so frequently mentioned by the theorists of insurgency. It goes without saying that with no masses to arouse, there were few hopes of a rapid spread of revolutionary fervour.

Moreover, the area penetrated by Masetti's force was about 1,500 kilometres away from Buenos Aires, and possessed no vital economic resources that could be held hostage by the *guerrilleros*. For all the difference their presence made, Masetti's band could have continued forever in their isolated forest haunts. If they wished to make any sort of political impact, or to engage the Army, or even to seek sustenance, the guerrilla fighters had no choice but to emerge from their forest sanctuary and come out into the open. Even for those who know them well, Salta's forests are inhospitable. The lush vegetation is misleading, for water is hard to find. Wild fruits and tubers can be highly toxic, as Masetti's Cuban companions discovered when they picked what they believed to be a local variety of the edible Cuban fruit *malanga* and fed it to the party. They were all seized with violent convulsions, and many never fully recovered from the effects of the poisoning. And then there is the ubiquitous *polvorín,* a tiny insect which burrows under the skin causing infections that can cause paralysis and the most fearful pain.

The ravages caused by aimless wandering in the forest, with weapons at the ready but no enemy to engage, soon began to wear down the morale of the guerrilla band. Their thwarted yearning for battle in the cause of revolution began to get twisted into internal bickering and intolerance of minor failings among themselves. When one young recruit, whose recurrent bouts of asthma were beginning to turn into a burden for the group on their training marches, suggested that it might be best if he were allowed to leave, their frustrated heroism found a perverse release: they set up a 'revolutionary tribunal' to try their hapless comrade for attempted desertion, found him guilty and sentenced him to die before a firing squad. It was not long before another similar incident took place. This time it was a former bank clerk who fell foul of the revolutionary principles upheld by the People's Guerrilla Army. A man whose initial zeal had led him to extract his toenails to enable him to march long hours without hindrance, he was charged with negligence in the handling of arms, insubordination and offences against revolutionary morale. He too was tried and shot.

Then came the ultimate disaster. The *guerrilleros'* carelessness in procuring supplies — they showed themselves openly to local villagers in their olive-green battledress, ostentatiously waving wads of cash — and in recruiting adherents in the capital made it an easy task for the security forces to locate them and make leisurely plans for their suppression. They did not rush the Army to engage them, but instead mobilised the Gendarmería Nacional, which was formed entirely of professionals hardened in frontier encounters with drug traffickers and smugglers. The gendarmes unobtrusively encircled the area where Masetti's presence had been reported. Then two agents provocateurs infiltrated the band.

No sooner had the two undercover agents been received into the People's Guerrilla Army and been issued with weapons, than they engineered a shoot-out with a gendarme patrol, in which one of the *guerrilleros* was injured. Masetti's men panicked. They dispersed and fled, only to be overcome by the forest (three starved to death) or to fall into the hands of the waiting gendarmes. Ricardo Rojo, a lawyer who later took up the captured guerrilla fighters' defence, described the episode in a chapter of his biography of Guevara. 'Fourteen men', he said, 'were already in the hands of the gendarmes, who tortured them in the bloodiest and most humiliating fashion. Five of them were dragged by the hair and had their faces shoved into the entrails of those who had already died, amid laughter and threats of the worst kind.' Only two of the insurgents, including the Cuban Hermes Peña, saw the fulfilment of their dream of engaging the security forces in combat. Surrounded by the gendarmes they fired off the automatic rifle and the revolver they shared against their assailants, and then were shot themselves. The gendarmes lost one man. Masetti vanished into the forest, never to be seen again.

Down in Buenos Aires, the news did not long hold people's interest. Illia's government had imposed exchange controls and declared an amnesty for twenty-one *colorado* officers who had been dismissed the previous year, and had proudly announced that the rate of inflation had actually dropped for two months running. But even these events paled before the signs of a crisis looming on the labour front. The CGT announced the imminent application of the 'second stage' of its struggle plan, the *Plan de Lucha*, reiterating that it would include the takeover by workers of factories throughout the country. And two *peronista* union leaders placed the campaign in a decidedly political context: Juan Carlos Loholaberry announced that Perón would be returning to Argentina before 1964 was out, and Andrés Framini, the triumphant but frustrated candidate for the governorship of Buenos Aires province, added that the exiled leader would be visiting Egypt and China on his way home, an oblique hint at the left-wing, pro-Third World coloration the more radicalised *peronistas* wished to imprint on their leader's return.

The *Plan de Lucha* got into gear in mid-May. Within a matter of days the first handful of factories were 'occupied' by striking workers; then the movement spread to 300 industrial establishments, and by the end of the month, with 1,200 factories taken over to the tune of screaming newspaper headlines, the country seemed to be besieged by an unstoppable wave of union militancy. It seemed almost inevitable that the Army would step in to restore order, or at least that the Illia administration would be forced to call in military assistance. Yet Illia confounded all expectations. Refusing to be drawn into an open confrontation with the *peronista* unions, he even refrained from ordering the police to intervene. Instead he coolly gave instructions for court proceedings to be instituted against 119 union leaders, which he followed by the promulgation of a law establishing a new, higher minimum wage and by decreeing a wide-ranging price freeze. He then sat back to let the storm blow over.

Strikes and occupations continued for another month, punctuated by ingeniously effective demonstrations, in which the CGT released into the most fashionable thoroughfares of the capital a flood of pigs, hens gaudily decorated with anti-government slogans, and tortoises (symbols of the Illia administration's 'slowness'). But by the end of June the

second stage of the *Plan de Lucha* was over, and the government had not
been dislodged.

It was not that the Army had remained completely impervious to the
events. On the contrary, the military hierarchy had been rattled by the
Plan de Lucha and by what they interpreted as the government's pusil-
lanimous reaction to the unions' open flouting of the law. And they
were particularly sensitive to any hint of a return to the *peronista* past.
They were incensed at the news that the Archbishop of La Plata had
travelled to Madrid to confer with Perón, and by former President
Arturo Frondizi's public announcement that he knew the whereabouts
of Evita Perón's embalmed body, which the military had secretly spirited
away after the 1955 coup. Although Illia had limited his promised vindication of the displaced *colorado* officers to a very restricted amnesty, and
took great pains to assure Army leaders of his wishes for good relations
between government and the military, they remained convinced that
sooner or later a bid would be made to interfere politically in the military
establishment. They were also worried by the government's apparent
lack of concern at the threat of subversion from the left, and indignant at
its decision to abstain from the vote in which the Organisation of
American States, following the lead given by the United States, instituted sanctions against Cuba.

The animosity between government and military became evident in a
multitude of ways. While the Army Commander-in-Chief, General
Juan Carlos Onganía, remained deliberately silent on political issues, he
obliquely drew attention on his travels abroad — to Taiwan and the
United States — to his differences with the government over foreign
policy and the attitude to be taken towards Communism. Unofficial
Army spokesmen let the public know, through controlled 'leaks' to the
press, that if *peronismo* were to score an important victory when the time
came to renew the legislature, in 1975, the military 'might have to step
in'. And one of the rising stars of the Army hierarchy, Alejandro
Agustín Lanusse, stated for the record that the Army was decidedly
opposed to Perón's return to Argentina.

By August 1964 *el retorno* (the return) had become the central theme of
Argentine politics. A number of prominent *peronista* leaders — Alberto
Iturbe, Andrés Framini, Delia Parodi, Juan Mena, Augusto
Vandor — travelled to Madrid with the ostensible purpose of preparing
the trip. At first, however, it seemed as if the Spanish authorities would
abort the project. Their police prevented Iturbe from holding a press
conference to announce *el retorno*, and Héctor Villalón, a businessman

linked to the 'revolutionary' wing of *peronismo*, made headlines by announcing that the entire operation had failed and that he, Villalón, was resigning from the *peronista* movement. Soon afterwards, Vandor, a leader of the 'metalworkers' union, made his way back to Buenos Aires, convincing many that *el retorno* was indeed off.

Yet within a matter of weeks the *retorno* fever had reached a new peak. Soon after Congress formally lifted the ban on *peronismo* (and on Communism), the *peronistas* took to the streets to call for their leader's homecoming. At first sight, the occasion they chose was an unlikely one; they timed their demonstrations to coincide with a state visit to Argentina by General de Gaulle, greeting the French statesman with chants of '*De Gaulle, Perón, un solo corazón*' ('De Gaulle, Perón, a single heart'). However nonsensical it might have seemed in terms of the respective political outlooks of the two men, the allegory was inescapable: like de Gaulle, Perón too would make a triumphant return from a long, apparently hopeless exile. The police did their best to suppress the demonstrations, which only enhanced their effect by provoking clashes that ended in numerous arrests, including that of Vandor.

Throughout the *peronista* movement the word spread that Perón would be home, one way or another, in time to celebrate with his supporters the historic date of 17 October, the annual memorial of the mobilisation which in 1945 cleared the way for Perón's accession to the Presidency. No longer proscribed by law and wildly enthused by this expectation, the 17 October rally, held at Plaza Once in Buenos Aires, attracted the largest multitude in years. Perón was not there in person, but a tape-recorded message promised that he would arrive soon, and the crowd's mood was almost triumphant as they attempted to march through the city, in defiance of police orders. Scuffles and clashes, barrages of tear-gas and water jets, flash demonstrations and baton charges continued well into the night.

Forty-three days later, as evening fell on the outskirts of Madrid, the police guarding the Perón residence paid little attention as the old leader's wife said her good-byes to two visiting *peronista* leaders, Delia Parodi and Jorge Antonio, and waved as they drove away in Perón's grey Mercedes. The General, they had heard, was unwell and had remained upstairs watching television. In actual fact, Perón was curled up in the boot of the Mercedes, where he would remain for a three-kilometre drive, at the end of which he was transferred to another car. The small party drove to a hostel outside the city, where a number of leading *peronistas* were waiting. They stretched their dinner until shortly before

midnight, then split up for the last leg of their journey, to the airport of
Barajas. The entire first-class compartment of an Iberia plane had been
booked for them, and Perón was able to reach it undetected thanks to the
complicity of the Chief of Spain's Army General Staff, who arranged for
a van to drive him in through a service entrance. They were airborne
half-an-hour after midnight: *el retorno* was under way.

But it was never completed. When the plane made its scheduled stop
at Rio de Janeiro, Brazil, it was surrounded by troops. Politely but
firmly, the travellers were informed that they would not be allowed to
continue their journey, and that the flight would be turned back.

Predictably enough, having thwarted Perón's return, the Illia administration had to face a renewed wave of strikes, stoppages and demonstrations, plus a smattering of terrorist bomb attacks, from the enraged
peronistas. To make matters worse, the conflict with the Army leaders
became more acute, and Illia was forced to accept the dismissal of a sympathetic General, Jorge Rosas, when General Onganía objected to his
'political' misdemeanours. Elections for the renovation of the legislature
had been scheduled for March 1965, and all eyes turned to a number of
previous provincial contests to gauge the possible outcome.

The first signs fuelled the government's optimism. The UCRP, now
competing in elections untarnished by proscriptions, won in the northeastern province of Formosa, and then again in La Rioja, in the northwest. A third contest, in the province of Catamarca, was somewhat
more sobering, though hardly depressing: the UCRP collected more
votes, but the *peronistas* gained more seats in the provincial legislature.
But these were small, relatively unpopulated provinces, and no amount
of wishful extrapolation could serve as a basis for accurate predictions of
the electoral behaviour of the more populous districts.

When the national legislative elections were finally held, the impact of
peronismo's return to legality was unmistakable. Attracting more than a
third of the vote, the *peronistas* increased their presence in the Chamber of
Deputies from the seventeen seats originally held by *neoperonista*
legislators, to fifty-two, which made them the second largest bloc in
Congress. All other parties (with the sole exception of a tiny provincial
grouping from Corrientes) lost seats in the *peronista* advance. This
included the UCRP, whose seats decreased from seventy-two to
seventy. Few commentators paused to remark that the ruling party had
in fact increased its share of the vote, from under 25 to over 28 per cent.
Indeed, the rejoicing on one side and the fear and resentment on the other

at the unmistakable *peronista* victory almost entirely obscured the fact that, in a free contest, just under two-thirds of the electorate had revealed itself as non-*peronista*, and just over half of these, split into a host of parties that were still undergoing processes of fragmentation, had voted neither for the government nor for the *peronistas*.

The country had certainly not been 'de-peronised' as hoped by the die-hard *antiperonistas*, but Illia certainly seemed to have fared better than his predecessors, military or civilian, in demonstrating that proscriptive measures were not the only way to forestall the re-peronisation of Argentina. One can speculate as to whether Perón's presence in Argentina would have made a difference; probably the answer is a guarded yes. Only weeks after the March 1965 elections, events would began to unfold which would reveal strong centrifugal tendencies within *peronismo*, with many strong leaders of union extraction — Augusto Vandor at their head — openly bidding for control of the movement in direct defiance of the directives relayed by Perón through his 'delegates'. The conflict was, of course, conducted in the name of 'true' *peronismo*, and was thus only possible in the physical absence of *el Líder* himself. The Radical government was banking on the intensification of internal strife within the *peronista* movement, and believed that competition for elected office would bring this about. Only two things could patch over the cracks in *peronismo*, and turn it again into a homogeneous force. One was Perón's return to Argentina, which had been prevented. The other was a military coup.

To a large extent, Illia's government was trying to play democracy by the book. The lifting of the ban on *peronismo* was, in Radical eyes, the only practicable form of washing away their own government's original sin, the illegitimacy engendered by the proscription of *peronismo*. Eschewing wholesale repression, even in the face of extreme provocation by the *peronista* unions, was a further token of their sincerity in this respect. This, of course, did not mean that the Radicals had renounced politicking, or decided not to take the fullest possible advantage of the fact that they were in power. On the contrary, the Radicals were rightly seen as the most 'political' of animals in the traditional sense. Strictly, theirs was the only political grouping in the country organised along party lines, in a pyramidal structure resting on a wide base of neighbour-hood *comités* (although *peronismo* had adopted the legal form of a party for electoral purposes, the *peronistas* themselves insisted that they embodied a 'movement', and thus were something bigger than a mere party).

Patronage and the traffic in political favours were very much the life-blood of the Radical party. And chicanery, trickery and skilful manoeuvring were resorted to whenever possible to weaken or neutralise their adversaries. The division of *peronismo* was fostered and encouraged by every means at the Radical government's disposal. Yet there was a tacit acceptance of a number of basic rules; there was, on the whole, sub-mission to the checks and balances embodied in Congress and the judiciary.

Much of the rest of Argentina's political world, however, was operating on a different wavelength. The years of *peronismo*'s absence from power had created a 'parallel' political system, unforeseen by the nineteenth-century makers of the Constitution, in which the powerful union movement, the armed forces and the business associations, as 'factors of power', negotiated the terms of political co-existence or con-frontation in the country. If elections entered the picture, the large *peronista* vote was there as a key commodity to be bought, sold or stored away. When elections played no part in the game, there was the mainly *peronista* union machinery to be wielded as a weapon. Although many a politician, *peronista* and non-*peronista* alike, was to learn painfully that the *peronista* workers were hardly a soulless, zombie mass, the temptation to play with them in complicated games of power arithmetic seemed almost impossible to resist.

Much the same could be said of the Army: 'knocking at the doors of the barracks' had become, even for the Radicals when they were out of power, an integral part of Argentina's 'parallel' political system. Such was the pervasiveness of this 'parallel' political structure that it actually swallowed up some segments of the formerly party-oriented political élite. The Conservatives were the first to give up on electoral struggle; after a number of splits and re-naming exercises, they vanished into the emerging reservoir of 'pressure groups', specialising in the provision of Economy and Finance Ministers at times of crisis. The nationalists, espe-cially those of the pseudo-aristocratic, ultramontane Catholic variety bordering on Fascism, had never managed to set up a sizeable party of their own; they were the original 'pressure group' or 'powerhouse', ever-ready to embark on an exercise of *copamiento* (take-over) of ideolo-gically formless political movements or of accidental, aimless governments.

The Illia years saw the passage to this shadowy political hinterland of the Frondizi-Frigerio group. Theirs was not a sudden shift — indeed, in the mid-term elections Frondizi's followers still managed to hold a substantial number of seats in Congress, but their leadership was already heavily involved in attempts to influence the military, the unions and the business élites towards a 'national revolution' that conceded only tactical relevance to the electoral system.

From the pressure groups came a barrage of hard-hitting, mostly fallacious propaganda messages about the Illia administration: that the President lacked decisiveness; that the Radicals were so engrossed in prospective electioneering that they had little time left for their administrative duties in government; that the government was lethargic and slow; that the economy was stagnating; that there was no firm response to threats against public order; that, just as in the time of Yrigoyen, the Radicals had confused the nation with their party, and had ended by ruling, most shortsightedly, only for themselves. This image, or composite of images, was reinforced by political humour, and particularly by the cartoonists, who were enjoying a rare spell of freedom from official censorship. Playing on Illia's habit of actually living in the Casa Rosada during the week, and of occasionally walking out alone, unprotected, to the plaza to feed the pigeons, he was portrayed systematically as a sleepy-eyed old man with a pigeon on his head. This — meant originally to symbolise his peace-loving nature — was later used to ridicule him. More bitingly, others had popularised the image of Illia as a tortoise, *la Tortuga*; stories made the rounds of Illia as the President who ruled through two folders on his desk, containing respectively the problems that time would solve and the problems time had already solved.

Attacks by the press on the Illia government became relentless, and into them crept an insidious lateral message: the idealisation of the military, and particularly of the *azul* leadership, as men of order and power with a vision; men inclined to produce a revised version of Perón's Army-unions-business entente, geared now to the rapid modernisation of an Argentina, the true realisation of whose greatness had long been postponed. Ironically, this idealisation of the Army spread across the entire political spectrum, from the far Right to the Trotskyite Left. Argentines were reminded of the Army's role, as embodied in General Mosconi, in the development of that touchstone of progress, the oil industry; and of the Army's contribution, through the less·deserving General Savio, to the construction of another touchstone, the steel industry. Even the Air Force, lacking a comparable figure, was blessed by the adoption of a civilian aviation pioneer, Jorge Newbery, whose image was militarised by association.

This campaign took place with the aid of a qualitative change in the

Argentine media. Television, having overcome its first bumbling decade, was becoming increasingly sophisticated, more 'Yankified', especially under the influence of a handful of Cubans who had fled Castro's revolution. The staid old newspapers, La Nación and La Prensa, were beginning to make long-delayed concessions to changing times in their format and style. And a newcomer had erupted on the scene, captivating the imagination of the highly-politicised Argentine readership: the weekly newsmagazine on the model of Time and Newsweek. Playing heavily to the passion of the Buenos Aires porteño for being 'the man in the know', the newsmagazines, departing from the florid, heavy style of the traditional journals, began to feed the country a rich diet of 'inside information' and 'behind-the-scenes' reports. First came Primera Plana, with a penchant for neologisms that soon degenerated into snobbism; then its competitor, Confirmado, deliberately adopting a colloquial, 'popular' style. These magazines were ideal vehicles for politics, and right from their inception they were used politically.

Both these new publications were created, one after the other, by the same man, the publishing entrepreneur who was to leave his mark on a whole generation of Argentine journalists: Jacobo Timerman. A tough, acid journalist himself, he had already displayed his talent for knowing intuitively what the public wanted, and his instinct for the jugular, as senior editor of the newspaper El Mundo and on television. His was anything but spectator journalism. Timerman not only campaigned but actually got involved in the thick of events. His task was more than merely reporting on history in the making; it was also that of helping to shape it. In a more institutionally structured society, he would have been the prototypical exponent of the press as Fourth Power; in the Argentina of the day, he made his new, influential segment of the press — perhaps inenvitably — a servomechanism of the pressure groups that operated in the 'parallel' political system.

Timerman loved the role of the hard-nosed, street-wise, almost cynical press baron. He acted it out with gusto, leaving a trail of deliberately provocative pronouncements on the realpolitik of journalism. 'Sell out?' he once responded to an accusation; 'like Xerox I have discovered that it is more profitable to rent oneself out!' As the super man-in-the-know who informed the aspiring man-in-the-know, he was sought out by generals, politicians, union leaders, businessmen. But the awe he inspired was not universally matched by trust or respect. Indeed the 'cynical' image he cultivated, coupled with the fact that he was a Russian-born Jew, made him ideal fodder for the streak of anti-Semitism that ran through nationalist political circles, while his success made him a target for many more in Buenos Aires, which is notoriously merciless to those of its inhabitants who make it to the top on merit. Timerman attracted accusations of opportunism, of shady business practices, and of involvement in many more conspiracies, political and entrepreneurial, than even he had heard of.

Timerman hardly ever 'softened' his image enough to reveal the ideals governing his immersion in politics, almost as if he felt that this would impair the efficacy of his tough-guy approach. His language, or rather the language of his publications, was basically that of developmentalism, Frondizi-style. Rapid industrialisation, particularly in 'basic' sectors, was the criterion against which all performance was measured. Inflation was regrettable, as were public deficits, but ultimately they were mere symptoms of more deep-seated ills which could only be cured by 'structural transformation'. Politically, the key problem was the 'integration' of *peronismo* in a mature society. Democracy was a commendable idea, but other things came first; the pursuit of 'formal' democracy was a red herring, and it was evident that Argentina's constitutionally-enshrined democratic institutions were mere transplants of European and North American experience, adopted without regard to the country's own history and traditions. This was the basic message, and it was rounded off with a more sophisticated version of that appeal, so popular in the 1930s, to the armed forces as the only institutions capable of bringing about the necessary transformation with the concurrence of all the major 'factors of power'.

'Let's manufacture intelligent generals' is one of the sayings attributed to Timerman. As the story goes, the technique consisted basically in attributing perceptive quotes to leading figures in the Army. The inevitable congratulations from those reading these pronouncements would not only insure against denials; they would actually lead the officer in question actively to seek a diet of well-phrased ideas in the pages of the newsmagazines. Timerman apocrypha are abundant, and as hard to confirm as most of the 'inside stories' he himself published. What cold facts show is that the magazines he created became vehicles for the promotion of Army leaders, for the systematic denunciation of the Illia government, and for formulating an updated version of the 'national security' rationale which in the 1940s had committed the military to promoting Argentina's first bout of industrialisation. One recurrent figure on the covers of *Primera Plana* and *Confirmado* was that of General Juan Carlos Onganía.

Onganía had been drifting steadily away from his original advocacy of military 'professionalism' and constitutionalism to a position of virtually justifying military resistance to the will of the elected authorities — a thoroughly political act — in the name of preserving the Army's 'apoliticism'. He began to see himself, as Commander-in-Chief, as the only guarantor of the Army's integrity, and the government's attempts to assert its authority as a campaign 'to destroy the Army'. Under Onganía, for the first time, the Army's General Staff did not limit its activities to the perennial updating of hypothetical war plans — they began to prepare, also, a host of contingency plans for running the government of Argentina. And Onganía himself began to perform as a military diplomat, often journeying abroad and holding forth to foreign audiences on what amounted to an alternate foreign policy for Argentina, and even for the whole of Latin America. His key contribution in this sphere was the notion of 'ideological frontiers': instead of their traditional role of defending their countries' physical boundaries, Onganía saw Latin America's armies as holding a far more undefinable line against the advances of 'international Communism'. And in this mission he envisaged close co-operation between the armies of Argentina and Brazil — the two largest and most industrialised nations of South America — as the keystone.

Onganía's doctrine of 'ideological frontiers' fitted in perfectly with Washington's designs for the hemisphere, although those close to Onganía would advance the curious argument that his scheme was actually an independent alternative to US policies. Roberto Roth, later one of Onganía's closest civilian aides, wrote, 'The United States were bent on transforming the South American armies into *gendarmeries* for the maintenance of public order, a thesis shared by important sectors of the Radical government. [Onganía] had managed to impose, at least officially, the opposite doctrine. [. . .] But through attrition, and lack of interest and understanding, a continuation of the Radical attitude would have led to the *gendarme* Army.' The paradox was solved through recourse to the rationale of developmentalism: structural change and rapid development would eliminate the root causes of Communist subversion, but the autonomous development of the Latin American nations — so went the argument — was actually being blocked, or at least discouraged, by the United States. But the fact remained that Onganía's 'ideological frontiers' seemed closer to Washington's Cold War approach to Latin American affairs than to the policies of the Illia administration, which made quite a show of distancing itself from anything that sounded like US interventionism in the hemisphere.

The differences between government and military over foreign policy flared out into the open soon after the March elections. The United States invaded the Dominican Republic to quell a rebellion that was attempting to restore to power the constitutional President, Juan Bosch. The reason invoked was that the rebel movement was reported to be controlled by Communists. Immediately after the invasion, Washington tried to legitimise its action by coaxing its partners in the Organisation of American States to make it an inter-American venture, and even to organise an OAS military force which would disguise the unilateral nature of US intervention. Many Latin American governments dutifully complied, despatching token units to the Caribbean. The Argentine military, fully expecting their government to do likewise, set about organising their own 'Caribbean Brigade'. The government was not of a single mind on the matter, but a number of high-ranking officials assured the Generals that an Argentine military presence in the Dominican Republic was a certainty. The CGT organised a mass rally against intervention in the Caribbean; in front of Congress shots were fired and petrol bombs hurled as the demonstration turned into a battleground between members of the right-wing Tacuara movement and the Communists. Two died in the fracas. The chairman of the Chamber of Deputies announced publicly that no Argentine troops would be sent to the Dominican Republic; the Under-Secretary of Foreign Affairs resigned in a huff, and military disaffection reached a new peak.

The squall had not passed when two journeys began that were to have dramatic consequences. From Madrid, sporting the title of personal delegate of Perón, his third wife, Isabelita Martínez, set off for Argentina via New York and Asunción. Soon afterwards, the Army Commander, General Onganía, departed on a grand tour of Spain, West Germany, Italy and Brazil. The latter trip was quickly completed, but on its last leg, in Brazil, Onganía stunned Argentina by hinting at an anti-Communist alliance between Argentina and Brazil, the first stage in the implementation of his theory of the new 'ideological frontiers' of the hemisphere. The UCRP promptly responded by accusing the General of meddling in politics, and the War Secretary, General Ignacio Avalos, resigned just as Isabelita Perón arrived in Buenos Aires. The opportunity had appeared for the Illia administration to rid itself of its troublesome Army commander.

There was nothing subtle about the chosen procedure. Illia made it known that his choice to replace the departed Avalos was General Eduardo Castro Sánchez, a serving officer who was junior to Onganía. The Commander-in-Chief, in no uncertain terms, said that he would find this intolerable. Castro Sánchez's appointment went through, and Onganía resigned. In his place the government appointed General Pascual Pistarini. Strictly, there was nothing irregular in the manoeuvre, but the *azul* Army leaders saw it as confirmation of their worst suspicions about the Illia administration. It was, they felt, the beginning of the long-expected Radical bid to 'politicise' the Army.

Isabelita Perón's presence in the country, meanwhile, led to another spate of *peronista* activism. Unauthorised demonstrations multiplied and were met with stiff police repression. Demonstrators were arrested by the score, and in one incident three were killed. More important, however, a serious split emerged within the ranks of *peronismo*. The *peronista* unions, still known as 'the 62', divided into two bands. One, led by José Alonso, declared its allegiance to Isabelita and adopted the name *De Pie Junto a Perón* (Standing next to Perón). The other, commanded by Augusto Vandor, paradoxically named itself *Leales a Perón* (Loyal to Perón), although its obvious *raison d'être* was its resistance to the dictates of Perón's personal delegate. Alonso lost his position as head of the CGT, and failed in an attempt to halt the tide of *vandorismo* by producing a letter from Perón that authorised the 'elimination' of Vandor from the *peronista* movement. Against the backdrop of this internecine power struggle, turbulence spread through the union movement. Strike followed strike, and acts of sabotage began to be reported in power utilities and steel plants. In the province of Tucumán the caneworkers struck and, borrowing a page from the *Plan de Lucha*, occupied the sugar mills and held managers hostage. The threat of a paralysing railway strike led the government to commandeer private buses and, in an uncharacteristic loss of nerve, to issue orders to the armed forces to stand by to intervene in the event of a major breakdown of order.

The extent of the feud within *peronismo* dawned upon everyone when elections were held in the province of Mendoza. Split into three squabbling factions, the *peronistas* lost miserably to the Radicals and Conservatives. Yet the feud not only continued but actually seemed to grow in violence and bitterness. In a shoot-out in the industrial city of Avellaneda, on the southern rim of Buenos Aires, a union leader close to Vandor, Rosendo García, was murdered along with two others. Vandor thundered publicly that more blood would flow.

Only days earlier, President Illia had delivered his 'state of the nation' message to Congress. He pointed out that his government had initially set itself the task of pacifying the country and normalising its institutions, of ruling without recourse to state of siege regulations or the holding of political prisoners, and tolerating the kind of pluralism that was manifest in the fact that opposition parties held power in several provinces of the republic. He claimed that in the thirty-two months of his Presidency, most of these aims had been realised. Contradicting assertions by the opposition that he had allowed the economy to stagnate and the social situation to deteriorate, Illia pointed to the statistical record. The economy as a whole had grown by 10.3 per cent in 1964 and 9.1 per cent in 1965; the manufacturing sector — whose alleged 'paralysis' figured prominently in most criticism of the regime — had expanded by 18.9 per cent in 1964 and 13.8 per cent in 1965. On the social front, the respective rises in real wages had been 7 and 5.1 per cent, and the rate of unemployment had dropped from 8.8 to 5.2 per cent of the labour force. His own party aside, few Congressmen heeded the President; instead his budget was rejected and one drawn up by the opposition was pushed through.

Towards the end of May, when the soldiers were celebrating Army day, their Commander-in-Chief, General Pascual Pistarini, delivered a strong speech in which he actually blamed the government for *peronismo*'s comeback. 'Freedom', he said, 'is jeopardised when, for the sake of convenience, decisions are delayed, encouraging the persistence of outmoded totalitarian myths . . . that generate both disappointment and frustration in everyone.' The Defence Minister, a UCRP politician, attempted to avert confrontation by producing a toned-down interpretation of Pistarini's outburst, and the War Minister, General Castro Sánchez, made a public statement flatly contradicting the Commander-in-Chief. But everyone knew that a coup was in the air. High-level meetings began to follow each other at a frantic pace. The armed forces tried to impose upon the government a purge of alleged Communists in high places. Top-ranking Air Force officers were dismissed for making political statements. Through a third party, Illia tried to halt the tide by appealing to Onganía to name a War Minister of his choice, but the message was never delivered — the chosen go-between had long been involved in a conspiracy to overthrow the government.

Then the commander of the Third Army Corps, General Carlos Augusto Caro, and the War Minister, General Castro Sánchez, held a none-too-secret meeting with three *peronista* Congressmen to discuss possible ways out of the crisis. The Army Commander, General

Pistarini, reacted to the news by ordering Caro relieved of his command and placed under arrest. President Illia, in turn, ordered the dismissal of General Pistarini. He had intended to announce the decision in a radio and television broadcast to the nation, but it was too late. The coup was already under way. In the early hours of the morning of 28 June 1966, General Mario Fonseca entered the headquarters of the Federal Police and informed the Chief that he was relieved of his post. Almost instantly, Army troops began to occupy radio and television stations, and armed units began to move into positions encircling the Casa Rosada. The movements were noticed by a young Lieutenant of the Presidential guard regiment, the Granaderos. He did not hesitate: he ordered the mere thirty soldiers under his command to man defensive positions, and informed his commanding officer, Colonel Marcelo de Elía, who alerted his regiment to prepare for a march on the Casa Rosada at the first sign of hostilities breaking out.

The Army entrusted General Julio Alsogaray, commander of the First Army Corps, with the task of securing the capture of the Casa Rosada. His attempts to persuade the Granaderos to abandon the President to his fate were a total failure. As the morning of the 28th dawned, Alsogaray turned up in the Casa Rosada with a retinue of five colonels and two civilians. He was ushered to Illia's office. The President, busy putting his signature on photographs for a handful of partisans around him, did not look up. Alsogaray strode to the desk, swept away the photographs and said, 'I have come on behalf of the armed forces to request your resignation.'

'The armed forces', replied the President, 'are represented by me. You are making use of a force that should be at the service of the Constitution and the law, and you cannot invoke a representation which is not yours.'

'Very well,' said Alsogaray. 'If that is the way you want it, I ask you to leave on behalf of the force under my command.'

'If you have that force,' said Illia, 'go and get it!'

But as Alsogaray left, Illia sent word to the Presidential guard that they were relieved of their duty to defend him.

The Casa Rosada began to be occupied by the military, but still Illia did not budge from his office. Finally, a squad of the Guardia de Infantería, the riot unit of the Federal Police, was ordered to dislodge the President, taking care to do him no personal harm. This they achieved by gently pushing the ring of young Radicals, who had protectively surrounded Illia, out of his office and into the street. Illia haughtily refused the offer of the Presidential limousine to drive him home.

Instead, he hailed a taxi and disappeared into the night.

The country was informed that the government had been taken over by the Junta of Commanders-in-Chief, with the purpose of carrying out the *Revolución Argentina*, the Argentine Revolution. Hours later, a new communiqué stated that the Junta had appointed a new President: General Juan Carlos Onganía.

16
A MILITARY MILLENNIUM
(1966–1968)

When Juan Carlos Onganía was sworn in as President, a number of trade union leaders, mostly belonging to the faction headed by Augusto Vandor, were present as honoured guests. This fuelled much speculation about the imminence of another Army-union entente similar to the one that had laid the foundations for *peronismo*. More immediately, however, it was read by Vandor and his followers as a tacit admission by the Onganía regime that the unions occupied an important position in the country's real power structure.

From afar, Lyndon B. Johnson issued a statement regretting the coup, and his government severed diplomatic relations with Argentina. At home, the displaced Radicals voiced some opposition, while the Left and the radicalised students castigated the new regime as yet another chapter in what they saw as the Pentagon's master-plan for repression in Latin America.

But the country as a whole remained quiet. The uninterested passivity of the majority and the vocal support voiced by a number of minorities hoping for a slice of the cake were all too readily construed by officialdom as signs of a widespread consensus operating in the new government's favour. Most of Argentina, to borrow a phrase much publicised by political commentators at the time, had given the Onganía government a 'blank cheque'.

However much hindsight might cast a flattering light on the deposed Illia administration, the propaganda campaign that had created the climate for the coup had not been so successful for nothing. It had struck a responsive chord in many people by criticising the permanence of 'the same old faces' in the higher echelons of the country's political parties. In an Argentina impatient for rapid change and frustrated by the poorly-understood obstacles that periodically brought to a halt the spurts of economic growth, it actually did seem that a government like Illia's, intent on conciliation and institutionalisation, was 'slow', and that the convolutions of the parliamentary process merely reflected the lack of urgency and of executive capacity of a Congress excessively preoccupied with

272

matters electoral. With the *peronista-antiperonista* rift still thwarting the integration of society, and with the *peronista* unions still capable of disrupting or preventing the normal conduct of government yet unable to take all the power into their own hands, the argument that a strong central force was needed to pull the country together appealed to many.

Beyond the small circle of those who actively promoted and executed the coup, there were those who went further than this visceral rejection of the Illia government's brand of democratisation. Quite a few were persuaded that parliamentary democracy as adapted from the Anglo-Saxon models did not fit the peculiar conditions created by Argentina's history, and was even more inadequate for the task of structural transformation needed to wrest the country from the grip of underdevelopment. There was, however, no universal agreement on the precise extent of this condemnation of democracy. Some read it as a merely temporary failing. In their view, Argentina was 'not yet ready for democracy': it was a matter first of actually building up the state, of establishing an orderly, efficient society, and only then of indulging in the luxury of democratic rule. (It is easy to see how this view dovetails with the economic 'liberal' axiom that the cake must first be baked before any thought is given to sharing it out.) Others took a more radical view, advocating either the adoption of corporate representation or the construction of a 'democracy of the masses', strongly nationalistic in character, on the foundations of a new convenant between the armed forces, the unions and 'national' industry. And there were, of course, multiple variations to these basic themes.

Whether or not, as rather elementary Marxist analysts strove to demonstrate, these political proposals immediately reflected the underlying economic interests of different groups in society is open to question. What is important is that by the time Onganía became President, a number of some such assumptions were common currency in Argentine political circles. It was widely accepted, for instance, that there was a considerable community of interest between the working classes and the small- and medium-sized entrepreneurs whose activities were directed mainly towards the domestic market. In the same scheme, these common interests were seen as opposed to those of the 'agro-export' sectors: the landowners, cattle-breeders and grain producers, who were seen as allied with the bankers, the local subsidiaries and affiliates of foreign companies, and the larger Argentine-owned business concerns with overseas links. It was further assumed that the interests of the former group found their correlate in policy packages that combined a measure of protectionism, exchange controls, heavy state intervention in the running of the economy, progressive income distribution and advanced social legislation, while the latter group would find it in free market policies, an open attitude towards foreign investment, a roll-back of state intervention, strict financial discipline, and a 'tough' disposition towards union demands. As to the purely political sphere, the latter were seen as formally adhering to democratic principles — after a period of enlightened authoritarianism — while the former insisted on 'real' democracy, regardless of the institutional forms involved.

Fitting the armed forces into this scenario has always proved a difficult task for students of Argentine political life, and the many and varied offerings available owe more to the political wishes of their authors than to rigorous examination of fact. Nonetheless, a widely-held view was that the military performed the role of 'arbiters' in the circular struggle for power between these broad alliances and sub-alliances discernible in Argentine society. They acted, in popular parlance, as 'tie-breakers'. The image of Argentina as engaged in a circular struggle between powerful forces that cancel each other out, yet are unable to achieve hegemony, is a favourite to this day. One scholar, Guillermo O'Donnell, has cogently argued that the 'joker' in this pack is the sector of Argentine-owned big business, the only one able to profit both from the expansionist policies favoured by the unions/small national business entente, and from the financial-austerity-cum-open-market approach of their opponents. Indeed, O'Donnell has suggested that most major political changes have accompanied the shifts in this sector's alliances with one or the other side. In the specific case of the Onganía administration, O'Donnell suggests that Argentine-owned big business, quite atypically, after having joined forces with the farmers to oppose Illia, decided to sever that link and make an attempt to run the country on their own.

If there was anything the new government needed, over and above the 'blank cheque' granted by the population at large, it was some sort of approval from the exiled Juan Domingo Perón; some sign that his followers, at least initially, would abstain from overt confrontation. Perón was kept well informed of the preparations for the coup. Three days before Illia was ousted, an encoded telegram was received at Perón's residence, the Quinta 17 de Octubre, in the residential Puerta de Hierro district of Madrid. It said: 'Arriving in Madrid between 28th and 29th but will probably advance journey by twenty-four hours.' It signalled the probable timing of the coup itself. The day before Illia was removed from the Casa Rosada, Perón granted an exclusive interview to an

Argentine journalist, Tomás Eloy Martínez, of the weekly news magazine *Primera Plana*, which was already preparing a special edition for publication the moment the military moved.

Perón was cagey about Onganía (whose appointment as President was still twenty-four hours in the future). 'I do not know Onganía well enough,' he said. 'He is a man who speaks very little, and is therefore hard to define. It is my impression that he is a good soldier; I know that he is patriotic, well-intentioned and honest, and these are essential qualifications for a political man. I recognise in Onganía the qualities needed to command the Army. If Onganía behaves in the political sphere in the same way as he has done in the military sphere, the country could do well.'

Then he added: 'I sympathise with the military movement because the new government has ended a catastrophic situation. As an Argentine I would have supported any man who put an end to the corruption of the Illia government. [. . .] The man who put an end to all this must command my sympathies, of course, but I do not know if this will last into the future. The present government's defect is that it does not know exactly what it wants, and it will be interesting to see what happens when they untie the package, because even they do not know what they'll find inside.'

Perón issued a call for unity and for prompt, clean elections. Not, he said, that he wanted to profit from them himself: 'I am already beyond good and evil. I have already been everything anyone can wish to be in my country, which is why I can speak unbound by earthly considerations [*descarnadamente*].' Yet Perón did not limit himself to offering free advice; behind the expressions of goodwill there came a very explicit threat. 'The time has come', he said, 'for the Argentines to reach an agreement. If not, the time will have come to take up arms and fight. The path of unity is increasingly difficult; the path of arms increasingly easy. [. . .] I have had many offers of arms and troops, but I have refused them so as not to sell my soul to the devil, and in order not to cause bloodshed. [. . .] This is our last chance, which is why we need greatness from this new government. Should this not happen, we will end up in a civil war, and we shall all have to take part in that war. May God illuminate Onganía and his boys [*muchachos*], and may those boys know how to grasp the hand that Fortune is extending in their direction.'

The men who inspired and executed the 1966 coup were convinced that they were engaged in a momentous task. They were the founding fathers of a new republic, though they carefully avoided using this phrase, because it recalled too vividly the ultramontane Catholic proposals behind General Uriburu's coup in 1930. 'New Argentina' had already been pre-empted by Perón. Arturo Frondizi, who had been vying for the position of major ideologue of the movement, had been calling for *the* 'National Revolution' — so that too was out. Anticipating the verdict of history, they chose to name their venture the *Revolución Argentina*, signalling their expectation that posterity would remember it in the same light as the French Revolution, the Russian Revolution, the Mexican Revolution, even the Cuban Revolution. Mariano Grondona, a pundit who had been, under President Guido, the country's youngest Under-Secretary of the Interior, and who had taken upon himself the task of discerning the historic transcendence of each successive government, suggested that those who had executed this *Revolución Argentina* were called to perform a unifying task similar to that of Julio Argentino Roca in the 1880s.

The Commanders-in-Chief of the three services had history in mind when they deposed Arturo Illia and called Juan Carlos Onganía to the Presidency. Not for them the drabness of mere decrees: the instrument of Illia's ouster was called *Acta de la Revolución Argentina*. Following the tradition of attaching an explanatory 'message' to every law and a carefully laboured list of 'considerations' to every decree, the *Acta* carried a long preamble, stating that the military had taken this drastic step after 'one last, comprehensive analysis of the general situation in the country, and of the multiple causes that have given rise to the dramatic and dangerous emergency the Republic is living through'.

'This survey', they went on to say, 'makes it clear that the exceedingly bad management of public affairs by the present government, a culmination of many other errors made by those who preceded them in the last decades, of structural deficiencies and of the application of systems and techniques that are inadequate to contemporary realities, has caused the breakdown of the Argentine people's spiritual unity, widespread disappointment and scepticism, apathy and the loss of national sentiment, chronic deterioration of economic and financial activity, the rupture of the principle of authority and an absence of order and discipline that translate into deep social disturbances and a notorious disregard for law and justice. All this has created propitious circumstances for a subtle and aggressive Marxist penetration of all spheres of national life, and has built up a climate favourable to extremist outbursts that place the Nation in danger of falling to the advances of totalitarian collectivism.'

The *Acta* then decreed the ouster of the President, the Vice-President and all provincial governors and vice-governors; dissolved Congress and all provincial legislatures; fired the Supreme Court and the Procurator-General; dissolved all political parties; and modified the Constitution by adding to it a 'Statute of the Argentine Revolution'. The Revolutionary Junta dissolved itself after appointing a new Supreme Court and installing General Onganía as President, with powers both executive and legislative. 'The armed forces', they proclaimed, 'do not govern or co-govern.'

There was none of the usual commitment to rapid restoration of elected rule; no term was set to the task of 'transformation and modernisation' they were taking upon themselves. 'It is not a matter of calendars,' they announced, 'but of the fulfilment of our objectives.' Some officials hinted to friendly journalists that this meant at least a decade. Onganía himself was reported as seeing the 'Argentine Revolution' unfolding in three successive stages: 'the economic time, the social time, and the political time'.

Formally, as Annex III to the 'Statute of the Argentine Revolution', the military published their 'Political Objectives'. In inimitable barracks prose, the document stated:

I. GENERAL OBJECTIVE

To consolidate spiritual and moral values; to elevate cultural, educational, scientific and technical levels; to eliminate the deeprooted causes of present economic stagnation; to achieve adequate labour relations; to ensure social welfare and to affirm our spiritual tradition inspired in the ideals of freedom and dignity of the human person, which are the patrimony of Western Christian civilisation, as a means to re-establish an authentic representative democracy ruled by order within the confines of the law, of justice and of the common good, and all of this to re-orient the country along the path of greatness and to project it abroad.

II. PARTICULAR OBJECTIVES

A. IN THE SPHERE OF FOREIGN POLICY

1. Firmly to maintain the sovereignty of the Nation, defending its territorial integrity, spiritual values, style of life and the great moral aims that conform the essence of nationality.

2. To develop a foreign policy inspired by the best of our history, executed in continuity with its traditions and international commitments, and guided by a moderate, well-reasoned conception of its future; to sum up, a foreign policy that affirms its faith in the greatness of the Nation's mission.

3. To assume with irrevocable decision, of its own free will, according to its

origins and destiny, the commitment to partake of the defence of the free Western Christian world.

4. To contribute with our best energies to the attainment of the international common good and to preserve friendly relations between peoples, based on a true peace and affirmed by the international juridical organisations.

B. IN THE SPHERE OF DOMESTIC POLICY

1. To promote a spirit of concord, solidarity and tolerance between Argentines; to restore in the country the concept of authority, the sense of respect for the law and the reign of true justice, in a republican regime in which the exercise of individual duties, rights and freedoms will be fully guaranteed.

2. To promote the consolidation of a national culture inspired essentially by the country's traditions, but open to the universal experiences proper to the Western Christian civilisation to which it belongs.

C. IN THE SPHERE OF ECONOMIC POLICY

1. To eliminate the deep-rooted causes that have led the country to its present stagnation.

2. To establish bases and conditions that will render feasible a great economic expansion and an authentic, self-sustained development through the full utilisation, at the highest possible level of yield, of the country's human and natural resources.

3. To ensure access to the availability of more goods and services for all those who are willing to make a sustained effort to obtain them, with the ultimate aim of procuring for the inhabitants of the Republic the greatest freedom, prosperity and security compatible with order, social discipline and the country's real possibilities.

D. IN THE SPHERE OF LABOUR POLICY

To reach a fair balance between the interests of the Nation, labour and the enterprise, maintaining the corresponding organisations within the specific frame of their proper functions.

E. IN THE SPHERE OF SOCIAL WELFARE POLICY

To create conditions for the growing social welfare of the population, developing social security, elevating to the maximum possible the levels of health and facilitating access to dignified housing.

F. IN THE SPHERE OF SECURITY POLICY

To attain the integral aptitude necessary to ensure the attainment of the objectives in the other spheres.

In plain language, the 'Argentine Revolution' was proposing whole-hearted alignment with the West, hard work, law and order, and the depoliticisation of the *peronista*-dominated unions. Much of the abstruse wording of the 'Political Objectives' represented compromises between the catchphrases of the different pressure-groups bidding for a leading role in the new regime.

With party politics out of the way, political activity would, as is usual in these cases, revolve around the management of the economy and the relations between government and unions. The main contenders for this key area were the followers of Arturo Frondizi and the disciples of Alvaro Alsogaray. Their rivalry was described in public debate as an option between 'structuralism' and 'monetarism'; between granting priority to the infrastructure necessary for rapid development and attending first to monetary stability and financial health.

Alsogaray had the inside track: most of the planning for the coup had been conducted by his brother, General Julio Alsogaray, and he himself had been called upon to offer advice in the field of economic policy. Indeed, many believed that Alsogaray's appointment as Minister of the Economy would be almost automatic. Yet when Onganía chose a relatively obscure businessman, Jorge Néstor Salimei, for the job, it was not seen as a defeat for Alsogaray, but as a shrewd tactical move. Salimei had frequented the Instituto de Economía de Mercado, Alsogaray's eco-nomic policy think-tank, and was readily seen as little more than an executor of Alsogaray's proposals, though one who would not provoke as much opposition as Alsogaray himself. The word quickly got around that Alsogaray had been kept in reserve for a more immediately impor-tant role: that of representing the new régime in the *de rigueur* pilgrimage to the financial centres of the Northern hemisphere, to ensure the neces-sary flow of resources for this brave new surge of development.

Frondizi was out, excluded at least from the crucial Ministry of the Economy. But not completely out. There was still the constellation of National Councils set up by the new government to map out in detail how the objectives of the 'Revolution' would be attained: the National Development Council, the National Security Council, the National Council for Science and Technology. Frondizi's 'developmentalists' put their sights on the first two, hoping to be able to dictate economic policy, and hence the shape of the new republic, from above. And there were the State Secretariats, only formally included within Salimei's jurisdiction (Secretaries were appointed independently, not as a team under the leadership of the Minister): Industry, Commerce, Agriculture, Mining, Transport, Communications. And the host of state-owned enterprises: the oil company, the gas company, the coal company, the meat board, the grains board, the utilities.

Salimei's command of the key area of economic policy was far from complete. Even without considering the inroads made or attempted by the 'developmentalists', the Central Bank had evaded his grasp, having been entrusted to a team of men loosely known as 'Social Christians'. Thus, what at first seemed to be a victory for Alsogaray was almost instantly turned into a small tactical advantage over his rivals. And even that seemed to vanish as it became evident that Salimei had a mind and a will of his own.

The mishmash of tendencies at work within the government was reflected, in one way or another, within Onganía himself. In the purely political field, he saw his task as that of giving the country a period of peace and growth during which it could overcome the '*peronista-antiperonista* antinomy'. The armed forces, in his view, could now settle down into the 'professionalist' role he had advocated, as Commander-in-Chief, five years earlier. As for the political long term, Onganía had no clearly-defined project, although he had taken to heart some of the arguments put forward by his nationalist friends, to the effect that perhaps Argentina had adopted too slavishly an Anglo-Saxon model of democracy that did not quite fit local traditions and circumstances. The political ministry, the Ministry of the Interior, had been entrusted to nationalists, as had the staffing of Presidential advisory bodies.

Onganía was a devout Catholic, but had not remained wholly immune to the winds of change sweeping through the church in the 1960s. Indeed, he was known to be affiliated to *cursillismo*, a movement of personal renewal in the faith perhaps best decribed as a conservative precursor of the charismatics. Well-read in the social teachings of the church, he openly adhered to the principle of 'subsidiarity' as the factor governing relations between state and community: the state, according to that principle, should only take upon itself, apart from its regulatory role, those activities ordered towards the common good which private persons or associations could not, or would not, do on their own. Understood passively or restrictively, as had so often been done in the past, 'subsidiarity' could easily become indistinguishable from laissez-faire — hence much of the affinity Onganía felt for the arguments put forward by Alsogaray as the prophet of a 'social market economy'. Understood in a more active, militant frame of mind, 'subsidiarity' could embrace the entire range of state interventionism — hence Onganía's parallel sympathy for the 'Social Christians' and for the grandiose development schemes being hatched by 'Conade', the National Development Council. And at this end of the spectrum, Onganía's inclinations were reinforced by the Army's 'national security doctrine', which he himself had helped to expand.

Onganía believed in a strong Presidency, and heartily agreed with those of his advisers who maintained that Argentina's system of government had wrested away much of the President's effective power, reducing him to rubber-stamping decisions and proposed legislation produced by his ministers. And as the 'Argentine Revolution' had endowed the Presidency with legislative as well as executive faculties, they saw a clear danger that this transfer of power to the ministries would increase rather than decrease. With differently motivated pressure-groups carving out their respective niches in the ministries and State Secretariats, it was an ominous prospect.

Onganía's solution to the problem was the enlargement of the President's own establishment, recruiting trusted specialists and experts for a new Legal and Technical Secretariat, whose role it would be to scrutinise and assess every single piece of paper passed on by the ministries for the President's signature. The various National Councils reported directly to the President, as did the team set up to achieve the rapid rationalisation and drastic slimming of Argentina's huge public administration.

The Onganía regime did not find it too difficult to staff the administration. Hosts of young Argentines in their twenties or thirties were standing by, more than willing to fill vacancies as under-secretaries, directors-general and heads of department in the ministries and state-owned enterprises. They were, in more than one sense, the Frondizi generation — not necessarily because they shared his views (which many did), but because they were the first fruits of the 'developmentalist' expectations his government had generated, and of the innovations he had set in motion in higher education by ending the state's monopoly on university teaching. These young men, and their masters in the higher echelons of the administration, came later to be described as 'technocrats'. Indeed they represented a change in the educational qualifications expected of high-ranking public officials. Hitherto the state apparatus had fed on the *bachilleres*, the graduates of the nineteenth-century

French-style secondary school system, and it had been ruled by *doctores*. The latter were only exceptionally authors of doctoral theses: besides physicians, dentists and veterinary surgeons, in Argentina the title *doctor* is liberally applied to lawyers, and these — the most abundant harvest of the universities — had flocked to fill positions of leadership in the political parties, and the choicest slots in the country's government.

During the brief Frondizi era, much had been made of the inadequacy of an educational system which churned out lawyers and physicians by the hundred in a country preparing for the great leap forward towards rapid industry-based development. One of the key motives for the legalisation of private universities was the hope that, in close contact with the demands of business and industry, the new institutions would offer courses and curricula to train the youth in the less prestigious but eminently practical and vitally necessary disciplines required by the 'developmentalist' crusade. To a certain extent it worked, but the broader response was one of 'modernisation' of the status-linked careers. Some engineering and technical careers were certainly enriched, and commercial and managerial training had its prestige elevated, but the main product of this period was an avalanche of aspiring economists, sociologists, political scientists and psychologists.

This was hardly surprising, for the new private universities could more easily embark upon these paths than upon the 'harder' disciplines that called for huge investment in equipment and physical installations. And the state universities found it equally easy to follow suit.

By the time Onganía arrived on the scene, four years after Frondizi's ouster, the youths who had responded to these new opportunities were already graduates. Everywhere there seemed to be scores of *licenciados*, eager to prove themselves and their 'modern' skills and outlooks.

For all the prior planning, the new government did not seem to be in a hurry to get its 'Revolution' under way. The first couple of weeks were taken up with the appointment of new officials, while other forces, domestic and external, cleared the decks for action. Perón's wife Isabelita abruptly ended her sojourn in Argentina and headed back to Madrid. The United States announced its recognition of the new authorities and the resumption of diplomatic relations, while the Minister of the Interior, Enrique Martínez Paz, served official notice on all and sundry that the 'Argentine Revolution' had no deadlines and could well last a full decade.

Then action began, giving the people their first taste of what they could expect from their new rulers. The first decision of any importance was the closure of the satirical magazine *Tía Vicenta*, for having dared to adorn its cover with a caricature depicting Onganía as a walrus. The next, calculated to show the government's determination, was the order to bulldoze the popular grills on Buenos Aires' Avenida Costanera, the riverfront avenue where the *porteños* had grown used to gorging themselves on juicy steaks, roasted entrails and huge *chorizo* sandwiches. Still known by their old name of *carritos*, or little carts, recalling the days when they operated out of trailers, the grills had taken root along the Costanera, becoming regular restaurants — but obstinately refusing to comply with municipal regulations. Hardly a major issue but, in the absence of any other, it allowed the government to make a show of toughness.

Only days later, the same toughness was directed towards a far larger target: the universities. Shielded by their precious autonomy, the institutions of higher learning were seen by the military as hotbeds of seditious thought, and by nationalists as enclaves of foreign influence, disconnected from the real needs and aspirations of the country. The government announced the *de facto* cessation of university autonomy, appointing federal trustees to run them. Not surprisingly, the students launched a protest movement, occupying the university buildings. Unlike its predecessors, the Onganía government did not take the student reaction lying down: police armed with tear gas and batons took the buildings by assault, bruising protesters by the score and arresting them by the hundred. Not even members of the faculty were spared in what came to be known as 'the night of the long batons', the first link in a chain of repression that forced many academics into exile and led the international academic community to ostracise Argentina for several years. Within Argentina itself, this hamfisted first approach to university policy sowed the seeds of a movement of student dissent that was to grow in intensity throughout the years of military rule. Indeed, before the government was three months old, the student protesters already had their first martyr: twenty-four-year-old Santiago Pampillón, shot by the police during a demonstration in Córdoba.

If the government's commitment of upholding 'the principle of authority' was not found wanting in its treatment of irreverent humorists, recalcitrant *carrito* proprietors and seditious students, it did not fare too well in its first confrontation with the unions. The first union whose annual wage agreement came up for renewal was none other than that of Augusto Vandor's metalworkers. Heedless of the government's calls for restraint, they not only pressed ahead with their claims, but actually took to the streets. After a vicious little clash with the police in the industrial district of Barracas, the government switched suddenly to conciliation. Within days a satisfactory agreement had been hammered out, and a great show was made of inviting Augusto Vandor to the Casa Rosada for its formal signing.

In the Ministry of the Economy, Jorge Salimei fired off, in time-honoured style, by decreeing a devaluation that took the quotation of the US dollar from 202 to 215 pesos, and announcing that it was his intention to move towards a wholly free exchange market. Beyond that, the new government's proposals hardly lived up to their 'revolutionary' billing. On the whole, they added up to little more than a tough-talking house-cleaning operation. Salimei himself chose to make his first stand by announcing a complete overhaul of one of the economy's longest standing problems: the sugar industry in the province of Tucumán. Ever since Perón's days, the industry had been functioning under special legislation, ostensibly designed to protect the small cane-growers from the greed of the large mills. They were paid according to the tonnage of cane they delivered, regardless of their actual sugar content; not surprisingly, with sales virtually guaranteed, this led to an inordinate expansion of sugar-cane growing, well beyond the most suitable lands and into marginal terrain. Quite naturally, this did not make for economic results, and many of the mills were only kept in operation by government largesse. Chronic financial constraints kept wages low and working conditions primitive for a large number of mainly seasonal workers, making Tucumán a perennial hotbed of social discontent that had already erupted into violence several times.

Salimei's solution was a government takeover of those mills that were in worst shape, as a prelude to a major reorganisation of the industry. Closures, he made it quite clear, were unavoidable. Under pressure to show rapid results, Salimei railroaded Onganía into signing the necessary legislation. It soon emerged, however, that the list of mills targeted for government takeover had been prepared over-hastily: it included several companies in good health and left out a number that were on the brink of collapse. Furthermore, no measures were taken to create new sources of employment in place of those being slated for elimination, and anxiety spread rapidly through Tucumán, generating protest movements and even a higly-publicised 'March to Buenos Aires'.

In other areas as well, the Onganía government announced its intention to tackle the economy's most notorious 'white elephants': the railway system, still shouldering a huge, chronic deficit almost a decade after Arturo Frondizi's government had performed drastic surgery on dozens of uneconomic lines; the state apparatus, grossly overstaffed, riddled with irregularities such as multiple job-holding and a proliferation of 'special commissions' surviving long after the reasons for their creation had been forgotten; and the port of Buenos Aires, weighed down by restrictive practices that had already earned it a reputation as a 'dirty port'. And, of course, there was the question of the oil industry, which the Onganía administration was committed to opening once again to foreign participation, in a complete reversal of the Illia administration's nationalistic approach.

Before anything could get under way in any of these fields, however, the government had to face an embarrassing challenge from an unexpected quarter. It was not, as in earlier cases, a direct challenge to its authority, but to its nationalistic leanings and its commitment to affirm Argentina's sovereignty over its entire territory.

Prince Philip had just arrived in Buenos Aires for a visit that was to include much social contact with Argentina's 100,000-strong British community, and a fair amount of polo-playing — a passion the Prince shared with General Onganía. No sooner had the visit begun than it was shattered by news that an armed group had hijacked a domestic Aerolíneas Argentinas flight and diverted it to Port Stanley, capital of the Malvinas or Falkland Islands. To make matters worse, one of the passengers on the hijacked plane was the Governor of Tierra de Fuego: his full title was Governor of Tierra del Fuego *and the Islands of the South Atlantic*, and the Malvinas, on paper at least, were part of his jurisdiction. The gunmen, who called themselves Grupo Cóndor, put the Governor in the awkward bind of being invited formally to repossess the Malvinas and to call on Buenos Aires for military backing of this improvised 'invasion'. The leader of the Grupo Cóndor was a young man called Dardo Cabo, an action-minded nationalist, son of a trade union leader; he had once been prominent in a right-wing goon squad known as Movimiento Nueva Argentina and more recently was the man in charge of Isabelita Perón's bodyguard during her visit to Argentina.

Enthusiasts in Buenos Aires greeted the news by shooting — harmlessly — at the apartments where Prince Philip was in temporary residence. But Onganía disowned the escapade, and in Port Stanley the Governor of Tierra del Fuego refused the honour his captors were offering him. They were left with no choice but to surrender to the British authorities, who lost little time in repatriating them to

Argentina, where they were promptly thrown in prison.

From Madrid, without making any direct reference to the event, Perón cut short his honeymoon with Argentina's military rulers, describing Onganía as 'a reactionary and a *gorila*'. Predictably, that year's celebration of *peronismo*'s major anniversary, 17 October, turned into a violent confrontation with the police and ended with clouds of tear-gas hanging low over Plaza Once. The very next day, protesting at the government's announced reorganisation of the port of Buenos Aires, the dockworkers went out on a strike that was to last for two full months. Within a few days they were followed by the railwaymen, who struck in opposition to the announced restructuring of the entire rail system. On their heels the CGT, claiming that the cost of living had risen by one-third in the first eleven months of the year, called a one-day general strike.

Salimei, with little except widespread dissatisfaction to show for his five months in office, felt compelled to decree yet another devaluation, pushing the price of the US dollar to 255 pesos. In the political area of government, Enrique Martínez Paz was under fire for having passed legislation that severely restricted the right of *habeas corpus* and all but eliminated the judges' ability to grant injunctions against administrative decisions. Onganía's Legal and Technical Under-Secretary, Roberto Roth, who had opposed these measures, recalls having said to a colleague at the time: 'With this text one day we will find ourselves in prison.' In his memoirs of this period, published in 1980, Roth added: 'My words were prophetic. Three years later, during the Lanusse government, I was in prison, claiming an ineffectual *habeas corpus*.'

More immediately, however, these developments exacerbated the impatience which leading Army officers had already been voicing privately. Unwilling to question Onganía himself, they concentrated their criticism on his two leading ministers — and were eagerly joined by most of the pressure-groups, who saw a new opportunity opening for the placement of their own people in key government positions.

Onganía made another display of authority, ordering the replacement of the Army Commander-in-Chief, General Pascual Pistarini, by General Julio Alsogaray. It was his way of reminding the generals that in the *Revolución Argentina*, as they had proclaimed earlier, 'the armed forces do not govern or co-govern.' Having made his point, he allowed a fortnight to pass, then demanded the resignations of his entire cabinet, six months to the day after his inauguration as President. Before the year was out he had appointed the successors to the two key ministries: Guillermo Borda at Interior, and Adalbert Krieger Vasena at Economics.

The day after Adalbert Krieger Vasena was appointed Economics Minister, New Year's Day of 1967, Fidel Castro in distant Havana was delivering one of his usual lengthy harangues to the Cuban people. Towards the end he had inserted a paragraph which caught the imagination of his listeners; a greeting to Che Guevara 'wherever he may be'. Throughout the Americas, intelligence officers monitoring the broadcast discounted the reference as a hypocritical propaganda ploy: Guevara had dropped out of sight in 1965, abandoning his official position in the Cuban government, obviously having incurred the disfavour of his former comrades. Everyone *knew* that Guevara was either a prisoner, or an internal exile, or even dead. There had been many rumours of Guevara sightings throughout the world since his vanishing act — and just as many reports stating categorically that he had been killed.

Officially, Che's last words had been the letter he had written sometime in mid-1965 and which Castro had read publicly in a speech in October of that year:

Other nations are calling for the aid of my modest efforts. I can do what you are unable to do because of your responsibility as leader of Cuba.

I want it to be known that I do this with a mixture of joy and sorrow: here I leave behind the purest of my hopes for building, and the dearest of my loved ones, and I leave a people who have accepted me as their son. This deeply pains a part of my spirit. In new fields of battle I will bear the faith you instilled in me, the revolutionary spirit of my people, the feeling that I am fulfilling the most sacred of duties: to fight against imperialism wherever it may be. This comforts me and more than compensates for my regrets.

Guevara's departure from Cuba officialdom had indeed taken place under the shadow of disfavour. At first he chose for himself a destiny of stoical anonymity: he would return to the everyday life of the working man, adding his efforts to the Cuban goal of achieving a larger sugar harvest. Guevara made a sincere effort at 'self-criticism', the Marxist equivalent of confession, but his attempts at penance did not last long. Just how his change of heart took place is not known, nor has anyone described the steps he took to convince the Cuban leadership that he had a role to play as a *guerrillero* errant. But by the time his letter to Castro was written, the Cuban G-2 (secret police) was busy planting abroad a cover story to deflect attention from Guevara's real movements. The government of the Dominican Republic was fed the tale that Guevara had infiltrated their country in April of that year, during the rebellion led by Colonel Francisco Caamaño, and had been killed in a street fight.

In the mean time, Che left Cuba secretly for Cairo, then travelled on to Brazzaville. There he took command of a unit of Cuban soldiers whose mission was to provide for President Alphonse Massamba-Débat the skilled firepower he needed to match the mercenary units recruited by Moise Tshombe. Guevara remained in the Congo until February 1966, when he was recalled to Havana. There are two versions of why Castro decided to call a halt to this first projection of Cuban foreign policy into Africa. The first attributes it to Cuba having finally come down on the Soviet side in the growing Sino-Soviet split, and to China having threatened to uncover the Guevara mission. The second attributes it more directly to a change of course by Moscow, parallel to its decision to withdraw support from insurrectionist movements in Latin America.

Whatever Moscow's wishes might have been, the fact is that almost as soon as Guevara was back in Havana he immersed himself in a project that openly challenged Soviet policy in Latin America: the launching of a guerrilla war from a *foco* situated somewhere near the point where Bolivia meets Argentina and Paraguay — in other words, a new attempt at the venture of Guevara's disciple Masetti in 1963.

This was hardly a maverick operation. Guevara was given a team of fifteen Cuban veterans, most of whom had fought under his orders during the war against Batista. Six of them already held the rank of *comandante*, the highest in the Cuban army; one was a member of the Cuban Communist Party's Central Committee; another had been second-in-command of the G-2; and yet another had held Vice-Ministerial rank.

In August 1966 the first three members of the party arrived in Cochabamba, Bolivia, to prepare the ground. In mid-September Guevara himself, his beard shaven, his passport identifying him as a Uruguayan businessman, flew from Havana to Madrid, and from there to São Paulo in Brazil. He finished the journey by bus, via Corumbá and Puerto Suárez. By December the team was complete. They set up their headquarters in a farm in Ñancahuazu, near the southeastern oil town of Camiri. Local contacts were activated, and feelers were put out to engage the co-operation of Bolivia's Communist Party.

The Bolivian Communists, firmly entrenched in a pro-Moscow line, were reluctant to have anything to do with armed insurrection. Moreover, they felt uneasy at Guevara's declared intention to seek alliances, as well, with other left-wing factions, of Trotskyite and pro-Peking leanings. Nonetheless, the Secretary-General of the Party, Mario Monge, felt sufficiently attracted to Guevara's plan to suggest a compromise. Monge would resign his official position with the Party, in order not to compromise it openly with a breach of Moscow's directives, but in exchange he demanded from Guevara the leadership, political and military, of the insurrection. Guevara refused. Suddenly, he and his men were alone, cut off from the support they had expected from the militant miners of the Bolivian highlands, bereft of the communications and supply lines they had counted on in the cities, and stranded in an inhospitable area larger than Britain but with a mere 340,000 inhabitants. Again, as in Masetti's ill-fated venture, this was hardly the sea of people into which the *guerrilleros* could merge like the proverbial fish.

The day after Monge's refusal, Guevara and his small band huddled round their radio set to hear a broadcast from Havana. Fidel Castro's voice came across the waves, saying, 'We send a particularly warm message, which comes from the very depths of our beings, from the affection born in the very heart of battle, to Comandante Guevara and his comrades, wherever they may be right now.

'The imperialists', added Castro, 'have already killed Che many times and in many places, but we hope that one day, when imperialism least expects it, Comandante Guevara will be reborn from his ashes, like the phoenix, bearing the arms of the *guerrillero* and of the doer of good; we expect someday to receive very concrete news of Che.'

One of the first members of Onganía's entourage to learn of Krieger Vasena's plans for Argentina's economy was Roberto Roth, the Legal and Technical Under-Secretary at the Presidency. In his memoirs he writes:

That [Krieger] would devalue was no secret; the surprise would be by how much. In order to contain rises in domestic prices, he would introduce export taxes, reckoning there would be enough left to stimulate agriculture. These export taxes would cover the budget deficit while he set in motion a plan of public works with international credit. Renewed confidence in the country and the stability of the peso would contribute to a return of departed capital, which would help to balance the payments position. Also, in order to contain costs, he would keep wages frozen after granting an initial nominal raise. There would be an increase in tariffs for public services in order to ease the weight on the federal budget of the deficits of the state-owned companies. He would reach a standby agreement with the [International] Monetary Fund to deter any run on the peso, which would not take place during the first year but might occur in the second if he did not manage completely to restrain the deficit. He would have to print money at first, but trusted his ability to reabsorb the emission with Treasury bonds and by delaying payments. He would keep the money supply in check by restricting credit, for which he would allow interest rates to rise.

Roth's reaction was far from enthusiastic: 'The Minister's plan corresponded to classical economic doctrine, but did not differ greatly from what we had several times tried out unsuccessfully. One could argue in its favour that he could count on something his predecessors had lacked: quiet on the labour front and absence of important political pressures. But it was doubtful that this could determine the difference between failure and success, which had been linked conceptually with the elimination of the budget deficit.'

The public at large did not see all of Krieger's plan at once. First he announced his budget for 1967, calling for 'sacrifices' from the population. Former President Arturo Frondizi was the first to react, castigating not Krieger but Onganía himself for putting monetary stability before development. A few days later, after unveiling more details, including the scale of external borrowing he envisaged, Krieger found himself suddenly under attack from the conservative newspaper *La Prensa*. His plan, said the paper, was no more than a collection of 'generalisations couched in the typical language of CEPAL [the UN's Economic Commission for Latin America], in a fragmentary and reiterative fashion. [. . .] It is evident that in its preparation a fundamental truth has been overlooked: that what has scared capital — ours and foreign — away from the country is precisely inflation; and that in order to attract it back again we must start by containing inflation.' Surprisingly enough, the newspaper that usually voiced Frondizi's ideas, *Clarín*, issued forth in qualified support of Krieger's policies. 'There can be no doubt', said *Clarín*, 'that these policies differ fundamentally from those favoured by the agro-import sectors, who advocate measures of monetary stabilisation at the expense of deepening the present recession and of the massive unemployment of hundreds of thousands of people.' Completing the range of reactions, the CGT produced a condemnatory document stating that everything that had transpired since June 1966 'has only served to prove to us workers yet again that the defence of our condition of wage-earners and of the great national and popular interests is on the opposite side of the street to the present military government.'

It was only two months later, during Easter, that Krieger finished unveiling his scheme, with a mammoth devaluation that took the quotation of the US dollar up to 350 pesos (his predecessor, Jorge Néstor Salimei, had found the dollar costing 202 pesos and left it at 255). He slapped heavy export taxes on agricultural products, a move which certainly helped his budgetary calculations and prevented a massive and quite gratuitous transfer of income to the farmers, as well as checking the traditional 'drag effect' of Argentine devaluations on domestic prices, but which also earned him the enmity of the powerful farming sector. In the coming months the farmers would not hesitate to play their full arsenal of 'de-stabilising' tricks, alleging insufficiently high prices and excessive taxation as reasons for the disruption of the cattle-breeding and grains production cycles. Krieger made no bones about the fact that his devalution had gone well beyond what could have been justified in terms of 'catching up with inflation' or 'restoring competitiveness'.

'The transcendental measure', he explained, 'of setting a new parity for the Argentine peso of 350 pesos per dollar, or the equivalent in other currencies, ensures, because of its magnitude, that there will never be any more devaluations.'

A couple of days later, Krieger publicly announced that wages would be frozen. There was no immediate outburst from the unions. Already in early March the CGT had attempted to pre-empt the finalisation of his policy package by announcing a new *Plan de Lucha*, including twenty-four- and forty-eight-hour general strikes. The government riposted by claiming that the police had discovered a 'terrorist plan' scheduled to coincide with the CGT's action, and publicly announced that it was severing its relations with the CGT. Activists were arrested, and in at least one case (that of a young *peronista* called Jorge Eduardo Rulli, fully corroborated five years later) severe torture was used. Then came a frontal attack on the unions: the railwaymen and sugarcane cutters had their bank accounts frozen; the metal-workers, textile workers, telephonists and chemical industry workers had their legal standing withdrawn and then their funds frozen as well. A week later, just before Krieger's wage freeze was announced, the Secretary of Labour called in the bruised union bosses to extract promises of good behaviour in exchange for a 'resumption of relations' between the government and the CGT.

It was a calm if sullen Buenos Aires that read in the newspapers of 17 April a letter sent by Che Guevara to the Tricontinental in Havana, forecasting: 'New uprisings shall take place in these [. . .] countries of Our America, as has already happened in Bolivia, and they shall continue to grow in the midst of all the hardships inherent to this dangerous profession of being modern revolutionaries. [. . .] America, a forgotten continent in the last liberation struggles, is now beginning to make itself heard through the Tricontinental and, in the voice of the vanguard of its peoples, the Cuban Revolution, will today have a task of much greater relevance: creating a Second or a Third Vietnam, or the Second *and* the Third Vietnams of the world.'

The rhetoric of Guevara's letter was not quite matched by the reality of his guerrilla campaign in Bolivia. His first casualties had been victims of the hostile environment: one man had fallen down a ravine and two were swept away by a mountain torrent. Food had run out and they had been forced to hunt and forage for their sustenance. Their first contact with the peasant population had led to their being reported to the authorities, and soon troops were pouring into the region, throwing a wide circle around the area where armed and uniformed men were known to be marauding. The first two encounters with Bolivia's army, ambushes in which Guevara's men had the advantage of surprise, were guerrilla victories. Prisoners taken by the *guerrilleros* and later released became responsible for an additional but hollow propaganda victory: the soldiers, in order to justify their defeat, greatly magnified the numbers of the guerrilla band. But this did not earn Guevara any practical help. The Bolivian Communists belatedly announced their support for Guevara's 'Army of National Liberation', but kept support merely verbal. On the other hand, the growing evidence that Guevara and a handful of Cubans were leading the insurrection strengthened the hand of Guevara's enemies. Bolivia's large populist party, the Movimiento Nacionalista Revolucionario, though opposed to the ruling military régime, called on all Bolivians to oppose 'foreign intervention'. The Bolivian military despatched an envoy to Buenos Aires to secure military assistance, while the United States deployed Green Berets in Bolivia to speed up the training of that country's élite corps of Rangers.

To make matters worse, two persons on whom Guevara had counted as contacts, even propagandists, in the outside world — the Frenchman Régis Debray and the Argentine Ciro Bustos — had been arrested by the Bolivian military as they tried to slip out of the battle zone.

The events in Bolivia certainly created more of a stir in Argentine left-wing circles than the Masetti adventure had ever done, but apart from some imperceptible tightening of security, there were few ripples elsewhere in society.

Indeed, the country's political life seemed to have slid into a morass of banality, mainly concerned with the in-fighting in the higher echelons of the Onganía administration, which in four months saw the resignation of three Secretaries of State, the Mayor of Buenos Aires and the Governor of the province of Córdoba. Only this last event was to have any lasting consequences, since the new Governor, Carlos Caballero, came to power with very determined ideas on the future political structure of his province. Visible opposition to the government was left to the Radicals: former President Illia managed to get himself arrested once, for publicly comparing his ouster to an armed robbery, and was later hosed down by the fire brigade for attempting to place a wreath at the Monument to the Flag in the city of Rosario. The government, however, saw adversaries further afield: a television programme was shut down when a presenter allowed himself a 'pro-Cuban' comment; two popular burlesque theatres were temporarily closed for 'indecency'; a number of people were dragged off to police stations for 'a decent haircut'; high-ranking police officials became personally involved in a campaign of 'moralisation' which included regulating how much light there should be in night-clubs and conducting raids on the *hoteles alojamiento*, where assignations were made possible by moderate hourly fees.

Amid all this petty repression, it is only hindsight that allows the singling out of one minor incident as an indicator that something new was developing on the Argentine political scene. The event was the brief arrest, during a demonstration in front of Buenos Aires' Metropolitan Cathedral, of one Juan García Elorrio. What had got him into the régime's bad books was that he edited a magazine called *Cristianismo y Revolución* (Christianity and Revolution). It was one of the few visible signs of the effort under way in nominally Catholic Argentina to marry the teachings of Christianity with the revolution advocated by the Left and with the revised view of *peronismo*'s role as the representative party of the masses. Most political commentators, involved as they were in bigger things, had little time for this apparently fringe pursuit, except perhaps when they needed a 'curiosity' to liven up their pages. In high places few were paying attention to it; the general public was almost completely unaware that it was taking place.

The main incubators of this coming together of new ideas were the universities, where from their first blundering incursion the authorities had been oblivious to what was really happening in the students' minds. Ten years later, also with the advantage of hindsight, General Alejandro Agustín Lanusse would write:

The country had given birth to what came to be known as 'the new opposition'. The hegemonic ideology of this new opposition was no longer that of the Radicals, the Socialists, the Liberals, or even the Communists in the traditional sense of the word. It was . . . a youthful opposition that tried to add up all the sectors who opposed the liberal system, and particularly the liberal economic system. This youthful opposition saw no antagonism between Catholicism and Marxism, nor between Nationalism and Marxism. True enough, Radicals, Socialists, orthodox *peronistas*, Liberals and Party-line Communists also took part. [. . .] But to that traditional, foreseeable opposition had been added two novel facets: a Catholicism that leaned towards the Left and towards *peronismo*, and which in many cases had emerged from classical nationalism, and a neo-Anarchism that advocated the violent destruction of structures without explicitly proposing a replacement model.

At the time, however, it was oversight, not hindsight, that ruled the behaviour of the Onganía administration. Krieger still occupied the centre-stage, signing up foreign credit by the hundreds of millions of dollars, getting long-delayed public works programmes under way, announcing a new Hydrocarbons Law that reopened Argentina's oil industry to foreign participation, drawing up sets of incentives to attract foreign investment. Big companies seemed willing to come in: Renault of France bought up Argentina's largest automobile concern, Ford bought up a local steel company. Smaller, locally-owned industries were not doing so well; high interest rates were forcing their backs to the wall, and the devalued peso made them attractive targets for takeovers by anyone who had hard currency to invest and the financial capacity to survive in the harsher, efficiency-oriented climate created by Krieger's policies. A new word began to creep into the Argentine political lexicon: *desnacionalización*, de-nationalisation. It began to be seen as the inevitable corollary of the path Krieger had chosen, and soon became one of the most frequent barbs hurled at Krieger's *liberals* by the *nationalist* faction in the administration, centred on the Minister of the Interior and the Presidential establishment.

Krieger began to be attacked, as well, for allegedly favouring foreign interests in Argentina's beef and grains trade, and for allowing them to block initiatives that would have allowed Argentina a more autonomous development in key areas of the economy. Within a few months the CGT was clamouring publicly that 'the economy is controlled by foreign monopolies' as Krieger announced yet another budget of 'sacrifice'. Then Arturo Frondizi joined in the fray, issuing one of his already classic doomsday condemnations of Krieger's policies.

While the anti-Krieger campaign was still in its infancy, in October 1967, Buenos Aires was shaken by a dramatic report: Che Guevara had been killed in Bolivia.

After their two initial successes against the Army, Guevara's forces had had no choice but to try to break out of their inaccessible base area. They split up and began long, difficult treks in search of places where at least they might have the chance of recruiting more insurgents. They were to claim only one more victory: the fleeting occupation of a small town. From then on the noose formed by the unwelcoming terrain, a hostile people and the highly trained Bolivian Rangers tightened inexorably. One of the two columns was all but decimated in an Army ambush; the stragglers were trapped soon afterwards. Che's own group lasted a little longer, but was eventually cornered in a canyon with no way out. Guevara put up a fierce fight, but received massive injuries. He was taken alive, only to be shot in captivity on orders from La Paz. The last the world saw of him was the badly focussed picture of his half-dressed body lying on a table, his eyes wide open in an awesome yet oddly peaceful stare.

The realisation did not reach everyone at the same time, but it was clear that not only Guevara had died in the Bolivian hinterland. Also dead was the notion that the Cuban experience, at least when interpreted as a formula for rural guerrilla warfare, could be repeated at will anywhere in Latin America.

17

'CORDOBAZO'
(1968–1969)

By mid-1968 the Secretary of Industry, Raúl Jorge Peyceré, was publicly admitting that *desnacionalización* was a problem, and announcing that special legislation would be drawn up and credit facilities offered to prevent it. The promises, however, made less impact on the public than a lengthy report published by the news-weekly *Primera Plana*, which detailed the full extent of the foreign takeover process.

Weeks earlier, Onganía himself had given signs that the criticism was beginning to be felt. He called a meeting of the highest-ranking officials in the civil administration and the armed services and exhorted them to a *profundización*, a 'deepening' of the Revolution. Among the nationalist members of the administration, this was interpreted as an oblique censure of Krieger's 'liberal' team, which was precisely being accused of holding up major projects. They also interpreted it as a call to start working in earnest on the design for new institutional structures throughout the country. The President's message was rapidly relayed down the line. The Commander-in-Chief of the Army, General Julio Alsogaray, called together forty-eight leading generals to tell them, in no uncertain terms, that Onganía was 'dissatisfied with the process'.

Despite Onganía's determination to keep the Army out of politics, many of the generals were already grumbling quite openly. On the one hand, they were uneasy about the whole question of *desnacionalización* and about what they saw as an unhealthy closeness to big business of leading figures in Krieger's team. On the other, they worried about the erosion of the government's image through its involvement in petty repression. The government's prestige had only recently taken a public battering in a couple of court cases against publishers. Back in October 1967 the government had ordered the closure of a confidential news-sheet called *Prensa Confidencial* and of the well-known nationalist newspaper, *Azul y Blanco*. The editor of *Prensa Confidencial*, Jorge Vago, took his case to court, but without waiting for the judicial decision, he promptly resumed publication under a new name, *Prensa Libre*. Within days, this too was closed down by government order. Vago responded by reappearing under yet another name, *Prensa Nueva*. Again the government closed him down. In late November, the Appeals Court ruled that the closures of *Prensa Confidencial* and *Prensa Libre* had been unconstitutional. Days later a judge ordered the lifting of the ban on *Azul y Blanco*. The government refused to comply and both cases went to the Supreme Court; Vago was soon publishing again, under the title *El Cívico*, which was closed down in April 1968. Only days after this latest reassertion of government determination, the Supreme Court ordered the government to lift the bans on *Azul y Blanco*, *Prensa Confidencial* and *Prensa Libre*. Admitting errors or defeat, however, was hardly the Onganía administration's style, and the Minister of the Interior, Dr Borda, showed no signs of compunction when he proclaimed, some time later, that Argentina enjoyed 'complete press freedom' — a statement Onganía repeated to the annual convention of the Inter-American Press Association.

If there was unease and grumbling in the higher echelons of the Army, outright anger was brewing among the trade unions. The government kept insisting that it would not allow the formal reconstitution of the CGT 'along the lines of the past', and a number of major unions remained under earlier interdicts, either without any legal standing or with their affairs in the hands of government-appointed trustees. In March 1968 the union leaders responded to a call for a 'Normalising Congress'. From the outset there was a quarrel over the admission of delegates from the unions under government sanction. Augusto Vandor's faction, allied on this occasion with his erstwhile rival José Alonso, felt that admitting them would virtually guarantee non-recognition of the CGT by the government. When the Congress went ahead and recognised the sanctioned unions, Vandor's faction withdrew its nine members from the fifteen-member committee which had been set up to oversee the 'normalisation' of the Confederation.

The Congress proceeded to elect a new leadership, headed by Raimundo Ongaro of the printers' union. Ongaro had earned himself, in a political press still unused to the idea of a union leader who was both a militant Catholic and a left-winger, the scornful sobriquet of 'mystic'. In fact he was the first figure of nationwide prominence to emerge from the ranks of that 'new opposition' that was bringing together post-Vatican II Catholic thinking with left-wing political proposals in a nationalist, *peronista* frame. Not surprisingly, the manifesto produced by the CGT Congress quotes abundantly from papal encyclicals like *Mater et Magistra, Pacem in Terris* and *Populorum Progressio*, saying that they 'encourage us towards the social and moral revolution that will enable mankind to liberate itself from all forms of oppression'. The bishops of Latin America had not yet met in their celebrated Medellín Conference, where they were to commit the hemispheric church to 'liberation'; the school of thought that would come to be known as 'liberation theology' was still in the future; yet here, in the thick of social and political confrontation, Catholic laymen were attempting to put these things into practice. Among the clergy, although Argentina boasted a ten-year-old worker-priest movement, the first organised expression of this shift in Catholic thinking and practice, the Movimiento de Sacerdotes para el Tercer Mundo (Movement of Priests for the Third World) did not formally come into existence until two months after the CGT Congress. The episcopate, as a body, was still obstinately conservative, though since 1965 bishops like Antonio Quarracino, Jerónimo Podesta and Alberto Devoto had begun to acquire a reputation for social involvement and for tolerating, if not encouraging, the more radical of their priests (Podestá, indeed, was deprived in 1967 of his diocese, the industrial city of Avellaneda, because of his outspokenness on social issues).

The union faction led by Vandor decided to ignore the Congress. Invoking its majority on the 'normalising' committee, it formally convened the ruling body of the CGT and decreed the suspension of all the unions that had taken part in the Congress. It called for 'authentic solidarity and national unity, banishing reactionary infiltrations that are inimical to the Argentine being', and added, 'The Government must be the vertex of understanding and the executor of this mandate which could prove to be historic.' Thus there came to be, once again, two CGTs. Ongaro's, formally calling itself CGT de los Argentinos, became known as CGT-Paseo Colón, after the street in which its headquarters were located. In the same vein, Vandor's faction was known as CGT-Azopardo.

Although the CGT-Azopardo had bent over backwards to gain government sympathy, none was forthcoming, at least towards anything claiming to be an organised CGT. As soon as this sank in, there was yet another split in the union movement, with a group of 'participationists' hiving themselves off in order to seek a separate understanding with the authorities.

Ongaro's CGT-Paseo Colón, on the other hand, chose confrontation from the outset. Recalling Alvaro Alsogaray's fateful 'winter' slogan, it described the situation as follows:

They asked us to hold on through the winter; we have done so through ten winters. They ask us to rationalise; thus we lose the conquests obtained by our grandfathers. And when there is no further humiliation left to suffer and no further injustice to be perpetrated against us, we are ironically asked to 'participate'. [. . .] One-and-a-half million unemployed and under-employed are the measure of this system and of this government which no one has elected. The working class is living through its bitterest hour. Wage agreements suspended, the right to strike annulled, conquests trampled underfoot, unions under government trustees, others without legal standing, wages frozen. . . . The oppression of the working class goes hand in hand with the liquidation of national industry, the sell-out of all our resources, submission to international financial organisations.

The First of May, Labour Day, gave the CGT-Paseo Colón its first opportunity to test its strength. Rallies and demonstrations were held in La Matanza (an industrial suburb of Buenos Aires), Rosario and Tucumán. Though not overwhelming, they were impressive enough for the authorities to start taking notice. May 1968, of course, was the month of the student rebellion in Paris, when Daniel Cohn-Bendit and Rudi Dutschke became household names. In Argentina it was an unusually quiet month, a fact which later led many to find in the Parisian May the source of inspiration for later rebellion in the country. Later, Perón himself was to say, 'It all started in May 1968 in Paris.' And stretching credulity a bit, he would add, 'I was there in the barricades, and I saw it.' One man who actually was there, the veteran Peruvian leader Víctor Raúl Haya de la Torre, was able to set the 'events of May' in their proper perspective. The black and red banners of Paris had moved him to tears because they reminded him only too vividly of the early 1920s, when as a student he became one of the leaders of the university reform, a movement that had started in the Argentine city of Córdoba. Indeed, one of the documents that circulated freely among the rebel students of Paris was a reprint of the Córdoba manifesto.

When the present-day students of Argentina began to move, their demands and aspirations were far removed from those of their European counterparts. And they moved soon. On 14 June they came out on strike throughout the country, clashing with the police in Buenos Aires, La Plata, Córdoba and Tucumán. Only days had passed when the police were called out again to disperse protest demonstrations on the second anniversary of the *Revolución Argentina*. And before June was out the students of Córdoba twice gained the streets; on each occasion police reaction was vicious, and on each a student was wounded by police gunfire.

Córdoba was rapidly becoming the centre of anti-government feeling.

Not only was the provincial capital a university city; its environs were also the most important seat of Argentina's auto industry, and home of two large unions, the metalworkers led by Elpidio Torres and the power workers led by Agustín Tosco, which had earned themselves the reputation of being among the most radical in the country.

Since September 1967 the Governor of Córdoba had been Carlos Caballero, a man close to the Interior Minister, Guillermo Borda, and like him widely classified as a nationalist of the right-wing variety. Caballero was among those who had taken Onganía's call for a 'deepening of the Revolution' to mean that the time was ripe to start creating new institutional structures. 'Participation', as denounced by Ongaro's CGT, had become the most important catchword within the administration: the idea was clearly to attempt a widening of the government's political base by attracting to it, if only in a consultative capacity, prominent members of the local communities. Political parties and their leaders were anathema, so the government began to seek out its partners in the business and professional associations, and among the 'participationist' unions. Caballero's formula, hardly original, was the creation, in his province, of an 'Economic and Social Council', vaguely inspired by the French model. The Council would be formed by representatives of the different sectors of society: business, the professions, labour. Its role would be purely advisory; the government would not be bound by the advice proffered, and the Council would only hold forth on issues chosen by the government. As a share of the decision-making process, it was not a very appealing offer. But it was not its unattractiveness that many found objectionable. There was a growing suspicion that, in the minds of many of Onganía's officials, if not of the President himself, 'participation' was not the first stepping-stone along the way back to democracy, or even a future aid to the functioning of a party-based representative system, but actually a substitute for it. And in this light, with the added factor of the nationalist background of its proponents, 'participation' began to look uncomfortably like corporativism, even perhaps Fascism.

Fears in this sense were being openly voiced by the banned political parties, and it was widely known that they were shared by two of the country's most prominent generals: the Commander-in-Chief, Julio Alsogaray, and the head of the Córdoba-based Third Army Corps, Alejandro Agustín Lanusse. This line of criticism became so intense that Interior Minister Borda felt compelled to issue a public statement, flatly declaring that the projected Economic and Social Council in Córdoba 'is not corporativist' in intent. This allayed few fears, so Onganía himself went on the record stating that 'the *Revolución Argentina* is not Fascist.'

At this point, Onganía acted again to remind the men in uniform of the principle that 'the armed forces do not govern or co–govern.' On 23 August 1968 he announced that the three Commanders-in-Chief, General Julio Alsogaray, Admiral Benigno Varela and Brigadier Adolfo Alvarez, were relieved of their duties. Their replacements were to be General Lanusse for the Army, Admiral Pedro Gnavi for the Navy, and Brigadier Jorge Martínez Zuviría for the Air Force. It was the second time that Onganía had asserted the authority of his very *sui generis* Presidency over those who had given him his mandate. The changes were accepted by the officer corps, whose mood was best captured by an Army man who commented, 'Onganía behaves like Franco with the civilians, but towards the Army he adopts the attitude of a Swiss President.'

A month later the Onganía government had another opportunity to show that it was firmly in command of the situation: the security forces reported that they had uncovered and disbanded a *peronista* group, led by Envar El Kadre, that had attempted to set up a rural guerrilla *foco* in Taco Ralo, province of Tucumán. A confident calm descended on the government as 1968 came to a close, unperturbed by major incidents except for a bid by the oil workers to organise a major strike (the union was promptly placed under the supervision of a government trustee), and a sign that movement might be beginning on Argentina's longstanding dispute with Britain over the Malvinas (Falkland) islands, when Lord Chalfont, a minister at the British Foreign Office, arrived in Port Stanley to sound out the islanders on their hopes for the future. At the year-end, Adalbert Krieger Vasena presented his budget without the usual call for more sacrifice, announcing instead the beginning of 'an era of prosperity', while Onganía reserved for himself the announcement of the prize the union bosses had long been demanding: the resumption, in 1969, of free collective wage bargaining.

The optimistic mood continued into January, when a proud Onganía laid the foundation stone of one of Argentina's most heralded, and most delayed, major development projects: the El Chocón-Cerros Colorados hydroelectric complex, which from the province of Neuquén, over 1,200 kilometres southwest of Buenos Aires, would finally ease the energy shortage that held tight reins on growth in the country's industrial belt. Yet if any of this enthusiasm had spread beyond the confines of the government itself, it was soon dampened. News came of protest marches by unemployed workers at a sugar mill in Santa Fe; of a strike in a major industrial concern; of a banned march followed by a hunger strike at another sugar mill, this time in Tucumán; of the brief, surreptitious arrest of Raimundo Ongaro by the Tucumán police; of the detention of yet more would-be *guerrilleros* in the northwestern province of Jujuy. Then Onganía, in his habitual deadpan style, proceeded to dash a double set of hopes: he told businessmen that there was still a long time to go before the Revolution entered the 'political time'; and he reiterated to the union leaders that the CGT would not be allowed to re-organise 'along the lines of the past'.

The church hierarchy, under pressure from the government, began to take official cognisance of the winds of change sweeping through their flock. The Archbishop-Coadjutor of Buenos Aires, Juan Carlos Aramburu, ordered his priests to abstain from political activity, an injunction clearly aimed at the nascent 'Movement of Priests for the Third World'. In Rosario, twenty-eight priests resigned when their Archbishop, Guillermo Bolatti, attempted to rein them in; in Villa Ocampo the parish church gave refuge to unemployed demonstrators after they had briefly taken over the municipality. The Cardinal Archbishop of Buenos Aires and Primate of Argentina, Antonio Caggiano, thundered out against 'rebel priests' and proclaimed that the church in Argentina was undergoing 'a crisis of faith'. Yet in the aftermath of the Medellín Conference, more bishops were drifting towards the side of the socially committed. From Tucumán Mgr Juan Carlos Ferro openly accused the government of not fulfilling its promises to the province. And when the entire episcopate met, towards the end of April, at San Miguel, they produced a document highly critical of the situation in Argentina, and declaring formal adherence to the conclusions and commitments reached by their peers from the rest of Latin America at Medellín.

Meanwhile, the country had been hit by a storm of unexpected virulence. It started on April 15, when an armed group attacked a guard post at Campo de Mayo, the largest military complex in Argentina. Days later, another armed group burst into the offices of Radio El Mundo, and only barely failed in their purpose of broadcasting a taped insurrectionist message. Almost without interruption, the attacks began to multiply. The laconic entries of a chronology prepared by Andrew Graham-Yooll, then the political editor of the *Buenos Aires Herald*, starkly portray the intensity of the blitz:

April 12. Attack, supposedly by *guerrilleros*, on a guard post at Aeroparque. Foiled by a sentry.

April 15. Attack on an armoury in Buenos Aires: a truckload of light-calibre weapons is stolen.

April 16. Commando attack on a guard post at Mar del Plata [naval] base.

April 18. Attack on shooting range at Villa María, Cóŕdoba: 12 rifles stolen.
Attack on a military post in Catamarca.
Attack on an armoury in Neuquén.
Attack on an Army communications post in Neuquén.

April 20. Commando attack on hospital sector of Río Santiago (naval) base: male nurse dies.

April 22. Report of *guerrillero* attacks on military posts in Magdalena, Salta and other parts of the country.

April 23. Carlos Caride and his companion, Aída Rosa Filipini, are captured after a shootout at an apartment on Calle Paraguay. Police officer Jorge Alfredo Mato is killed. Discovery announced there of a guerrilla cell.

May 4. Tucumán: discovery is announced of the cell of a guerrilla organisation.

Where had this outburst come from? Who were the authors of these attacks? Much later, official intelligence sources would attempt to explain this and future events as straightforward linear developments which could be traced back to Guevara's failed guerrilla campaign in Bolivia. According to these sources, three groups in Argentina had come together to form an 'Army of National Liberation' in support of Guevara's identically named organisation. The three were identified as the Partido Revolucionario de los Trabajadores (PRT), a Trotskyite coalition formed in 1965, which gave birth to the Ejército Revolucionario del Pueblo (ERP), one of Argentina's major guerrilla organisations. The second was the Partido Comunista Revolucionario (PCR), a breakaway faction of the Argentine Communist Party, whence emerged elements of two guerrilla organisations: Fuerzas Armadas de Liberación (FAL) and Fuerzas Armadas Revolucionarias (FAR). The third group, unnamed but presumably of *peronista* origins, gave birth to the Fuerzas Armadas Peronistas (FAP).

In fact, of all these organisations, only FAL and FAP were at the time in existence as anything more than embryos; the rest, plus others not even mentioned, were still struggling with the confused lead-up to actual organisation. Minor attacks were, of course, part of the would-be *guerrilleros*' training, as were some daring bank robberies, such as the February 1968 Boedo heist which yielded 65 million pesos (some $186,000), or the January 1969 hold-up at Escobar which yielded 72 million pesos (about $260,000). There was little, if any formal communication across this constellation of guerrilla and proto-guerrilla organisations; certainly the concentration of incidents throughout the country in April 1969 was not the product of any masterplan. Beyond the fringes of *peronismo*, the PRT was perhaps the organisation moving fastest and most methodically towards the creation of a military apparatus. Within *peronismo*, opinions and attitudes regarding armed action varied widely, as became evident when, in March 1969, a congress of groups and organisations calling themselves 'revolutionary' and '*peronista*' was convened in Córdoba.

The congress split three ways over tactics. Ongaro's CGT de los Argentinos called for concentration on militant union action; the rump of the oldest insurrectionist group, the Movimiento Revolucionario Peronista (MRP), together with a group led by Gustavo Rearte, battered by years of failure, pleaded for an effort to organise the working classes politically before launching armed rebellion; a third, multi-faceted coalition, which in the congress found its spokesman in José Sabino Navarro, a militant in Elpidio Torres' metalworkers union, advocated the immediate launching of an armed struggle. There was no consensus, and though Navarro seemed to carry the majority of the participants with him, he soon discovered that their support was no more than verbal.

The following weeks witnessed another series of incidents: the hijacking of a truckload of explosives, a petrol bomb attack against a farmer, a bomb explosion inside the Federal Police headquarters in Buenos Aires. But the centre-stage had already been occupied by another chain of events in which the protagonists were not the embryonic guerrilla organisations but the students.

It began in the University of the Northeast, in the city of Corrientes. The trigger, or more accurately the straw that broke the camel's back, was a decision by the government-appointed trustee to raise the prices for meals at the students' cafeteria. The students organised a protest march through the streets of Corrientes, and the police were sent out to disperse them. Repression proceeded rapidly from batons to tear-gas to gunfire: the day ended with Juan José Cabral, a twenty-two-year-old medical student, lying dead of a bullet wound. The following day people turned out by the thousands for Cabral's funeral, and demonstrations were held in sympathy throughout the country.

In Rosario, a protest demonstration was broken up brutally by the police: an economics student, twenty-two-year-old Ramón Alberto Bello, was hit by a police bullet and died the next day in hospital. Once again crowds flocked to the funeral, and angry demonstrations were held in all major cities. In Córdoba the authorities retaliated by closing down the university. On the fifth day after Cabral's death the students were still demonstrating: the Córdoba police blinded eighteen-year-old Elba Canelo in one eye with a badly-aimed tear-gas grenade; in Buenos Aires twenty were wounded and 160 arrested.

The sixth day saw the population of Rosario converging on the city centre in a 'March of Silence'. The police were ordered into action. Once again repression got out of hand: a fifteen-year-old metalworker, Luis Norberto Blanco, was killed by a police bullet in the back. As the mood of the crowd turned uglier, the police drew back, calling on the local Army garrison for aid. Within hours, after consultation with Buenos Aires, General Roberto Fonseca had declared the city an 'emergency zone' and ordered his troops to occupy it. The townspeople remained defiant, turning out in strength for Blanco's funeral, while the local branch of the CGT, putting aside its internal squabbles, united to call for a general strike. For the first time ever in Argentina, students and workers were making common cause. While General Fonseca's soldiers were busy arresting people by the score in Rosario, the students in far-away Salta, in the northwestern extremity of the country, were becoming more belligerent: they stormed the fashionable 20 de Febrero Club, the meeting-place for local high society, and burned it to the ground.

For the first time in most people's memory, the government ordered the cancellation in most cities of public festivities scheduled for 25 May, Argentina's National Day. Only by the 28th, thirteen days after Cabral's death in Corrientes, did the authorities feel sufficiently confident to pull the troops off the streets in Rosario. In their wake came the special military tribunals set up by executive order to try those arrested during the riots.

On 29 May, Juan Carlos Onganía and General Alejandro Agustín Lanusse rose early to attend the Army Day celebrations at the Colegio Militar in Campo de Mayo. In Córdoba at 9 o'clock in the morning the local delegate of SIDE, the state intelligence secretariat, was attracted to his office window by noise in the street below. He rushed to the telex machine and dashed off a three-word message to his Director in Buenos Aires, General Eduardo Señorans: 'Announced events beginning.'

When Colonel Conesa, the state intelligence delegate in Córdoba, looked out of his window, the sight that greeted him was a crowd larger than any the city had witnessed for years, chanting anti-government slogans and marching towards the town centre. It was an unusual crowd. Foreseeably, there were students by the score, but by their side, most unusually, there were workers from the motor-car industry. Even stranger, they were accompanied by people who obviously belonged to Cordoba's white-collar middle classes, and they were encouraged from the windows by habitually reticent housewives. This, the Colonel concluded, was what the security services had been fearing for the last couple of months, ever since a joint student-worker demonstration had been narrowly averted with some help from Buenos Aires. Governor Caballero and the intelligence services were convinced that this particular provincial government was the target of a wide-ranging conspiracy, and that sooner rather than later they would have to face the joint assault of Córdoba's more militant unions and of the Marxists infiltrated in the student movement. Time and again they had warned Buenos Aires; every time, the evidence they produced was considered unsatisfactory, particularly as the remedy Governor Caballero was advocating was the declaration of a state of siege and the preventive arrest of the alleged ring-leaders of the plot. What Caballero did get was a contingent of Federal Police to reinforce his unruly, underpaid provincial police force.

Yet the crowd that poured into the streets of Córdoba that 29 May was not composed only of the student and union activists they had been expecting. Almost all the political parties were out under their own banners, and encouragement was clearly coming from all quarters, even the affluent residential districts where demonstrations were usually greeted with shuttered windows.

The first to reach the town centre were the metalworkers. They were also the first to run into the provincial police, to suffer the first barrage of tear-gas grenades, and then the first volleys of gunfire. The first man to fall dead was a worker and a Radical, Máximo Mena.

The surge of the crowd proved uncontainable, and the provincial government closed down and abandoned one police station after another in the path of the demonstrators. By mid-morning, barricades were going up throughout the city, buses and cars were being overturned and set on fire, and the plate-glass windows of shops and company buildings were being smashed by rocks and petrol-bombs. The police pulled back towards the government palace and their headquarters in the old *cabildo*. Around mid-day a desperate call went out for the Army to move in and restore order. Once the orders had been issued by the Commander-in-Chief, General Lanusse, in Buenos Aires, Córdoba was declared an 'emergency zone', and Army broadcasts warned the population that troops were on their way, with instructions to act firmly against anyone still on the streets. At a quarter to four in the afternoon, General Jorge Raúl Carcagno led his paratroopers into the city.

The bulk of the crowd had already withdrawn as the demonstrations turned into all-out rioting. By the time the paratroopers reached the scene, they found only isolated pockets of protesters and scattered snipers who fired ineffectually from the rooftops before vanishing. Fires still burned in quarters that a beleaguered fire brigade had been unable to reach, and the odd looter flitted amid the shambles of the town centre. Yet it took another day, and the arrest of some 500 people, for the Army to re-establish complete calm in Córdoba. The government of Carlos Caballero' was at an end; General Carcagno was appointed in his stead, in his capacity as a serving officer, but only after the Minister of the Interior had accepted his conditions. 'I'll go,' Carcagno had said, 'but not only to restore order on the streets. I'll also go to re-establish dialogue.'

The Córdoba uprising, henceforth to be known as *el cordobazo* (by analogy to the *bogotazo*, the riots that had wrecked Bogotá, Colombia, in 1948), also signalled the end of the Krieger period. Onganía's entire cabinet was reshuffled. Borda was replaced at the Interior Ministry by General Francisco Imaz, and Krieger at the Ministry of the Economy by José María Dagnino Pastore, who most uncharacteristically started off by announcing that he was there merely to continue executing his predecessor's policies.

Yet the significance of the *cordobazo* went beyond a change of faces at the top. It marked a turning-point: for Onganía himself the beginning of a decline he would be unable to arrest; for the *Revolución Argentina* a call to attention that would persuade many of the leading figures in the Army that it might be well to start thinking of restoring civilian rule; for the opposition, both those who thought in terms of electoral competition and those who harboured hopes of armed insurrection, it became a symbol, a rallying-point, a sign that this armour-plated military régime was vulnerable.

Thus the *cordobazo* began to take root in Argentine political mythology, with a number of conflicting versions of its origins and ultimate significance. Onganía would continue to insist that it had all been the product of a subversive conspiracy, while his adversaries, including General Lanusse, openly attributed the event to wider-ranging civic dissatisfaction, in both the economic and the purely political fields. Among those close to Onganía, several have continued to hold that the *cordobazo* was actually fostered by General Lanusse, by deed (he was said to have had contacts, in his days as Commander of the 3rd Army Corps, with the radicalised union leaders who were later sentenced by military tribunals as instigators of the riots) or by omission (he was charged with having deliberately delayed the Army's intervention). His alleged aim: to displace Onganía from the Presidency. This theory is countered by those who claim that Onganía and Governor Caballero themselves had had a hand in causing the riots and attempting to involve the Army in a bloody exercise of repression. In this case the alleged motive was the need for an excuse to get rid of the 'liberal' wing of the government, represented by Krieger in the Ministry of the Economy and, in the eyes of the 'nationalists', by Lanusse in the Army. In his memoirs Lanusse claims not to give any credence to this last interpretation, though he does point out that one of Onganía's advisors, Diego Muñiz Barreto, later had close contacts with one of the guerrilla organisations, and that another, Alejandro Losada, wrote in 1970: 'We were all thinking of the country and, although we were engaged in a revolution, we saw that the economy was in the hands of the liberal group, that inflation had been checked, that credit had been expanded and interest rates had gone down. Something had to be done, because governments of equilibrium do not achieve anything. We had begun to put together the Party of the Argentine Revolution, because Perón was no longer wanted and Onganía could get support from the CGT. [. . .] Hitler knew how to raise the banner of the New Order. We had to create a similar situation, in which the population is overwhelmed by panic and confusion.'

The more radical opposition were later to read into the *cordobazo* a more complex ideological meaning: the reaction of the people against imperialism, against military dictatorship and against anti-worker economic policies. The riots, in this light, became a 'spontaneous uprising' of the masses.

In Córdoba, the newborn Movement of Priests for the Third World issued its analysis of the events: 'We are convinced that this was a spontaneous reaction of the people of Córdoba, who, just like the immense majority of their fellow-countrymen, are tired of oppression, of injustice, of the persecution directed against them by a privileged minority. [. . .] We maintain that what is at stake is not only material demands, but above all the growing will to assume common responsibility for the conduct of the country's affairs. [. . .] The absence, in all these popular reactions, of the traditional political banners leads us to believe, with some reason, that the definitive solution to the conflict cannot consist in a return to an electoralist regime.' The priests' formula for the future? A 'new order', a 'socialist society'.

Although Krieger's successor was one of the few Economy Ministers not to inaugurate his term of office by stating that the country was facing its worst-ever economic crisis, there was little if any applause for the achievements of the Krieger era. In his own terms, Krieger could have claimed a number of successes. He had effectively brought down the rate of inflation from about 30 per cent to 7.6 per cent. He had, as promised, trimmed the fiscal deficit by more than half; he had rebuilt the country's reserves of hard currency; and the economy as a whole had begun to show new signs of life, with a growth rate of over 7 per cent in 1968. During his thirty-month tenure of office, the number of motor vehicles in the country increased by more than half, and the public works programmes stimulated a 40 per cent growth in the production of cement. Statistics, as Krieger had underlined at the beginning of 1969, seemed to prove his case. Yet they did not tell the whole story. Most of the spurt of growth in the previous year had been led by exports, and they in turn had been boosted mainly by improved markets for beef and other agricultural products — in spite of the fact that agriculture's contribution to Argentina's gross domestic product had shrunk to a mere 12.6 per cent. And although inflation was down, the purchasing power of the average paypacket had begun to shrink too; in 1968 it did so by more than one-tenth. It was this last development that had been fuelling discontent on the labour front, where the absence of free wage bargaining and the high-handed treatment of union demands were already long-festering sores.

This discontent, moreover, had acquired political overtones when combined with another visible effect of Krieger's policies: the process known as *desnacionalización*. Indeed, so dominant was this dimension of the Krieger era that it virtually blotted out all other considerations. The issue had been mentioned in top-level conversations between the Army Commander-in-Chief, General Lanusse, and President Onganía. It had moved the Chief of the Federal Police to order a top-secret investigation, the results of which were gleefully pounced upon by the 'nationalist' faction in government. The police report showed that between early 1967 and mid-1968 thirty-two Argentine-owned companies had been taken over by foreign interests. More than half of the new owners were companies from the United States, but the buyers also included five from Spain, two from West Germany, and one each from Britain, Canada, Austria, France, Switzerland, Belgium and the Netherlands. Eleven of the companies taken over were banks.

The theme of *desnacionalización* was rapidly becoming the battle-cry of all opposition forces lying left of centre, but soon, almost without a perceptible change of gear, it became enmeshed in another issue of even greater political potency: that of the influence exerted over the country's economic policy by large foreign corporations, or *monopolios*, as they came to be known rather loosely. As the Krieger era came to an end, demands were already afoot for an investigation into the meat-packing industry, dominated by a pool of large, foreign-owned plants, at the head of which was the Compañía Swift de La Plata, a subsidiary of the US-based Deltec group. Rumours had been circulating quite openly of undue influence in securing government funds and in blocking the growth of the smaller, locally-owned packing plants. With the changes at the helm in the Ministry of the Economy, these demands found willing ears in the Secretariat of Agriculture. Krieger and his men began to be portrayed as having connived at keeping irregularities in the meat industry hidden from the public eye. And as the mood grew fouler, a retired Krieger imprudently provided what everyone took to be irrefutable proof of the wide-ranging conspiracy: he accepted an appointment to the board of Deltec.

But while these storms were only beginning to brew, the country was buffeted by a chain of traumatic events. Fifteen supermarkets of the Minimax chain were fire-bombed as a protest against the imminent arrival in Buenos Aires of Nelson Rockefeller. In broad daylight, on the streets of Buenos Aires, the police gunned down a left-wing militant, Emilio Mariano Jáuregui. From an unknown hiding-place 'somewhere in Buenos Aires' the leaders of Ongaro's CGT de los Argentinos announced a 'week of struggle' to start on 9 July, the anniversary of Argentina's independence. And there was something more in the wind: rumours of an impending re-unification of the CGT, astutely engineered by *el Lobo*, Augusto Vandor. All these separate strands were being woven into a fuse which would be set alight on 30 June.

Eight months earlier, Augusto Vandor had travelled to Madrid to patch up his relations with Juan Perón. The old man had readily forgiven and had seemed to give his blessing to Vandor as the authorised interlocutor, on behalf of the *peronista* unions, with Onganía's government (or with any general who might be seeking to overthrow Onganía).

Raimundo Ongaro's CGT de los Argentinos had not been able to attract the larger unions to its militant anti-government stance, but was visibly growing in popularity among the students, the youthful 'new opposition' and the radical clergy. Perón, in his best 'pendulum' tradition, did not let his new-found support for Vandor go to the extreme of excommunicating the radicals. Indeed, he managed to keep up a constant stream of statements which could be read as encouraging their combative attitude. At the time of the *cordobazo* Perón even earned himself a reprimand from the Spanish government for granting an interview to a Catholic newspaper in which he proclaimed, 'The people wish to participate in the destiny of the country and they reject military dictatorship.' He then added an ambiguous edge to his statement by warmly praising Castroism while simultaneously condemning Communism and Marxism.

Vandor decided that the time had come to obtain a more unequivocal mandate from *el Líder*. With a forged passport, he journeyed to Spain, where he closeted himself with Perón for two full days of discussions in an Alicante hotel. He emerged with the old man's approval for a plan which, it was hoped, would lead to the unification of the union movement and the striking of a new deal with the government. Vandor would return to Buenos Aires and announce the resignation of his men from the positions they held in the CGT; Ongaro would be invited to do likewise. The government would be offered a truce, in exchange for a commitment to re-start collective wage bargaining by September. At the same time, contacts would be intensified with the Army leaders known to be dissatisfied with Onganía's helmsmanship.

On the morning of 30 June, back in Buenos Aires, Vandor was still hard at work at his heavily guarded office in the UOM headquarters, trying to weave together the different parts of his strategy. Behind his electrically locked door, he was oblivious of the fact that a car had pulled up in the street outside, disgorging five men.

The driver had remained at the wheel; one of the disembarked passengers wandered a few steps, then stopped and lit a cigarette. The other four went straight to the UOM's doorway, rang the bell and started pounding the door for attention. When the door was inched open, they indentified themselves as agents of the Federal Police, come to serve a warrant on one of the union's employees. Asked for their credentials, they suddenly produced guns and forced their way in. As they rounded up the UOM personnel on the ground floor one of them began to shout, 'Where is *el Lobo*? Where is Vandor?'

Upstairs, hearing the commotion, Vandor released the electric lock on his office door and ran out to see what was happening. He was met by a volley of gunfire and fell, having been hit six times. One of the assailants placed a bomb between Vandor's legs, announcing that it would explode in three minutes. Brandishing their weapons, the assassins fled.

Two union officials managed to drag Vandor away before the bomb went off, blowing away a large portion of the ageing building. An ambulance was called and the wounded union leader was rushed to the UOM's own clinic. But it was too late: he was dead on arrival.

The news spread rapidly across Buenos Aires, stunning everyone. Onganía called an urgent meeting of the National Security Council, and within hours the country was being informed that a state of siege had been imposed. Outside, the police were already on the move. The headquarters of the CGT de los Argentinos was raided and its leading figures were hunted down and arrested. Ongaro and forty-two others were picked up as they held a meeting in a small town far away in the province of Córdoba. Private citizens, overcome by the sense of impending catastrophe, rushed to draw money out of the banks and stock up with food; by evening the shelves of the grocery stores were bare.

Within twenty-four hours more than 300 people had been arrested, and the Supreme Court was being bombarded with protests from the Lawyers' Association, claiming that many of their members who had attempted to obtain a *habeas corpus* had been thrown into the same prisons as their clients. Most of the detainees were union activists, but without any apparent logic the dragnet had also reached out to former members of the Illia government and even to a couple of leading intellectuals with no known political affiliation. The new Minister of the Interior, General Francisco Imaz, said: '[The disturbances] are not the consequence of political activity; we are facing a plan of subversion with a clearly identifiable ideology, which is attempting to change our form of life. [. . .] They are the result of the struggle between the two large blocs. [. . .] This is a struggle for the dominance of ideologies, which has arrived here in an attempt to force Argentina to change its style of life.' Onganía followed suit with the announcement of a new overall policy: 'We must now, without neglecting the anti-inflation drive or the process of stabilisation, think of the needier classes, of the popular classes, of the people with less resources.'

The clampdown was effective, but it hardly brought peace. The union movement, with one of its leaders dead and his main rival in prison, was not in a mood to welcome or even give credence to the government's new-found social sensitivity. Within the Army unease was spreading. The General Staff produced a position paper underlining the erosion of Onganía's image and calling for an end to the service's 'spectator role'.

Harsher assessments had begun to circulate among the officers in the form of mimeographed pamphlets, and a number of high-ranking generals were publicly known to be advocating a nationalist coup and hoping to attract the acquiescence if not the support of the *peronistas*. Onganía himself broke his 'professionalist' code by lending an ear to some of this conspiratorial talk, and found himself involved in a barely-contained confrontation with the Commander-in-Chief, General Lanusse, when the latter received reports that one of the President's interlocutors had started canvassing support among the regional commanders for a challenge to Lanusse's authority.

On the political front, sensing the government's weakness, the Radicals had begun to work on a plan for an orderly transition back to elected rule, but they were unable to break Onganía's steadfast determination not to have any dealings whatsoever with the political parties. Nonetheless, schemes for an electoral 'opening' began to proliferate, and one actually managed to make its way up the hierarchy of the Ministry of the Interior to General Imaz, but it too was haughtily thrown out by Onganía. Pressure began to mount on both President and Army Commander to come up with some sort of public hint at what the country's political future might be, and although Lanusse, backed by his General Staff, openly favoured some sort of electoral outcome, Onganía still demurred.

In September Rosario was again the scene of violent rioting, which once more was suppressed by Army occupation of the city. By early October the government was facing the prospect of a general strike called by all sectors of the union movement: Onganía's response was the announcement of a general wage increase, followed shortly after by the news that collective bargaining would not be allowed to include any discussion of wages, but would only address the more general issue of working conditions. Although the unions' response was muted, just over a month later Onganía was proffering an olive branch, in the form of an amnesty for the detainees and the lifting of government 'intervention' of the CGT. The Army General Staff, meanwhile, was already analysing a set of options which included the removal of Onganía from the Presidency and his replacement, either by the Army Commander-in-Chief or by another general who would exercise far more limited Presidential powers.

The new year of 1970 brought with it two novelties. The first one was expected: the introduction of the 'new peso', equivalent to 100 of the old ones, in a futile attempt to rid the inflation-wracked economy of the dizzying talk of tens and hundreds of thousands in minor transactions. The public grudgingly accepted this further demand on their arithmetical faculties, but doggedly continued to reckon in *pesos viejos*, 'old pesos'.

The second novelty, this time unexpected, was the sudden irruption on the political scene of the urban guerrillas. The festive season (the weeks stretching from Christmas Eve to the feast of the Epiphany, or of the Magi) was still in full swing when a group claiming to belong to the Fuerzas Armadas Peronistas (FAP) rode fully armed into a shantytown called Villa Piolín and began to distribute toys and sweets to the children, while a loudspeaker incessantly blared the tune of the *Marcha Peronista*. Only days later a second group attacked a guard post at Campo de Mayo and made away with weapons. From then onwards the will-o'-the-wisp appearances seemed to follow each other uninterruptedly: a Paraguayan consul kidnapped by the FAL; a guerrilla cell captured by the police in Luján; a FAP attack on a Maritime Police post in the delta of the river Paraná; an attack on a police station in Rosario; another in Córdoba; another in the Buenos Aires suburb of Villa Devoto; a narrowly averted bomb attack on the Federal Police headquarters in Buenos Aires. And interwoven with these visible guerrilla operations and their yield of stolen uniforms and guns came disquieting news of an unusual upsurge in major robberies: sixty-four of them in the first three months of the year, yielding a haul equivalent to slightly over one million US dollars.

Against this backdrop came another thunderclap: yet another of Arturo Frondizi's 'kiss-of-death' manifestos, aimed this time not against any of Onganía's ministers, but against the President himself. 'The National Movement *vis-à-vis* the Government's Failure' was its title. Said Frondizi: 'The hopes the country deposited in the government of Lieutenant-General Juan Carlos Onganía, mandatory of the Revolution, are now exhausted. In these almost four years, not only has the Revolution not been made, but the government has sold out to the Counter-Revolution. He accused the Onganía régime of having attempted to substitute 'pseudo-corporativism' for 'the revolutionary objective of creating the political base of the Revolution in a vast accord of the social sectors committed to a change of structures: the workers, the entrepreneurs, the politicians able to adapt themselves to the needs of the real country, the intelligentsia, the armed forces and the church.' Onganía, said Frondizi, had 'identified the Revolution with ideological obscurantism, the repression of ideas, the censorship of thought and art, the trivialisation of education and the maintenance of outdated institutions and pedagogic methods'. But his greatest sin had been postponing the modification of 'the old agro-import policies'.

On 27 May Onganía called a meeting of fifty-two senior generals to explain the outlines of his political plan. In front of a blackboard he subjected them to a classroom lecture. Lanusse takes up the story:

With great enthusiasm, General Onganía began to explain his points of view on representation. It was almost an aesthetic awakening: he spoke, he wrote, he began to draw graphs and pyramids. 'We have our policies in every field. Please excuse the didactic method I'm going to use. It has all been said before, but it is necessary to pause and to study the Argentine Revolution with some generosity. We have not become federalists just because of a long struggle but at the end of one. We are in a process in which four years mean nothing. The world is calling for change. Economic and social development must be determined by objectives, policies and plans; the same applies to political development,' he said.

In Onganía's view, what was needed was 'to organise the community through its structures'. If people were afraid of the power wielded by the CGT it was, in his opinion, because this power was not being opposed by any other. 'We wish to create other structures: the entrepreneurial structure and the professional or technical structure,' he said.

He then drew three triangles: one represented the technical-professional structure; another, the enterprises; the third was organised labour in the form of a unified CGT. The triangle representing the entrepreneurial organisations was divided by perpendicular lines: each segment represented a different sector. The community was represented by a perfect circle.

Then came another three triangles. 'We must', he said, 'create the leadership structure that is formed by: (a) the traditional, decision-making structure and (b) the planning structure, and (c) we are now creating the advisory structure. Only now have we managed to overcome the obstacles in the planning area. The Advisory System is being prepared, with sectoral commissions dealing with vertical issues (for example, the Potato Commission), and with councils dealing with horizontal issues (for example, the Economic and Social Council). These systems are interconnected but independent. The Advisory System supports Planning and also, sometimes, Decision-Making. The Advisory System is based on all the rest (CGT, entrepreneurs, etc.).'

Then came the second series of triangles. One triangle was 'Planning' and included the Security, Development and Science and Technology Councils. Another triangle was 'Advisory', with lines dividing it into horizontal segments: Economic and Social Council, Councils, Commissions. Issues could be dealt with vertically or horizontally. Then came the 'Decision-Making' triangle, crowned by a smaller triangle that said 'Cabinet', with a little flag on top, the President.

What Onganía could not figure out, as he said, was why the politicians showed no enthusiasm for this idea. 'Why are they not with us, if we have not yet clarified the way?' he asked. For him, the most natural thing in the world would have been, for example, that Ricardo Balbín should declare his support for this proposal, a support which should be forthcoming because no one had clarified just what the proposal was. Politics should be efficiency, and nothing was more efficient than this offering: 'The functioning of this system will give place to an equilibrium between the political parties. There will be a transfer, and it will give stability to politics, which tends to be rather unstable.' The generals could not disguise their disappointment.

There is, of course, another version of that strange meeting. Roberto Roth tells it thus:

When they asked [Onganía] about the government's political plan, he replied that it consisted in fulfilling the National Policies, which would soon be announced. Then came the key question: how long would it take to fulfil them? He gave the same old answer: ten to twenty years.

So far Lanusse had achieved what he wanted. As the questions had posed abstract issues, the answers were of the same nature, giving the impression of a ruler who was divorced from reality and from concrete problems, thinking only of his policies, of planning and of remaining in power for ten or twenty years. One more question trapped the President into his famous three pyramids.

These were a graphic representation Onganía used with those close to him to explain what was going to happen in the country once the state stopped making all decisions and responsibility devolved upon the provinces and municipalities. What was unique about them, and Lanusse knew it, was that no one understood them the first time round. With the generals seated a fair distance from the table where Onganía was drawing while he explained in terms they were unused to hear, such as 'participation', 'integration' and 'community', confusion was bound to reign supreme.

And so it happened. The moment Lanusse felt he had achieved the desired effect, he called the meeting to a close.

The following morning General Lanusse called on Onganía with a situation paper which bluntly underlined 'the existence of a deep internal crisis in the government, caused by the lack of firm leadership of the revolutionary process; the co-existence within the government of opposing factions and the absence of clearcut policies or sense of direction.' The document mentioned the failure of the Revolution's economic policies, the involvement of Ministers and Secretaries of State in shady dealings, the growing Deltec scandal — all set up against 'the evident aspiration of many Argentines, not all of whom are irresponsible, that a political plan should be produced to lead the Revolution towards a democratic outcome'. Onganía listened calmly. He must have known, though, that the next day, Army Day, would be used by Lanusse as an opportunity to state publicly his growing dissatisfaction with the President.

Lanusse chose to be elliptical when he addressed his comrades-in-arms and his President during the celebrations at the Colegio Militar. 'Together', he said, 'as so often throughout our history, it is time for us to launch forth with enthusiasm and patriotism to establish the bases of that great national project that will satisfy the aspirations of the citizenry and enable it to consolidate that ambitious aim of reconciling the advantages of progress with the privilege of liberty. This enterprise is opposed by those interests, domestic and foreign, that have profited from stagnation and from the divisions between Argentines. Also opposed to it are those who are committed to establishing in the country a régime alien to its democratic traditions, and who do not hesitate to appeal to violence in order to cause the collapse of the state.' Still Onganía remained calm.

When the formalities were over and they repaired to the study of the Colegio's Director for a glass of champagne, Onganía asked Lanusse for a frank opinion on how the generals had reacted to his lecture two days earlier. 'Personally', said Lanusse, 'my own conclusion left me profoundly disturbed. The generals drew varied conclusions, of course, but I could divide them into two groups: those who didn't understand what you were trying to say, and those who are in total disagreement with what you had to say.' The other two Commanders-in-Chief, Admiral Gnavi and Brigadier Rey, joined the conversation. Onganía offered to have another session with the generals, but after he had explained the same thing to the admirals and Air Force chiefs.

The exchange was brought to a halt by the sudden appearance of a flushed aide-de-camp, who rushed in with news of a major calamity. One of Argentina's former Presidents had been kidnapped.

It was just before nine in the morning on May 29, Army Day, and the first anniversary of the *cordobazo*. In the northern quarter of Buenos Aires, a distinguished residential area, a white Peugeot turned off the fashionable Avenida Santa Fe and into Calle Montevideo. Avoiding the roadworks in front of the Colegio Champagnat, a secondary school run by a religious order, it pulled into a garage offering parking space. Three men stepped out, leaving the driver at the wheel. Two of them wore Army uniform, with insignia indicating that one was a captain and the other a first lieutenant. The third man and the driver, in civilian clothes, wore their hair cut very close, like conscripts. They approached the garage attendant and politely asked if they could leave their car there, near the entrance, for a short while. He agreed. As the three men walked out of the garage, along the pavement and into the apartment block at Number 1053, a pickup pulled up across the road, in front of the Colegio Champagnat. A corporal of the Federal Police and a priest climbed out of the back; the driver, a rather flashy blonde, stayed at the wheel. The nearside doors of the pickup remained open; on the seats, within easy reach, lay machineguns and hand-grenades.

The three who had entered Montevideo 1053 got into the lift and went up to the seventh floor. The man in mufti remained there; the other two went up to the next storey. The Lieutenant rang the doorbell and both squared their shoulders and stood erect. When the door was opened by a pleasant-looking, middle-aged woman, they saluted sharply and the Captain said, 'Good morning, Señora. Is the General in?'

She explained he was still in the bath, but ushered them into the living room and offered them a cup of coffee while they waited. They would have to excuse her; she had some shopping to do.

After a long time he appeared: General Pedro Eugenio Aramburu, former President of the military régime that had ousted Perón in 1955 and currently a leading politician, engaged with little concealment in an attempt to secure a return to elected rule, for which purpose he had already begun negotiations with his erstwhile arch-enemy, Juan Domingo Perón. Over another cup of coffee they settled down to business. The Captain explained that they were there to offer him permanent Army security services, as the government had only recently, and rather inexplicably, withdrawn the police protection given as a matter of course to personages of his standing. The General was pleased. Conversation began to drift into small talk when the Lieutenant suddenly whipped open his short raincoat, producing a submachinegun and saying, 'General, you are coming with us!'

Aramburu offered no resistance. They trooped out, rode down in the lift, picking up the lookout they had left on the seventh floor, and walked out of the building to the waiting Peugeot. As they drove off, priest and policeman leapt into their pickup and followed.

Their first stop was just a few blocks away, near the Faculty of Law building; there they abandoned the Peugeot, and all crowded into the pickup. A few minutes later, divested of their disguises, they stopped to let off the blonde, the phoney Lieutenant and priest, and one of the short-haired youngsters. Their task was to get rid of the uniforms and prepare a communiqué for the press, informing Argentina that a new *peronista* organisation had kidnapped Aramburu in order to submit him to a 'revolutionary trial'. The charges: having ordered the execution of *peronista* rebels in 1956, having desecrated and spirited away the remains of Evita, having repressed *peronismo* and defamed its leaders, and having annulled the 'social conquests' of *peronismo*, restoring oligarchic rule and selling out the country to foreign interests.

The name chosen by the new organisation was 'Montoneros', the historic appellation of the motley armies mustered in the nineteenth century by the provincial *caudillos* to fight against the centralists of Buenos Aires.

The main party of kidnappers continued their journey, switching vehicles again near the city airport. They drove out of the federal district and into Buenos Aires province, along carefully chosen side-roads that avoided built-up areas. It was almost 6 o'clock in the evening when they reached the locality of Timote and drove into the Estancia La Celma, a farm belonging to the family of one of their company, Carlos Alberto Ramus. While Ramus distracted the unsuspecting foreman, the others bundled Aramburu into the main house and imprisoned him in a bedroom.

Back in Buenos Aires, for several hours the radio stations had been broadcasting news of 'the alleged kidnapping of Aramburu'. At Timote, as night fell, the 'revolutionary trial' began. It lasted two whole days. The outcome was relayed first to the press: Aramburu had been 'found guilty' of four charges which he admitted, and of another five which he denied; the 'Revolutionary Tribunal' had sentenced him to death by firing squad.

Aramburu himself was told of his fate a day later, just half-an-hour before the time set for his 'execution'. The former President was then marched down to the cellar. While one Montonero, upstairs, hammered on a shutter to drown the noise, another fired a 9mm. pistol at Aramburu's chest. His companion joined in with a .45 for the *coup de grace*. A blanket was thrown over the body as they dug a shallow grave for him in the earth floor of the cellar.

In Buenos Aires, the press received a small printed handbill which read, 'Perón returns. 1st June 1970. Communiqué No.4. To the People of the Nation: The leadership of Montoneros informs that today at 7 o'clock Pedro Eugenio Aramburu was executed. May God our Lord have mercy on his soul. Perón or Death! Long Live the Fatherland! Montoneros.'

This account of Aramburu's murder follows the lines of one published four years later by two of the participants, Mario Firmenich (the phoney policeman and the man whose hammering concealed the noise of the pistol shots) and Norma Arrostito (the bewigged 'flashy blonde' who drove the pickup), in the Montonero magazine *La Causa Peronista*. Many of Aramburu's friends and followers, however, have hinted broadly that this first public coup of the Montoneros was somehow aided and abetted by high-ranking officials in the Onganía government. In support of their theory, they point out that Firmenich had been a frequent visitor at the Ministry of the Interior; that the government had facilitated the kidnapping by withdrawing Aramburu's police guard, and later by failing to respond swiftly to news of the event (some government spokesmen openly suggested at the time that the kidnapping had been staged by Aramburu himself as a propaganda coup); that many of the younger officials in that administration later joined the Montoneros or worked closely with them; and that most of the alleged perpetrators of the crime were later killed either while 'resisting arrest' or while 'attempting to escape'.

But where had these Montoneros come from? They had, in fact, announced their existence to the world a couple of months earlier, but hardly anyone had taken any notice: verbal belligerence and promises of armed action were being issued by a host of small groups of the extreme Left and on the fringes of *peronismo*. And this, by any standards, was a small group: the original Montoneros numbered only twelve, and they had had to commit a full ten of their company to their first public exploit, the kidnapping and murder of Aramburu. Most of the original twelve came from a Catholic background; politically-minded, they had discovered their first link between religion and politics in the traditional frame of nationalism. Like many others, they had felt the impact of the Second Vatican Council and of the Medellín Conference, where the bishops of Latin America had announced their church's 'option for the poor' and commitment to '*liberación*', a term hitherto only to be found in the lexicon of the far Left. They had also felt the pull of those two other currents that had been swirling through Argentine politics since the early 1960s: the traditional Left's revision of its attitudes towards *peronismo*, and the adoption, by some segments of the old body of *peronistas*, of the doctrine of armed insurrection. One of the precursors of this small band, Fernando Abal Medina, had travelled to Cuba in 1967 and acquired the rudiments of guerrilla training. Another, Norma Arrostito, had come from the ranks of the Partido Comunista Revolucionario, a splinter of Argentina's staid Communist Party.

In their formative years, 1968 and 1969, the Montoneros-to-be devoted their efforts to study and to steeling themselves for armed revolutionary action. Remaining anonymous, they held up banks to secure funds for their budding organisation, and assaulted policemen to obtain their first arms and their first taste of confrontation with the security forces. In February 1969 they pulled off a major heist — the robbery of guns from the *Tiro Federal* (public shooting range) in Córdoba. Together with most of the Latin American Left, they were able to contrast the failure of Guevara's attempt to set up a rural guerrilla *foco* in Bolivia in 1967, as well as the aborted bid by radicalised *peronistas* to initiate rural insurgency in Taco Ralo in 1968, with the introduction of urban guerrilla tactics by Carlos Marighela in Brazil, and by the daredevil, Robin Hood-type Tupamaros in neighbouring Uruguay. By the time the *cordobazo* hit Argentina in 1969, the Montoneros-to-be (who did not take an active part in the riots as an organisation) had concluded that armed struggle in Argentina would take place in the cities.

18

DEEPENING THE REVOLUTION
(1969–1971)

The days following Aramburu's kidnapping witnessed a heightening of tensions between the military commanders and President Onganía. The service chiefs insisted that Onganía's explanations about the country's political future had been unsatisfactory; privately they began to consider ways and means of limiting the power they had given him, while publicly pressing him for a formal disavowal of any 'corporativist' intentions and for a clear indication of the path he would follow to re-establish institutional normality. Onganía argued and procrastinated, then in a fit of pique told the commanders that if they did not like the catalogue of 'national policies' his government had prepared, they themselves should get their heads together and come up with a better alternative. Yet when they indicated that they were thinking along the lines of dialogue with the political parties, Onganía again withdrew into his shell, reminding the commanders that it was he, Onganía, whom the armed forces had entrusted with running the government; suggestions from them would be precisely that and no more: suggestions. As a threatening rider, he added, 'The Commanders-in-Chief appointed me, but they cannot remove me. And if they were to ask me to resign, who knows if I would?' In strict formality, he was right: back in 1966 the Revolutionary Junta that had wrested power from Arturo Illia had dissolved itself after designating Onganía as President of the Republic. According to the rule-book they themselves had written, the Junta could only be reconvened in case of manifest inability to rule on the President's part. And although the military had a long record of disregard for rules, whoever they were written by, one of their most persistent traits was their devotion to sophistry — the compulsion to twist and turn facts in order to prove that they were always respecting, even protecting the very rules they were breaking. In Onganía's case they decided among themselves to consider the Revolutionary Junta reconvened *de facto* when the President requested from them the preparation of an alternative political plan.

One tense meeting followed another almost hourly for ten long days. Then, on the morning of 8 June, Onganía returned to the Casa Rosada from an official ceremony to find that the Commander-in-Chief of the Army, General Lanusse, had made public a statement announcing that no further 'blank cheques' would be issued in favour of the President, and that the Revolutionary Statute would be amended to give the service chiefs a greater say in government. The Navy followed suit almost instantly; the Air Force a couple of hours later. Onganía responded by relieving General Lanusse of his command, but only to hear, five minutes later, that the Junta of Commanders-in-Chief had publicly announced their decision to depose the President.

It was almost immediately clear that Army corps commanders throughout the country were backing General Lanusse, yet Onganía sat firm in the Casa Rosada, proclaiming 'The era of the coups and *planteos* has ended and will never return' and 'I will not resign just because they wave papers at me, but only when I see the troops deployed.' The area around the Casa Rosada was sealed off and plans began to be prepared to eject Onganía forcibly. Yet still he sat firm, issuing futile restatements of his authority, such as the decision to dismiss the Air Force commander, Brigadier Rey. As night fell, Onganía was obstinately clinging to the empty trappings of the Presidency. Just as he had promised, it was only when the troops were ordered to start closing in on the Casa Rosada that he relented. Half-an-hour before midnight, he crossed over to the Ministry of Defence, stormed into the room where the Commanders were meeting, and handed them a sheet of paper — which even then was not quite a resignation.

'The circumstances the country has lived through in these last few hours', Onganía had written, 'force me, under the pressure of arms, to step down from the position of President of the Republic. I assume total responsibility for everything that has happened since the beginning of the *Revolución Argentina*, at the same time as I charge my successors with the responsibility they shall have to answer for, both to the people and to history, for these recent events. May it be God's will that these irrevocable steps they have taken may be for the good of the Republic. As a citizen now, I once again exhort my people to union and concord, to build their destiny of greatness in peace. And may no one use the events of this sad night to divide the Argentines.'

The man who had envisaged a ten-year rule and a total transformation of Argentina's political system was gone, only days before the fourth anniversary of the *Revolución Argentina*. Power was again directly in the hands of the military chiefs, committed now to prevent the appearance of another Onganía, and convinced that somehow political life, with the parties as protagonists, should return to Argentina. Their immediate problem was the appointment of a successor, a man capable of running the government under close military scrutiny and of setting in motion the much-awaited political *salida*, the 'way out'. The idea of appointing a civilian flitted across the scene, but it presented formidable difficulties: either it had to be a man of some political weight, in which case it would be impossible to avoid the impression that the military were openly favouring a particular party or pressure group, or a relatively unknown figure, which would immediately create the impression of a puppet Presidency, with no real power of its own. In the military field, there were two obvious possibilities: Admiral Pedro Gnavi, who at the time was chairing the Junta of Commanders-in-Chief, and General Lanusse, the man most clearly identified in the public mind as the leader of military opposition to Onganía. Gnavi demurred; the Army was the senior force in Argentina, not the Navy, and the Army bore a special responsibility for the failed Onganía experiment. Lanusse proclaimed: 'I want to put an end, once and for all, to the custom of elevating the Army Commander-in-Chief to the Presidency.'

Someone floated the notion of seeking out a retired Army officer, but this seemed to present the same kind of problems as the discarded civilian option. Days were speeding past with no sign of a decision, creating the impression of a wholly improvised or, even worse, deadlocked military Junta that had acted precipitously, with no clear idea of what was to come next. It was fear of a further loss of prestige by the armed forces that finally forced the appearance of an 'outside' solution. Admiral Gnavi is credited with having picked out of the proverbial hat the name of General Roberto Marcelo Levingston, a senior Army intelligence officer posted abroad at the time as military attaché in Washington. Gnavi had done a stint with Levingston in the state intelligence service; Brigadier Rey had worked with him in the Joint General Staff; General Lanusse had had him as a subordinate at the Escuela Superior de Guerra, the Army's staff college. They all agreed quickly: Levingston seemed a good choice, not least because he had been out of the country, insulated from the tensions and in-fighting that had preceded Onganía's ouster.

Roberto Marcelo Levingston was installed as President twenty days after Onganía left the Casa Rosada. He took the job with severely curtailed powers: major legislative decisions were to be shared with the Junta of Commanders-in-Chief, and he was not even to appoint Ministers without their approval. Yet no sooner had Levingston settled into the Casa Rosada than he was issuing forth publicly with his own interpretation of these limitations. 'The President of the Nation, designated by the Junta of Commanders-in-Chief', he said, 'derives from the armed forces the foundations of his political power. The armed forces, in turn, derive it from the people from whom they emerge, whom they serve and with whom, consequently, they are intimately united. I, as President of the Nation, have total and exclusive responsibility for all executive acts. I do not share this power, I exercise it in its entirety, and it arises from the conditions under which I accepted this position. The participation of the armed forces is institutionalised through the Junta of Commanders-in-Chief, who share with me the legislative responsibilities. [. . .] There may well be doubts as to the possible limitations of my executive faculties. It must be understood, however, that I have not made the great sacrifice of retiring from active duty in the Army, which has been a lifetime vocation, in order to occupy a position that, if limited, would lower the dignity of the high functions I must carry out, of the uniform I wear, and of myself as a person.' A shiver of apprehension ran through military and political circles.

Day Thirteen of Levingston's Presidency was about to dawn in La Calera, a small township some 23 kilometres northwest of Córdoba city. Overhead lights flashing, a patrol car raced in and pulled up in front of the small police station. Out jumped three uniformed men. They rushed in, guns in hand; already inside, a young couple who had been apparently reporting some banal incident also drew weapons. After forcing the assembled policemen to chant the *peronista* march and tapping out on the station typewriter, 'Montoneros Group — Perón or Death — Eva Perón', they trussed up their captives and locked them in a back room. The band then rushed off to the telephone exchange, where they ripped out wires and smashed cabinets, cutting La Calera off from all communication with the outside world. Only five minutes later, a police jeep patrolling near the branch office of the Banco de Córdoba was rammed from behind by a pickup. When the dazed occupants scrambled out, they were held at gunpoint. The ·assailants, divided into two parties, then entered the bank and the town post office. As they set about the leisurely task of ransacking both institutions, an unsuspecting police patrol car drove into town, only to run into a hail of machine-gun bullets, the first and only shots fired during the raid. Twenty minutes later, the band of Montoneros left, taking with them a haul of some 10 million 'old' pesos.

The operation, planned and directed by Emilio Maza, Montoneros commander in Córdoba, was almost a carbon copy of the takeover of

Pando in Uruguay by that country's Tupamaros. The parallel would extend further: like the Uruguayan operation, initial success was to be followed by disaster in the retreat. With remarkable swiftness, the 2nd Army Corps set up a ring of roadblocks round the La Calera area; isolated members of the guerrilla band were picked up or shot before they even made it to their hideouts in Córdoba city. The first captures put the security forces on the scent of the group's urban bases, and by mid-day the police were storming a house in the Córdoba suburb of Los Naranjos, where they killed Emilio Maza, badly wounded Ignacio Vélez (one of the participants in the Aramburu kidnapping) and arrested another two Montoneros. A couple of hours and twelve police raids later, a full nine members of the raiding party had been taken.

At a stroke, half of the Montoneros' pompously labelled apparatus (on paper they boasted Departments of War, Psychological Action, Maintenance and Documents) had been all but wiped out. There remained the Buenos Aires unit, commanded by Fernando Abal Medina, and the small band of newcomers led by José Sabino Navarro, the young union activist from Córdoba who had formed his own armed organisation a year earlier and joined forces with the budding Montoneros in the first half of 1970. And even these remnants were not to remain immune from the aftermath of the La Calera operation. Over a few days, the documents captured in Córdoba and the interrogation of arrested Montoneros led to a chain of detentions, culminating in mid-July with the discovery of Aramburu's body in its cellar grave at Timote.

The Montoneros were not the only guerrilla group in existence, nor were they the largest. The days following the La Calera coup witnessed also a bombing attack on the Escuela Superior de Guerra, a string of *caño* explosions in the seaside resort of Mar del Plata and in the central city of Santa Fe, and an armed raid on the police station of Ferreyra, a town in Córdoba. And then, as July came to a close, what seemed to be yet another carbon copy of the Pando and La Calera operations: an armed raid on the township of Garín, in the province of Buenos Aires and not far from the capital.

The Garín raid was far more sophisticated and impressive than the attack on La Calera. Thirty-six guerrilla fighters took part, mobilised in five pickups and three passenger cars, all of which had been stolen for the occasion. Roadblocks were set up on the town's two access roads, a lookout post was established at the nearby junction with the Panamerican highway, the master telephone line was cut, the home of the town's only radio ham was occupied, as was the railway station; the police station was neutralised, and even the bar on the opposite side of the road from the bank they robbed was included among the raiders' targets. The entire operation took eleven minutes.

Codenamed 'Gabriela', the Garín raid had been planned by three men, Marcos Osatinski, Roberto Quieto and Carlos Olmedo, leaders of the FAR (Fuerzas Armadas Revolucionarias — Revolutionary Armed Forces), many of whose members had come from the Partido Comunista Revolucionario, a splinter of the Argentine Communist Party. FAR thus entered the stage, next to the older FAL and FAP groups which, with other smaller organisations, were already engaged in talks about possible joint actions.

Another newcomer was also preparing to emerge on the public scene. The Trotskyite Partido Revolucionario de los Trabajadores, in its Fifth Congress, formally decided to implement its First Operational Military Plan. The instrument chosen to carry it out was the ERP (Ejército Revolucionario del Pueblo — People's Revolutionary Army). Their reading of the situation, as expressed in Congress documents, was that conditions were ripe, if not for all-out insurgency, at least for an ideologically sound 'armed vanguard' to take the lead, avoiding both the 'right-wing opportunism' and the 'militaristic tendencies' they could detect among other armed organisations. 'The process of development of the revolutionary war', said the PRT, 'continues in its present stage of sustained ascent.' It continued:

We can affirm that since the beginning of this year this trend has not varied, which is very promising; we can also point to a rhythm (unplanned) of one action of national importance each month and a series of minor actions occurring daily. Quite logically, all of this has had an acute effect on the country as a whole, to the point that no one is unaware of the fact of the war. This does not mean that society as a whole feels itself to be an active part of the process, either in favour or against, but that the effects of the war have, every day, a greater impact on the daily life of the population, especially in the important urban centres and often in smaller townships. As far as active participation goes, the process is still a confrontation of vanguards; the revolutionary vanguard and what we could call the 'reactionary vanguard'.

The 'First Operational Military Plan' was itself brief and to the point:

Under present conditions any plan must be based on our concrete reality and not on our subjective wishes. Our present stage of development calls for two main tasks: *Armed Propaganda* and *the Creation of a Solid and Efficacious Military Structure*, which include obtaining money and armaments, and giving the whole of the Party a military capability. Within Armed Propaganda we include, as the main point, publicising our military acronym (ERP) and the Army's programme, through military actions of great repercussion, continuity and national scale, since isolated actions, no matter how big, if they lack a frame of similar actions in three or four regions of the country and a certain rhythm, are meaningless, because our acronym would become just one among five or six.

Within the creation of a military structure we consider the following priorities: *(a)* to obtain funds and armaments; *(b)* massively to toughen the military cells and the Party as a whole in military and resistance actions. We underline the convenience of carrying out the greatest possible number of disarmaments of isolated policemen, an action which allows, apart from the collection of arms, the testing of our *compañeros* in action, and which has political repercussions within the repressive apparatus; this kind of action must be carried out by all cells.

Such is the frame of our First Operational Plan, which will be developed in the following months through the following actions: (1) a series of military actions involving the expropriation of money, the capture of arms, the occupation of townships, the liberation of prisoners, and kidnappings, to be carried out by stages in different parts of the country, following a sequence we cannot foresee at this time; (2) interspersed with these, the continuity of minor resistance actions by all cells. The most important of these are those of capturing arms and distribution of foodstuffs. (3) Alongside demonstrations and mass mobilisations, the Army's military cells shall carry out simultaneous and complementary action; (4) a fundamental point for a correct political outcome of this plan is its propaganda exploitation. This will consist in an intelligent formulation and realisation of the propaganda of each concrete action and of our Army's acronym and programme. We must assess each action politically, carefully avoiding doubtful actions, and always choosing those that will be clearly popular; we must prepare good, sober communiqués, strictly adhering to the truth and with a clear political content within the lines established by the Army's programme. We must produce our own propaganda, painting slogans on walls, distributing leaflets etc., which is important for the people to become aware of the physical proximity of our military force; for them to realise that the combatants are near; that they could be any of the people among them; that it is not an isolated vanguard. As a general rule we must point out that armed propaganda actions will be excellent if they are carried out with our eyes fixed on the masses, with a 'line' of the masses, through perfect observation of people's reactions and states of mind. (5) The fundamental tactical recommendations of this plan are: *(a)* to prepare actions carefully, ensuring their success as far as possible. Take minimal risks by foreseeing possible consequences. Limit the risks of each action by carefully protecting the rest of the organisation. In action all details are fundamental; *(b)* to act with decision, audacity and serenity. Timidity, doubt, nervousness etc. are the main enemies of success and multiply the risks inherent to combat; *(c)* when facing difficulties, behave heroically. Go in willing to kill or to die. Revolutionary morale, the basis of our heroism, is our fundamental superiority in combat. Heroic comportment stimulates the imagination of the masses, awakening admiration, solidarity and a wish to emulate.

The population certainly were becoming more and more aware of the presence and activities of the armed groups, yet this was a far cry from seeing them as engaged in 'a process of revolutionary war'. The security forces themselves were confused, unable yet to bring together in their minds all the elements until recently found firmly in the ranks of right-wing nationalism, the radicalised Catholic youth, and the many splinters of the Argentine Left. Their belief, rooted in the experience of earlier years, was that the outbreak of terrorism could be contained by identify-ing and neutralising the handful of committed ringleaders they imagined to be orchestrating the whole effort. There was, to be sure, growing unease at the succession of minor *coups de main*, directed mainly against lone policemen on the beat, but there was no full realisation yet that these fitted into the recruitment and training patterns of very ambitious new guerrilla organisations.

And there was no real understanding of the effect these events were having on the 'new opposition', the generation left in the lurch by the political freeze imposed by the *Revolución Argentina*. Public and official awareness was still only advancing erratically, with such major shocks as the assassinations of Aramburu and Vandor, the takeovers of townships and the large bank heists. Shocks, it must be noted, which were not always accompanied by condemnation: the victims of murders, leaving aside the political élite, did not belong to sections of society that are par-ticularly loved, and there was more than a tinge of admiration, among a people ruled autocratically for four years, for the audacity of those who could thumb their noses at authority (in addition, bank robbers have never been among the most despised of criminals). To a large extent it was spectator shock, a focal point for morbid interest; not a reaction to any perceived threat to society as a whole or to the onlookers themselves, but rather a fascination with a contest taking place somewhere 'out there', in which both challengers and challenged were equally 'them' and not 'us'.

In the political field, the upsurge in armed confrontation was only too rapidly cast into existing categories. On the Right, few went beyond the ritual invocation of 'foreign-inspired subversion' as a justification for more and better instruments of repression: more complete and detailed 'anti-subversive' legislation, speedier and more expeditious court pro-cedures. The Left, or those of its spokesmen who were able to speak in public, spoke of 'the violence from below' emerging as a response to 'the violence from above'. The wide political centre played it safe, both expressing its distaste at individual acts of violence and preaching that it was no good to choose heightened repression as an answer: the proper response could only be 'an attack on the root causes of violence'. Perón, from Madrid, played his classic 'pendulum' in a novel fashion, no longer swinging from Right to Left but wielding all options simultaneously. Through the union leaders and the political wing of his movement he increased pressure on the government, and particularly on the military, calling alternately for a 'National Revolution' and for elections, all the while offering the country dire forecasts of civil war and chaos if his words were not heeded. At the same time he spoke to the youthful Left of his movement about *socialismo nacional* (literally 'national socialism', though in Spanish the phrase does not carry the same connotations as in English: Nazism is usually rendered *nacional-socialismo*) and heaped praise and encouragement on the 'special formations', a term he coined to give the impression that the many self-proclaimed *peronista* guerrilla groups were somehow part of a master scheme controlled ultimately by himself. In actual fact, the guerrilla groups acted with almost complete autonomy, having learnt from the union bosses the tactics of presenting Perón with *faits accomplis* and only calling upon him for overt support on selected occasions. In later years, for example, a leader of the *peronista* Left would boast of how, by murdering Aramburu, they had prevented Perón from 'swinging to the Right': *'el Viejo'*, he said, 'was quite ready to go along with Aramburu's proposals for an electoral agreement against Onganía.'

Indeed, among the guerrilla organisations, old and new, a debate had begun to rage over their exact role *vis-à-vis* the *peronista* movement as a whole, and by extension *vis-à-vis* Perón himself. One current of opinion, the *movimientistas*, held that the entire *peronista* movement with its alliance of social classes was the appropriate, indeed the only available vehicle for the 'national and social revolution', which in its current stage was basically an 'anti-imperialist' struggle: national liberation should come first, socialism would follow. Among the *movimientistas* there were those who genuinely believed that Perón had become committed to *socialismo nacional*, and that his many apparently contradictory postures were to be attributed entirely to his genius as a tactician. Others were not so convinced of this, but they felt that if the Left managed to conquer positions of importance within the *peronista* movement, Perón would have no choice but to heed them. And in order to conquer those key

position, a vital part of their struggle had to be the elimination of the
'traitors' within the *peronista* movement — meaning all those who were
willing to settle for an electoral outcome, plus the 'union bureacrats'
who limited their action to wage-bargaining rather than pressing for
revolutionary gains.

On the opposite side of the fence were the *alternativistas*, who
maintained that the *peronista* movement, as currently organised, was
a far cry from a revolutionary force. The main task, as they saw it,
would be to wrest away *peronismo*'s historic banners and create a new
vehicle, a truly revolutionary party. A common feature among *alternativistas* was the view that socialism could not wait for national liberation; that the anti-imperialist struggle was of necessity a struggle against
capitalism.

The debate, to a large extent, was couched in euphemisms, and proponents of one or the other approach could be found in virtually every
one of the armed organisations. If, however, attention is paid only to
dominant trends, organisations like Montoneros, and later the FAR,
could be identified as *movimientistas*, while the mood in the FAP was
more markedly *alternativista*. One of the ironies of this confrontation was
that, as a rule of thumb, *movimientismo* was more easily found among the
newcomers to the *peronista* fold, while *alternativismo* was quite popular
among some of the veterans of revolutionary *peronismo*, including many
survivors of the post-1955 'Resistance'.

Shocks, courtesy of this constellation of armed organisations,
continued throughout Levingston's first four months in the Presidency.
A major blow was the murder, in late August, of José Alonso, the
veteran *peronista* union leader who had long rivalled Vandor's control of
organised labour. One day in September, twenty-three bomb blasts
rocked a number of cities. Within a few weeks, the ERP raided a police
station in Rosario, killing two policemen; the FAL hijacked a com-
muter-loaded train in the Buenos Aires suburb of Bancalari; the FAP fire-
bombed the home of the US Air Force attaché in the residential district of
Martínez; and yet more bombs exploded in Buenos Aires, Rosario, Santa
Fe and Tucumán.

The security forces, however, were not just sitting tight. Arrests
related to the Aramburu case continued, while the trial of those already
indicted sped ahead. In early September a police patrol caught up with
Fernando Abal Medina, Montoneros commander in Buenos Aires and
the recognised overall head of the organisation, and Carlos Ramus; the
farm of a relative of his had been used for the 'revolutionary trial' and

murder of Aramburu. Both Abal Medina and Ramus were killed in a fierce gunfight.

The political analysts who had pictured Onganía's government as a balancing act between 'nationalists' and 'liberals' continued to seek the same pattern in Levingston's first cabinet. Fitting the new appointees into either category was no easy task — indeed in some cases it was impossible. The Commanders-in-Chief, eager to forestall the emergence of another Onganía, had carefully vetted every appointment. Signalling the fact that the *Revolución Argentina* was entering a more 'political' phase, they had picked men with greater political experience than their predecessors. The 'political' portfolio par excellence, the Ministry of the Interior, was entrusted to a retired Air Force officer, Brigadier Eduardo McLoughlin, who had been Air Force Minister under Aramburu and again under Guido, and had only just returned from a stint as ambassador in the United Kingdom. His antecedents placed him firmly within the 'liberal' camp, as did his declared commitment to the restoration of elected rule.

Unlike the previous administration, the crucial Ministry of the Economy was not given to any of the instantly recognisable 'liberals'. The man chosen for the job was Carlos Moyano Llerena, an economist known to be imbued with the social teachings of the Catholic church — which led analysts to place him, tentatively, as closer to the 'nationalist' line, until he surprised everyone by decreeing a devaluation of the peso 'for psychological reasons' and by announcing a programme that did not depart too noticeably from the broad policy lines established by his predecessors.

The Ministry of Foreign Affairs went to Luis María de Pablo Pardo, who had been Minister of the Interior under Lonardi: a nationalist, but of the more élitist variety. Social Welfare was entrusted to Francisco Manrique, a former Navy captain who had been Chief of Aramburu's Military Household before launching on a career as a maverick journalist. A close friend of General Lanusse, the Army commander, Manrique was seen as the leading 'liberal' of the administration. Public Works went to Aldo Ferrer, a well-known economist of nationalist inclinations who had won acclaim as Economy Minister of the province of Buenos Aires; the National Development Council to General (retired) Juan Enrique Guglialmelli, a declared *desarrollista*; and the Labour Secretariat to Juan Alejandro Luco, of *peronista* extraction.

Yet this was not, strictly, Levingston's cabinet: it was the service chief's cabinet, a fact of which the new President was painfully aware. Levingston's inaugural statement of executive independence from the Commanders had not been just a face-saving device. From the very beginning he started manoeuvring to neutralise their influence on the government. If ministerial appointments had had to be approved by the Commanders, the rest of the administrative hierarchy remained very much in Levingston's hands, and he lost no time in filling Under-Secretariats with people of his own choice. Nowhere was this more evident than in the Ministry of the Interior, where Levingston's man, Under-Secretary Enrique Gilardi Novaro, openly contradicted McLoughlin's emphasis on the need for a 'political plan', meaning a set of rules for a fairly prompt call to elections).

Levingston himself preferred to interpret the issue of political normalisation in a manner somewhat reminiscent of Onganía. In public statements, he listed a number of economic targets — mainly large public works — as indispensable prerequisites for any advance on the political front. Echoing Onganía, he called for 'a deepening [*profundización*] of the Revolution'. And as if the debate which had led to Onganía's ouster had never taken place, he insisted time and again that the dissolution of the political parties was 'irreversible'. The only concession he would make was the promise that the 'former political groupings' — the parties — would be consulted in a 'wide dialogue', but that they would be called upon, not as parties but as 'representing currents of opinion'.

The Commanders, in the meantime, were still thinking in terms of a conventional political outcome, and their staffs were kept busy churning out draft 'political plans'. They went as far as to reach agreement on some of the ground rules: electoral mandates were to be shortened from six to four years; they were also to be unified, i.e. made to run concurrently (thus eliminating what the soldiers thought was one of the drawbacks of electoralism: the distractions caused by mid-term polls). Finally, a variation of the French system of *ballotage* was to be adopted, whereby if no candidate to the Presidency secured a clear majority, there would be a run-off between the two contestants who had polled the most votes (thus, reasoned the soldiers, eliminating the possibility of a minority government, and giving the President-elect the advantage of a clear-cut majority mandate to legitimise his rule).

In Levingston's bid to neutralise his military overseers, he chose a cunning method to deal with the one area in which even he had conceded their role as ultimate arbiters: legislation. He simply swamped the Junta of Commanders-in-Chief with urgent requests for their judgment on a

massive array of widely-differing topics. This placed them in the
uncomfortable position of having to choose between merely cursory
examination of the matters put before them, or the risk of being accused
of 'holding up the march of the Revolution' by devoting too much time
to their proper consideration. One day he would ask the Commanders
for prompt delivery of an agreed draft 'political plan'; the next, he would
tell the nation that the final version would not be issued by the Presidency until mid-1971. Levingston's temperament was a useful aid in this
task of keeping the commanders off balance: prone to near-hysterical
tantrums, he often disrupted top-level meetings with the Junta by shouting accusations at them, blaming them for obscure plots aimed at under-
mining the President's authority. For far too long, the Commanders
played into his hands, responding to these outbursts with soothing
reassurances of their wholehearted support.

It took Levingston less than four months of unremitting harassment
to drive McLoughlin to resign from his post as Interior Minister. When
Economy Minister Moyano Llerena, for the sake of form, offered his
own resignation as well, Levingston shocked him by coolly replying,
'Well, now that you are no longer a Minister . . .' Levingston's following step was more of a gamble. Deliberately ignoring the agreement to
consult with the Commanders, he appointed men of his own choice to
the two key ministries: Aldo Ferrer was shunted from Public Works
to Economy; Arturo Cordón Aguirre, an Air Force man, to Interior.
The President was clearly and openly throwing his weight behind the
'nationalists' or, to be more precise, behind what was by then described
as the 'national and popular line', *línea nacional y popular*. The phrase
drew a distinction between these nationalists and their more élitist predecessors, associated in the public mind with ultramontane Catholicism
and with pseudo-corporativist schemes, who continued to be known as
nacionalistas.

'*Nacional y popular*' was an emotion-laden term which encompassed a
wide segment of the political spectrum: it was *peronismo*, plus several of
the offspring of the old Radical trunk and a faction of the Christian
Democrats. It was rapidly becoming a catchphrase of the youthful 'new
opposition' where *peronismo* and the Left were meeting. Vague though
its limits were, it suggested economic nationalism coupled with the
espousal of the interests of the salaried classes, of the 'popular majorities'.
Populist rather than formally democratic, mainline '*nacional y popular*'
was not necessarily committed to conventional electoral and parliamentary procedures.

Levingston did not, at this stage, openly espouse the *línea nacional y popular*. He had no real need to do so: political commentators, duly briefed in private by high government officials, were busy illuminating the manuscript for public consumption. Here was a double gamble: first, a challenge to the Junta, and more particularly to General Lanusse in his public persona as the 'arch-liberal' of the régime (in the coded language of Argentina in 1970, nothing was more opposed to the *línea nacional y popular* than the 'liberals'); and secondly, to the whole body politic — what Levingston was suggesting was that he would exercise the power he had been given on behalf of all those who identified with the *línea nacional y popular*, and that on the strength of that suggestion he had a claim on their allegiance.

The Junta did not pick up the gauntlet. On the contrary, they floated a plan which would have made Levingston the linchpin of their electoral schemes: they proposed to call a national referendum to give Levingston a clear four-year mandate as leader of a transitional administration, which would eventually hand over power to the politicians.

In the wider political context, the second part of Levingston's challenge was being studiously ignored. Only days before his cabinet shuffle, the CGT went out on a twenty-four-hour general strike. The appointment of Ferrer as Economy Minister did not defuse union hostility; within the month the CGT had called another general strike — for ten hours this time, but escalating to thirty-six hours in early November. In the mean time, the unmentioned key factor of all speculation about 'political plans' — Juan Domingo Perón — was unceremoniously thrust onstage in a fashion that reminded all and sundry that, despite everything, Argentina still phrased its political options in terms of that unresolved dilemma which six governments since 1955 had tried to bludgeon, decree, coax or freeze out of existence. The day before the *peronistas* engaged in their dogged annual attempt to celebrate their October revolution, General Lanusse chose an assembly of fellow-generals to proclaim publicly, '*Señor* Juan Domingo Perón, quite apart from the rights and wrongs of his exercise of public office, was opportunely disqualified, for very grave faults, by a Special Tribunal of Honour composed of five lieutenant-generals of the Nation . . . It is not my intention to re-stoke hatreds or to condemn a movement of opinion whose motives I respect. What I do wish is to define, without the shadow of a doubt, the opinion our Institution holds of a man who belonged to it until he was separated from our ranks for manifestly unbecoming conduct.' It was a resounding slap in the face of *peronismo*.

And it was returned, two days later, by Perón's new 'personal delegate' in Argentina, Jorge Daniel Paladino. 'Perón', he said curtly, 'will return before the end of the year.' There was no room for Levingston in the debate: it took place between the men who represented real power: Lanusse for the Army, Paladino for Perón.

Less than a month later, Perón followed up with a devastating back-hander. As the culmination of many weeks of secret negotiations, a meeting was held in Buenos Aires between *peronista* leaders and their peers of the Unión Cívica Radical del Pueblo, plus an assortment of minor figures representing the Unión Cívica Radical Bloquista, the Partido Conservador Popular, the Partido Demócrata Progresista, the Partido Socialista Argentino, and 'independent liberals'. All told, as was estimated by a General Staff officer quoted by General Lanusse, 'they represented between eight and ten million votes.' The conclave, calling itself *La Hora del Pueblo* ('The Hour of the People'), committed itself to struggling for a prompt return to elected rule. Few of those with memories stretching back a decade-and-a-half could fail to appreciate that this was an evocation of *La Hora de los Pueblos*, the title of a tract written by Perón shortly after his ouster and forecasting the utter defeat of those who had defeated him. Historic allusions apart, the message from the conclave was that the political parties were back in business, and did not need governmental approval to devise and implement their strategies. From his exile Perón interpreted the event far more brutally than the participants. 'In Argentina,' he said, 'there are only two parties: the rest are mere ornaments.' Implicitly, he was telling the military that with *peronistas* and Radicals embarked on the same course by common agreement, they could give up speculating about how the rest would react.

Sophisticates laughed the event off. After all, there was an impressive list of groupings which had kept well away from *La Hora del Pueblo*: the Conservatives, the 'Democratic Socialists', even Frondizi's *desarrollistas*, Oscar Alende's Intransigent Radicals, and the Communists — and the latter three were among the people Levingston was wooing with his *nacional y popular* insinuations. Perón's insulting simplification and the General Staff officer's down-to-earth arithmetic were equally ignored. Yet the death-knell of the military régime had just sounded.

One increasingly powerful political group that did not laugh off *La Hora del Pueblo* was the *peronista* Left. In their eyes this was a dangerous development, engineered by the 'traitors' in the *peronista* movement who were bent on seeking some form of accommodation with the régime rather than pursuing *peronismo*'s revolutionary destiny. That the event had obviously had Perón's blessing did not disturb this line of reasoning. After all, they argued, *El Viejo* had always been a brilliant tactician, and he was using the more conservative elements of *peronismo* to keep the military busy on another front, while the real business of creating the conditions for a revolutionary victory was left to the militant armed groups, Perón's 'special formations'. This was not just a collection of wild imaginings. The Montoneros had written to the exiled leader justifying their actions, and specifically the assassination of Aramburu, against accusations from the more orthodox *peronista* leaders that they were jeopardising Perón's strategy. And Perón had replied, reassuring them: his strategy, he said, far from being endangered by the actions of the 'special formations', was furthered by them; the campaign against the régime, he explained, must proceed on many fronts. They had given him the opportunity of claiming to be the mastermind behind the many unco-ordinated, highly autonomous actions of the guerrilla groups, and Perón had taken it. For Montoneros and the other armed organisations, what mattered was that he had given them his blessing, and in writing. That they had forced his hand was beside the point: they were doing no more than what the *peronista* union bosses had taught them — presenting Perón with *faits accomplis* and allowing him to take the credit for them. It was, of course, within the realms of possibility that Perón would refuse to take the bait, and disown them instead. But the experience of the past fifteen years indicated that Perón usually only disowned losers, or leaders who seemed to be gaining too much of a following in their own right. In late 1970, the Montoneros and the other 'special formations' did not fit into either category.

This hardnosed, cynical approach to Perón's overlordship was never voiced in public, and only rarely in private. It was papered over with two myths. One, shared with the guerrillas' rivals within the *peronista* movement, was that of Perón's tactical genius. And there was substance to it: Perón defined himself as a 'conductor' rather than a politician; unencumbered by the principles that limit the actions of the ideologues, Perón had proved himself a master of 'the art of the possible', if only by keeping himself and his movement at the very centre of Argentine politics for a full decade-and-a-half after being ejected from power.

The other myth, this time specific to the radical wing of the movement, was that there actually was a 'real Perón' behind all his confusing, often contradictory tactical moves. And this 'real Perón', they claimed, was the revolutionary, the man who spoke of *socialismo nacional* and compared himself to Mao Tse-tung. That he did not voice this commitment more openly and wholeheartedly was due, they explained, to the fact that he was constrained by the nature of his movement, with the union and political leaders it had inherited; Perón's true nature was conditioned and distorted by the 'circle of traitors' who hemmed him in. The *peronista* Left needed this myth, both to justify their declared allegiance to Perón and to rationalise their attacks on *peronista* union bosses and political chieftains. And many, if not all of them, actually came to believe it.

Guerrilla activity continued unabated throughout the rest of 1970. A high-ranking Federal Police officer was assassinated by the FAL; the FAR raided two banks, in Córdoba and La Plata; the FAP attacked a police station in Escobar, province of Buenos Aires; Montoneros made off with 8 million pesos from a Córdoba post office; and an unnamed group went as far as to shoot up one of the guard posts at the Presidential residence in Olivos. The anti-guerrilla campaign conducted by the security forces kept up a similar pace: massive search-and-arrest sweeps were carried out in the country's major cities; a Montonero plan for a La Calera-type takeover of the town of Ensenada, in Buenos Aires province, was thwarted by the timely arrest of the ringleaders; and sentences were passed on several of those who had been implicated in the Aramburu murder — eighteen years for Carlos Alberto Maguid, two to eight years for Ignacio Vélez, two years (suspended) for Fr Alberto Carbone. Norma Nélida Arrostito de Maguid, the phoney blonde in the operation, was set free.

The military were not entirely sure, even among themselves, of the precise nature of the guerrilla threat, or of what should constitute the most suitable response. During his brief stint as Minister of the Interior, Eduardo McLoughlin had attempted to outline an official policy towards *la violencia:* 'My main concern', he had said, 'is to rescue the sector that is close to violence — that is where something must be done. There is a minority, a small minority, that has embarked on this course of action: I do not believe we can convince that small minority. But around this minority there is a much wider circle of people, a very important sector of the youth, who may sympathise and share intellectual concerns with the nucleus which has chosen violence. We cannot afford to lose that youth. We must make them understand that violence is a utopia, that the debate of the late nineteenth and early twentieth century has exhausted the experience of violence. Fundamentally, that youth must be shown that its great concerns, often justified by very real situations of injustice, should be channelled along other routes — even if only so that they do not become counter-productive.'

General Lanusse, on the occasion of Aramburu's funeral, unfolded another line of official thinking. He said:

The full weight of justice, will fall inexorably on the material authors of this deed; on its instigators and on their accomplices. *However, public revenge must also reach those who, with their insidious preaching, sheltered by a freedom they violate day by day, help to encourage the use of violence to solve the grave problems faced by the country and its people. In their deceitful campaign they do not hesitate to use any means or arguments to move the good faith of public opinion, to erode the prestige of the forces of order and to justify the actions of those who, betraying even their most sacred responsibilities, contribute through their dissociative activity to encourage this new type of delinquency that has become the scourge of the country.*

In his memoirs of this period, however, Lanusse mentions an apparent consensus on the guerrilla issue, reaching from the higher echelons of the armed forces to President Levingston:

In the three services there was absolute clarity about the inconvenience and impossibility of establishing an open-ended reactionary dictatorship. On 31 July [1970], at a meeting of the National Security Council, it was President Levingston himself who categorically rejected that alternative: 'We shall not go in the direction in which they are pushing us. They want to drive us towards a dictatorship. But they shall not drive us to dictatorship.' The theory outlined on that occasion by Levingston broadly coincided with the Army's own appreciation of the situation: the country had been chosen by an international subversive conspiracy as the launching pad for a revolutionary war which aimed at reaching continental, or at least subcontinental proportions. If Argentina managed to contain the enemy and simultaneously attained constitutional normality, setting up a strong, efficient and modern democracy, backed by the majority of public opinion which identified with the system (from pro-government forces to the opposition), then the insurrection would retreat, not only in the country but in the entire area. But if the Republic should rely merely on force, with weak laws and weak rulers, subversion would spread, because it would have reached the political desideratum it sought, and any circumstantial tactical success by the forces of order would become relativised.

Late 1970 witnessed the appearance of two new accretions to the overall panorama of violence. The first was a very concrete notification to the public at large, in the form of two attempts to assassinate judges, that the extreme Right was joining in the fray. The perpetrators called themselves 'Alpha 66' (like the US-based terrorist grouping of anti-Communist Cuban exiles), but that meant very little: Argentina's extreme Right donned and doffed organisational titles to suit the need of the moment.

The second, which was not entirely without precedent, was the adoption of a new technique of repression, later to be known as 'disappearance', but in those days more baldly described as *secuestro*, kidnapping — the clandestine arrest formally denied by the authorities, which more often than not led to interrogation with torture, and to the death of the victim. The rationale behind these clandestine arrests was not always immediately apparent: some victims would have connections with trade union activities; others were known to have left-wing leanings; on yet others there was nothing to go on. In the early days, it was easy to keep track of the names, and not unsurprisingly they became powerful political symbols in opposition circles: Martins, Zenteno, Verd, Palacios, Maestre, Misetich, Licara. Néstor Martins and Nildo Zenteno were the first two of this chain, 'kidnapped' on 16 December 1970; a year later, the press totted up a twelve-month total of seventeen 'disappearances', and individual names began to give way to cold statistics.

Uncertainty as to the nature of the threat and the kind of response it merited overflowed into the soldiers' public assessment of the way they were coping with the guerrilla movements. In mid-November, only days after the government had had to resort again to the declaration of an emergency zone in face of a spate of demonstrations, compounded by a police strike, in the northwestern city of Catamarca, General Lanusse confidently proclaimed that 'extremism is in decline'. Thirty-six days later, he announced in a formal statement to the Army that the country was 'facing the most critical moment of the past hundred years'.

Meanwhile, Levingston continued to put into practice his own version of 'deepening the Revolution'. Under the guidance of Ferrer, the government began to adopt economic policies that did not differ greatly from what mainstream *peronistas* were proposing. The scandal that had linked former Economy Minister Krieger Vasena to Deltec became the trigger for a public airing of the way Argentina's economic establishment had allowed public credit policies, fiscal incentives and trade regulations to operate to the benefit of foreign companies. Overnight, it seemed as if everyone was openly discussing the stranglehold exercised by 'the monopolies' over all key aspects of Argentine economic life. The debate was highly political in tone, emphasising cases of personal corruption rather than analysing structural relationships; concentrating on the formulation of a demonology and the identification of the demons rather than translating the awareness of the country's external dependence into the concrete terms of the current political line-

up. In his own oblique fashion, Levingston was appealing to views held
in common by a wide segment of the population in an attempt to sidestep
party-political mediation, and to align behind his government a broad
'national and popular' movement that would make the whole question
of elections obsolete.

Perhaps unknowingly, he attempted to repeat Perón's technique for
the takeover of the unions, but in the purely political sphere. Pointedly
ignoring the top echelon of national political leaders, he issued an appeal
to the 'intermediate generation' — leaders of small provincial parties
and second-line personalities in the major groupings. Unlike Perón in his
day, Levingston had nothing as concrete as wage increases and better
working conditions to offer. The only enticement at his disposal was the
privilege of becoming a publicly recognised interlocutor of the military
government. Not surprisingly, even among the aspiring second line of
political leaders, there were not many who responded to his summons.
Among the few of any consequence who did was Oscar Alende, leader of
the Intransigent Radicals, runner-up to Arturo Illia in the 1963
elections, and the man under whose governorship of Buenos Aires province Aldo Ferrer had acquired much of his reputation. Alende's main
contribution to Levingston's efforts was to claim in public that the
'monopolies', through their agents infiltrated into high public positions,
were plotting the government's downfall. After an encounter with
Levingston, Alende said, 'it is symptomatic that just when an attempt is
being made to set in motion the National Revolution, we begin to see
manifestations of those representatives of foreign interests bent on toppl-
ing the government. That is why I went to see the President. It is at least
twenty years since the country last had a government with such a clear
position in defence of the national interest. This is why the conspiracy
wants to topple it *now* — because they reckon that if they leave it until
later, they will never topple it at all!'

The message was picked up by others throughout the country, and
began to be embroidered, a hint or allegation at a time, until its full
import became clear: what the country was witnessing was a covert but
deadly struggle between the defenders of the national interest, embodied
in Levingston's presidency, and the straw men of foreign domination,
the 'liberals', who resorted to the red herring of elections in order to
divert the course of the 'National Revolution'. No leading figure said so
explicitly, but it was impossible not to see the implication that none
other than General Lanusse was being cast in the role of arch-conspirator.

Levingston pressed on, alluding publicly to the election of Salvador

Allende in Chile and the emergence of the left-leaning régime of General
Juan José Torres in Bolivia as illustrations of the welcome anti-imperialist
mood sweeping the continent. Implicitly, he was saying that he would
lead Argentina in the same direction. He orchestrated the replacement of
provincial governors, and finally managed to provoke the resignation of
the Minister of Social Welfare, Francisco Manrique, the man considered
to be closest to Lanusse among the first-ranking members of the government (also a man with political ambitions of his own, which he had been
promoting very skilfully — dare one say in the fashion of Eva
Perón? — through the largesse of his ministry). In an official document
of the Presidency, Levingston launched a fairly open attack on those who
advocated a rapid restoration of elected rule:

When we have recovered the management of credit, assumed control over the
banks, opposed distortions in operations with our main export commodities,
nationalised energy etc., it is only natural to expect a stubborn resistance and a
growing offensive from those whose privileges have been curtailed. [. . .] This
reaction [becomes manifest] in many guises, including the alarmist rumour, the
twisting of news and facts, the malevolent creation of false expectations, all the
way to the incitement of rebellion, which above all aims at involving the armed
forces. And this happens because the affected interests will not succumb without
attempting — by all means at their disposal — to revert the process. *To this
action we must also add the intentional or unintentional contribution of those who press for
a premature electoral outcome, which would only lead us back — yet again — to one of
the grossest forms of fraud and deceit. They attempt to justify their urgency by attributing
covert designs to the political solution initiated by the government, when they know full
well that without consensus any political design is futile, and that with consensus it is
unnecessary, because political solutions will emerge naturally from the bosom of national
opinion.*

Lanusse did not counter-attack immediately; instead he turned
inwards, to the task of ensuring close personal contact with all Army
unit commanders, while he quietly suggested to the other two Commanders-in-Chief that the time had come to work out some mechanism
of 'closer co-ordination' between the Junta and the President. Beyond
the inner circle of government and armed forces, events seemed largely
unaffected by the confrontation. The guerrilla groups were stepping up
the scale of their operations, dynamiting a police station in Santa Fe,
raking in hauls of 88 million and 121 million pesos in holdups (the former
in the mountain resort of Bariloche, the latter in Yocsina, Córdoba),
continuing the 'training' attacks on policemen. The security forces were
also increasing the pressure: in a shootout in the Buenos Aires suburb of
Tigre, three leading figures of the FAR were killed — one of them,

Diego Ruy Frondizi, a nephew of the former President Arturo Frondizi. The political parties continued to ignore Levingston's call to 'dialogue', while the unions, and particularly the more militant ones of Córdoba, refused to let the 'national and popular' inclinations of the Economy Minister override the attention they demanded for immediate wage claims.

There was, in all this, a strong sense of *déja vu* — an impression that, after a lapse of only two years, the country had decided to re-enact the decline and fall of Onganía. This impression was strengthened by the fact that Córdoba was rapidly becoming, yet again, the hottest troublespot. Levingston had appointed as governor of that province a nationalist of the old school, José Camilo Uriburu, who had chosen a policy of confrontation with his restless students and workers. Unrest in his province, claimed Uriburu, was the product of a subversive conspiracy — in a colourful speech he likened this to a snake (*víbora*) which he boastfully promised to decapitate. The unions and students of Córdoba planned a series of strikes and demonstrations, and intelligence reports began to warn of the risk of another *cordobazo*, only this time better manipulated by the guerrilla organisations, which had grown in skill and strength. Governor Uriburu was urged to accept the declaration of an emergency zone as a preventive measure. He refused. From 12 to 15 March 1971 Córdoba was paralysed by strikes and overrun by angry demonstrators, who inevitably clashed with the security forces: two died, twenty were injured, close to three hundred were arrested. Only three days after the events (to be recalled as the *viborazo*, in memory of Uriburu's fateful speech) the Governor was removed and a state of emergency was declared.

Like his predecessor, Levingston openly criticised Lanusse's handling of the riots. But then the replay was suddenly telescoped. Led by Lanusse, the Junta decided to rewrite the rules, imposing further limitations on the President's autonomy. Five days after the *viborazo*, Levingston countered by dismissing Lanusse as Army Commander-in-Chief and appointing General Cáceres Monié in his place. Cáceres accepted, but only to reinstate Lanusse hours later. At two in the morning the Junta announced the dismissal of General Roberto Marcelo Levingston from the office of President, 248 days after he had taken office. By noon the following day, the highest office in the land had passed to the chairman of the Junta, General Alejandro Agustín Lanusse — the man who wanted to put an end to the custom of elevating the Army Commander-in-Chief to the Presidency.

19

'THE GREAT NATIONAL AGREEMENT'

(1971-1972)

Two ministers were sworn in almost immediately after Lanusse took over the Presidency. One was no surprise: Lanusse's friend Francisco Manrique, returning to Social Welfare. The other signalled an important departure for the military régime. For the key post of Minister of the Interior Lanusse chose a well-known politician, Arturo Mor Roig. He had been president of the Chamber of Deputies — the culmination of a thirty-five-year career in the Unión Cívica Radical — in the very government Lanusse had helped overthrow five years earlier. The military had overcome the fear of appearing to favour the Radicals by this appointment far more easily than the Radicals themselves had acquiesced in it. Mor Roig made it abundantly clear that he was severing all ties with his party, and apart from his reputation there was an important factor that made this claim credible: born in Catalonia, Mor Roig was barred by the Constitution from aspiring to the Presidency himself.

The new 'political' minister was an icon of the return to institutional normality promised by Lanusse. The President would have liked to go further, making his entire cabinet visibly representative of this intention by including a leading *peronista* as Minister of the Economy. Alfredo Gómez Morales and Antonio Cafiero had been sounded out, but when they consulted Perón he recommended refusal. So Aldo Ferrer was kept on at Economy, partly to give the lie to those who held that Levingston had been sacked because of the brave nationalistic policies of his minister.

Lanusse started out with a very clear scheme in his mind. He called it *Gran Acuerdo Nacional*, the Great National Agreement. Much as he would insist, again and again throughout his Presidency, that he was being perfectly straightforward about this scheme, he never actually spelt it out in public. That is, beyond the very general assertion that the only acceptable political solution was one which would arise from a broad national agreement, and the vague threat that neither he nor the armed forces would tolerate any outcome that represented 'a leap into the void'.

On the surface, it seemed evident enough that no overt proscriptions were on the cards. Within ten days of his accession to the Presidency, Lanusse issued a decree lifting the ban on party-political activity. Three months later, the country had a new statute governing the legalisation of political parties, establishing minimum membership requirements which were intended mainly to avoid the proliferation of mini-parties and to reduce the political spectrum to only three or four large parties. With the major parties within the loose grouping of *La Hora del Pueblo*, and the parties of the moderate left (including representatives of the left wings of *peronismo* and the UCR) in their own equally loose grouping called *Encuentro Nacional de los Argentinos* (National Encounter of the Argentines), there seemed to be something pretty close to a national agreement, at least on the desirability of an electoral outcome.

So what else was Lanusse wishing to include in his *Gran Acuerdo Nacional?* So vague was he about this in public that even in his memoirs of the period it is hard to find an unequivocal answer to that question. But there were enough hints in his speeches, in 'off-the-record' comments to journalists and in private conversations with generals, admirals and politicians, for most politically aware people to have few doubts about the main intended elements of the *Gran Acuerdo Nacional*.

The first thing Lanusse was seeking was agreement between the major parties on a candidate for the Presidency — who should, of course, enjoy the approval of the military. Next, there should be agreement on giving the military some kind of formal participation in the government arising from the election. Finally, there should be agreement on not granting an 'indiscriminate' amnesty to political prisoners — meaning that convicted terrorists should remain behind bars. These, clearly, were not terms which could be voiced too loudly, given the mood of the country at the time.

Any agreement regarding the Presidency required the approval of the great absent elector, Juan Domingo Perón. Within days of stepping into the Casa Rosada, Lanusse 'leaked' to the *New York Times* the message, duly published, that he was willing to speak to Perón. Journalists in Buenos Aires seeking confirmation were told by the Press Secretary: 'The President of the Nation is willing to listen to any constructive contribution tending towards the establishment of a real, authentic, modern, stable and efficient democracy, within the frame of the most complete respect for the republican, representative and federal system.' For the first time since 1955, a military ruler was willing to deal directly with the ultimate pariah of the system the military had created, the man whose political influence they had attempted to destroy by banning, persecuting, imprisoning and killing his followers; the man whose very name they had once tried to erase, and whom they had kept in exile for sixteen years. The event was all the more striking in that the ruler closing this circle was none other than Alejandro Agustín Lanusse, participant in an aborted uprising against Perón in 1951, imprisoned by Perón until his ouster — the epitome of the *antiperonista*.

This belated coming to terms with the political reality of Perón and *peronismo*, only five years after the military had taken power to abolish all party politics, had been forced upon them by the rising tide of popular unrest (with its dramatic outbursts such as the *cordobazo* and the *viborazo*). And by the fear that, in the absence of a political solution, this unrest would be capitalised by the practitioners of organised violence, the guerrilla organisations. It was a matter of opening the door to the more acceptable outcasts, in order to get the entire body politic to cast out the new, unacceptable threat. In Lanusse's own version, it was a matter of 'uniting adversaries in order to fight the enemy'. This was Perón 'as reinsurance against the radicalisation of the masses', in Rodolfo Terragno's phrase. The Left would speak of the appeal to Perón as 'the last card of the bourgeoisie' (that is, except the *peronista* Left, for whom that description applied not to Perón himself, but to the 'traitors' and 'union bureaucrats' within *peronismo*). 'The military', wrote the sociologist Liliana de Riz, 'were opening the doors of political power in order to make room for another contingent of the owner classes and to unite a power bloc capable of neutralising the radicalised popular masses.'

Attempting to negotiate with Perón, in Lanusse's view, meant in the first place removing all the constraints and obstacles imposed upon the old exile. Lifting the political ban was a relatively easy matter, but there were other barriers not so easily disposable. Chief among these were the handful of court cases brought against Perón after 1955, and which successive governments, invoking the independence of the judiciary, had been content to leave alive as a weapon of last resort to prevent Perón's return to Argentina. Now, under Lanusse, Perón's lawyers were allowed to invoke, unopposed, the statutes of limitations to have the pending suits thrown out, one after the other. First went the charge of rape, then that of treason, then that of contraband — a string of acquitals due to 'extinction of the cause'. Lanusse was convinced that Perón had no real intention of returning to Argentina, but he wanted to make it clear for all to see that if Perón remained abroad, it was of his own free choice, not because anyone was preventing his homecoming. Lanusse actually wanted to go a step further and make it clear that Perón could, if he so wished, be a candidate for the Presidency, but to persuade him that it was in everyone's interest for him freely to choose not to run. Perón's self-proscription was perhaps the most important target of Lanusse's *Gran Acuerdo Nacional*.

Official rehabilitation of Perón and *peronismo* would not have been complete without one act of reparation of great symbolic significance, which Lanusse announced within six months of becoming·President: the long-missing body of Eva Perón was returned to Perón in Madrid. After having been shunted around between closets and disused offices in buildings owned by state intelligence in Buenos Aires, Evita's body had been spirited away to a tiny graveyard in Italy, where it had lain buried, under an assumed name, during the years of Perón's exile. Now it would lie, unattended, in an upper room of the Quinta 17 de Octubre, Perón's Madrid residence, a grim symbol that the myths of a decade-and-a-half were being called to re-enter the concrete world of practical Argentine politics.

In Lanusse's book, 'uniting the adversaries in order to fight the enemy' meant striking back — hard — at the 'enemy', the guerrilla organisations. A new Law for the Repression of Terrorism was enacted, introducing stiffer penalties for a range of 'subversive' crimes. A special Federal Penal Chamber was established to mete out swift, exemplary punishment to those charged under the new legistation. Anti-guerrilla sweeps followed each other across the country with increasing frequency, as did 'preventive' arrests of people deemed to be close to the guerrillas, such as left-wing intellectuals and the more radical union leaders. Córdoba's Agustín Tosco and Raimundo Ongaro of the CGT de los Argentinos were soon behind bars. Socially and politically active priests met the same fate in Rosario and Córdoba. 'Disappearances' began to multiply, as well as allegations of torture and mistreatment of the detainees.

Lanusse was later to say, 'We did everything in our power to avoid a *dirty war*.' But at the time he adopted the attitude of the tough soldier, often callous in his dismissal of brutality in repression, as when he greeted the news that a demonstrator had received serious injuries from a police tear-gas grenade with the comment: 'Now these youngsters will begin to realise that we do not carry our weapons just for show.' Much the same was his reaction to one of the first 'kidnappings' or 'disappearances'. Only four days after Lanusse became President, the Army had suffered its first casualty from the officer corps: Lieutenant Mario César Asúa, killed when the FAR attacked a military truck in which he was travelling. Seventy-seven days later the sociologist Juan Pablo Maestre and his wife, Mirtha Misetich, were abducted by armed men. Maestre's body turned up the following day; his wife was never heard of again. Lanusse's version (emphasis added): 'In those days *it was discovered* that the sociologist Juan Pablo Maestre had been *actively linked* with the murder of Lieutenant Asúa. Maestre, a man of the FAR, was then *illegally abducted and murdered*. At his funeral, Bernardo Alberte [a retired *peronista* Army officer] did not hesitate to admit the criminal act committed by Maestre — clearing away the doubts of those who, even in the government, still doubted — or to praise the deed. [. . .] Maestre was not innocent, nor anything remotely approaching it, and none of us could allow ourselves to be disconcerted by the circumstance — which caused confusion at the time — that some of Maestre's most notorious friends had no contact at all with the guerrillas, but were actually advocates of opposite lines of thought. The 'vendetta' was not appropriate, but my statement (publicly condemning the murders of Asúa and Maestre) was not tantamount to an absolution of Maestre.' Lanusse clearly admits that Maestre's murder was a 'vendetta', a revenge killing, but carefully avoids mentioning who was responsible — presumably those who 'discovered' Maestre's 'active links' with the Asúa killing.

There were successes in the anti-guerrilla campaign. A training camp was discovered in Córdoba and a 'field hospital' in the Buenos Aires township of Ramos Mejia. Guerrilla leaders like Roberto Quieto of the FAR and Luis Enrique Pujals of the ERP were captured and imprisoned, together with many more minor figures. A shootout at Ferreyra, Córdoba, in November between security forces and members of the FAR and the FAP left a toll of four guerrilla fighters dead, five injured and an undisclosed number under arrest. In Rosario, with characteristic hyperbole, the military authorities claimed to have destroyed '85 per cent of the subversive apparatus'.

Yet it was hardly disputable that it was the guerrilla organisations who retained the initiative, growing in strength and operational ability, and becoming increasingly bold in their public challenge to military rule. The ERP went as far as to hold two successive press conferences under the noses of the security forces. Two daring jailbreaks in June, in Córdoba and Buenos Aires, freed ten women guerrilla fighters; in

September, fourteen *guerrilleros* were sprung from the Villa Urquiza prison in Tucumán (though four were later recaptured), in an operation that cost the lives of five prison guards. *Copamientos* (brief occupations) of townships and villages continued: San Jerónimo Norte and Santa Clara de Saguier in the province of Santa Fe, Gonnet in the province of Buenos Aires. A bank raid in the Buenos Aires suburb of Villa Ballester yielded half a million pesos. In typical Montonero operations, two country clubs (in Córdoba and Tucumán) and a golf club (in San Nicolás) were dynamited after the access roads had been blocked off with signs reading 'Halt! Mined Zone.'

For all this escalation of guerrilla activity, the armed bands were not the only challengers of Lanusse's *Gran Acuerdo Nacional*. Within days of Lanusse's accession to the Presidency, his predecessor Juan Carlos Onganía was issuing in public a dire warning that if the government's course were not rectified, 'it is easy to foresee dark hours in our institutional future, which will force us to assume greater responsibilities to safeguard the Nation and its Armed Forces.' Translation: a nationalist coup was in the offing.

The coup attempt surfaced a few weeks later, its leader General Eduardo Rafael Labanca, whom Lanusse had eased out of the service back in 1969 when he had caught him plotting with President Onganía to pull off a nationalist-populist coup against the Army commander. Labanca issued a call 'to all the Argentines throughout the Fatherland who struggle for the National and Popular Revolution', signing himself 'Commander of Troops and Leader of the National Revolution'. Although Labanca had earlier had a sympathetic hearing from a potpourri of right-wing nationalists, left-wing *peronistas* and radical union leaders, his call to an uprising found no echo among the 'men with the irons', the military unit commanders. The coup did not get off the ground.

A second bid was made six months later, when a couple of regiments in the cities of Azul and Olavarría, in the centre of Buenos Aires province, actually rebelled, their commanding officers calling on their comrades to follow suit. Lanusse responded by ordering four regiments under the commander of the Tenth Infantry Brigade (ironically, Labanca's last command) to encircle and crush the rebels. Simultaneously, a massive propaganda campaign successfully painted the uprising as an 'obscurantist' plot to prevent the people from expressing themselves freely in elections. The Azul-Olavarría revolution was over within the day. It was to be the last such attempt. Lanusse concluded years later with hindsight that his easy success against these plots did not prove entirely beneficial. The lesson assimilated by the politicians, he said, was that there was no real danger of a coup against Lanusse; therefore, they no longer needed to temporise with the military. Just before the Azul-Olavarría uprising, Lanusse had given the parties yet another of the things they had been demanding: the electoral calendar. The formal call to elections would be issued in October 1972; polling day would be 25 March 1973; and the newly-elected authorities would take office on 25 May 1973.

Lanusse did not reverse the policies initiated under Levingston, not even those which seemed most obviously designed, under the banner of the 'national and popular line', to build for the government a political following of its own . On the contrary, he emphasised them. For all his identification in the public mind as the 'arch-liberal' of the régime, he had — even before arriving at the Presidency — spelled out to his fellow Commanders-in-Chief his commitment to nationalist economic policies. 'It will be necessary', he had said, 'to tend towards the nationalisation of the economy — which must not be confused with statism — in order to attain a greater freedom of action for decision-making in this field, to orient the entire system in the exclusive service of the national interest, and to conquer effective economic independence. [. . .] It will also be necessary to channel the benefits of economic growth towards an equitable distribution of the wealth generated by the common effort, paying attention, first of all, to the demands of the neediest sectors.'

However, once he felt he had made the point that Levingston had not been ousted because the 'monopolies' objected to his economic policies, he got rid of the Economy Minister, Aldo Ferrer. This he did about two months after taking power, and once he had become convinced that there was no hope of obtaining Perón's acquiescence in the appointment of a *peronista* to the economic portfolio. The procedure Lanusse chose was unusual, but in keeping with his determination to show that the era had ended in which, in the absence of open party-political activity, real politics was conducted through the Ministry of the Economy. Lanusse abolished this super-ministry, and upgraded the Secretariats previously under its jurisdiction. For the Ministry of Finance he chose a man with a background not unlike Ferrer's: Juan Quilici, of *desarrollista* extraction, who had gained his experience in the field in the provincial government of Santa Fe. However, he seemed to be repeating the old balancing act when he appointed Carlos Brignone, clearly identified with the 'liberals', to the chairmanship of the Central Bank. But it was to be a temporary arrangement.

In the spirit of the *Gran Acuerdo Nacional* he was promoting, Lanusse attempted to draw into the task of formulating economic policy both the unions, as represented by the CGT, and the entrepreneurs. And as his interlocutors among the latter, rather than turning to that pillar of the establishment the Unión Industrial Argentina in which the larger companies — subsidiaries of foreign firms and those autochtonous enterprises most closely linked to the agrarian sector — were grouped, Lanusse turned to the Confederación General Económica (CGE), the body born in the earlier Perón years to represent the small and medium-sized 'national' businesses (though some were by now not quite so small), and led by José Ber Gelbard.

The wooing of the unions did not prove an easy task, and Lanusse had to face one general strike before he was able to launch what he called a 'social truce' (a blanket wage increase, plus rises in pensions and family subsidies, accompanied by a wide-ranging freeze on prices); and yet another general strike before he managed to get on speaking terms with the union bosses, José Rucci, the secretary-general of the CGT, and Rogelio Coria, head of the *peronista* union bloc that still went by the old name of 'the 62'. Lanusse and the union bosses had an interest in common: both felt threatened by the upsurge of radical militancy among the rank-and-file union membership, which was developing along lines parallel to that of the youthful *peronista* Left, and hence also parallel to that of the guerrilla organisations, whose panoply of enemies had by now been distilled to a triad: 'the military dictatorship', the 'traitors' within the *peronista* leadership, and the 'union bureaucrats'.

Winning over the CGE was not very much easier. Echoing the CGT's two general strikes, the 'national' entrepreneurs had organised a 'national day of protest' by business, and then, in a masterstroke engineered by Gelbard, obtained a 'multi-party agreement' on the broad outlines of a desirable economic policy package, and then a more specific agreement on the same subject with the CGT, before responding openly to Lanusse's overtures.

Yet Lanusse ploughed ahead, announcing the de-centralisation of the state apparatus, starting with the transfer of the National Development Bank to the province of Córdoba; setting up an Economic and Social Council; and floating the idea of actually implementing a forgotten provision of the Constitution — worker participation in the manage-ment and profits of business. His Social Welfare Minister, Francisco

Manrique (another member of the government seen as a 'liberal', which, it must be recalled yet again, in Argentina means conservative), attempted to solve the long-lasting sore of the Tucumán sugar industry by handing over the 'intervened' sugar mills to workers' co-operatives. And to crown it all, Lanusse set himself the task of reversing one of Onganía's most cherished creatures: the foreign policy based on the notion of 'ideological frontiers'. Reaffirming Argentina's role as a Latin American and an Andean nation, Lanusse travelled abroad for meetings with Chile's Salvador Allende and with Perú's General Francisco Velasco Alvarado, leader of a left-leaning military régime which Argentina's 'national and popular line' had long hailed as the proper model for their own soldiers. In Lima, Lanusse went as far as to define his government as 'left-of-centre'. Once the new foreign policy had been designed and launched, Lanusse jettisoned de Pablo Pardo and brought back Eduardo McLoughlin as his Foreign Minister.

One thing Lanusse refused to do. Despite mounting pressure from all over the political spectrum, and even from some of his closest friends, he would not announce publicly that he himself was not in the running for the Presidency in the elections he had promised. His own explanation, which he never ceased to repeat, even years after returning to private life, was that this was a necessary tactical choice: had he announced his self-proscription, he argued, his would clearly have been a 'lame-duck' administration, bereft of the power needed to coax or bully all parties, and particularly Perón, into the *Gran Acuerdo Nacional* he envisaged. These protestations were greeted with much scepticism. It seemed only too obvious, to friend and foe alike, that Lanusse had tailored his proposed *Gran Acuerdo Nacional* to fit only one purpose: his own candidacy for the Presidency. In most people's minds, the agreed candidacy Lanusse was trying to extract from *peronistas* and non-*peronistas*, from labour and business, was none other than his own.

From his headquarters in Madrid — rapidly becoming a place of pilgrimage for Argentine politicians of all colorations — Perón saw the danger all too clearly. When his 'personal delegate' in Argentina, Jorge Daniel Paladino, seemed to be drifting too close to Lanusse, Perón abruptly fired him, appointing in his place that most loyal of his followers, Héctor José Campora, the dentist who had held the rubber-stamp position of president of the Chamber of Deputies, and who had almost been killed in 1955 when Perón called him over to the Casa Rosada, failing to mention that the place was being evacuated in anti-cipation of the bombing planned by anti-*peronista* Navy plotters. The

CGT leaders were also summoned to Madrid for a dressing-down, Rogelio Coria of 'the 62' coming in for the harshest treatment, both in private and in public — to the delight of the *peronista* Left. Perón's classical 'pendulum' tactics now began to look more like a pincer movement: he openly encouraged the guerrillas, the 'special formations' as he called them, at the same time as he called on all political parties to join the *peronistas* in a Frente Cívico de Liberación Nacional ('Civic National Liberation Front'); in other words, he was responding to Lanusse's proposal of a *Gran Acuerdo Nacional* with one of his own creation. And then the bombshell: he announced publicly that Lanusse had sent emissaries to try to negotiate an electoral pact with him, Perón.

The news stunned many in Argentina, not least the service chiefs, who had been kept in the dark about any contacts between Lanusse and Perón, direct or indirect. There was not much choice but to confirm that the contacts had taken place, first through a laconic statement by the Argentine ambassador in Spain, later by releasing the transcript of the conversations between one of Lanusse's aides, Colonel Cornicelli, and Perón. The first newspaper to run a leaked version of the tapes was *La Opinión*, a daily which had been launched only months earlier by that untiring innovator Jacobo Timerman. Modelled on France's *Le Monde*, the paper had brought together many of Argentina's most talented journalists, and was giving Buenos Aires a heady daily ration of independent, irreverent and inquisitive commentary, reflecting almost every shade of political opinion that lay left of centre. Timerman's partner in the venture, unknown to all but a few at the time, was a young banker with a penchant for politics, currently acting as an Under-Secretary below Francisco Manrique in the Ministry of Social Welfare: David Graiver. On its own, *La Opinión* had already become an exciting political event, although it was not to move to centre-stage for another four years. At that particular point in time, what is worth recording is that its published version of the Cornicelli tapes did not bear out Perón's allegations.

What the steady stream of visitors to Madrid was bringing back was a peculiar version of Perón's circumstances. At seventy-seven, and having undergone a number of operations, he was said to be delicate in health, his old propensity to lung ailments accentuated by the passing of the years. A friend described him as still intellectually fresh and alert, but with his will weakened. And in most of the stories filtered across the Atlantic, this weakening of the will had its counterpart in the alleged iron control exercised over his activities by his wife Isabelita and even more by his personal secretary José López Rega.

Lopecito, as Perón called him, was a relative newcomer to the old man's entourage. He had no history at all within the *peronista* movement: until 1962 he had served in the Federal Police, in the lowest rank (though, in accordance with existing regulations, he was promoted corporal on retirement for the purpose of calculating his pension). He had been an unusual policeman. By the year of his retirement a 740-page book was published which López Rega had been writing while off-duty. Its title was *Astrología esotérica* (Esoteric Astrology) and in rambling, often impenetrably obscure lauguage it developed strange theories about the colours of names and countries, and the importance of different forms of music on national traits. The jacket of the book promised a whole string of further productions by the same author: *Génesis de la nueva era* (Genesis of the New Age), *El hombre, un mundo desconocido* (Man, an Unknown World), *Tratado de canto, impostación y arte escénico* (Treatise on Singing, Voice Control and Scenic Art), *El libro de los desheredados* (The Book of the Disinherited), and *Libro madre del éxito: predicciones y guía diaria válida hasta el año 2000* (Mother Book of Success: Predictions and Daily Guide valid until the Year 2000). It is not known if he ever got around to publishing or even writing any of these, but there have been reports of his continued interest in matters esoteric, including his alleged membership of a secret lodge called Anael, in which he was known by the name Daniel.

Little is known for certain of how López Rega managed to attach himself to Perón, except that it happened in 1966 and, according to the most popular myth, that he made his entrée as a male nurse. On the evidence of people close to Perón at the time, in the early years López Rega spent a lot of his time 'doing business for the General'. There is also evidence that on more than one occasion he invoked Perón's name to do business behind his back, and a recurrent version has him obsessed with gaining access to the legendary 'Perón fortune'. With the ideal background for the role of mystery man, López Rega was bound to become the subject of all kinds of speculation and rumour-mongering. What is verifiable is that only six years after appearing from nowhere, he had become a power to be reckoned with at the Quinta 17 de Octubre, in control of that most valuable asset — access to Perón. López Rega decided who could get in to speak with him, spoke publicly on his behalf, chaperoned his wife. Soon not a few of the pilgrims seeking to woo the old man's favour concluded that the first necessary step was to gain the favour of his personal secretary and gatekeeper. The era of López Rega the power-broker had begun.

The youths with the guns were determined to give the military government no respite. A thriller-style weekend heist by the ERP cleaned out 400 million pesos (about US$850,000) from the National Development Bank, just a few hundred yards from the Casa Rosada. In three days in March, assassins shot down a former police chief in Tucumán, a leader of the railwaymen's union, and a leader of the new Conservative party only recently founded by Alvaro Alsogaray. Then the ERP carried out their most notorious kidnapping; the victim was Oberdan Sallustro, head of the powerful Fiat motor company in Argentina. Less than a month passed before the Sallustro kidnapping turned from daring exploit to tragedy. A party of police checking out a suspect house in the Buenos Aires suburb of Villa Lugano was unexpectedly greeted with gunfire. Help was called, and within minutes hundreds of police converged on the area. A fierce but brief gunbattle ensued. Then the shooting from the house ceased. A woman emerged and surrendered; her companions had fled through an unwatched alley at the back. When the police entered the house they found the corpse of Oberdan Sallustro, riddled with bullets. That same morning, in Rosario, the car carrying the local Army Corps commander, General Juan Carlos Sánchez, was boxed in by a pickup in the city centre. As the General's car swerved to a halt, another car drew up alongside, and from an open roof-hatch General Sánchez was machine-gunned to death. The assassination had another, unwanted victim: a woman newsvendor who happened to be plying her trade in the line of fire.

The murders of Sallustro and Sánchez deeply shocked the country's establishment. The guerrilla fighters had struck down a leading industrialist and one of the Army's most celebrated generals. Even Perón, from Madrid, joined in the condemation of the killings. Few at the time paused to reflect that in fact that bloody 10 April 1972 was signalling that the guerrillas had begun to lose the war against the government. Apart from their usual sweeping, boastful statements, the military had not made the point clearly in public. Perhaps they were unaware of just how deeply they had managed to strike into the guerrilla organisations; perhaps they thought it prudent not to make public the full extent of the growth in numbers and sophistication that had taken place in the armed bands. They had, of course, reported individual successes and arrests, but they had not revealed publicly the importance of their discoveries and of the guerrilla fighters they had captured. What should have been noticeable, however, was that the scale of the guerrilla operations had been shrinking rapidly over the recent months, until they were reduced to strikes that required few trained fighters; to bombings and assassinations — the lowest, most rudimentary form of terrorist activity.

The efficacy of the security forces, and particularly of the police, had been improving apace. Alongside the massive dragnets, the indiscriminate arrests, the swift and brutal repression of public protest, and the increasing use of torture, the more cerebral techniques of investigation and detection had been refined. Working back from kidnappings or major guerrilla strikes, the patient scouring of records of real estate transactions, of unusual movements of money, of suddenly altered living patterns (instead of the knee-jerk identification of beards and long hair with potential subversive activity, police began to look for conversion to short hair and jacket-and-tie as a more likely giveaway of the new guerrilla recruit), the anti-guerrilla units began to unearth 'people's prisons', safe houses, makeshift field hospitals, stashes of armaments. And guerrilla fighters. Many of the top leaders of the ERP and a large number of the more seasoned 'combatants' of FAR and the Montoneros were arrested and imprisoned. Indeed, the assassination of General Sánchez was actually a revenge killing, a recognition, guerrilla-style, of the savage efficiency with which this General, who had spent most of his career as a professor at the War School, had decimated the guerrilla organisations in the Rosario area.

Opposition from the left, however, was not confined to the violent action of the guerrilla organisations. The Juventud Peronista (JP — *Peronista* Youth) had been growing swiftly, much more so than the armed groups, as an above-surface, openly political movement. Strictly, there were several groups claiming the title Juventud Peronista, but the faction that had attracted most adherents was the one on the left, which shared the same rhetoric with the Montoneros, and substituted verbal aggressiveness for bullets and bombs. Mainly based on the middle classes, the JP sprouted wings in the labour movement and in the *villas miseria*, the shanty-towns. Claiming as their own the history of popular uprisings all the way back to the *cordobazo* in 1969, appropriating the victims of repression as their martyrs, incorporating all the hagiography of the *peronista* resistance since 1955, and appealing to a suitably edited version of Evita's more radical pronouncements, the JP presented itself as the heir to *peronismo's* true revolutionary essence. Their lexicon was not the traditional one of *justicialismo* and the Third Position, but one which rested on the pillars of *socialismo nacional*, of anti-imperialism and of liberation. The JP had tapped a vast reservoir of long-frustrated demands for political participation and social justice, of revulsion against the hypocrisy of a system that for almost two decades suppressed the will of the majority in the name of democracy. And it articulated this pent-up energy with the lack of restraint nurtured among the young by the short-sighted military-imposed freeze on politics. Quite unexpectedly, the JP revealed itself as a superb agent of mobilisation, easily attracting huge, enthusiastic crowds to call for an end to the military dictatorship and for the return of Perón. Picking up the *peronista* tradition of expressing political slogans in chant, while dancing to the beat of large drums, their rallies resounded to the rhythm of

> *Si Evita viviera*
> *sería Montonera*

(If Evita were alive/she would be a Montonera);
or the more directly ideological:

> *Perón, Evita,*
> *la patria socialista*

(Perón, Evita/the socialist Fatherland).

The mobilising capacity of the young left-wingers caused much anxiety among the union bosses and the right wing of the movement. Soon the 'orthodox' *peronistas* were devoting more time to castigating the 'infiltrators' within *peronismo* than their obvious rivals, the military. Union goon squads were sent to break up JP rallies; a union-backed Juventud Peronista de la República Argentina was created to respond to the radicals with the alternative chant

> *Perón, Evita,*
> *la patria peronista*

(Perón, Evita/the *peronista* Fatherland).

In July 1972, in an interview with a Spanish newspaper, Perón said, 'I do not return [to Argentina] because in matters of leadership I am a professional. I have devoted my entire life to the study of leadership, and it is not foreseeable that I should fail in any of its basics. There is a principle or rule of leadership which says that the strategic command must never be in the tactical field of operations, because there it would be influenced by immediate events, taking part in them and losing sight of the whole picture.' Lanusse interpreted this as meaning that Perón had decided not to return at all. Addressing an assembly of military men at the Colegio Militar, he launched a direct challenge to the old leader. 'Nothing', said Lanusse, 'can replace the physical presence of a commander.' And then he added the insulting punchline: 'Perón does not return *porque no le da el cuero* [because he hasn't the guts for it].'

More formally, Lanusse laid down the rules of the game for the forth-coming elections. No one, he decreed, could be a candidate if he did not reside continuously in the country from 25 August 1972 to polling day. No one could be a candidate, either, who continued to hold government office after 25 August. The message was clear: if Perón did not return before that date, he would proscribe himself. Equally, however, Lanusse would proscribe himself if he held on to the Presidency beyond the dead-line.

The scramble began immediately. There was at last the serious pos-sibility that Perón might not be in the running, which meant that the *peronista* vote would once again be up for grabs. In the first days of August, Francisco Manrique resigned his post as Minister of Social Welfare, with the clear intention of becoming a Presidential candidate. The ambassador in Brazil, General Osiris Villegas, resigned his post and returned to Argentina, convinced that he would be called upon to play the role of replacement candidate. And the Commander-in-Chief of the Air Force, Brigadier Carlos Rey, helped muddy the waters even more by stating publicly that he meant to step into the Presidency in January, when his turn arrived to chair the Junta of Commanders-in-Chief.

Only five days before the deadline, however, the suspense was broken by an event which first left the country gasping at the daring shown, then in horror at its sequel. In the southern province of Chubut, there was a mass break-out from the isolated Rawson prison. Twenty-five of the more prominent and seasoned guerrilla detainees escaped and drove 20 miles to Trelew airport. A commercial jet airliner, hijacked by other guerrilla fighters, landed to take away six of them, including the leaders of the ERP and the FAR, Mario Roberto Santucho and Roberto Quieto. The diversion of a second airliner foiled the getaway of the other nine-teen, who were taken into custody in a naval air base not far from the field. Seven days later the news reached Buenos Aires that all but three of the recaptured prisoners have been shot dead by naval personnel during the night. There were two versions of the mass killings. The Navy said it happened when the prisoners, during a routine inspection in the middle of the night, attempted to overpower the armed guards and escape. The guards responded by opening fire. The survivors maintained rather that they were all taken out and lined up against a wall; then the guards opened fire at pointblank range and did not cease until all the prisoners were lying on the ground. That there were any survivors at all, they said, had depended on their being given up for dead long enough for other, uninvolved naval officers to arrive on the scene. Very few people believed the official version; but for political Argentina the event would henceforth be known as 'the Trelew massacre'.

The deadline for the candidates came and went, and Perón had not returned to Argentina. Lanusse was still in the Presidency. If the rules were to be respected, the leading figures in the political contest had ruled themselves out. The scene was set for the final act, and no one had any inkling of what was in the script.

20

ALL AGAINST THE MILITARY
(1972–1973)

The tableau suited Perón beautifully: himself and Lanusse on centre-stage; a hazy but threatening background of guerrilla actions and radical mobilisations; the politicians in the wings, hoping to pick up the pieces after the big showdown; the vast majority as audience, held in thrall by an ever more obscure plot in which the climax kept on being delayed. Perón's main aim was to polarise the political options completely; to reduce them to a test of power between himself and the military, played not according to Lanusse's rules but to his own. The 'self-proscription' gambit was a key element in this strategy. Its first fruits were already evident: Lanusse had matched Perón's moves and ruled himself out of the electoral contest — but whereas Lanusse had no reliable proxy to carry on in his name, Perón had a huge political movement ready to do his bidding. Lanusse's only hope of rescuing his *Gran Acuerdo Nacional* was that Perón might pursue even further the line of 'self-proscription', ruling out not only his own candidature but also that of any member of the *peronista* movement. In these circumstances, if Perón were willing to bargain, there was an outside chance that the *peronista* vote might be swung behind some nominee acceptable both to him and to Lanusse. This, as Perón knew well, was an option a number of leading politicians were keeping in mind. And as long as they continued to do so, they would carefully avoid antagonising the *peronistas*. Perón even offered them the rationale for this unusual way of entering an electoral contest, and in a variety of forms to suit different ideological emphases. 'No party', he said, 'is our enemy — the enemy is the military dictatorship.' Or again, 'The only confrontation here is between the people and the armed forces.' And for the more radically minded, 'The struggle is between revolution and counter-revolution.'

In a very real sense, Perón was playing on the store of guilt politicians had accumulated over a decade-and-a-half for their part in the proscription and persecution of *peronismo*. Their commitment to the restoration of democracy was quite rightly translated into a commitment to oppose any new exclusion of *peronismo*. And if it seemed that the 'hidden

360

agenda' of the *Gran Acuerdo Nacional* was yet another scheme to cheat the *peronistas* of power, then Perón could count on virtually all other parties to oppose the military on his behalf. For this he had to engage in highly risky brinkmanship. The rules laid down by Lanusse had to be continually and deliberately flouted, the military had to be taunted till they came close to exploding; *peronismo* had to act as if it were constantly courting a ban. This was the period in which Perón — still very much the general who was well aware of Army susceptibilities — came up with his best anti-military insults. 'These military', he said, 'are not soldiers; they are a bunch of gangsters.' 'The only thing a military man is good for is to fill the space between the cap and the horse.' 'What are military officers but secondary students with four years of gymnastics?' This, of course, was minor provocation, but it was effectively magnified by the glee with which it was picked up and repeated in political circles.

Far more provocative was Perón's build-up of the radicalised Juventud Peronista youth movement and of the 'special formations', the guerrilla organisations. A place was found on the ruling council of *peronismo* for a representative of the Juventud Peronista, Rodolfo Galimberti, who immediately set the tone by proclaiming in a press interview, 'Political power comes from the barrel of a rifle.' Soon afterwards, Perón appointed Juan Manuel Abal Medina (brother of Fernando, founder of the Montoneros) as Secretary-General of the movement. To all and sundry Perón announced that the time had come for *trasvasamiento generacional* ('generational transfusion') within *peronismo*. He also picked up the Radicals' rhetoric about 'union bureaucrats': 'In union action,' he said, 'there is a lot of bureaucracy. No one has experienced that more painfully than myself. I have seen them, the union leaders, defect at the most decisive moments of our political history. The union leaders have the illusion that they run the show, but this is not so; union action is only for the defence of professional interests and cannot go any further. Politically there is very little that they run.'

At the same time, however, Perón managed to put himself across as the great conciliator, as the only person capable of bridging the gap between management and labour, of bringing all sectors together for 'national reconstruction'. In October 1972 he made a big show of sending his faithful delegate, Héctor Cámpora, on an official visit to the Junta bearing a decalogue entitled 'Minimal Bases for an Agreement of National Reconstruction'. It was a safe bet, as it did not differ from the proposals already put forward by the CGT and the CGE, and approved by *La Hora del Pueblo*.

The message was somewhat less than subliminal: with Perón in charge, this was the sort of reasonableness that could be expected; without him, there would be no holding back the young radicals, enemies of the military, of the capitalists and of the union bosses. Big business seized this reassurance eagerly; now they too had a 'real Perón' of their own, a figure opposite in every conceivable way to the 'real Perón' of the *peronista* Left.

Altogether, Perón's strategy was highly effective: it bound most rival political forces into an expectant truce, it sharply curtailed the union bosses' ability to pursue autonomous courses of action, and it neutralised most of the opposition that could have been expected from the business community. And with hindsight, it is possible to see yet another side-effect which was not at all evident at the time: it tied down many of the best, most dedicated talents of the country's 'new opposition', either in the ghetto of guerrilla activity or in the heady carnival of mass rallies and marches — well away from the task of proselytising and securing an organised base at union grassroots level or among the population at large.

Only a few small political parties launched forth into the campaign under their own banners, eschewing calculations about an eventual proscription of *peronismo*. The fiercely *antiperonista* Democratic Socialists (who elsewhere would have been more readily identified as conservatives) nominated seventy-three-year-old Américo Ghioldi to head their slate. Alvaro Alsogaray's latest neo-conservative creation, Nueva Fuerza, picked an unknown newcomer, Julio Roberto Chamizo, to run in a campaign based on a barrage of agency-designed advertising. On the Left, the minuscule Partido Socialista de los Trabajadores selected Juan Carlos Coral, and the equally small, but ideologically potent Frente de Izquierda Popular decided to run their chief ideologue, Jorge Abelardo Ramos. Apart from Alsogaray's aspirations to become the new electoral vehicle for the centrist middle classes, none of these groupings had any illusions of gaining more than minimal representation in Congress, and perhaps the odd municipal or provincial coup.

A notch higher were the hopes of three new 'alliances', whose eyes were set on the possibility of capitalising on an eventual proscription of *peronismo*. First in the field among these was Francisco Manrique, Lanusse's former Minister of Social Welfare, with his Alianza Popular Federalista, an *ad hoc* collection of small provincial parties plus the shell of the *neoperonista* Unión Popular and the uneasy concurrence of the Santa Fe-based Partido Demócrata Progresista (who offered him his running-mate, Rafael Martínez Raymonda). Manrique's closeness to Lanusse (they were personal friends of long standing) initially led many to assume that his candidature was fostered by the military government, and to fear that the electoral process might be tampered with in his favour. In actual fact, perhaps because of this widespread impression, Manrique's attempts to set up a viable electoral organisation were initially obstructed quite deliberately by Presidency officials. But it was not long before another candidate appeared as a far more likely government favourite: Brigadier Ezequiel Martínez, another close associate of Lanusse who left his offices in the Presidency to head the Alianza Republicana Federal, which began to seek support among the same provincial parties that were being courted by Manrique. If Martínez was not the vehicle for some government-inspired electoral scheme, then at the very least he was part of a 'spoiling' operation designed to undercut Manrique's chances.

Both Manrique and Martínez were political outsiders; neither had played the electoral game before. The third 'alliance' to appear on the scene, however, was very much a product of the political establishment. Led by Oscar Alende of the Partido Intransigente (one of the three fragments of the old Radical trunk), the Alianza Popular Revolucionaria had attracted the support of a faction of the old Christian Democratic party (Horacio Sueldo's Partido Revolucionario Cristiano), of Udelpa (the party originally formed around Pedro Eugenio Aramburu and now, led by Héctor Sandler, shifting towards a more populist stance) and of Argentina's 80,000-strong Communist Party. Alende had originally joined Perón's 'Civic National Liberation Front', but broke away to offer a more consistent left-wing alternative.

In the mean time, the Unión Cívica Radical, the country's second-largest party since the mid-1940s, was the only party resorting to formal party-political procedures to choose its Presidential candidate. The contenders were the sixty-eight-year-old centrist Ricardo Balbín, the party's perennial Presidential hopeful since 1951, and the forty-five-year-old Raúl Alfonsín, leader of a left-of-centre 'movement for renewal and change'. In their own good time, and by a narrow margin, the Radicals settled on Balbín.

Perón had managed to polarise the political scene in terms of 'the people versus the military dictatorship'. Other, longer-running factors had led the bulk of the body politic to phrase its options in terms of 'liberation versus dependence'. Only a very few on the far right of the spectrum failed to adopt this schema. For the rest, however, the words had a wide range of meaning and led to a variety of policy approaches, from the advocacy of a revolution that would sweep away capitalism, together with the shackles of imperialism, to less rousing, more technically intricate formulas to overcome the economy's external vulnerability and curtail the dominant influence of foreign business interests. If there was a common denominator, it was a commitment to nationalistic economic policies, with a high degree of state intervention, and to a sharply progressive redistribution of income, within the overall frame of a more Latin-American-minded, Third-World-oriented foreign policy. In its less strident form, this consensus could be found expressed in almost identical terms in the draft platforms prepared by one of the *peronista* think-tanks, by the Unión Cívica Radical, and by the economic policy team of Manrique's Alianza Popular Federalista. (More than coincidence, this was attributable to the presence in all three parties of members of the Grupo Diamand, an influential think-tank led by the economist-industrialist Marcelo Diamand, which had been peddling alternative economic policies since the early 1960s.) Almost identical too were the various renderings of the more radical version of this consensus, stretching across the board from Alende's Alianza Popular Revolucionaria to the Juventud Peronista and the Montoneros. An outside observer would have had no difficulty in finding strong elements of this consensus, in its more moderate form, among the policies of the Lanusse government.

Save at the extremes, the difference between emphases on these common themes ran not between, but across the political parties and groupings. Indeed, *peronismo* could be said to contain the extremes as well. As for the major groupings, what separated Argentina into parties was not issues as such, or the means proposed to deal with them, but the less easily manageable question of 'identification with the people' — 'the people' being that large mass which insisted on feeling, over and above any explicit formulation of policies, that its interests were best represented by *peronismo*. In the 1940s, the link between *peronismo* and the interests of Argentina's working classes and budding industries had been clear and immediate; in the early 1970s the identity persisted as a matter of faith — of commemoration and hope, strengthened by rejection of what the intervening years had had to offer. And a good part of that rejection was directed at those who, in the interim period, had reduced politics to the task of persecuting, suppressing, defrauding or hijacking the *peronista* masses.

On the Left and among the more 'combative' of the older *peronistas*, a myth had been growing of the imminence of an event which would make all the real and imagined machinations of Lanusse's *Gran Acuerdo Nacional* irrelevant. It was a romantic vision: with no obstacles now barring Perón's return, he would come back, and the moment he stepped again on Argentine soil, the people would rally to his call in an overwhelming human tide that would sweep away the military government and all its works. It would be a repetition of that day twenty-seven years earlier, in 1945, when the mere presence of the people marching upon the capital and concentrating in front of the Casa Rosada sufficed to free Perón from detention, to cow his adversaries into retreat, and to set in motion the process that first led him to the Presidency. It would be another 17 October 1945, but on a far grander scale. Recalling the *cordobazo* of 1969, when a popular eruption signalled the beginning of the end for Onganía's régime, a name had already been chosen for this new mass phenomenon the enthusiasts envisaged: *argentinazo*, the Argentina-wide popular coup. And the date on which this would occur was only too obvious: the anniversary of that first *peronista* revolution, 17 October 1972.

Preparations were clearly under way for Perón's return. Shortly after Héctor Cámpora gave the Junta Perón's 'national reconstruction' plan, he travelled to Madrid with a delegation of *peronista* union bosses. But there was no call to the *peronista* rank and file to start mobilising for the great event; no propaganda campaign to start setting the scene. Instead, Perón held a press conference in Madrid, full of calls for conciliation and studiously omitting any reference to the anticipated great reunion on 17 October. As if on cue, the government in Buenos Aires announced that it had detected 'points of agreement' with Perón's statements.

Cámpora and his companions returned to Buenos Aires on the eve of 17 October: no Perón, still no call to mobilise. Instead, Cámpora rushed off to closet himself with the Junta, and revealed nothing of what was said when he emerged from the meeting. The 17th dawned, and there was no Perón to preside over the *peronista* rallies. Instead of the *argentinazo*, the day brought the formal announcement of the call to elections, the promulgation of a law establishing a new prison régime for political detainees, the assassination of a high-ranking police officer in the province of Buenos Aires, and a string of bomb explosions in several cities.

Soon Cámpora was off on another trip to Madrid. This time, he announced on his return that Perón would be back in the country before November was out. A couple of days later the date was set: 17 November. And still no call for mass mobilisation.

On the great day, no *peronista* supporters were allowed anywhere near Ezeiza airport; the entire area and its access routes were cordoned off by the military. Perón was led to the airport hotel, and as the hours dragged on into the night, it began to seem as if they were going to keep him there. Mutterings spread through *peronista* circles that *el Líder* was a prisoner. But the prime concern of the military was not that a Perón suddenly let loose would spark off an uncontrollable uprising — that had already been negotiated away with Cámpora and the union leaders. They were, however, worried about his personal safety; about the possibility that someone might attempt to assassinate him or, even worse, succeed. That, they were sure, would have been a real detonator of events impossible to foresee. The situation was not without its ironies: back in the Joint General Staff, an admiral charged with the intelligence aspects of Perón's security paced his room musing, 'We are all mad! First they tell me to go and kill him; now they tell me to make sure he isn't killed!' The admiral was recalling his days as a lieutenant, when he took part in one of the failed clandestine operations to assassinate Perón.

But there was no intention to keep Perón quarantined at Ezeiza airport. Although later it seemed like an eternity, it was only hours before he was transferred to the house the movement had bought him, on Gaspar Campos street in the suburb of Vicente López, only a few blocks away from the residence he had occupied as President. There too security was tight, and only with great reluctance and greater care were the militants of the *peronista* youth eventually allowed to gather in front of Perón's window, to serenade him with their rhythmic chants:

> *Hay que cantar,*
> *hay que cantar,*
> *hay que cantar,*
> *fuerte,*
> *para que oiga el General*

(We must all sing,/ we must all sing,/ we must all sing,/ loudly,/ so the General can hear).

> *Atención, atención,*
> *aquí llega un Montonero*
> *y su nombre es Juan Perón*

(Attention, attention,/ here arrives a Montonero,/ and his name is Juan Perón).

> *Buenos días, General,*
> *su custodia personal*

(Good morning, General,/ here's your personal bodyguard).

For all the three days of parading and chanting, Perón made it clear that his main business was not with the youth. He did grant an audience to a delegation of the Juventud Peronista, and made the right sort and amount of encouraging noises in their presence, but his targets were the political establishment, the military, and the population at large. His first statements on arrival set the tone: 'I have come', he said, 'as a token of peace.' And more to the point: 'There will be time for violence later.'

One by one, Perón met the political leaders, most of whom had at one time or another been his enemies. Special attention was reserved for Ricardo Balbín, leader of the Unión Cívica Radical. The praise heaped by Perón on the leader of the UCR did not spare Balbín the indignity of having to leave the house at Gaspar Campos by clambering over the back garden wall, to avoid the chanting enthusiasts blocking the street at the front. Then Perón called all party leaders to a meeting intended mainly as a show of force for the benefit of the military. Everyone from the centre leftwards attended the gathering; only Francisco Manrique made a show of announcing that he would not attend even if invited — he was not, but he did earn himself some biting remarks from Perón, who publicly dismissed him as a political nonentity. Little of what was said at the multi-party meeting went beyond circumstantial rhetoric; what mattered from Perón's point of view was that the meeting took place at all. What the gathering provided, also, was an opportunity for an open clash, on the streets, between the left and right wings of *peronismo*; one of many tests to determine who was to call the tune for the restoration of *peronista* rule. As confrontations go, the clash was inconclusive; only by taking several steps back was it possible to note that the radical youth did not manage to dominate in the streets, where they were strongest, and that there was a barely bridgeable chasm between their chanted demands and the language Perón was speaking inside with the country's political establishment.

The Army conceded the significance of the multi-party meeting by announcing, through General Alcides López Aufranc, that there was no intention of modifying the residency clause that prevented Perón from running as a candidate.

Perón took his time to knit together his electoral strategy. On 6 December it was tacitly conceded that the 'Civic National Liberation Front' was no longer in existence. In its place emerged a tighter alliance, the Frente Justicialista de Liberación (*Justicialista* Liberation Front, soon to be known by its acronym, Frejuli). Apart from the *peronistas*, the

Frejuli included Frondizi's Movimiento de Integración y Desarrollo, the Partido Conservador Popular led by Vicente Solano Lima, the Partido Popular Cristiano (a splinter of the old Christian Democratic party), and a fraction of socialists. The vehicle was ready, but what was by no means clear was whom it would carry as Presidential candidate. The union bosses insisted that Perón should defy Lanusse's ban, and that the Frejuli should submit his nomination to the electoral authorities. The left-wing *peronista* youth were equally adamant that the only acceptable candidate was Perón himself. The other members of the alliance counselled caution. It is said that Perón, old and ailing as he was, saw through these various proposals with the greatest of ease: the union bosses he suspected of seeking an outright ban, not only on Perón but on the Frejuli as well, because this would leave them masters of the situation and able to negotiate a candidate with the military; the left-wingers he also suspected of seeking a blanket proscription, but as the perfect excuse for a call to insurrection; and finally, his allies' motives were the most transparent of all, as each and every one of them would be a potential candidate with Perón out of the running.

Always the master-tactician, Perón decided that there was nothing to lose by waiting. In mid-December, it was announced that the old man was leaving the country, and still no word about *his* candidate. He was heading for Paraguay, to a hero's welcome in the place that first harboured him when he began his exile seventeen years before. Speculation spread that he would set up his headquarters in Asunción, and conduct the campaign from there. Indeed the first act seemed to confirm this assumption: from Asunción he despatched Héctor Cámpora back to Buenos Aires with *the order*, his long-awaited decision on the Frejuli's candidates. It was a bombshell. No insistence on his own candidacy; no selection of a leading *peronista* politician, or a prominent union boss, or any of the more prestigious figures from among the allied parties. Perón's candidate was none other that the quintessentially loyal Héctor Cámpora, chosen for the same reason that had inspired his earlier appointment as 'personal delegate': that without any political weight of his own, he could be relied upon to do Perón's bidding. As his running mate, Perón selected a non-*peronista*, Vicente Solano Lima, the seventy-one-year-old leader of the tiny Partido Conservador Popular. And together with *the order* came the news that Perón would not be setting up his command post in Paraguay. He was headed back to Madrid, by way of Lima.

The union bosses were aghast, and did not bother to hide their displeasure. The *peronista* youth and Montoneros were at first confused, but did not take long to take their cue from the unions' reaction. They rushed to adopt Cámpora in the name of 'loyalty', a ploy that reinforced, by way of contrast, their argument that the 'union bureaucrats' were really traitors to the movement. To the left wing of *peronismo* Cámpora became *el Tío*, 'the Uncle'; to Cámpora the Left became an enticing offer of the one thing he had always lacked, a political power-base of his own. From Perón's point of view, this outcome was all benefit. Whatever schemes the union bosses might have been hatching with Lanusse on the strength of Perón's proscription had been foiled; the radicalised youth had been deflected from insurrection to elections, and in the process they provided the political wherewithal for the advancement of Cámpora's candidacy, in the absence of union support (indeed, as Perón correctly surmised, a second move on the checkerboard would also bring the chastised union leaders back into the game, if only for fear of losing all control of the movement to their adversaries on the Left).

Perón had not, however, ceased entirely to play on the brink of self-proscription of *peronismo*. Technically at least, when he picked Cámpora he had chosen a man unable to run under Lanusse's rules. The 'residence clause' built into the electoral legislation had indeed been aimed at ruling out Perón himself, on the correct assumption that he would not be back in Argentina by 25 August. But it also stated that eligibility to run depended on the candidate *residing continuously* in the country between that date and polling day. With his trips abroad, Cámpora — according to the strict letter of the law — had already disqualified himself. The military government was handed a tough dilemma: either it applied its own rules, which would be interpreted as confirmation of widespread fears about its proscriptive intentions (and might provoke unforeseen reactions from the *peronista* masses), or it would look the other way, conceding yet again that Perón alone was setting the rules of the game. From Madrid and in public, Perón was scornfully confident that the military would give way. 'Cámpora', he said, 'is a bitter pill for them to swallow, but Licastro [a former lieutenant who had been drummed out of the Army for openly professing to be a *peronista*, and had since become one of the rising stars on the Left of the movement] is even more bitter. Licastro is the youth, and they are already half afraid of the youth.'

In his memoirs, Lanusse later confirmed that he had suffered a tactical beating. 'Legally', he wrote, 'Cámpora could not be a candidate to the Presidency of the Nation: he had violated express provisions with his trips abroad. But the impression we had was that Perón had come up with this name precisely so we would veto it. With the veto, he would be replaced by a more irritative candidate (from Julián Licastro to Rodolfo Galimberti, through anyone who might prove unpalatable to the government), and this left the armed forces with only two options: either suspending the elections or flatly proscribing *peronismo*. In the event, we left things as they were.'

The union bosses were also given a taste of what they could expect if they did not play along. When the time came to adopt candidates to Congress, the *Peronista* Youth figured prominently among the appointees; the union hierarchy not at all. Indeed the only candidates drawn from organised labour were representatives of the 'combative' unions, politically close to the radical youth. And from Madrid Perón spoke openly in condemnation of the union bosses who were 'accepting money' from the military government. He singled out for particularly harsh criticism one of the Left's favourite targets: Rogelio Coria, leader of the builders' union and a prominent figure of the '62' *peronista* unions. Yet the attack on the union bosses was conducted in true Perón style, leaving them a clear escape route. Far from extending his criticism to Coria's constant partner in dealings with the government — José Rucci, leader of the powerful metalworkers' union and secretary-general of the CGT —, he described Rucci as a paradigm of loyalty and a guarantor of true *peronista* discipline among organised labour.

By the time Cámpora's candidacy had been duly accepted by the electoral authorities, in January 1973, the union hierarchy had thrown in the towel. They turned up *en masse* to the official launch of the *peronista* election campaign at Cámpora's home-town of San Andrés de Giles, in Buenos Aires province. There, for the first time, they shared the platform with their rivals of the radicalised youth and joined in yet another open provocation of the military. Breaking Lanusse's unwritten rule that campaigning politicians were, if not to condemn, at least to remain aloof from the armed 'subversives', speakers abounded in open praise for the Montoneros and other 'special formations'. The chanting youths ominously recalled that the secretary-general of the *peronista* movement, Juan Manuel Abal Medina, was the brother of a founder of Montoneros, Fernando Luis Abal Medina, who had been killed by the security forces.

> *Abal ... Medina,*
> *el nombre de tu hermano*
> *es fusil en la Argentina*
> (Abal . . . Medina/ your brother's name/ is a rifle in Argentina).

And signalling to Lanusse and the military that their partial observance of the electoral rules, and the candidacy of *el Tío* Cámpora, amounted to little more than an elaborate charade, they danced to the sound of:

> Qué lindo, qué lindo,
> qué lindo que va a ser,
> el Tío en el gobierno,
> y Perón en el poder.

(How nice, how nice,/ how nice it's going to be,/ with Uncle in the government,/ and Perón in power).

The refrain was picked up as the leading slogan for the *peronista* campaign: *Cámpora al gobierno, Perón al poder* ('Cámpora to government, Perón to power'). It is not that the government was unaware that this was precisely Perón's intention all along, but to have it rubbed in in this fashion outraged the Army chiefs. Casting aside their earlier caution, they ordered the Procurator-General to take legal action against the Frejuli for blatant infringement of the electoral legislation, and Lanusse thundered that participation by unions in the rally could lead to the loss of their legal standing. It was the nearest they came to being provoked into proscribing the *peronistas*, and although they later regained their composure and allowed these threats to fade away, the effect of this outburst was to leave the threat of proscription hanging in the air. This, in turn, only prolonged the hands-off policy adopted by the other contenders by keeping alive the hope that at the eleventh hour they might be able to pick up the *peronista* vote. The Junta compounded this by suddenly announcing that Perón himself would be banned from returning to Argentina until after a new, elected government had been installed in power.

The six-and-a-half months between the 25 August deadline that ruled out the candidacies of Lanusse and Perón, and the elections on 11 March 1973 saw no diminution of action by the guerrilla bands. Not a single week went by without news of some exploit, the horror of individual events somewhat dulled by their frequency, but replaced by a growing sense, if not of personal insecurity, at least of chronic unease at the apparent inevitability of violence as part of everyday life. Kidnappings multiplied, in an escalation both of the prominence of the victims and of the size of reported ransom payments. Among the score or so of abductions were those of the president of Philips Argentina, the general manager of the Anglo meat-packing plant, a top executive of

ITT — and Isidoro Graiver, member of a well-known banking family from La Plata, whose brother David was Jacobo Timerman's partner in the newspaper *La Opinión* as well as a fund-raiser for his old boss, presidential candidate Francisco Manrique. These connections were known only to a few at the time, but even among them they were not considered especially remarkable. Graiver's kidnapping fitted the general pattern, and the fact that no ransom payment was announced was simply attributed to the natural reticence of bankers. Some years later these connections and the consequences of that abduction would be partly disinterred by a military investigator to prove that even in 1972 Argentina was the target of a vast subversive conspiracy that reached well beyond the youths bearing arms, into the heart of the business community.

Bomb attacks continued too, from the Left against the Sheraton hotel, a country club, the home of a young Army officer; from the Right against the homes of a writer and of a lawyer who specialised in defending political prisoners. There were casualties all round: the armed forces lost a rear-admiral and a lieutenant of Army intelligence; the ERP lost one of its leaders in Tucumán, Ramón Rosa Jiménez; the FAR saw the failure of an attack on a military convoy, and the dispersal and arrest of a cell led by the well-known writer Francisco Urondo; the trade unions and the police suffered frequent losses.

Most of the guerrilla operations were simple, 'easy' strikes. The only major coup was an attack by the ERP on the barracks of a Communications battalion in February 1973, which yielded them a haul of two anti-aircraft guns and over a hundred hand weapons. For the rest, it was quite obvious that the available organisational resources were being concentrated on the kidnappings, in an effort clearly aimed at replenishing their war chests.

The military were relatively satisfied that the campaign was going their way. In this half-year they had unearthed another 'people's prison' and put another forty-odd *guerrilleros* behind bars, among them not a few who were key figures in their respective organisations. They had managed to track down, capture and put on trial some of the participants in the assassination of General Sánchez. But they faced the prospect, with elections in the offing, of having to lift the state of siege regulations which gave them a free hand inasmuch as they suspended constitutional guarantees. So they added yet another item to the formidable array of repressive legislation in force: a bill allowing the military to take part in counter-insurgency operations even without the umbrella of the state of siege.

This was Law Number 20,032, the 8,301st since the Illia government passed its last major piece of legislation in early 1966 — and the tail-end of the *Revolución Argentina* still had another 348 laws to come. In their six years in power, the military had promulgated more than two-thirds as many laws as had preceded them since the foundation of the legal system — a nightmare even for lawyers and a daunting legacy for the legislators-to-be.

For all the disquiet caused by the noisy presence of the *peronista* Left, heralding the imminent establishment of *la Patria socialista* ('the socialist Fatherland'), for all the unease which would normally have accompanied the spectacle of Perón meeting a delegation of the Viet Cong in Paris, the *peronista* electoral campaign was lavishly funded, a sign not only of the willing disbursement of union funds but of massive campaign contributions from private business. José Ber Gelbard, the leader of the CGE, continually crossing to Madrid for consultations with Perón and his immediate entourage, acted as the movement's ambassador to the business sector. His message was one that businessmen were only too eager to hear: that only Perón could call the young radicals to heel, and that this was precisely what he intended to do as soon as victory was secured at the polls. He portrayed Perón the realist, a man with business acumen whose long years in Europe had given him the necessary contacts to attract to Argentina a massive inflow of European investment capital; a man whose Third World credentials and connections would enable him to entice Arab money across the water. Independence from economic imperialism was not a matter of shutting out foreign investment but of diversifying its sources; what really mattered for business was a credibly stable government, and that could only be guaranteed by Perón. The businessmen, local and foreign, responded generously. One foreign chamber of commerce carried its support to the extreme of threatening to dismiss the Argentine editor of its magazine if he continued to campaign for a candidate other than Perón (he resisted, but was not actually fired until after the election results were in).

The youthful Left of *peronismo* were clearly the political driving force of the campaign, and Cámpora rewarded them with positions of influence and a number of candidatures, to Congress and to several provincial governorships. The union bosses did their utmost not to leave the field entirely free for the Left, but they had obviously lost much ground with their late start. Command of the campaign, however, was not the same as command of the movement, or of its plans for government. This remained in Madrid, and was mediated by the Right of the movement, a none-too-solid alliance in which the leading figures were José López Rega and the CGE's José Ber Gelbard, with José Rucci's CGT as a somewhat reluctant third partner.

Barring last-minute proscription, the end-result was never in doubt: *peronismo* would carry the bulk of the vote. The only outside hope remaining to Perón's adversaries was that he might not collect enough votes to carry the election in the first round, and that in the ensuing run-off between the two candidates with the most votes, the opposition would rally against him.

In the event, the Frejuli came just short of winning the first round, with 49.5 per cent of the vote instead of the requisite 51 per cent. Second in line came Balbín's UCR, with 21.3 per cent, followed by an unexpected third: the untried Manrique, with 14.9 per cent. The arithmetic did not allow any hopes of upsetting this outcome in a second round; at the very least Perón would get the combined votes of the non-*peronista* Left, an 8% that amply sufficed for victory. So the UCR instantly conceded defeat, renouncing the run-off. While Manrique was still toying with the idea of demanding the run-off himself, on the grounds that by UCR default he had been left in the position of candidate with the second largest number of votes, Lanusse proclaimed the Frejuli victor. As the *peronistas* had always maintained, in free elections they would win comfortably. It had taken seventeen years to prove the point, with an electorate in which over a third of the voters had been under ten years of age when Perón was ousted in 1955. The elections had been won, and the eruption of *peronista* euphoria on the streets of every major city in the country almost obscured the fact that there were still seventy-five difficult days ahead before the first part of the campaign slogan — *Cámpora al gobierno* — would become a reality.

There was no more than a four-day truce after the elections. Violence erupted again with a shootout between police and Montoneros at the home of the deceased *guerrillero* Mariano Pujadas. And from then on, barely two days at a time would pass without news of some guerrilla coup. Publicly at least, the Montoneros were the least active: the exploits to which they admitted were the hijacking of a truckload of minerals and the assassination in early April of Colonel Héctor Alberto Iribarren, chief of intelligence of the 3rd Army Corps in Córdoba. To a large extent this reflected the fact that the Montoneros had not yet recovered fully from the impact of repression. More visibly back on its feet was the FAR.

Towards the end of March they briefly occupied the Cordoban town of Villa Alende; in early April they raided the courts of law in the Buenos Aires suburb of San Isidro, making away with arms and documents, and towards the end of that month, for propaganda purposes, they staged the 'occupation' of three railway stations on a suburban line leading south of the capital.

But it was the ERP — by now divided into two factions — that returned with a vengeance, displaying unprecedented operational capacity throughout the country. In only thirteen days ERP guerrilla units raided and gutted a police station on a main access route to the capital; occupied the country's first nuclear power plant at Atucha (leaving it unharmed); overran two police stations on Maciel island just outside Buenos Aires; occupied a factory in Santa Fe; placed a bomb inside Navy headquarters (the conscript who carried out the bombing killed himself in the process), and abducted Rear-Admiral Francisco Agustín Alemán, a former chief of Navy intelligence.

ERP actions escalated in the second half of March. They destroyed Army aircraft in a raid on the San Justo airfield, publicly flaunted their 'interrogation' of Rear-Admiral Alemán in a film distributed to TV stations in Buenos Aires, killed policemen and stole their weapons, occupied the town of Ingeniero Maschwitz in Buenos Aires province, briefly took over a clinic and a school, and abducted the interim chief of the Gendarmería, Commander Jacobo Nasif. Then, on 30 March, they struck in the very heart of Buenos Aires city. At nine in the morning, Rear-Admiral Hermes Quijada, a naval airman who had gained popularity with his flight over the South Pole, stepped out of his home in the distinguished northern quarter of the capital. With him was his chauffeur and bodyguard. They walked swiftly to the nearby garage to pick up the Admiral's white Dodge GTX. Following their usual pattern, they both sat in the front, Quijada with a submachinegun at the ready on his lap. For some time Quijada had lived with the certainty that one or another of the guerrilla groups would try to kill him — they held him ultimately responsible for the 'Trelew massacre' at the Almirante Zar naval airbase in August 1972, when sixteen of their comrades had been shot while in detention. Only a few weeks earlier, Quijada had been describing his security precautions to a former comrade in arms, Francisco Manrique. 'I've got it all figured out,' he said. 'The only way they can kill me is by coming abreast of my car and shooting me through the window.' That day, he turned into Calle Junín and headed down-town; it was slow but easy going for the first four blocks, but a red light forced him to stop just short of Calle Cangallo, boxed in by the traffic. A motorcycle wove its way through the halted cars, and as it came abreast of the trapped Dodge, a young man riding pillion emptied a pistol at Quijada. The chauffeur, injured as well, managed to fire his own sidearm at the assassin, fatally wounding him (his body was found days later in a city apartment).

The Navy high command were shocked and infuriated. All available admirals were summoned to an emergency meeting. The mood was ugly: this was the second of their number to be killed by guerrillas in the last four months, and another was being held by the ERP. The General Staffs of the three services were also called to crisis meetings, and throughout the country officers hurried to their bases, openly anticipating something drastic, perhaps even a coup which would prevent the elected authorities from taking office. The realisation that this was precisely the ERP's aim held the military in check — but only just.

Cámpora was away in Madrid, in consultation with Perón. Lanusse sent him a telegram, via the Argentine embassy, virtually summoning him back to the country for 'very urgent' discussions on 'matters related to the internal security of the Nation'. Perón made sure that the reply was instant: Cámpora would return on the first flight. The President-elect had already been having a rough time in Madrid on account of the antics of his left-wing supporters: only a fortnight earlier, the representative of the *Peronista* Youth on the movement's supreme council, Rodolfo Galimberti, had proclaimed that the new government would not only investigate the armed forces for their performance in power, but would also set up an armed popular militia.

A similar suggestion back in 1955 had been one of the reasons invoked by the military for overthrowing Juan Domingo Perón. In 1973 the idea was not only equally offensive to the military, but also alarming: unlike 1955, there were now in Argentina armed bands who would eagerly step into the role of officially-sanctioned militias. Yet the military had managed to contain their reaction to Galimberti's announcement: in public, General Alcides López Aufranc stated coolly that the armed forces simply would not tolerate the formation of militias; privately, the message was relayed to Perón in much stronger terms. Perón, already under pressure from the Right of his movement, dismissed Galimberti from the supreme council and subjected Cámpora to a stern dressing-down. They were few who took much notice at the time, but this event marked the turning-point in the fortunes of the youthful Left of the *peronista* movement.

The assassination of Quijada disguised the nature of the backlash from the Right. After all, the perpetrators were not *peronistas* but the Trotskyites of the ERP, for whom, unlike the Montoneros and the FAR, the elected *peronista* government was not the first step on the road to liberation, but 'the last card of the bourgeoisie'. Thus it was not hard to accept, even to encourage a military crackdown (particularly if the alternative seemed to be a coup).

Lanusse's reaction was harsh indeed. A decree was issued giving kidnappers a five-hour ultimatum to produce their victims or inform the authorities of their whereabouts. Non-compliance would mean incurring the death penalty, as would the possession of firearms or explosives. Five provinces (Buenos Aires, Santa Fe, Córdoba, Mendoza and Tucumán) were declared 'emergency zones' in which justice would be meted out summarily by special military tribunals. Within days the forces had geared up for massive anti-guerrilla sweeps throughout the country. Censorship was imposed on all news concerning guerrilla activity.

The guerrilla groups retreated underground, emerging only a few times for small hit-and-run raids. Within less than ten days the government felt confident enough to lift the 'emergency zone' regulations in Mendoza, Tucumán and part of Buenos Aires province. With only three days to go before handing over power to the new government, on 22 May they lifted the state of siege, which had been in force since the *cordobazo* of 1969. That same day the ERP surfaced again, in La Plata, to assassinate Dirk Kloosterman, a leader of the auto mechanics' union.

What the military crackdown did not affect at all was the wave of kidnappings for ransom, for which the guerrilla groups did not usually claim credit, but in which all of them, including the *peronista* organisations, were actively engaged. Many of the abductions were not even reported by the victims or their families, who preferred to pay quietly and avoid the attentions of the security forces. At least twelve, however, did reach public notice in the seventy-five days between the elections and the inauguration of the new government, and it was known that large ransoms were paid for the release of Kodak Argentina's general manager and of the director of Nobleza, one of the country's largest tobacco manufacturers. When a top executive of Ford Motors Argentina was injured in a shooting, the public also became aware of another guerrilla-managed racket that had remained unmentioned for months, though it had already reached enormous proportions: the extortion of 'protection' money from large business concerns, in exchange for leaving their installations and their executives alone.

Right up the last minute, Lanusse felt it necessary to keep issuing public warnings against any coup attempt by disgruntled officers, promising to resist them with force if necessary. In his farewell speech to the Generals at the Colegio Militar, he insisted that there would be no justification for a coup as long as the Constitution was being respected. There was reason enough for Lanusse's vigilance. A month before the elections, the Generals, and later the commanders of the three services, had publicly committed themselves to a five-point programme which was meant to remain in force for the ensuing four years. For the military, two of the five points were crucial: one of them committed them to securing participation for themselves in the next civilian government; the other stated that they would 'reject the application of indiscriminate amnesties for those who face trial or who have been sentenced for the commission of crimes connected with subversion and terrorism.' The elected authorities, to the growing despair of the soldiers, were just as committed to keeping the military in the place assigned to them by the Constitution — out of government — and to granting an 'ample and generous amnesty' for those accused of political crimes.

In the intervening months there had been some heart-searching among politicians as to the scope of the amnesty. Legislators with juridical experience had been arguing, in none-too-loud a voice, that while it made sense to amnesty the members of the *peronista* guerrilla organisations — whose stated objective was the restoration of a legitimate government and whose recourse to armed struggle would cease with the inauguration of the new authorities — the same did not apply to the ERP, whose avowed intention was to continue the struggle against the constitutionally elected government. Others pointed out that in the tradition of Argentine jurisprudence, eligibility for amnesty did not extend to those who had been sentenced for committing *crímenes atroces* — 'atrocious crimes', a phrase that included murder. The debate among the legislators-elect did not get very far once it became clear that the *peronistas* intended to take their lead from the Left, and proclaim a general amnesty. Smaller blocs of legislators shied away even from making points of principle, reasoning that in any case they would not affect the result, but that they would be offering themselves up as targets for the men with the guns.

And the great day came. The multitude covered the Plaza de Mayo in front of the Casa Rosada, and huge banners proclaimed the presence of FAR and Montoneros. The rhythmic chants jubilantly bade farewell to the military:

> *Se van, se van*
> *y nunca volverán*
(They're going, they're going/ never to return).
And they ushered in the utopianism of the new era:

> *Qué lindo, qué lindo,*
> *qué lindo que va a ser,*
> *el Hospital de Niños*
> *en el Sheraton Hotel*
(How nice, how nice,/ how nice it's going to be, /the Hospital for Children/ in the Sheraton Hotel).

The scheduled military parade was cancelled after a number of incidents: ERP men snatching guns from cadets, chanting demonstrators mobbing the soldiers who were raising the flag in front of Army headquarters to celebrate the 163rd anniversary of the first rising against Spanish rule. The doors of the Casa Rosada were bolted tight when over-enthusiastic activists started clamouring for admission. Insults and spittle rained upon military officers and the Cardinal Archbishop of Buenos Aires as they approached the building. Inside, a sour-faced Junta had to tolerate the presence of Presidents Salvador Allende of Chile and Osvaldo Dorticós of Cuba, gleefully greeted as *compañeros* (comrades) by the *peronista* Left.

The ceremony proceeded as planned. Héctor Cámpora was sworn in as the first *peronista* President in eighteen years and Vicente Solano Lima as his Vice-President, followed by the ministers — a motley crew representing the toeholds gained by the different factions on the shaky power structure of the new régime. The Left had taken the most political ministries, with their proxies Esteban Righi in Interior, Juan Carlos Puig in Foreign Relations and Jorge Alberto Taiana in Culture and Education. The bastion of the far Right was the ministry of Social Welfare, entrusted to *el Brujo* (the warlock) José López Rega. The unions had gained the Labour ministry for one of their own, Ricardo Otero; the CGE's José Ber Gelbard had conquered his expected prize, the Ministry of the Economy; Defence and Justice had gone to two mildly conservative 'orthodox' *peronistas*, Angel Federico Robledo and Antonio Juan Benítez.

With the new government, a new team of service commanders took over. The Army was entrusted to General Jorge Raúl Carcagno, the paratrooper of *cordobazo* renown, who was already making himself a new reputation as a populist. The new Navy chief was Vice-Admiral Carlos Alvarez and the Air Force commander Brigadier Héctor Luis Fautario; both were political nonentities.

The first item on Cámpora's agenda, which admitted of no delay, was the amnesty for the military government's political prisoners.

21
CÁMPORA TO GOVERNMENT
(May-October 1973)

Cámpora's inaugural address to Congress openly recognised his government's debt to the youthful radical wing of the *peronista* movement. 'At the most decisive moments', he said, 'a marvellous youth, with the decision and courage of the most vibrant national epics, knew how to oppose the blind, sickly passions of a delirious oligarchy. How can we say that this victory does not also belong to them, when they gave everything — family, friends, goods, even life — for the ideal of a *justicialista* Fatherland! If it had not been for them, perhaps the agony of the régime would have been prolonged, and with it the disintegration of our heritage and the misfortune of the humble.'

'That is why', added Cámpora, picking up one of the radical slogans *(La sangre derramada jamás será negociada*, The blood we have spilt will never be negotiated), 'the blood that was spilt, the affronts to flesh and spirit, the mockery piled on the just, shall not be negotiated.' But this was only partly what they wanted to hear. Cámpora had carefully avoided choosing between rival slogans *(Patria socialista* versus *Patria peronista)*, and the rest of his address contained, not the blueprint for revolution expected by the left-wingers but a fleshed-out version of the economic programme prepared by the businessmen of the CGE. In their eyes, the keystone of the programme, 'concertation' between labour and business, was no more than an attempt to paper over the reality of conflicting class interests; the new foreign investment code, similar in inspiration to the one adopted years earlier by the Andean Pact, did not affect the capacity of the multinationals to survive as a dominant feature of the country's economic life; the agrarian law, with its heavy taxation of the 'potential yield' of the land, did not go far enough in the direction of destroying the powerbase of the landed oligarchy. The misgivings of the *peronista* Left, however, were not voiced openly. To borrow Richard Gillespie's felicitous description — 'The Social Pact, which formed the foundation of Perón's plan for "National Reconstruction", was condemned by the Marxist Left who saw it as an attempt at a national reconstruction of capitalism, which indeed it was. For the Montoneros,

381

however, with their "stages" approach to revolution, the Pact was the "superstructural expression of the class alliance between the workers and the small and medium national entrepreneurs", with these classes being "the social base of the National Liberation Front." ' It is interesting to note that six years later the economic programme announced by Cámpora would be cited in an official document as evidence of 'economic subversion' — part of a global subversive conspiracy against Argentina.

The youth were being reminded of the precise role they had played in Perón's strategy, that of instruments of electoral victory on Perón's own terms. The 'generational transfusion' had not been meant to go all the way to making them and their radical proposals the backbone of the new government. The government's programme was Perón's own, not theirs. Their response was to find ways to rationalise their acceptance of this programme in public, as a necessary first step towards the achievement of their own aims, while keeping alive their most potent tool, mass mobilisation, and using it to force their way into positions of power in the new administration, and to pressure the government into following their lead on specific issues. The first test case was the amnesty for political prisoners, which became a three-sided race from the moment the newly-elected Congressmen took their seats.

The Chamber of Deputies rushed approval of the amnesty bill without any debate to speak of, and sent it up to the Senate for equally hasty treatment. In the meantime, the *peronista* youth and the guerrilla organisations, wary of delays and juridical niceties that might limit the extent of the amnesty (an unnecessary worry, since a cowed Congress had already decided to make it indiscriminate and automatic), massed their followers in front of the prisons to clamour for the instant liberation of the 'soldiers of Perón'. There were clashes at the largest concentration, in front of the Villa Devoto prison in a suburb of Buenos Aires, and two demonstrators were killed. On 26 May the Senate gave its approval to the amnesty bill, but already President Cámpora, fearful of an eruption of violence, had decided not to wait on the formalities of promulgation by the Executive: he went ahead, on the strength of Presidential privilege, and granted political prisoners a blanket pardon. Security in the prisons was already crumbling, as detainees — political prisoners and common criminals alike — mutinied against the guards, and warders decided not to wait for official notification before opening the gates. There was jubilation in the streets as the prisoners streamed out, and at the metropolitan airport as the first plane-loads of pardoned detainees arrived from prisons in the south of the country. The episode did not end with the liberation of the political prisoners, as a dozen common criminals — including a notorious international drug trafficker — took advantage of the confusion to slip out of Villa Devoto, fifty others staged a mass jailbreak in Córdoba, and mutinies spread to other gaols throughout the country. This created a new, wholly unexpected political problem, which a harrassed and confused government swept away a few days later through mass commutation of sentences for petty crimes.

Together with the amnesty bill, Congress approved two other Bills effectively dismantling the apparatus of repressive legislation built up over the years by the military régime. One wiped out all the modifications introduced by the military in the country's Penal Code; the other rescinded thirteen special laws (creation of the special Federal Penal Chamber for crimes of subversion, establishment of special régimes for prison life, authorisation of the use of the armed forces in anti-guerrilla operations and to run the prisons, plus a mass of procedural detail).

The release of the political prisoners was a first, important victory for the Left, and seemed to prove that mobilisation carried more weight than the newly-restored institutional mechanisms. The momentum was kept up. Takeovers and occupations were engineered in public offices and businesses, demanding worker and employee participation, which initially, in the absence of any clearer aims, expressed itself as a demand for the right to veto official appointees and to dismiss officials on the grounds that they were *gorilas*, agents of the multinationals, or enemies of *peronista* orthodoxy as re-defined by the Left. Only the first few takeovers had required minimal planning and organisation; their example, plus what appeared to be government unwillingness or impotence to halt them, triggered a wave of spontaneous, imitative occupations. There was something of a bully's carnival in this largely aimless exercise of 'people's power' — in many cases the political content of the takeovers seemed exhausted after senior officials had been forced to hop while chanting *'El que no salta es un gorilón'* (The one who doesn't hop is a great *gorila*). In other cases the occupations had a harder, nastier edge: the Minister of Public Works, Horacio Zubiri, felt compelled to resign when his Ministry became totally unmanageable; in the universities — subjected to 'intervention' by the new government on 29 May — professors and lecturers were hounded into resignation, curricula were thrown out, academic requirements waived, and the buildings turned into permanent forums covered with gaudy graffiti proclaiming the dawning liberation.

At Federal Police headquarters, orders were issued to disband the hated DIPA (Department for Police Investigations of Anti-democratic Activities) and to destroy the files on suspected and convicted 'subversives' — an order known to have been foiled by the secreting of duplicates. Senior police officers were assembled to hear a lecture by Interior Minister Esteban Righi about 'the end of the era of repression of the people'.

It was as if a revolution had taken place on 25 May — only it had not. The right wing of *peronismo* was also moving swiftly to secure its own hold on positions of power. Its centre of operations was José López Rega's Ministry of Social Welfare, and the job of organising a counter-offensive against the Left was entrusted to a retired colonel, Jorge Osinde, an old-time *peronista* who had been given the innocuous-sounding post of Under-Secretary for Sports. Apart from its mainline occupation with pensions, housing, health, protection of minors and community promotion, the Ministry of Social Welfare was entrusted with the war against drug trafficking, an activity which gave it access to funds, including US aid, which could be spent quite legally on the acquisition of arms. This allowed Osinde to organise a small army of bodyguards, whose popular appellation of *argelinos* (Algerians) hinted at the role played by another of the hidden organisers of the *peronista* Right. This was Ciro Ahumada, a former Army captain who had been dismissed the service after his part in a *peronista* uprising in the 1950s. Ahumada had since become an expert in guerrilla warfare; he would often claim, rather vaguely, that during his years of exile he had 'fought with Ben Bella in Algeria'. His contacts and acquaintances certainly included former members of the French OAS, and in the early 1970s he was back in Argentina representing French business interests.

One of Ahumada's favourite textbooks was *Elementos y métodos de la guerrilla comunista* (Elements and Methods of Communist Guerrilla Warfare), a Spanish translation of a book by the Croatian Colonel Ivan Štir, which concluded thus:

The turn has come for the territory farthest from the front line, the virgin territory of Latin America, rearguard of the free world. The Communist waves arrive with optimism at the Latin American shores, confident that they will soon dominate the young American republics of the Southern Hemisphere. This is their last objective. [. . .] If this effort is broken, it will represent the long-awaited retreat of Communism towards the epicentre where it was born. This is a Communist charge behind the backs of the free world, and this charge must be repealed in order to be able to move, finally, into the counter-attack. [. . .] The peoples of Latin America must prepare for this decisive struggle, which is not only theirs, but that of the entire free world, which must aid these peoples to carry out their historic duty. After the historic moment of their epic struggles for liberation, this will be their second most important historic duty . . .

Štir's formula for this historic campaign included

installing in power a decidedly anti-Communist government, backed by parties of the same ideological base as a common denominator; increasing the severity of the measures which directly or indirectly punish guerrilla and Communist activity; planning a convenient propaganda campaign to clarify the aims of the Communists and the guerrillas, imposing the conviction that 'to be a Communist represents a public shame, cultural backwardness and personal irresponsibility'; activating and increasing the state's security personnel, identifying the material and moral aid, internal or external, received by the guerrillas, and suppressing it; eliminating from the armed security forces, from national and private institutions, all Communists and suspects . . . .

If Ahumada had any formal base at all, it was his office as security boss at YPF, the state's oil corporation, although he was usually hard to find there, as were the other members of the informal network of 'security' men in the state enterprises and government agencies. Ahumada was widely believed to have been the recruiter of the *argelinos* at Social Welfare, and the coordinator of the fraternity of retired officers and subalterns from the armed forces and the police appointed to security posts throughout the administration.

Both sides continued to expand their power bases in government well into June. Montoneros and FAR held a press conference to announce that they had left armed struggle behind, but stood ready to defend 'the government of the people'. Mario Firmenich, publicly appearing as head of the Montoneros, used the occasion to try to dispel fears of a rift between Perón and themselves. 'There is no difference', he said, 'between *patria peronista* and *patria socialista*.' The very same day the ERP also held a press conference, their leader Mario Roberto Santucho solemnly proclaiming that the guerrilla struggle would continue until power was conquered. Guerrilla actions, however, were few, and consisted mainly of more kidnappings to build up the war chests.

In mid-June Cámpora was ready to fly to Madrid to fetch Perón for his definitive homecoming. The few remaining accoutrements had been dealt with in the now usual speedy style: the Argentine embassy in Madrid had already delivered Perón his first Argentine passport in eighteen years; the Presidency had announced the imminent restitution of his military rank — Lieutenant-General — and the right to wear his uniform.

And, as if oblivious to the power struggle going on around them,

Economy Minister José Gelbard and CGT chief José Rucci had gone ahead with the public signing of the 'Act of National Commitment', in which a two-year wage truce was granted by the unions in exchange for an immediate across-the-board rise and a freeze of prices, as well as the promise to implement a package of nineteen economic reform laws: (1) a tax on the 'potential yield' of agricultural land, (2) 'buy Argentine' regulations, (3) a freeze on rural evictions, (4) an agrarian transformation programme, (5) penalisation of tax fraud, (6) industrial promotion, (7) creation of the Corporation of Small and Medium Enterprises, (8) creation of the Corporation of State Enterprises, (9) nationalisation of the export trade in grains and beef, (10) nationalisation of bank deposits, (11) elimination of para-banking financial companies, (12) foreign investment rules, (13) regionalisation of credit, (14) creation of a registry of foreign agents, (15) mining promotion, (16) regulation of the transfer of national enterprises, (17) a 'social interest' housing programme, (18) conservation of natural resources, and (19) regulation of idle or deficiently exploited land. The package, together with the Act, went to Congress on 8 June.

As Cámpora flew out, amid rumours — far too promptly denied by officials — that Perón was mightily displeased with the Executive's inability to curb the youth, the secretary-general of the *peronista* movement, Juan Manuel Abal Medina, issued a call for the occupations of public buildings and business premises to cease. Two days later the CGE, clearly speaking on behalf of Economy Minister Gelbard, published a strong condemnation of the occupations. On 17 June, the Ministry of the Interior, in a long-winded communiqué claiming that the government was not shutting out the people, made it an order: occupations were to cease forthwith.

The significance of the order and the implications of its fulfilment were obscured by the fact that everyone's attention had already been diverted elsewhere — to the preparations for Perón's reception. It was to be a grand occasion, an historic meeting of the leader with the multitudes. The CGT created the frame for the event by announcing a countrywide stoppage until the day after Perón's arrival. Unions and government set about providing travel facilities and improvised accommodation so that people could come from the farthest reaches of the republic. And close to the top of the unwritten agenda was the determination by both Left and Right that this would be the one occasion on which the mobilising power of each could be demonstrated in the open, before the eyes of the whole country and, more important, before the eyes of Perón. Millions were expected, and an appropriate venue was chosen to fit them all: a section of the motorway leading to Ezeiza airport, flanked by a wide expanse of parkland. On both sides, the organisational effort was impressive. The *Peronista* Youth devised a succession of marches, with columns converging from different points in the capital and Buenos Aires province, banners held high — a river of people which would pour into the meeting ground, engulfing the main platform. The Right were responsible for the logistics of the main event itself: the location of the platform with its bullet-proof glass cabin; the network of loudspeakers and radio and TV link-ups; the first aid centres; and, of course, the allocation of space to the different parties, with pride of place reserved for the unions.

Days before the event, Colonel Osinde started planning the security aspects of the giant rally. Teams of bodyguards from the ministries and the unions were lined up and armed as if for war, with submachineguns, shotguns and pistols. And the word was passed down the line that vigilance and preparedness would have to be extreme, because intelligence reports suggested that the Left were planning to assassinate Perón. The security apparatus was in place on the night of 19 June. People were already arriving and camping out to await the big moment.

Vast crowds thronged into the area throughout the morning of 20 June. The atmosphere was that of a giant picnic with people of all ages beaming in anticipation of the great celebration, often bursting into song to the sound of big drums. Most of the crowd remained oblivious of the first incident at mid-day, next to the central platform, when there was a brief outbreak of shooting between the occupants of a jeep and members of the provincial police. Two policemen and three civilians were injured, and the police chief reacted by ordering all patrol cars out of the vicinity. In remoter areas, policemen were set upon and divested of their arms by unidentified groups. At about half-past-two, a huge column bearing banners of the *Peronista* Youth and Montoneros wove its way through the crowd towards the central platform, seemingly intent on taking up a position directly in front of where Perón would be. They were not far off when shooting broke out. Versions differ as to where it started, but within minutes there was pandemonium, with people scurrying for cover as shots were fired in both directions. Security men with shotguns and submachineguns fanned out from the platform, and the marchers retreated under withering fire. It was not so much a battle as a series of skirmishes, with the heavily armed bands of the Right sweeping through the neighbouring copses and buildings seeking their targets.

Suspects were roughly carried to the central platform for interrogation, or whisked away by car to the nearby airport hotel, where Osinde personally directed an improvised torture centre. Others, less fortunate, were lynched; literally torn limb from limb or hung from the trees.

Still the crowd did not leave. At four-thirty it was hysterically announced from the platform that there were snipers in the trees, and the first hail of bullets that ripped through the branches started a new, prolonged exchange that for the first time began to clear the area of terrified, confused onlookers. Perón's plane had already been diverted from its original destination, Ezeiza airport, to the more distant Air Force base of Morón. Until the last minute not even the officials gathered on the landing strip were informed of the change in plans, and then, with clashes spreading to the airport itself, only to be allowed an undignified scramble for airplanes hastily commissioned for a flight to Morón.

The obstinate, dejected stragglers at the motorway venue were not told that Perón would not be going there until half-past-five, when a helicopter had already whisked him away to the Presidential residence in Olivos. There had been millions at Ezeiza; not as many as the publicised six million, but certainly close to two. The millions more who had been following the events on TV were not shown pictures of the disturbances, then or later; only a few sound broadcasts conveyed the enormity of the confrontation. Casualty figures varied enormously: 13, 25, 100 dead; 100, 374, 500 wounded. The Left, who suffered the greatest number of losses (apart from the mass of innocent bystanders), insisted that the whole thing had been a carefully laid ambush, devised by Osinde and Ahumada, who had been spotted and photographed directing operations on the platform. The Right stuck to their story of a plot to murder Perón, and pointed as proof to the fact that their rivals had been armed and willing to fight. Official reports later mentioned the active participation of the non-*peronista* guerrillas, the ERP, to add substance to this claim. In any case, the Right had struck pre-emptively and with brutal thoroughness. The great carnival, a larger version of the historic 17 October 1945, had gone sour. Instead, Ezeiza had witnessed the first major battle of a war, still undeclared but certainly started with official sanction.

A day went by and night fell, one of the coldest of the year, before a stunned country got its first real sight, on TV, of a haggard Perón. He spoke slowly, his voice seemingly hoarser than usual. But there was no doubting the meaning of his message. He said:

Perhaps the beginning of our action may have seemed indecisive or lacking in precision. But we must keep in mind the circumstances in which we began. [. . .] We have a revolution to carry out, but for it to be valid it must be one of peaceful reconstruction, without costing the life of a single Argentine. [. . .] We must return to legal and constitutional order as the only guarantee of liberty and justice. There cannot be exclusive enclaves of any sort within the administration, and those who accept the responsibility of public office must demand the authority needed to defend it with dignity . . . .

There are no new labels to describe our doctrine and our ideology . . . It is not by shouting 'My Life for Perón' that one builds the Fatherland, but by maintaining our creed. The old *peronistas* know this. Nor is it ignored by our boys who raise revolutionary banners. Those with unconfessable aims, however much they may cover their false designs with deceitful shouting or scatter-brained fighting, cannot fool anyone. Those who do not share our principles, if they respect the verdict of the polls, have an honest path to follow in their struggle, which must be for the good and the greatness of the Fatherland, not for its disgrace. Those who naïvely think they can hijack our movement or wrest away the power which the people have reconquered, are mistaken. No dissembling and no covering up, however ingenious, can deceive a people that has suffered as much as ours and that is animated by a firm will to win. For these reasons I wish to warn those who attempt to infiltrate the ranks of the people or the state that they have chosen the wrong path. . .

To our covert, hidden or dissembling enemies, my advice is to cease and desist, because when the peoples run out of patience, they tend to bring down chastisement like thunder.

Unable to escape Perón's words, the unofficial organ of the Montoneros, *El Descamisado*, lamely riposted that it was not they who were departing from the true *peronista* creed, 'but the same people who have permanently betrayed the people and Perón; those who refused to support Cámpora's candidacy as ordered by the General; those who on Wednesday the 20th occupied the airport so that the General's airplane could not land, and who shot up the people so that Perón could not attend the rally.'

The youth did not turn tail at Perón's condemnatory words. Instead they organised a march of thousands to parade down to his residence, protesting their loyalty. Going against López Rega's express advice, Perón acknowledged the importance of the demonstration by inviting a group of youth leaders to step inside for a chat. He listened patiently while they essayed their arguments that others, and not they, were betraying the General and the movement. Then he sent them off with a few vaguely encouraging words which, however, did not basically alter what he had said before: that the youth must get in line. The radical *peronista* press played up the meeting for all it was worth, as proof that they had not been excommunicated.

At about this time the government, and more specifically José Ber Gelbard, Minister of the Economy, was granted full anti-imperialist credentials by the most unimpeachable source: the US embassy. For days the US chargé d'affaires, Max Krebs, had been putting pressure on Gelbard and on a number of Congressmen to withdraw the economic reform package which had been submitted to the legislature. Krebs made the mistake of conducting much of his lobbying in writing, thus giving Gelbard the perfect opportunity, when he judged the time to be ripe, to go public waving documentary evidence of this hamfisted attempt at US interference in the workings of Argentina's institutions. Gelbard had already been billing his policy package as a recipe for the 'rupture of dependence', under the slogan 'National Unity and Reconstruction with Social Justice for Liberation'. Krebs appeared on the scene as the best possible corroboration of these claims — which were played to the hilt by Gelbard and his supporters as a refutation of the Left's allegations that this was anything but a revolutionary anti-imperialist government.

Of the major newspapers, the ultra-conservative La Prensa had already been damning Gelbard's programme as unworkable; the conservative La Nación was still managing to be cautiously non-committal; and Clarín, reflecting the Frondizi-Frigerio line, had adopted a stance of 'critical support' in which there was more than a hint that the government's aims would be better served with the economic policies of desarrollismo. The only paper that appeared as a staunch supporter of Gelbard was Jacobo Timerman's La Opinión, which used the Krebs incident to portray the Minister as pitted against an unholy de facto alliance of the cattle-ranchers of the Sociedad Rural, the 'Marxist guerrillas' (interpreted at the time as meaning the ERP), the 'classist' trade unions, and the US embassy.

It suited many at the time to identify left-wing subversion with the Trotskyite ERP. Their hand was seen behind the continuing wave of abductions for ransom (at least a dozen were recorded in the last week of June), and their leader Roberto Mario Santucho had had the double effrontery, in an open press conference, of describing Perón as old, incompetent and non-revolutionary, and of announcing that his organisation would keep up the armed struggle. Two Buenos Aires television channels were fined for running excerpts of this press conference, and the incident led to a summons from the President's Press Secretary to the heads of all newspapers and radio and television stations to hear a barely disguised order from Perón not to publish any further information about the ERP.

The extreme right wing of *peronismo*, however, tended to make no distinction between the ERP and the *peronista* guerrilla organisations or, for that matter, the vast array of left-wing factions, within the *peronista* youth and the trade union movement. Indeed, their embryonic war was directed far more against the latter groups, and among them, against their more vocal, visible and less violence-prone exponents, than against the ERP 'combatants', who were usually, in any case, acting clandestinely, out of their reach. On the Left of *peronismo*, the common slogans and chants of rallies and marches tended to obscure the fact that there was a wide range of ideological expression at work. This went — to use current points of reference — from quite close to the attitudes embodied in the Gelbard programme to the radical proposals of the Montoneros and FAR guerrillas. The groups on the Left were by no means all committed to an armed assault on power, yet publicly they all shared a marked reluctance to disown the strong-arm tactics of the guerrilla organisations — even a propensity to glorify their deeds and to provide them with cover and alibis. The constellation of left-wing groupings that attracted the ire of the Right included the Juventud Peronista and its recently-sprouted labour branch, Juventud Trabajadora Peronista; the resuscitated secondary-school association Unión de Estudiantes Secundarios; Peronismo de Base, mainly an ideological power-house which had made some inroads in white-collar unions; the 'classist' rebel unions of Córdoba; and the FAR, FAP and Montoneros guerrilla organisations. Within the political establishment they had conquered positions of influence in the Ministries of the Interior and Foreign Relations, in the provincial governments of Buenos Aires, Córdoba, Mendoza and Catamarca, and in the universities.

Their adversaries on the Right included the '62' *peronista* unions, the Juventud Sindical Argentina, Juventud Peronista de la República Argentina, Alianza Libertadora Nacionalista, Comando de Organización, and Comandos Agrupados de la Resistencia Peronista. There was also the shadowy network of tough, fanatically anti-Communist 'security' men that spread out from López Rega's Ministry of Social Welfare to several minor government agencies and state enterprises.

The ministries and agencies in Gelbard's economic fiefdom were seen from the Left as part of the right-wing cabal, and certainly when dealing with the challenge from the Left before Perón, Gelbard and López Rega sought support from each other. Still, the *peronista* Right viewed Gelbard and his team with suspicion.

By the end of June the right-wingers were pursuing their offensive with vigour. They had engineered takeovers in several key radio stations and were actively stirring confrontation in the provinces of Buenos Aires and Córdoba, and in the universities. And they were busy, too, heightening the evident unease of high-ranking military officers at what they portrayed as unchecked, anarchic advances by the Left. Military unease there undoubtedly was (only days after Perón's arrival yet another high-ranking officer, Navy Commander Alberto González Riesco, had been murdered by guerrillas as he drove to work), but there was little military inclination to intervene. The events of 20 June at Ezeiza, which had marked the public emergence of a heavily-armed, organised Right (as murderous as the guerrillas, if not more) determined to settle the power struggle by force, were not viewed with particular apprehension. An admiral (destined for a key role in years to come) dismissed a journalist's anxiety at this development saying, 'You are missing the point. These chaps will do our dirty work for us, and when the time comes for us to take over again, we'll get rid of them together with the remaining Reds.'

Nor was Perón anxious to get the military involved at this stage. In early July he set about showing his own determination to re-establish order and strengthen the state, instructing Cámpora to push through Congress, at full speed, a tough bill penalising the possession of arms and explosives. Yet he stopped short of putting the full weight of his authority behind a major crackdown on the Left. They still served a purpose, as a powerful motive for his next political move, already being planned in a series of meetings with Gelbard and López Rega: the replacement of Cámpora in the Presidency by none other than himself, as the only person capable of stopping the country from sliding into chaos. And this step required military acquiescence.

Many analysts and participants close to the events have maintained that Perón had been truly reluctant to return to Argentina, apart from his yearning to end his years there, his role in history having already been vindicated by the re-establishment of *peronista* rule. Different people, but most frequently López Rega and Gelbard, have been credited with persuading Perón that his presence was politically indispensable. Even when he eventually agreed, the argument goes, he saw his role as that of the father-figure, removed from the daily chores of running his movement and the government. Again, López Rega, Gelbard and the union bosses are believed to have convinced Perón that his dream of a reconciled Argentina, with a strong state and renewed confidence in its international role, could only be secured with himself at the helm.

This fits with the image of the ailing old man favoured by the *anti-peronistas* and privately shared by the youthful *peronista* Left, though the latter expressed it elliptically by maintaining that Perón's actions could only be explained in terms of his having been 'fenced in' by the López Rega clique and the *vandoristas* of the trade union bureaucracy, and cut off from 'the people' — in direct contact with whom, they held, Perón would come alive as the true revolutionary leader of the masses. The unspoken key element of the 'fenced in' theory is that it presupposed a Perón unable to discern that he was being manipulated, or too weak-willed to assert himself and break out.

Yet there are factors that argue against this vision of Perón as the reluctant victim of circumstances and pressures. For one thing, his role as ultimate arbiter within his movement was one which he had carefully built up and consolidated through the years, preventing and frustrating the emergence of leaders who could command a following in their own right, playing one faction off against the other, obstructing the institutionalisation of his movement along traditional party lines in favour of the looser notion of a 'movement' wholly dependent for its cohesion on himself. The other factor is Perón's recurrent use, throughout his career, of the same political tactics: the feigned reluctance, the simulated weariness at the obduracy of warring factions, the gesture of resigning in hurt or disgust or despair, only to relent at the last minute, agreeing to sacrifice himself a while longer when all around him — preferably by tens of thousands in a public square — pleaded with him to reconsider.

In mid-1973, the *mise-en-scène* was prepared swiftly. The conservative *peronista* newspaper *Mayoría* ominously warned that the country was suffering the effects of a 'vacuum of power'. From a prominent union leader of Buenos Aires province, Victorio Calabró, came the pronouncement: 'Now that Perón is in the country, no one but he should be President.' On 10 July, Perón met General Carcagno, the Army commander, for a 'soldier-to-soldier' talk. The purpose: to secure the forces' agreement to the removal of Cámpora from office. The public sign of Army approval came the next day: at long last, the decrees were signed returning Perón his rank and uniform, of which an Army 'Tribunal of Honour' had divested him in 1955 on a charge of 'manifest unworthiness'. Opposition leader Ricardo Balbín of the UCR was informed personally by Perón. Then followed hurried meetings with the commanders of the Navy and Air Force, while behind the scenes the third in line to the Presidential succession, Senate leader Alejandro Díaz Bialet, was persuaded to take an unscheduled trip abroad. The decision was then communicated to Cámpora and his cabinet.

The next day, 13 July, all radio and television broadcasts were linked up to the official network, and information was kept to a minimum until the bombshell, anticipated already by the unfailing Buenos Aires rumour mills: Cámpora and Solano Lima had resigned, and in the absence of Díaz Bialet, the Presidency had been handed over to the fourth in line, the leader of the Chamber of Deputies, Raúl Lastiri. Following established custom, the ministers tendered their resignations. All were rejected, except for two: those of the ministers considered allies of the youthful Left, Esteban Righi (Interior) and Juan Carlos Puig (Foreign Relations). They were instantly replaced by two safe 'old' *peronistas*, Benito Llambí and Alberto Vignes.

Cámpora had gone after ruling for forty-nine days, and the way was now clear for elections which would undoubtedly fulfil the *peronista* dream of seeing Perón back in the Casa Rosada. Few had doubted that somehow, sometime, this would be bound to happen. For the *peronistas*, after all, this was what it had all been about. The Catholic journal *Criterio* wrote:

The logical thing would have been to celebrate the occasion with drums and cymbals. Yet Friday the 13th was a day of grave faces because all those who hovered around the seat of power knew that the official version of events was designed for the consumption of the faithful people, and not to provide the real explanation. [. . .] How was it that Cámpora and the youth miscalculated the situation? In believing that the group surrounding Perón was using him, and not the other way round; in believing that Perón is a prisoner forcibly isolated from 'his people'; in believing that, in Perón's eyes, López Rega is a traitor and Osinde a murderer; in believing, finally, that they [Cámpora and the youth] were called to administer the leader's charisma. In a movement that professes 'verticalism', that sort of mistake is paid for dearly. But here it was not only an internal faction of *peronismo* that lost; the country lost too, because institutions cannot be played with as unscrupulously as this.

The leader of the left-wing faction of the UCR, Raúl Alfonsín, thundered that what had happened was 'a coup of the Right'. Perón dismissed this, and the few other opposition voices raised in criticism, by proclaiming 'With Balbín at my side, I will go anywhere!'

Never was the word 'accidental' used more aptly to describe a Presidency than in the case of Raúl Lastiri. An advertising salesman for a Buenos Aires magazine, with no known political past, he was caught up in the whirlwind of a resurgent *peronismo* during the Lanusse era, after he left his wife and flung himself into a romance (eventually leading to his second marriage) with a young colleague called Norma, who happened to be the daughter of José López Rega. López Rega, then in charge of Perón's household in Madrid, at first disapproved of the match, and it took much persuasion by their friends to achieve reconciliation between father and daughter. It is said that López Rega finally relented when he was told that Lastiri was terminally ill, and that it would be cruel to impose on his daughter the distress of estrangement from her father on top of the loss of her lover. The occasion was marked by a pilgrimage of the couple to the Madrid residence, an event which hardly went unnoticed by those seeking favour with the man who controlled access to Perón. On returning to Argentina, Lastiri found himself courted and co-opted into *peronista* political circles. When elections approached, he was quite matter-of-factly included among the *peronista* candidates to Congress, in a safe enough position to guarantee him a seat. And when the time came, what better, safer choice than the son-in-law of 'Lopecito' for the delicate job of presiding over the Chamber of Deputies? Within weeks, this far-from-affluent newcomer to the political scene found himself being rewarded by 'first-hour *peronistas*' (among them a businessman who had had his factory shut down by the Perón administration in the 1950s) for his 'long years of deprivation in the struggle for the cause' with the gift of a full tailor-made wardrobe and of a comfortable apartment in Buenos Aires (another apartment in the same building went to his mother-in-law and the ground floor business premises to his father-in-law). And he, Raúl Lastiri, was — though he never dreamt that it would be more than a formality — fourth in line to succeed the President in case of the death, resignation or disability of the other three.

The main purpose of Lastiri's elevation to the Presidency was fulfilled seven days after his designation, when he formally announced the calendar for Perón's restoration to power: elections on 23 September, handover of the sash and baton on 12 October. Yet the ninety-one days of his unexpected mandate were to prove exceptionally testing, and for all his inexperience and the obvious limitations of his role, he managed to acquit himself with reasonable competence.

If there was one subject that remained taboo to *peronistas* of all colorations, it was that of Perón's advanced age and infirmity. Speculation on this matter, from whichever quarter it came, was angrily anathematised as *gorila*, unspeakably *antiperonista* (at a time when almost everyone took great care not to be seen as *antiperonista*). So it was that in approaching the most delicate *peronista* decision of this new electoral round, the selection of a Vice-Presidential candidate, the constitutionally intended role of the Vice-President (to replace the President should he die or become incapacitated) was never once brought into consideration. The matter did, however, become the focal point for arduous internal competition. Perón's choice of a running mate would be the clearest, most unequivocal expression of his future direction, of whether he was going to swing his movement to the Left or to the Right. Even the least publicly committed of those considered eligible for the job was carefully scrutinised. The date for the convention to proclaim the slate was set for 4 August, and despite the welter of speculation and rumour, no hint of the outcome was forthcoming. The suspense lasted right up to the moment when the gathering started. Then came the word: Perón had decided on Isabelita, his wife.

He had leapt over the horns of his dilemma and produced the one name which guaranteed no dissent or debate. He could not know it at the time, but in so doing he had sealed the fate of his movement for years to come. The decision that had been intended to avoid division merely forced it underground. *El Descamisado*, the organ of the *peronista* Left, wailed in a banner headline, 'Why Isabel?' Clinging to the belief in an 'isolated' Perón, the paper's editor Dardo Cabo wrote: 'Isabel has been the General's companion; we owe her affection for all these years in which she has filled our Chief's life with kindness. It is not because of her that we do not understand. [. . .] Allow us, General, after eighteen years as your soldiers, to express our confusion at this order. [. . .] We do not agree with it, but we remain silent, disciplined and trustful, and we shall carry it out. But we do not agree, leaving aside *compañera* Isabel herself, who deserves our respect and of whom we know that she does not intend to replace anyone, who has made her humility clear, and of whom we know that she is a soldier of yours. What we do not understand is . . . a line of conduct, a project of national unity which we feel endangered. [. . .] These are not the shouts of *provocateurs* who come to destroy, playing the enemy's game. Today more than ever we will be faithful to the instruction given us by Evita; we will be closer than ever to our General; we will not abandon him even if they come along cutting throats; and we will do as he orders. Of that you can be sure.'

The right wing of *peronismo* was overjoyed: the Left was in retreat.

However, only days later, the non-*peronista* Left struck hard, at the very heart of Buenos Aires. Shortly after midnight on 6 September, a van pulled up at the gates of the Comando de Sanidad Militar, headquarters of the Army medical corps. When its occupants announced that they were delivering a load of supplies, the van was ushered in. Suddenly, one of the conscripts on guard trained his gun on his comrades and disarmed them, as out of the van poured a uniformed ERP commando unit. They made straight for the guardhouse, where a lieutenant and a lance-corporal attempted to resist, but were shot down. After securing the installations, they unhurriedly set about raiding the arms depot.

Unknown to the attackers, two conscripts had slipped out of the compound and rushed to report the raid to the nearest police station. Within minutes the police had cordoned off the area, while across the city eighty men of the 1st Infantry Regiment and the 101st Battalion of Intelligence and Military Police were speedily mobilised for action. Before day broke the Army had ringed the compound, training machineguns and recoilless anti-tank guns on gates and windows. At 5.20 an officer used a loud-hailer to call on the guerrillas to surrender. Their answer was a volley of gunfire, to which the soldiers responded with a heavy barrage that sent the defenders scurrying back to the inner buildings.

Lieutenant-Colonel Raúl Duarte Ardoy, the Regiment's second-in-command, picked a handful of men and led them round the back of the compound to scale a wall and attempt an assault from the rear. As Duarte Ardoy forced open a back door of the Comando de Sanidad, he was shot in the stomach. His men retreated, carrying him with them.

Out in front, an officer gave the *guerrilleros* an ultimatum: either they surrendered within ten minutes, or the troops would overrun the Comando. After the briefest of pauses, the ERP men surrendered. Duarte Ardoy was already dying in hospital.

The guerrilla attack shook the military and the government. An immediate crackdown on the ERP was ordered, beginning with the arrest of Pedro Luis Cazes Camero, editor of *El Combatiente* (organ of the Partido Revolucionario de los Trabajadores, the ERP's parent party) and of *Estrella Roja* (the ERP's own paper). No sooner had this happened that an ERP faction abducted one of the managers of the daily newspaper *Clarín*. In exchange for freeing him, they demanded that the newspaper publish a front-page advertisement violently attacking López Rega, Gelbard and the union bosses. *Clarín* complied, and although the manager was released, the newspaper's premises were raided by an armed gang, who shot up the place before setting it on fire. The attackers were easily identified as men of the Unión Obrera Metalúrgica, the metal-workers' union.

Then came the elections. As expected, Perón won, with 61.8 per cent of the vote, followed by Balbín with 24.4 per cent and Manrique with 12.2 per cent. It was as if, in delayed action, the electorate were explaining what it would have done in March had there been a run-off. The non-*peronista* left-wing vote swung behind Perón; the right-wing vote went to Balbín rather than Manrique, who actually lost part of what he had gained in March. And almost the whole electorate chose between those three candidates; only 1.6 per cent of the vote went elsewhere, against 14.3 per cent in March.

There was jubilation among the *peronistas*, but not as much as in March, and certainly not as much as had been expected to mark the return of Perón to the Presidency.

The very day after the polls, the government issued a decree declaring the ERP illegal, and appointed a new chief of the Federal Police: retired General Miguel Angel Iñiguez, an old-time *peronista* who had been an inveterate plotter of revolts against military régimes in the 1950s and '60s. Iñiguez would find his plate full within hours of taking over his new post with a promise 'to guarantee the peace that the Argentine people have conquered through the ballot boxes'.

Mid-day of Tuesday 25 September, in the suburban district of Flores. José Rucci, secretary-general of the CGT, steps out of an unassuming house (one of the many secret places in which he had taken to sleeping on alternate nights). One of his bodyguards is already at the wheel of his car, the other at his side. Nothing seems amiss until, from nowhere, a smoke grenade arcs towards the windscreen, shattering it on impact. At that, the entire area round the car is raked with gunfire; the booming of a riot gun from a first-storey hoarding across the road, the rattle of sub-machineguns from a car showroom down the street and from the rooftop of the Maimonides Sephardic school next door. Rucci's body is riddled before he hits the ground. The driver is dead, slumped over the wheel. The other bodyguard, also injured, manages to slide under a parked car and loose a few hopeless shots at the unseen assailants. In a few minutes it is all over.

This was not the only incident of violence that day. Six men, brandishing submachineguns, had made away with a billion pesos' worth of goods from a warehouse at Ezeiza airport. A woman who had just finished tending the wounds of a criminal on the run was shot dead by him. A body found in a railway shed in Rosario, with head disfigured by two dum-dum bullets, was identified as Bautista Nava, of the Juventud Peronista. Police arrested one kidnapper in Buenos Aires, six in Córdoba, but there was no news of five other kidnap victims.

Rucci's assassination certainly found its way into the conversations of the politically-minded, together with the latest developments in Chile, where Salvador Allende's government had been ended thirteen days earlier by a bloody military coup. On this day the news from Chile was that the military there were rounding up Uruguayan exiles and shipping them back to Uruguay. But many more conversations turned to the evening match between Belgrano and Huracán football clubs in Córdoba; to how uninspiring the previous day's soccer victory over Bolivia had been; to the forthcoming world championship bout between local heavyweight Ringo Bonavena and George Foreman; to Carlos Monzón's coming encounter with the Frenchman Claude Bouttier; to Jorge Ahumada's victory by points over the Puerto Rican José González. Horse racing was normal in Palermo, but was interrupted at six in the evening in La Plata, as a sign of respect for Rucci. For the same reason, the Lottery of Mendoza decided to postpone its 8 million peso draw for one week.

For most, life in Buenos Aires that day was as usual. The Luna Park offered *Beriozhka*, a Russian dance spectacle by a troupe from the Bolshoi. The capital's twenty theatres presented a choice that ranged from Tchaikovsky at the Colón to Bertolt Brecht at the *Embassy* to burlesque at the Maipo. The sixty-one cinemas were as full as ever, with crowds flocking to see Costa Gavras' *State of Siege*, Pasolini's *Decameron*, Eisenstein's *October*, Zeffirelli's *Brother Sun, Sister Moon*, Roger Moore in *Live and Let Die*, Burt Lancaster and Alain Delon in *Skorpio*, Steve McQueen and Ail McGraw in *The Getaway*, Ingmar Bergman's *Cries and Whispers*, Edward Fox in *Day of the Jackal* and a couple of dozen other imported films. The lovers of local films could choose from the traditional fare, such as Luis Sandrini's latest comedy *Today it's my Wife's Turn*, or a couple of the more recent highly political productions, Fernando Solanas' *La hora de los hornos* ('The hour of the furnaces' — banned while the military were in power) and Jorge Cedrón's *Operación Masacre* (based on Rodolfo Walsh's book on the executions of 1956). The hundreds of restaurants, pizzerias and bars were full; the stalls along the Costanera avenue attracted the same number of people as usual with their aroma of sizzling beef. The night-clubs and *boîtes* — Mau-Mau still the most fashionable — kept going until the early hours of the morning.

For all the horror of the killings and the knowledge that armed men were stalking each other, for all the increase in police visibility (18,000 of them cast a dragnet over the suburb of Mataderos that night), Buenos Aires was still a city in which the streets could be walked at night.

The political reaction to Rucci's murder was one of shock. All sectors of the *peronista* movement, all political parties, expressed their revulsion. Dardo Cabo wrote in *El Descamisado*: 'All sectors of the Movement, including the Juventud Peronista and the Juventud Trabajadora Peronista, even the Juventud Universitaria Peronista; sectors from which came the harshest criticism of the methods Rucci used, have lamented this violence that put an end to the life of the CGT's secretary.' A day after the death of Rucci, the Right assassinated Enrique Grynberg, overtly a member of Juventud Peronista; at his funeral the coffin was placed under the Montoneros and FAR flags.

The ERP-22, one of the factions of the Trotskyite guerrillas, issued a communiqué denying any involvement in Rucci's death (a year later, Montoneros claimed responsibility for the killing). For publishing it, the daily newspaper *El Mundo* was shut down for three days, and television Channel 9 was fined. The press, particularly that of the Left, seemed to have moved into the line of fire. In the twenty-three days remaining before Perón's inauguration, bombs exploded in the offices of the newspaper *La Capital* in Mar del Plata and Rosario, gunmen raided *El Norte* of San Nicolás, injuring a journalist, the police confiscated an issue of *Avanzada Socialista* (organ of the Partido Socialista de los Trabajadores) in Tucumán, a bomb injured eight visitors to the offices of *Militancia* (an organ of Peronismo de Base). The government joined in the fray too; only days after announcing that it was sending the tax inspectors to examine the books of the private television stations, it abruptly cancelled the concessions for three television channels in Buenos Aires, one in Mendoza and one in Mar del Plata. Right-wing organisations which staged takeovers of the companies involved were complimented on their public-spirited action.

Suddenly it was 12 October 1973, and Juan Domingo Perón was being sworn in as President of Argentina for the third time in his life. As on the previous occasions, he wore his uniform: no longer the splendid gold-braided blue of the 1940s and '50s, but a more businesslike green.

22
PERÓN TO POWER
(1973–1976)

Perón's immediate aim was to strengthen the state. This was not an end in itself, but the necessary first step towards the fulfilment of one of his oldest dreams: an Argentina fully realising its potential, material and human, and moving to take its rightful place as a leading nation in Latin America and in the Third World as a whole. The main instrument to achieve Perón's purpose was the 'social compact', or more precisely a string of social compacts: between business and unions, between the federal government and the provinces, between the state and the agricultural sector, between the state and its enterprises. Conflicting interests, wherever they were to be found, would be settled round the negotiating table, and the settlements would be solemn and public. An important pre-requisite of this scheme was that the parties sitting round the different negotiating tables should be invested with as much legitimacy as they could possibly muster; only this could make the compacts enforceable.

His old creations, the CGT and the CGE, were obviously the vital pillars of this edifice. With Gelbard running the economy, it was an easy matter both to keep the CGE on the government's side and, within a very short while, to coax the rival Unión Industrial Argentina to cast aside its separate identity and merge with the Confederación General de la Industria (the CGE's industrial branch). The same did not happen with the farmers; the CGE's Confederación General de la Producción never managed to subsume the Sociedad Rural Argentina, the association of the country's largest landowners.

On the labour front, the CGT was challenged by the Marxist-led 'classist' unions of Córdoba, by what was left of Raimundo Ongaro's radical Christian influence, and by growing shop-floor militancy led by the *peronista* Left and particularly by the Juventud Trabajadora Peronista and Peronismo de Base. (The Montoneros guerrillas did not engage in union activism, but tried — not very successfully — to gain influence in the labour movement by selectively supporting strikes with the threat of armed action.) Therefore, the CGT needed reinforcing. This Perón promptly did, with a new 'Law of Professional Associations' that greatly enhanced the powers of the national union leaders and centralised the labour movement even more sharply that before. The length of the national leaders' mandates was doubled, from two to four years, and they were granted the faculty of 'intervening' in local branches and of overruling union decisions taken at factory level. No one was left in any doubt that this meant the beginning of a campaign to decapitate the rebel unions and nip in the bud the growth of shop-floor activism.

Perón concentrated on the broad outlines of his project, and on power politics when it was being played by large numbers or close to the centre of power (namely himself). He did not concern himself with the details of implementation; indeed, whenever he descended in conversation or in speeches to this level, he revealed that his grasp of the factors involved was decidedly infirm. 'I will keep away from economics,' he said, soon after re-entering the Casa Rosada, 'because that is a very complicated subject. You will not catch me saying yes or no, for that would lend itself to all sorts of interpretations.' But Perón could not resist 'saying yes or no' about almost everything. Even more than in the 1940s and '50s, he became the President-lecturer, expounding frequently and at great length before captive audiences — the union leaders, the heads of business associations, senior civil servants — on his vision of the future. His old ideas of the 'organised community' were dusted off and presented in their new guise of 'integrated democracy', with promises of corporate representation running in tandem with political parliamentarianism:

In organised communities people struggle for their interests. We are not going to play a game of chance among gypsies: it is interests that are paramount and it is interests that must be defended. In order to defend them we need organised communities, and this does not mean that we should have forty political parties. That would be a policy for disorganisation. There are other, non-political factors of power which must be made to weigh decisively in the life of the community. [. . .] Man expresses himself also in his condition as an intellectual worker, a businessman, a priest, et cetera. And as such he must participate in another kind of Chamber: the Council for National Projects which we shall create, aiming its efforts solely at that great task in which the whole country must become involved.

It was, in essence, the same idea for which Onganía had been anathematised as a 'corporatist' (only in this case, peronistas would say, it was being proposed with the people, not against them).

Perón also addressed himself to another favourite topic: 'continentalism'. After securing an 'organised community' at home, the formula went, the next necessary step was Latin American integration. This was an urgent task because, he said, 'the year 2000 will find us united or dominated.'

Most of his partisans, of whatever coloration, preferred not to listen too closely when Perón broached the subject of the economy. The industrialists of the CGE, and particularly Gelbard (whose programme was based largely on the redistribution of income away from the still effortlessly wealthy agricultural sector), found no comfort in Perón's view that Argentina had already achieved an adequate balance between countryside and city. The unions (and again the Gelbard team, who pinned many immediate hopes of expansion on the enlargement of the domestic market through income redistribution) were hardly exhilarated by Perón's adoption of the old conservative maxim that wealth had to be created before anyone could aspire to a larger slice of the cake. It is worth noting that *per capita* production in Argentina had been rising steadily (with only two hiccups, at the beginning and end of the Frondizi administration, which did not disturb the long-term trend) since the 1952 crisis, and by 1973 it stood almost 75 per cent higher than two decades before. On the other hand, the wage-earners' share of national income, which had peaked at 51 per cent in 1954, with Perón in power, had shrunk by at least 20 per cent in the following five years, then to inch forward roughly at the same rate as *per capita* production until 1968 — on the eve of the *cordobazo* — when it started shrinking again, most sharply in the last year of military rule.

Nor was the Left enthusiastic about Perón's definition of his government's role: 'The only thing that the *justicialista* government guarantees is that there will be no injustice in sharing out the benefits, and that each and every Argentine should have access to property, to dignity, to happiness.'

As for practicalities, on taking power Perón limited himself to a blanket approval of everything done so far by Gelbard, assuring the country that nothing would change. But Gelbard's programme was already running into difficulties. Inflation had been held in check, even apparently reversed, but by means of rigid price controls, rather ham-fistedly applied, and enforceable only in the higher reaches of industry, where accounting could easily be scrutinised. The big firms, in turn, demanded compliance from their medium-sized suppliers, sandwiching these between the official ceilings and the uncontrolled behaviour of their myriad small suppliers of small components, who demanded market values under threat of switching to more profitable lines of business. This was compounded by the 'scatterbomb' technique of import controls, which ignored industry's pleas for pragmatic selectivity in favour of simple rules for broad categories of products. Ridiculous bottlenecks appeared throughout the economy, as when the local subsidiary of Chrysler was forced to withhold delivery of its $6,000 cars because they lacked speedometers, delivery of which was in turn prevented by the lack of a transistor element worth about 40 cents because its importation had fallen foul of the official controls. To make matters worse, the sharp decline in the rate of inflation had taken interest rates from markedly negative values to sharply positive ones, discouraging the credit purchases which were expected to fuel the reactivation of the domestic market and placing a great strain on the finances of industry and commerce.

Defects in the official price controls also led to the loss of a vital opportunity to capitalise on the country's relatively comfortable external position. The price set for wheat was deemed unsatisfactory by scores of *chacareros* (small farmers), who switched to other crops. At a time of booming world prices for wheat, Argentina was not only unable to rake in a windfall; it was actually forced to import wheat to ensure domestic supplies. Nature added its own adverse contribution, in the form of massive flooding of the *pampas*, particularly severe in the areas devoted to fattening the herds — the country's other great export-earner. Prospects for 1974 were even grimmer, with one of the lowest-ever sowings of grains, and the beef industry out of kilter. Butchers began to rebel, periodically shutting down Buenos Aires' central market and neighbourhood shops, and more permanently joining the black market that was already spreading to other areas of supply.

Then came OPEC's first oil price shock, and the contry felt in very concrete terms the effects of not having closed the relatively small gap between local oil production and full self-sufficiency. For all the work put into the development of hydroelectricity, more than two-thirds of Argentina's power generation was still oil-fuelled. And the international ricochet of the higher oil prices was also felt, in the form of more expensive raw materials, intermediate products and capital goods for industry. Instead of gritting his teeth and passing the higher prices on to the final user, Gelbard played for time, granting special exchange treatment to importers for the sake of maintaining his officially-fixed domestic price levels.

The reason for this was a powerful one. The CGT had warned him that any upward adjustment of prices would have to be matched with wage increases. Granting this would have tarnished the image of rock-solid stability the government was hoping to attach to that cornerstone of the 'social compact' scheme, the agreement between unions, business and the state (apart from upsetting all of Gelbard's calculations for the next two years). Resisting it would mean ditching the agreement entirely, and this was even more unthinkable.

And there was no question of persuading the union bosses to withdraw their demands. If they were to stand a chance in their campaign against the rebel unions and the radical shop-floor activists, they needed at least to appear as defenders of the wage-packet. The labour scene was far from quiet; even with a *peronista* government, even with Perón himself as President, strikes were being recorded at the inordinately high rate of thirty-odd a month. The vast majority, so far, were motivated by protests against working conditions or against dismissals — containable issues, the union bosses reckoned, as long as they were not reinforced by the more explosive one of a falling pay-packet.

Gelbard was also having trouble of a different kind in Congress. In committee, his carefully interlocked package of economic reform bills was being pulled apart and degraded. Key aspects of the laws on foreign investment, industrial promotion and the import-export régime were being thrown out, their importance never understood, or replaced with less technical but more politically appealing formulas. The one pleasant surprise — the signals coming from the Sociedad Rural Argentina that it was willing to live with his tax on the 'potential yield' of the land — was a mirage. This unexpected tolerance was being expressed by leaders of the *Rural* whose activities were not concentrated wholly, or even largely, in agriculture, but were heavily involved in finance and even in industry. Had Gelbard watched more closely, he would have noticed that this attitude was not shared by CARBAP, the *Rural*'s affiliate that represented the most powerful 'pure' farming group in the country, those of the flatland provinces of Buenos Aires and La Pampa. And CARBAP's opposition would be skilfully translated into a filibuster, upheld by very reasonable technical arguments, to delay passage of that law indefinitely.

It was not that Gelbard's programme lacked critics. There was the Left, *peronista* and non-*peronista*, claiming from the heights of ideological abstraction that Gelbard's scheme did not differ substantially from the one attempted six years earlier by Adalbert Krieger Vasena, under Onganía (the same similarities, suprisingly, were detected by the conservative newspaper *La Nación*, but here they were motives for praise).

But the Left's opinion was to be discounted. There was also the ultra-conservative *La Prensa*, trotting out its much-used arsenal of condemnations against state interventionism and interference with the workings of the market. But opposition from *La Prensa* was predictable, and therefore also to be discounted. Moreover, the Gelbard team fell all too readily into the same sophistry as the Frondizi government in the late 1950s and early 1960s: simultaneous attacks from the Right and the Left, they said, only proved that they were on the right track.

Discreet but more acutely critical representations were being made from within the CGE itself, by the Confederación General de la Industria, by some of the people who had drafted Gelbard's policy package, by exporters, by the small farmers of the Federación Agraria Argentina. But these were not meant for public airing: it was *gorila* to mention black markets and supply bottlenecks, mistakes in implementation, or Perón's vagueness about the economic viability of his project. Julio Broner, head of the CGE since Gelbard had moved on to the Ministry of the Economy, aptly summed up the dominant attitude: 'People must learn to distinguish between constructive criticism and those who criticise the management of the economy.' (One small weekly that breached this consensus, *El Observador*, was forced out of circulation when the Ministry of the Economy put pressure on advertisers to withdraw their custom.)

Gelbard was not unaware of the hurdles ahead, but he felt confident that he could eventually turn the situation around, so he played for time. Printing money was, in the circumstances, an attractive choice for the time being, but the waiting period was to be extended indefinitely, and Gelbard's decisions of late 1974 were already locking the Argentine economy into a self-destruct mechanism.

Late 1974 was also the time when the ERP made a fateful decision: to shift towards rural guerrilla operations, opening a front in Tucumán province, and to start planning assaults on major military targets. And it was the time when the right-wing gunmen, after the car of Senator Hipólito Solari Yrigoyen (UCR) had been blown up, decided to adopt the name Alianza Anticomunista Argentina or AAA (never more than a public label, it had been used once before, some years earlier, by a group that tried to abduct a Soviet diplomat).

And it was also the time when one of the larger units of the left-wing Juventud Peronista, Regional I, led by Juan Carlos Dante Gullo, tried to demonstrate that the youth were not only able but willing to get involved in constructive work. They organised hundreds of volunteers to work alongside Army units in salvage and reconstruction work in the areas most severely damaged by the recent floods. For a time, once the Army's initial apprehensions had been overcome, it seemed as if they had succeeded in exorcising the demonic image they had gained in military eyes. The chief of Army operations in the area, one Colonel Albano Harguindeguy, was full of praise for the selfless dedication of the youth. The Commander-in-Chief, General Jorge Raúl Carcagno, who had already been cultivating a populist image with his slogan of 'Army-People unity', was equally enthusiastic. But it was too late.

General Carcagno was soon to lose his job as Army chief. Some attributed Perón's decision to replace him to the fact that Carcagno had become tainted by association with the Cámpora administration, that he had been too willing to 'peronise' himself, and that this was not what Perón wanted to see in the Army of his 'organised community'. This seemed to be confirmed by Perón's choice of a replacement, General Leandro Enrique Anaya, who in the current jargon of political analysts was described as a representative in politics of *profesionalismo prescindente*, 'the professionalism that does not take sides'. But there were also those who interpreted the move differently, as more in keeping with Perón's old habit of preventing the emergence of figures enjoying too much popularity — and a general who seemed to be finding favour with the radical youth was certainly one such figure.

And the campaign against the Left was already on its irreversible way. Completing a full circle from a year earlier, when he used the radical youth to overcome resistance to his electoral plans by the 'defection-prone bureaucrats' of the CGT, Perón now proclaimed, 'The CGT can rest safe and secure with the leadership it has, *even though some fools say that they are bureaucrats.* [. . .] I know these leaders, not from now, but from thirty years back.'

When the ERP guerrillas launched a large force against the barracks of the 10th Armoured Cavalry Regiment in Azul (killing the commander, Colonel Camilo Gay, and his wife, and abducting and later murdering Lieutenant-Colonel, Jorge Roberto Ibarzábal, before being repulsed), Perón took advantage of the occasion to demand the resignation of the governor of Buenos Aires province, Oscar Bidegain, seen as too close to the radical youth. Bidegain was replaced by Victorio Calabró, a union stalwart, who promptly started purging the provincial administration of suspected left-wingers. The attack on Azul led Perón to change his line on the ERP, whom he had hitherto dismissed as a minor 'police matter': 'This is no longer a matter of gangs of delinquents,' he said, 'but of an organised group, acting under foreign direction and with foreign aims, attacking the state and its institutions. [. . .] Annihilating this criminal terrorism as soon as possible is a task for all of us who desire a just, free and sovereign Fatherland.' He followed this instantly by pushing through Congress a bill reforming the Penal Code — basically reinstating the 'subversive' crimes, requiring severe penalties, that the Cámpora administration had thrown out on the very day of its accession to power. The newspaper *El Mundo* was withdrawn from circulation for publishing an ERP communiqué on the Azul coup, while the right-wing gangs which operated from the shadows took matters further, bombing a printing press in Buenos Aires, and the premises of the newspaper *La Capital* of Rosario.

Perón now openly directed his wrath at the radical youth of his own movement: 'The youth, just the same as all Argentines, have the right to think and feel as they please. This is an inalienable right of the individual in a democracy, which is what we are defending. What is unacceptable is saying that we are one thing when we are possibly another. Those who wish to go on fighting are going to be beyond the law, because there is no fighting any longer in this country. If there is any fighting to be done, I will decree mobilisation and this will end rapidly; we'll call on all to fight in an organised fashion, wearing the uniforms and bearing the arms of the Nation. [. . .] The problem now is to see who are *justicialistas* among the youth, and who are not.' And then came formal excommunication, when he addressed the dissenters: 'What are you doing in *Justicialismo*? If I were a Communist, I would go to the Communist Party!' *El Descamisado*'s editor, Dardo Cabo, spokesman for the left-wing youth, retorted: 'Why didn't they tell us earlier, when we were fighting against Lanusse, that we had to join another party? No one has the right to throw us out! No one has the right to dismiss us!'

The campaign to drive out leftists from all positions of influence moved on, in a highly unusual fashion, to Córdoba. There the Chief of Police, retired Colonel Domingo Antonio Navarro, took it upon himself to dislodge the governor, Ricardo Obregón Cano, and his deputy, Atilio López, by means of an armed police coup. Instead of moving against this blatant act of sedition and reinstating the deposed officials, President Perón validated the rebellion and appointed a federal trustee to run the province.

In March the labour front counter-attacked. The metalworkers of the Acíndar steelworks at Villa Constitución downed tools for the reinstatement of three dismissed shop stewards and for the right to elect their own regional authorities, which had been postponed for four years already by the national union leadership. The union bosses in Buenos Aires responded by expelling the strike leaders, but other factories in the area came out in sympathy with them. The Labour ministry intervened, containing the conflict by ordering a settlement in the strikers' favour. Perón moved swiftly, too, to avert a threat of further labour unrest, this time for higher wages, by decreeing a blanket rise which only barely bought acquiescence from the CGT while further upsetting Gelbard's scheme. This sign of vulnerability prompted the radical youth to try to recover lost ground with the one weapon still at their command, their ability to put people on the streets.

On May Day the Juventud Peronista and Montoneros turned out in full strength, by the tens of thousands, to attend the mass rally called by Perón in front of the Casa Rosada. On their own they filled almost a third of the square. This was the magic moment they had awaited for so long, an opportunity of direct contact, of dialogue between the Leader and his people. This was a leap over the 'fence' they imagined López Rega and the union bureaucrats had set up around Perón. It was an axiom of *peronista* theory, encouraged by Perón himself, that the Leader would respond to the demands of the masses. In the best *peronista* tradition, the 'dialogue' was conducted by interrupting Perón's speech — as usual dotted with appropriate pauses — with thunderous chanting and waving of banners. This May Day they sang:

> *Si Evita viviera*
> *sería Montonera!*
> (If Evita were alive/ she would be a Montonera!)

> *Asamblea popular;*
> *no queremos carnaval!*
> (Popular assembly;/ we don't want Carnival!)

> *Qué pasa?*
> *Qué pasa?*
> *Qué pasa, General,*
> *que está lleno de gorilas*
> *el gobierno popular?*
> (What's the matter?/ What's the matter, General,/ that the people's government/ is so full of *gorilas*?)

The Leader responded. He was almost apoplectic. 'In spite of those stupid ones who are shouting', he fumed, 'the unions have remained sound for twenty-one years — and now it turns out that some beardless youths claim more merit than those who worked for twenty years!' He called them *idiotas útiles* (useful idiots, the Spanish-language equivalent of Trotsky's *poputchiki* or 'fellow travellers'), and 'mercenaries in foreign pay'. His rage increased when the youths, without waiting to hear the end, turned their backs on him and marched out of the square, drums beating, banners waving, the chants resounding even more loudly, 'It's the people walking out!' Television cameras were hurriedly averted, new angles were sought so that the public in their homes would not see the huge, insulting bare patch in the Plaza de Mayo. Perón thundered, 'Let everyone go to his combat station, for if these reprobates do not desist, then *we* will begin!'

It was a rhetorical promise, for *they* had already begun. The right-wingers now had everything they needed: confirmation from Perón himself that the radical youth of *peronismo* was the same thing as the outlawed ERP — foreign mercenaries, people who belonged in the Communist Party — and the government was unequivocally on their side. The authorities shut down *El Mundo, El Descamisado* and *Militancia*, all by executive fiat (in the ensuing weeks the government would ignore court rulings against it, as well as the rising groundswell of protest from all quarters of the opposition against these and other attacks on the press).

The mass of the population seemed to have been made incapable of shock by the succession of acts of violence; stupefied into a fatalistic acceptance of the fact that strife, violent strife, would be with them until the balance tilted decisively in favour of one faction or another. Yet they would soon discover that there remained some capacity for horror, and for apprehension at the promise of worse to come.

On 10 May 1974 it was already dark when Father Carlos Mugica finished saying Mass. The scion of a distinguished family, this priest had given up a promising career in the church (as the Archbishop's secretary he was being groomed from an early age for a high positon in the Argentine hierarchy) to go and minister to the people of Buenos Aires' largest shantytown, which sprawled between the Retiro railway terminal and the port. He was one of the founders and leaders of the Third World Priests movement, which sought to put into practice the church's 'preferential option for the poor'. From an early advocacy of a socialist future for Argentina, Mugica and his movement had shifted to support for *peronismo*, although he refused an offer to run as a Frejuli candidate for Congress, and later spurned an appointment at the Ministry of Social Welfare when he found himself in disagreement with López Rega's paternalistic approach to the problem of the shantytowns,

the *villas miseria*. Mugica, who had been very close to the radical *peronista*
youth, had lately become concerned at the split between them and Perón.
After the May Day fracas, he had swung the Third World Priests solidly
behind Perón and plunged headlong into the task of persuading the
youth to set aside their differences with the old man. For this purpose he
had even decided to return to journalism, asking Jacobo Timerman to
give him back his old column at *La Opinión*. A couple of days earlier he
had delivered his first article.

As Mugica stepped out on to the pavement, chatting to some par-
ishioners, a figure came out of the shadows and opened fire on him with a
submachinegun at point-blank range. Mugica did not die instantly.
Another priest managed to rush to his side and administer the last rites.
He caught his last words: 'Now we must be closer to the people than
ever.'

No-one claimed credit for the assassination. The Left blamed it on the
Right. The Right blamed it on the Left. Timerman recalled a recent conversation in which Mugica had spoken of having received death threats
from Montoneros, 'though on reflection', he added, 'he seemed more
concerned about [Montonero leader] Firmenich's safety than his own.'
A prominent independent politician, Basilio Serrano, said, 'This is the
first time we have witnessed a murder designed solely to provoke'. Five
years later, a military government published a heavy tome entitled *El
terrorismo en la Argentina* which listed Mugica's death, not under 'Persons
murdered by terrorist delinquency' (i.e. the Left) but under 'Delinquent
acts executed by the AAA and other extremist elements'.

That same month, the Army commander, General Anaya, proclaimed
that he was ready to place his services at the government's disposal in the
war against subversion. The first Army units were quietly mobilised,
next to the Federal Police and the Gendarmería, to fight the ERP in
Tucumán.

Within days, the enormity of Mugica's murder was eclipsed by
another fear. Perón, it was rumoured, was gravely ill. At first there were
the usual angry reactions from the *peronistas*, who considered it almost
blasphemous to mention Perón's health, let alone speculate about it.
Because everything revolved around Perón's presence at the helm, this
was the one thing *peronistas* refused most steadfastly to contemplate. It
had been for so long one of the dearest hopes of the *antiperonistas* that
Perón would die, and with him his movement, that the subject itself was
rejected as *gorila*. Yet this time, although official confirmation was slow
in emerging, the creeping numbness caused by the whispered news

seemed to testify to its truth. After Perón, what? Reluctantly, painfully, the forbidden question began to circulate, but there did not seem to be either the imagination or the will to provide an answer. A shiver ran through the body politic as Isabelita was summoned back, in the middle of a European tour, to stand in for the bedridden President. Then, all too soon, on the first day of July 1974, Perón was dead.

The three days of mourning dragged on interminably, with newspapers forced by the printers' union to publish only stories about Perón's death and reactions to it at home and abroad, and reminiscences or panegyrics about Perón's life. Even now, there was extreme reluctance to let him go. The numbness was driven home by page after page in the newspapers carrying the same government advertisement (the only difference being the title of the government agency in whose name it was inserted):

'I came to the country to launch a process of National Liberation; I came to the country to unite the Argentines' (Lt.-Gen. Perón, before the People gathered on 12 June in Plaza de Mayo). The State Secretariat of _____ shares in the pain afflicting the Argentine People at the death of the Most Excellent Señor President of the Nation, Lieutenant-General Don Juan Domingo Perón.

At this time of grief, when all sectors of the country unite to bid farewell to the mortal remains of him who was their Leader beyond any partisan banner or partiality, the Secretariat underlines the responsibility of all Argentines to solidify National Unity in order to complete the process of Reconstruction and Liberation, as proposed and initiated by General Perón. This is the legacy left to his People by the Leader who passed into immortality on 1 July 1974.

The road ahead is clear and allows of no deviation: it was mapped out by the National Constitution and by the will of the Republic's citizens. It is total support for the administration now initiated by the Most Excellent Señora President of the Nation, Doña *María Estela Martínez de Perón*. Her task begins amid the greatest of sorrows, but also with great stimuli: the exemplary memory of General Perón and the trust of her People.

Isabelita took office, bolstered by a massive show of support from all political parties whose leaders, from Ricardo Balbín all the way down the popularity scale, swallowed their misgivings about the lady's ability to rule and their hearty dislike of her and her unavoidable shadow, José López Rega, for the sake of preserving the fragile edifice of recently restored constitutional rule. Then reality returned.

Isabelita's government was barely into its second week when the nation went into mourning again. Arturo Mor Roig, who had been Minister of the Interior under Lanusse and retired after having completed his task of piloting the country back to elected rule, was assassinated as he sat down to lunch in a restaurant at San Justo, outside Buenos Aires. Initial newspaper reports identified the assassins with the euphemism imposed by official censorship: 'an extremist organisation declared illegal', meaning the ERP. Later, however, the crime — a pointless revenge killing — was attributed to Montoneros.

From that moment on, it was virtually open war. The ERP unit operating already in Tucumán decided to test its fighters in an incursion against the 17th Paratroop Regiment in the neighbouring province of Catamarca, hoping to make off with a haul of some 300 rifles. On their way they were surprised by the provincial police, and after an armed clash in which three *guerrilleros* were killed and two policemen injured, the raiders fled. Police and Army units fanned out over a wide area, reaching into the department of Famaillá in Tucumán (one of the ERP's rural base areas), and within the day had captured thirteen members of the guerrilla party. Almost simultaneously, another large ERP unit launched an assault against the Army explosives factory in Villa María, province of Córdoba. Although here too the attack was detected in its preparatory stages and provincial police engaged the guerrillas before they had reached their objective, the ERP men pushed on, achieving their purpose of raiding the factory's arsenal and making off with a large haul of military equipment. In their retreat they took as hostages a captain (released soon afterwards, badly mauled) and a major, later murdered. In the encounter the attackers lost at least three men and the provincial police one.

The government responded by passing a Law of National Security, which stiffened penalties for crimes of subversion, and by re-imposing the state of siege. In a parallel action, the AAA launched a wave of political killings, choosing their victims from among known left-wing politicians and intellectuals, and among student and union activists. In the ten days following 31 July they killed five people, including Rodolfo Ortega Peña, a national deputy identified with Peronismo de Base. In September there were seven killings, including the former deputy governor of Córdoba, Atilio López; the former police chief of Buenos Aires province (and one of the few survivors of the botched illegal executions of 1956), Julio Troxler; and Silvio Frondizi, a brother of the former President Arturo Frondizi. A pattern began to emerge in the operations of the right-wing murder squads. Armed men claiming to belong to the police or one of the security forces would abduct their victims, from their homes or in the streets, and drive away in unmarked cars, often the sturdy Ford Falcons. Unusually for the heavily guarded and patrolled Argentina of the day, the areas where the abductions took place were conspicuously lacking in police presence. The bodies would appear hours or days later, lying in parks or rubbish dumps. Twenty more right-wing killings were reported before the end of 1974, increasing in gruesomeness (bodies charred, or with visible signs of torture, or with their hands cut off) as they did in numbers, and — a new twist — the victims began to be drawn from the Chilean exile community.

Within the union movement, the latter half of 1974 saw the intensification of the campaign by the CGT bosses against the leaders of rebel unions. Within weeks René Salamanca lost control of the Córdoba metalworkers, Agustín Tosco of the Córdoba electricians, Raimundo Ongaro of the graphic workers in Buenos Aires, Guillán of the telephonists. Keeping step with the union bosses, the federal government purged the provincial government of all remaining suspected left-wingers. One after the other, Isabelita ousted governors Martínez Baca of Mendoza, Cepernic of Santa Cruz, Ragone of Salta, Mott of Catamarca. Throughout the country, the press media were subjected to intense pressure, in the form of threats, suspensions or closures by the government, or in the more fearsome form of bomb attacks, abductions and death threats by the AAA and allied right-wing groups.

Escalation by the Right was matched by escalation from the Left. Montoneros continued with abductions for enormous ransoms (that of the brothers Born, heads of one of Argentina's largest grain exporting concerns, yielded no less that US$60 million) and with highly spectacular assassinations: within weeks the chief of the Federal Police, Comissioner Alberto Villar, was blown up together with his wife as he set off for a cruise in a launch, and his successor, Commissioner Margaride, narrowly escaped death when a landmine exploded prematurely under his car. The ERP, however, continued to build up its forces in two departments of Tucumán and to conduct minor raids throughout the country.

In the midst of all this, Isabelita dumped Gelbard from the Economy Ministry, replacing him with an old-time *peronista*, Alfredo Gómez Morales, who had sorted out the crisis faced by the second *peronista* administration in 1952. Gelbard could claim credit for two years of considerable economic growth (5.8 per cent in 1973 and 6.3 per cent in 1974), for having cut back unemployment by almost two-thirds while he was in office, and for having increased the wage-earners' share of the national income to 42 per cent, very near the range of the Perón administration of the 1950s. But inflation was clearly picking up speed (reaching an annual rate of about 40 per cent by the time he was removed from his post), and the peso had become grossly overvalued, stimulating imports and playing havoc with the plans to promote exports of manufactured goods (one of Gelbard's achievements had been the opening of a number of new markets, including Cuba, which he entered against the express wishes of the United States, selling US-designed but Argentine-built motor vehicles). Investment was drying up, and the unions were getting restless. Shortly after taking office, Gómez Morales threw them a sop in the form of a 15 per cent wage rise, but this was soon gobbled up by the inexorable, now uncontrolled rise in prices. He devalued the peso, but in spite of the magnitude of the cut (the price of the US dollar rose by 50 per cent) it did not succeed in curing the imbalance already created by inflation.

Within a few months, Gómez Morales had to face a second Villa Constitución strike that lasted two whole months and threatened at times to spread to the entire metalworking sector. No sooner was this over than he had to face the CGT's annual bout of wage bargaining. He argued for restraint, but Isabelita overruled him for pressing political reasons — she badly needed to keep the unions on her side. She granted the unions a 38 per cent wage increase, and Gómez Morales resigned.

The war, meanwhile, was increasing in intensity. In late 1974 the Montoneros leadership suddenly announced that they were going underground to continue the fight against the régime. So sudden was the announcement that it caught thousands of members of 'surface' organisations unprepared, leaving them exposed to reprisals from the government as well as from the right-wing armed bands. Politically-motivated killings began to multiply at an overwhelming rate. Newspapers no longer paid attention to 'minor' abuses of authority or human rights violations such as abductions if the victims were set free alive. The public verdict in those cases was that 'nothing had happened', even though the victim, as was often the case, had been tortured in the process — something that had become 'normal'.

The deaths quickly became mere statistics. Later military figures recorded forty-four political murders between March 1973 and July 1974 (the month Perón died) and 284 between then and March 1976. Of the latter figure, ninety-four cases are listed as attributable to the AAA and other right-wing groups, between May 1974 and April 1975 — the count being inexplicably interrupted at this point. The Catholic magazine *Criterio* listed 501 political killings in the year following Perón's death, while Amnesty International, in different sets of figures, mentions over 300 political killings in 1974 alone, and 461 between July 1974 and June 1975 — pointing out that of the latter figure two-thirds were attributable to the right-wing murder squads. In yet another set of figures, Amnesty International's Annual Report for 1975-6 mentions the AAA as being responsible for more than 2,000 deaths since 1973, and for more than 133 abductions in 1975.

The *peronista* Left had coined a term to describe the Isabelita administration: *brujovandorismo*. If translatable at all, it would be something like 'warlock-Vandorism', the alliance of the 'warlock' López Rega (alluding to his penchant for the occult) and of the union bosses, identified as heirs of Augusto Timoteo Vandor. López Rega's star had certainly risen fast. In addition to the Ministry of Social Welfare, he had secured an appointment as 'private secretary' to the President — in effect, the power behind the throne. One of his aims was to involve the military as much as possible in the war against the Left. The first step was to hand over to them the sole responsibility for operations against the ERP in Tucumán; this went into effect in February 1975, aided by a complete news blackout (indeed the Presidential decree authorising military involvement describes the Presidential Press Secretariat's role in the operation as that of carrying out 'the necessary psychological action'). The next step was to be the creation of a National Security Council, which would give the military overall control, countrywide, of 'anti-subversive' operations. This project was enthusiastically supported by the Commander-in-Chief of the Navy, Admiral Emilio Massera, who moved into the breach when the Army high command, though approving the idea in principle, refused to appoint an Army man for the task. Massera tried to persuade an old friend, an admiral posted abroad, to take on the job, and when the latter refused, packed him off into premature retirement.

The next man to lose his job was the Army Commander-in-Chief, General Anaya, who was replaced by General Alberto Numa Laplane, a proponent of 'integrated professionalism' — meaning closer identification of the armed forces with the government in power. It was at about this time that Alfredo Gómez Morales resigned as Minister of the Economy, and López Rega moved into that breach as well, securing the appointment for one of his cronies, Celestino Rodrigo.

Though already punch-drunk from the buffeting by daily, barely comprehensible acts of violence, the country was left breathless by the enormity of the measures Rodrigo, without warning, pulled out of his hat. He decreed a devaluation that increased the price of the US dollar by

100 per cent, doubled the officially-set prices for fuels and public services, and announced sweeping budget cuts, the freeing of prices and a tight lid on wage increases. This policy package and several of its intended adjuncts (better official prices for agriculture, giving incentives to private investment, curbing the power of the national unions), was the mirror-image of a plan which had been prepared over the previous weeks by a team of conservative economists, commissioned by some high-ranking military men in the expectation of a coup.

What the Rodrigo plan did achieve was the break-up of the two components of *brujovandorismo*. The union bosses indignantly withdrew their acceptance of the wage offer that had led Gómez Morales to resign. The new minister offered to increase it to 45 per cent, but was sharply rebuffed: the unions demanded free bargaining. When it was conceded, the negotiations produced agreements on rises ranging from 80 to 200 per cent. The unions organised a massive demonstration to press Isabelita into ratifying the agreements. She appeared to agree, then suddenly annulled the results of the negotiations and offered instead a blanket rise of 50 per cent, to be followed a year later by another 15 per cent. For the first time, that creature of Perón, the CGT, struck against the government, with a tacit addendum to its wage demands: the resignations of López Rega and Rodrigo. The unexpected union challenge bolstered the demands, already gaining ground in Congress, that López Rega should be called to account for a number of blatant instances of corruption and for the previously unspoken but widely held assumption that he was personally responsible for the direction of the AAA murder squads. Isabelita appealed for support from the Army, but her 'integrated professional' commander, General Numa Laplane, refused to intervene.

Isabelita buckled under the pressure. She ratified the freely negotiated wage settlements, giving inflation a momentous boost as well as driving a number of firms to the wall. She jettisoned Rodrigo, but did not give in to Congressional demands to hand over López Rega. Instead she relieved him of his positions as minister and Private Secretary to the President, and gave him an undefined posting abroad. In the ensuing cabinet reshuffle, she pursued López Rega's policy line of drawing the armed forces into closer involvement with the government by appointing a serving colonel, Vicente Damasco, as her new Minister of the Interior. This sparked off a row in the Army, with the generals giving Colonel Damasco an ultimatum: to resign his post as minister or retire from active duty within two months. Damasco chose to stay on as minister, and the Army hierarchy vented its spleen instead on the Commander-in-

Chief, General Numa Laplane, forcing him to resign. No sooner had the new Commander-in-Chief, General Jorge Rafael Videla, taken over than he pressed Damasco into leaving his cabinet post.

The strain was too much for the President. She requested leave of absence on grounds of ill-health, and was duly replaced by the leader of the Senate, Italo Luder. During his brief interlude in power, Luder formally announced the military takeover of the war against subversion, and attempted, with the aid of Antonio Cafiero in the Ministry of the Economy, to find a 'gradualist' way out of the economic debacle. The project floundered on the CGT's inability to get its members to stomach a 'social truce' which would have implied postponing wage demands and banning strikes. Pressure from the grassroots was aggravated by the fact that the guerrilla groups were using the threat of armed action to settle industrial disputes.

Confounding those who hoped she was gone for good, Isabelita returned to the Casa Rosada, cocking a snook at Congressional demands that she too should be brought to account for her involvement in misuse of public funds. The *peronista* bloc in Congress was by now deeply split, and it began to seem as if Isabelita could no longer count on an automatic majority. The CGT was also split, with an apparent majority in favour of finding a way to remove Isabelita from office. She conceded the difficulty of her position by agreeing to bring forward the date for the next Presidential elections to October 1976. In December 1975 she survived a coup attempt by a nationalist Air Force officer, Brigadier Jesús Capellini, but it was widely felt that this was just a temporary reprieve. Almost everyone had become convinced by then that a military coup was inevitable, and that the Brigadier had merely jumped the gun.

Meanwhile the underground war was fast approaching a turning-point. In August the Montoneros had achieved an important propaganda coup by striking at the heart of the military counter-insurgency operations in Tucumán. They blew up a Hercules transport plane as it was taking off, killing six soldiers of the Gendarmería and injuring another twelve. In early October they mounted the largest and most ambitious operation in their history: an attack on an infantry regiment in the northeastern province of Formosa, deploying seven guerrilla 'platoons' for an assault on the barracks to capture weaponry, a simultaneous assault on a prison to free incarcerated comrades, and the hijacking of a Boeing 737 to secure their getaway by flying across two provinces and making a forced landing on a farm. The attack was repulsed, and the Montoneros lost at least sixteen of their guerrillas, although the retreat was carried out as planned. The Montoneros boasted in a communiqué that 'with this action our Organisation begins to develop a regular Army . . . which will allow the conquest of power in the Fatherland,' but this was their last major engagement. From then onwards, clearly under pressure from the security forces, they returned to more rudimentary terrorist actions, such as the assassination a month later of yet another chief of the Federal Police, General Jorge Cáceres Monié, together with his wife.

The ERP surfaced again in December 1975 for a major attack on an Army arsenal in Monte Chingolo, south of Buenos Aires. A hundred or more guerrilla fighters were deployed for this operation, which was repelled after they had lost almost half their men. For the ERP too, this was the last major engagement before reverting to minor terrorist actions. The Army had broken the back of the ERP's rural guerrilla units in Tucumán, and by the end of 1975 considered that all it had left to do in the area was to mop up the stragglers. This, however, was not announced publicly — a deliberate act of policy by the military, as high-ranking officers were to admit some years later.

Isabelita had only ten more months to go before the electorate, in which the key feature was a profoundly divided *peronismo*, was to issue its verdict. Congress, only barely deadlocked in her favour, echoed with demands for investigations into official corruption, all the way up to the President herself. The country's prisons were full, with over 3,000 political detainees over and above the common criminal population. The major guerrilla organisations were, according to the military, in retreat, and the military themselves were in complete charge of all counter-insurgency activities. The clandestine abduction-and-murder operations were still continuing on a large scale, but at some point since López Rega's departure those shadowy armed gangs that had once been known as AAA had been co-opted by the military.

A number of politicians toyed with the idea of getting Italo Luder, as leader of the Senate, to convene an assembly of both chambers of Congress to impeach and remove Isabelita as a first step towards cleaning up the government and reaching election day with at least the country's institutions in order. Luder himself thought the venture hopeless, apart from being of doubtful constitutionality. He was convinced that the military had already made up their minds, and were just awaiting the appropriate moment to move and depose the government. A parallel suggestion was made to the military by Isabelita, now surrounded by a new, conservative cabinet: that Congress should be dissolved and that she should continue as the figurehead President of a new régime, run in practice by the military themselves. The idea did not prosper.

Inflation was running at more than 300 per cent in a year; production was dropping sharply. The image of economic chaos was compounded by the cattlebreeders' decision to withhold their stock from the markets, followed by the industrialists' decision to stage a countrywide lockout. The Executive and Congress were deadlocked, making no attempt to grapple with the economy or to act against corruption. The fear of the guerrilla threat was still alive. When the usual harbinger of coups, the evening newspaper *La Razón*, started running a series under the headline 'The Political Crisis', the picture was complete: everyone knew that a military takeover was just around the corner.

In the last few weeks, however, anticipation of the coup began to produce, ahead of schedule, one of the most predictable effects of military rule in Argentina — a gradual closing of *peronista* ranks — if not this time behind their leader, at least in face of the challenge from without. Ahead would lie, yet again, the years of proscription, but when they ended — as end they must — the country would find once more that *peronismo* had been preserved for yet another round.

Night had fallen on 23 March 1976 when President María Estela Martínez de Perón drove from the Casa Rosada to the metropolitan airport, whence a helicopter would carry her home to the residence at Olivos. When she stepped out of her car, an Air Force officer approached her, saluted, and politely informed her that she was no longer President. The sixth *peronista* administration since 1946 faded away without a whimper.

23
THE PROCESS
(1976–1980)

It all suddenly stopped: the unremitting barrage of news about guerrilla attacks, murders, explosions, bodies found by the roadside; the cliff-hanging suspense surrounding the triangular conflict between Presidency, Congress and the unions; the frustrating spectacle of unbridled corruption in the upper reaches of government; the fatalistic dread that runaway inflation would continue to soar while production continued to plunge. Quietly, effortlessly — with no upheaval, no cataclysm, not even a ripple of resistance — it just stopped. The television screens, the radio broadcasts, the front pages of newspapers did not quite go blank; instead they abruptly switched from tension and turmoil to the aseptic calm of military announcements and proclamations. There were many who heaved a sigh of relief. The soldiers had stepped in; they would crack a few heads and re-establish order, 'normalcy'.

The three service Commanders — General Jorge Rafael Videla for the Army, Admiral Emilio Eduardo Massera for the Navy and Brigadier Orlando R. Agosti for the Air Force — installed themselves as the supreme power. General Videla, as head of the senior service, was given the title of President. They did not choose a pompous title for the régime they were inaugurating. This was not to be a *Revolución Libertadora* as in 1955, or a *Revolución Argentina* as in 1966. Indeed it was not to be a *Revolución* at all. The Junta, in a subdued style, announced that they were embarking on a 'process of national reorganisation', and this instantly became the anodyne name for their rule: *el Proceso*. Their targets were simple: to eliminate the subversive threat, to eradicate corruption, to straighten out the economic chaos. The man heading the government, General Videla, had already been 'sold' as the quiet, honest, austere professional; a convinced democrat who represented moderation — in contrast to the 'hardliners' and 'extremists' among the generals, admirals and brigadiers.

It was predictable that the military government would announce tough measures. This they did on the very first day. The death penalty was announced for anyone who killed or injured personnel of the security

421

forces, or attacked public utilities. Those caught in the act and refusing to desist could be shot on the spot; those who surrendered would be tried summarily by a military tribunal, behind closed doors, and defended by a military officer. Breaching the peace would be punishable by an eight-year prison sentence; offending the dignity and decorum of the military by ten years. All penalties for subversive crimes were increased, and the age of criminal responsibility was lowered from eighteen to sixteen. And there was more. Forty-eight organisations were declared illegal, political parties were dissolved, and political activity became punishable by imprisonment. Unions were taken over and industrial action was all but banned. Troublesome exiles and refugees would be deported. Associating with the wrong people and 'instigating' any of the new forms of criminal activity carried prison sentences of up to twelve and six years respectively. And as the crowning element in the package, the press was muzzled, banned from 'defending, divulging or propagating' anything said by illegal organisations or by 'persons or groups notoriously dedicated to subversive activities or to terrorism' (on pain of indefinite detention), or anything that might 'disrupt, prejudice or lessen the prestige or the activities of the armed forces' (on pain of a ten-year prison sentence). News media were specifically banned from carrying any 'reports, comments or references' about terrorist activities, abductions, the discovery of bodies, deaths of terrorists or security personnel, 'disappearances' — unless they were announced by an official source.

The news blackout that had erased Tucumán from the map now blotted out the whole country. It all looked like a harsher version of 1966; the soldiers in power with a larger, harder stick to brandish as a deterrent. But it was more than that, and not only because of the presence of bigger, better-organised and evidently more determined guerrilla organisations. The military had changed too. Over the previous few years they had acquired something that Argentina's armed forces had scarcely known since the days before Perón's birth, when the Army had marched to war in Paraguay: they had acquired a real enemy. In the past they had known isolated acts of terrorism, even a brief flurry of terrorist activity, directed against political targets; they had known the occasional bombing of a barracks, the rare attack on a military man; they had experienced uprisings by other members of the military, and being called upon to quell street riots. But in the 1970s, for the first time, they had come up against people bent on attacking them systematically, even at times head-on; people with the effrontery to believe that they could defeat Argentina's military establishment by force of arms. And their reaction had been a mixed one; on the one hand the reflex of hurt pride, of offended disbelief that anyone should refuse to be deterred by their might; on the other the elation at having, at long last, a real enemy — someone who made sense of the long years of training, the military mystique, the long sacrificial years of barrack boredom; someone who enabled the professional soldier to test his own mettle, his skill, his self-abnegation and patriotism.

This particular enemy posed a series of problems to the Argentine military. At first they had attempted to dismiss the guerrillas, denying them both political and military legitimacy, describing them as common criminals, and as such worthy only of consideration as a matter for the police. Yet the police had not been able to contain them and the military had taken the task upon themselves. Twice they had done so: during the latter part of the *Revolución Argentina* and during the latter part of the Isabelita administration. Hate — the professional hatred of the enemy — demanded that denigration of him should continue; self-respect demanded that he should be given greater stature. So the guerrillas became demonised; the few thousand armed fighters began to be portrayed as merely the tip of a huge iceberg, which consisted not only of the 'surface' organisations of the Left but a vast subversive conspiracy which, said the military, had already taken hold of every aspect of life in Argentina. There was the 'ideological subversion' that pervaded the universities, the press, the arts, and some professions like psychiatry and sociology; there was the 'economic subversion' detectable in the adoption of policies aimed at destroying the national economy; there was infiltration of the state apparatus, and an orchestrated campaign to destroy family and morals, to falsify history and to corrode all traditional values.

Even that was not enough. Behind the university students and lecturers and young trade unionists who had taken up arms, the soldiers persuaded themselves that they saw the hidden hand of the foreigner. Argentina, they said, had been targeted for destruction by 'international subversion' — a vague category in which Marxism was a key factor but the actual presence of the Soviet Union was never claimed, and in which a demonic Cuba was often mentioned in the same breath as Libya. Most of the invective was saved for the 'infiltrators' in the White House, the US and European press corps, the Catholic church. This, they proclaimed, was war. In fact, it was the beginning of the third world war, and Argentina (just like neighbouring Chile and Uruguay before her) would be a decisive battlefield.

'National security' had finally reached its maximum expression, having been transplanted from those military doctrines, originating in the northern hemisphere, that gave birth to the notion of total war. In an Argentina unaffected by wars of its own, it had taken root in the 1940s, under the guise of military involvement in industrialisation on grounds of national security. It had become enmeshed with the role the military had already begun to assume as arbiters or 'tie-breakers' on the political scene; introducing to the military staff colleges first economics, then development theory and finally the study of public administration techniques; expanding the role of the military as entrepreneurs (to the point that the Army's corporation, *Fabricaciones Militares*, had become the largest industrial conglomerate in the country); and leading, by the mid-1960s, to unsurprised acceptance of the fact that the Army General Staff had extended its brief from the traditional task of periodically revamping war plans to the more ambitious task of preparing plans of government. By then the soldiers were only a step away from seeing themselves, not merely as a part of the state apparatus, but as its most permanent and pure part — indeed, as the very embodiment of the state.

There was nothing unusual about Argentine military doctrine in its strict sense. The old Prussian model favoured by the Army and the British model preferred by the Navy had given way, in the postwar years, to the influence of the United States. Even counter-insurgency doctrine, developed in the wake of the Cuban revolution, was fairly orthodox, emphasising the primacy of politics, aiming at the isolation and neutralisation of the insurgents, and at 'winning over' the hearts and minds of rest of the population (though exposure to French and US missions, to veterans of Indochina and Special Forces instructors, had led too easily to the acceptance and later the adoption of ruthless interrogation methods). But in the mid-1970s something snapped. The response to the new enemy began to be predicated, not in terms of isolation and neutralisation, not with the old military aim of forcing the enemy to do one's will, but in terms of total annihilation. And the enemy who had to be annihilated was not just the man with the gun or bomb in his hand, nor the one who actively supported the fighter by harbouring or feeding him, but also the person who created the environment for subversion — a wide category which could easily include any kind of critic or dissident.

The military régime that took power on 24 March 1976 had not only the subversive threat on its agenda. The crusade was also going to envelop the economy with similar totality. The country's economic ills were attributed to over three decades of demagoguery, to the corrosive illusion of protectionism and autarky, and to the spread of state interventionism into almost every sphere of activity. This, they maintained, had deformed and distorted the workings of the market, fostering the growth of inefficient industries, penalising the one genuinely competitive sector — agriculture — granting inordinate power to organised labour, and rewarding the speculator and the corrupt. All this was to be swept away: the state's economic apparatus was to be dismantled, paring it down to the barest minimum compatible with its legitimate regulatory role; the unions would be put in their places; protectionist barriers would be hacked down, letting an 'open' economy select, as harshly as might be necessary, those fit enough to survive; finances would be 'made healthy' by allowing interest rates to rise to whatever levels the market might dictate. However painful it might be, what the country needed was economic *sinceramiento*, an honest acceptance of reality.

'We shall transform an economy of speculation into an economy of production,' said the man chosen to command this aspect of *el Proceso*, José Alfredo Martínez de Hoz. The new Minister of the Economy came from an old Argentine family, resident in the country since the end of the eighteenth century. One of his landowning ancestors was among the founders of Argentina's Jockey Club; another, of the Sociedad Rural. He himself was a cattle-rancher, captain of industry (chairman of the private steel-manufacturing company, Acíndar) and financier, director on a dozen boards, senior partner of one of the most prestigious law firms in Buenos Aires. He was no stranger to public office: under Aramburu he was Minister of the Economy in the province of Salta and president of the National Grains Board; under Guido First Secretary of Agriculture, then Minister of the Economy. And the team he chose to help him run the economy drew heavily from the ranks of veterans of the Krieger Vasena experiment of 1966. As early as May 1975, several of them had been preparing plans for the moment when a military régime would oust Isabelita and call upon them to set things straight. There was, in their proposals, nothing radically new: diagnosis and remedy were the same old package that Argentina's 'liberals' had been trotting out periodically since the 1950s. What was different was the context. Whenever this package had been tried in the past, political and social considerations had forced the dulling of its sharpest edges, and whenever elections had appeared on the horizon, it had been abandoned completely. This time there were no constraints.

Martínez de Hoz moved without delay. Holding a firm clamp on wages, he freed prices, with the immediate effect that most of the population saw its purchasing power drop immediately almost by half. The exchange market was unified, interest rates were allowed to drift upwards (though, oddly, deposits continued to be guaranteed by the state, even when this sparked off a cut-throat competition by financial institutions). With exports performing well and the country's international reserves on the rise, the new team was elated as the inflation rate, after the initial price shock, dropped by over two-thirds, and it began to seem as if 1977 would be a year of positive growth. As in 1966, bankers abroad were pleased, and this promised the new régime the kind of acceptance that translates into ready availability of credit and, they hoped, the kind of 'genuine' investment the country needed. So the economy was 'opened' by removing constraints on the movement of capital, and import tariffs were lowered. That the result included a drastic lowering of living standards for the country's wage-earners was dismissed as an inevitable side-effect of *sinceramiento*.

What the cloak of press censorship barely managed to disguise was that *el Proceso* was launched with a bloodbath. In the two weeks that followed the coup, killings by the shadowy groups which raced around in unmarked cars rose to over a hundred, while arrests took place by the thousand. The military authorities spoke publicly of armed clashes with the 'bands of subversive Marxist delinquents' and of arrests, but did not seem to be applying their own draconian legislation, which called for summary trials and for execution by firing squad within twenty-four hours of sentence being passed. A weird, unreal pattern began to emerge, transmitted by rumour or clandestine newssheet. In the clashes reported by the military, the death rate among the 'subversives' was inordinately high, with less than one in every thirty casualties merely being injured, while on the side of the security forces twice as many were being reported injured as killed in action. And increasingly the arrests seemed to have been carried out by phantoms. People dragged away from their homes or offices, or picked up in broad daylight on the streets, were suddenly nowhere to be found. Enquiries by relatives and friends at police and military headquarters drew blanks: the persons being enquired after were not officially under arrest.

Penetrating the fog of these unreported, unadmitted detentions was made more difficult by the complexity of the new power structure created by the military to wage their war. Real authority was vested in the regional commanders, who operated with the autonomy of war leaders in the field. Each in his own fiefdom was supreme, reporting only to his superiors in his own branch of the service; a tangled, overlapping network that led upwards, not to a single national authority, but to three separate authorities — the Commander-in-Chief of each of the armed services who made up the ruling Junta. This decentralisation and autonomy, at the other end of the scale, meant enormous power in the hands of very junior officers, each secure in the knowledge that no one could really tell under whose instructions he was acting.

The war was not entirely one-sided. Though battered before the coup, the guerrilla organisations maintained a capacity to carry out deadly and spectacular terrorist strikes. In the nine months after the military take-over, they murdered at least four prominent company executives, yet another chief of the Federal Police and an Air Force vice-commodore. They also struck at the heart of the security apparatus. In July, a bomb exploded at Federal Police headquarters, in the Superintendence of Federal Security, killing twenty-two and wounding sixty; in October another bomb blew up in the Círculo Militar, the Army officers' club, wounding fifty; and in December a third explosion, in the Planning Under-Secretariat of the Defence Ministry, killed fourteen and wounded twenty.

But the military were bent on keeping it a grossly unequal confrontation, in which the stakes would become progressively higher for their opponents. Their response to the bomb attacks was massive reprisals in the form of revenge killings. Right after the attack on Federal Police headquarters, seventy suspected 'subversives' were taken from their places of detention and shot; a similar attack on the Police Department in the capital of Buenos Aires province was matched by fifty-five executions; the Defence Ministry bomb led to thirty killings; and the assassination of a colonel on New Year's Day 1977 to forty.

Many of the leading figures of the ERP, including their chief Mario Roberto Santucho, and of the Montoneros and the Juventud Peronista, such as Marcos Osatinsky, Hugo Vaca Narvaja and Dardo Cabo, were killed in the first ten months, some secretly after months in detenion. Norma Nélida Arrostito, one of the kidnappers of former President Aramburu, was reported killed in December 1977, but was actually kept alive for months of interrogation by Navy men who wished to discover some evidence which would prove the Onganía government's involvement in that infamous killing.

The statistics of death became ever more mind-numbing. When an

Amnesty International mission visited Argentina in November 1976, they were given official figures recording 1,354 killings since the beginning of the year. Of these, 200 were policemen, military personnel and businessmen — typical guerrilla targets — and only 391 were identified by the authorities as guerrilla fighters; the other categories, widely believed to be victims of the security forces, included 151 'unkown', twenty-eight trade union leaders, fifteen students and university teachers, twelve politicians and nine priests.

The church was hit hard by the war against 'subversion'. In July two priests and nine cathechists were arrested in the industrial suburb of Avellaneda and later released after being threatened with death; the body of another catechist of this group, detained days earlier, was dumped in the city. In the suburb of Belgrano, three priests and two seminarians were found shot after a visit by men claiming to be from state intelligence. In August, Bishop Enrique Angelelli of La Rioja, travelling with documents about the killing of two priests of his diocese (after arrest by people claiming to be from the Federal Police), was killed when his car was forced off a mountain road. The same mouth the Archbishop of Córdoba saved a priest and five seminarians who had been carried off by unidentified armed men — when he intervened, the police admitted to holding them.

The scientific and academic communities were also targeted for repression. In April five scientists from the Atomic Energy Commission were arrested and held for seven months, during which they were subjected to torture. In July, claiming to have discovered a plan of 'ideological and socio-cultural infiltration', the Army raided the Universidad Nacional del Sur at Bahía Blanca, arresting seventeen professors and ordering the capture of another thirty-one who were not then on the campus. Psychiatrists were persecuted and gaoled on the grounds that their therapy helped to maintain the morale of urban guerrilla fighters who had gone underground.

The press, though in the main held in check by fear (self-censorship replaced outright censorship quite early), was badly mauled. Closures of publications, temporary and definitive, alternated dizzyingly with arrests of editors and journalists, official and clandestine, while others were intimidated by bombings or telephoned death threats. Openly dissident publications very soon disappeared, and scores of journalists left the country. Only two of the surviving newspapers, both with small circulations but considerable prestige, braved the official ban and continued to publish news of human rights violations, of 'disappearances' and unexplained deaths. One was the English-language *Buenos Aires Herald*, an enthusiastic supporter of Martínez de Hoz's economic policies. The other was Jacobo Timerman's *La Opinión*, earlier one of the most outspoken critics of the guerrilla organisations, apart from having been one of the leading advocates of the military ouster of the Isabelita Perón government. Both papers resisted enormous pressures from the military. The *Herald's* political editor, Andrew Graham-Yooll, left the country under threat of death; the editor, Robert Cox, followed some time later, but under his successor, James Neilsen, the paper stuck to its line. *La Opinión* met a different fate.

First, a new partner of the publishing company, Edgardo Sajón (who had been President Lanusse's press secretary), 'disappeared', never to be seen again. Then Timerman himself was abducted, though the ensuing furore led the government to admit that he was being held. The military authorities hoped to pin on him a charge of involvement with the guerrillas. They announced the discovery that his main partner at *La Opinión*, David Graiver (who had died a year earlier in a plane crash), had been laundering Montonero money, acquired through kidnappings and heists, through his family bank. There was the suggestion that this had been the 'ransom' demanded for the release of Isidoro Graiver, kidnapped by the Montoneros two years before. The implication was that *La Opinión* had actually been funded by Montonero money, and had played a key role in a wide-ranging subversive conspiracy which by now the military investigators felt they could trace, through Graiver's business and political associations, all the way to the former Minister of the Economy, José Ber Gelbard. The fantasy did not take long to collapse, but Timerman was held for more than forty months and was savagely and repeatedly tortured. He encountered one of the more sinister developments of what the military already called their 'dirty war': the adoption of elements of Nazi ideology, complete with a strain of sadistic anti-Semitism, by many elements of the armed forces. Though cleared by military courts and with his release ordered by the Supreme Court, Timerman was only freed after enormous international pressure, and then after he had been stripped of his property without compensation and had his Argentine citizenship revoked. His book *Prisoner Without Name, Cell Without Number* later became one of the classic exposés of secret detention and torture under the Argentine military.

The journalists and academics, priests, scientists and politicians, had at least the benefit of their prominence, which attracted international support for their cases. Most of the victims, however, did not enjoy that

privilege. Well over half of Argentina's 'disappeared' after 24 March
1976 — a host estimated at anything between 6,000 and 30,000
— were ordinary employees and workers, often with a record of grass-
roots union militancy. It was at this point that the war being waged by
the military had its most obvious point of contact with the drastic
economic turnaround engineered by Martínez de Hoz. Political scientists
coined a word for it: de-mobilisation. This meant breaking the back of
union militancy (as well as of political resistance in any form or colour)
by the most ruthless use of force and terror.

The main instrument of terror was the 'disappearance', the unacknow-
ledged abduction by faceless, nameless armed gangs. But the 'disappearance' itself, the act of abduction, was no more than the gateway to
a huge military underworld. No one was safe from 'disappearing'. If the
arrest party did not find its 'target', others would be taken instead:
parents, children, relatives. If anyone happened to be with a 'target' at
the moment of arrest, the likelihood was that that person would be
abducted as well. Inquiring after the fate of a 'disappeared' person often
led to the 'disappearance' of the inquirer, and this happened many times
to lawyers pursuing a hopeless *habeas corpus*. Looting would follow an
abduction as a matter of course.

Torture was the first stage following the 'disappearance.' The
application of electric prods to the most sensitive parts of the
body — lips, eyes, nipples, genitals — was the staple item. They called
it *la máquina*, 'the machine'. There was also immersion until the victim
was near suffocation: *el submarino*, 'the submarine'. And beatings. And
rape. The first session of torture was just for 'softening up'; interrogation might not follow for weeks, or it might never happen at all. In
between came the long period of being 'boarded up', or hooded, unable
to see or to communicate — only able to hear as others were put through
la máquina.

When interrogation was over, prisoners began to be streamed off. The
few lucky ones would be released, or transferred to regular prisons to
await trial by a military tribunal or simply to remain in detention at the
Executive's pleasure. The others would move around from one
clandestine detention centre to another, awaiting a further selection, for
what was also called 'transfer' — illegal execution. The myth was
created of work camps and 're-education' centres in the interior, healthy
places after the overcrowded, barely endurable detention centres. These,
allegedly, were the places to which people would be 'transferred'. Some

were simply taken out and shot, to be reported as 'killed while trying to escape', or to swell the statistics of those announced as killed in armed clashes with the security forces, or simply to be taken, by the truckload, for burial in graves marked NN (the official acronym for 'unknown') in out-of-the-way municipal cemeteries. Some were slated for the 'naval solution': to be flown over the estuary of the River Plate, close to the Uruguayan side, where strong currents were expected to carry the bodies out to sea (a system which showed its unreliability when twenty-five bodies, bearing the marks of torture, were washed ashore in Uruguay between March and October 1976). Others were weighted and sunk to the bottom of lakes (like those found by fishermen in Buenos Aires province) or of reservoirs (like those found by a skin-diver near the San Roque dam in Córdoba province). Yet others were disposed of in a government animal virology unit in Buenos Aires province, which had two large digestors for making the carcasses of experimentally infected cattle innocuous.

This was happening on an enormous scale. On average, one out of every 300 families was touched by 'disappearance', arrest or violent death. The only two newspapers which spoke about 'disappearances' did not mention what lay behind them. The rest of the press remained completely silent, as did the politicians, and the great mass of the population preferred not to know — the facts were too hard to bear. It was far easier to adopt the lame, contradictory rationalisations produced by the government, particularly when the question of the 'disappeared' became a major issue abroad. It was, said the government at first, no more than a huge calumny, part of an 'anti-Argentine' campaign orchestrated abroad by 'international terrorism' — a description which hardly fitted the major news media of the United States and Europe. The 'so-called disappeared', they added, were really no more than terrorists who had gone into hiding, or fled the country, or been killed by their own comrades. And to cover the many rough edges of this explanation, they went on to add, in knowing fashion, 'People must remember that this has been a dirty war.' This message was all too eagerly repeated by the media in Argentina, and particularly by one of the largest publishing houses, Editorial Atlántida, which put its stable of mass-circulation magazines, plus a news-weekly created for the purpose, to work as an enthusiastic propaganda machine for *el Proceso*.

As the military changed their tune under the pressure of increasing evidence, so too did the press, neither of them bothering to paper over the blatant discrepancies between new and earlier explanations. Thus the time came when the military began to admit the possibility of 'some excesses'. Thus, too they went on to peddle the story that the atrocities had been committed by 'freelancers' who had reacted 'spontaneously' to left-wing terrorism. Later they even accepted that there might have been some excessive zeal by junior commanders, whose autonomy in the field put them almost beyond the control of their superiors. Many of Argentina's large middle class were willing to accept these explanations at face value. Enticed by official propaganda, they developed a perverse line of defence which twisted the situation around to the point where being a victim was proof of guilt, though guilt of a vague, undefined kind. If someone was arrested, or killed, or 'disappeared', the instant reaction was, 'Well, he must have done *something*!'

A passage from Andrew Graham-Yooll's *Portrait of an Exile* illustrates the deep fear that induced such ready acceptance of government propaganda:

The car coasted to the curb moving apace with my steps on the pavement. It nosed ahead slowly. Into the vision line of the corner of one eye moved the bonnet; then the brilliance of the windshield came into scope. A glance around brought the sight of the small dark hole of the muzzle of a gun resting on the window frame aimed at me.

Knees reacted first; they did not bend properly. Guilt, due to the existence of a follower, gave rise to the feeling, the certainty, that each awkward step was as noticeable as the impeded gait of a severely handicapped person. My feet trod with short hurried steps on a cushion of air, hesitant whether to touch the ground, to run or slow down, without a suitable order from me. The men in the car were watching me . . . . The man at the wheel called out something about my beard and added a remark that ended in an oath.

I began to turn my head, slowly, stiffly.

The car drove away. It was not me they wanted this time.

Little, if any at all, of what happened had been the work of uncontrolled freelancers or over-zealous junior commanders. Later, in 1980, Amnesty International published the testimony of former prisoners who described in great detail the network of clandestine detention centres, and the highly organised way in which the *patotas* or abduction brigades of the 'tactical groups' filed in writing their 'target requisition forms' to the regional commands, obtained the 'liberation' (clearing-out of police units) of the areas in which they intended to operate, filled a daily register of detainees on quadruplicate forms, and finally, just before the 'transfer' of each prisoner, filed a 'final resolution of case' form in which the grades 'dangerous' and 'extremely dangerous' spelled execution, while 'potentially dangerous' might just mean freedom.

Over sixty-one clandestine detention centres throughout the country have been identified, some within military units, others in derelict or condemned buildings, others in premises commandeered for the purpose. The most notorious internationally was the Escuela de Mecánica de la Armada, a school for naval ratings, known among other things as the 'maternity' unit where pregnant prisoners were delivered of their babies — these were given to childless couples within Argentina and, in at least one case, in neighbouring Chile. In central Buenos Aires there was the Club Atlético, close to the intersection of the Avenida Independencia and Paseo Colón. Also in the city, in its western quarter, was Olimpo, and the garage of Automotores Orletti, in Floresta. In the environs of Buenos Aires was La Atómica, on land owned by the Atomic Energy Commission near Ezeiza airport. All told, there were over forty centres in the Greater Buenos Aires alone. In the interior, the best known were La Perla and La Rivera in Córdoba. Many of these *ad hoc* prisons, their mission fulfilled and their inmates relocated or killed, were demolished or reconverted to other uses after 1978.

Two-thirds of all the 'disappearances' recorded by the Committee for the Defence of Human Rights in the Southern Cone, based in São Paulo, Brazil, took place in the Greater Buenos Aires area. Most of them were in the first two years of *el Proceso*: over 3,600 in 1976, over 2,800 in 1977. Thereafter, numbers dropped sharply: 895 in 1978, 155 in 1979, 46 in 1980 and beyond — but 'disappearances' never stopped altogether.

By the end of 1977 Martínez de Hoz could claim to have achieved a modest growth rate of 4.9 per cent — the first upward swing since 1975. His balance of payments looked good, and he had drastically trimmed back the budget deficit. Yet inflation had refused to shrink any further — indeed it had accelerated again to an annual 140 per cent — and with wages still squeezed, the only thing he could think of doing was to adopt a policy of tight money. The seeds of destruction of his dream had already been sown. By refraining from devaluation as inflation accelerated, his 'open market' policy was beginning to work in one direction only, that of a wild import-spending spree. Local industries were made doubly uncompetitive by the lowering of tariffs and by the creeping over-valuation of the peso. And now, with real interest rates rising rapidly, their finances were being squeezed beyond their limits of tolerance. As the market became flooded with cheap imported goods,

companies started going to the wall, and the country began to witness
ever new records in the number of bankruptcies.

In 1978 politics helped to make matters worse. The year began on a
sour note, with the military government rejecting out of hand a British-
sponsored arbitration in the long-running dispute with Chile over the
Beagle channel, south of Tierra del Fuego. The issue involved not only
the possession of three tiny islands — Picton, Nueva and Lennox — but
also the more vexed question of whether, in breach of a nineteenth-
century treaty, Chile was to gain shores on the Atlantic — which meant
gaining also a 200-mile exclusive economic zone, which would affect
future claims on disputed Antarctic territories. The arbitrators found in
Chile's favour, and Argentina, alleging that they had overstepped their
brief, refused to accept the award. Presidents Videla and Pinochet
managed to agree on a temporary freeze of the dispute, but tempers were
running high in the Argentine armed forces, and as time passed and it
seemed as if the Chileans had decided to act on the strength of the award,
sabres began to rattle.

However, there were other important things to attend to first. The
military had decided to consolidate their régime, institutionalising the
Presidency with a three-year mandate and carving up jurisdictions
between the Junta and the President. Videla retired from active duty but
retained the Presidency, while General Roberto Eduardo Viola took over
as Commander-in-Chief of the Army. There began to be talk of an
imminent political thaw. The military confidently claimed that they had
'decapitated' the guerrilla movements, and were preparing to show
the world that they had achieved stable conditions in which the Argentine people were content. The occasion was to be the event all
Argentines — great devotees of soccer — had long been awaiting: the
celebration of the World Cup championship in Argentina. Many
millions of dollars were poured into preparations for the event: refurbishing stadiums, introducing colour television, hiring public relations con-
sultants to counteract the bad press *el Proceso* had received abroad on
account of its human rights record. When the time came, the contest
was not sabotaged, as feared, by remnants of the guerrilla groups, and
the government, aided by the fact that the Argentine team won the cup,
was able to exhibit a jubilant, flag-waving population feasting in the
streets.

But the carnival was about soccer, not about the achievements of the
military régime. This became evident only weeks after the soccer
victory, when Buenos Aires played unwilling host to the Inter-American

Commission on Human Rights, come to investigate the myriad allegations against the military rulers. A massive propaganda campaign was
mounted by the government to demonstrate popular approval of what
the soldiers had done, 'dirty war' and all. Advertisements were taken in
the press and posters were plastered on the streets, proclaiming *Somos
derechos y humanos'* ('We are righteous and humane' — a rather sick pun
on *derechos humanos*, human rights). Yet people flocked by the thousand
to testify before the Commission, unloading tale after tale of horror.
Later diplomatic efforts by the Argentine government managed to delay
publication of the report, but not to suppress it (allegedly the published
version lacks an appendix which names the people identified as responsible for a number of human rights violations).

The World Cup spending spree was hardly over when the military
government was again disbursing hundreds of millions of dollars for a far
less festive purpose: preparations for war with Chile. Conversations
with the Chileans over the Beagle channel seemed to be getting nowhere, and in Buenos Aires the generals and admirals and brigadiers were
clamouring for military action. As winter turned to spring, Argentines
began to wake up to the fact that this was not just another of the usual
bouts of military posturing over the old border dispute. The military
were placing orders for fuel tanks to be built in a hurry all over
Patagonia. Army units left their barracks and headed south, as reservists
were placed on call. Activity at naval and Air Force bases became
feverish, and all along the border with Chile, particularly in the southern
provinces, anti-aircraft batteries began to be sited in back gardens and
orchards. A blackout and air raid drill raised the temperature to fever
pitch as the year was ending, and indeed probes and forays and minor
skirmishes were already taking place, although the public of both
countries were kept in ignorance. Eleventh-hour intervention by the
Vatican prevented an open outbreak of hostilities, and in January the
Foreign Ministers of Argentina and Chile were agreeing in Montevideo
to submit the dispute to papal mediation.

Although the exact amount of money spent was not revealed it was
one of the factors that accelerated Argentina's rapid slide into indebtedness over the following years, when the country's balance of payments
moved sharply into the red and production slumped, plunging
Argentina into the worst and longest recession in anyone's memory. The
peso became grossly overvalued, further fuelling the spending sprees
abroad by the affluent, while strongly positive interest rates attracted all
sorts of short-term speculation. Argentina moved rapidly into a state of

fantasy, its capital city becoming the most expensive in the world, its affluent citizens buying up swathes of real estate in Uruguay, Brazil and Florida, inflation still roaring ahead at 140 per cent, and production declining fast in tandem with it.

It was in this atmosphere that controls began to be relaxed on the press and on political activities. The parties as such continued to be banned, but the politicians were very much in evidence, and their reappearance evoked memories of a decade earlier. Right-of-centre forces such as those of Manrique and the host of provincial parties which had once supported him rallied around the figure of General Viola, the Army commander slated to replace Videla in the Presidency. After a long silence, the politicians began to sound a critical note, and as in the days of the *Revolución Argentina*, they delivered their criticism obliquely, choosing the obvious target: Martínez de Hoz, whose programme was floundering badly. The theme of a political 'way out', *la salida política*, began to gain strength, as officials were flying the old kites: the formation of a government party, the preparation of a careful electoral calendar, and staging elections one level at a time from the municipalities upwards. Journalists and politicians began to test the limits of the new tolerance, and the theme of the 'disappeared' moved into the pages of the hitherto silent major daily newspapers.

Yet despite the similarities, this was not the same as the early 1970s. Certainly many of the old dilemmas had reappeared, and again the country had a great number of young people of voting age who had had no exposure at all to politics; if anything, they had been insulated from politics more completely than their predecessors. Again the party-political freeze had perpetuated the old leadership structures in the parties; the same people were still there, and they had nothing new to say. But there was no Perón on the horizon, waiting to return as a saviour after a long exile. And this time the influence of the military on society was far more pervasive. There were soldiers not only throughout the public administration, but also on the boards of private companies and in managerial positions everywhere. The taint of corruption and reckless speculation that accompanied the collapse of Argentina's leading private bank, followed by the near-collapse of several others, inevitably left its mark on the military, apart from signalling that the days of Martínez de Hoz were numbered.

Decomposition had clearly set in by late 1979, when General Luciano Menéndez attempted, from his base in Córdoba, to lead a rebellion of hardliners intent on putting back the clock, reinstating a full ban on political activity, and stamping out what he saw as a re-emergence of subversion: the growing demand for an official explanation on the plight of the thousands of 'disappeared' persons. The revolt was crushed almost as soon as it was declared, but it reminded the country that the military would have a great deal at stake in any eventual return to political normality. The message was relayed down the line: the one thing the military would not tolerate was any attempt to call them to account for the 'dirty war'. It was stated unequivocally that there could not be a repetition of Nuremberg in Argentina. This view was shared by all in the military establishment, 'hardliners' and 'moderates' alike. 'You must remember', said a former and future Presidential candidate Francisco Manrique to a group of Argentine expatriates in London, 'that "hardliners" were the ones who actually did the killing, and "moderates" those who ordered them to kill.' Most of the political leaders who had already initiated conversations with the military were quite willing to go along with the soldiers' proviso, to the extent of finding some face-saving formula which would allow the military to take collective responsibility for what had happened in a very general, unspecific fashion, avoiding any case-by-case investigation which would start revealing the chain of individual responsibilities in the whole sordid affair.

Yet even as this condition was stated, it became hard for anyone to consider it as realistic. No guarantees offered by the political leaders could possibly take account of what hundreds of elected Congressmen would do the moment their chamber was in session. This was realised in some quarters of the armed forces, most notably in the Navy, the service with the blackest human rights record in the outside world, thanks to the notoriety achieved by the Escuela de Mecánica de la Armada when one of its 'tactical group' officers, Lieutenant Alfredo Astiz, was publicly linked with the abduction and torture of two French nuns, and with the murder of a Swedish national.

The Navy commander, Emilio Massera, had already begun to nurture political ambitions of his own. A ruthless intriguer in the pursuit of his service career, he was an easy socialiser, and once in power he struck up good relationships with a number of *peronista* union leaders. This, say his critics, led him to fancy himself as a sort of latter-day Perón: he began to adopt a distinctly populist attitude in public, and to distance himself from his peers in the Junta. Massera himself had been mentioned by a number of human rights organisations as personally involved in the ugliest aspects of repression following the coup, and he set out to modify that image. He began to travel widely abroad, making contacts with Argentines in exile (whose numbers had been increased by well over 200,000 in recent years) and even, according to several independent accounts, meeting Montonero leader Mario Firmenich. Massera's line was that the blame for the worst excesses of the 'dirty war' could be laid at the Army's door, and that he had tried to redress the balance by freeing a number of political prisoners (which he did).

With Massera's defection the inter-service unity, which had been the strength of the Junta, all but vanished. The economic adventure launched by Martínez de Hoz, with whose fate Videla had insistently identified that of the entire military government, was all but defunct. Almost all sectors of the country were now openly opposed to the government; of its early allies in the business community, by mid-1980 only the larger banks, local and foreign, remained sympathetic to it. Moreover, isolation at home was compounded by international isolation.

Despite the role in which the Argentine Junta saw itself — as defender of the West in a World War III which had already begun — the West remained extremely aloof. In most cases the Junta's methods were considered embarrassing, if not totally unacceptable. In the most vital case of the United States, the Junta clashed head-on with President Carter's human rights policy. Profoundly hurt by this rejection, which it attributed to incomprehension of conditions in Argentina (and, frequently, to the presence of a number of 'Marxists' surrounding Carter), the military in Buenos Aires stuck to their guns. Adopting a pragmatic air, they tried to console themselves with the fact that their Economy Minister, Martínez de Hoz, was highly esteemed by the world's bankers — that, they maintained, was what really counted. The only real friends the Junta started out with were the like-minded military governments of Chile and Uruguay, although the only area in which this was translated into real co-operation was that of repression, each allowing the other's secret police to operate in their territories, and on more than one occasion providing mutual assistance in the disposal of unwanted bodies (several Uruguayan and Chilean politicians were murdered in Argentina, and there were a number of reported cases of cross-border body dumping). But friendship with Chile turned to enmity in 1978 over the Beagle channel, and Argentina shifted to strengthening its traditional ties with Chile's old enemies, Bolivia and Perú. In mid-1980 the Argentine military found themselves aiding General Luis García Meza of Bolivia to stage a coup against the recently-restored civilian administration.

Beyond their immediate neighbours, the violently anti-Marxist Argentine military found themselves befriending the Soviet Union, which soon became one of Argentina's most important export markets, particularly for grain. In 1979, the prospect of a Conservative victory in the United Kingdom wildly excited the Junta, who saw Mrs Thatcher (with her tough anti-Communism and affinity with the economics of Martínez de Hoz) as a like-minded person and a probable ally. Margaret Thatcher probably got a better pre-election press campaign from the media in Argentina than from the Conservative newspapers in Britain, and there was jubilation in Buenos Aires at her electoral triumph. But there were few gains in this for Argentina, except for the increased access of their large naval purchasing mission to advanced British military technology. Here was no great change, since this access had never been cut off by the Callaghan government. (Labour hostility to the Argentine military régime was mainly verbal; under Labour, for example, Britain was no more welcoming to Argentine refugees than under Thatcher.)

If Argentina's 'defence of the West' was largely cold-shouldered by the West, it was clearly detested by many nations in the Third World, which saw it as yet another example of Argentina's recurrent propensity to place itself in a category apart and to shun solidarity with other developing nations.

The Argentine Junta's isolation became symbolically complete when an obscure but indefatigable human rights campaigner named Adolfo Pérez Esquivel, once an inmate of the Junta's gaols, was awarded the 1980 Nobel Peace Prize. He was Argentina's fourth Nobel prize winner, and the second to receive the Peace award (his predecessor, Carlos Saavedra Lamas, was given it in 1936 for helping to end the Chaco war between Bolivia and Paraguay). But there was little rejoicing over the event in Buenos Aires: it appeared to be not only a sign of international rejection of the Junta and its works, but a reminder that it would be impossible to sweep the issue of the 'disappeared' under the carpet.

In October 1980, in the face of that sign and that reminder, the Junta of Commanders-in-Chief designated General Roberto Eduardo Viola as the second President of *el Proceso*, and Argentina's thirty-fifth ruler in 100 years.

EPILOGUE
(1981–84)

General Viola had to wait almost five months between his selection as Videla's successor and his actual accession to power. These were exciting times for Argentina's military rulers, apparently full of promise. Ronald Reagan had been elected President of the United States, his inauguration marking the end of international isolation for the soldiers in Buenos Aires. The rhetoric of key figures in Reagan's entourage, such as Jeane Kirkpatrick (appointed ambassador to the United Nations), closely matched some of the older themes of *el Proceso*. After suppressing the left-wing guerrilla movements within Argentina, the military had kept alive the spectre of the 'international subversive threat' by pointing to the way Nicaragua's *sandinista* régime was evolving, and to the spread of insurgency in El Salvador and Guatemala. They maintained that the threat they had eradicated in the southern extreme of the hemisphere was growing, unchecked, in the Caribbean and Central America. Kirkpatrick concurred — indeed one of her theses that had endeared her to Reagan during his election campaign was a distinction between 'authoritarian' governments (like those of Chile and Argentina) which the United States should prefer as allies, and 'totalitarian' governments (like those of Cuba and Nicaragua) which it should oppose at all costs.

Ronald Reagan arrived at the White House committed to halt the spread of 'totalitarian' influence in Central America, and the generals in Argentina offered to help him in this task. Within two months of Reagan's inauguration, Argentina's President-designate, General Roberto Viola, was given a red-carpet welcome in Washington. Soon afterwards, a stream of US envoys, civilian and military, descended upon Buenos Aires, where they were hosted by the new Commander-in-Chief of the Army, General Leopoldo Fortunato Galtieri, a tall, rugged, tough-talking man of fifty-five who had taken to emulating actor George Scott's screen interpretation of General Patton, to the delight of his guests.

Far more than Viola, Galtieri won the hearts of the 'anti-totalitarian' crusaders in Reagan's team. The friendship they struck up was not all partying and backslapping: Galtieri was soon taken up on his offer to provide military support for the US effort in Central America. Already in the last months of the Carter administration, the CIA had been quietly authorised to initiate covert action against the *sandinista* régime in Nicaragua and to interdict support from Cuba and Nicaragua to the insurgents in El Salvador. Now Galtieri came up with the means to escalate that campaign without any visible involvement of US forces. Argentine intelligence and counter-insurgency experts were flown to El Salvador and Guatemala, to share the expertise they had acquired during Argentina's 'dirty war'. A larger contingent — perhaps fifty-strong — was despatched to Honduras, to train a force of Nicaraguan exiles in the techniques of irregular warfare, with the aim of launching cross-border raids and sabotage operations against the *sandinistas*.

In the mean time Viola, already installed in the Casa Rosada, was having a hard time. After the Martínez de Hoz experiment, it was inevitable that the new Minister of the Economy, Lorenzo Sigaut, would face a daunting task of whittling down the gross over-valuation of the peso, restoring some sanity to relative prices in the domestic economy, and reactivating production — all in a context of stubbornly high inflation, an unrelenting tide of bankruptcies and a foreign debt spiralling upwards with uncomfortably short maturities and astronomic interest rates. Hamstrung by the perceived need to maintain some sort of continuity with previous policies and to avoid violent upsets, Sigaut's measures kept falling short of what was needed, and kept having to be repeated. This created the impression of aimlessness and lack of resolve in what politicians and union leaders alike saw as the crumbling edifice of *el Proceso*. As criticism in the press grew more daring, and dissent began to be expressed more openly, Viola began to gain among his military peers a reputation for being too 'soft', and for pursuing too recklessly a path to political 'normalisation' which the forces still viewed with great apprehension.

Rumours of a coup by the 'hardliners' began to surface early in Viola's Presidency. The Army Commander, General Galtieri, raised the matter with his North American hosts on his two visits to the United States in 1981, and their advice weighed heavily on the course chosen by the plotters. By November, the date of his second visit, Galtieri had already expanded the agenda of Argentine-US co-operation. He had trotted out, once again, the old right-wing dream of a South Atlantic Alliance, envisaged as an anti-Communist entente between the military régimes of South America's Southern Cone and South Africa, with the blessing of the United States. He had agreed, too, that Argentina would distance itself from the Non-Aligned Movement (whose president at the time was Fidel Castro). In exchange, he sought from Washington the lifting of the arms embargo in force since the days of Jimmy Carter, and sympathy with another longstanding Argentine aim: the recovery of the Malvinas, or Falkland Islands, before 1983 — the 150th anniversary of their occupation by Britain. This last quest had a practical side to it; a commitment to recover the Malvinas was necessary to secure the acquiescence of Admiral Jorge Isaac Anaya, Commander-in-Chief of the Navy, in a coup in which Galtieri might take the Presidency without relinquishing command of the Army. On 22 December 1981, Galtieri ousted Viola and was himself appointed President by the other two members of the Junta. He retained his position as Commander-in-Chief of the Army.

The Malvinas issue had never been far from the surface since the military took power in March 1976. In December that year Argentina obtained passage by the United Nations General Assembly of Resolution 31/49, expressing gratitude to Argentina for its efforts 'to facilitate the process of decolonisation and to promote the wellbeing of the population of the Islands', and urging Britain and Argentina — for the third time — to expedite negotiations. That same month, Argentina installed a naval scientific station on Southern Thule, an island claimed by Britain in the South Sandwich group. It was the first move in a chess match devised by Admiral Massera: if Britain attempted to evict the Argentines from Southern Thule, Argentina would retaliate by removing the British Antarctic Survey team from Grytviken in South Georgia. If further British action followed, the Malvinas would be invaded. In the event, Britain kept the incident quiet, only informing its public more than a year later.

On the diplomatic front, Britain continued to play for time — its delaying tactics transparent to the Argentine government and particularly to the man watching most closely: Admiral Jorge Isaac Anaya, then head of the large Argentine naval mission in London. Talks were scheduled for December 1977, against such a foul mood in Buenos Aires that Britain feared an aggressive reaction as soon as the Argentines became aware that there was nothing concrete on offer. Britain secretly despatched two frigates and a nuclear submarine to the area, but nothing happened.

Procrastination continued over the next four years, but Britain began to scale down its presence in the South Atlantic, as if it were letting the whole matter go by default. The only Royal Navy vessel in the area,

HMS *Endurance*, was to be removed after the summer run of 1981–2; the British Antarctic Survey station at Grytviken was marked out for closure; and there was a clear refusal by the government to reverse legislation that had deprived many Falkland Islanders of full British citizenship. In September 1981 Argentina served notice that it expected the next round of talks to be the last. British intelligence and the Foreign Office reckoned that the most they could hope for before Argentina turned to action was one more bout of avoiding concessions on sovereignty over the islands. Talks were scheduled for late February 1982, in New York.

When Galtieri stepped into the Presidency on 22 December 1981, he appointed as his Foreign Minister Nicanor Costa Méndez, the man who in General Onganía's days had gone along with the British suggestion that the Malvinas might be won over by 'seduction' — only to discover that this was one more in a long series of delaying tactics. By this time, Admiral Anaya was already putting the finishing touches to his plan of completing the recovery of the Malvinas by the end of 1982. Militarily, it was in its essentials an updating of Massera's Southern Thule ploy of 1976. Four days before Galtieri's inauguration, the icebreaker ARA *Almirante Irízar* had sailed into Leith habour on St Peter's Island in South Georgia. On board were a civilian, Constantino Davidoff (armed with a contract to dismantle an abandoned whaling station there), and a high-ranking Navy officer, Captain Trombetta, Chief of the Antarctic Squadron, who like Anaya had made the acquaintance of the British from a senior position in the naval mission in London. Davidoff was there to inspect his scrap metal, and Trombetta to test British reactions by pointedly not requesting clearance from the British commander at Grytviken, down the coast. It took nineteen days for that reaction to emerge in Buenos Aires, in the form of a diplomatic protest.

The end-of-February talks in New York fell well short of Argentine expectations. Already the press was full of belligerent noises; now the Foreign Ministry hinted broadly that Argentina was considering means other than diplomatic ones to regain the islands.

On 19 March the Argentine naval transport vessel *Bahía Buen Suceso* landed Davidoff's workers at Leith. A day later HMS *Endurance* sailed from Port Stanley with a party of marines on board and orders to evict the scrap merchants — but was diverted to Grytviken to await the outcome of diplomatic exchanges. The *Bahía Buen Suceso* sailed out of territorial waters on March 21, but four nights later another Argentine vessel, the *Bahía Paraíso*, slipped into Leith under cover of darkness and disembarked a party of Argentine marines, with orders to resist any attempt at eviction. Two missile-carrying corvettes, ARA *Granville* and ARA *Drummond*, were despatched to stations off the islands. And when reports arrived from London that Britain had sent a nuclear submarine south, the Argentine fleet was ordered to close in on the Malvinas. On 2 April 1982 the first Argentine marines went ashore.

Seventy-three days later, the Malvinas were back in British hands. The brief intervening war has been written about in extraordinary profusion, yet two years after its end — as this epilogue is written — several of the most important issues it raised still lack a definitive answer. The war itself does not fall within the brief of this book. It is impossible, however, not to mention some of its consequences.

Galtieri did not survive defeat. His comrades-in-arms replaced him with another General, Reynaldo Bignone, who was charged with guiding the country back to elected rule as speedily as possible, making only half-hearted attempts at securing some say for the military in the future régime, and only barely giving the impression of an orderly withdrawal. Elections were called for October 1983, and most political analysts took it for granted that this meant yet another repetition of the cycle into which the country had been locked since the 1950s. The *peronistas*, they predicted, would once again win.

The *peronistas* did not risk fielding Isabelita Perón as their candidate, but instead picked one of the most moderate of their leading figures: Italo Luder, who as acting president of the Senate had stood in for Isabelita during her absence from the Casa Rosada shortly before the 1976 coup. The Unión Cívica Radical nominated an untried man, Raúl Alfonsín (see above, pp. 363 and 394), who ran a campaign curiously reminiscent of the one which took Hipólito Yrigoyen to the Presidency, emphasising the need to return to the rule of the Constitution and the law. Alfonsín accused the *peronistas*, and particularly the union bosses, of having celebrated a secret pact with the military, trading military acceptance of an elected *peronista* government for *peronista* assurances that the excesses and abuses of the 'dirty war' would not be investigated too energetically. Indeed the military attempted to formalise their immunity by passing a law granting an amnesty for all acts committed 'in the line of duty' during their rule. All parties — the *peronistas* included — rejected it, and no evidence was ever offered for the existence of the *pacto militar-sindical* denounced by Alfonsín.

The election results shocked everyone. Not only did Alfonsín win, but he did so with a majority only equalled in the past by Yrigoyen and

Perón. In December 1983 he took office, and almost instantly dismissed half the country's generals and placed the military firmly under civilian control. The Supreme Council of the Armed Forces — the highest court-martial in the land — was ordered to institute legal proceedings against those responsible for the large-scale abuses of human rights in the years of military rule (orders were also issued for the arrest of known terrorists still at large). Within his first hundred days in office, the men responsible for the Malvinas war — General Galtieri, Admiral Anaya and Brigadier Lami Dozo — were behind bars.

At the time of writing these lines, it is too early to do more than record these few facts. The country inherited by Alfonsín was in a mess, with inflation running at over 300% and an external debt estimated at US$43,000 million; 600,000 people were unemployed and 1½ million underemployed. Even worse than the economic indicators, the population was reeling under the shock of having allowed itself, finally, to take cognisance of the horrors which some Argentines had inflicted on others, and which many more had pretended not to see.

SOURCES

Chapter 1 (1880–95)

1. Alvarez (G.) *El tronco de oro*. Neuquén, 1968.
2. Auzon (E.), *Historia de la revolución de julio de 1890*. Buenos Aires, 1890.
3. Balestra (J.), *El Noventa: una evolución polítoca argentina*. Buenos Aires, 1935.
4. Bialet Massé (J.), *El estado de las clases obreras argentinas*. Córdoba, 1968.
5. Bortnik (R.), *Breve historia de las luchas sociales en la Argentina*. Buenos Aires, 1974.
6. Carlevari (I.J.F.), *La Argentina: geografía humana y económica*. Buenos Aires, 1972.
7. Dingskirchen (J.), *Algunas observaciones sobre la disciplina del Ejército Argentino*. Buenos Aires, 1892.
8. Di Tella (T.S.) *et al.*, *Argentina, sociedad de masas*. Buenos Aires, 1965.
9. Graham (W.), *English Influence in the Argentine Republic*. Buenos Aires, 1890.
10. Guillén (A.), *La oligarquía en la crisis de la economía argentina*. Buenos Aires, 1956.
11. Hernández (J.), *Martín Fierro*. Buenos Aires, 1952.
12. Hernández Arregui (J.J.), *Qué es el ser nacional? La conciencia histórica hispanoamericana*. Buenos Aires, 1963.
13. Irazusta (R.) & Irazusta (J.), *La Argentina y el imperialismo británico*. Buenos Aires, 1934.
14. Iscaro (R.), *Historia del movimiento sindical*. Buenos Aires, 1973.
15. Lloyd (R.), ed., *Twentieth Century Impressions of Argentina: Its History, People, Commerce, Industries and Resources*. London, 1911.
16. López, (V.F.), *Historia de la República Argentina*. Buenos Aires, 1911.
17. Martínez Estrada (E.), *Radiografía de la Pampa*. Buenos Aires, 1961.
18. Morris (F.), *The forced currency and gold contracts*. London, 1886.
19. Muniz (R.), *Los indios pampas*. Buenos Aires, 1966.
20. Nellar (G.) *et al.*, *Reseña histórica y orgánica del Ejército Argentino*. Buenos Aires, 1971.
21. Ortega Peña (R.) & Duhalde (E.L.), *Baring Brothers y la historia política argentina*. Buenos Aires, 1973.
22. Palacios (A.), *Nuestra América y el imperialismo*. Buenos Aires, 1961.
23. Pavón Pereyra (E.), *Vida de Perón*. Buenos Aires, 1965.
24. Pinedo (F.), *La Argentina en un cono de sombra*. Buenos Aires, 1968.
25. Power (J.), *The Land We Live in*. Buenos Aires, 1891.
26. Quebracho (*pseud.* Justo, L.), *Pampas y lanzas; fundamentos histórico-económico-sociales de la nacionalidad y de la conciencia nacional argentina*. Buenos Aires, 1962.
27. Quesada (E.), *La deuda argentina: su unificación*. Buenos Aires, 1895.

28. Ramos (J.A.), *Historia de la nación latinamericana*. Buenos Aires, 1968.
29. Ramos (J.A.), *Revolución y contrarrevolución en la Argentina*. Buenos Aires, 1961.
30. Romero (J.L.), *Las ideas políticas en Argentina*. Mexico, 1946.
31. Senén González (S.), *Breve historia del sindicalismo argentino 1857-1974*. Buenos Aires, 1974.
32. Sindicato Luz y Fuerza. *Cien años contra el país*. Buenos Aires, 1970.
NEWSPAPERS, PERIODICALS AND JOURNALS: *Diario de Sesiones, La Prensa*.

Chapter 2 (1895-1916)

33. Acosta (A.), *El Dr Hipólito Irigoyen*. Buenos Aires, 1918.
34. Bortnik, op. cit. (5).
35. Centeno (F.), *Virutas históricas 1810-1928*. Buenos Aires, 1929.
36. Di Tella, op. cit. (8).
37. Guillén, op. cit. (10).
38. Hammerton (J.A.), *The Real Argentine*. New York, 1915.
39. Iscaro, op. cit. (14).
40. Koebel (W.H.), *Argentina, Past and Present*. London, 1910.
41. Lloyd, op. cit. (15).
42. Lix Klett (C.) *Estudios sobre producción, comercio y finanzas de la República*. Buenos Aires, 1900.
43. López, op. cit. (16).
44. Luca de Tena (T.), Calvo (L.), Peicovich (E.) ed., *Yo, Juan Domingo Perón: relato autobiográfico*. Barcelona, 1976.
45. Nellar, op. cit. (20).
46. MacCorquodale (D.), *The Argentine Re-visited 1881-1906*. Glasgow, 1909.
47. Máspero Castro (A.), *País rico, pueblo y gobierno pobres: Estudio económico-social sobre la situación actual en la República Argentina*. Buenos Aires, 1917.
48. Palacios, op. cit. (22).
49. Pavón Pereyra, op. cit. (23).
50. Pinedo (F.), *Siglo y medio de economía argentina*. Mexico, 1961.
51. Pinedo, op. cit. (24).
52. Ramos Mejía (J.M.), *Las multitudes argentinas*. Madrid, 1912.
53. Ramos, op. cit. (29).
54. Romero, op. cit. (30).
55. Williams (J.H.), *Argentine International Trade under Inconvertible Paper Money 1880-1900*. Cambridge (Mass.), 1920.
56. Sindicato Luz y Fuerza, op. cit. (32).
57. Yrigoyen (H.), *Discursos, Escritos y Polémicas 1878-1922*. Buenos Aires, 1923.
58. Yrigoyen (H.), *Hipólito Irigoyen 1878-1933: Documentación histórica de 55 años de actuacion por la democracia y las instituciones*. Buenos Aires, 1934.

NEWSPAPERS, PERIODICALS AND JOURNALS: *Diario de Sesiones, La Nación, La Prensa*.

INTERVIEWS AND PERSONAL COMMUNICATIONS: Alfredo Palacios, Federico Pinedo.

Chapter 3 (1916–30)

59. Alende (O.), *1930–1982: Complot contra la democracia*. Buenos Aires, 1982.
60. Bortnik, op. cit. (5).
61. Almenara (S.), *La tiranía de Uriburu*. Buenos Aires, 1932.
62. Cossio (C.), *La revolución del 6 de septiembre*. Buenos Aires, 1933.
63. Crawkes (J.B.), *533 días de historia argentina: 6 de septiembre de 1930–20 de febrero de 1932*. Buenos Aires, 1932.
64. Del Mazo (G.), *La función argentina en el mundo*. Buenos Aires, 1955.
65. Ferrer (A.), *Nacionalismo y orden constitucional*. Mexico, 1981.
66. Ferrero (R.A.), 'Julito Roca y el complot de 1922' in *Todo es Historia*. Buenos Aires, Nov. 1972.
67. Frondizi (A.), *Petróleo y política: Contribución al estudio de la historia económica argentina y de las relaciones entre el imperialismo y la vida política nacional*. Buenos Aires, 1959.
68. Iscaro, op. cit. (14).
69. Koebel (W.H.), *The New Argentina*. London, 1923.
70. Luca de Tena, op. cit. (44).
71. Main (M.), *Evita: The Woman with the Whip*. London, 1977.
72. Máspero Castro, op. cit. (47).
73. Oritz Pereyra (M.), *La tercera emancipación: actualidad económica y social de la República Argentina*. Buenos Aires, 1926.
74. Palacios, op. cit. (22).
75. Pavón Pereyra, op. cit. (23).
76. Peters (H.E.), *The Foreign Debt of the Argentine Republic*. Baltimore, 1934.
77. Perón (J.D.), *Tres revoluciones militares*. Buenos Aires, 1963.
78. Pinedo, op. cit. (50).
79. Potash (R.A.), *El ejército y la política argentina 1928–1945*. Buenos Aires, 1981.
80. Quesada (J.A.), *Orígenes de la revolución del 6 de septiembre de 1930. La campaña presidencial de 1928. La agitación popular de 1930*. Buenos Aires, 1931.
81. Ramos, op. cit. (29).
82. Reyna Almandos (L.), *La demagogia radical y la tiranía*. Buenos Aires, 1920.
83. Sarobe (J.M.), *Memorias sobre la revolución del 6 de septiembre de 1930*. Buenos Aires, 1957.
84. Senén González, op. cit. (31).
85. Sindicato Luz y Fuerza, op. cit. (32).
86. Viale Ledesma (S.), *6 de septiembre: el pueblo, el ejército y la revolución*. Buenos Aires, 1931.

87. Villafañe (B.), *Irigoyen, el último dictador*. Buenos Aires, 1922.
88. Viñas (D.), *En la Semana Trágica*. Buenos Aires, 1966.
89. Williams, op. cit. (55).
90. Yrigoyen, op. cit. (57).
91. Yrigoyen, op. cit. (58).
NEWSPAPERS, PERIODICALS AND JOURNALS: *Crítica, Época, La Fronda, La Nueva República, La Prensa*.
INTERVIEWS AND PERSONAL COMMUNICATIONS: Juan José Arévalo, Víctor Raúl Haya de la Torre, Alfredo Palacios, Federico Pinedo.

Chapter 4 (1930–45)

92. Alende, op. cit. (59).
93. Almenara, op. cit. (61).
94. Barnes (J.), *Eva Perón*. London, 1978.
95. Crawkes, op. cit. (63).
96. Fayt (C.S.), *La naturaleza del peronismo*. Buenos Aires, 1967.
97. Ferrer, op. cit. (65).
98. Hernández Arregui, op. cit. (12).
99. Lanús (A.), *Campo minado*. Buenos Aires, 1942.
100. Lastra (B.), *Bajo el signo nacionalista*. Buenos Aires, 1944.
101. Lipset (S.M.), & Solari (A.), ed., *Elites in Latin America*. New York, 1967.
102. Luca de Tena, op. cit. (44).
103. Main, op. cit. (91).
104. Martínez Estrada (E.), *Qué es esto? Catilinaria*. Buenos Aires, 1956.
105. Ordóñez (M.V.) *et al.*, *Perón frente a la verdad*. Buenos Aires, 1945.
106. Pavón Pereyra, op. cit. (23).
107. Perón (E.), *La razón de mi vida*. Buenos Aires, 1952.
108. Perón, op. cit. (77).
109. Pinedo, op. cit. (50).
110. Potash, op. cit. (79).
111. Ramos, op. cit. (29).
112. Sánchez Sorondo (M.), *La revolución que anunciamos*, Buenos Aires, 1945.
113. Santander (S.), *Técnica de una traición*. Montevideo, 1953.
114. Senén González, op. cit. (31).
115. Sindicato Luz y Fuerza, op. cit. (32).
116. Torres (J.L.), *La década infame*. Buenos Aires, 1945.
117. Tussie (D.A.) & Federman (A.M.), 'La última montonera radical', *Todo es Historia*, Buenos Aires, Nov. 1972.
NEWSPAPERS, PERIODICALS AND JOURNALS: *Crítica, Deutsche La Plata Zeitung, Época, La Nación, La Nueva República, La Prensa, La Vanguardia*.
INTERVIEWS AND PERSONAL COMMUNICATIONS: Enrique Oliva.

Chapter 5 (1945–46)

118. Alende, op. cit. (59).
119. Barnes, op. cit. (94).
120. Bortnik, op. cit. (5).
121. Cochran (T.C.) & Reina (R.E.), *Espíritu de empresa en la Argentina.* Buenos Aires, 1965.
122. Colom (E.), *17 de Octubre: La revolución de los descamisados.* Buenos Aires, 1946.
123. Fayt, op. cit. (96).
124. Fraser (N.) & Navarro (M.), *Eva Perón.* London, 1980.
125. Gambini (H.), *El 17 de Octubre.* Buenos Aires, 1971.
126. Gambini (H.), *El peronismo y la Iglesia.* Buenos Aires, 1971.
127. Gambini (H.), *El primer gobierno peronista.* Buenos Aires, 1971.
128. Giussani (P.), *28 días que conmovieron al país* in 'Extra'. Buenos Aires, Aug. 1965.
129. Irazusta (J.), *Perón y la crisis argentina.* Buenos Aires, 1956.
130. Iscaro, op. cit. (14).
131. Kelly (D.), *El poder detrás del trono.* Buenos Aires, 1962.
132. Luca de Tena, op. cit. (44).
133. Main, op. cit. (71).
134. Martínez Estrada, op. cit. (104).
135. Pavón Pereyra, op. cit. (23).
136. Perelman (A.), *Cómo hicimos el 17 de Octubre.* Buenos Aires, 1961.
137. Perón, op. cit. (107).
138. Perón, op. cit. (77).
139. Potash, op. cit. (79).
140. Ramos, op. cit. (28).
141. Ramos, op. cit. (29).
142. Santander, op. cit. (113).
143. Senén González, op. cit. (31).
144. Sindicato Luz y Fuerza, op. cit. (32).
145. Taylor (J.M.), *Evita Perón: The Myths of a Woman.* Oxford, 1979.
146. US Department of State, *Consultation Among the American Capitals With Respect to the Argentine Situation.* Washington, 1946.
147. Whitaker (A.P.), *La Argentina y los Estados Unidos.* Buenos Aires, 1956.

NEWSPAPERS, PERIODICALS AND JOURNALS: *Crítica, Democracia, Época, La Nación, La Prensa, Tribuna.*

INTERVIEWS AND PERSONAL COMMUNICATIONS: John William Cooke, Arturo Jauretche.

Chapter 6 (1946–51)

148. Argentine Republic, *Declaración de la Independencia Económica*. Buenos Aires, 1947.
149. Briano (J.P.), *Geopolítica y geoestrategia americana*. Buenos Aires, 1966.
150. Ciria (A.), Partidos y poder en la Argentina moderna. Buenos Aires, 1964.
151. Cochran & Reina, op. cit. (121).
152. Diamand (M.), *Doctrinas económicas, desarrollo e independencia*. Buenos Aires, 1973.
153. Fraser & Navarro, op. cit. (124).
154. Gambini, op. cit. (127).
155. Irazusta, op. cit. (129).
156. Iscaro, op. cit. (14).
157. Kirkpatrick (J.), *Leader and Vanguard in a Mass Society: A Study of Peronist Argentina*. Cambridge (Mass.), 1971.
158. Luca de Tena, op. cit. (44).
159. Lucero (F.), *El precio de la lealtad*. Buenos Aires, 1959.
160. Oddone (J.), *Gremialismo proletario argentino*. Buenos Aires, 1949.
161. Olivieri (A.O.), *Dos veces rebelde: Memorias julio 1945–abril 1957*. Buenos Aires, 1957.
162. Pavón Pereyra, op. cit. (23).
163. Portnoy (L.), *La realidad argentina en el siglo XX: Análisis crítico de la economía*. Mexico, 1961.
164. Potash (R.), *The Army and Politics in Argentina 1945–62*. Stanford, 1980.
165. Senén González, op. cit. (31).
166. Taylor, op. cit. (145).
167. Tussie (D.A.) & Federman (A.M.), 'El golpe de Menéndez' in *Todo es Historia*. Buenos Aires, Nov. 1972.
168. Whitaker, op. cit. (147).

NEWSPAPERS, PERIODICALS AND JOURNALS: *Buenos Aires Herald, Democracia, El Mundo, La Razón, Noticias Gráficas*.
INTERVIEWS AND PERSONAL COMMUNICATIONS: Gabriel González Videla.

Chapter 7 (1946–51)

169. Alende, op. cit. (59).
170. Argentine Republic, *Constitución de la Nación Argentina*. Buenos Aires, 1950.
171. Barnes, op. cit. (94).
172. Fayt, op. cit. (96).
173. Frondizi, op. cit. (67).
174. Gambini, op. cit. (126).
175. Diamand, op. cit. (152).
176. Fraser & Navarro, op. cit. (124).
177. Iscaro, op. cit. (14).

178. Kirkpatrick, op. cit. (157).
179. Luca de Tena, op. cit. (44).
180. Potash, op. cit. (164).
181. Taylor, op. cit. (145).
182. Whitaker, op. cit. (147).

NEWSPAPERS, PERIODICALS AND JOURNALS: *Buenos Aires Herald, Crítica, Democracia, El Mundo, La Nación, La Prensa, La Razón, Noticias Gráficas.*

INTERVIEWS AND PERSONAL COMMUNICATIONS: John William Cooke, Ricardo Franke, José Ber Gelbard, Alfredo Gómez Morales, Enrique Oliva, Jorge Sábato.

Chapter 8 (1952-55)

183. Alende, op. cit. (59).
184. Barnes, op. cit. (94).
185. Busacca (S.), *La Democracia Cristiana en busca del país.* Buenos Aires, 1958.
186. Ciria, op. cit. (150).
187. Del Carril (B.), *Crónica interna de la Revolución Libertadora.* Buenos Aires, 1959.
188. Fraser & Navarro, op. cit. (124).
189. Frondizi, op. cit. (67).
190. Gambini, op. cit. (126).
191. Irazusta, op. cit. (129).
192. Jauretche (A.), *Los profetas del odio y la yapa: La colonización pedagógica.* Buenos Aires, 1967.
193. Kennedy (J.J.), *Catholicism, Nationalism and Democracy in Argentina.* Notre Dame (Indiana), 1959.
194. Kirkpatrick, op. cit. (157).
195. Luca de Tena, op. cit. (44).
196. Lucero, op. cit. (159).
197. Marsal (P.), *Perón y la Iglesia.* Buenos Aires, 1955.
198. Mercier Vega (L.), *Autopsia de Perón: Balance del peronismo.* Barcelona, 1975.
199. Olivieri, op. cit. (161).
200. Pavón Pereyra, op. cit. (23).
201. Potash, op. cit. (164).
202. Ramos, op. cit. (29).
203. Senén González, op. cit. (31).
204. Taylor, op. cit. (145).

NEWSPAPERS, PERIODICALS AND JOURNALS: *Buenos Aires Herald, Clarín, Democracia, El Pueblo, La Nación, La Prensa, Leoplán.*

INTERVIEWS AND PERSONAL COMMUNICATIONS: Ricardo Franke, José Ber Gelbard, Alfredo Gómez Morales, Arturo Jauretche, Ruth Monjardín de Masci, Jorge Sábato.

Chapter 9 (1955)

205. Alende, op. cit. (59).
206. Barnes, op. cit. (94).
207. Bortnik, op. cit. (5).
208. Busacca, op. cit. (185).
209. del Carril, op. cit. (187).
210. Fayt, op. cit. (96).
211. Fraser & Navarro, op. cit. (124).
212. Frondizi, op. cit. (67).
213. Gambini, op. cit. (126).
214. Iscaro, op. cit. (14).
215. Jauretche, op. cit. (192).
216. Kennedy, op. cit. (193).
217. Lonardi (M.), *Mi padre y la Revolución del 55*. Buenos Aires, 1980.
218. Lucero, op. cit. (159).
219. Marsal, op. cit. (197).
220. Mercier Vega, op. cit. (199).
221. Olivieri, op. cit. (161).
222. Pavón Pereyra, op. cit. (23).
223. Perón (J.D.), *Del poder al exilio*. Buenos Aires, 1973.
224. Perón (J.D.), *La fuerza es el derecho de las bestias*. 1958.
225. Perón, op. cit. (77).
226. Potash, op. cit. (64).
227. Ramos, op. cit. (29).
228. Senén González, op. cit. (31).
NEWSPAPERS, PERIODICALS AND JOURNALS: *Buenos Aires Herald, Clarín, La Nación*.
INTERVIEWS AND PERSONAL COMMUNICATIONS: Ricardo Franke, Arturo Jauretche.

Chapter 10 (1955)

229. Alende, op. cit. (59).
230. Ciria, op. cit. (150).
231. del Carril, op. cit. (187).
232. Ferrer, op. cit. (65).
233. Graham-Yooll (A.), 'Chronology 1955–76' (typescript).
234. Jauretche, op. cit. (192).
235. Lonardi (L.E.), *Dios es justo*. Buenos Aires, 1958.
236. Lonardi, op. cit. (217).
237. Luca de Tena, op. cit. (44).
238. Mercier Vega, op. cit. (199).

239. Pavón Pereyra, op. cit. (23).
240. Perón, op. cit. (223).
241. Potash, op. cit. (164).
242. Rock (D.) ed., *Argentina in the Twentieth Century.* Pittsburgh (Pa.) 1975.
243. Rouquié (A.), *Pouvoir militaire et société politique en Republique Argentine,* Paris, 1978.
244. Senén González, op. cit. (31).
NEWSPAPERS, PERIODICALS AND JOURNALS: *Buenos Aires Herald, Critero, La Prensa.*
INTERVIEWS AND PERSONAL COMMUNICATIONS: Ricardo Franke, Arturo Jauretche, Juan Carlos Herken, Raúl Prebisch, Jorge Sabato, Omar Torrijos.

Chapter 11 (1955-58)

245. Alende, op. cit. (59).
246. Bortnik, op. cit. (5).
247. Ciria, op. cit. (150).
248. Ferrer, op. cit. (65).
249. Frondizi (A.), *Estrategia y tactica del Movimiento Nacional.* Buenos Aires, 1964.
250. Frondizi, op. cit. (67).
251. Graham-Yooll, op. cit. (233).
252. Iscaro, op. cit. (14).
253. Luca de Tena, op. cit. (44).
254. Mercier Vega, op. cit. (199).
255. Pandolfi (R.), *Frondizi por él mismo.* Buenos Aires, 1968.
256. Pavón Pereyra, op. cit. (23).
257. Potash, op. cit. (164).
258. Rock, op. cit. (242).
259. Rouquié, op. cit. (243).
260. Senén González, op. cit. (31).
261. Silberstein (E.), *Los ministros de economia.* Buenos Aires, 1982.
262. Walsh (R.), *Caso Satanowsky.* Buenos Aires, 1973.
263. Walsh (R.), *Operación Masacre.* Buenos Aires, 1969.
NEWSPAPERS, PERIODICALS AND JOURNALS: *Clarin, Qué, La Prensa.*
INTERVIEWS AND PERSONAL COMMUNICATIONS: Ricardo Balbín, John William Cooke, Francisco Manrique, Ruth Monjardin de Masci, Enrique Olivia, Raúl Prebisch, Rodolfo Walsh.

Chapter 12 (1958-61)

264. Alende, op. cit. (59).
265. Bortnik, op. cit. (5).
266. Ciria, op. cit. (150).

267. Diamand, op. cit. (152).
268. Di Tella (G.) & Zymelman (M.) *Etapas del desarrollo económico argentina.* Buenos Aires, 1964.
269. Frondizi, op. cit. (249).
270. Frondizi, op. cit. (66).
271. Frondizi (S.), *Bases y puntos de partida para una solución popular.* Buenos Aires, 1961.
272. Graham-Yooll, op. cit. (233).
273. Iscaro, op. cit. (14).
274. O'Donnell (G.A.), *Modernización y autoritarismo.* Buenos Aires, 1972.
275. Pandolfi, op. cit. (255).
276. Pavón Pereyra, op. cit. (23).
277. Perón (J.D.) & Cooke (J.W.), *Correspondencia.* Buenos Aires, 1973.
278. Potash, op. cit. (164).
279. Ramos, op. cit. (28).
280. Rojo (R.), *Che Guevara: vie et mort d'un ami.* Paris, 1968.
281. Rouquié, op. cit. (243).
282. Senén González (S.), *El sindicalismo después de Perón.* Buenos Aires, 1971.
283. Senén González, op. cit. (31).
284. Silberstein, op. cit. (261).

NEWSPAPERS, PERIODICALS AND JOURNALS: *Clarin, Qué, La Razón.*

INTERVIEWS AND PERSONAL COMMUNICATIONS: Quito Burgos, John William Cooke, Marcelo Diamand, Arturo Jauretche, Jorge Abelardo Ramos.

Chapter 13 (1961–62)

285. Alende, op. cit. (59).
286. Ferrer, op. cit. (65).
287. Frondizi, op. cit. (249).
288. Graham-Yooll, op. cit. (233).
289. Guevara (E.), *La guerra de guerrillas.* Havana, 1960.
290. Guevara (E.), *Reminiscences of the Cuban Revolutionary War.* London, 1968.
291. Guevara (E.), *Venceremos! The Speeches and Writings of Ernesto Che Guevara.* (John Gerassi, ed.), London, 1968.
292. O'Donnell, op. cit. (274).
293. Pandolfi, op. cit. (255).
294. Potash, op. cit. (164).
295. Ramos, op. cit. (28).
296. Rojo, op. cit. (280).
297. Rouquié, op. cit. (243).
298. Villegas (O.G.), *Guerra revolucionaria comunista.* Buenos Aires, 1963.

NEWSPAPERS, PERIODICALS AND JOURNALS: *Buenos Aires Herald, Clarín, La Razón, La Vanguardia*.
INTERVIEWS AND PERSONAL COMMUNICATIONS: Ciro Ahumada, Marcelo Diamand, Santiago Diaz, Francisco Manrique, Enrique Olivia, Jorge Sábato.

Chapter 14 (1962–63)

299. Diamand, op. cit. (152).
300. Ferrer, op. cit. (64).
301. Graham-Yooll, op. cit. (233).
302. O'Donnell, op. cit. (274).
303. Potash (R.A.), *The Impact of Professionalism on the Twentieth Century Argentine military.* Amherst, 1977.
304. Rouquié, op. cit. (243).
305. Senén González, op. cit. (282).
306. Silberstein, op. cit. (261).
307. Torre (J.C.) & Senén González (S.), *Ejército y sindicatos.* Buenos Aires, 1969.

NEWSPAPERS, PERIODICALS AND JOURNALS: *Análisis, Economic Survey, La Nación, La Prensa, Review of the River Plate.*
INTERVIEWS AND PERSONAL COMMUNICATIONS: Gustavo Rearte.

Chapter 15 (1963–66)

308. Alende, op. cit. (59).
309. Alfonsin (R.), *La cuestión argentina.* Buenos Aires, 1980.
310. Bortnik, op. cit. (5).
311. Briano, op. cit. (149).
312. Crawley (E.), *Subversión y seguridad: La curestión de la guerra de guerrillas en el contexto argentino.* Buenos Aires, 1970.
313. Debray (R.) *Revolución en la revolución?* Havana, 1967.
314. Graham-Yooll, op. cit. (233).
315. Iscaro, op. cit. (14).
316. O'Donnell, op. cit. (274).
317. Potash, op. cit. (303).
318. Ramos, op. cit. (28).
319. Roth (R.), *Los años de Ongania: Relato de un testigo.* Buenos Aires, 1980.
320. Rouquié, op. cit. (243).
321. Senén González, op. cit. (31).
322. Senén González, op. cit. (282).
323. Shils (E.) *et al., Los militares y los países en desarrollo.* Buenos Aires, 1967.
324. Torre & Senén González, op. cit. (307).

NEWSPAPERS, PERIODICALS AND JOURNALS: *Análisis, Confirmado, La Nación, La Prensa, Primera Plana.*
INTERVIEWS AND PERSONAL COMMUNICATIONS: Marcelo Diamand, Ruth Monjardin de Masci, Jacobo Timerman, Jorge Sábato, Osiris Villegas.

Chapter 16 (1966–68)

325. Alfonsín, op. cit. (309).
326. Argentine Republic, *Acta de la Revolución Argentina.* Buenos Aires, 1966.
327. Crawley, op. cit. (312).
328. Eggers Lan (C.), *Cristianismo y nueva ideologia.* Buenos Aires, 1968.
329. Graham-Yooll, op. cit. (233).
330. Guevara (E.), *El diario del Che Guevara en Bolivia.* Havana, 1968.
331. Guevara, op. cit. (291).
332. Lanusse (A.A.), *Mi testimonio.* Buenos Aires, 1977.
333. Mayol (A.) *et al., Los católicos postconciliares en la Argentina* 1963–1969. Buenos Aires, 1970.
334. Rojo, op. cit. (280).
335. Roth, op. cit. (319).
336. Rouquié, op. cit. (243).
337. Senén González, op. cit. (282).
338. Silberstein, op. cit. (261).
339. Torre & Senén González, op. cit. (307).

NEWSPAPERS, PERIODICALS AND JOURNALS: *Clarín, Confirmado, Cristianismo y Revolución, La Prensa, Primera Plana, Review of the River Plate.*
INTERVIEWS AND PERSONAL COMMUNICATIONS: Carlos Brignone, Nicanor Costa Méndez, Marcelo Diamand, Victor Raúl Haya de la Torre, Adalbert Krieger Vasena, Lorenzo Pepe, Jorge Néstor Salimei, Héctor Zalduendo.

Chapter 17 (1968–69)

340. Argentine Republic, *El Terrorismo en la Argentina*, Buenos Aires, 1979.
341. Bortnik, op. cit. (5).
342. Buntig (A.J.), *El catolicismo popular en la Argentina.* Buenos Aires, 1969.
343. Cholvis (F.), *Esencia de la economía latinoamericana.* Buenos Aires, 1971.
344. Delich (F.), *Crisis y protesta social: Córdoba 1969–73.* Buenos Aires, 1974.
345. Genta (G.B.), *Seguridad y desarrollo: Reflexiones sobre el temor en la Argentina.* Buenos Aires, 1970.
346. Graham-Yooll, op. cit. (233).
347. Imaz (J.L.), *Los que mandan.* Albany, 1970.
348. Iscaro, op. cit. (14).
349. Lanusse, op. cit. (332).
350. Mayol, op. cit. (333).

351. Mercier Vega, op. cit. (198).
352. Rock, op. cit., (242).
353. Rouquié, op. cit. (243).
354. Roth, op. cit. (319).
355. Senén González, op. cit. (31).
356. Torre & Senén González, op. cit. (307).

NEWSPAPERS, PERIODICALS AND JOURNALS: *Clarín, Economic Survey, La Causa Peronista, La Prensa.*

INTERVIEWS AND PERSONAL COMMUNICATIONS: Marcelo Diamand, Héctor Fernández Mendy, José Teófilo Goyret, Francisco Manrique, Carlos Mugica, Raúl J. Peyceré, Jorge Sábato.

Chapter 18 (1969–71)

357. Alende, op. cit. (59).
358. Argentine Republic, op. cit. (340).
359. Bortnik, op. cit. (5).
360. Centro de Estudios de la Realidad Argentina, *Claves para la interpretación de la realidad argentina.* Buenos Aires, 1972.
361. CEPAL, *La distribución del ingreso en América Latina.* New York, 1970.
362. Delich, op. cit. (344).
363. De Riz (L.), *Retorno y derrumbe: El último gobierno peronista.* Mexico, 1981.
364. Diamand, op. cit. (152).
365. Ducantzeiler (G.), *Syndicats et politique en Argentine 1955–1973.* Montreal, 1980.
366. Ferrer, op. cit. (65).
367. Garcia Belsunce (H.A.), *Trece años en la politica económica argentina, 1966–1978.* Buenos Aires, 1978.
368. Genta, op. cit. (345).
369. Graham-Yooll, op. cit. (233).
370. Guglialmelli (J.E.), *120 dias en el gobierno.* Buenos Aires, 1971.
371. Herrera Vegas (J.H.), *Una nueva república.* Buenos Aires, 1971.
372. Lanusse, op. cit. (332).
373. O'Donnell, op. cit. (274).
374. Roth, op. cit. (319).
375. Rouquié, op. cit. (243).
376. Senén González, op. cit. (282).
377. Silberstein, op. cit. (261).

NEWSPAPERS, PERIODICALS AND JOURNALS: *Buenos Aires Herald, Clarín, La Nación, Review of the River Plate.*

INTERVIEWS AND PERSONAL COMMUNICATIONS: Ricardo Balbín, Aldo Ferrer, Juan Enrique Guglialmelli, Francisco Manrique.

Chapter 19 (1971-72)

378. Argentine Republic, op. cit. (340).
379. Bortnik, op. cit. (5).
380. Delich, op. cit. (344).
381. De Riz, op. cit. (363).
382. Ducantzeiler, op. cit. (365).
383. Gillespie (R.), 'Peronism and Left Militarism: The Montoneros' *Bulletin of the Society for Latin American Studies*, London, 1979.
384. Garcia Belsunce, op. cit. (367).
385. Graham-Yooll, op. cit. (233).
386. Lanusse, op. cit. (332).
387. Luca de Tena, op. cit. (44).
388. Mercier Vega, op. cit. (198).
389. Mugica (C.), *Peronismo y cristianismo*. Buenos Aires, 1973.
390. Peicovich (E.) *El último Perón*. Madrid, 1975.
391. Rouquié, op. cit. (243).
392. Senén González, op. cit. (31).

NEWSPAPERS, PERIODICALS AND JOURNALS: *Clarín, Cuestionario, La Opinión, La Prensa.*

INTERVIEWS AND PERSONAL COMMUNICATIONS: Ricardo Balbín, Ricardo Franke, José Ber Gelbard, Alejandro Agustín Lanusse, Francisco Manrique.

Chapter 20 (1972-73)

393. Argentine Republic, op. cit. (340).
394. Bortnik, op. cit. (5).
395. De Riz, op. cit. (363).
396. Ducantzeiler, op. cit. (365).
397. Gillespie, op. cit. (383).
398. Graham-Yooll, op. cit. (233).
399. Iscaro, op. cit. (14).
400. Lanusse, op. cit. (332).
401. Luca de Tena, op. cit. (44).
402. Munck (R.), 'The Crisis of Late Peronism and the Working Class' *Bulletin of the Society for Latin American Studies*, London, 1979.
403. Peicovich, op. cit. (390).
404. Rouquié, op. cit. (243).
405. Terragno (R.H.), *Muerte y resurrección de los politicos*. Buenos Aires, 1981.
406. Senén González, op. cit. (31).

NEWSPAPERS, PERIODICALS AND JOURNALS: *Clarín, Cuestionario, Economic Survey, El Descamisado, La Opinión, Mercado.*

INTERVIEWS AND PERSONAL COMMUNICATIONS: Ricardo Balbín, Marcelo Diamand, Ricardo Franke, David Graiver, Francisco Manrique, Ruth Monjardin de Masci.

Chapter 21 (May–Oct. 1973)

407. Argentine Republic, op. cit. (340).

408. De Riz, op. cit. (363).

409. Di Tella (G.), *Argentina Under Perón*. London, 1983.

410. Ducantzeiler, op. cit. (365).

411. Gelbard (J.B.), *Política económica y social. Ruptura de la dependencia. Unidad y reconstrucción nacional con justicia social para la liberación*. Buenos Aires, 1973.

412. Gillespie, op. cit. (383).

413. Graham-Yooll (A.), *The Press in Argentina 1973–1978*. London, 1979.

414. Graham-Yooll, op. cit. (233).

415. Munck, op. cit. (402).

416. Puig (J.C.) *et al.*, *De la dependencia a la liberación: Política exterior de América Latina*. Buenos Aires, 1973.

417. Terragno (R.H.), *Contratapas*. Buenos Aires, 1976.

418. Terragno, op. cit. (405).

NEWSPAPERS, PERIODICALS AND JOURNALS: *Clarín, Criterio, Cuestionario, El Combatiente, El Descamisado, El Mundo, El Observador, Estrella Roja, La Nación, La Opinión, Mayoría, Militancia*.

INTERVIEWS AND PERSONAL COMMUNICATIONS: Ciro Ahumada, Ricardo Franke, Emilio E. Massera.

Chapter 22 (1973–76)

419. Alende, op. cit. (59).

420. Argentine Republic, op. cit. (340).

421. Bortnik, op. cit. (5).

422. De Riz, op. cit. (363).

423. Di Tella, op. cit. (409).

424. Garcia Belsunce, op. cit. (367).

425. Gillespie, op. cit. (383).

426. Graham-Yooll, op. cit. (233).

427. Graham-Yooll, op. cit. (413).

428. Luder (I.A.) *El proceso argentino*. Buenos Aires, 1977.

429. Munck, op. cit. (404).

430. Perón (J.D.), *La comunidad organizada: con un apendice de actualización doctrinaria*. Buenos Aires, 1974.

431. Rouquié, op. cit. (243).

432. Terragno, op. cit. (417).

NEWSPAPERS, PERIODICALS AND JOURNALS: *Buenos Aires Herald, Clarín, Criterio, Cuestionario, El Descamisado, El Observador, La Nación, La Opinión*.

INTERVIEWS AND PERSONAL COMMUNICATIONS: Ciro Ahumada, Alberto Camarasa, Marcelo Diamand, Ricardo Franke, Francisco Manrique, Carlos Mugica.

Chapter 23 (1976–80)

433. Alende, op. cit. (59).
434. Amnesty International, *Report of an Amnesty International Mission to Argentina*. London, 1977.
435. Amnesty International, *Testimony on Secret Detention Camps in Argentina*. London, 1979.
436. Amnesty International, *The Disappeared of Argentina*. London, 1979.
437. Argentine Republic, op. cit. (340).
438. Catholic Institute for International Relations, *Death and Violence in Argentina*. London, 1976.
439. Comité de Defensa de Derechos Humanos en el Cono Sur, *Disappeared in Argentina*. São Paulo, 1982.
440. Garcia Belsunce, op. cit., (367).
441. Graham-Yooll, (A.), *Portrait of an Exile*. London, 1981.
442. Graham-Yooll, op. cit. (413).
443. Kahn (H.), *Doy fe*. Buenos Aires, 1979.
444. López Salvatierra (G.F.), *La dinamita de Pérez Esquivel en la Argentina*. Buenos Aires, 1980.
445. Martínez de Hoz (J.A.), *Bases para una Argentina moderna 1976–1980*. Buenos Aires, 1981.
446. Massera (E.), *El camino de la democracia*. Buenos Aires, 1979.
447. Massera (E.), *Entre la guerra y la democracia*. Buenos Aires, 1981.
448. Timerman (J.), *Prisoner Without Name, Cell Without a Number*. London, 1981.
449. Varela-Cid (E.), ed., *Juicio de residencia a Martinez de Hoz*. Buenos Aires, 1981.
450. Waldmann (P.) & Garzón Valdés (E.), ed., *El poder militar en la Argentina 1976–1981*. Frankfurt, 1982.
451. Zinn (R.), *Cuatro años después de la segunda fundación de la República*. Buenos Aires, 1980.

NEWSPAPERS, PERIODICALS AND JOURNALS: *Buenos Aires Herald, Cuestionario, Gente, La Nación, Para Tí, Siete Días, Somos.*

INTERVIEWS AND PERSONAL COMMUNICATIONS: Julio Algañaraz, José Teófilo Goyret, Cristina Guzmán de Andreussi, José A. Martínez de Hoz, Emilio E. Massera, Jorge Sábato, Jacobo Timerman.

INDEX